JOHN EVELYN

JOHN EVELYN
LIVING FOR INGENUITY

GILLIAN DARLEY

YALE UNIVERSITY PRESS
NEW HAVEN AND LONDON

For information about this and other Yale University Press publications, please contact:
U.S. Office: sales.press@yale.edu   www.yalebooks.com
Europe Office: sales@yaleup.co.uk   www.yaleup.co.uk

Set in Caslon by J&L Composition, Filey, North Yorkshire
Printed in Great Britain by St Edmundsbury Press Ltd, Bury St Edmunds

Library of Congress Cataloging-in-Publication Data

Darley, Gillian.
  John Evelyn: living for ingenuity/Gillian Darley.
    p. cm.
  Includes bibliographical references (p.   ) and index.
  ISBN 0–300–11227–0 (alk. paper)
1. Evelyn, John, 1620–1706. 2. Authors, English—Early modern, 1500–1700—Biography. 3. Diarists—Great Britain—Biography. 4. Gardeners—Great Britain—Biography. 5. Great Britain—History—Stuarts, 1603–1714—Biography. 6. Great Britain—Court and courtiers—Biography.   I. Title
  PR3433.E5Z63 2006
  828'.403—dc22
  [B]

                                                                2006020724

A catalogue record for this book is available from the British Library.

10 9 8 7 6 5 4 3 2 1

For Susannah

Ex Libris Evelyni emptus apud Toun
16: Junij 1644: pret: 2:
Omnia Explorate, Meliora Retinete.

Dominus providebit.

Contents

John Evelyn's Works   ix

Note on Sources   x

Introduction   xi

Chapter 1   Early Years   1

Chapter 2   The Fruits of Travel   19

Chapter 3   'Out of the Garden into Paradice'   37

Chapter 4   'Sweete Mrs Eveling'   56

Chapter 5   'A very great Alarme'   77

Chapter 6   'I am exceedingly happy heere'   93

Chapter 7   Wise Men Possessing Themselves in Patience   113

Chapter 8   Planting Cabbages and Blotting Paper   136

Chapter 9   Restoration   155

Chapter 10   City and Country   175

Chapter 11   The Active Life   192

Chapter 12   Paris and London   214

Chapter 13   Perpetual Motion   233

Chapter 14   Endeavour to Submit   254

Chapter 15   An Absolute Philosopher   279

Abbreviations   307

Notes   308

Select Bibliography   352

Index   358

Acknowledgements   381

Photographic Acknowledgements   383

John Evelyn's Works (published in his lifetime, excluding most pamphlets and tracts)

Of Liberty and Servitude (translation from the French, 1649)

The State of France (1652)

An Essay on the First Book of T Lucretius Carus, De Rerum Natura (verse translation from the Latin, 1656)

The French Gardiner (translation from the French, 1658)

The Golden Book of St John Chrysostom (translation from the Greek, 1659)

A Character of England (1659)

Fumifugium (1661)

Instructions Concerning Erecting of a Library (translation from the French, 1661)

Sculptura (1662)

Sylva (1664, 1670, 1679, 1706 (in latter edition spelled 'Silva'))

Pomona (1664, printed with *Sylva*, above)

Kalendarium Hortense (1664, published in *Sylva*, then separately from 1666 onwards)

Parallel of Architecture (translation from the French, 1664)

Publick Employment and An Active Life Prefer'd to Solitude (1667)

Idea of the Perfection of Painting (translation from the French, 1668)

Navigation and Commerce (1674)

Discourse of Earth (1676, with the *Kalendarium*, later editions with *Sylva*; 1706 edition retitled 'Terra')

The Compleat Gard'ner (translation from the French, 1693)

Numismata (1697)

Acetaria (1699)

Note on Sources

In transcribing from manuscript material I have followed the convention of expanding any contracted words, retaining spelling and obvious capitalisation (when legible). I have not italicised, either from underscored words or phrases in manuscript or in contemporary printed works. The prefix '[LB]' before the two letter-book volumes (BL Add Ms 78298, 78299) denotes the copybooks which Evelyn made and which, when compared to the letters which were sent, often show significant variations. In some cases, there is no proof that the letters in the letter-books were ever sent. It will also be seen that some manuscripts are given folio numbers, others not. This relects the fact that the archive was undergoing foliation and binding thoughout the period in which I worked on the papers; I have incorporated folio numbers where they were available. Since spelling of proper names is often arbitrary in this period, I have, when in doubt, followed that form used in the *ODNB*.

Introduction

In the early 1800s John Evelyn's last linear descendant was dead and his elderly widow had been befriended by a light-fingered librarian called William Upcott whose address, Autograph Cottage, should have been warning enough. With William Bray, her lawyer and a reputable Surrey antiquarian, they began to sort through material from the mouldering shelves and cupboards at Wotton House. First came Evelyn's journals, his 'Kalendarium', tucked away in a drawer of his finest continental cabinet, which were published in 1818. Until then, John 'Sylva' Evelyn, as his family referred to him, was known entirely for his book on trees.

The Victorians fell upon Evelyn with delight. Fuller editions of Evelyn's diary and correspondence were published, as were previously unseen papers such as a history of religion and a hagiography of his platonic beloved Margaret Blagge; everything accentuated his exceptional piety, his discretion and steely morality. When a Victorian history painter (E.M. Ward) showed Charles II trysting with Nell Gwyn, John Evelyn was standing disapprovingly in the shadows. Evelyn, or at least the late nineteenth-century version, did not appeal to the new brooms of the twentieth century. Virginia Woolf, writing in 1920, the tercentenary of his birth, described the diary as 'the uninspired work of a good man', but suspected he was censorious and patronising.[1] Yet this is the man who reduced a group of friends, amongst them Samuel Pepys, to helpless laughter as he babbled nonsense at them and who, when his pet project to build a hospital at Chatham for sick and aged seamen in the king's navy looked as if it might succeed, wrote to his wife that he was 'half pulled to pieces for joy'.[2] Evelyn's voice, reported by Pepys, fearing that the flagrant decadence at court they both descried would bring a second Commonwealth or describing the duke of York's mistress, Lady Denham, as 'bitchering' is, like that heard in his less formal letters, surprisingly frank.

John Evelyn's name is now increasingly familiar, yet as a flesh-and-blood man he still seems as shadowy as the figure in Ward's painting. Ubiquitous whenever a neat quote on the seventeenth century is required, he emerges from his 'diaries' (by design, I suppose) 'a little pale in character, perpetually elusive'.[3] But his massive archive, which arrived at the British Library as late as 1995, suggested to me that there might be more to say about him.

And so there is. With his papers, colour begins to bleed into the sepia image, contradictions start to upset assertions, uncertainties to shake convictions. He left many clues, not all of which I can solve. My privilege, working on the archive as it emerged into view, now online and catalogued, has been to see another face of John Evelyn. A more complex and interesting figure than the Victorians found steps forward, a man with astonishing 'hospitality of mind', whose hunger for knowledge allowed him to embrace new ideas and distant horizons until the very end of his life.

His wife, Mary, is virtually invisible in the diary but was by his side for almost sixty years, first at Sayes Court, her own family's house next to Deptford dockyard, and from the 1690s, at the Evelyn family home, Wotton House in the Surrey Hills. She was a woman of acute intelligence and tangible warmth. They survived together into old age, overcoming personal and financial difficulties, growing ever closer in what became a perfect companionate marriage, validated by his growing appreciation of her qualities of mind and capabilities. Their well-recorded life is our good fortune, as is Evelyn's reluctance to dispose of any written document, whether hers or his. Preserving their papers, his library and possessions as far as was possible, Evelyn (though an advocate of regular 'purges') ensured later generations could gain a window on seventeenth-century life from the kitchen to the court. Ever the patriarch, he inspired his grandson Jack, the future Sir John Evelyn Bt, by his example, and subsequent generations took their responsibilities seriously. The world-wide dispersal of Evelyn's print collection and what remained of the extensive library, as well as furniture and paintings, prompted by the subdivision of the estate between heirs in the 1970s, made a mockery of their conscientious stewardship.

Evelyn's papers reveal a curiosity which rebukes our own ignorance and narrow-mindedness, a public spirit and competence which challenge our apathy. By our standards, his was a small yet limitless world, impossibly distant in its foundations in classical learning, hope of spiritual redemption and ambitions for universal knowledge. John Evelyn's motto was *Omnia explorate, meliora retinete* (look into everything, keep the best). His voluminous papers include letter-books, commonplace books, lists and catalogues, sermon notes and personal devotions, manuals to guide the young, incomplete manuscripts and miscellaneous correspondence (much of it in copybooks, embellished for later eyes) covering some eighty years of public and private life. Yet Evelyn had a surprising degree of self-knowledge and no one can fail to sympathise as, like the sorcerer's apprentice in *Fantasia*, he tried to contain the tidal wave of material washing over him, especially for his unpublished labour of love, his great work on gardening, the *Elysium Britannicum*.

My object in trying to scale the foothills of such a mountain of material has been to look beyond the 'diarist'.[4] Evelyn told his grandson, the admirable Jack Evelyn, to take notes of what he read and not depend on memory alone; a commonplace book or collection was essential, 'no man being able to build anything whatever without the help [of] others'. Evelyn's first translation was published before he was thirty, his last work just after his death fifty-five years later.[5] He translated work from French, Latin and Greek, in both verse and prose, composed pamphlets and tracts and wrote a number of authoritative books as well as those he never completed. And there were (are?) secrets: a box that he frequently reminded Mary Evelyn no one must see. He was not an entirely original thinker and probably received more help than he acknowledged: seventeenth-century authorship was frequently uncertain (or obscured) and literary conventions and practices very different from our own. If Evelyn did not always remember to give credit where credit was due, he was following where many had gone before. In any case, the wider project was the point.

According to Stephen Switzer it is thanks to Evelyn 'that Gardening can speak proper English'.[6] But outside the confines of the flower border, the vegetable garden, the orchard, the park and the wooded estate, and far beyond the English-speaking world, he helped prepare the ground for Diderot's *Encyclopédie*, Johnson's *Dictionary*, the British Museum and the rational Georgian rebuilding of London, Bath or Edinburgh. His hand can be seen equally behind the setting up of public libraries, the establishment of twentieth-century town and country planning legislation and the popularity of vegetarianism (the 'herby-diet') in the twenty-first century. The Virgilian motto around the milled rim of the current pound coin, *Decus et tutamen* (ornament and protect), was his choice.

In his 'hole' at Sayes Court, working deep into the night, he gathered information and ideas and put them together, to the best of his ability and as an avid collector of knowledge, making surprising, even visionary, connections. In *Fumifugium* he envisaged a London in which smoky industrial premises were separated from residential areas by a scented green belt. He expanded further on the ideas when he advocated a rebuilt London after the 1666 fire. In old age, he envisioned his nation, created from stock as diverse as Romans and Saxons, and gathered into a bouquet,

cull'd and compos'd, not from any one single Beauty of the flowry-Parterre, but from the Rose and the Lily, the Jasmine, Tuberose and the rest. . . . so the Inclinations of the English seem to result from the great Variety of the People; which as so many glorious Flowers from time to time, have been transplanted into our British Elysium: Few Nations that I know of under Heaven (in so short a time) consisting of so many Ingredients, by Revolutions, and Successions.[7]

Until the foundation of the Royal Society Evelyn worked on his chosen topics in relative isolation, urged on by assorted fellow spirits and subscribing to the then-current model of the reluctant author, 'yielding to the requests of my friends'.[8] As an early and stalwart Fellow, he then happily became part of a wider collaboration dedicated to the advancement of useful knowledge, to which all contributed according to their particular strengths.[9] Fittingly they were known as the 'ingenious' – enquiring men. He found himself in the company of great experimental scientists and bookish divines, statesmen and mechanical geniuses. Together they advanced a common project, in the face of continual schisms and catastrophes which made everything unsure – even books could disappear in a column of flame, as they did in September 1666.

In decades of continually adjusting loyalties and beliefs, Evelyn rarely lost a friend and his exchanges of letters with the Catholic convert Samuel Tuke or the public servant Samuel Pepys show the man who can seem to be a sermonising pedant slipping into the shadows behind the lively-minded man of the world. Evelyn advances, zigzagging between Oxford and Surrey, Holland, France and Italy, London and Deptford, through the reigns of five English monarchs, a republic and a protectorate, sometimes a very private virtuoso (in the original sense of a connoisseur of objects of 'vertu'), at other times an entirely honest and conscientious servant of the state. Horace Walpole saw his life as a perfect combination of 'inquiry, study, curiosity, instruction and benevolence'.[10]

Evelyn told Pepys: 'It is not imaginable to such as have not tried, what labour an Historian (that would be exact) is condemn'd to: He must read all, good, and bad, and remove a world of rubbish before he can lay the foundation.'[11] Writing a life of John Evelyn in a moderate-sized single volume has often felt daunting, but my encouragement came from his own attitude – always 'living for ingenuity'.

CHAPTER 1

Early Years

Wotton House in Surrey represents the book ends of John Evelyn's life, where he spent his infancy and early childhood, and late old age. From 1625 until 1699, when Evelyn inherited the house and estate from his older brother George, he was no more than a visitor, an invited (and sometimes paying) guest, at his family seat, that 'old extravagant house', as he described it to his friend Samuel Pepys.[1]

Inheritance, a shared past given (and explained) to subsequent generations, was at the core of Evelyn's sense of himself. The manor of Wotton only became family property in 1579, forty years before his birth. In the event his grandfather George did not live there long before settling the estate on his son Richard in 1595.[2] But Evelyns root quickly; below the North Downs lay the little parish church to which their mortuary chapel was added and where, in a room over the porch, John Evelyn's education began. His own son John came to share his pleasure in this continuity and, when his elderly parents were allocated an apartment in the house by his uncle George, wrote tenderly: 'I confesse had I bin born there, as you were, I should have a secret satisfaction in returning and as it were taking possession of my Birthplace; I was allways touch'd with delight when I came in view of Wotton.'[3]

Folded away between the Surrey Hills and North Downs, Wotton House was a rambling Tudor mansion of brick and tile, girded by a moat, a comfortable, hospitable house of a kind then familiar in the English southern counties. It was a confection of gabled roofs and mullioned windows, latticed glazing and cut-brick chimneys; such asymmetry and irregularity had lent itself easily to small alterations and additions over generations. The core of the (old) house can easily be made out from higher ground, still marked by the original roofs and chimneys. Barns and outhouses huddled close, giving the impression of a little hamlet tucked away in its secluded wooded valley, cut by watercourses and rutted tracks.

As a young man in the early 1640s, Evelyn sketched the house, aware that the current incendiary atmosphere might spoil, even obliterate, its untouched calm. He had made a record of Wotton, he said, 'before my brother changed it', for although the turmoil of the civil wars greatly unsettled his family, the house in the event remained unscathed. On his drawing of the south front he marked the upper 'chamber window to the roome where I was borne'. In front of the house he marked out the formal patterned compartments of a Tudor knot garden which ended at the moat, on which were swans and a swan house. There was a summer house, brick-paved paths, a 'pheasant garden', while 'here now is the fountain' and 'there a mound of trees'. Behind a coppice was the 'upper garden' and a barn, close to the house, for no one then objected to the smell of horses or the sound of flails as Evelyn remembered. Another view, from the north, showed a variety of outhouses and farm buildings with rabbits frolicking in the foreground.

Although he never drew the interior, in a commonplace book Evelyn described a typical old-fashioned, hospitable English gentry house. It was Wotton in every detail. A grassy courtyard, flanked by stables and barns, announced a sequence of gatehouse, porch and then an 'ample hall' with tall windows, separated from the buttery by a screen. Instead of a separate drawing room (introduced in his lifetime), the large bay windows were curtained 'a good way from the window so as when drawn men were as private from the rest of the company as in a closet'. Heavy cushions padded the window seats and the secluded space became an ideal place to conduct business, away from the eye of the household.[4] A Tudor house with unwieldy principal rooms needed such adjustments to provide mid-seventeenth-century levels of comfort, practicality and privacy.

Beyond the immediate surroundings, which suggested a pastoral setting, the area was heavily industrialised. Only a generation earlier, the family wealth had come not from land but from manufacture, for the Evelyns held a monopoly on gunpowder. John Evelyn turned this background to his own advantage (quickly distancing himself from the mores of the rural gentry) and it strongly coloured his views. Many years later he wrote, with the authority of a member of the Council of Trade and Plantations: 'It is a greate mistake to thinke Commerce & Merchandise a diminution to the dignity of gentlemen; unless the honour we derive from bloud or rapine be preferrable to what is gotten by honest Industry.' To be a merchant 'brings us in as well as carries out so many usefull things for Life. And as to other Trades, I see no reason it should the more dishonour to sell a yard of silke or cloth than hoggs or sheepe.'[5] From his youth, he lost no opportunity to flag up his own situation, even if the Evelyns' considerable estates ensured that, as a scion of the landed gentry, he was in the top echelons of rural society.

1 Garden front of Wotton House drawn by Evelyn, *c*. 1700. He was born in the upper room between the two pairs of double chimneys.

Along the fast-flowing streams and waterways that had cut the valleys of north-west Surrey were dozens of water-powered mills, much of their output devoted to arming the country, its militias and navy. The Tillingbourne, the watercourse nearest Wotton, powered mills producing gunpowder as well as brass, wire and other commodities. Timber, for charcoal, was well husbanded and the woods flourished. Evelyn remembered: 'I have heard my own Father (whose Estate was none of the least wooded in England) affirm that a Forge and some other Mills, which he furnished with much Fuel were a means of maintaining and improving his woods.'[6] Saltpetre was the main ingredient in gunpowder, made from an incendiary recipe combining black earth, animal excrement, lime and ash. Dovecotes were the best source for nitre (although in the 1630s citizens were requested to store their own urine for a year, in case of shortage) and legal disputes continually raged over unauthorised entry to them and the digging-up of pigeonhouse floors.[7] Gunpowder was a milled concoction of roughly two-thirds saltpetre to one-third each of charcoal and sulphur, the latter the only imported ingredient. George Evelyn, John's grandfather, was awarded his first gunpowder contract in the 1560s.

Royal letters patent were granted in 1589 to him, his son John and a Richard Hill, for gunpowder mills at various Surrey locations. Their monopoly made it the only county with authorised powder mills. The contract was with the Commissioners for Saltpetre and Gunpowder on behalf of the Lords of the Admiralty, but government supply carried potentially onerous penalties, a £50 fine being levied every time they defaulted on monthly deliveries to the Tower of London. When George died in 1603, in his late seventies, he sat at the centre of a web of estates and profitable gunpowder mills which were now divided between four of his sons (he had fathered twenty-four children by two wives). The eldest, Thomas, inherited Long Ditton, the original Evelyn property. When Robert (to whom came the mills at Godstone) left for Virginia in 1609 he referred to the 'in-supportable losses' of the business. Nevertheless, given this opportunity to do so, John confidently added his brother's share to his holding at Kingston and expanded the works. It was this uncle who continued in the trade until the family monopoly was removed in 1636 – but by then the Evelyns were major landowners.[8] The extravagance of the next generation led to Sir John's Godstone estate being frittered away, helping to confirm Evelyn's strong views about the pitfalls of a privileged rural life, lived without purpose or programme.[9]

Richard Evelyn, the father of the diarist, was their younger half-brother. After inheriting Wotton in 1595 he quickly expanded his holdings, acquiring at least seven neighbouring manors in the parish, in Abinger and as far as Dorking, including Leith Hill, a good vantage point from which to survey his land. His son believed he owned timber worth around £4,000 a year.[10] Even allowing for filial exaggeration, there was money in those hills. Richard appears to have had no financial interest in the Wotton mills, which ceased production in 1625. They were probably Hill's.

The iron of the nearby weald, smelted with local charcoal, had made Surrey in effect the ordnance capital of England. Accessible from London, peppered with royal palaces past and present, the county was of the highest possible political significance. With the outbreak of civil war in 1641 came a huge increase in demand for gunpowder, now supplied from locations across south-eastern England.[11]

The dangerous and intrusive nature of gunpowder had made the vicinity of working mills unappealing. In July 1636, a close neighbour Thomas Howard, earl of Arundel, wrote from Bohemia to Sir Francis Windebank, secretary of state that he was 'sorry to hear Mr Comptroller should incline to have a powder-mill spoil my poor cottage at Aldbury [Albury], the only recreation of me and my poor family; which I am resolved to oppose as *pro aris et focis* being the greatest indignity, I think, ever offered to any, especially in publick employment'. The king's message was that Howard had no reason to worry.[12]

By the time of Evelyn's birth, his father was a pillar of the Surrey gentry, conscientiously supporting charitable institutions, among them the grammar school and almshouses in Guildford. Evelyn always emphasised the public responsibilities that came with good fortune, and his father was his model.

From 1621 he sat as a justice of the peace – according to his son, a notably humane one – and took his turn as high sheriff. His duties were typically those expected of the county elite, a self-perpetuating oligarchy. As one historian has expressed it succinctly, the art of governing (in both the pre-war and Restoration periods) depended on the coincidence of interest between the gentry and the Crown.[13] A gentleman's honour carried with it considerable obligations. Different branches of grandfather George's spreading family were at the apex of Surrey life by the mid-century, though their allegiances diverged during the Commonwealth.

Evelyn paints a vivid, affectionate portrait of his father. The physical opposite of his etiolated, pale and sharp-featured son, Richard Evelyn was short, thick-set and high-coloured with 'a Sanguine Complexion, mix'd with a dash of Choler'. His 'extraordinarily quick & piercing' eyes were set below a generous forehead and thick wavy hair 'inclining to light'. He was becoming grey at the temples by the age of thirty, though his fashionably pointed beard remained brown. He ate and drank sparingly and was a man of few words, though very hospitable. 'Discreetely severe; yet liberall upon all just occasions both to his Children, strangers, and servants', he had a good knowledge of Latin and was 'more than ordinarily knowing' in municipal legal matters, as befitted a JP. Further, he was 'a studious decliner of Honors and Titles', having turned down a knighthood in 1630. (He was fined for this, such refusals providing one of the king's more unorthodox sources of revenue.)[14] His son continued that tradition on more than one occasion.[15]

Richard's wife, Eleanor (or Ellen) Stansfield, an only child born in 1598, was a striking woman, with hair and eyes 'of a lovely black', a 'browne complexion' and a good figure.[16] But she was a withdrawn, if not depressive, person, 'inclyn'd to a religious Melancholy, or pious sadnesse'. Her appearance seems at odds with her disposition, but in her only known portrait there is a touch of John's slightly foxy look. Perhaps it was her upbringing, a solitary child in the household of a strongly puritan father, that formed her sombre character. Following the couple's marriage in St Saviour's, Southwark, in January 1614, five children were born within eight years: two daughters and three sons, Elizabeth, Jane, George, John and Richard. Unusually, all survived to adulthood (and two into their late eighties). As he showed in his drawing, Evelyn was born in a first-floor room overlooking the gardens but soon, 'in reguard of my Mothers weaknesse, or rather costome of persons of quality', was sent out to a comely wet nurse, the wife of a local tenant. He stayed with the family, 'in a most sweete place towards the hills, flanked with wood, and refreshed with streames', until early 1622, when he was about eighteen months old. In the diary he sketched in early influences, his liking for solitude, his love of gardens and woods, tastes that all too neatly matched the man he became.[17]

The family of Evelyn's maternal grandfather (and godfather), John Stansfield, came from the north of England, but Stansfield himself was born in Lewes in Sussex in the 1550s. His shipping business operated from Newhaven, at the mouth of the Ouse, where he owned extensive water meadows and grazing lands on the estuary. The cargoes included iron heading for the West Country, as well as wheat for Marseille and lead for Newfoundland. He traded with London and ports in northern France and the Netherlands. The ships came back laden with coal from Milford Haven, salt from La Rochelle, almonds from Malaga and stoneware from Rotterdam, which he then distributed across the south of England. Among the vessels registered at Newhaven was the *Eleanor Stansfield*, the name of both his wife and daughter.[18] Evelyn's maternal grandmother, Eleanor Comber, died in 1613 and her family's lands at Cliffe, on the other side of the Ouse from Lewes, together with a handsome portfolio of holdings scattered through East Sussex, all bought with the profits generated by the Stansfield merchant fleet, would later pass into the Evelyn family.

In 1625 a ferocious return of the plague, centred as usual on London and adjacent towns, convinced Richard and Eleanor Evelyn to send John (and perhaps his sister Jane) to live with their grandfather in East Sussex, well away from infection. When he assumed responsibility for his grandchildren, John Stansfield was well over seventy and his second wife, Jane (born Michell), at least fifty. In February 1628 Stansfield died. His will, proved by his only daughter and executor, requested that he be buried in his birthplace, Lewes. The bequests reveal his strong puritan beliefs and his charitable impulses. Among the Evelyn papers is a little book, a panegyric written by John Sampson, who had been financially supported by Stansfield during his years at Corpus Christi, Oxford.[19]

While the parish church at Cliffe, with its communion table laden with valuable church plate railed off to the east end and the rector officiating from the chancel clad in fine vestments, represented the Laudian tendency of its incumbent and some of its parishioners, John Stansfield's was a very different faith, strongly puritan and without ritual. Episcopalian Anglicanism – with its emphasis on the 1559 Book of Common Prayer, sacraments and expensive church furnishings, that proliferation of 'crucifixes, altars, images, organs and what else' about which Evelyn's grandmother warned him when he arrived at Oxford – smacked of creeping Catholicism.[20]

When Stansfield bought the deanery, church lands and benefice of South Malling from the Sackville estate in 1623, he ensured that the minister shared his views. Just before his death, he took his grandson to lay the foundation stone of the rebuilt little church, dedicated to St Michael, which looks across the water meadows and the Ouse towards Lewes. According to Evelyn, the building and endowment were 'almost wholy at the Charge of my Grandfather', who left an annual £20 towards it.[21] Stansfield's support was for Protestantism pure and unadorned.

His twelve-page will shows his wealth. His granddaughters, Elizabeth and Jane, received £500 on marriage or at the age of twenty-one. The residue of the estate went to his only child, Eleanor, for 'I know she hath a wise and understanding husband, and able to mannage farr greater matters than theis are'. Richard Evelyn's care of his Surrey estates, along with the steady and religious character his son described, reassured his father-in-law.[22]

Stansfield's death did not change the domestic arrangements. Evelyn's step-grandmother, Jane, was much loved by the family and she was, in large measure, to be John's mother-figure during his formative years. In 1628 he began Latin lessons with a Frenchman, M. Citolin, and enjoyed drawing, which his father, who followed his progress with an eagle eye, albeit from a distance, soon began to consider a waste of valuable time.

By 1630 Jane Stansfield had married again. William Newton, her late husband's executor, was a widowed barrister with a son and a daughter of his own, who willingly assumed the position of paterfamilias to the young Evelyns. The new Mrs Newton moved house a few hundred yards along the valley, from Cliffe to Southover. In 1572 Newton's father, also William, had built a substantial gabled stone house just outside and below the hefty flint walls enclosing Lewes. The builders incorporated quantities of the fine-quality stone that lay around the site of the ruined Lewes priory and carved the Newton crest to the left of the entrance. The house overlooked a landscape of water meadows, held between the heavy knees of the South Downs – after wooded Surrey, it must have looked almost bleak.

Behind and above the house a warren of streets wrapped itself tightly around the crag on which Lewes castle stood. Compared to residences within the town walls, Southover House (later known as Southover Grange) had a generous garden and was on a comfortable scale. The rooms were built around a double-height panelled hall, off which a handsome oak staircase ascended by several turns to the first floor. Above was a range of attic bedrooms with dormer windows. The arrangements were not unlike those at Wotton, although on a smaller scale. The household must have had an exceptionally warm atmosphere; Jane Evelyn who, like her siblings, often visited the elderly couple afterwards, wrote that she had been 'made wondrous much of both by my grandfather and grandmother'.[23]

Very close to the house was Southover Free School, founded more than a century earlier by Agnes Morley.[24] There, in 1631, Evelyn began his formal education. He periodically complained that his schooling had been deficient but the Free School was well regarded, good enough for the son of the leading local puritan, Robert Morley of Glynde, whose son, Harbert (or Herbert) Morley, four years older than Evelyn, became a friend.[25] Another was the pedantic Robert Heath, with whom Evelyn corresponded for years – usually in Latin or Italian.

Richard Evelyn intended that the twelve-year-old should attend Eton – 'better to be unborn than untaught' was his maxim – but John was alarmed by the school's disciplinarian regime and opposed the idea, presumably supported by his grandparents. He claimed he later regretted his decision but the telling point in the episode is the respect accorded to his wishes. Whatever the educational limitations of a small provincial day school, its administration was certainly much gentler than that of the great public school.[26] By now his father suspected (no doubt correctly) that life at Southover was not particularly rigorous. Richard Evelyn had chosen Eton, at least partly, to wean his son away 'from my fondnesse of my too indulgent Grand-mother'. But it was too late; his step-grandparents' household, regardless of the fact that neither was actually a blood relative, was home. After a visit to Wotton in October 1631, Evelyn realised that it was the first time his parents had ever seen all their children together under the same roof.

His schoolmaster for those seven years, Dr Edward Snatt, seems to have been a light-hearted character. Evelyn's sister Jane commented that John would not 'want for mirth' when travelling back to London with him. In later years, the Evelyns remained in touch with him and his family, even helping them financially, and Evelyn regularly sent him his new publications. Snatt's son William, like his father, also a churchman and an enthusiastic grower of fruit trees, wrote in 1668: 'if the dead have any knowledge of affairs here below, your greatly obliging kindness to the necessitous son cannot but be hugely acceptable to the defunct father'.[27]

In the guidance John Evelyn offered his grandson Evelyn admitted that the regime at Eton had changed a great deal since his day, offering 'something above that of most ordinary Country Gents who commonly unlearne and abolish all they had learn'd at schole, university, &c'. Since he considered that his own education had been deficient, in reaction he had overburdened his children with learning and directives. Now he was eager that his (Etonian) grandson and even Jack's as yet unborn children benefit from his experience. Their studies should extend well beyond the confines of the classic Aristotelian subject matter, 'the so long domineering methods and jargon of the schools' as he described it elsewhere, and embrace those topics 'more for use & life than speculation onely', such as natural philosophy, mathematics, anatomy, medicine and chemistry.[28]

Aged ten, Evelyn began to keep a journal of sorts, the genesis of his diary 'in imitation of what I had seen my Father do'. The almanac entries were later amended, deleted and expanded.[29] At this time he combined distant child-hood memories with new entries on major events, such as the plague which led to his move to Sussex, the murder of the duke of Buckingham in 1628 and the celebratory jubilee which marked the birth of the prince of Wales in 1630. Evelyn could never resist embellishing personal memories with fact.

Alongside such matters of national importance, he also recorded events such as his sister Elizabeth's wedding to Edward Darcy in the autumn of 1632. She was a good catch, with her inheritance from her grandfather and a marriage portion of £6,000. When, two years later, she died after giving birth to a daughter Elizabeth (who did not survive), she was, wrote Evelyn, freed from 'the worst of men', who had 'little deserved so excellent a person'.[30]

At Wotton, the double blow was the beginning of the end for Evelyn's mother: 'the visible cause of her indisposition proceeded from griefe'. She fell ill with a high fever and in September the children were summoned to her deathbed, whence she dispensed pious advice and embraced them one by one. She also sent for her servants, who were 'infinitely affect[ed]'. Despite the attentions of three doctors over several weeks and the application of Sir Sanders Duncomb's 'celebrated & famous powder', she died on 29 September 1635, aged thirty-seven, after twenty-two years of marriage.

Eleanor Evelyn was buried near her daughter in 'our Dormitory', as Evelyn called it, at the north-east corner of Wotton parish church. The interment was at night, reducing the numbers of mourners, 'but with no meane Ceremony'.[31] She had asked that money be spent on the poor rather than on her funeral since, Evelyn surmised, 'she feared, God had not a little punish'd her, for the pomp, and expense of my Sisters'. But the real extravagance (some £1,000) had occurred during her husband's year as high sheriff of Surrey and Sussex in 1633–4, for which he had dug deep into the family's pockets to support a huge retinue and pay for the prodigious entertainments required. Evelyn argued that his father was simply doing what was expected of him, but the recent tendency had been to reduce the trappings of office, bringing the honoured position within the means of a wider range of rural gentry.[32]

After his mother's funeral, Evelyn returned to Lewes and Southover Free School, accompanied by his younger brother Richard, as she had requested. George, educated at Guildford Grammar School, had by this time been at Oxford for a year, matriculating at Trinity College in October 1634. His education reflected his position as eldest son and heir, representing the Evelyns of Wotton on a wider stage. Central to his children's education was Richard Evelyn's emphasis upon his family's duty; George prayed that God might bless their studies 'that hereafter we may be beneficiall to our Countrey'.[33] When he wrote to ask his father for money, since they were performing a play – 'an occasion of expense to me by reason of friends which come' – he promised not to 'consume my money idly, but uppon good grounds'. Richard Evelyn sent £2 but cautioned his heir to be 'carefull of your behavyer, for you are in a publicke place and many eyes are uppon you'. He warned him not to fall victim to drink and flattery, and encouraged him to study hard, which 'will doo you good when other things will faile'. George wrote in a careful hand and, on occasion, in a literary style. A letter after his mother's death is interspersed with lengthy quotes from Horace.[34]

George reported that 'Mr Outred desireth me to study the Mathematickes for he saith twill doe me much good'. William Oughtred, the greatest mathematician of his day who invented the 'x' sign for multiplication and the slide rule, had the living at Albury, dividing his time between Surrey and rooms provided for him at Arundel House in London, in return for tutoring the earl of Arundel's second son, William Howard. George, no academic, was finding the subject 'a hard studdy in initio but afterwards it wilbe very pleasant when one comes to the knowledge of them'. At college, a Fellow was helping him; they would start with arithmetic, and then progress to geometry and astronomy.[35]

At Christmas 1635 his father wrote to tell John that he would soon be joining his brother at university: 'I would willingly have you goe this year the Candelmas before he comes awaye for he may doe you much good at your first coming & you will have much benefitt.' With three sons born at convenient intervals from one another, each could assist the next. Studying hard, Evelyn's father wrote, would enable him to get sooner to university, 'a joye to me & a credit to your selfe'. Richard Evelyn was still worried about his son's penchant for art since 'painting & such like things will doe you noo good heereafter'. If he wanted to continue with 'studyes of Limning' then he should wait until he settled at Oxford, 'till they may doe you lesse hurt in your study & be more proper for you'. He ended his letter with domestic advice, perhaps feeling that his motherless sons needed guidance. He, Richard and Dick Hunt, their servant, must order themselves new suits for which he had already sent the material, although the buttons, silk and trim had been forgotten. They must keep their clothes clean and 'play the good husbands & laye the old bye till winter'; after his recent heavy expenditure, economy was a priority.[36]

Richard Evelyn also entered his sons for the Bar. On 17 February 1636 John and George Evelyn were admitted to the Middle Temple, the former 'though absent and as yet at Schoole'.[37] Evelyn later recalled that George entered 'as gent: of the best quality did, tho' with no intention to study the Law as a Profession'.[38] In old age, Evelyn pointed his grandson's own (as yet unborn) sons towards 'some honest course ... having reguard to there Inclynations, be it Law, physick, Merchand or the Church'. He told his own son that he had nothing but scorn for 'those Gentlemen (of what state or fortune soever) that take not to some calling or other, or at least fit themselves for it, if there be occasion'.[39]

This was the moment when Evelyn chose his motto, *Omnia explorate, meliora retinete*, writing it and the date on the cover of a grammar book.[40] From then on, every volume he owned, every manuscript or bundle of notes he drafted, would bear these ringing words, evidence of his life's mission to grasp the known and knowable. Later he sometimes added a pentacle, the five-pointed star that came to acquire such personal significance for him.[41]

By Easter 1637 Richard Evelyn had decided that John should go up to Oxford at Whitsun, marking the end of the long contented years of his childhood and early youth. He had lived in Lewes for almost twelve years. The regularity with which Evelyn returned afterwards to his step-grandparents in Lewes and the continued contact with Snatt are testament to his strong attachment. Richard Evelyn thanked Newton for 'your love & kindness always to my children'.[42]

Expense was a constant worry. In his third year George had spent £30 alone on two suits, 'one . . . a blacke satin doublett and black cloth breeches, the other a white satin doublett and scarlett hoase'. He reassured his father that he had otherwise been extremely frugal – 'I have spent none of it in riot or toyes' – but he needed another £6. The fine tailoring was probably in honour of the king and queen's visit in late September 1636, with their cousins, the exiled elector palatine Frederick Henry, and his brother Rupert. They were guests of Archbishop Laud, chancellor of Oxford University since 1629. George described the occasion, the dignitaries in their robes of scarlet 'and 60 other townsmen all in blacke satin doubletts and in old fashion jacketts'. There were speeches and presentations, a Bible for the king, Camden's *Britannia* for the queen and 'Croke's Politicks' for the prince. Scholars lined the street, arranged according to their degrees, as the party headed to Christ Church, the most elite of colleges and a royal foundation. There were church services, an honorary degree for Prince Rupert, numerous plays (one judged too solemn and obscure for the court audience) and ceremonial banquets.[43] Laud's Canterbury quadrangle at St John's College was inaugurated. The event was orchestrated to show the strength of the monarchy, Charles I having ruled without Parliament since 1629, and of Laud's church. Oxford was Laud's fiefdom, and his dominance over the king was sowing the seeds of catastrophe.

George undertook to find his serious younger brother a suitable tutor. A university tutor stood effectively *in loco parentis* to the student, taking responsibility for his behaviour, religious observance, education and even spending money. The situation offered an opportunity to forge contacts with influential families who might, in the future, have patronage to offer, such as livings in their gift or travelling tutorships to France or Italy. The son of the recent high sheriff of Surrey and Sussex was a good catch.

At Trinity, the Evelyns had already discounted George Bathurst, whose younger brother Ralph, tipped for eminence, had neither time nor space to tutor more students. The elder brother was an embryologist and mathematician who tended to put the modern before the ancient, which was not to George Evelyn's liking. 'Of Logicke and humanity he litile readeth which I know to be true, for what I have gott of either of them hath beene by my owne industrie.'[44] Evelyn was later mortified to realise that he had been denied access to a broader curriculum including the natural sciences, because of his brother's prejudice, so typical of the prevailing view. Edward Hyde, the future Lord Chancellor Clarendon, warned his youngest son's tutor Seth Ward, 'not to infuse any Mathematics into him, for fear they should render him unfit to be a Politician'.[45] Even in the late 1660s the inquiring lawyer and pioneering autobiographer, Roger North, at Cambridge, found that the 'New Philosofy was a sort of heresie'.[46] English conservatism and philistinism, as well as religious scruples, fought the new sciences and Lorenzo Magalotti, when visiting London in his capacity as secretary to a Florentine scientific academy, found it 'prejudicial' in London 'to pass for a philosopher and mathematician'. A widow of whom the personable Italian had hopes was told (by a rival) that he was one such, 'and it was as so much poison to me, for from that time on I was considered a platonic lover'.[47]

Conventional Aristotelian education was defined by the formal 'schools' of Rhetoric, Greek and Logic. The study of Divinity was undertaken in the college chapel. Considering, later in life, the deficiencies of the old academic regime Evelyn wholeheartedly agreed with the philosopher John Locke's dismissal of rhetoric and the schools 'so fruitlessly retain'd in Universities'. He had not even been taught Greek well, admitting his 'owne defects in the Greeke tongue and knowledge of its usefulnesse'.[48] Yet, given his tenacity, these obstacles were to prove the grit in Evelyn's oyster shell.

The tutor finally chosen for him was George Bradshaw of Balliol, 'well spoken of in the University'. But although Evelyn later learned that he was 'a person of disloyal Principles' he appeared 'far otherwise whilst I was his pupil', even if he was not a very stimulating intellectual guide.[49] Letters between his father and Bradshaw, prior to Evelyn's matriculation, were typical of those between any parent and teacher, not meant for the eye of the student. The tutor reassures his father that he will live under his own roof 'for the better preventing of ill companye'. At academically conventional Balliol (which had until recently been a notoriously unruly college) the 'government', assured Bradshaw, is now so good that he can safely enter as a Fellow Commoner, a more lenient and privileged status, at a cost of £5 extra, payable in books or plate. Bishop Laud's new statutes regulated all students rigorously in their personal, religious and academic behaviour. When the sixteen-year-old Evelyn matriculated on 19 May 1637 and was admitted Fellow Commoner to Balliol College, the Master was the largely absentee Dr Parkhurst, a royal chaplain.[50] Conscientious Evelyn hoped to learn there 'all that I had neglected or but perfunctorily gaind'. George told his father he was looking forward to his brother's company and promised to encourage his studies but left soon after, before taking his degree, at the time an expensive and largely unnecessary process. He passed his books and linen on to John.

Although several of the natural philosophers Evelyn came to know from the mid-1650s onwards were his contemporaries at university, he remains surprisingly silent about his Oxford years and companions. We probably glimpse him, anonymous (but identifiable) as one of Walter Charleton's fellow students, 'discoursing freely and calmly of some Argument or other in Philosophy', but in his writings he hardly alludes to his university years, as if revealing their details would detract from the crucial contacts and experiences that he obtained abroad afterwards.[51] Fortunately, in view of his tutor's short-comings, Evelyn found a mentor at Balliol. James Thicknesse, 'then a Young man of the Foundation, afterwards fellow of the house', would become a trav-elling companion and close friend. His 'learned and friendly Conversation' largely replaced the desultory attentions of Bradshaw.[52] The conventions of male friendship were set within the formal framework of kinship, patronage and intellectual fellowship, but the tone of Thicknesse's letters, warm and bantering, speaks of familiarity and mutual understanding.[53]

Evelyn certainly bore no resemblance to Dr John Earle's caricature of the privileged university student who 'endures not to be mistaken for a scholar', spends brief periods reading 'some short history' with his tutor, and when in the library 'studies arms and books of honour, and turns a gentleman critick in pedigrees'.[54] Undergraduates were judged by 'disputation', so that a successful student needed debating skills and powers of oratory. Obadiah Walker, a contemporary, considered that such formal argument brings 'a ques-tion to a point, and discovers the very center and knot of the difficulty'.[55] Evelyn's first experience, an alarming baptism of fire for a boy of hardly seven-teen, came in December 1637: 'I offerd at my first exercise in the Hall, and answered myne Opponent: and upon the 11th following declaymed in the Chapell before the Master, Fellows, and Scholars according to the Custome. The 15th after, I first of all Oppos'd in the Hall.'[56] Apart from these oral skills, the ambitious student displayed his learning in a commonplace book: as Francis Bacon put it, 'a Substantiall and Learned digest of Common-Places is a Solid and a good aide to memory'.[57] The amassing of pertinent material from ancient Greek philosophers to modern thinkers and divines was an essential mental underpinning and Evelyn was soon collecting such precious nuggets, as he continued to do throughout his life.

As a freshman with more than average interest in his surroundings, Evelyn explored Oxford thoroughly but, on writing up the diary later, could find no record of what he had seen. The town he grew to know so well was mostly stone-built (with timber framing beneath), a labyrinth of streets fronted by gabled houses, the medieval college quadrangles tucked away behind great wooden gates. Recent expansion in the number of scholars required new colleges to be built and existing ones to be extended. Their jewels were the libraries and chapels, many recently embellished by Laud. Typically, Evelyn listened to sermons in his college chapel now resplendent with new paving and stained glass, its golden lectern a crowned eagle. In 1621 Henry Danvers, earl of Danby, had funded the creation of a Physic Garden, the walls and handsome classical entrance gates of which were completed by 1633. But behind them the grounds remained bare, for all the money had gone before they could be planted. The first curator, Jacob Boburt, was appointed in 1642.

Evelyn's progress at university was monitored closely. Edward Snatt wrote to Richard Evelyn that he was delighted to hear that John was settled, while William Newton was impressed that he troubled to write to his grandparents since 'between young & old there is little . . . that way'. Newton reminded the young scholar of the importance of his studies: 'now is the time for you to gett learning & goodness.' As for religion, if it 'be not gotten in youth, it is for the most parte, not gotten'. There were worries in Lewes about the lavish trappings of college chapels: 'as it was once said they had wooden chalices but golden ministers anciently, but now they have wooden ministers but golden chalices, so it may be said of your university, that you have glorious buildings and outsides far beyond those of old, but not such sound scholars as heretofore.' Newton counselled him to 'care not for flaunting preachers, but resort to such plain teachers where the hope of grace may be wrought in one's heart'.[58]

Despite his years in his grandparents' puritan household, Evelyn was solidly Church of England. Having taken his first communion in the college chapel (although he was not confirmed until December 1639), he found the established Church 'in the greatest splendor it had ever ben since the Reformation which made it envied, without any just cause'.[59] Behind the glitter, it was splintering: Archbishop Laud's Arminianism, with its emphasis on ceremony and rejection of the harsher doctrines of Calvinism (from which it had broken away), was distrusted by many, who saw it as Catholicism creeping in through the back door.

The clearest indication of the pull of his grandparents' practice against the Anglicanism of Wotton and Oxford comes in a letter written in 1651. His cousin Thomas Keightley was on the brink of conversion to Catholicism and Evelyn strenuously tried to dissuade him, offering his own experience. Keightley knew 'what my Education hath bin; and how freely I have lived from compulsion, though I have wrestled with infinite temptations, enjoyed much Liberty, frequent in doubts, and reluctances as to matters of Conscience'. He was, therefore, well placed to advise that no one should take 'their Religion on Trust'.[60]

His father enjoyed hearing from his son but was not happy for him to go to dancing school; dancing, like drawing, was a frivolous occupation for which he did not have time, although he was allowed to take music lessons. Evelyn needed no parental admonitions about drunkenness (there were several hundred alehouses in Oxford), gambling, womanising or keeping bad company. The worst that happened to him was a tumble from a table on which he was standing to watch a comedy, which lost him several weeks of study. Bradshaw's messages to his family were largely to reassure them but he toed the party line: 'As for his drawing and painting I shall be care[ful] to see him use it as his recreation, not as his businesse.'[61]

At the end of his first university year, Evelyn's tutor lent him a horse to get home quickly and, in words bound to give satisfaction in Surrey, reported that Evelyn was 'of a very stayd and studious disposition, nor can I finde ought to dislike or accuse of him'.[62] Every summer Evelyn undertook a tour of part of his own country, as well as family visits to Lewes, providing evidence of a catholic taste in architecture which ranged from military structures to Gothic churches. In 1638, he and his brother Richard went to Portsmouth to admire the fortifications ('a greate rarity in England [in] those Halcion days') before crossing to the Isle of Wight. They returned to Wotton via the 'faire Cathedrall' at Chichester.[63]

Evelyn was finding university life alarmingly expensive. After a year, his father gave him responsibility for his own funds but suggested that he remain up for the vacation, 'for now is the tyme to doe yourselfe good . . . you will finde the benefitt heereafter'.[64] He was always welcome to come home for a change of air, for as his father wrote, 'I would not have you think my love or affection are any whitt lessen'd.' In January 1640 he heard that Richard was coming to join him at Balliol.[65] Just as George had helped him, he now helped his younger brother settle in and shared his lodgings and books.

He had more in common with Richard, who was more ambitious and intellectually adventurous than George. During the civil wars John's carefree situation on the Continent would contrast with Richard's responsibilities at home, and bring tensions into their relationship. But at university, respectively aged eighteen and sixteen years old, they re-established their close childhood ties, first nurtured under their grandparents' roof in Sussex. They sat together at table and John bought Richard a plate engraved with the family arms. Roger North worried about brothers entering the same profession, 'because one will certainly overtop, and like over-forward plants drip and mortify the other', but his family, just like the Evelyns, offered ample proof of the strength of the bonds between brothers in their formative years.[66]

At Wotton, Richard Evelyn senior's health was failing. He began 1640 by adjusting his will, lest there be no male issue in the family, perhaps foreseeing the threat of civil war.[67] By March he was so ill that he called his sons home from Oxford. John was considering coming down for good, encouraged by George. 'You cannot imagine Sir what an extasie of joy I harbour in me . . . my father's resolutions are to send for you at Easter, this your tutor can dictate to you.' George also told him of his forthcoming marriage, which he must keep secret. Mary Caldwell 'was a match desired of my mother . . . and now of my father', and so he had the satisfaction of fulfilling the wishes of both the dead and the living.[68]

In April 1640 it was Evelyn's turn to quit Oxford before graduation, an easy decision since his time at university had been 'of very small benefit to me'. Having settled Richard in, he was ready to leave. He joined George at the Middle Temple in London, where they saw the elaborate procession marking the opening of the Short Parliament on 13 April, 'the King circl'd with his royal diademe, and the affections of his People'. By the time he had moved into his rooms in early June, the brief return to parliamentary rule was over, unsustainable in the face of the king's obduracy.

Their 'very handsome apparrtiment' was in Hall Court, high up on the fourth of five floors and offering views towards the river, over the City and probably to the fields north of London. The building, with shops below, had been recently constructed on the site of some run-down premises at considerable expense.[69] Richard Evelyn spent £145 'to purchasse our present lives, and assignements afterwards' but Evelyn did not warm to the law and his frequent visits to his ailing father at Wotton proved disruptive.

In May 1640, George and Mary Caldwell were married and 'part of the nuptials' celebrated at Albury. Thomas Howard, 2nd earl of Arundel, had recently bought the Surrey estate, just five miles from Wotton, from the Duncombes, the bride's relatives. Richard Evelyn had been a trustee in the transaction. Albury would come to play a highly significant role in Evelyn's life.

Richard Evelyn's illness was a series of crises. In September he was well enough to take the waters at Bath but an acute episode sent the brothers rushing west after him. He returned to Wotton, sick but still able to move around the rooms. In honour of the new Mrs George Evelyn, the house was being smartened up, there were painters and upholsterers at work, and hangings were fitted.[70] The changes added interior comfort and charm to a house that had become run down, but more extensive renovation could not be considered while George's invalid father was alive.

From the Temple, Evelyn observed the instability in London, the 'frequent disorders, and greate insolencies'. In October the king appeared to reassert his tattered command, riding through London in a stupendous cavalcade, but by November the Long Parliament had opened, and the monarch's authority, after a decade of high-handed misrule, was ebbing fast. Perhaps somewhat out of touch now, Richard Evelyn expressed himself pleased that Parliament 'goes on so well, god graunt it maye . . . that he [the king] may have the glory of it & wee the benefitt'. He sent his son £5 with a caution. 'Money is hard to come by . . . be carefull, how you disburse it.'[71] It was the last letter Evelyn ever received from his father.

Richard Evelyn died on Christmas Eve 1640, an 'excellent man, and indulgent parent'. The funeral was held at night, as his wife's had been, and he was interred beside her in the mausoleum at Wotton. The practice of nocturnal burial was growing in popularity with the gentry, in an effort to keep the ceremony more intimate and less extravagant. As former sheriff of the county, his funeral could have been a grandiose public event, far beyond the pocket or inclination of his mourning family. The candles and torches required for night burials might have suggested Catholic ritual but his position put him beyond suspicion.[72]

'Thus we were bereft of both our Parents in a period when we most of all stood in neede of their Counsell and assistance,' wrote Evelyn. The young man felt unprepared for what was ahead, and later looked back on his 'raw, vaine, uncertaine and very unwary inclination' when faced by the 'most prodigious hazards, that ever the Youth of England saw'.[73] But were he considering a literary future, Thicknesse's response to a play he had shown him was hardly encouraging; he carefully avoided comment. Later, Pepys thought Evelyn's plays were 'not as he conceits them' and perhaps even the author himself came to realise that they were facile: his unperformed, unpublished comedy *The Originals* includes the self-mocking line 'any pert boy who's been to university, passed an Easter term in town & a month in Tunbridge, can turn up a play'.[74]

George asked him for an epitaph for their father's monument, which was much more Evelyn's style, and was impressed by the results: 'I cannot but admire the smoothness & worth of your Penn.' George's responsibilities now lay firmly in Surrey and he quickly began to find the countryside in winter and the unmitigated company of their neighbours depressing.[75] As the inheritor of Wotton, he was anchored there at a time of unprecedented uncertainty for the landed gentry.

John inherited £4,000, equal to the value of Wotton, as well as his mother's land at South Malling which he could oversee adequately from London. His guardian was a cousin, Robert Hatton, an executor of Richard Evelyn's will and a sergeant at law (a senior barrister), who later became treasurer of the Middle Temple, the highest office of the Inn.[76] Richard inherited Baynards, near Ewhurst. Their sister also became a woman of property, inheriting a farm in Sussex and £2,000. She asked John to help her find a trustworthy, neatly dressed person with clear handwriting (her own was unusually educated) to deal with 'those Littell rents & monies I shall have'. In her mid-twenties and unmarried, she said that if the candidate could teach her to sing and play the organ 'I shall like him much the better'. She would pay a salary of £10.[77]

They all missed their father's guidance and support. Forty years later Evelyn wrote to his own son, who was showing signs of becoming the sort of idle, drunken country gentleman, passing his time in 'wretched emptinesse', that he most despised. There were, by then, several of his kind in the family. Evelyn reminded him that 'my Father dyed when I was hardly twenty, before I could either have the experience or the Counsel which is given you'.[78] But, arguably, Richard Evelyn's early death brought his son more freedom and certainly more wealth than he might otherwise have enjoyed.

CHAPTER 2

The Fruits of Travel

In the summer of 1641 every institution in England was under threat. What had started as angry rumblings against Charles I's religious and political misjudgements now turned into confrontation. The Scots were on a war footing. The earl of Strafford's execution for treason in May sounded alarm bells (a 'fatal Stroake, which sever'd the wisest head in England').[1] Continental Europe was hardly peaceful but it was still navigable.

Evelyn was a fervent disciple of the philosopher and statesman Francis Bacon and echoed his emphasis on the crucial importance of wide personal experience in youth 'the seed-time in which the foundation of all noble things is to be laid' especially travel, which 'must crowne all'.[2] Evelyn's own departure from England was, however, propelled by the 'ill & Ominos face of the Publique at home'.[3] Hearing of his plans, James Thicknesse sent him 'Mr Stoakes booke of vaulting', as a distraction and reminder of their time in Oxford. William Stokes's illustrated handbook of esoteric horseplay showed young blades leaping over their mounts at implausible angles.

Evelyn knew it was not enough for a son of the nobility to 'be taught to dance, and to ride, to speak languages and wear his clothes with a good grace', but that he should also learn about 'men, customs, courts and disciplines', such is 'the fruit of travel'.[4] Bacon had taught him that the traveller must be well prepared and have a programme of learning in mind, 'for else young men shall be hooded'.[5]

When John Milton received 'the melancholy intelligence . . . of the civil commotions in England' in Naples in 1638, his own pleasurable continental journey suddenly seemed self-indulgent. He did not rush home but he was sensitised by the extremes of freedom and autocratic rule that he saw around him.[6] Evelyn, more gently awakened by his father's careful guidance, realised that privileges abroad led to responsibilities at home. An educated member of the gentry must contribute towards the wider good of the state, especially

2 Horseplay in Leiden, engraved by W. Swanenburg, 1610. An esoteric art for the
nobility but not for Evelyn.

now; this was Cicero's counsel when he reproached 'a Gentleman for being
solicitous about his Fish-ponds, when the Common-wealth was in danger'.[7]

But for the moment there was little for Evelyn to do at home, either in
Surrey or Sussex. As a second son he was relieved of the heavy responsibilities of primogeniture, in particular the maintenance of the family estate. But
since his older sister would not inherit and George might die at any time, this
could prove no more than a temporary respite. For Evelyn, approaching his
majority at a moment when every institution in the country was threatened
by change, dissolution or even revolution, foreign travel offered pause,
instructive distraction and, potentially, an eventual sense of purpose. Evelyn
recalled later that his guardian had encouraged him to go, hoping that he
would build up or at least preserve 'for my Elder Brother, as my owne Sake,
the little fortune that I had, lying mingled with his in the parliaments quarters & neere London'.[8] The journey might also offer glancing military
engagements, enough at any rate for a reluctant soldier like John Evelyn.
Troops were bivouacked across northern Europe, a reminder of the interminable war between Protestants and Catholics that had been spluttering on
since 1621. Bored English officers in their fortified encampments were always
happy to welcome passing volunteers, for social rather than military reasons.

Evelyn's journey to the Low Countries was neither a prolonged exile nor a Grand Tour, but rather a leave of absence. But why did he choose such a relatively unusual destination for an English gentleman? The path to France and Italy and, in politically clement times, to Spain was comparatively well trodden. A visit to the United Provinces and the Spanish Netherlands suggested an interest (or closer involvement) in trade and intellectual, political and religious matters. An explanation lay in his grandfather's extensive trade links with the enviably prosperous states across the North Sea, the immediate backdrop to his childhood.

For Evelyn mainland Europe represented a 'terrestial cabinet' from which he should make a considered selection. As Bacon said: 'if you will have a young man to put his travel into a little room, and in short time to gather much, this you must do.'[9] The 'divided Provinces' formed an ideal introduction to and 'synopsis' of the rest of Europe, from which to absorb that 'Ethicall and Morall part of Travel which embellisheth a Gentleman . . . [leading] to the profit, and Emolument of his own Country at his Return'.[10] Evelyn was also aware that his Surrey neighbour Thomas Howard, earl of Arundel, was heading in that direction and dreamed of joining his train.

As captain general of the king's forces in Scotland, Arundel had overseen their humiliating climbdown when faced with the Covenanters in 1638–9 and now, in spring 1641, as high steward, he was presiding over his close friend Strafford's trial, opening the wounds caused by his own father's trial and execution. At the same time, as master of protocol at court, he was responsible for housing the young prince of Orange and his suite of some four hundred attendants, come to claim the hand of the nine-year-old Mary, the princess royal.[11] The ceremonies attending their match provided a grotesque counterpoint to the trial, at which (as Evelyn later mused) a man was sentenced to death for transgressing a law that had not yet been passed and that was almost immediately repealed. The earl's next painful duty was to accompany the terminally ill Marie de Médicis, the queen mother, to Flushing.

Denied his dukedom of Norfolk and approaching sixty, Arundel was preparing to leave the political stage. In June 1641 Evelyn sat for his portrait, a parting gift for his sister Jane, and it may have been then that the idea of joining the earl overseas emerged, in a studio at Arundel House. Hendrick van der Borcht the Younger was a refugee from the Thirty Years War, a protégé of the earl who had been sent to Italy to learn at the knee of Arundel's agent. Since his return to England in late 1637, Van der Borcht had been curator of his patron's collections but continued to carry out his own commissions and deal in works of art. Working alongside him at Arundel House was

Wenceslaus Hollar, also rescued from the turbulence of central Europe by Arundel, who knew the Low Countries equally well. A little sketchbook of Hollar's drawings, including some of Amsterdam and Leiden, contains Evelyn's inscription, dated 1641.[12] Between them, Van der Borcht and Hollar were capable of pointing Evelyn towards everything that might interest him there. The sittings must have served as planning sessions for his prospective tour.

The finished portrait shows Evelyn, aged almost twenty-one, in a half-length seated pose. There are two versions. In one the solemn, long-nosed sitter awkwardly holds a drawing, and a landscape can be glimpsed behind him, while in the other he is indoors with a book. His hair (his own) is long and dark, falling around a pale and intense face, brightened only by the scalloped lace of his shirt, which is covered by a simple cloak. In the outdoor portrait, he is dressed in a fine slashed satin outfit. The attributes chosen point, respectively, to his love of art and of the life of the mind. John Evelyn was already known in his family as 'the Philosopher'; Dr Johnson defines a philosopher as 'A man deep in knowledge, either moral or natural'.

The bookish Evelyn had vague but not inconsiderable ambitions which a link to the Arundel 'court' – a microcosm of European intellectual and artistic life – would serve well. When younger, the earl had been patron to dozens of scholars and artists, among them Peter Paul Rubens, Anthony van Dyck, Franciscus Junius, Henry Peacham, William Camden and Inigo Jones. He was, through a network of agents and his own discerning eye and intellect, an unmatched collector of antiquities, books and manuscripts, natural curiosities and Old Master paintings and drawings, many of which were also engraved by Wenceslaus Hollar. Evelyn may have already begun to collect his work. Many years later, Hollar turned to him when attempting to be confirmed as 'ichnographer royal', citing 'his kindness whilst in the service of his late patron, Thomas Earl of Arundel'.[13]

Arundel House, a rambling Tudor Thames-side mansion, more village than palace, provided accommodation for men such as Hollar, Van der Borcht and William Oughtred, and acted as an informal academy, a meeting place of like minds which stretched out across the English Channel and back into the early seventeenth century, with Latin serving as its scholarly *lingua franca*.[14] Evelyn, after the frustrations of his incomplete formal education, was irresistibly drawn to this world of fresh intellectual possibilities.

On 16 July 1641 his new life began. Evelyn and John Caryll, a cousin of his sister-in-law Mary and of Oughtred who also, since 1610, had had the living at Albury, arrived at Gravesend armed with their passes.[15] Calm weather left them idling for several days and, passing the time locally, they went to Chatham. In the dockyard was the jewel of the fleet, the *Sovereign of the Seas*, double the tonnage of any previous ship of the English navy and built for an astounding £40,000. The prodigious vessel, 'for burthen, defense and ornament the richest that ever spread cloth before the Wind', was built using taxes raised without parliamentary sanction but legalised by the judiciary. Peter Pett's great gaudy ship epitomised the profligacy and high-handedness in financial affairs that would soon bring the monarchy down ('it cost his Majestie the affections of his Subjects,' Evelyn would write), and symbolised the tensions between the king and Parliament, just as Strafford's execution had shown the frailty of English justice under political pressure.[16] Then, suddenly, the wind got up and Evelyn and Caryll were on their way to Flushing, sailing on a Dutch vessel protected by a flotilla of smaller craft. Sporadic hostilities between the Dutch and the Spanish, the tail end of the Thirty Years War which dragged on until 1648, put every vessel at risk.

Evelyn's account of the Netherlands, the United Provinces and Flanders, is largely his own. The emphases point to his interests and preoccupations at a time in his life for which there is very little other available evidence. As the scholarly editor of the diary, Esmond de Beer, discovered, the majority of Evelyn's entries relating to his travels depended on existing or, in some cases, later topographical accounts, reflecting the fact that the diary was written decades later, guided by brief notes, almanac entries or correspondence. Sometimes Evelyn reveals a source by repeating errors or describing buildings or works of art which were not there at the time he visited or, alternatively, in repeated coincidences between a printed account and his own. De Beer believed that the main bound volume of the diary, the 'Kalendarium', was not begun until after 1660 while more than two-thirds dated from around 1680. But in the passages relating to this journey, the heightened language and the close and original observations show Evelyn's arrival in Holland to be one of the turning points of his life, his first taste of mainland Europe and an introduction to an enlightened nation which had built itself upon merchant enterprise.[17]

Novice travellers inevitably encountered many practical difficulties – the frustrations involved in gaining passes between one jurisdiction and the next, the avoidance of areas where hostile forces were engaged and the simple difficulty of obtaining money from home. Bills of exchange had to be collected at a given place and time, and a broken appointment or even a misspelled name might force the traveller to double back or to press on in the hope of finding a fellow countryman to provide emergency funds.

But if they were apprehensive, Evelyn and Caryll were reassured by their first impression of Flushing, which, although a frontier post, was 'pretty and neate'. From the moment Evelyn set foot on Dutch soil, he found the

architecture of the Low Countries a revelation, in style and emphasis so
unlike that of England. Every town had a handsome 'state-house' and their
squares focused as much upon commercial weigh-houses, merchants' premises and exchanges for goods and products as on churches, almshouses and
hospitals. Material prosperity brought with it civic, moral and religious
responsibilities for the mercantile elite. The administration was in the hands
of city councils headed by regents.

Across the United Provinces the affluent citizens of the republic had
rejected the mongrel architectural style of the previous century, which
combined the mullions and crow-stepped gables of medieval northern
Europe with the ornamental flourishes of the Flemish Renaissance. Their
new buildings were symmetrical and classical, adapted from those in the
pages of pirated editions of the treatises of Vignola, Serlio and, above all,
Scamozzi. It was a confident architecture mirroring an intelligent merit-
ocracy, not a jaded autocracy. By contrast, England could boast scarcely a
handful of classical buildings.

Each town they passed through was a model of urbanity; streets, canal sides
and public walkways along the walls were well laid out, shaded by ubiquitous
lime trees. Even the country roads were decently made and paved, unlike the
muddy, rutted tracks of England. En route to Dordrecht, Evelyn's wagon
driver, seeing that his passenger, unaccustomed to travelling fast (at about ten
miles an hour) on a hard surface, had developed a painful stitch, stopped to
minister to his disorder by pressing a lump of couch grass to his side, under
his doublet. It worked and the idea for an ingenious compress may still lie
somewhere among Evelyn's long lists of efficient and useful medicinal recipes.

The landscape that met the travellers on arrival was dotted with the ruins
of settlements that had been overrun by the sea, then revealed again as the
land was reclaimed from the water. The degree to which these people had
manifestly shaped and constructed their own country, using a panoply of
machinery (horse mills, pumps, Archimedean screws, buckets and water
wheels) all devoted to the task of drainage and earth-moving, was extraordinary to English eyes. The same spirit of invention was on show in private
gardens, with ingenious hydraulics and musical apparatus. Even quite small
country houses or villas boasted remarkable gardens, such as Ryswick,
belonging to the House of Orange, built in 1634.

Reaching Rotterdam, Evelyn and Caryll sought out Erasmus's birthplace
and statue, admired the principal buildings including the Bourse, the
merchants' Exchange, before taking a regular canal boat service (at walking
pace) to The Hague, via Delft, where the handsome frontage of Hendrik de
Keyser's Senate House, built in 1620, caught Evelyn's attention, with its
'stately Portico, supported with very choyce Pillars of black-marble' cut from

a single block. The classical style served the purposes of commerce and government equally.

The Hague was home to the widowed sister of the English monarch, Elizabeth, the so-called 'Winter Queen' of Bohemia who had lived there for more than twenty years. Nine years a widow, she remained in mourning for her husband Frederick, the deposed Elector Palatine. Evelyn and Caryll arrived on one of the queen's many fast days and found the presence room hung entirely in black velvet. Several of her children were there, including Princess Elizabeth, a formidable girl who corresponded with René Descartes and was the dedicatee of his *Principia Philosophiae*, and Princess Louise, an accomplished painter and pupil of Gerard Honthorst, who eventually became a Catholic nun but supported her uncle's cause as she was best able.[18] Although the queen had refused her brother's invitation to return to England, for all her studied neutrality her court soon became a marshalling yard and conduit for money and support for the royalist cause and a refuge for prominent exiles. Soon her son Prince Rupert would be the commander of the royalist cavalry. At the time of Evelyn's visit, the former lord keeper Sir John Finch was there, fleeing impeachment by Parliament over the affair of the *Sovereign of the Seas*.

At The Hague Evelyn saw (although he did not record) the finest examples of the Dutch classical school of architecture anywhere in the country, epitomised by the Mauritshuis, designed by Jacob van Campen, assisted by Pieter Post, and completed only five years earlier. Here giant pilasters, slender sash windows and restrained ornament embellished the relatively modest house of a general, a member of the ruling House of Nassau. Nearby, Constantyjn Huygens, the polymath secretary to the stadtholder, had built himself a house which, he told Rubens proudly, recalled 'l'Architecture ancienne'.

The Low Countries offered Evelyn and Caryll the opportunity to taste something of the military life, but on a field of battle that was largely quiescent. The standard form of warfare in this theatre was the siege, requiring a different form of soldiery: vigilance rather than confrontation. The two 'volunteers' joined Captain Apsley's regiment in their camp on the Maas outside the village of Gennep, where the castle had been in Spanish hands since 1636. After a two-month siege led by the stadtholder Frederick Henry, prince of Orange and leader of the United Provinces, the fortress had just fallen to the Dutch who were assisted by English and French forces. A detailed map, unsigned but dated that year, shows the lines of approach of the besiegers and the exceptional complexity of the multiple bastions and angled defences which they faced. The main body of the fortification stood on the bank of the river, opposite a lesser secondary defensive site on a tributary. The drawing is in the hand of Bernard de Gomme, the young Dutchman who under Prince Rupert's patronage became the leading military engineer in England.[19]

On arrival, Evelyn and Caryll found the men listening to thanksgiving sermons and firing their cannons in celebration. Captain Honywood, taking Apsley's command in his absence, was related by marriage to Evelyn and ensured that his duty as a night watchman was not too onerous, obliging him only to trail a pike until relieved by a company of French soldiers. During the day Evelyn rode out from an exceptionally well-appointed tent to visit interesting buildings in the locality and, ever the autodidact, to take note of the impressive fortifications and machinery, in particular the stadholder's own invention, the 'Wheele-bridg', a kind of proto-Bailey bridge. The atmosphere was demob happy, awash with relaxed English cavaliers and their ladies, cheered by 'more wine than was needful'. Later, Evelyn criticised the laxity of life in military camps, expressing his surprise that the gentry still preferred to send their sons 'to seeke their miserable fortune in the Field then in the Citty'.[20] The gunpowder-maker's grandson was a purposeful, peaceable fellow. Having witnessed 'the Confusion of Armys, and method of Seiges', Evelyn could see no point in extending his Dutch military experiment. It was stifling hot under canvas by day and the river fogs swirled in at night. After ten days, he turned his back on military life and discomfort.

His brother George's letters reminded him to buy pictures for Wotton, assuring him that he would send more bills of exchange if needed. Despite Evelyn's advice to hold off while the market was unduly inflated, George persisted: 'pray buy me a good one to hang over my Chimnie in the Dining Roome.' In fact, Evelyn found a plentiful supply (and bought several) at the annual Rotterdam market, where there were enormous numbers of 'clownish' paintings, landscapes and 'Drolleries' (presumably genre subjects) which Evelyn claimed were bought by farmers speculatively and were now being resold at considerable profit.[21]

In August George reported the king was making his way to Scotland and smallpox had returned to London. The earl of Arundel had finally left for Flanders with Marie de Médicis.[22] The queen mother had delayed so long in Kent that his countess, Alathea Howard, had gone ahead to settle in Antwerp, where the earl joined her in 1643.[23] George now told his brother that Arundel was intending to remain abroad for at least a year and to travel further afield: 'you cannot gaine a better opportunity to answer your desires & wait on him.'[24]

As Evelyn traversed the United Provinces he missed little. At a menagerie in Rotterdam he noted his impressions of an elephant and a pelican, the former remarkable for the properties of its trunk or 'proboscis', the latter for its concertinaed bill. Arriving in Amsterdam on the Sabbath, Evelyn hurried to a synagogue service. This experience of Judaic ritual intrigued him greatly, for the Jews were still prohibited from residing in England. The theologian in Evelyn observed with close interest their 'Ceremonies, Ornaments, Lamps, Law, and Scholes [which] afforded matter for my wonder and enquiry'; in the galleries above, the women kept their heads well covered.

After the service he went beyond the city walls to the Portuguese Jewish cemetery, 'a spacious field' of elaborately lettered gravestones where he noticed beneath the cracked paving of one tomb that the body was surrounded by books. Evelyn found a stick and prised several pages out through the chink in the stone, the beautifully wrought Hebrew characters still discernible though damaged by age and exposure.[25] Later he learned that such burial practices indicated a learned man or rabbi. He was impressed by a religion that so honoured its holy texts – particularly at a time when the Anglican Book of Common Prayer was under threat. The next day in Amsterdam Evelyn rang the changes with a visit to the English Reformed church.

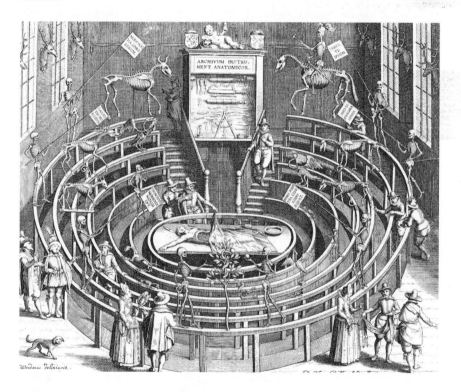

3 The anatomy theatre at Leiden University (1610). During the warmer months it became a museum of natural curiosities.

The efficiently run Dutch hospitals, workhouses and asylums would be on his mind when he was considering how to provide for sick and wounded men in his own country more than twenty years later, ironically enough during the Second Dutch War. In this admirable country it seemed that only the lepers were still poor and needy, confined on islands well away from the healthy populace and receiving alms from passing boats in floating boxes.[26]

In early September Evelyn and Caryll matriculated at the university of Leiden, reciting their names, ages, dates of birth and intended faculty. They were accepted in 'Mat. et Histor.', instructed to abide by the university's rules and regulations and issued, on payment, with a ticket. In reality, this was a practical exercise in tax avoidance; now they were 'Excise-free'.[27] Nevertheless, the university, dating from 1575, the first in the Protestant provinces, was of considerable interest to Evelyn. The anatomy school was founded in 1594, housed in the apse of a former Catholic church. Used for anatomical studies during the cool months, provided there was a supply of criminals' cadavers available for dissection, the rest of the year it served as a museum of natural rarities, which is how Evelyn saw it. Among ethnographic objects from all over the world he could admire rare Egyptian funerary arte-facts including severed limbs, the skeletons of species ranging from the whale to the spider, rare volumes devoted to plants, known as herbals, and a remark-able print collection, including Goltzius's salutary series showing the four guises of the physician – God, angel, man and devil.[28] As a testament to the medical skills available in Leiden, there was also a portrait of a peasant who had swallowed a seven-inch knife while trying to make himself vomit after a heavy meal, and who had survived the subsequent operation to remove it. The blade was displayed alongside.

Nearby was Leiden's sixteenth-century botanical garden. It offered, in a tiny compass, a perfect epitome of the natural world as then known, the plants (just catalogued) complemented by galleries of curiosities brought home from the new territories, thanks to the Dutch East India Company.

In this important university city, a breezy port on the Rhine, the most substantial new town houses stood on the Rapenburg, the main canal, the work of city architect Arent van s' Gravesande. Their impressive frontages were dominated by giant orders of pilasters, reaching from basement to eaves, with the principal rooms set high above ground level, a sensible precaution in a country at the mercy of the sea. The same man also built the Wool Hall (the city's wealth came from textiles) and its first Protestant church. This genera-tion of Dutch architects designed as if the classical treatises at their elbow were illustrated by chunky woodcuts, rather than fine engravings, as many were. Their architectural vocabulary and use of ornament was feisty, even crude; early seventeenth-century Holland was not a place for the self-effacing or the exquisite.

For a lover of the book and a devotee of print such as Evelyn, the names of many Dutch towns were synonymous with the great presses, the lifeblood of the pan-European Republic of Letters. Leiden was the home of Elsevier's printing works, the finest in Europe, while in Haarlem Evelyn tried to track down a monument to the putative father of typography, Laurence Coster. In Amsterdam he explored the book-, print- and map-sellers' area of town, visiting both Blaeu's and Hondius's establishments, at the latter admiring the 'wonderfull Imprimery, where so many Rolling, & other presses are perpetualy at worke'. (In Antwerp he bought books from Plantin's works, simply to have the name represented in his library.) It was the pulsing energy and plurality of Amsterdam – its commercial vitality making it the Hong Kong or Shanghai of its day – that overwhelmed and excited him.

Amsterdam was at the heart of mercantile Europe. Every aspect of trade in goods and knowledge was laid out before him. He wandered from shop to shop, marvelling at rare editions and atlases and the curiosities imported from Dutch territories to be seen at the headquarters of the East India Company, the Oost-Indisch Huis. There, a wider world was illuminated by 'precious spices & other rare druggs, which have set all the world together by the Eares for the possession, from both the Indies; (a Sight, not to be paralleled, or over vallued)'. Bursting from the pages of the normally reticent diary, Evelyn's voice thrills to the world suggested by Amsterdam's bookstalls and shops, offering a first taste of an unimaginably wide universe. This prodigious city, where people could worship as they pleased and 'every new-fangle [was] acceptable', demonstrated the potential for human industry, application and imagination. Amsterdam's population had expanded fivefold in the past seventy years, and had gained affluent and able new citizens from the Spanish Netherlands, the Protestants of Antwerp and Flanders. Even the very ground on which the city stood had been largely regained from the sea 'with vast Expense, & fitted for the most busy Concourse of Trafiquers, & people of Commerce, beyond any place or Mart in the world'.

In early September Evelyn visited The Hague to order a suit of armour, together with 'the harnasse of a horseman'. Perhaps this was equipment he might need to travel with Arundel. Soon after he witnessed Marie de Médicis's arrival at Dordrecht, attended by the earl. The cumbersome train was finally en route for Cologne. In view of her ill health and reputation as an interfering and extravagant liability, her reception was a sad, low-key business, as Evelyn observed, nothing 'befitting the greateness of her Person, but an universal discontent, which accompany'd that unlucky Woman whereever she went'. It was in poignant contrast to her lavish arrival at Harwich three years earlier, when the exiled French queen regent had come to visit her son-in-law and daughter attended by a court of six hundred. Since then she had been vilified, an irritant in the volatile political and religious atmosphere in which any link to the Catholic monarchies of Europe was unwelcome. Arundel appeared to have reached the end of his journey, so Evelyn's harness and suit of armour may have proved an unwarranted extravagance.

His experience of the United Provinces, brief as it was, had a great impact on Evelyn. Looking back, he considered that their achievement, without any of the natural resources taken for granted by neighbouring countries, hinged upon social and economic factors: 'their Admission of Foreigners, Increase of Hands, Encouraging Manufactures, Free, and Open Ports, Low Customes, Tolleration of Religions, Natural Frugality, and Indefatigable Industry'.[29] He wrote these perceptive words from the vantage point of the Council for Trade and Plantations and after years as a commissioner for the sick and wounded and prisoners of war, during which the Dutch had been the enemy. Nothing ever persuaded him to harbour an enmity for such an admirable nation.

The final leg of the journey took them to the provinces of Brabant and Flanders, which had been sheltering under the flag of Spain and the Habsburgs for the last fifty years. The journey involved bad weather, inadequate ports and more bureaucracy. The border was governed by the usual petty tyrants, including one who rejected Evelyn's valid pass when he refused to proffer a bribe. He threw it under the table 'and bad me try whether I could get to Antwerp without it'. Eventually Evelyn and his companion were allowed to travel between 'these two jealous States'.

After the orderly buildings of Protestant Holland, the architecture of Antwerp and the Counter-Reformation Spanish Netherlands was ebulliently Baroque. Evelyn was impressed by the principal Jesuit church, as he also was by the organisation of the Jesuit school, facilities ranging from punishment blocks for miscreants to an aviary and menagerie for pupils' amusement 'at times of remission'. Both music and mathematics were taught. Evelyn's admiration for the Jesuits' educational and intellectual achievements always vied with his implacable hatred of their proselytising, idolatry and record of persecution. He spent one evening with the Duarte family, the Portuguese Jewish musicians who became close friends of William and Margaret Cavendish when they lived in Rubens's house in the mid-1640s. Then Evelyn and Caryll liaised with Arundel, travelling in luxury from Brussels to Ghent in his coach and six.

The Spanish Netherlands equalled its northern neighbour with complex fortifications as well as harbours, dykes, canals and drainage schemes of extraordinary engineering skill and ingenuity, something Evelyn never forgot. His other abiding memory, of both countries, was the quality of the public spaces: tree-shaded walkways, such as those he had admired in Antwerp, with its 'delicious shades and walkes of stately Trees', and immaculately brick-paved streets such as the Keisersgracht in Amsterdam, which looked like 'a Citty in a Forest', with its neat, flat-fronted gabled brick houses rising above the ranks of lime trees. Even the houseboats between Antwerp and Brussels were kept beautifully: 'few houses on land enjoy'd better accommodation . . . kept so sweet and polite, as nothing could be more refreshing.'[30] After the mud and ordure of London thoroughfares, overhung by ramshackle medieval houses, these merchant cities, marshalled obediently around the banks of their canals and rivers, came as a revelation. Evelyn never forgot the orderly towns with their handsome public institutions and innumerable places of worship, reflections of an enviable sense of civic and social responsibility. Their seats of learning were fed by a vital intellectual world of print and spoken word, innovative engineering kept land and sea in equilibrium and everything was underwritten by continually growing prosperity, the fruit of a vital overseas trade.

From Ostend to Dunkirk Evelyn and Caryll travelled along the hard sandy shore and, still with Arundel, embarked for England on an ordinary packet boat. Their departure was marked by a thirteen-gun salute from the fort; they could only muster three in reply. On arrival in Dover Evelyn made straight for Canterbury. The cathedral was, as he put it later, 'now in greatest splendor', for the wonderful stained-glass windows they admired were shattered within three years, 'demolish'd by the Phanatiques'. Back again in Gravesend they took a light craft upriver, catching up with then overtaking the cumbersome water convoy carrying Earl Marshal Arundel and disembarking at two in the morning at Arundel Stairs where goodbyes were said.

The man whom the twenty-one-year-old Evelyn now considered his mentor, was the premier earl in the kingdom and the greatest patron of the age, despite his years, poor health, diminished political status and unsound finances. Arundel encouraged him, being 'allwayes kind to me upon all occa-sions'.[31] Years later in the pages of *Sculptura* Evelyn quoted him as saying that 'one who could not Designe a little, would never make an honest man'. After his father's discouragement, this was music to Evelyn's ears. Arundel must have seen promise in the earnest youth, even a potential recruit to his circle. Evelyn had hardly returned to Wotton when he hurried off again to Albury, where the earl 'first told us of the Massacre in Ireland & consequent rebellion'.

That Christmas Evelyn was master of revels at Middle Temple (perhaps at Robert Hatton's instigation), the last time such festivities were allowed. The unruly feasts that used to mark the occasion in the Inns of Court had already been suppressed, 'musicke, gaming or any publique noise or show' having been

HENRY VAN DER BORCHT PEINCTRE.

4 Hendrick van der Borcht, Evelyn's portraitist and friend was a print publisher who acted as an agent for the earl and countess of Arundel.

forbidden. In their place Evelyn set up a series of bronzed plaster busts of the caesars in Middle Temple Hall, an improving, yet decorative, effect to impress the young lawyers.[32] Arundel's Dutch-born librarian Franciscus Junius argued that classical statuary offered great men as an example.[33] With the Arundel marbles ranged in Inigo Jones's classical gallery nearby, Evelyn may also have been paying homage to his patron.

Some insight into Evelyn's state of mind at this time comes from his later letters to his son, John, who was much the same age in 1680 and was, his father felt, in danger of wasting his time. Evelyn suggested he read the classic authors and other histories, study 'municipal laws' and translate a useful book: 'when you are weary of one thing, passe to another.' His advice came from personal experience, he told his son – Evelyn dreaded boredom and was always avid for 'things of which I am ignorant to informe my self in'.[34] His lifelong difficulty was setting himself limits.

In England the political temperature was rising. In late February 1642, Queen Henrietta Maria headed to Holland, taking her daughter Mary and her jewels, in a desperate search of funds. Since the princess royal was now the daughter-in-law of the stadtholder, the House of Orange was her best hope of support. The party's escorts were the earl of Arundel and Lord Goring, vice-chamberlain of the royal household. Once arrived in the Netherlands, Arundel went to Antwerp. His exile had begun.

Meanwhile the king and his sons were in the north. Sir John Hotham refused Charles I and his five hundred horsemen access to Hull. Parliament stated that the king was acting beyond his authority in branding Hotham a traitor. When the Nineteen Propositions reached Charles in York, reducing his powers to those of little more than an onlooker, as he put it, the war of words between king and Parliament intensified. Skirmishes and feints pointed to imminent civil war. A friend of Evelyn's commented: 'Things are come to a strange height amongst us.'[35] John Evelyn took his brothers on a pilgrimage to St Albans, to the church and ruins of 'old Verulame, where the L: Chancelor Bacons contemplative monument is the sole ornament worth remembering'.[36] That summer the family took their regular 'journey of pleasure' to Lewes, where their step-grandparents provided happy memories of childhood security.

That autumn saw the first engagements in the civil wars. Evelyn witnessed the siege of Portsmouth, where on 9 October 1642 Goring's son handed the city over to the parliamentary forces of William Waller before heading into exile in France. On the way back to Wotton, Evelyn made a careful note of the reassuring relics in Winchester: 'Castle, Schole, Church [cathedral] & K Arthyrs round table; but especialy the Church and its Saxon Kings Monuments.'

In late October came the Battle of Edgehill, a massive engagement with Prince Rupert heading his own forces in support of the king. But instead of seizing advantage and marching on London, as Rupert had proposed, Charles fatally retreated to Oxford and made just one further attempt to capture the capital when the prince briefly took Brentford. There, on 14 November, possibly clad in the helmet and armour he had ordered abroad, Evelyn put in another short military appearance but found he had arrived too late: 'just at the retreate; but was not permitted to stay longer'. He claimed that he told absolutely no one of his adventure.[37]

Compared to many of his contemporaries, Evelyn's overt involvement in royalist politics was minimal and sporadic, giving him the advantage of remaining an unmarked man.[38] Even at the height of the first civil war he was free to travel wherever and whenever he chose, and at this time he decided to go abroad again, this time with his godmother's son. On 16 March 1643 the

House of Commons ordered 'That Mr Wm. Keightley and Mr. Jo. Evelyn shall have Mr Speaker's Warrant to pass into France, with one Servant'.[39]

Before he too left England for Antwerp at the end of 1642, taking what he could of Arundel's collection with him, Hendrick van der Borcht had visited Wotton – no doubt a pleasant break from the melancholy business of packing up Albury. He found Evelyn there and sold his 'verie good friend' a water-colour landscape, a 'little tempest' and a 'boy of bronze', priced between ten and thirty shillings each. George bought an Adoration for seven pounds which, the dealer told him, in better times might have sold for more than ten as well as some smaller (and cheaper) seascapes. The Evelyns were putting family funds into transportable artefacts – as John's guardian had suggested. Afterwards Van der Borcht quickly wrote to Evelyn asking for payment, apologetic at being so pressing for 'if times wheare otherwise or that I did not goe away, I should not trouble you so much about it'. On the journey back to London, Van der Borcht was alarmed to meet soldiers marching from Kingston. Arundel was still unsure of his own eventual destination once he left Antwerp, although it seemed likely to be Italy.[40] In April Van der Borcht wrote again, from Alkmaar. He was sorry to have missed Evelyn in Italy, assuming that he had already left England as planned.

But that spring neither events nor portents augured well for a journey. One night Evelyn saw a great cloud, illuminated as if by the moon, in the shape of a sword; it pointed north. Meanwhile Henrietta Maria had left her place of shelter in The Hague and landed near Bridlington in North Yorkshire.[41] With the court now trapped in Oxford Evelyn saw nothing but disaster ahead; he and his brothers were likely to be 'expos'd to Ruine'. The same message came from every corner; his schoolfriend Herbert Morley wrote from Rye of the 'miserably distressed kingdome'.

In the event Evelyn decided to remain at Wotton, 'resolving to possesse my selfe in some quiet if it might be, in a tyme of so great jealousy'. He passed the time gardening, making 'stews & receptacles for Fish, and built a little study over a Cascade, to passe my Malencholy houres shaded there with Trees, & silent Enough'. These were the precursors of the ambitious gardens and water effects to come, 'the Occasion of my Bro: vast Expence'.[42] Evelyn had never made a garden before and he patently enjoyed the business of diverting streams and engineering water effects – for ornamental rather than industrial purposes. He was busy drawing too and some of the results survive, including one of the little 'garden room or hermitage' as he termed it.[43]

The garden at Wotton was no more than a sketch towards later work, but Evelyn showed marked originality in the way he combined water and shelter, creating a private place for thoughtful withdrawal rather than for social prom-enading or effect. Purposefully immersing himself in drawing, hydraulics and

5 Albury Park, etched by Wenceslaus Hollar in 1645. Evelyn did not succeed in buying it in 1652 but later redesigned the Italianate garden for Henry Howard.

gardening (though only a few miles from the gunpowder mills that were arming the opposing forces), Evelyn worried that he might become one of those rustic wits who, in John Aubrey's delightful metaphor, became wrapped in moss.[44]

That summer Evelyn went to see Sir John Harrison's Balls Park, a handsome new brick house possibly built by Nicholas Stone, the Dutch architect Hendrick de Keyser's son-in-law, and so the nearest thing to Dutch classical architecture on English soil. Other visits constituted something of a royalist pilgrimage: he went twice to see the home of Elizabeth I's favourite, Hatfield House, 'inferior to few for its Architecture then in England', surrounded by gardens and vineyards, and also explored the royal palace of Theobalds Park, all but demolished in 1651. Having seen 'furious & zelous people demolish the stately Crosse in Cheapeside', he was aware that the artefacts and buildings of the church and monarchy were becoming increasingly vulnerable. The flurry of visits to sites of antiquarian, historical and architectural interest suggests that it was beginning to feel like a race against time.

The previous November the Committee for Advance of Money was given parliamentary powers to borrow funds that would, in theory, be repaid with 8 per cent interest. To begin with, assessments were confined to property within twenty miles of London but the net was bound to widen soon.[45] The following summer Evelyn refused to sign the Solemn League and Covenant, implying his opposition to Presbyterianism.[46]

In 1643 Hendrick van der Borcht published Wenceslaus Hollar's engraving of Sir Anthony van Dyck's self-portrait and dedicated it to Evelyn, whom he described as a lover and patron of the arts. The print testified to the friendship between the engraver, publisher and dedicatee, all linked to the earl of Arundel. In the portrait, Van Dyck, Charles I's court painter, is pointing to a sunflower, symbol of the king. The meaning was unmistakable.[47]

Up to this point Evelyn may have signalled his royalist credentials more by default than specific action. Continually shuttling between Wotton and London, he had not been able to 'evade the doing of very unhandsome things', as he wrote elliptically. Finally, in November, Evelyn secured another pass for France and set out, accompanied by James Thicknesse. This journey had the makings of a prolonged self-imposed exile.

CHAPTER 3

'Out of the Garden into Paradice'

John Evelyn was good company on a journey. His Balliol friend James
Thicknesse, with whom he was going to France, liked the way he seemed
to engage with everything – 'your observation of places of Manners of Men',
as he said. When they were apart he had imagined their conversations,
'censuring with you Somethings, extolling of others'.[1] Effusive and demon-
strative and, as a college Fellow, bound to remain a bachelor, Thicknesse was
an honorary member of the Evelyn family. Abroad, the balance between them
subtly shifted, with Evelyn taking the lead. They must learn to write French
'congruously' and speak it intelligently. Travellers should not 'meerly run
abroad' but learn about things 'Mechanically curious and usefull' as well as
about government and politics.[2] On the latter count, there was plenty to
discuss. As the young men toiled across the sinister marshes of the Pas de
Calais in the short dark days of late November, they were inevitably aware of
the effects of long-lasting conflict in Europe. In Abbeville, prosperous
gunsmiths were the beneficiaries of a seemingly endless war between the
French and the Spanish.

Reaching the cathedral of St Denis, its spires almost at the gates of Paris,
they explored the 'Dormitory' of the French monarchy. In the crypt below,
King Louis XIII's catafalque lay heavily draped in black velvet. Arriving in
Paris, Evelyn and Thicknesse took rooms at the Ville-de-Venise on rue de
Bussy, in the Faubourg Saint-Germain. Seventeenth-century travellers moved
together, in packs determined by nationality, guided by the same books which
pointed them to choice sites and suitable lodgings.[3] For the latest information
and useful contacts, Bacon had suggested that new arrivals in a foreign city
should look up 'secretaries and employed men of ambassadors'. The English
Resident, Richard Browne, lived close by, on the rue Taranne (later lost
beneath the boulevard Saint-Germain), and they went to meet him.[4]

A swelling tide of exiles from the civil war was washing up on French
shores and Browne's welcoming household provided a reassuring sense of

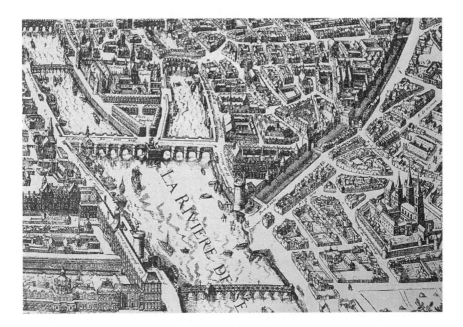

6 Paris in the 1630s showing the pont Neuf and behind it the place Dauphine. Outside the walls (bottom right) is the Abbey of S. Germain, close to the rue Taranne where Evelyn lived with the Brownes from 1649 to 1650.

English domesticity as well as a meeting place for compatriots, including those on covert political business. Browne's family consisted of his wife, Elizabeth, daughter, Mary (Mall), and son, Richard (Dick).[5] A fatherly man, he acted as an intermediary between the generations, his consular duties extending to settling financial and other difficulties for errant young men. His postbag was always filled with letters from concerned parents.

The king's representative in Paris came from a distinguished line of courtiers who had served both Elizabeth I and James I. Aged twelve he had acted in a royal masque for Queen Anne and his youth was spent as a roving diplomatic secretary, serving ambassador Isaac Wake successively at the court of Savoy in Turin, in Venice and finally in Paris.[6] Back in England, Browne purchased a post as a clerk of the council in 1641, only to be sent back to Paris as acting Resident, an initial posting of eighteen months eventually stretching to nineteen years.[7] It may have been Browne who suggested that Evelyn join the procession taking Charles I's new ambassador, George Goring (father of the royalist soldier), to an audience with the five-year-old Louis XIV and his mother, the regent, the redoubtable Spanish Habsburg Anne of Austria, his thrilling introduction to french royal ceremonial.[8]

To any royalist arriving in France at such a moment of uncertainty in English affairs, the absolute ascendancy of the monarchy must have appeared remarkable. Following his father's death in spring 1643, the child had opened his reign with a state entry into Paris and a *lit de justice* – a meeting with his supreme court, the Parlement. There was a shift in the balance of power at court, but merely to different shoulders. Louis XIII's minister of state, Richelieu, who died in 1642, had been replaced by another wily cardinal, the Italian Giulio Mazarini, a Jesuit-educated lawyer made a cardinal by Pope Urban VIII as a reward for 'diplomatic services'. The Gallicised first minister Mazarin was the new king's godfather, some said his natural father. Louis *le Dieudonné*, as he was known, had been born to his parents after two decades of childlessness, providing an apparently miraculous riposte to the ambitions of his uncle, Gaston d'Orléans. Hardly more than a toddler on his accession, Louis XIV was immediately awarded the attributes of a warrior king, depicted in armour or enthroned, holding the instruments of power, even shown congratulating a victorious general.[9]

When he became familiar with Paris, Evelyn considered that it was above all 'the Streets, Suburbs, and common buildings' that made it the match of any city in Europe.[10] The dense mesh of medieval lanes, belted in by the heavy city wall, was intermittently ripped open: a square, the place Royale (later des Vosges), a triangle, the place Dauphine (laid out specifically for artisans), a river crossing unencumbered by shops and houses, the pont Neuf, all set new standards of urban elegance which had, the Piazza at Covent Garden apart, no match in London.[11] The work had been begun by Henri IV, who remodelled the Louvre and engaged the municipality, merchant and trading interests and the court in a wider modernisation project. Behind such eye-catching constructions, promoted in maps and engravings, lay a programme of city-wide civic and social reform, the incremental improvement of streets, quays and the water system, and the introduction of building regulations. There were new hospitals, universities, churches and markets, while the great *hôtels particuliers* were the marks of success for men who had achieved immense power and wealth.[12] The city palaces of power-brokers such as Sully and Richelieu had no equivalent in London. Until Louis XIV moved the court out to Versailles in 1682, the transformation continued. Compared to sorry London, recently abandoned by the king, Paris seemed a proud city, a seat of government and a model of enlightened urban planning and architecture.

In the new year Evelyn moved to lodgings on the rue de Seine on the Left Bank, again in the Faubourg Saint-Germain, just outside the city walls where they met the river at the tour de Nèsle. The street was (and is) a long narrow tunnel, many of its tall houses swelling contentedly at the waist, as if well-fed. The glimpse of the water that Evelyn caught as he walked north had not yet been obscured by the riverside Collège des Quatre Nations. Far from the troubles at home, Evelyn and Thicknesse explored Paris tirelessly,

investigating its commerce, court, learning, religion, art and daily life. They
delved into markets and stalls along the river, where Evelyn made his first
book and print purchases, inscribed 'Coll. Evelynus Parisii 1643', and, always,
his Latin motto, *Omnia explorate, meliora retinete*.[13]

In spring 1644, Jane Evelyn wrote to her brother to ask for a more recent
portrait and he sent a watercolour by Louis van der Bruggen.[14] The picture
has not survived but Evelyn was no longer the hesitant youth who had sat to
Van der Borcht. He told his sister he had been too busy to write regularly. Jane
was forgiving: 'pray lett not the thoughts of our troubles disturbe your peace.'
All remained quiet at Wotton.[15] In fact, the calm was superficial and the
conditions for the landed gentry in England were deteriorating fast.
Parliamentary confiscation of estates still remained largely only a threat but
the burden of heavy taxation and falling rents, loss of crops and damage to
property were penalties enough. Where a landowner was also required to
quarter troops and horses, as at Wotton, his plight was worse still.

In late February 1644 William Ducie, a colleague from the Middle Temple,
had written to Evelyn, hoping that 'you finde in France all that contentment
& pleasure you expected there' and reporting the news from England. In
the north the marquess of Newcastle was heading towards confrontation
with the Scottish army (who backed Parliament), three thousand of the
king's forces were heading for Sussex and Surrey and Prince Rupert was
following with more. 'Believe it Sir you may thinke your selfe happy to be
out of the Calamaties that are like to befall us in the kingdome this next
summer.'[16]

As the days lengthened, Evelyn, with Thicknesse and their friends,
ventured beyond the city walls to visit parks and gardens to which he would
return, time and again. In the diary Evelyn describes these gardens very much
in his own voice, fleshing out notes made on the spot or soon after. As he later
told Sir Thomas Browne, where horticulture was concerned, 'I have observed
so many particularities as, happly, others descend not to.' They began at St
Cloud, its terraces giving a bird's-eye view of distant Paris, as they still do, the
huge park ornamented by fountains, pools, grottos, cascades and groves.
Cardinal Richelieu's immense garden at Rueil, nearby, was an even more
impressive affair, with sculptures, water features and 'Walkes of vast lengthes',
all beautifully maintained. In February the evergreens were impressive and
unfamiliar to an English eye. Immersed there, Evelyn lost track of time:
'viewing of this Paradise made us bring night to St Germains.'[17]

At St Germain-en-Laye the two royal summer palaces, old and new, dominated a ridge of low hills west of Paris, about as far away as Windsor from
London.[18] The old château was a 'mix'd Structure', an irregular Gothic
moated castle with later additions, while almost on the escarpment was

Henri IV's new palace (the birthplace of Louis XIV), an extended classical pavilion. In front, 'six incomparable Terraces' cascaded down the hillside to the Seine, undercut by grottos, with artificially lit hydraulic figures and elaborate waterworks inside. The upper terrace stretched half a mile.[18] The French gardens that most appealed to Evelyn and that he wrote about later were essentially Italianate.[19]

Back in the city, Evelyn was swept up in a round of visits to art galleries. On this occasion he was not tamely following guide-book suggestions but was led by his portraitist, now friend, Hendrick van der Borcht, who was in Paris accompanying Henry Frederick Howard, Lord Mowbray, the earl of Arundel's eldest surviving son.[20] Arundel himself had been trying to secure passes for France from Browne, ostensibly to visit the baths at Bourbon, but his precarious finances, a sick granddaughter and his own worsening health delayed him in Antwerp.[21] He passed through Paris and later thanked the Resident for all his help.[22]

From Evelyn's point of view, Van der Borcht was an ideal guide, with his eye for the masterpieces of Italian and northern European art and his open-sesames from Arundel. They began with a visit to the duc de Liancourt's collection in a handsome *hôtel* on the rue de Seine, where they enjoyed the undivided attention of their host, who even asked his wife to leave her dressing room so that they could see its contents.[23] The state rooms contained paintings by Raphael, Michelangelo, Leonardo, Mantegna and Dürer as well as Poussin, whose Parisian patron the duke was. Over the next two days they visited three more collections.[24]

A week later Evelyn went with Van der Borcht to Fontainebleau: the Hampton Court of France, as he termed it. The rugged landscape and the untamed forest gave the journey a certain excitement. Recalling the trip later, Van der Borcht asked if Evelyn could send him 'anie little draftes of your ouwne of the habits of gentlewomen of severall Places. Mr hollar will make them in Print, and make mention that you are the designer of them.'[25] There is no evidence that he was able to oblige, but it proves that Evelyn was still busy drawing, his father's injunctions as distant as the civil war.

But the most memorable of all Evelyn's visits during that first stay in Paris was to Pierre Morin's famous nursery garden. He was taken there by an unidentified friend in April, the optimum moment to enjoy the 'Tulips, Anemonies, Raunculus's, Crocus's &c. . . . held for the rarest in the World' on which Morin's reputation rested. The friend may have been Richard Browne himself, a keen horticulturist. Morin's garden was almost next to his house. The Parisian nurseryman who had supplied the great plantsman John Tradescant the Elder with rare cultivars now became Evelyn's botanical mentor, later commemorated in his own garden.[26]

The set-piece of Morin's garden was an oval flowerbed or parterre laid out as a daisy, each petal edged in box, which Evelyn described as 'an exact Oval figure planted with Cypresse, cutt flat & set as even as a Wall'. Another Englishman with an eye for gardens, Richard Symonds, sketched it and provided a key to the main features.[27] Evelyn gathered that Morin's wealth came from sales of a shrub he had brought from Provence, 'wherewith all walls are lyned'. *Rhamnus alaternus*, or Italian buckthorn, was an evergreen plant which Evelyn promoted at every opportunity and later claimed to have introduced to England.

Morin had another interest that endeared him to Evelyn: 'from an ordinary Gardner, [he] is ariv'd to be one of the most skillfull & Curious Persons of France for his rare collection of Shells, Flowers & Insects.' Like his English colleague Tradescant in Lambeth, he had created a personal museum. Living 'in a kind of Hermitage', he was surrounded by porcelain and prints as well as the *pièce de résistance*, his butterfly display.

In mid-April Evelyn, still with Thicknesse, headed to Tours to escape the expense and incessant social demands of Paris. The towns of the Loire were favoured by English exiles as quiet places to learn the language and observe French life more calmly. When his old school friend Robert Heath sent him his observations on French habits, Evelyn scribbled tartly 'this gentleman had not been in France'. Two of Evelyn's exercise books survive, one inscribed 'Turoniis' and dated 18 September 1644 (probably the date on which he left) and containing notes on the pronunciation and meaning of words, some translated from French into Latin, as well as pencil doodles, proof that even Evelyn's attention sometimes wandered.[28]

Evelyn told his sister that he had found a congenial teacher and she replied, saying that she wished she could join him. For Jane in Surrey, there were no such pleasurable opportunities. Her reality was daily privation and uncertainty, with no idea of what might lie ahead as Parliament and king confronted one another. She feared for the future since neither side seemed strong. In addition, brother George had been widowed after four years of marriage. Burdened young with the family estate, Jane reported that he was relieved that his only son, also George, had survived a serious illness.

Many were deciding not to stay and chance the uncertain political climate in England. William Keightley, with whom Evelyn had earlier planned to travel to France, arrived in Paris in July with his brother Thomas. They turned to him for practical help but, having found them a *pension* in Tours and provided them with 'exercises', he moved smartly on. At the Lion d'Or in Lyons, Evelyn and Thicknesse joined a larger party for the journey south. Lyons was his first, agreeable taste of the Midi, a stone-built city embraced by vineyards. Travelling on down the Rhône to Avignon, they stopped to look at both the Palace of the Popes and the synagogue.

To go further, to Italy, travellers had to procure a 'bill of health', showing them to be plague-free. The next leg of their journey, from Cannes to Genoa by water, was hazardous; the captain's fear of capture by Spaniards, who 'frequently catch a French Prize, as they creepe by these shores', meant that he 'ply'd both sayles & Oares to get under protection of a Genoeze-Gally that passed'. As they left its shelter, the weather immediately worsened. Trying to shorten the distance (since they had already agreed payment), the captain turned out to sea and met the full force of the wind. Evelyn was worried to see two Irish priests hearing confessions; even the captain was 'giving us for gon'. Then, just as bailing out the swamped boat began to seem impossible, the wind dropped and they sailed euphorically on to Genoa, basking in the scented breezes now drifting across the water, 'the peculiar joys of Italy, in the natural perfumes of Orange, Citron, & Jassmine', and celebrating their narrow escape.[29]

From time to time on his travels Evelyn encountered buildings which may have been already familiar to him from the page. The château of Chambord on the Loire was discussed in Palladio's *Quattro Libri* while Rubens's *Palazzi di Genova* was the seventeenth-century architectural amateur's guide to the handsome town houses along the Strada Nuova (later Via Garibaldi), Genoa's principal street. One contemporary noted that here 'ordinary houses are out of countenance and dare not appear in this street, where every house is a pallace and every pallace as beautifull as marble pillars and painting can make it'.[30] The steep gardens were oases of citrus and pomegranate trees, statuary and water features; though limited by the precipitous ground, they were highly ornamented and full of plants unfamiliar to the northern eye, such as cypress and myrtle. An eleven-mile-long wall encircled the town, as well as a six hundred-foot mole to protect the harbour. Genoa, a spectacularly affluent merchant city close to the border with France and overlooking the contested seas from which its wealth came, was a rich prize and kept itself well guarded.

Arriving in Pisa in mid-October 1644 (at which point Thicknesse went to Siena with other English friends), Evelyn met up, as planned, with Thomas Henshaw, who had arrived via Spain and Holland. Henshaw, a couple of years older than Evelyn, had fought with the royalist forces at York before being taken prisoner. His permit to leave the country was conditional on his not rejoining the king's army and he was now one of many former soldiers making the best of enforced exile. Evelyn and he would travel together for most of the next year. Henshaw's background was unusual, both his parents being described as 'chemists'.[31] After matriculating at University College, Oxford in 1634, he studied mathematics with William Oughtred at Albury.[32] It may well have been in Surrey that he and Evelyn met. A shared interest in

Montis Vesuvij Fauces et voraga, sive Barathrum internum

7 A figure (left) looks into the bubbling crater at Vesuvius; Evelyn's etching probably
shows his friend Thomas Henshaw, with whom he travelled to Naples.

books, prints and antiquities, as well as in chemistry and the natural sciences,
made them perfectly matched travelling companions.

In Florence they lodged on the Piazza Santo Spirito, not far from the
Palazzo Pitti and the impressive Boboli Gardens which unfolded behind.
Characteristically combining a tour of 'the most memorable buildings &
Curiositys of this noble Citty' with a glimpse of its most profitable trade, the
manufacture of damask, velvet and silk fabrics, Evelyn also ordered himself a
cabinet, now to be seen at the Victoria and Albert Museum in London.
Francis Bacon had ordained that the 'philosopher', in addition to a library,
garden and laboratory, should have 'a goodly huge cabinet, wherein [should
be] whatsoever the hand of man by exquisite art or engine hath made rare in
stuff, form or motion'.[33] Such a cabinet should be both a beautiful artefact and
a rich hoard of memories. Since Evelyn would not be returning to the city for
at least six months, the craftsman had ample time to turn his wishes into a
fine piece.[34]

Evelyn and Henshaw continued their journey south. Other members of the
group who had travelled from France to Italy had fanned out but they all
remained in touch; Evelyn's letters are the 'veins which convey you to us,'
wrote one from Siena.

Arrival in Rome was a memorable moment; many a Grand Tourist remembered their very hour of arrival, and Evelyn was no exception: 'I came to ROME on the 4th of November 1644 about 5 at night.' His brother Richard knew he had longed to see Rome and was envious to think of him there, 'whear you see that saying verified, *tempora mutantur* and where I confesse is the only place I can imagine to please my melancholy humor and busie my wandering fancy by reason of the vast number of Antiquities, a thing I have alwayes delighted'.

Despite the sense of having arrived at the heart of the classical world, Evelyn was met by a hail of bad news from home. Richard reported a 'sudden alteration at Wotton'. After quartering soldiers for some time, George had closed up the house and gone to his chambers in the Middle Temple until times improved. At least five of their Surrey gentry neighbours had also left their estates, faced by falling rents and rising taxes. The coach horses were sold and only his servants Dick Hunt and George Downe had gone with him to London. The cook and the boy had left, as had the falconer, leaving only a handful of staff in the house. George planned to lay off the farm workers shortly 'and hire men by the weeke to doe his businesse'. In his letter Richard apologises for troubling his brother but knows he would want to be kept informed. Since October he had stayed nowhere longer than three days.[35]

Jane's circumstances were the clearest sign of their family troubles, perhaps exacerbated by George's role as a commissioner for assessment and sequestrations in Surrey. She had become housekeeper to the widow of a member of the king's bedchamber who lived in Twickenham. She considered herself fortunate: 'necessity has no law for . . . there are now so few houskeepers and thos that doe will not Bord.' None of their friends had offered to help her but 'so long as I [can live] with out them I will no seeke them'. Her plight touched Evelyn. The brothers had a tender relationship with their surviving sister and in the draft of his reply he revealed how far away and helpless he felt. In fact, despite her frail health ('the sharpnes of the Ayre . . . agrees not with my thin body'), Jane was to be very happy there, her employer becoming a personal friend.[36]

On the wider front, Richard reported that the king's emissaries had come to London from Oxford (where the court now was) to negotiate with Parliament. He planned to return to Baynards, his own estate, and stay there quietly with his servant.

Brother, you cannot image how ioyfull I was at that passage in youre letter where you speake of shortning your iourney, but saddnd againe, when you write of two yeares more travaile, none could be more gladd of youre returne then my selfe, especially we now being all parted, but I confesse the times are such that I cannot invite you over for as yet I can perceive nothing but ruine.[37]

Soon after Evelyn heard of the burning of Oxford, with the loss of more than three hundred houses and a church. What went through his mind when he received these letters? The news made him indecisive but still did not persuade him to alter his travel plans and return to join the king's forces.

Jane was glad to hear that Evelyn had reached Rome: 'you tell mee you are com out of the garden into Paradice.'[38] Yet the peaceful papal city had not long ago been dangerous territory for Protestants. In Rome the English lodged around the Piazza di Spagna or the Quattro Fontane. Evelyn chose to stay in a Frenchman's house reached by a steep path through long grass up to the church of Trinità dei Monti and the Villa Medici. There were no Spanish Steps yet.

New arrivals, Catholic or not, were assured a warm welcome at the English College, the Jesuit training school. Evelyn had the advantage of various introductions from the earl of Arundel, including one to the Benedictine abbot and poet Patrick Cary, brother of Lucius, Viscount Falkland, the central figure in the influential Great Tew intellectual circle of the 1630s. Later Cary, who was equally hospitable to the puritan poet and political radical John Milton, returned to England, renounced his faith and married.

By coincidence, just as a new monarch had been the focus of attention in Paris when Evelyn was there, so Rome was caught up in celebration for the new pope. Pope Urban VIII, a Barberini, had died in the summer. During the subsequent hiatus, the *sede vacante*, Rome had been convulsed with riots as a result of antagonisms between rival French and Spanish interests. The new pope, Innocent X, a Pamphili, had strong ties with, but was not financially dependent on, the Spanish. He was crowned a month to the day before Evelyn arrived.[39] For a traveller whose ear was attuned to matters of government and power, his timing was immaculate.

Evelyn was longing to buy books and works of art but repeated reminders came from home that he must be frugal. Nevertheless, well-chosen purchases might become saleable commodities in the hard times ahead. He later claimed that £300 a year had purchased 'my severall Masters, Mathematics, Musique, Languages etc. besides a Servant or two, and the amassing of no inconsiderable Collection too of Pictures, Medaills, and other trifles'.[40]

In Siena, Thicknesse found Evelyn's letters to be almost as good as his company: 'so lively that I enjoy Rome at Siena . . . you call to mind the ages past and their Heroick actions and never putt foot to ground but in the footstepps of a Caesar.' He and a friend were eager to join him; could Evelyn find them lodgings, ideally in a bookseller's house? Like anyone heading for an unfamiliar city, Thicknesse was worried about getting lost. 'The entrance into Rome perplexes me much, pray Sir direct me what to do.'[41]

The early days of November hurtled by, if Evelyn's diary is any guide, in an exhausting if predictable round of visits. Originally he had not intended to spend much time in Rome but found it so 'approportionata all mio Genio', so congenial, that he extended his stay and began to learn the language.[42] As he immersed himself in Roman architecture, perhaps with Palladio's *Quattro Libri* to hand, he found himself poorly equipped to record the ruins and 'Modern structures, al'Antique' for himself. Evelyn later told his son that he had very little grasp of mathematics, such as Oughtred's method of the 'Algebraic, and Cartesian way', and hoped John, then in Paris, would study Euclid, for 'I exceedingly deplore my not cultivating them with more sedulity, when I had the opportunity'.[43]

The first building Evelyn visited in Rome, the Palazzo Farnese, which he believed (wrongly) to be entirely the work of Michelangelo exemplified the debt the Renaissance owed to classical antiquity. Roger Pratt, a lawyer turned architect with whom he shared lodgings there, considered it to be the best of all the Roman palazzi. Inside were the stupendous Farnese antique bronzes of Hercules and Flora.[44] The collision of ancient and modern in Rome gives an electrifying charge, nowhere more so than on the Campidoglio, where the Capitol, with all its late Renaissance urban panache, looks down on the Forum. But the vestiges of imperial Rome were hard to discern and, even with a better grasp of Euclidean geometry, Evelyn would have been hard-pressed to measure the major monuments accurately. In the Forum, known long since as the Campo Vaccino (cattle market), the temples and triumphal arches were obscured by a clutter of houses, churches, chapels and vegetation, adhering to them, barnacle-like, as they sank into the silt of the centuries. Above, on the Palatine and Aventine hills stood the ruined playground of the imperial city, now punctuated by Christian churches.

In hidden corners within the mostly medieval fabric, Counter-Reformation churches and cloisters were being shoehorned into the heart of the city. None was more exquisite than Carlo Borromini's San Carlo alle Quattro Fontane, 'all of a new white stone, & of an excellent oval designe'. Below was a crypt, with pilasters on an identical plan. Also by Borromini was San Ivo, begun in 1642, buried within the university of the Sapienza, but announced by a majestic portico. Confronted with new and unfamiliar architecture, Evelyn was surprisingly open-minded, apparently as taken with the contradictory and exuberant forms of the Baroque as he had been with the bold simplicity of Dutch classicism. There is little evidence in Pratt's notebooks that he was interested in Baroque architecture; Evelyn's enthusiasm seems to have been his own.[45] While they were in Rome, St Peter's, the

8 John Evelyn's etching of 1649 showing the Roman Forum setting off his dedication to Thomas Henshaw.

ceremonial church of the papacy, was causing considerable alarm. One of Bernini's twin *campanili* was fissured with alarming cracks and deep shafts were being sunk to investigate the suspected faulty foundations.[46]

Evelyn and Henshaw's guide to one important Baroque building, the Jesuit church of the Gesù, was a German, Father Athanasius Kircher, who also showed off the dispensary, laboratory and gardens to his guests. Finally he took them down a hall hung with pictures of Jesuit martyrs to his own study. Here the hospitable cleric 'with Dutch patience shew'd us his perpetual motions, Catoptrics, Magnetical experiments, Modells, and a thousand other crotchets & devises'.[47] The meeting was a revelation for both Evelyn and Henshaw.

Kircher had arrived in Rome in 1635 from Avignon, where he had been a protégé of the antiquarian and virtuoso Nicolas-Claude Fabri de Peiresc. Appointed professor of mathematics at the Collegio Romano in 1635, he built up a reputation as a Prospero-like figure, sitting at the hub of intertwined investigative programmes into phenomena of every sort. Despite growing doubts about the quality of his scholarship and signs of mendacity (contrary to his claims, he had never visited the Orient), he was a leading collector and interpreter of the novel, the arcane and the exotic, a man who could link papal Rome and Jesuit missionary networks with the intellectual world of northern Europe.[48] For religious reasons, Kircher remained a closet Copernican, yet Pope Urban VIII, who condemned Galileo to trial by the Inquisition in 1633 for his heretical views about the solar system, visited Kircher's collection in 1640, suggesting official approval. His nephew, Cardinal Francesco Barberini, one of three cardinals who refused to sign the sentence upon Galileo, was a strenuous protector of Kircher's intellectual independence.

By the time Evelyn and Henshaw arrived, calling upon Athanasius Kircher was *de rigueur* for Grand Tourists. Robert Boyle, for all his distaste for Jesuits, regretted he had not seen Kircher's hydraulic organ and Richard Lassels recommended several visits to his room, so 'full of admirable curiosities and experiences both mathematicall, magneticall, and hydraulick'.[49] Visitors had to submit themselves to the priest's prankish humour. He had installed a speaking tube through which guests announced themselves and down which came his disconcertingly disembodied voice in answer. Kircher's cramped room at the Collegium Romanum was not yet properly speaking a museum, rather an esoteric cave of curiosities. Henshaw, brought up among alchemical treatises and manuscripts, and taught by William Backhouse and Oughtred, was on familiar ground. Evelyn, less well prepared, attended Kircher's lecture on Euclid and bought several of his books. By the time of his death in 1680, Kircher had published over forty titles and his crowded study had long since been enlarged into a museum.[50]

The *cavaliere* Cassiano dal Pozzo's collection on the Via dei Chiavari was a more sophisticated and well-organised display than Kircher's chaotic roomful. Dal Pozzo, a central figure in the intellectual circles around Urban VIII and whose correspondents included Rubens and Peiresc, employed Nicolas Poussin to copy antique sculpture and became his principal patron during the Frenchman's long stay in Rome until 1640. His 'museo cartaceo' (museum on paper) consisted largely of copy drawings, arranged in two parts, *res humanae* and *res divinae*, ranging from fine art and antiquities to natural history. While admiring his library, hung with portraits of famous literary figures, Evelyn was particularly taken by 'his rare collection of the Antique Bassirelievos about Rome' all meticulously recorded in albums.[51] The collection, much of which later came into the possession of George III after being bought by the architect James Adam from Cardinal Albani, may have prompted Evelyn to commission the twenty-year-old Carlo Maratti (perhaps in the hope that he had found another Poussin?) to copy some bas-reliefs on the Capitol. Maratti was the first in a distinguished line of young artists whom Evelyn patronised early in their careers.[52]

At the public gallery in the Villa Borghese, Evelyn found two striking new sculptures by Gianlorenzo Bernini. They are still there today. One shows the young David with his sling, the other the pursuit of Daphne by Apollo; both were, Evelyn effused, 'observable for the incomparable Candor of the stone, & art of the statuary plainely stupendious'. Bravely, Evelyn attempted to capture Daphne's marble flesh melting into foliage in verse:

> Chast Daphne's limbs into the Laurel shoote,
> Whilst her swift feete the amorous Center roote;
> How the rude bark invades her virgin Snow,
> And does to that well timber'd body grow![53]

As well as individual works of art and architecture, Evelyn admired the way in which major streets or processional routes met or intersected in Rome, marked by eye-catchers. Antique trophies, sometimes Roman columns but more usually Egyptian obelisks, conjured up the impossibly distant world of Thebes or commemorated steely rulers such as Caligula or Julius Caesar. They were focal points in the formal reconfiguration of Rome in the late sixteenth century. Sixtus V erected four obelisks: one in the piazza outside St Peter's (not yet embraced by Bernini's colonnades), inscribed to Julius Caesar and topped by a cross; one outside the benediction loggia at San Giovanni in Laterano; another behind Santa Maria Maggiore; and the fourth in the Piazza del Popolo.[54] In 1643 Kircher had published his *Lingua Aegyptiaca Restituta* and Evelyn was intrigued that the 'recondite & abstruse learning' of the Egyptians could be conveyed by these hermetic symbols, 'serpents, men, owles, falcons, Oxen, Instruments, &c'. Kircher's room was full of models of obelisks, lettered carefully in the arcane codified language which he claimed – falsely – to have deciphered. Innocent X would soon add another obelisk to the collection, in the Piazza Navona, and Kircher published it.

On 23 November 1644 Evelyn stood high on the steps of the Ara Coeli to watch the stupendous procession which marked the official inauguration of Innocent X. It wound from the Vatican to San Giovanni in Laterano. He had witnessed elaborate ceremonial in Paris but this, featuring the papal house-hold in their rich and colourful liveries mounted on horses or mules according to rank, was in a class of its own. There were two immense temporary triumphal arches, of 'boards, cloath &c painted & fram'd on the suddaine, but as to outward appearance solid and very stately'. The decorations between the Arch of Titus and the Colosseum were set up by the Jews 'in testimony of gratitude for their protection under the Papal state'. The celebrations ended with dramatic figurative fireworks, including depictions of the papal arms. Tapers lit every window, 'put into lanterns or sconces of severall colour'd oyl'd papers, that the wind may not annoy them', and the Castel Sant'Angelo was transformed into a 'Pyramid of lights'.[55]

Christmas Eve marked the zenith of Catholic observance, an astonishing sight for an Anglican of simple tastes like Evelyn. 'I did nothing all this night but go from Church to Church in admiration at the multitude of sceanes, & Pageantry which the Friers had with all industry & craft set out to catch the devout women & superstitious sort of people with.'[56] Every church had a carved Nativity. The Jesuits of the English College invited their countrymen to celebrate 'their great feast of Tho: of Canterbury' with them and watch the students act an Italian comedy for the benefit of the cardinals. Robert Boyle would pretend to be French when he was in Rome, to avoid the 'distracting Intrusions & importunitys of English Jesuits', but Evelyn was less fastidious.[57] His opposition to the Jesuits was largely doctrinal and historical, but he always admired their intellectual curiosity (and the excellence of their Latin teaching). It was at the English College that Evelyn heard, early in the new year, of Archbishop Laud's execution. He was puzzled that English Catholics celebrated his fall, since, as he wrote to a churchman fifty years later, Laud's so-called crime was 'being Popishly affected'.[58]

After the ceremonies marking Epiphany Evelyn attended one of the monthly sermons to the Jews, who were compelled to attend this uncomfortable (and fruitless) exercise. He recorded their angry faces, the 'spitting, humming, coughing & motion [so great], that it is almost impossible they should heare a word, nor are there any converted except it be very rarely'. Perhaps it was viewing this farce that tempted him into the ghetto, where he watched, uncomfortably, a seven-year-old boy being circumcised.[59]

The Vatican had proved difficult of access and it was not until January that Evelyn was able to visit the papal apartments, the Sistine Chapel and the Vatican Library. The latter, decorated with 'Emblemes, Figurs, Diagramms, and the like learned inventions found out by the Wit, & Industry of famous Men', he considered pointed up the limitations of the Bodleian Library, ornamented by meaningless grotesques.[60] At the Vatican, as in Cassiano de Pozzo's library, men of letters and fathers of the church stood guard over the valuable library, its books stored in presses rather than on open shelves, the most precious 'shew'd to the curious onely'. The esteem in which Catholics held learning was highly appealing to Evelyn.

Following the custom, Henshaw and Evelyn timed their travels south to Naples to coincide with carnival. On their arrival they found the city's always exuberant street life further enlivened by thousands of 'registred sinners', courtesans 'who pay a tax to the state for the Costome of their bodys'. Evelyn described them, breathlessly, in 'all their naturall & artificiall beauty' and how they 'play, sing, feigne, compliment, & by a thousand studied devices seeke to inveagle foolish young persons'. Syphilis might await those who strayed; 'some of our Company did purchase their repentance at a deare rate, after their returne'.[61]

Visitors to Naples typically spent three days on the journey there and back and five in the city and surroundings. Neither Pompeii nor Herculaneum had yet been excavated, so expeditions beyond the walls were to the Phlegrean Fields, Posilippo, Cumae and, of course, Vesuvius. The climb to the volcano, still active after its 1631 eruption, was punishing but thrilling. Although Kircher's book on vulcanology had not yet appeared, he must have conveyed his passion for the subject to his visitors in Rome.[62] Here was a natural phenomenon that offered a window into the bowels of the earth.

Approaching by mule, they 'alighted, crawling up the rest of the proclivity, with extraordinary difficulty, now with our feete & hands, not without many untoward slipps'. Bruised and messy from the brimstone and pumice (a piece of which Evelyn pocketed), they reached the summit, from which they could see Naples and far beyond. Evelyn ventured to the edge: 'I layd my selfe on my belly to looke over & into that most frightfull & terrible Vorago [gulf] a stupendious pit . . . continually vomiting a foggy exhalation, & ejecting huge stones with an impetuous noise & roaring, like the report of many musquets discharging.' It was, he told an Italian friend, a truly terrifying spectacle. The eddies from the depths of the great chasm gave onlookers an added frisson since the most recent eruption had engulfed and destroyed the entire land-scape below them, towns, villages, vineyards, fields and gardens. The descent through a valley of fresh ash, the remnants of what the volcano had just spewed out, was much easier than the ascent. At the Phlegrean Fields, the ground painted acid-green by the sulphur, they had another reminder of the intense subterranean activity in this area. Equally thrilling were the visible links to classical antiquity particularly Posilippo with its crypt and what was believed to be Virgil's tomb, a place of pilgrimage to a reader of the *Aeneid* or the *Georgics* and a setting which Evelyn was to recreate later – far away in Surrey.

While there Evelyn drew a set of landscapes: Naples seen from Vesuvius, the crater and peaks of the volcano, Cape Terracina and the Tres Tabernae. These were to become familiar scenes in the eighteenth century, but they were still fresh in the 1640s. When he engraved them in Paris in 1649, Evelyn dedicated the set, published under the name of his amanuensis Richard

Hoare, to Henshaw, very probably the behatted figure he showed looking into the crater at Vesuvius.[63]

A week later they were back in Rome, having travelled by road to avoid the risk from Turkish pirates at sea. Carnival continued; riderless horses raced down the Corso, their spurs hanging loose, followed by races 'of Asses, of Bufalos, of Naked Men'. Then came the sobriety of Lent. The days leading up to Easter ceremonies were divided between the two papal churches, St Peter's and San Giovanni in Laterano. Evelyn, already a connoisseur of the art of the pulpit, enjoyed the formulaic but theatrical sermons at St Peter's, 'full of Italian Eloquence, & action'. The processions reached their peak with the 'heathnish pomp' of the night-time flagellants late in Holy Week (a practice suppressed early in the eighteenth century).

The new pope traversed the city, one day blessing golden roses for 'severall greate Princes' and the next washing the feet of the poor. Evelyn ran 'from Church to Church', marvelling at so much 'buisy devotion, greate silence, and unimaginable Superstition'.[64] Then, after the guns of Castel Sant'Angelo had sounded a welcome to the risen Christ, Innocent X celebrated his first Easter Sunday Mass, blessing the crowd from a loggia above the doors of St Peter's. Next month, through the good offices of the anglophile Cardinal Francesco Barberini (who was sent into exile soon after) Evelyn was invited to witness a papal ceremony and found himself invited 'to kisse his Toe, that is his embrodr'd Slipper, two Cardinals holding up his Vest and Surplice, so as sufficiently bless'd with his thumb & two fingers for that day I returnd home to dinner'. Despite the ironic tone of the diary entry, written long afterwards, Evelyn cannot disguise how bedazzled he was to find himself at the feet of the temporal and spiritual head of the Catholic Church. A few years later, while attempting to persuade Thomas Keightley not to convert to Catholicism, he conceded that one reason for his own stay in Rome was to explore 'the verity of things' since he had 'sometyme bin (I confesse) so farr in admiration of the Discipline of the Roman Church; as (if the Doctrine had bin as tempting) . . . to have resolved upon a farther Communion with her'.[65]

By now Evelyn was comfortable in the city, knowing his way round, speaking the language with confidence and, despite himself, somewhat seduced by Catholicism. As in Paris, there were literary and scientific academies 'where the Witts of the Towne meete on certaine daies, to recite poems & prevaricate on several Subjects &c.' He attended a gathering of the so-called *Umoristi*. But these circles also attracted those who preyed upon the suggestible. Almost fifty years later Henshaw told the Royal Society that in Rome 'he had seen a Mountebank, that had a ring, in which there was a stone like a Toad-stone, upon which putting a clear liquor like water, there arose a flame not unlike that of a small wax candle, which burnt a considerable time. The same attested by Mr Evelyn.' By then old men, Henshaw and Evelyn confessed that they had both been thoroughly hoodwinked at the time.[66]

As the weather became warmer, Evelyn wandered in the gardens of Villa Medici and Villa Borghese, shaded with evergreens and cooled by fountains and 'murmuring rivulets trickling downe the declining Walkes'. The papal palace at the Quirinale (like the Vatican) had a notable garden: 'I am told the Gardner is annualy alow'd 2000 scudi for the keeping it: Here I observ'd the glorious hedges of myrtle above a mans height; others of Laurell, Oranges, nay of Ivy, & Juniper.' Waterworks, cascades, grottos, hydraulic organs and the usual array of automata completed the picture.

He and Henshaw also travelled out to the parks and gardens up in the cooler hills where the nobility and grandees spent their summers. The remains of the Temple of Fortune at Palestrina caught their eye, its long terraces visible on the distant hillside. Of the more modern gardens, Villa Aldobrandini at Frascati and the Villa d'Este at Tivoli, which they visited on different days, were the most impressive – their dramatic settings intensified by the hand of man. More extensive than the Roman gardens, they showed the same happy balance between architectural structure, the forms (natural or contrived) of the landscape and restrained indigenous planting. At the 'delicious' cardinal's villa, 'a horrid Cascade' emptied into a 'Theater of Water', below which was a grotto full of water-driven singing birds and other 'surprising inventions'. The unwary visitor was bound to come out wet to the skin – such gardens were designed as much for hilarity as for quiet appreciation. At Tivoli, the villa on its summit crowned four descending gardens with torrents of water pouring down them, springing out from hundreds of fountains and spouts or disgorging into pools and water-stairs.[67]

But however impressive the waterworks, grottos and massed ranks of sculpture, Evelyn's abiding memory of these gardens was of their cool, dense foliage. Evergreens provided year-round substance, always the unifying feature in his own garden and those he laid out. In the English climate yews, hollies and laurels replaced Mediterranean myrtles and cypresses, smooth turf took the place of fine mosaic paving, but he hoarded his treasured Italian memories – the elements provided by splashing and glittering water, scented air, strong sunlight and deep shadow, long vistas and secret places.

Evelyn's departure from Rome was so precipitate that even Henshaw was taken by surprise. With just two days' notice, he told him, he could have gone too. But Evelyn's funds had run out and Collyer, the Livorno merchant handling both his letters of credit and the transportation of their trunks, was about to leave for England. He may also have had word from Padua: the earl of Arundel had been in poor health for some years and Evelyn was worried that he might never see him again. After going to Livorno and Florence, he headed for Bologna, a city under papal control. As always, he looked for a viewpoint, in this case the hilltop church and convent of San Michele in Bosco, so fresh and lovely that he envied the friars their good fortune. From there he thought he could see 'almost as far as Venice itself'.[68]

CHAPTER 4

'Sweete Mrs Eveling'

Sailing by night across the marshes towards Ferrara, Evelyn read by the light of a handful of phosphorescent glow worms. His first impressions of Venice were utterly devoid of any such enchantment, soured by long delays, first at the hands of health officials and then of customs men. Evelyn was hurrying to be there for Ascension Day, in late May 1644, to see the strange and moving ceremony of the Venetians' annual marriage to the sea, solemnised by the doge throwing a ring into the waters.[1]

The republic, its fortunes based upon seafaring and trade, had lasted longer 'than any of the foure antient Monarchies' and continued, he noted, 'in great State, welth & glory'.[2] Only the constant threat from the Turks (they were about to seize Crete from the Venetians) clouded the horizon. Machiavelli had celebrated Venice as a modern city-state in which engaged citizens enjoyed their liberties, and this remained the case more than a century later, offering a political model even English royalists might want to consider.[3]

The vitality of the city, a cornucopia of art and architecture with its jostling waterways and teeming streets proffering temptation, was the strongest possible contrast to Rome, a 'proud & imperial Citty in her duste & Ruines' brought down by 'Time & Barbaritie'. Evelyn allowed himself to be happily seduced. Henshaw, the friend through whose eyes we sometimes see aspects of the diarist that he did not choose to reveal himself, congratulated 'Sweet Mr Evelyn' on dealing with 'the pleasant daungers of Venice, which have bin able to give a temptation to so resolved a chastition as yours'. Evelyn wrote back teasingly, now that their roles were reversed: 'Pray be not unmindfull of your friends, do not loose us altogether, and burie us among the learned rubbish you so admire at Rome.'[4]

Henshaw was perhaps a little surprised that Evelyn found Venice so much to his taste. He planned to join him there but meanwhile, in the oppressive heat, had changed lodgings, moving to 'one of the best and freshest appartements in Rome', which he shared with seventeen-year-old Henry Howard,

Arundel's grandson, whom he was currently accompanying. They were enjoying themselves 'as well as wee can', especially on the Roman feast day of saints Peter and Paul, when music and spectacular illuminations filled the night air. Henshaw kept Evelyn informed about their compatriots' comings and goings, but the most magnificent travellers of all, the Villiers brothers, were still awaited he told him. George, 2nd duke of Buckingham and his brother Francis, aged respectively nineteen and seventeen, living regally in the shadow of their murdered father, were progressing slowly southwards. Currently they were 'delayed at Genoa because his governor Mr Alesbury is shot in the chest by some accident'.[5] They eventually reached Padua in mid-July when their party all matriculated at the university on the same day, but it took another six months for the cumbersome caravan to reach Rome, by then including Andrew Marvell.[6]

Well in advance, like an early swallow announcing summer, 'Sir Kenelm begins to appear now, a rich coach a stately Pallace, six staffiers and bobs to his horses'. Sir Kenelm Digby provided an intriguing link back to the vanished world of the lavish court of Charles I and Buckingham. Pretentious in his *équipe*, ducking and weaving between Catholicism and Anglicanism, he also epitomised the virtuoso, learning by snatches and publishing at intervals. He was currently Queen Henrietta Maria's papal envoy. Later on Evelyn dismissed him as 'an errant mountebank', a man who changed his religion as often as his costume and held conflicting views on alchemy and natural philosophy, but in the 1640s and '50s he still admired him enormously, asking Henshaw to give him his 'humble services'.

Henshaw had been to see Father Kircher, as promised, taking Evelyn's careful copy of some hieroglyphics: 'he was ravished at the sight of it he beg'd it before it was offred, and was so earnest with mee that instead of the copie I was fayne to give him my Originall.' Kircher promised to acknowledge them both in his forthcoming book on hieroglyphics when 'wee shall both bee made immortall'.[7] But when it was published there was no mention of Evelyn and Henshaw was only cited in passing. The wily but tireless priest was expert at milking the ingenuous visitors who came to sit at his feet. These admirers ensured him a constant supply of material which he consumed and carelessly exploited.

Henshaw also checked on young Carlo Maratti's progress with his various commissions for Evelyn. Evelyn had requested several books on Jesuit theology while Henshaw wanted Evelyn to purchase Galileo's dialogues and titles on the religion of the ancient Romans and Egyptian artefacts for him, 'all curious and rare, if you can find any of them pray buy it for mee and keep it till I come'. Both men were captivated by a heady mix of the new science and theology. In the midst of their high-minded discourse, Evelyn sent

Henshaw a pastoral poem (as he had earlier given Thicknesse a sight of his play). Henshaw replied that Evelyn might have to describe himself as a Catholic, it had pleased so many readers in Rome, only to be rebuked for showing it. Before turning north, Henshaw arranged for some of their trophies to be packed and sent to England, 'where I hope we may one day enjoy both one-another and them'.[8] Even apart, they operated in easy tandem, two instinctive *virtuosi*, enquiring and acquisitive.

Henshaw's news from home could hardly have been worse for royalist sympathisers or former cavaliers such as himself: 'Wee are all heer at our wits ends since wee receivd the sad news, the King bled and wounded in two places, the Duke of Richmond and four thousand taken prisoners; bags & baggage with a traine of 15 peeces of artillery & the Royall Standard lost.' However inaccurate his report was in detail, Naseby was a major defeat for the royalists at the hands of Cromwell's New Model Army. The old order was under serious threat. The nature of power and citizenship, despotism and liberty, suddenly became burning topics and the Venetian Republic was a good place to consider the alternatives. The young prince of Wales whom Evelyn had met in the House of Lords four years earlier was now a terrified fugitive in the West Country.

Across Europe exiles struggled to affirm or shift their religious allegiances. Evelyn was repeatedly shocked by conversions in his own circle, tending to blame the proselytiser rather than the proselyte. Henshaw witnessed one poignant episode at first hand. His 'dear Padrone', Henry Howard, had gone 'post from hence with expresse Letters of the Popes to fetch his brother Philip either by faire meanes or by force out of the monastery of Domenicans at Cremona'. From Padua, the enraged earl of Arundel, himself an (expedient) convert to the Church of England, enlisted the help of Cardinal Francesco Barberini and Sir Kenelm Digby. The eighteen-year-old was brought dramatically back to Rome, away from the influence of an Irish friar, but remained steadfast in his faith. In 1675 he became the first new English cardinal for a century.

Meanwhile James Thicknesse, already at Padua University, offered Evelyn two lower rooms at his own lodgings, as large and cool as he wanted.[9] The pair also hatched a plan to avoid the sweltering summer heat. As Evelyn told Henshaw: 'we have (the last weeke) taken our Cabine in a Vessel at Venice, which is bound for the Levant.' They planned to go to Alexandria, pay 'our devotions at Jerusalem' and return by Constantinople. Enterprising travellers were increasingly tempted by the prospect of exotic sights, experiences and acquisitions. But sadly for Evelyn the journey was aborted when their boat was requisitioned for likely action against the Turks. Otherwise, life continued with 'the usual reciprocations betweene Padoa and Venice, Venice and Padoa (and now and then a little baite on the sweete Brenta)'.[10] Hendrick van der Borcht, by now far away in Antwerp with the countess of Arundel, imagined Evelyn hurrying out to the 'island of St George' to see 'the rare great picture of Veronese and the goodly Pictures of Titian at Frari and other Places'.[11]

The first time Evelyn recorded going to Padua from Venice was for the feast day of St Anthony of Padua on 13 June 1645, a focus for pilgrimage ever since the Portuguese-born saint had been buried there. The canal boats went past delicious villas and country retreats, many designed by Palladio and his successor Scamozzi, and showing just how freely and to what effect the classical canons of architecture could be adjusted. No less interesting to Evelyn, many orchards were watered by systems of reservoirs, sluices and locks; mechanical ingenuity was transforming the countryside. Back in Venice he investigated the Arsenal, the industrial powerhouse of the republic, and then made a round of the city's most notable churches. Venice balanced mercantile and spiritual interests, to the obvious benefit of its citizens. In Padua he noted the Monte di Pietà, 'a continual banque of mony, to assist the poorer sort, upon any paune, & at reasonable Interest'.[12]

In July Evelyn returned again to Padua at the invitation of the earl of Arundel, who found himself confined by poor health and family tragedy. In 1645 his eldest grandson, also Thomas, who had been studying in Utrecht, came to join his family and fell sick. He never recovered and remained insane for the rest of his life, though he took the family's reclaimed title of 5th duke of Norfolk at the Restoration. He died in Padua in 1677.[13]

Among the hidden treasures that Arundel showed Evelyn during this memorable visit was Ammanati's gargantuan statue of Hercules, the same height as Michelangelo's *David*, which stood, then as now, hidden in the courtyard of the Palazzo Mantoa, close to the Eremitani and the Palazzo Foscari all'Arena. They also visited another treasure behind high walls, the miniature buildings of the Odeo (casino) and Loggia which had been built in the 1520s by Luigi Alvise Cornaro, author of the *Trattato de la Vita Sobria* (1558) and Palladio's patron. Was Evelyn struck by the neat symmetry that brought him there with Inigo Jones's first patron?

The Loggia was the first building on the classical antique model in northern Italy, while the tiny Odeo was an acoustically perfect music room at the heart of a series of tiny Renaissance rooms each painted and stuccoed according to different themes, often combining the motifs of classical antiquity with those of the Christian era.[14] Here the virtuous Cornaro had famously held his enlightened *salon*, offering music, theatre and intellectual discourse to a select audience. In Paris in 1651 Evelyn would see the boy-king Louis XIV perform in a ballet, in which a chariot of singers 'representing Cornaro & Temperance . . . was overthrowne by Bacchus & his Revellers'.[15]

In mid-September Evelyn matriculated at the university. He wrote (in good Italian) to an Italian friend, describing the town slowly coming back to life after the summer. Students converged on the ancient university, Galileo's *alma mater*, from countries as far apart as Greece, Poland, Scotland and Malta. The armorial bearings of the cream of the aristocracy still encrust the vaults and walls of the double-colonnaded quadrangle. But the register records men of all ages, nationalities and conditions, many in political or religious exile. Thirty years later at Padua, a professor's daughter, a student of philosophy called Elena Piscopia, became the first female university graduate in the world. Beyond papal control, Padua University represented intellectual freedom.

Some students, like Evelyn, were planning to remain a few weeks, others merely matriculated. He reported that the audience for the formal orations was very sparse although courses had begun. In Venice 'il Turco fa il Diavolo' (the Turk makes mischief) and in England the news could not be worse for the king, he told his regular Italian correspondent.[16] Now James Thicknesse, Evelyn's 'dear friend & until now constant fellow traveller', was called home unexpectedly; henceforth, they would remain bound by the 'passionate conventions of the familiar letter'.[17] In early October Henshaw and Francis Bramston, nicknamed the 'little lord chief justice', the diminutive son of Charles I's lord chief justice, finally caught up with Evelyn, who hurried back to Venice to act the cicerone. They attended a virtuoso performance by 'la Figliola', who sang and played several instruments, as if born 'senz ossi ne ditti' (without bones in her fingers). It was like being on Mount Parnassus.[18] The three shared lodgings in Padua on the Via Cesare Battista (now the Via San Francesco), a long arcaded street south-east of the university.

An intriguing figure arrived in Padua that winter. The poet-politician Edmund Waller matriculated at the university on 25 January 1646. As a young man he had been one of the Great Tew circle, introduced by Dr George Morley, later bishop of Winchester, who encouraged him to turn his verbal dexterity into verse.[19] Waller inherited his estate near Beaconsfield in 1616, sitting in the Commons in the 1620s and again in the early 1640s, in both the Short and Long Parliaments, where he was an adept in debate, arguing for reform but remaining a royalist. The so-called 'Waller's Plot' arose from his attempt to set up (with his brother-in-law and others) a party of moderates to bridge the divisions between king and Parliament, and involved a scheme to seize the City and deliver it to the king's forces.[20] Upon his arrest in May 1643 Waller was thought to have named his fellow conspirators, earning himself the scorn of many. Burnet famously described him as exhibiting 'a degree of flexibility unusual even in a poet'.[21] After eighteen months' imprisonment and payment of a fine of £10,000 (scarcely denting his fortune), he arrived in

9 Thomas Howard, 2nd earl of Arundel seen in his forties, engraved portrait by Lucas Vorsterman, undated but after 1625.

France with his son and nephew, who were briefly tutored by the political philosopher Thomas Hobbes. Waller was preparing for further travel; as Hobbes wrote to him in Calais: 'I believe you pass much of yours [time] in meditating how you may to your Contentment (and without blame) passe the seas.'[22] He was witty, erudite and worldly-wise, almost a generation older than Evelyn and his friends, and, inevitably, somewhat notorious.

Waller's poetry and discourse had often served a political purpose, overt or covert. He was Oliver Cromwell's cousin and was also related to John Hampden, and throughout the Interregnum he penned numerous panegyrics, switching his allegiance and often disguising his political message by metaphor or symbolism but always deploying his famous charm. 'Her face is so smooth that the eye slides off it, / Smooth as Waller's verse,' wrote the duke of Buckingham.[23] The man whom Evelyn met was, as described by Aubrey, thin and 'not at all robust'. He had a small oval face with a high, wrinkled forehead but his main features were his eyes, 'popping out and working'. He had a hot temper and was 'something magesteriall'.[24] Evelyn, nursing literary ambitions and unsure how to make himself useful to the royalist cause, was magnetised by his political and intellectual sophistication. Waller was a generous, engaging mentor and, the earl of Arundel apart, the man whose advice he followed most closely in the coming years.

Carnival drew Evelyn back to Venice where, as he had been the previous year in Rome and Naples, he was caught up in the celebrations, dodging eggs 'fill'd with sweete Waters' as well as heavier, deadlier missiles: enraged bulls charging down the alleys pursued by Venetian young bloods. He found fancy dress a great leveller – there was no way of knowing whether your companion was an aristocrat or a shopkeeper. But the greatest delight of carnival was the activity, both theatre and music, from *commedia dell'arte* to opera, from street rehearsal to concert performance. Monteverdi's *Coronation of Poppea* was performed that year, possibly one of 'three noble Operas' he heard, as well as a recital by the incomparable Anna Renzi, singing with her eunuch and accompanied by a harpsichordist.[25]

Back in Padua for Lent, Evelyn embarked upon a month-long study of human physiology. In the university's claustrophobic anatomy theatre, Evelyn spent every morning watching, in succession, 'a Woman, a Child, & a Man dissected, with all the manual operations of the Chirurgion upon the humane body'. Shaped like an elliptical funnel, the narrowest point or spout of the theatre was a tiny basement, and this is where the dissections took place. As many as two hundred students crammed together to watch, lining a spiral ramp that coiled its way upwards, wrapped about by an ornamental walnut balustrade. In the afternoons the 'young Gentlemen Travellers', as Evelyn termed them, observed operations on the poor at the main hospital, San Francesco. Surgeons demonstrated a series of repulsive procedures: 'Trepanning, Launcing, Salivating, Sweating etc.' Evelyn suspected the female patients were whores.

Following in the footsteps of distinguished physicians like William Harvey, who had studied in Padua between 1599 and 1602, there were a number of *bona fide* students training in medicine alongside the many amateurs who swelled their ranks briefly. Since 1632, the chair of anatomy had been held by the German professor Johann Vesling, well known thanks to his widely translated book *Syntagma Anatomicum* (1641). The anatomy course was the best in Europe and, of the English physicians studying there, two became Evelyn's particular friends: George Rogers, later president of the Royal College of Physicians; and George Joyliffe, who helped discover the lymphatic system before dying young.[26] Both Vesling and Rogers were honoured with poems by Waller.

Vesling lectured and demonstrated 'simples' grown in the botanical garden, the first in the world, founded in 1545. The study of medicine and the skills of the apothecary were complementary. Their design prompted by the discovery of the New World, the botanical gardens were laid out as at Leiden, in four quadrants, each representing a continent. At Padua some attempt had even been made to plant according to the orientation of the gardens – cedar and cypress were to the east. Though the collections were still somewhat random, they epitomised God's creation within a measured and confined space. Usually a menagerie or aviary and a selection of mineral and geological specimens recalled a cabinet of natural curiosities. For Evelyn, 'philosophical-medical' gardens demonstrated 'a rich & noble compendium of what the whole globe of the Earth has flourishing' and allowed experiment, breeding, study and, above all, contemplation of God's universe.[27] The Padua garden was, appropriately enough, overlooked by the clustered 'five handsome Cupolas leaded' of San Antonio.

Evelyn asked Vesling's permission to take a representative sample of medicinal plants to dry and paste into an album. His *hortus hyemalis* (winter garden) opens with a bleeding heart pierced by arrows, his motto and an epigram from Ovid. Each example was named in both Latin and English and, in the early pages, he also added descriptions. The herbarium was a desiccated personal reminder of a flourishing garden, an aide-mémoire for a questing horticulturist, a popular way of collecting specimens for study. A little later Evelyn turned to George Joyliffe for help. The physician, like many of his peers also a knowledgeable botanist, wrote from Sussex that he had 'taken a catalogue of all the Latin names and viewing the plants themselves by them ere I adioyned the English' he had found several duplications and a number of wrong names. He offered to correct the errors.[28] Nomenclature remained a problem until the taxonomy of flora was resolved later in the century. Evelyn's herbarium was a source of great pride to him and was one of the prized possessions he showed to Pepys when he first visited Sayes Court.[29]

Evelyn also bought a set of 'tables', as he referred to them, prepared by Vesling's assistant, Giovanni Leoni. Having discovered that Leoni was leaving for Poland, he obtained three boards on which were mounted the arteries,

veins and nervous system, dried relics from dissections.[30] The gruesome specimens were the anatomical equivalent of his herbarium. Here was useful
evidence, however faltering, towards an understanding of the workings of the
human body at a time when even distinctions between male and female physiology were still unclear. For William Harvey nature was 'the best and most
faithful interpreter of her own secrets, and what she presents either more
briefly or obscurely in one department, that she explains more fully and
clearly in another'. Further careful examination led to insight, a 'kind of image
or reflection of the omnipotent Creator himself'.[31] Evelyn was pursuing an
intensive programme of his own devising, continually investigating new
topics but alert to the divine provenance of everything.

By Easter, he was ready to leave Padua and added his medical trophies to
the acquisitions he was shipping home. Once they were aboard he lost track
of the ship, which was diverted to Holland (he discovered later), arriving in
London in 1649. The tables were 'the first of that kind [that] had ben ever
seene in our Country, & for ought I know, in the World' and, over fifty years
later, finely engraved, they were published under the auspices of the Royal
Society.[32]

On his last morning in Padua he breakfasted with the earl of Arundel. It
proved a poignant encounter.

> I tooke leave of him in his bed, where I left that greate & excellent Man in
> teares upon some private discourse of the crosses had befaln his Illustrious
> family: particularly the undutifullnesse of his Grandson Philips turning
> Dominican Frier (since Cardinal of Norfolke), the unkindnesse of the
> Countesse, now in Holland. The miserie of his Countrie, now embroild in
> a Civil War etc.

He asked Evelyn to deliver messages in England for him, hoping that Sir
Richard Onslow would keep an eye on Albury and instructing his steward to
report 'howe my water & all thinges are at Alberry, & that he will have greate
care that agaynest the Gallery & House, store of Roses, Chesimine wodbines
& the like sweetes be plantes'.[33] He then provided an itinerary for his onward
journey and asked him to write, gestures of trust and friendship that proved
Arundel's high regard for him.

After months spent in the company of the grandees of Padua and Venice,
Evelyn may have been becoming self-important. John Abdy, a relative of
Bramston's, felt his letters were increasingly formal: 'I thought our friendship
so happily begunne and soe long continued at Padova and our freedome . . .
in all our affaires at Venice would not have suffered such a style . . . but you
are the patterne of civility and I shall studie to copie from you.'[34] When

Evelyn left Venice he was seen off by a group of friends, among whom was one of Hugo Grotius's sons – with the exception of Francis Bacon, no writer is more prominent in Evelyn's commonplace collection than the Dutch ecumenical thinker.[35] Then, bearing an elaborately worded pass in Latin that gave them access to Spanish territories (such as Milan), he and his two companions, the by now ubiquitous Edmund Waller and a Captain Wray, travelling with 'a huge filthy Curr' (an English water spaniel), set off. Arundel's instructions covered both architecture and helpful personal contacts. Most of his suggestions concerned Milan, but on the way he directed them to Palladio's work in Vicenza, especially the theatre and the many unfinished private palaces.[36] The best, and most complete, was 'The Pallace called the Rotonda' a mile outside town, but to Evelyn's regret his companions caused him to miss it. At Verona, they visited the Roman arena and the Giusti gardens as recommended. At the border with Spanish territories, the inspecting officers 'finding we were onely Gentlemen Travellers dismissd us for a small reward'. Once in Milan they ascended the cathedral, 'an ill designe of Gothick Architecture' but 'worth one's paines of going up to the top,' in order to see the elaborate carving on the roof. They also viewed the priceless manuscripts in the Ambrosiana Library, kept in 'a little place made of wanscote'. Then, after a tragic accident, during which their Scottish host was killed by his rearing horse, they left in a hurry, nervous that the authorities might want to question them. There was no more time for the earl's recommendations and soon Evelyn turned his back on Italy for ever.

The party headed across the Lombard Plain for the Simplon Pass. Although it was May, the Alps were under unseasonably heavy snow as they struggled up through 'very steepe, craggy, & dangerous passages', an intimidating landscape so unlike the artificial drama of the cascades at Tivoli. Even the mountain people, disfigured by goitres, seemed sinister. The atmosphere infected his companions; the temperamental captain threatened to shoot his horse, which had slipped off the precipitous path, rather than let their Swiss guide catch the animal and risk him stealing his baggage. The climate of suspicion was heightened by a night spent in a mountain inn where the ghoulish heads of bears, wolves and foxes were nailed to the doors. Another night was spent in the foothills, where the bedding 'made such a Crackling, & did so prick my skin through the tick, that I could not sleepe'. In *Sylva*, his book on trees, he celebrated the comforts of (frost-bitten) beech leaves as a favourite Swiss mattress stuffing so perhaps these had been chestnut leaves, used by Italians. The suddenly pleasant descent to the prosperous Rhône Valley and the first sight of the calm waters of Lake Geneva came as a welcome relief.

Almost immediately Evelyn was struck down by smallpox and for five weeks in May and June he remained gravely ill. He could not have known that, having survived, he would have gained immunity for life. As he convalesced, Evelyn explored Geneva, for even the aftermath of a near-fatal illness did not stop him rooting around the bookshops and examining the fine watches and gun mechanisms crafted in the city. Waller and Wray stayed with him throughout. Their hosts were kindness itself and the captain passed his time by falling in love with their daughter.

Once Evelyn had recovered, they headed back to Lyons and Paris, a cheerful, leisurely journey marred only by the loss of Evelyn's dog, a faithful spaniel. Waller's presence guaranteed that things remained lively, and also offered an opportunity for Evelyn to discuss his future with his worldly friend – no one knew better what his options might realistically be.

In England Thicknesse was surprised to hear of Evelyn's illness, imagining he had an iron constitution: 'I am afraid those nocturnal lucubrationes of Padova & the unaccustomed cold of the Alpes have seiz'd on you as cold on glasses, (but God forbid) the danger of cracking.' He used a metaphor for the situation at home: the kingdom was a shipwreck, from which two passengers swam cheerfully away with a plank, only to be hit by an empty barrel. 'The presbyter & independent have now the board betweene them', and if they are not drowned, all may end peacefully.[37]

In Paris Evelyn received a letter from Arundel.

Mr Eveline I am very glad to heare you passed soe well your sicknes in your iorney, I hope by this time you with good Mr Waller are in Englande, & hope you will there remember me that I may hope to see my poore little Cottage of Alleberrye to my comforte, I had a conserve for snowe there which did not hold it well, I desire it might be amended, & an other made to keepe Ice in, you see I still continue to troble you. I pray for all happines to you as beinge your assured frende.[38]

But Evelyn did not return to England in time to pass on the earl's wishes and Arundel never saw Albury again. That autumn he died and his heart was buried in the cloister at Padua. The difficulties of his Catholic countess Alathea (born a Shrewsbury, she brought immense wealth into the marriage) continued. Her son Lord Mowbray contested his father's will until his own death in 1652.[39] For Arundel, Albury represented calm and refuge, and he hoped that a house, with a library and laboratory, might be built near the church for six 'honest unmarried men'.[40] Although nothing came of it, the idea of this little college may have caught Evelyn's attention.

Back in Paris, Evelyn relaxed or, as he characteristically put it, wasted time. Thicknesse wrote to him at the Ville-de-Venise, a convenient *poste restante*, telling him that Oxford had been reduced to a home for beasts: 'Ho travato in B[alliol] C[ollege] duoi cani, tre gatti, gli maschi e femini . . . quanti furono in arca di Noe' (Noah's Ark). That October, Thicknesse told him, was the moment to see honest men falling as fast as leaves.[41] But Evelyn was not worrying unduly about the situation at home – these were the months 'in my whole life I spent most idly'.[42]

Paris was, more than ever, at the centre of interlocking intellectual circles based in France and the Low Countries, eager to welcome new contributors to their project. They included many exiles from England, especially after the arrival of the prince of Wales, the future Charles II, in July 1646. Thomas Hobbes, his mathematics tutor, sat poised uncomfortably between his court affiliations and his increasingly contentious published views. The author of *De Cive* wanted his portrait and the inscription 'Academic Tutor to his Serene Highness the Prince of Wales' removed from the volume. It seemed impolitic, while the English monarchy was so troubled, to publish a political theory 'which offends the opinions of almost everyone' and which bore the apparent imprimatur of the heir to the throne.[43] But Samuel Sorbière, physician and aspiring man of letters, reassured him that England was fortunate to have a future king 'full of wisdom and imbued with your teachings'.

Waller was now in Rouen. He and Evelyn corresponded regularly despite what may have been a veiled warning from Thicknesse referring to the 'W' affair.[44] They planned to go to Spain that autumn. Waller would send his son back to England, after which 'I shall be the more free to wayt on you to Spaine'. He thought they would make 'a compatible & agreable company'. A Mr Fisher and John Digby were also joining them. Now Waller turned to practicalities: the former ambassador to Madrid, the earl of Arundel's friend Sir Arthur Hopton, was staying in his lodgings and 'I am every day learning such things as may be of use'. Despite Hopton's financial plight and his advanced age, the always generous Waller also hoped that he might obtain patronage for Evelyn via Hopton's nephew, Ralph, now in the suite of the prince of Wales. The older man had received great kindness from the Brownes after he left Madrid in 1645, which he was eager to repay, telling Waller that he thought highly of Evelyn.[45]

The hand of Arundel can be detected behind the Spanish venture. Referring to himself as 'your very affectionate friend', he wrote to an unnamed correspondent (surely Evelyn), asking to be kept informed of his whereabouts and for news of Waller. He also enclosed a letter to 'Signore Ettenhard', an art dealer who was also the Spanish king's superintendent of revenue, asking that he show the visitor the 'most notable things' in Madrid.

This clandestine exchange suggests that Arundel may have been preparing a deal involving works of art as a source of funds for the beleaguered monarchy. But Waller's correspondence was going astray or being read. Since the 'poor English have no safety on earth or water', he decided to pull out.[46]

If he was under surveillance, Waller preferred to remain in northern France, offering to buy Evelyn local curiosities for his cabinet. He had intended to write to him in French but 'I love to say what ever comes first to my mynde & in French I can not write without thinking on it'.[47] Evelyn's French was now better than Waller's who sent him his own translation of a poem for correction, adding 'there you have more french then ever I writt before as I beleeve you will perceave by my spelling.'[48]

Waller supported and encouraged Evelyn in everything from his financial dealings to his literary ambitions. He hoped 'the muses' were still visiting him and, though 'your lute can only entertain those in the same chamber, but if you touch that other string it may be heard many miles'. By this time Waller was clearly encouraging Evelyn into print and praised an (unspecified) translation into verse: 'if I were not now past it & so less fond of the reputation for poetry than I have been I should both fear & envy you.'[49]

Waller, according to Aubrey, found writing to order difficult but 'when the Fitt comes upon him, he does it easily'.[50] It seems probable that he introduced Evelyn to Hobbes, if not yet in person, then at least on the page. Waller had hoped to translate the elegantly argued *De Cive* into English but stood back when he realised that Hobbes was planning to do it himself.[51] It must have been now, in the winter of 1646–7, that Evelyn first considered translating a slim French volume published in 1643 dealing with the relationship between the courtier and his master, *Of Liberty and Servitude*. The author was François de la Mothe le Vayer, a scholar, historiographer and pedagogue who had been patronised by Richelieu and who now addressed himself to Mazarin. He was known to Hobbes and, like him, had spent an uneasy period tutoring princes.[52]

Paris was the perfect arena for Evelyn at this stage. Encouraged by a widening circle of advisors and confidants, he was finding his way. Drama and poetry were not his *métier*, but translation provided an ideal springboard into a life of letters. His library, well stocked with titles bought in Rome, Venice and Paris, was expanding and he began to consider how to manage and categorise his books. A recently reissued volume, *Advis pour dresser une bibliothèque* (1627, 1644) by Gabriel Naudé, the man entrusted with building up Mazarin's exceptional book collection and who Evelyn met in person, celebrated the idea of a universal library to which the 'public' had access. As Evelyn was to put it in his translation of that work: 'nothing . . . renders a Library more recommendable, then when every man findes in it that which he is in search of.' Evelyn was also becoming a discerning print collector. But he was vulnerable to those who offered intellectual sweets on the street. Later he warned against those Frenchmen who claimed to 'render any man an exact and perfect Philosopher, Divine, Orator, Chynmist; or to teach him all Languages, and indeed, what not, within the space of a month or two'.[53]

Evelyn was intrigued by chemistry and saw it within a wider scheme: 'the End is to perfect, and prepare medicines for the benefit of mans body also mettals, beesids the discovering of many seacrets of Nature both delightful & profitable.'[54] Those 'secrets' ranged from the chemical process required 'to make the depuration, fusion, spirit, and oyle of Nitre, or Salt-peter' to homely recipes for diet and good health such as 'Mr Waller's remedy' for troubles with the lungs and spitting, a concoction of honey, rose-water and an egg, to be eaten first thing in the day with walnuts. Evelyn was following Niçaise Le Fèvre's course. Le Fèvre was a Huguenot, recently arrived in Paris, who taught popular chemistry to mostly overseas students.[55] He drew heavily on the work of his patron, Samuel du Clos, the king's physician, and on that of the eminent Dutch chemist Johann Rudolf Glauber. Le Fèvre identified three strands in chemistry – philosophy, medicine and pharmacology. In a notebook begun in 1646 Evelyn also recorded his studies with 'my master monsieur Bartlet'. Neither Le Fèvre's nor Anibal Barlet's courses were yet published or translated and it occurred to him that an accessible chemistry manual might 'Benefit my Country'.[56]

The one person with whom he could discuss this, Thomas Henshaw, had been derailed by illness, exacerbated by poor medical treatment in Venice. At this time Henshaw described himself as pale as Lazarus or Sir Andrew Aguecheek, but said that he had found a more competent doctor – 'an honest Israelite of the Ghetto' – who, he hoped, would 'rub mee over the chops with his red hat & shortly give me a good colour again' (a reference to the red hats that Jews were required to wear). Francis Bramston and Dr George Rogers had gone on ahead to Padua.[57] The political situation was worsening in the Venetian Republic, with the Turks menacing its boundaries. The seventeenth-century Grand Tourist had to be ready to move on smartly to avoid civil wars and wider conflicts.

With his head down in the laboratory and his eye fixed on opportunities for publication, Evelyn must have been glad to hear that Henshaw was tired of 'this pilgrim's life of counting steeples' and planning to turn for home. He had abandoned a journey east to Cairo and Jerusalem, believing that peace was imminent in England: 'so advantageous an opportunity is never to bee hoped for againe.' He would be in Paris soon to exchange news with Evelyn and 'bee an admirer with the rest of your freinds of those accomplishments you dayly acquire'. He enjoyed Evelyn's account of his journey (sadly lost) which with its 'lively description' of places and 'judicious Essay uppon each thing worth note' had also demonstrated that 'dangers and troubles are much more frequent in travell then pleasures and satisfactions'. He was pleased that Evelyn was prolonging his stay in Paris, although he felt he should soon return to England 'for your own interest'. They could go back together, or 'any other design you please to propose'. In the meantime he hoped that no new friends now 'either extrude mee or precede mee'.[58] Had Henshaw, writing in the spring of 1647, already heard about the accomplished young daughter of the Resident?

Since Evelyn's previous stay in Paris, the expatriate English community had been swelled by the court of Henrietta Maria, which had arrived late in 1644. Charles I's queen was given apartments at the Louvre by her sister-in-law, Anne of Austria, and a pension of 1,200 francs per day, with use of the royal summer palace at St Germain-en-Laye for the hottest months. At the Louvre her confidant, Lord Jermyn, had a suite nearby and his sister was a lady-in-waiting. Jermyn's secretary was Abraham Cowley, the poet, and others such as William Davenant and John Denham helped to give the court a literary flavour.[59] The Catholic queen was manipulative, setting exile against exile, but her court reinforced the links between Paris and the English king, to the Resident's advantage. When Jermyn arrived in Paris he wrote, probably to Sir Edward Nicholas, immediately: 'One thing I must recommend to you, Sir, Richard Brown [sic] starves; it will be shameful in the Queen's presence to see him in the poverty he is. Pray speak to the King [that] he may have something sent him.'[60] Even at the best of times, the peripatetic life of the king's overseas representatives left them overlooked and often unremunerated. Furthermore, they were often passed over when they eventually returned home.

The Resident's house was a homing point for all royalists who came to Paris, whether exiles or passing travellers. His immediate circle numbered clerics, diplomats, courtiers and envoys. Browne was part of a human safety net stretching between The Hague and Brussels, Madrid and Rome, ready to catch those adrift. Subject to pressure from every direction and vulnerable to all kinds of disinformation, the (now unpaid) envoys were required to interpret the current situation and react to intelligence. Often, in the absence of ambassadors, they became solitary *chargés d'affaires*.

In a more emblematic role, the Resident maintained Anglican observance, holding services from the Book of Common Prayer and offering communion, baptisms, marriages and funerals in his chapel, and establishing links with the Huguenots in their chapel at Charenton, which Evelyn so admired, enjoying the music and setting, the psalms sung in a barrel-vaulted, galleried 'temple'. Between 1598 and 1685, when the revocation of the Edict of Nantes expelled the Huguenot community, they became a sizeable minority in France. Browne's predecessor, Lord Scudamore, had refused to speak French or visit Charenton but steadfastly provided a chapel 'adorned according to the newe devise, so that manie Papists there said they were at the English masse'.[61] In fact, it was no more than a room set aside in the Resident's house, furnished appropriately. Dr John Cosin, a Laudian who had been exiled in 1644, usually conducted the services and was chaplain to the Protestants in the royal household at the Louvre, a theological bulwark against what he termed Henrietta Maria's 'Romanising efforts'. Cosin established good relations with the clergy and congregation at Charenton, but Browne's own friendliness with the Huguenots was later to be misinterpreted and brought him trouble.

The Resident's wife was immensely active, the heart of the establishment on the rue Taranne. For instance, Elizabeth Browne received boxes of local grapes, 'a greate White Furr to cover a Bedd', gloves, ribbons and a pair of scarlet silk stockings with garters from Sir Ralph Verney in Blois as thanks for her (unspecified) help. When Margaret Lucas married William Cavendish, the marquess of Newcastle, in their chapel in 1645, Elizabeth played the role of mother of the bride. This kindness led Margaret Cavendish to promise her a gift of £1,000 once their fortunes were restored.

The prince of Wales's arrival from Jersey established a second English court in France, his advisors trying to keep him at a distance from his mother and her coterie at the Louvre, at least for the winter months. From July 1646 until June 1648, Charles was based entirely at St Germain-en-Laye, where his chaplains were Dr Richard Steward and Dr John Earle, the latter a distinguished classicist and, according to Dr Gilbert Burnet, 'the man of all the Clergy for whom the King had the greatest esteem . . . So he, who had a secret pleasure in finding out any thing that lessened a man esteemed eminent for piety, yet had a value for him beyond all the men of his order.'[62] The prince's non-spiritual care was in the hands of several impressive instructors, including Hobbes.

Evelyn's diary skates with unusual brevity and vagueness over his months back in Paris, during which he began to consider asking for the hand of the Resident's daughter, twelve-year-old Mary Browne. Her father was a man after his own heart, a knowledgeable enthusiast for gardens and books, as Evelyn had already discovered, while her mother made their house 'not only an hospital, but an asylum to all our persecuted and afflicted countrymen'. Evelyn would have been a regular congregant in the Resident's chapel, and so had a good opportunity to renew the acquaintance begun three years earlier. Later, in semi-fictional terms, Evelyn described a couple whose

Onely daughter . . . besides the pretynesse & innocence of her youth . . . had something mi-thought, in her that pleasd me in a Gravity I had not observd in so tender a bud; for I could call her Woman for nothing, byt her early steadines, & that at the age of playing with babies, she would be at her Book, her needle, Drawing of pictures, casting [?] Accompts & Undertook to Govern the house. I tooke notice that she began to discourse not Impertinently, was gay enough for my humor & one I believ'd that might one day grow-up to be the agreable companion of an honest-man.[63]

By early 1647 Evelyn's interest in Mary was obvious to all though he was not her only suitor. In early February, Thomas Keightley wrote to Evelyn ('Worthy Cosin') noting 'it was time for a private Cavalier to purchase that flower in the Bud, which when Blown would have bin reserv'd for Princes'. Mary had taken him into her confidence and 'you would hardly endure to see such deepe symptoms of languishing for your Companye in your Mistress's face'. In the light of this, he was reluctantly supporting Evelyn's suit rather than his own, especially since 'you seeme to apologise to mee'. Having ceded his claim, he writes that he is now 'endeavouring to please & beautifye her in whom I am confident you chiefly plan to advance your own Content & Happiness'. A different light falls on the episode in a later letter from the impoverished royalist courtier Sir Endymion Porter to Richard Browne: 'I feare Tom will make it doomes daye for Mr Eveling or him (if they meete) for marrieing his mistres'.[64] He seemed to imply that the usurped Keightley might challenge Evelyn to a duel – but Porter was a notorious gossip and far away in Brussels.

In summer 1647 George too had plans for marriage. His second wife was Lady Mary Cotton, a young childless widow. They were marrying privately and since Evelyn could not be there, George asked whether he would consider composing a poem for the occasion, as he had for his first wedding. He felt hopeful of a resolution between the army and Parliament and told his brother that the king was at Lord Craven's house at Caversham, near Reading, where Cromwell and he had met a number of times: 'They allow freedom to all men to come to Court, and divers of his owne party have had . . . liberty to wait upon his Majestie.' Despite the strictures upon the established church, the king still had his chaplains. George hoped that this optimistic news would persuade Evelyn home.[65]

At a time when marriages could be contracted from seven years old, and the legal age for marriage was twelve, Evelyn's good relations with Mary's parents gave him an advantage over his 'rival'. He had the means to alleviate their financial crisis as Keightley probably did not, for only two years later Evelyn was lending money to Keightley's brother Thomas. Evelyn claimed that he had got to know Browne better after he had helped him following a robbery, at which point he began to court his daughter, whom he had 'set my affections on'. Mary was effectively French, despite her English parentage, and the girl to whom Evelyn became betrothed that summer, a not exceptional state of affairs at the period, was to mature into a remarkable woman. His later description of her – 'the best Wife in the World, Sweete, and (though not charming) agreable and as she grew up, pious, loyal & of so just a temper' – hardly does her justice.[66]

The friendship with Richard Browne, only fifteen years his senior, gave Evelyn both a father-figure and a friend, even a dependant, for he was a surprisingly unworldly man who was happy to take financial advice from his son-in-law. With no support from the Crown 'he mortgag'd all his paternal estate' and by the mid-1640s he was seeking a position with the Levant Company in Constantinople with the help of his cousin George Tuke and others. Letters suggesting, first, that he was assured of the post, and then that it had been taken by someone else, kept him on tenterhooks. With the failure of that lifeline, the Evelyn family now came to his aid.

At the time of his betrothal John Evelyn was twenty-six. Their union would not be physically consummated for some time, and Evelyn's choice of an under-age bride ensured him a chaste wife. His contribution to the Resident's finances could be organised as soon as he returned to England, which he now resolved to do. By his action, he had jeopardised the family estate, which may explain his initial reluctance to tell his brothers about the marriage – leaving them to hear the news from others and after the event. An alliance with the only daughter of a man deep in debt – even if through no fault of his own – was an unwelcome drain on his own family's resources but he assumed that the Crown would eventually rectify the situation and that the current transactions would therefore be in its long-term interest. His eye was set on future prospects and potential patronage. Where Mary was concerned, he was well schooled in the norms of patriarchy and believed that he could mould his bride into an ideal wife, an attitude borne out by their early letters, which are more suggestive of those between school master and pupil than young lovers. The eventual harmony of their nearly sixty-year marriage, during which Mary became his wife, lover and friend, in his words, is all the more exceptional set against this awkward start.

So in early June 1647 'we concluded about my marriage' and went out to St Germain-en-Laye, the prince of Wales's quarters, to ask Dr Earle to perform the ceremony in Paris. The charming, erudite cleric was his first choice over Dr Cosin. Evelyn and Mary were married at around midday on 27 June, 'some few select friends being present', in the Brownes' chapel. It was Corpus Christi, a feast day, and the narrow, funnel-like streets of Paris had been transformed into oriental tents while the scent of blossoms overwhelmed less salubrious smells.

Among those present were William and Margaret Cavendish, the earl and countess of Newcastle, who had been married there two years earlier. The earl composed a rather risqué poem for Evelyn to mark the occasion, making great play upon the fact that his bride was still a child, for whom he would have to wait.

> Thy Inclosd Bewtious lilly shees so faire
> Not spotted or yett sullid with the Ayre
> A Virgin White Rose in the Budd thy owne
> No love yett Breath'd on her, so far from Blowne
> No Plum or Apricock or wooly Peach
> But fruite of frutes that's yett beyond thy reach
> A Preserved Virgin in a Cristall Boxe
> Transparent but yett under Naturs locks
> No opning it but with the Key of Tyme.

The full version of the (unpublished) poem, with its references to colts and stallions, scabbards and swords, suggests that Evelyn cannot have been entirely prim. The middle-aged, worldly Cavendish wished him well, while commiserating that he must 'see a Growing Aprill many hours/ Before a May where thou mayst gaither flowrs'.[67]

Congratulations came from across the royalist diaspora, including from Edmund Waller in Rouen enclosing Lord Hopton's good wishes, who shared his own view that 'the match betwixt you & your Excellent Lady was the fittest and happiest for both that could have been contrived'.[68] From Brussels, Endymion Porter sent his regards to Evelyn and to the sweet 'Zagala' (gypsy) of Deptford. The following month he wrote again to Browne: 'tell Mr Eveling that I wish his Epilogue maye bee as happie as the Prologue of his love was, and that sweete Mrs Eveling maye bring us daintie granchildren to playe with when we are wearie att courte'.[69] Browne's cousin James Stephens wrote to him from Spain, offering congratulations but wondering who the bridegroom might be. The unexpected news had refreshed him in the burning heat, he said. Before long Stephens and Evelyn would become close friends. Meanwhile James Thicknesse had been to Wotton, where he was able to tell Evelyn's family about his betrothal, prompting George to write in August, having heard of the 'civility and sweetnes of this your other halfe'.[70]

For Thicknesse, Mary could be a 'second sister', as Evelyn put it. He and Evelyn had originally met the Browne family in Paris in November 1643 and he was disappointed to have missed the wedding. 'Though my head is bad, my Hart is good and the newes of your happy choyse gave me much quiett to my thoughts, the best part of my life, and content being lockt up in your good Fortune.' He would tell their mutual friends about Mary, 'her unparallelld perfections ... that (j'en scais quos) of a Sweete solid behaviour, wise Melancholy and gallant Education have rendred her a jewell only for your purchase. Indeed her mind is all Virtue, her Body all English beauty, excepting her tongue, and that's perfect French.'

Elizabeth Browne also deserved praise, 'since she perfected that in your fayre Mistress which only Nature began and wrott all those noble characters in that spotless table of her mind'. Thicknesse also sent his fond regards to Browne. Evelyn, he said, fully deserved such a wife: 'your dayly pursuite after virtue, and noble actions must give the world satisfaction in that particular.' He imagined Evelyn did not often think of him but he hoped to be remembered fondly. Thicknesse thought it a good moment to return; the royalist army had moved away from London, leaving 'as faire weather now as you are like to have this 12 months'. He believed that the king would be restored. In the meantime, 'Your fame, that is your forerunner and harbinger for so noble & accomplisht a person (as we shall find you) has renderd me extremly passion- ate to enjoy you and draw out of your fountains'. But if he did decide to come home, Thicknesse advised him to 'leave your Virtue behind you, or else to keepe it close hid in your Brest, for should you divulge it here, it might bring you in question before a Committee. A Virtuous Man & a reall freind are as strange a sight here, as to find a serious Frenchman in France.'[71]

Some weeks after his marriage and having settled his will, Evelyn took Thicknesse's advice and left for England to play a role in his family's affairs. He travelled to the coast with Waller, via Rouen and Dieppe to St Valéry-sur-Somme, where they stayed overnight to discuss some 'business'. Evelyn then embarked at Calais for Dover. From Deptford, William Peters, Browne's faithful steward, wrote: 'We doo with a greate deale of impatience expect the arrival of the young gentleman that wee may have the honour to kiss his hand and wait on him heare.' Browne had asked him to keep the marriage secret.[72]

There had been little to tempt the staunchly royalist and enduringly Anglican Evelyn to return to England except his obligations to his family and Browne. But Edmund Waller was also urging him back to 'advance that affayre which will be much better treated by some trusty person present there then it can be by letters'. The development of a self-powered engine was the philosopher's stone of mid-seventeenth-century mechanics: some were even stockpiling patents in the hope of an eventual breakthrough.[73] Waller appears to have drawn Evelyn (and Browne) into an international treasure hunt via an intermediary, William Frizell, a former agent for the earl of Arundel as well as Charles I, 'than whom no man better understood the Value of Pictures'.[74]

The correspondence between Evelyn, Browne and Frizell suggests that they were attempting to secure an English patent for a novel water-raising wheel and boring device and Evelyn had advanced Frizell two large sums 'upon pawne and other covenants', four hundred French livres in February 1647 and six hundred in April.[75] Such an engine, which might potentially be used for the drainage of mines and marshes, construction and the provision of clean water supplies, had so far proved elusive. Heavy investment in a working prototype was needed but all development had to be pursued in extreme secrecy, before any profit might be reaped.

One of many patents had been tried out in England in 1645 (after initial registration at The Hague in 1639) but the results 'so much disheartened our inventor, who as yet had not quite perfected his work, that he went abroad, and sold his Patent and models'. If there was profit in such an invention, 'Parliament (in this their time of seekinge the Peoples loue) woulde appointe a Committee for the examininge & rewardinge of Ingenuities & purchasinge them for publike vse', as Sir Cheney Culpeper, much involved in trade and new inventions on behalf of Parliament, wrote to Samuel Hartlib, the latter soon to be an important figure in Evelyn's life.[76]

Whoever secured the successful patent would gain great wealth. By the summer of 1647 Frizell claimed they had 'perfected the worke to our great content and satisfaction, and will be of the most use and benefit to all Christendom of anie thing that ere was invented'. The engine in question was

wholly changed from my first work, which I had once totally given over in dispaire, and parted thence to Amsterdam much perplexed and almost mad I should faile upon so faire a probabillitie, when it pleased god to direct my thought to remove the difficultie that puzled us in the tryall, on which I immediately returnd to Dort [Dordrecht] where it performed as I could wish and expected.

Frizell, in Rotterdam, was worried how to transport the model safely to France but his friend and fellow investor Caspar Caltoff was, he said, developing it 'with much curiositie and skill'. William Corderoy of Rotterdam, another investor, would pay for the patent and first public tests. Frizell had promised that Evelyn would make up the remainder of the sum. An emissary was going to London. Secrecy was all, advised Frizell. 'In the meane time be silent of anie thing toucheing what's past of this business for it must be at the same time after some goode worke undertaken, alike publish'd in all places of which wee shall still correspond to advise the time by letter.'[77] When Evelyn departed for London, leaving his bride safely in the care of her family, he believed that they were well ahead in the race to develop the engine.

CHAPTER 5

'A very great Alarme'

Evelyn returned to England in October 1647 unencumbered and confused. He had lost his bearings, the monarchy and the established church were gone, his marriage was still no more than a contractual obligation, and he was neither academically nor politically engaged. Despite his impeccable contacts in mainland Europe, he knew few people in London: his mentors were either dead or overseas. His own prospects and duties, a second son with no major responsibility for the family estate, remained uncertain. The usual paths to patronage, by purchase, influence or inheritance, were no longer open. But he had transactions begun in Paris to continue and missions to accomplish; a well-connected but obscure young man, who had taken part in no royalist engagements, could be useful.

From his chambers at the Middle Temple, he could watch, listen and maintain a regular correspondence with his father-in-law in Paris. In letters written partly in cypher and signed 'Aplanos', and addressed to 'Mr Peeters' or 'Robert Kibble', he reported on 'our business' (largely his finances) as well as on the increasingly unsettling situation at home.[1] Browne appreciated the letters, 'entertaininge, soe ample, soe discreete and soe well penned an account of all that was to bee, or could bee written, as that you have thereby fully shew'd your capacity in greater matters then the little affaires of a poore, unfortunate (though truly lovinge) father in law'.[2]

The king was now under house arrest at Hampton Court, where he was accompanied by his chaplain, Jeremy Taylor, and overseen by a relative of Cromwell's. His visitors included his children as well as Cromwell himself, who was still trying to secure an agreement that would satisfy those who were growing impatient, such as John Lilburne, the head of the Levellers. In mid-October, Evelyn went to the palace on Browne's behalf bearing papers and reports from France. Although the king was still surprisingly accessible, 'multitudes' coming to court, the circumstances were strange. Evelyn's only audience with Charles I must have been shocking, if for no other reason than the king's surprising demeanour. He seemed calm, 'as if he were altogether unconcerned with all those rigours of his adverse fortune'; presumably 'his confidence that God will vindicate his cause is that which makes him ride out this storm with so much assurance'. But, Evelyn added, they must accept reality in Paris and 'not be offended if they laugh at you at London for all appearances of any suddayne settlement are as yet in so greate a mist'.

Nevertheless, Evelyn wondered if the lack of unity in the army, the 'madness' of the country, the fury in the City of London and the untrustworthiness of Parliament might play in the king's favour. The numerous schisms, between Presbyterian and Independent, between Scots and English, between the army and Parliament (and the splintering factions in all of these), suggested that if the king did regain control it would be by default. Some were already worrying that he might not forgive them for disloyal actions. Whatever occurred, Evelyn wrote to Browne, he could not see the king leading his army northwards from its current quarters since Charles was said rarely to venture out of doors at all.[3] The royal insouciance was an illusion.

Evelyn stayed to see the king dine and then returned via Thames Ditton, delivering Browne's papers to John Ashburnham. Despite their outward show of normality, Ashburnham, Colonel William Legge and a third courtier, Sir John Berkeley, were in fact currently plotting the king's disastrous escape. By the time Evelyn's letter reached Paris, Charles I was under arrest at Carisbrooke Castle, held 'in straiter custody in the Isle of Wight than ever he was at Hampton Court'.

Seeing him again after a four-year absence, Evelyn's family and friends must have found him changed, but no fashionable fop. He told Browne: 'I was expected all ribbon, feather, and romanco, which has turned much to my account', adding, self-consciously, 'though better spoken from another'.[4] His younger brother Richard was looking forward to spending time with him; hearing about his travels would be some compensation for his own lost opportunities. But Evelyn's first port of call was Wotton where George and his new wife, the young widow Lady Cotton, were keeping the old standards up, the household running at full strength once again. He was received with the kind of warmth that he might have expected from a father, as he put it.

Since 1645 George had been member of Parliament for Reigate, a so-called 'recruiter' brought in to bring up the numbers, lowered by death and defection. To be eligible, he must never have taken up arms against Parliament and to have subscribed to the Solemn League and Covenant. He continued to sit in the Long Parliament until Pride's Purge, and the creation of the Rump, three years later.[5] Wotton had been assessed for a loan payment of £500 under the requirements of the Committee for Advance but, himself a county commissioner since 1643, George was at an advantage. By September 1645 he had loaned £200; thereafter he was asked for no more, even though his assessment was doubled soon after.[6] During the civil war years he had been a commissioner for sequestrations, ordinance and militia, at most a passive royalist, though as his brother's banker he may have become, inadvertently, more deeply involved.[7] He now planned to spend the winter in London with Evelyn, in their chambers, well away from Surrey where the army was widely quartered, provoking civil unrest.

Evelyn's other promise to Browne had been to deal with Sayes Court, the Browne family house in Deptford. At first sight it was depressing but even then may have showed potential. A half-timbered Elizabethan manor house, it had become run down owing to the long absences and uncertain fortunes of the family.[8] Nor were the surroundings promising. There was no frontage onto the Thames and the house stood uncomfortably close to the naval dockyard, an expanding, even encroaching, industrial site to the immediate north – noisy, polluted and smoky. The town of Deptford was to the west.

Browne's father, Christopher, clerk of the greencloth and member of Queen Elizabeth's household, had been given a Crown lease on the house in 1604, his wife's family, the Gonsons, having been treasurers of the navy for two generations. On his death in 1646, William Prettyman, Elizabeth Browne's brother, was appointed executor and, in theory, took charge of the estate.[9] There was no sign of him when Evelyn called but William Peters, the steward, gave him a warm welcome, 'constrayned mee to stay all night and thene accompanied mee to London . . . I like the place exceedingly well for a retreat from this town and shall so farr make use of the liberty you give mee, as to visit it often and transplant some things thither till I have made mine owne fitt to receive mee.'[10]

Christopher Browne had taken good care of the gardens. There were mature ash trees and a raised turf feature, a mount which offered a view over the remains of a patterned Tudor knot garden and a well-established orchard. In March 1642 he was busily laying turf, carefully avoiding the shade of the ash trees, and digging the orchard and mount. By midsummer he wrote to his son in Paris with evident pleasure, describing how he had 'fringed the skyrtes of the gravell walkes with pynkes and violets, but imbroydered also the borders with varieties of herbes and flowers'. Easterly winds tended to punish the exposed site: that year the damask roses were damaged as well as the walnut trees and mulberries but, by way of compensation, the soft fruit promised well.[11]

For all its drawbacks, Sayes Court was a welcome refuge for Evelyn and the garden had possibilities. Evelyn's letters to Browne, who was glad that he was

making use of 'our cottage', were often addressed 'from your Villa'. On New
Year's Day he updated him on progress.

> I have now furnished mee a chamber with hangins bed sheetes etc. very
> handsome, for my retreate at your villa, that so I may no longer be a trouble
> to my Uncle [Prettyman] having (all this time) shut him out of his owne
> lodging; it is that next your studdey, wher I have replaced all your bookes
> in order (as I shall shortly better enforme you) having for mine divertisse-
> ment taken a compleate catalogue of them and I then [hope?] we shall
> conferr together.

Sorting out Browne's library was an act of friendship and intellectual
companionship. Sayes Court, convenient for travelling to London (by water)
but nonetheless at a safe distance away, had potential as a villa, the classical
retreat of a lettered man.[12]

In London, Evelyn was busy with errands from France; he delivered a
package to Lady Hanmer but failed to find Mrs Earle at home. Wives often
returned alone better to deal with the authorities, compound their estates and
pay the necessary fines, taking back funds or saleable objects to ease their lives
in France or the Low Countries. In the Brownes' circle, Mary Verney and
Margaret Cavendish spent time in England in 1646–7 while Anne Fanshawe
continually travelled backwards and forwards. Dr and Mrs Earle spent nine
years apart and Sir Edward Hyde, the prince of Wales' closest advisor, saw
little of his family for years, even though his wife moved to Antwerp and his
daughter Anne to The Hague where she was maid of honour to Mary Stuart
and a particular favourite at that court. His son Henry worked with him as a
copyist and decipherer: 'as secret as he ought to be', as his father put it.

Evelyn was still keeping an eye on Frizell's scheme for a perpetual motion
engine, and had found two letters waiting for him in London 'by which you
will understand unto what a period he has brought the designe & how he
sollicits my fathers assistance therin.' He suggested Browne take Waller's
advice as to the extent of his own involvement but Evelyn himself was going
to pursue the matter further: 'if there be such probable advantages as hee
assures us there are, I know noe reason why I should quit myne interest
therin.' If the business was worth 'stirring' he had someone to help him,
'an excellent instrument to see myne interest improved'. The person he had
in mind had 'insight into affairs of that nature' and though very poor
was honest.[13] His visits to London instrument-makers and the booksellers
congregated around St Paul's Cathedral brought him into contact with like-
minded useful people. Such establishments functioned as meeting places and
information exchanges as much as shops.

From Paris Browne wrote to Evelyn telling him that he had helped Frizell 'by puttinge him in the way of getting his Patent sealed' and, with Waller, they had met and agreed to proceed, if Evelyn would pay a third of the expenses needed 'for bringinge the Ingineer that hath perfected the Invention out of Holland and for makinge a small engine here for the experiment, which hee saith will nott amount in all to above six score pounds'. If this proved successful, the engineer would build a full-scale version, and Evelyn would have a quarter share in it. 'But if you thinke nott good to hazard this sume, then uppon your relinquishinge your totall interest, hee will pay in the hundred pistolls, retire his pawns and cancell his promise to you.' He asked Evelyn to consider the proposal and reply.[14]

Samuel Hartlib, the man to whom almost all paths in science led, knew Frizell's secret; he may even have been Evelyn's candidate for 'stirring' the project. 'One Frisel a Scotchman whose chiefe excellency lyes in judging of statues told Mr Robinson 3 Years agoe that hee had invented now a *Perpetuus Motus* and gives out now that hee hath imparted the secret to Kalthof . . . Sir Endimion Porter is also interested in it,' he wrote.[15] For many years Caspar Calthoff (Kalthof)'s patron was Edward Somerset, the marquess of Worcester, who called him an 'unparalleled workman for trust and skill'.[16] Hartlib's mention of both Robinson and Porter — one a key figure in trade affairs under the Commonwealth and the other a venerable member of the exiled English court — suggests the value of such a machine to whichever side could secure exclusive rights to it.

Evelyn appears not to have added to his initial investment with Frizell, but Calthoff spent time in France in mid-1649, having secured a patent from the States General.[17] He returned to Dordrecht to find his valuable model, 'son ouvrage d'eau', burned out, but he persisted and was still there in February 1652. After the Restoration, Robert Hooke told Robert Boyle he had seen the earl of Worcester's 'water-commanding engine', a hydraulic device, at Vauxhall. However, by then Calthoff himself was making fun of it and Hooke thought it 'one of the perpetual motion fallacies'.

These machines, which fascinated, promised much and never delivered, consumed many fortunes and dashed many exalted hopes. After Samuel Pepys's father-in-law, Alexandre St Michel, returned to Paris following his service with the English forces in the Pas de Calais, his son recorded that he 'grew ffull of wheemsis, and Propositions, (of Perpetuall Motions etc) to Kings, Princes and others, which soaked his pockett, and brought all our ffamely soe low'.[18] Later, Roger North referred to his own 'diseas', caught by all who dabbled in 'mechanicks': the belief that he had found 'a perpetuall movement. And was wonderful earnest and positive in it, and half wild to be putting it to experiment.' Only his elder brother Francis, who had already 'bin sick of the same infirmity' and suffered the failure of his invention, convinced him that it was futile.[19]

The art market was far safer and Evelyn busily shipped pictures and cases of unidentified objects to France as security against loans or even for sale.[20] He was knowledgeable and by now had a well-trained eye. With his brothers' help, Evelyn had taken responsibility for Browne's finances, setting up elaborate and often circular land transactions, involving large sums secured by mortgage or bond. Since his return to London, 'many gallant seates & reasonable purchasses have bin offered mee, I shall peruse the particulars & proceede as my friends advise mee'. That spring he seriously toyed with buying Bolney Court, near Henley, but decided that the times were too uncertain and taxes too high. By then, Evelyn was showing every sign of settling down in Deptford.

Throughout the summer of 1648, the height of the second civil war, the Evelyn brothers were busy sorting out their financial affairs, buying and selling land (including grandfather Stansfield's benefice at South Malling) with apparent ease.[21] As the year ground on, Evelyn tried to use his resources to best effect but, he wrote somewhat tartly to Browne, if his scheme (the machine?) had worked out, the proceeds would have been helpful. Once he could have raised £10,000 from friends, but now their funds had been disposed of elsewhere.[22] Such were Browne's difficulties at this time that even twenty pounds was enough to 'relieve' him. Closer to home, the family tried to get funds to their former schoolmaster, Dr Edward Snatt, a victim of the puritans of Lewes.

Some of Parliament's measures against the Church of England were deemed excessive. Evelyn reported to Browne that the sale of bishops' lands was 'virulently in agitation but none that I can heare off buys them'. Even 'puritan priests' were dissuading their parishioners from dealing in church lands, and the day before draconian proposals to sell all land belonging to deans and chapters had failed. Only Catholics were forbidden their liturgy and, despite nominal restrictions, private use of the Book of Common Prayer continued. As far as new sources of money were concerned, Parliament had now turned its attention to the City.

Evelyn's letters to Browne as the monarchy fought its ineffective rearguard action and the church was driven underground are crisp and factual, a punctilious and careful correspondence. For almost two years he kept his father-in-law as fully informed as he could. At New Year 1649 he told him he was now getting good 'intelligence' from Holland. Evelyn received and conveyed messages and tried to deal with Browne's parlous financial situation, for which his father-in-law had little energy and less aptitude.[23] But Evelyn felt himself without clear purpose. Browne realised he felt adrift and hoped that Evelyn's 'Iliads, that is some negociations worthy of you, and more proportionable to your abilities will in due time occurre to you'.

Evelyn had no ready-made circle, as did those who had been educated at Westminster or Eton, while the friends he had made in France and Italy who had now returned to England were widely scattered. Friendship with two physicians provided a lifeline to that world of the mind, experiment and enquiry that Evelyn hungered after. George Joyliffe was a discoverer of the lymphatic system and a keen botanist while Jasper Needham was a bibliophile with artist friends, one of whom had engraved William Harvey's portrait from a marble bust: 'I am sure it is exactly like him for I saw him sit for it.'[24] Evelyn had a high regard for English medical prowess and wrote that he would rather put his life into the hands of a physician in his own country 'then to a whole Colledge of these French Leaches'.[25] In Evelyn's scheme for a rebuilt City of London after the Great Fire, the College of Physicians was accorded an importance secondary only to St Paul's Cathedral.

In London Evelyn toyed with taking up law, then withdrew again to his books, building up a sense of himself as a literary man, but still unable to settle on a direction. From time to time he visited art collections and gardens and even saw a tragedy performed in a brief window between parliamentary ordinances against the theatre.[26] These were uneasy, distracted months – for the nation as for every individual.

In the summer Richard Evelyn married Elizabeth Mynne, who, as her father's only heir, inherited the family house, Woodcote at Epsom, to which belonged 'those medicinal Wells, that rise in the adjoyning Common'.[27] The Evelyn portfolio of Surrey estates had grown again. Later in the year George's wife gave birth to a daughter, Mary. Both of these new additions would in the future become thorns in the family's side. Jane Evelyn had also married; her husband was a handsome outspoken barrister called William Glanville, whom Evelyn remembered as 'a great friend when he took a fancy, and as great an enemy when he took displeasure; subject to great passions, positive, well-spoken, of good natural parts'.[28] Evelyn hoped that the couple might keep him company at Sayes Court and help with expenses but there is no evidence that they did so.

In a sign of heightened nervousness, all references in the correspondence between Evelyn and his father-in-law referring to important figures were now made in cypher, lest the letters be intercepted. When Henshaw returned he would be able to tell him all the news from Paris, Browne wrote. George Evelyn, as a sitting member of Parliament, provided full reports of both the House and the court. In his letters Evelyn carefully emphasised his brother's loyalty, for his involvement in sequestration and other parliamentary moves may have worried Browne, especially as Evelyn had told him that many people were playing on both sides. His letters, he said, would be brief since the news was so grim; nothing more had been done 'towards the undoing of his Majestie because I thinke they have him as low as they can desyre him to be'. Parliament intended to manage the kingdom without him. Evelyn surmised that after they had purged the Upper House and corralled their lordships into the lower chamber, there would be a grand committee of some twenty or thirty men. 'I heard a Greate one say (by chance this day) that they would make Whitehall another manner of society'; apartments would be offered to leading figures of the committee and 'it is not unlikely but there shall be their Court'. He described the wider picture: a high official in charge of each county, standing militia and in shire towns some kind of 'public' administration determining all legal matters. Law digests would be published encouraging every man to be his own advocate, while anything tainted by royal or episcopal association since the Norman Conquest would be confiscated. In the meantime cruel taxes and oppression were the rule.[29]

Evelyn remained available for 'any honnest employment wherein I may save my party' and determined to carry on, despite financial worries, but if conditions became desperate he would 'transplant my selfe into some more propitious climate'. He does not enlarge on his likely destination. His cousin George Evelyn, who had ventured to Maryland in the 1630s (and whose dubious activities there may not have been fully known within the family), was back in England.[30] He often visited Wotton and advised George on the embellishment of the house and gardens; later he went to Ireland.

Evelyn had heard rumours from France of the prince of Wales's illness and of riots in Paris but advised the Brownes to stay put. Whatever the troubles of the French monarchy in the civil wars of the Fronde (named after a child's sling for throwing stones), those in England ran deeper: 'by your last I perceived things were likely to accomodate more speedily then with us.' He apologised for seldom sending good news.

Outside London, Evelyn depended on second-hand information and unreliable gossip, such as the recent reports from Wales or the rumours (soon disproved) that the king had escaped from Carisbrooke Castle. But it was true that the duke of York had disappeared from St James's Palace, slipping out through the palace garden in women's clothing one night and taking ship for Holland.

The rebel army was now quartered in Whitehall, 'strangely bold, excessively merry & seemingly confident'. No one knew if the three thousand men were preparing to disarm or to plunder – the City feared the worst. The mayor had issued a summons, 'whereupon the whole citie, and your sonne (to his best capacity) put themselves upon a posture of deffence, and so stand at this present'.[31] Evelyn makes no mention of the episode in the diary.

Colonel Fairfax was constable of the Tower and Cromwell had been victorious on the Welsh borders, taking several thousand prisoners 'bag and baggage'. In the north 'the turne must now be very suddayne'; everything was conjecture and suspense, Evelyn told Browne, but 'so long as I write to you (not to St Germans) I shall give you truth.' Their personal communication could be much franker than anything sent via the English court. He did, however, spare him the news that the Kentish forces had briefly reassembled at Broomfield, next to Sayes Court. Then, unknown to Evelyn, the Fronde severed communications. Eventually, and reassuringly, Browne re-established contact, thanking him for his letters 'containing (as allways of late) fears and hopes'; but fear had overtaken hope.

The high drama of that summer was provided by the siege of Colchester, which lasted from early June until August. For a while royalist tenacity suggested that the country might swing back to the side of the monarch, but such optimism was short-lived. The siege ended in surrender on 28 August 1648. Sir Charles Lucas (Margaret Cavendish's father) and another commander had been shot dead; two of the Brownes' relatives were caught up in the grim business; James Stephens's house was burned out, as was much of the town, while Samuel Tuke, once a roving diplomat and now a royalist commander, was prominent on the losing side. With other survivors, Tuke fled overseas, where he would remain for eleven years.

Evelyn pressed Browne for more news from Paris, especially about how 'our Court' is constituted after 'this last alteration' – the arrival of the prince of Wales from The Hague.[32] Word came back that the French Parlement was dealing with government abuses and the king's revenue, but that it had no money for the new visitor. The queen's court was a shadow of its former self: of the principal courtiers, only Lord Jermyn was now at St Germain, the others remaining in Paris. (Evelyn had just been to see Henrietta Maria's palace at Greenwich, finding it in a miserable state and in Parliament hands.)

Evelyn had little time to dwell on his marriage or to think about his bride, 'who seemes now to have forgotten me', but he did commission a portrait of himself for her.[33] Initially it was to have been a miniature, but then Evelyn realised that Isaac Oliver was dead, and the other great miniaturists – Hoskins, Johnson and the rest – were absent. Instead, Robert Walker's full-sized portrait depicted a ghostly, distracted figure in a shift, a skull before him. The melancholy philosopher was a persona chosen to demonstrate his virtue. While they were apart, Evelyn explained, Mary must be content with 'la naïfe posture de la Maladie dont je suis tourmenté'. The Greek inscription above his head read 'Repentance is the beginning of wisdom', while the paper on the table carried stoical sentiments from Seneca.[34]

William Prettyman acted as courier – all who crossed the Channel found themselves laden with messages, goods and, doubtless, saleable objects. Now Evelyn hoped to receive Mary's portrait ('that shadow of my deare selfe') since the one he had was 'not altogether so like the subject as I have often wished'. He hoped his own portrait 'will serve to assure you, how intirely I love you, as well as put you in mind constantly to pursue those serious, and necessary papers . . . I have filled with some observations, not unworthy your perusall.' He assures her that the rich, beautiful and passionate women in London hold no attraction for him, for he wants a wife suitable 'to my own inclynation'.

Behaving more like a suitor than a husband, Evelyn compiled a little book for Mary. She must tell no one about it. 'Instructions Oeconomique' was beautifully bound, with gilded pages and marbled endpapers, a pen-and-ink frontispiece showing a seated woman with a cornucopia, and even a contents page and index. Transcribed in elegant, tiny calligraphy by Richard Hoare, his secretary of the 'dextrous pen', it was addressed to 'The present Mistress of my youth, the hopeful Companion of my riper Yeares and the Future Nurse of my old Age'. In the section 'on the conjugall' he told her that he preferred a virgin to a widow, who would have to be broken from the manners and customs of her late husband. He invoked scenes of peace and perfection including Seneca's fishponds and the Garden of Eden. Some pages were in French and there were recipes and poems; it was both a personal version of the conduct books currently in vogue and an intimate commonplace book.[35]

In a later letter to Sir Kenrick Eyton, in what may have been a metaphor for the political situation, Evelyn revealed something of his courtship: 'Virgin Ladys like forts and Castles, must be won by Approches, and stratagem, and lines of Circumvallations, and we are not strangers to the difficulties (we are told) you have gon through.'[36] Evelyn, more than twice Mary's age, may have had double her experience of the world but she was impressively accomplished, with fluent French and a good understanding of Italian. Her drawing master, the younger Alexandre du Guernier told Evelyn that 'Mademoiselle' was getting more skilled by the day.[37] She was drawing after the manner of Abraham Bosse and on his return Evelyn would discover 'elle poura faire un portrait d'après le naturel'. Elizabeth Browne was proud of Mary's talents and despite misgivings at losing her daughter to Evelyn in the future, was happy, she wrote to him, to put his happiness first.

Evelyn reported the Scots to be offering new terms and perhaps a faint hope of restoring the king, although it involved disbanding all armies and 'settling Religion according to Covenant'. Prince Rupert was said to be at Yarmouth, then in Holland. Not even the identities of the members of the king's inner court were known Evelyn noticed that a dead man's name had appeared on a list of royal advisors.[38] In need of relaxation, he left the sphere of gossip and rumour and, after haymaking in Deptford with Richard and his new sister-in-law, went to Sussex to check on his properties and, no doubt, visit his step-grandmother.

By the time Evelyn wrote to Browne ('By now you may have a stomache to the Newes') the king was demurring over Parliament's propositions, and the House, George had reported, was expected to declare against the army. Some favoured putting the king and his sons on trial; others planned to install Henry, duke of Gloucester as a puppet ruler. The 'old fox' Cromwell was waiting. 'Thus Sir you see what a blacke Curtayne there is suddaynely drawne over our hopes & how much the sceane is changed since I had last the opportunity to render you intelligence.' But they must not despair. Perhaps surprisingly, Evelyn rationalised that if all were levelled, everyone would have decent shares. For his own part, he reassured Browne, nothing could 'impeach my Loyalty at home'.[39]

Evelyn discovered that his Italian purchases were on their way home. His treasured medical tables were going with Prince Rupert himself to Holland. 'The Veynes which I purchased in Italy . . . are now in the powre of his highnesse who hath the shippe.' Did Browne have a contact there, 'so I might not lose them'? Meanwhile the ubiquitous Sir Kenelm Digby had reached Calais. Lady Fanshawe, on her way to England again, this time with Mrs Waller, listened to his fantastic tales over dinner, 'all of them passed with great applause and wonder of the French then at table; but the concluding one was, that barnacles, a bird in Jersey, was first a shell-fish in appearance, and from that, sticking upon old wood, became in time a bird. After some consideration, they unanimously burst out into laughter, believing it altogether false.'[40] William Keightley had returned to marry, having left his brother in Rome, and Sir Richard Fanshawe, the envoy between the prince of Wales at The Hague and the marquess of Ormonde in Ireland, was heading there with crucial letters.

The army was 'as thick as bees' around London. The king had been taken off the Isle of Wight, for which 'wee are in a very greate Alarme'. Now the world watched, Evelyn wrote, 'in expectation of the bloady trajedie which is now drawing to a catastrophe'. The Fronde too provided its own terrors and the parallels were not lost on the main players. Writing to Ormonde, Sir Edward Nicholas considered that the accommodation between the French king and the 'parliamentaries of Paris', offering the people everything they asked, was 'à la mode d'Angleterre'.[41]

As news of the situation in England reached the exiles in France, their own situation was worsening too. Sir Thomas Hanmer wrote to Browne from Angers. He was not surprised by the sad news from England and wished him and his family 'recompenses equall to your constancy in your suffrings. I admire you above all men living that can swim soe many years against soe furious a streame and that certainly without the help of bladders, I believe the Court of this country supports you but weakly.' But Hanmer, now a horticulturist rather than the politician of earlier times, could not resist a request. Would Browne get the names of the best sort of anemones at the lowest prices, which 'may be had at any season of the yeare, and I thinke you know the man that hath the best choyce of Anemons & Ranunculus'.[42] Browne must have happily exchanged the tensions of his office for the pleasures of an agreeable afternoon in Pierre Morin's nursery garden.

In contrast, Evelyn was losing his nerve and by December was more seriously contemplating emigration. 'I wish you could advise mee how I might prevent an absolute ruine as to some parte of my fortune which I would most willingly dispose off in some more peacable & soober corner of the earth.' Many would join him, he told his father-in-law, 'even of the best of my friends in England, who have thoughts of leaving this place in a very short tyme if those proceedings continued. Sir I am alltogether confused & sad for the misery that is come upon us.' Meanwhile, he again distracted himself 'hanging a chamb: in your Villa, where I am going to set up my rest (after Xmas) till you otherwise dispose of mee; having now in a manner settled all myne affayres'.[43]

By New Year the news was worse. The king was at Windsor, 'restrayned under many boults and a strong guard', addressed as plain Charles Stuart without the ceremony, as Evelyn termed it, of 'knee or hatt'. He refuted every charge: not answering to Parliament, setting up his standard, making war against his people and offering support to the Irish rebels. In England they wondered why he had not asked the queen of France to mediate and Evelyn beseeched Browne to let her know how little time remained and, he told him, he was also in touch with Holland. But the letter ends ominously. 'Seriously Sir they intend to destroy his Majestie having now amongst them men of such desperat principles . . . . All is naught, all is naught, believe it.' His letter ends with a drawing of an executioner's block.[44]

Ten days later the army seized power, the House of Lords was abolished and a hand-picked judiciary was put in place, any twenty of whom could determine matters in the 'painted chamber'. Charles Stuart was to be tried by the sound of the trumpet. The Commons had ordered a new seal, with the arms of England and Ireland and the inscription 'the first year of the peoples freedome' on one side, and on the reverse an engraving of Parliament.[45]

On the eve of Charles I's execution, Evelyn wrote to Browne again. Ten days earlier, the king had been taken from Windsor to a prison in St James's. In Whitehall a court was constructed for his trial, the 'Kings bench & Chancery in Westminster Hall being made into our greate Court with

scaffolds on both sides'. After a week of confused proceedings, with adjourn-
ments and the king's continual challenge to the authority of the proceedings,
he was sentenced to death. 'Alas! – – he is gon – – –.' Evelyn's prose became
tangled as he tried to convey what he termed the king's imminent martyrdom,
greater than any except for that of 'our Saviour himself'.[46] No help had been
forthcoming from the French, who were deep in their own problems, despite
the pleas of Henrietta Maria and the prince of Wales (currently in The
Hague). Prince Rupert was at sea. As a metaphor for the bleakness of the
moment, Evelyn noted that the Thames was frozen over. On the day of
the execution, 30 January 1649, he fasted in Deptford.

It fell to George to describe the gruesome event to him:

They have this day between twelve & one of the clock executed the king:
it was done upon a Scaffold erected on purpose over against the banquetting house in White Hall. The king come out of the banquetting house
upon the Scaffold. He carried himself very carefully & died very resolved,
he spoke some half hour to the people; the substance [of which] I cannot
yet learn; . . . by to morrow we shall have it in print.

Having handed his gloves to the bishop of London, Charles submitted to
his fate. 'The execution was disguised; his head was strucke off at one blow &
after wards held up to the people & the usual words uttered behold the head
of a traytor. Sir I am sorry to be the sad messenger of this day's tragedy; it is
now past & we must submit.'[47] Soon stories began to circulate about the royal
children, Henry aged eight and Elizabeth aged thirteen, tucking mementoes
of their father into their clothing as they left the scaffold.

Almost simultaneously Paris fell under siege, as the wars of the Fronde,
initially a conflict centred upon the hated Cardinal Mazarin's taxation
proposals, entered a new phase. They continued intermittently for four
years, descending eventually into a squabble between different factions
of the nobility and court. Browne was offered the chance to escape with the
royal household, which fled to St Germain-en-Laye in mid-January. Evelyn
wrote that he would not have judged him harshly had he accepted the invitation. But he knew that Richard Browne, upholder of the Anglican service
and lodestar for the exiled community, was not a man to run from
trouble. Henrietta Maria also remained in Paris, becoming a pensioner of
the French royal family.[48] Her son James came from The Hague and was with
her when she received the news of Charles's execution a fortnight after the
event.

At this seemingly terminal moment for the English monarchy, Evelyn
decided to break cover in print. His first small publication was a translation

of François de la Mothe le Vayers, *Of Liberty and Servitude* (1649), which
discussed the fate of courtiers and was dedicated to 'George Evelyn of Wotton
in the county of Surrey' – a first clue to the man behind the authorial initials
on the title-page.[49] In the dedication, purportedly written in Paris in March
1647, he announced to his brother that publication was a stage 'which I shall
prove to frequent but as Gentlemen who sometimes write Plaies, not often'.
There was a short Latin prefatory poem, naming Evelyn, by Alexander Ross,
an elderly Scottish cleric, both anti-Copernican and Laudian. Ross's immense
output included the first riposte to Hobbes's *Leviathan* (1651) and he may
have been employed by Evelyn's printer, Gabriel Bedell, to add *gravitas* to an
otherwise obscure work.[50] Now Ross became a friend.

'Fortune [has] no dominion over the Operations of our Soules,' ran
Evelyn's translation, yet 'is it not a thing most strange, that we find so few
men who are free?' The hunger for favour always intervened. The original
author lambasted 'the servitude of the court' and courtiers who conformed 'to
the inclinations of Princes', giving up the best years of their lives in the faint
hope of future reward or elevation. To enter the service of a great man was
comparable to a long sea voyage; a few return rich but many perish – Evelyn
was thinking of his father-in-law's travails.

The original was written in 1643, just after Richelieu's death. De la Mothe
le Vayer's authorial address was to Mazarin, appropriately enough taking up a
discussion that had been reanimated by Montaigne and Machiavelli but that
went back to the classical distinction between kingship and tyranny. The
author was one of a close group known as the 'libertins érudits' which also
included both Gassendi and Naudé. Evelyn carefully positioned his first
published translation within the radical European political debate but more
importantly, within a defined intellectual circle. Waller was acquainted with
de la Mothe le Vayer, and he may have been behind Evelyn's choice of text, a
surprisingly liberal discourse upon power and its ill effects. Evelyn was also to
meet Naudé in person. When the translation was published, in January 1649,
Evelyn claimed he was 'severely threaten'd' for the preface. But despite its
royalist tenor, there is no evidence that he was.[51]

Following the regicide, 'the last breath & period of all Religion, Liberty &
comon humanity in these Kingdoms', England was no place to be – but nor was
France.[52] Where could they go, away from 'these birds of prey', he asked
Browne. Ireland and the distant plantations offered no refuge now. Brussels
was an option and there were 'safe bankers toward Holland' – he noted
Antwerp and Rotterdam in the margin. He had friends in the exile community
who might help them and he would happily share everything he had with
Browne. His father-in-law must reply quickly and secretly, since every action
was now suspect. 'Sir this is the last addvice that will be worth giving you here-

after from mee & if in what I have already donne, then was little valuable, yet my good will was better then my capacity.'[53] Once again Browne's letters ceased, and Evelyn heard reports of famine in France. Resolved to go abroad, he put the Deptford estate in William Prettyman's hands.

Then Browne's letters began to arrive again from Paris. The Fronde seemed over, the result of a truce between the parties. 'How kind you were nott to lett us know our danger, till there was no more cause of fear,' Browne wrote. In early March 1649 word came from the court in The Hague. Browne's credentials could be renewed if he sent a document 'with the stile and addresse the late king then used'. He had not been forgotten and, though he might be sent away from Paris, his posting would not be 'across the seas'. He suggested that Evelyn return to France.[54]

'Of this improvisall invitement from you, I did nothing dreame off, neither was it my determinaction to see Paris (though happly some parte of France or Holland) till more particularly encouraged by you,' replied Evelyn. He was ready for 'any motion or long absence (if so necessity require)' and at the end of the legal term at the Inns of Court, 'I shall put myself in a posture to be suddainly with you' and would arrange for friends to continue to send intelligence to Paris.[55]

He must have been wondering how he and Mary, now an adolescent girl, would find one another following so long an interval – despite their letters and portraits, they were virtual strangers after two years apart. But shared interests would ease their awkwardness and he went 'to Putney and other places of the Thames to take prospects in crayon, to carry into France, where I thought to have them engraved'. Unfortunately these sketches have not survived, nor have the etchings. Evelyn had already been working on a set of imaginary landscapes, published after he had gone. There is no indication who taught him to etch.

That summer his 'Italian Collection' arrived, above all the treasured anatomical 'Tables'. Their odyssey had lasted four years. (The eminent doctor Charles Scarburgh was eager to secure the valuable material for the College of Physicians, but Evelyn would only agree to loan them for a year.) They would be published in 1700, just three years before Evelyn's death, by a distinguished surgeon, William Cowper. Evelyn 'disposed of some valuable goodes' and 'Inventoried my Moveables, that had hitherto ben dispers'd for feare of Plundering'. Elsewhere, memories were being erased as the king's statues were toppled from the portico of St Paul's Cathedral and from the Exchange, and, in Evelyn's words, 'Un-king-ship proclaim'd'.[56] From time to time he encountered the human flotsam of recent events, such as the half-Spanish courtier Sir Endymion Porter, a defeated old man back in London who died that August.

Nor was Paris yet 'free from palpitations'. The king had been ordered to stay in the city. Browne wanted Prettyman to send money to 'redeem my jewells as soone as hee can, in regard the party that hath them in pawne is goinge for good and all into Italy', or if easier, make the transaction through Holland or Flanders. Evelyn spent much of June arranging Browne's finances with his brother George and Prettyman. The brothers had undertaken to buy the Warley estate for £2,500 and, once the purchase was finalised, went to Essex in George's coach and four, their merriment, and perhaps ostentation, impressing the tenants who came to the manorial court.

If Evelyn was to be away, he needed someone to deal with the booksellers for him. Jasper Needham, still in Cambridge, was deputed. Evelyn asked him to bind anything not in loose sheets with good margins. Needham suggested that the printer Bedell should tell him 'what the presse brings forth worth your cognizance' rather than receiving every new title since 'our presses are so fruitfull and teeming that all the postes in London are become most learned blockheads'. While he could point to certain exceptions, for 'judiciary, Astrologers, Conjurers, Lyrick Moderne poets, Dispensatories etc this is levelling and laying all common'. He adds: 'the intollerable scab of translations is become so epidemicall [they] . . . take much from the industry of gaining the learned tongues', and then corrects himself hurriedly, perhaps remembering to whom he was writing, saying they could be 'an excellent advance to learning if well done and with good choice'.[57]

As Evelyn told Browne, he was 'a little given to bookes. I shall have now tyme to reduce my studyes into a method'. In Paris he would be able to transcribe 'some things (yet in embrio)'. He planned to take his amanuensis, Richard Hoare, and with his help he could fill commonplace books, copy texts and prepare catalogues. Hoare was a 'jewel' who could act as Browne's secretary and even tutor young Dick, although 'his person is not very gratious, the small pox having quite put out one of his Eyes'.[58] Browne tartly suggested that Hoare learn French first. Meanwhile he gave Evelyn free rein to organise their financial affairs as he thought best.

Browne's position as the representative of the monarch made it difficult for Evelyn to get a pass to leave England but in late June he succeeded 'under the Seale of State & Presidents hand with exceeding difficulty, strict examination & great jealosie'.[59] In France, Browne assured him, he would have no difficulties as long as he avoided Dieppe. Before leaving England, Evelyn attended the wedding of his sister Jane's companion to William Peters, the steward at Sayes Court, a further tie between the two families. Elizabeth Browne assured him a hearty welcome in Paris and made him promise that he 'thinke not of a second seperation'.

CHAPTER 6

'I am exceedingly happy heere'

In 1649 Thomas Rowlett published a set of etchings made by Evelyn: five imaginary renderings of vaguely Dutch or northern French landscapes, one showing Tobias and the Angel.[1] His first try at print-making was dedicated to Lady Isabella Thynne, the daughter of Henry Rich, earl of Holland, who was executed soon after Charles I. A famous beauty painted by Van Dyck, she had been one of Dr George Morley's 'elect ladies' at Oxford, as remembered by John Aubrey and was the subject of Edmund Waller's poem 'Lines on my Lady Isabella Playing on the Lute'. While she was parted from her husband, there were rumours of a liaison with the marquess of Ormonde. She was in the king's train as he went to Breda in 1650 and later, in France, acted as a link in the chain between John Denham, by then in Poland raising money from Scottish subjects of the king, and the court of Henrietta Maria.[2] Lady Isabella was a highly effective agent, who used her own cypher and who passed undetected because of her gender.[3] Women could come and go with fewer questions asked than their male counterparts.

Evelyn and Richard Hoare sailed back to France that summer with Lady Catherine Scott, daughter of the former ambassador George Goring, the earl of Norwich. She too was parted from her husband and engaged in secret missions. It was said that she was Prince Rupert's mistress. Was Evelyn's dedication to Lady Isabella, published only after he was safely out of the country, designed to flag up his credentials within royalist circles, pointing to his availability within the intelligence networks?

Back in Paris, after an exceptionally rough crossing during which his ship was chased by pirates, Evelyn was given a warm, even ceremonial welcome after his almost two-year absence. First, he and Mary took communion together, renewing their vows. Their betrothal was now a marriage in every sense. When his own son was about to marry, Evelyn urged the couple to receive the Holy Sacrament together at the first possible moment: 'the reason why so many men and women live unquietly after marriage, is much to be imputed to their want of seriously & reverentially considering how solemne a vowe they engage themselves into.'[4] He also advised sensitivity to a woman's preferences: a young married couple may be granted some sexual liberties but always based on decency and moderation. Evelyn's own approach was guided by Mary's extreme youth and innocence.

Her wardrobe for the occasion, including a blue satin gown trimmed with twenty pistoles' worth of lace, a gift from her mother, turned out to be unwearable. During the long months of wearing mourning dress for Charles I, the adolescent Mary had grown considerably – a development unnoticed, apparently, by her dressmakers.[5]

Now Mary and Evelyn had to learn to be at ease alone together and he took her out to Maisons, on the Seine, now nearing completion. Built by René de Longueil, a judge and powerful figure in both court and Parlement, who was to become Louis XIV's finance minister, Maisons was a testament to married love. Longueil's wife Madeleine had brought a substantial fortune with her which enabled the couple to patronise François Mansart, the rising classical architect. She had died in 1636, before the foundations of the new château were even laid, and her widower never remarried. Their entwined initials, 'R' and 'M', were carved everywhere at Maisons. It may have been the romantic associations of the beautiful country house, as much as Mansart's accomplishments or the extent and quality of the landscape, that first drew the young Evelyns there.

Back in the Faubourg Saint-Germain, the Resident's house with its improvised chapel had one foot in the country, another in the city. Some twenty years later Mary Evelyn directed her brother-in-law William Glanville there: 'when you walke to the Charity if you enquire for the Rue Tarrene you may see how pleasantly our house was situated.' In these weeks, while Paris was experiencing a lull in its own storms, it became Evelyn's home. When he writes to Jane to congratulate her on her pregnancy, he apologises for writing rarely but 'letters are more propper to contract then preserve friendshipp, especially amongst relations so neere as ours'. His new liveliness speaks both of his affection for his sister but also of the happiness he was finding as the honoured son of the Browne family, walking in the Tuileries, his wife on his arm. Preparations were afoot for the cold months; squealing hogs below his windows were 'under the knife for winter provision', reminding him to ask Jane about Wotton specialities such as a pork dish he recalled as 'folks pudding' as well as the recipe for syrup of violets and for 'surfeit water'. He had recently become 'a greate collector of such curiosities' and would be happy to send her recipes in exchange. 'I am exceedingly happy heere, as happy as I can wish to be, till I have the blessing to enjoy my friends in England, which I feare will be a late one.'[6]

Evelyn's gamble on the person Mary might become as she matured had been shrewd. The acute intelligence and independence of mind that she had shown from their earliest meetings meant that, despite her husband's often heavy-handed tutorials, she quickly became his equal (and even superior) in some areas, his supportive partner in others. Never complaisant, she remained a wry and fond observer of her husband's continual pursuit of knowledge, and often his assistant. More at home in French than English, she already showed signs of becoming an accomplished miniaturist and painter, while the overlap between kitchen and laboratory, medicine cabinet and herb garden, was letting her develop expertise in that department – the recipes Evelyn requested from his sister were probably for Mary and her mother. Before long Evelyn's wife became renowned for her skill in distilling essences and plant oils, her kitchen a source of famously good conserves and preserves. These activities fed Evelyn's interests; later he wrote to ask his sister for their grand-mother's green salve for wounds and another for burns, since 'I am furnishing a large booke of Receipts'.

In time, with wide reading and theatregoing, Mary became a noted stylist, both conversationally and on the page, a witty correspondent who more than held her own with a wide and admiring circle of both male and female friends.[7] As their son's tutor said later: 'you performe that in a silent closset which whole courts & Theaters would unanimously applaud.' When at Jane's request Evelyn reported on French court fashion, he found few novelties except that 'they dresse their locks so farr backward that the tipps of their eares may be seene; or just as if they were marching against a gentle wind', thinking the effect was flattering. The dry wit of the description sounds like Mary's.

Although Evelyn had come to claim his bride, he also hoped to make himself useful to the exiled royalists. Hardly had he arrived than Evelyn began a weekly correspondence with a 'Thomas White' or Mr Eaton.[8] Meanwhile young Charles Stuart was making his way back to Paris via Breda, Antwerp and Brussels, virtually penniless and politically adrift. Lord Hatton was deputed to look for lodgings for Sir Edward Nicholas, with 'an eye to cheapnes as well as conveniencie'.[9] Nicholas, the oldest of the court circle, had been Charles I's secretary of state and now reassumed the role. He was a family friend as well as a colleague of Browne's. Evelyn's father-in-law assured him that his house was his and 'all shall be ready for your reception'.[10]

Soon after arriving in Paris, Evelyn had dined with Nicholas as well as Sir Edward Hyde, the elderly Francis Cottington, George Carteret (governor of Jersey) and Dr Earle, effectively the entire inner circle of the king's advisors, recently converged in Paris from Jersey, The Hague and Antwerp. Presumably Evelyn was being debriefed and given instructions. Hyde and

O: IOHANNI EVELINO GENE.° ANGLO, ARTIS PICTV
tori & Admiratori Maximo, Amico & Patrono fuo fideliſsimo
Dnī Anthony van Dyck, Equitis Effigiem, manu eius propria delineatam
nceſsao Hollar Bohemo, in hac forma aqua forti æri inſculptam, Obſeruantiæ erg
Henric, van der Borcht iun. D.D.D. A° 1644.

10 Wenceslaus Hollar's 1644 etching after Sir Anthony van Dyck's self portrait, published by Van der Borcht and dedicated to Evelyn. The sunflower signifies his royalist allegiances.

Earle had been close friends ever since their days together at Great Tew; other members of that set – Waller, Hobbes and George Morley – were also in France. During the current uncertainties, they must have concurred with James Stephens's view that the young king in exile was 'the polar starre that's pointed to, by the needle of my hopes and affections'.[11]

Charles's advisors had argued against his return to France and his mother's sphere of influence. Hyde foresaw 'that for some time the Queen will govern all'.[12] A mature nineteen-year-old, Charles seemed to signal independence by rejecting her candidates for his council of state and standing his ground, but at the same time he was moving towards accommodation with the Scots, as his mother desired. Hardly had Louis XIV returned to Paris from Compiègne in mid-August than Charles and his retinue – bound to be a liability to whomever offered them hospitality in Europe – sailed back to Jersey. Before he left, Evelyn presented himself at St Germain-en-Laye, sharing a carriage with the royal mistress, Lucy Walter, 'a browne, beautifull, bold, but insipid creature'. A few months earlier she had given birth to a son, James, later to become duke of Monmouth.

Faced by disaster in Ireland where Cromwell was driving all before him, the new king of Scotland (and Jersey) now turned north. Hyde and Cottington left for Madrid. Many saw that the Scottish Presbyterians held Charles and his mother in their thrall – somewhat ironically, given that she was a Catholic who not long before had been pleading with Pope Urban VIII for financial support. The French Protestants, with their chapel at Charenton, were the natural allies of the Anglicans but might also be seen as a stalking horse for the Presbyterians. The Resident was just a pebble in a turbulent stream, and vulnerable to rumours or accusations of tendentious leanings; he was soon to be accused of overfamiliarity with the Huguenots.

The English court remained in deep mourning, though few went to the lengths of the marquess of Ormonde, who dressed exactly as the late king had done. The ladies, Evelyn told Jane, 'never misse frequenting our chappell every Sunday and Hollyday where wee have either Dr Morley, or Dr Cosens without fayle who give us excellent sermons, and duely administer the sacrament, beesides our Altar furniture &c (which lately cost £80 being all of damask) is exceeding decent'. So, despite its 'persecution at home, the Church of England is not utterly lost abroad'.[13] But there was no financial support, as Hatton told Nicholas: 'I am glad the King will write to the Louvre concerning the Church of England, but I wish you would get him to put in a word or two that Deane Cosens might have some pay, for they give him not a penny.' Every groom and lackey was paid, yet the chaplain received only four pistoles, 'intended as a scorne; and we heare they are now ashamed of the designe of putting downe the service, but have found a neater way of starving out their parson and they thinke the congregation will dissolve quietly'.[14]

As son-in-law of the Resident, Evelyn was occasionally presented at the French court, which offered a startling contrast to the English party's penury. Accompanying Browne in November, he had an audience with Louis XIV and his mother at the Palais Royal and afterwards explored Richelieu's palace, with its portrait gallery of the illustrious, Bernini's statues and 'good modern paintings'. Outside, they noticed the boy-king was now engrossed in a bull-baiting.[15]

Once Charles's plans in Scotland gathered momentum, Browne began to receive a weekly letter from Robert Long, his private secretary, a man he particularly disliked. Charles's advisors worried the old guard: 'God helpe us, when Hamilton, Mr Long, Newcastle and Buckingham rule in Council,' Hatton wrote to Nicholas; even the rule of his mother was preferable, 'for naturall affection and education might have pleaded for that, whereas there can be noe excuse for this'.[16] Now Charles summoned the Covenanters to meet him. The Treaty of Breda, by which the Scots were granted their religious wishes in return for their support, was finalised in March 1650.

On the first anniversary of the 'sad memory of this fatal month', in January 1650, Philip Packer, a family friend and contemporary from Oxford, reported to Evelyn that he was not prepared to compromise by changing all allegiances just to save 'his safety or fortune, att the damnable price of privacy or disloyalty'. Not everyone was so resolute. Packer, of Groombridge in Kent, was glad that Evelyn intended to visit England, but thought he was wise to stay where he was for the moment, with his bride, for the 'heliotropicall' times made it hard to know if people were flying closer to the sun or the clouds. He was relieved to know that his friend was in France, in 'freedome & safety'.[17] In republican England, Evelyn heard, 'no body tells Truth for feare of a Sequestration'.

Evelyn ('Smyth') had been exchanging letters with 'Tho: White'. This, apparently, was Kenrick Eyton, a friend of George Evelyn and Philip Packer (whom Evelyn had met in the Low Countries). 'Aiton' appears among Sir Edward Nicholas's contacts who had their own cyphers. After the Restoration he lived in Wales, becoming a judge and MP. Eyton frequently mentions reporting to an unnamed 'Chiefe' but the object and status of their exchange remains unclear and it was officially interrupted in late January 1650. Evelyn's side of the correspondence has not survived; the first of his own copy letters was dated February 1650, innocuously offering his congratulations on Eyton's marriage, the second promised that, from now, he would write short, anodyne letters, 'to save Charges, and prevent the cold Sweate, which I find my last put some-body into; by telling him nothing but who makes love to whom; when ther's a Ball at Court, and a New pupet play at Mademoyselles, together with a few sprinklings of the Mode for the Ladys, and so make up the paquet'.[18] At New Year, Lady Catherine Scott told him it was 'a large steppe to health to be out of England a place more horridd was never lived in', while George advised his brother to be circumspect, 'in regard of the danger men are liable to', regarding sending intelligence from France.[19] Richard Evelyn even wondered about joining his brother there; he could 'pack uppe and be [with] you at any time without much trouble, which cannot so conveniently be effected in a settled posture . . . should you resolve for England and I were worthy to advise you . . . live in London, and there as private as may be for the country is not habitable.' The situation seemed unlikely to change and his 'condition is as various as the tymes'. In fact, Richard stayed, glad that Evelyn had approved 'all that I have done in relation to your business in Sussex'. The interest was coming in and in late 1649 he sent Browne £200.[20]

The Evelyns were now funding the king's Resident in Paris. Richard cautioned his brother not to trust anyone, whether friends or merchants, with large sums of money, implying that Evelyn should be his own courier. That New Year news came that his step-grandmother Jane Newton had died; Evelyn was sad, for 'she had a most tender care of me during my childhood, & was a Woman of Extraordinary charity & piety'. However, her death released him from paying rent of £60 per year on her behalf.[21]

By the spring, Richard, acting as intermediary between his brothers in their financial transactions and frequently charged with errands at Deptford or Lewes, was growing irritated. Evelyn's ability to ignore complaints and duck out of harm's way exasperated his family and friends. Thomas Henshaw still dreamed of their pleasant time together in Paris, but

> were you not . . . one whom I unfainedly love and esteeme, I could very much envy the happy occasion, and the good convenience you have of being there whilst wee live heer expos'd to all kind of misery, and daunger and every day in feare of worse, for if the Treaty at Bredah succeed, which thes our states begin to suspect, that wight [man] which doth not cordially and effectually ioyne with them, must at the best not eat or which is worse not drinke or breathe but out of a prison.[22]

Charles's capitulation to the Scots had filled the English gentry with dread and he began to lose support at home.

Well away from these worries, and with his ambitions to be a royalist intermediary in abeyance, Evelyn now found himself on the fringes of a congenial group of secretaries and emissaries around the court at the Louvre. Among them were the poets Abraham Cowley, Henry Jermyn's secretary at the court of Henrietta Maria since 1644, and John Denham, a busy intelligence officer. Mary's cousin Samuel Tuke, a hero of the siege of Colchester and now a royalist agent with his own cypher, was in the suite of James, Duke of York. He had literary ambitions of his own and from time to time came to Paris from The Hague. He and Evelyn explored the gardens of the Île de France and were soon bound together by Tuke's affection for Mary, whom he adored 'above al the Women in the World but with soe fautless a passion that it can never offend the respect I have for her, nor my friendship to you'.[23]

Edmund Waller was based in Rouen, but was often in Paris. In the summer of 1649 he told Browne he was looking for a translation of the 'late king's book', the *Eikon Basilike*, and hoped to see him and his son-in-law soon.[24] When in the city Waller lived splendidly, in marked contrast to most of his exiled compatriots. When Sir Richard Fanshawe travelled with him to Paris, he found him excellent company and eloquent 'upon all the subjects imaginable'. Fanshawe – diplomat, translator and poet – had been the prince of Wales's secretary for war since 1644, and had been at his side in Oxford, Exeter and Jersey. Earlier he had returned to England to compound his estate and raise money for his master, always 'upon thorns' for fear of discovery.[25]

The new learning and the exchange of information within interlocking circles of correspondents were thriving, energised by a free-floating intellectual community and the continual comings-and-goings from England, Scotland and the Low Countries which made Paris the hub of Europe. Latin was the *lingua franca*, dissolving linguistic barriers and ensuring that the leading figures in an international 'Republic of Letters' could converse freely on the page. Regardless of their different nationalities Grotius, Bacon and Peiresc were common property. From Paris Thomas Hobbes wrote to Gassendi (in the south of France, at Digne), to Samuel Sorbière in The Hague and to Charles Cavendish, living with his brother and sister-in-law, the earl and countess of Newcastle, in Antwerp. René Descartes and Christiaan Huygens were at the heart of further exchanges from Holland. By way of contrast, James Stephens, confined to 'my hermitage' in the English countryside, felt cut off and unable to respond in kind to the 'copious and exact' report on French affairs his cousin Evelyn sent him.

One place that drew English aspirants together to this world of new knowledge was the Jardin des Plantes, the royal botanical garden, which Evelyn knew from his previous visit. Abraham Bosse's superlative engraved 'perspective horizontale' of 1641 shows the garden, its walled and irregular site containing formal areas for display and botanical investigation and, beyond that, a varied landscape, including a mount, a marshy area and an elaborate parterre, as well as 'meadows, growne Wood, & Upland, both artificial and naturall'. The garden was for the cultivation of 'simples' as well as for pleasure, highly contrived and surprisingly naturalistic by turn. Behind its walls Thomas Hobbes, Sir Kenelm Digby and William Petty had all embarked on chemistry courses. Evelyn followed that given by the newly appointed Scottish curator and professor of botany, Dr Davisson, who enjoyed extensive premises along the rue St Victor.[26] James Stephens was envious: 'I hope to see you shortly graduated in the highest forme of Philosophers: especially having the advantage of such an elaboratory in the

house with you.' If he came to join Evelyn in Paris, he would 'be very ambitious of some one of the meaner offices . . . the keeping of fires, . . . retorts or
blowing of the bellowes'.[27]

Nor had Evelyn abandoned his anatomical studies. His friend from Padua,
the physician George Joyliffe, was currently staying with Richard Evelyn, and
Evelyn asked if they could obtain a skeleton for him. Joyliffe, later Pepys's
doctor, reported back. Although it was allegedly possible to obtain a cadaver
through the assizes, it proved difficult. Even in London the professional
charter of physicians and surgeons erected so many obstacles that the only
way was 'surreptitiously by private and particular favour which at length I
design'd by contracting an intimacy with the new lecturer of that hall . . . &
some inferior officers, that so I might privily be possessed of the bones of that
body whose musculous parts had been publickly shown in an Anatomicall
administration'. Just as the plan came to fruition and they laid hands on it, a
'Grandee' of the medical establishment whisked it away for his own purposes.
It had taken a fortnight – all to no avail.[28] Since the exemplary Charité
hospital, founded by Marie de Médicis and run by a prior and thirty-eight
Augustinian monks, was close to Browne's house, Evelyn observed operations
there including a child being 'cut' for a kidney stone. He was interested in the
physiological effects, testing the limits of human endurance rather than the
surgery itself.

Dr Joyliffe, an esteemed botanist, had no more luck finding plants and
seeds for Evelyn.[29] He tracked down the 'ablest man about London for skill
that way and one who had command of Mr Tradescant's garden and others of
note', only to find him dying of consumption.[30]

Then the calm of Parisian life was suddenly disturbed when the wars of the
Fronde broke out yet again. An episode that Evelyn marked with a special
anniversary prayer occurred after a bucolic day in the countryside. Evelyn, his
in-laws and three students at Del Campo's riding academy, the marquess of
Ormonde's sons, Lord Ossory and Lord Richard Butler, and Lord Philip
Stanhope were set upon.[31] A mob appeared, armed with 'gunns, swords, staves
& forks' and throwing stones. Ossory's companions tried to defend him.
Several of the party were injured, including Lady Browne, despite her
husband's efforts to shield her with his cloak. Eventually, after a stand-off, the
combatants realised they had captured 'persons of qualitie' rather than the
'Burghers of Paris' they had taken them for.

The unprovoked attack upon the English Resident and his aristocratic
charges quickly blew up into a diplomatic incident. Evelyn gave thanks for
their fortuitous delivery from 'the violence of implacable men'.[32] He
remarked, with evident satisfaction, that the gallant Ossory had felt in greater
danger there than 'in all the Conflicts he was ever in at sea, or land'.[33]

The affair revealed the febrile atmosphere in France. The exiles had other worries too. In May 1650 Dean Cosins heard that Charles was about to forbid the use of the Book of Common Prayer in services at the Louvre and in the Resident's chapel, apparently at the request of the French queen regent. Henrietta Maria told Hyde she was troubled by the edict, since Protestants 'deserved well from her' and she was beholden to them. The chapel was increasingly important, becoming the centre for Anglican ordinations, 'there being so few Bishops left in England'. Despite Charles's failure to offer his support, it was, in Evelyn's words, a 'Little Britain and a kind of Sanctuary'.[34]

Evelyn could count himself an adoptive Parisian by now and he had several favourite retreats in the city. One was the Palais du Luxembourg, built for Marie de Médicis by Salomon de Brosse. Since 1644 it had been the home of the erudite Gaston, duc d'Orléans, whose 'exquisite skill in Medailes, Topical memory, and extraordinary knowledge in Plants' allowed him to be considered by antiquaries and botanists as 'their Prince'.[35] The botanist duke's impressive town garden (he had another at Blois, overseen by a Scot, Robert Morison) consisted of stupendous box 'embroidery' parterres, the water that played in their midst being brought by aqueduct from Arcueil, and a garden of simples. Much of it was public, with unusual features such as tall hornbeam hedges, an icehouse and a tortoise garden. Evelyn noted the variety of citizens who were attracted to it: 'Gallants & Ladys' as well as 'studious Scholars . . . [and] jolly Citizens; some sitting & lying on the Grasse, others, running & jumping, some playing at bowles, and ball, others dancing and singing: and all this without the least disturbance, by reason of the amplitude of the place.' No gardeners were to be seen in this cheerful public paradise and yet it was all in perfect order.[36]

Like Browne, Evelyn would always be an outsider in the socially nuanced world of the Anglo-French nobility, but in domestic and intellectual terms his situation in Paris was ideal. He was at the centre of a loving family, in a marriage that was growing in ease and affection. He could continue as a practising Anglican, improve his French, enjoy the music and painting that so pleased Mary and extend his expertise in chemistry, physiology and horticulture. He was becoming a bibliophile, encouraged by his father-in-law's love of books and fine bindings.[37] Surrounded by stimulating company, he was close to the epicentre of continental intellectual life. Now he had to find an endeavour worthy of his ambitions.

It may have been at this time that Evelyn's friends suggested that he undertake a task that would test him to the limit – the translation of Lucretius's *De rerum natura*. This most difficult of classical texts, with its celebration of Epicurean philosophy and the heretical notion of atomism, was yet to be mastered in English. Pierre Gassendi had discussed it, albeit in Latin.[38] He argued that if Epicureanism could be given a Christian gloss it would a worthy antidote to Aristotelianism. In 1650 a French prose translation of Lucretius' six books appeared, made by a cleric, the abbé de Marolles. Now his literary godfathers, Browne, Waller, Fanshawe and Wase (now living under Browne's roof), set Evelyn a stern test: to translate the notoriously difficult and rarely studied poem into English verse.[39]

It was probably an early draft to which Alexander Ross referred in July 1651, when he thanked Evelyn for sending a 'translation, the beginning whereof I have yesternight and this morning perused; but sometime will be requisite to peruse it all with judgment'. He had marked up some of the pages, which he wanted to discuss with him.[40] Although at first sight an unlikely choice of adjudicator, Ross had previously attempted to provide a Christian reading of Roman philosophers and poets, notably in his *Virgilius Evangelizans* (1634).[41] He was thus a suitable person to offer Evelyn reassurance on that score.

During these precious months in Paris, Evelyn was in the grip of what he later admitted to be 'the unsatiable coveting to exhaust all that should, or can be said upon every head'.[42] The tendency that he also confessed to his son, the irresistible need to ferret out the new and accumulate information (whether to stave off tedium or depression he never makes clear), now became very evident.

Hendrick van der Borcht had re-established contact, writing from Amsterdam, having belatedly heard of Evelyn's marriage.[43] He sent congratulations and was delighted that his wife had a 'good inclination unto the art of designing and miniature, it must needs bee a great Pleasure for you'. How he wished he lived nearer 'so that I might be able to showe some little helpe', but he was still in the service of the countess of Arundel, who, he explained, 'hath her dwelling most heer at amsterdam'.[44] Then he passed to Evelyn's print collection: he could arrange a good price with Wenceslaus Hollar for some prints – 'they have no certaine numb[er] he adding continually unto them'.

By now Evelyn had found an artistic father-figure in France, the Protestant engraver Abraham Bosse, who had just begun to teach perspective at the Académie des Arts, where he was a rare theoretician among the artists. When, in the summer of 1650, Evelyn decided it was finally safe enough to visit England again, he commissioned Robert Nanteuil, three years his junior and still little known, to draw himself, his wife and Sir Richard and Lady Browne.[45] In this set of four exquisite pencil portraits, Mary appears a self-possessed, pretty girl, while Evelyn, wrapped in a cloak and seen at a slight angle, has a look of quick intelligence and kindliness. He gave Nanteuil a commission to engrave his own portrait, for twenty pistoles (£12), and adjusted his will, a sensible precaution before setting out on what was bound to be an uncertain journey.

While Evelyn was away, Richard Hoare kept an eye on his artistic affairs, as well as on the progress of his wife's music. He reported that Nanteuil had begun the plate, but would 'grave the Face last, wherefore you may not expect a proofe as soone as you thought'.[46] Evelyn is Nanteuil's only English subject among his engraved portraits; exiles more usually turned to their compatriot William Faithorne, who worked with Bosse.[47] Evelyn distributed the engraving of himself to several of his closest friends, including Tuke, Packer and Needham, and, many years later, Pepys.[48]

Evelyn's first glimpses of the English Commonwealth, proclaimed the month before, were of the military as they overran the Surrey countryside, commandeering horses at will and, in London, of 'pulpets full of novices and novelties'. An earlier returnee had observed that, with Cromwell in power, back from Ireland, 'the best of men is removed, yet the worke is not finished'.[49] He looked in on Sayes Court and made some financial arrangements, possibly buying paintings to sell later on, before a round of family visits, seeing his new nephew William Glanville and taking a chilly plunge into the pond at Wotton, a reminder of childhood pleasures. While there, George enlisted his help for his ambitious plans for Wotton. Now with a daughter and the prospect of a growing family, and perhaps sensing calmer times ahead, George was hoping his well-informed and widely travelled brother could propel the musty old family seat into the vanguard of style.

After Evelyn had returned to Paris in mid-August, George wrote regularly with requests. He wanted a fashionable cabinet, observing that the furnishings at Wotton required a lighter touch, and he began to nurture grandiose schemes (so far only on paper) for the gardens, a project first prompted by his peripatetic cousin Captain George from America. George Evelyn shared his brother's liking for evergreen planting 'to cover all my bancks'. Their cousin had suggested flattening the top of the hill behind the house and making a bowling green below. 'I intend to make upon my hill a very spatious Grotty & fountaines below, my water & ground being apt for these things. If you can collect for me some curious shells or stones or pebbles . . . I mean to make it very Naturall.' But in the present circumstances he doubted 'my estate will make me any way capable of so handsome a designe'.[50]

Unusually Evelyn's diary notes a letter written on 3 January 1651 to George, 'directing him concerning his Garden at Wotton & Fountaines'; he clearly wanted to record his role in the design.[51] Unfortunately the letter itself is lost but George was obviously delighted with it. 'Sir you have furnished me with such instructions in this affaire, that it bespeake you a great observer of all things.' He had asked a West Indies merchant to find coral, exotic rocks and shells for the grotto but 'you have very rightly observed the more natural or wilde it is invented the best . . . for such a design & for natural greens as Ivy & the like'. But in this domestic pipe dream there was always a gulf between imagination and available funds, as George acknowledged.

In September he reported that he had perfected it: 'the only thing that is wanting will be moneys.' The 'Ladys vote' had been for a garden with a fountain (fed by running water) rather than a bowling green, but he will not go further without 'your approbation & advise', particularly on how to design 'varietys of waterworkes'. However, 'I have almost levelled [the] hill behind the house & built my walls'. There was also to be an aviary, 'to be built with small change'. Although he hoped for choice flowers and 'verdure', they were at the mercy of an ignorant elderly gardener. George was relieved that his brother approved the plans, 'though I believe they will come shor[t] of expectations'. Their cousin had not yet provided a detailed drawing, being 'unwilling to present you with imperfections', but in any case he had always intended to be guided, said George, by 'your better genius'.[52]

Evelyn had returned to find 'Paris, & indeede all France, full of Loyall fugitives'. On 2 October Dr Richard Steward, latterly dean of St Paul's and a royal chaplain, preached in front of Charles. 'God would certainly avenge his Saints, however deferr'd: . . . yet we must not think of selfe revenge, or go on in luxurie.' In July 1651 Dr Earle's sermon, in the presence of the duke of York, suggested that 'the want of Peace in England was, our making slight of the Law of God &c'. A month later he took up the theme again: 'it was better to be humble & penitent Malefactors, than profane & wicked Loyalists, inveighing against the vicious lives of severall of the Kings party.' His passionate words reduced the congregation to tears.[53]

Samuel Tuke wrote from The Hague, worrying about his new friend's future. 'Dear Cousin spare so much time from your bookes & business as to advise mee how you designe to Rowle in this World for . . . I am most affectionately concerned for your Well being.'[54] While at Spa and Aachen he had been reading 'Mr Hobbs his politiques & pretend to have studied him so well that I may assume the stile of his disciple; Since hee was translated in French (which is a language the layman better master) I have recomended him to manie of my aquaintances'. Could Evelyn send him more of Hobbes's writings?

The Evelyns marked their first anniversary together by returning, on 5 September (also the birthday of King Louis XIV), to see Maisons, now complete, 'to take a more exact view of a place formerly so pleasant to me'. The exterior of creamy stone was symmetrical and classically erudite, and the interior was handsomely carved, especially the main stair. The estate boasted an elm avenue which crossed the river and continued at great length, and the outer court, with its splendid stable block was enclosed by iron gates and walls. An entire village had been razed to make way for the park. Long after, Evelyn recalled the landscape of the 'incomparable' Maisons in *Elysium Britannicum*. The feature that caught his eye above all was the artificial harbour, created on the Seine by 'cutting the bankes like a Harbour or Bay into a part of the Garden', a device that he tried to introduce in London, first at Greenwich, then at Chelsea.[55] In fact, 'to take it alltogether, the Meadows, Walkes, River, forest, Corne-grounds & Vineyards, I hardly saw anything in Italy exceede it'.[56]

Though most of Evelyn's time was spent at home with his wife (whose first pregnancy ended in a miscarriage in May 1651), he enjoyed himself with the young men from the academies such as Philip Stanhope, with whom he confessed to drinking 'too liberaly'. Over the winter, the Resident's household was caught up in a round of balls and entertainments, operas and concerts. There were visits to private collections and gardens, while the 'noble Academists' invited their compatriots to witness their prowess on horseback.

Mostly importantly, though, Evelyn remained in regular contact with the literary men at court and his own, well-read intellectual circle, Tuke, Fanshawe and Waller. In Paris between 1649 and early 1652, Evelyn was buying books at an unprecedented rate, his growing library amounting to 'a serious arsenal of book-learning' which ranged from the classical authorities to modern science and which he soon began to organise by category and catalogue with Hoare's help. He also compiled collections of sermons, commonplaces and miscellanea, including medical recipes. Gathering together material from France and further afield, the results of his efforts were to be 'abnormally cosmopolitan', as Michael Hunter has written.[57] In addition to all this activity, Evelyn's mentors were identifying a range of suitable topics and texts for him to translate once he returned to England – with a French-speaking wife at his side.

Unsurprisingly Richard Evelyn had begun to see his brother's enjoyment of Paris as being, to some extent, at his expense. Writing just before Christmas 1650, he was

> glad of your felicity in your cabinett enioyments abroad & know these peaceable and innocent contentments [illeg.] your Phansy, nor can I blame you . . . . You I perceive are not without thoughts of your country and ffriends and . . . a settlement at home, though it be [to] the preiudice of that quiet you enjoy for naturall affection hath a power beyond all conveniencyes whatever.[58]

The signal from home was that his honeymoon had lasted long enough.

But outside the comfortable house in which he was amassing his books and papers, political and religious upheavals were taking place on every side. *Parlement* had exiled Mazarin and France had been plunged again into political chaos. Then, within a few months of one another, two young Englishmen in Evelyn's close circle converted to Catholicism. One was his cousin Thomas Keightley, the other Dean Cosin's own son, John. Evelyn strenuously attempted to dissuade them. Having thoughtfully rejected the puritan faith of his grandparents, Evelyn was proud of the care and rigour with which he had formed his religious views. No one should take their religion on trust; it was his own experiments with the freedom to choose and exercise doubt, even to toy with Catholicism, that had brought him to such a conclusion. His own intense introspection and investigation of spiritual matters, fed by his reading, had led him to an observant and essentially private, even domestic, Anglicanism, entirely at odds with the dogma and proselytism of Roman Catholicism, as he saw it. But he had little more sympathy with the Calvinism now ascendant in the Commonwealth and greatly feared the Quakers.[59]

Philip Packer had tipped Evelyn off about 'our lost friend in Italy' while hoping that Keightley was not 'nearer the Church of Roome [*sic*] then the Gates'. He was glad that Evelyn was trying to argue him out of his inclinations. 'Your charitable indeavours to return him, before he be to farr confirmed in his eternall ruine, hath added to my Hope.'[60] On the feast of the Annunciation Evelyn composed a long letter telling Keightley of his own flirtation with the Roman Catholic faith before discovering that 'the mettal is foul mixed, and all is not gold that glisters'. He must not hurry. 'Reade our Writers, consult our Doctors, frequent the Religious' before making your choice, he advised him, and wondered if Keightley was deserting 'our Church' because of 'the present calamity' – in which case he should take a longer view. The Church of England was an article of faith for those who hoped for the restoration of the monarchy. 'Judge you the truth of a Religion because it flourishes? Turne Mussellman; suspect you the Persecuted? Renounc[e] Christianity. Those that will live piously must suffer it. The church of the Jewes was once without Temple without Priest, without Altar, and without Sacrifice, and yet as deare to God as ever.' The Catholic Church is, in Evelyn's view, 'Sacrilegious, Idolatrous, Rebelious, Impure, and infinitely Superstitious'. There might be scant reason to remain in the Church of England under the current circumstances beyond 'an affection to the Truth', but that, for Evelyn, is conclusive enough. Evelyn claimed that his choice of the Anglican Church, with its unimpeachable episcopalian pedigree, was the result of protracted thought, having compared 'the religious Pretences of the severall Parties' for some fifteen years. At the end of that time, he said: 'I found no Rest, but in the boosome of my old Mother, the Church of England

... I found in her alone the Golden Meane, neither too streite, nor to Wide, but of a just dimension and admirable Constitution.'[61]

That summer the unreprentent Keightley appeared in Paris, 'newly made a Proselyte at Rome'. Evelyn's persuasive powers – if in fact he ever sent the letter, which may have been largely composed for his own benefit – had failed. Soon he heard that Keightley's brother William had followed suit.

There was pliancy wherever Evelyn looked. During 1651 Edmund Waller received his pardon from the Rump and prepared to go home to his Buckinghamshire house, Hall Barn, having buried his daughter, Mary Evelyn's godchild, in Paris.[62] He showed signs of moving towards his cousin Oliver Cromwell's regime. If the country followed the Machiavellian centrist model that Packer and Evelyn discussed in their letters, peace obtained through order, might even Evelyn drift that way?

He was intrigued by the views of Thomas Hobbes. Later Evelyn claimed 'long acquaintance' with this man who was old enough to have taken dictation from Francis Bacon and translated his essays into Latin, and who was held in great esteem in France and the Low Countries.* Hobbes's *De Cive,* first published anonymously in Latin in 1642, was translated as *Philosophical Rudiments concerning Government and Society* in 1651. Its frontispiece showed three emblematic figures: Religion topped the pyramid, with Dominion and Liberty to either side of a roundel showing the author. Hobbes, now identified as the author, promised to discuss 'the duties of men, First as Men, then as Subjects, Lastly, as Christians', and proposed to take the constituent parts of civil government apart – as if they were a watch, as he put it – to illustrate the essential qualities of a 'well-grounded State'. Despite the difficulties and contradictions of his position, Hobbes believed 'coercive power' necessary to control the innate distrust of man for man. The 'warre of all against all' paradoxically extended equally to the state and to religion, as his French circle immediately observed – imagining the work to be by Descartes.

Having initially conceived of a trilogy concerning logic (*De Corpore*), man (*De Homine*) and, finally, society and citizenship (*De Cive*), Hobbes finally decided to begin with the last at a time when the country was 'boyling hot with questions' as it slid into civil war. Now, ten years later, a copy of Hobbes's stimulating text was before Evelyn, in English, as he pondered the face and forms of power, both in England and France. Better still, that autumn Evelyn found himself beside Hobbes himself, watching from his window 'the whole equipage & glorious Cavalcade' which two days after his thirteenth birthday carried Louis XIV 'like a young Apollo ... in a sute so coverd with rich embrodry, that one could perceive nothing of the stuff under it' to *Parlement.*

*Hobbes was born in 1588.

As he progressed through the streets of Paris, the young king waved his hat to the crowds, who shouted back 'vive le roi'.[63]

On 7 September 1651, having come of age, Louis XIV formally took over the reins of power from his mother, designating her his 'chef de mon conseil'. A heady period of tournaments and ballets followed, brightened by extravagant new fashions. Soon after, Louis left for the provinces to continue his long war of attrition against the insurgent nobility. Almost a decade earlier Evelyn had seen the tiny Louis XIV carrying out his first official duties. Now supreme power was vested in the young monarch, the personification of the divine right of kings. Evelyn would come to despise Louis XIV as his regime became synonymous with tyranny, corruption, religious oppression and treachery, but in 1651 he believed he was in the presence of a great monarch at the opening of his reign. To have witnessed the moment at Hobbes's side was, Evelyn realised with hindsight, extraordinary. By the time Hobbes had returned to England and retirement, a few weeks later, his radical observations on power in *Leviathan* had attracted the opprobrium of two different authorities, the French clerical hierarchy and the English exiled court, for his perceived atheism and political disloyalty respectively. Evelyn met Hobbes in England at least once, in 1655.[64]

The best course for those who returned to England was decent obscurity. Thomas Henshaw kept his head down, buried in studies of alchemy and mathematics in Kensington, at that time a village far west of London. He asked Evelyn to send him engravings of antiquities and architecture, anything 'of Antiquitie, erudition or art', including 'the best crucifixions' – he believed there was one by Michelangelo – but urged him to ignore the latter if it seemed too 'popish or prejudicial to other things that are brought along with it'.[65] He suspected letters were being 'opened and supervis'd by our superiors, according to the moderne custome of this commonwealth'.

Henshaw was flattered to find himself the dedicatee of the set of six small etchings of Italy which Evelyn had arranged for his secretary Richard Hoare to publish in Paris in 1649: 'You have made mee strangely proud', he wrote

to have my name prefix'd to the first publicke endeavour of your Burin, when you have so many freinds that so much better deserve that honour, when it would have been a sufficient happines for mee to have those places which I once view'd with so much pleasure and delight in your company brought againe before my eyes by the skill of your hand.

The prints, carefully topographical although hesitantly executed, were a reminder of their journey together, south of Rome in the early weeks of 1645, and a testimonial to their firm friendship. Only one drawing has survived, that showing a view of Naples from Vesuvius. The most spirited is of the crater itself, with stylised plumes of smoke, dramatic shadows and in the foregound a man (Henshaw?) looking down into the boiling vortex from the shelter of a rock. Henshaw also sent messages to the Brownes, assuring them he would 'never bee unmindful of their great civility & favour to mee', and to Mary, asking Evelyn to kiss each of her 'white musicall hands . . . with which she doth such miracles, both with pen & pencill'.[66]

By the end of his stay in Paris, with the laboratory set up for him in Browne's house, Evelyn felt he had mastered chemistry and covered 'the whole & perfect Course of this Resolutive Arte'. He continued to toy with translating Le Fèvre's lectures, which retained the distinction between theoretical and practical chemistry that Evelyn found so reassuring, 'the science of nature itselfe'.[67] Niçaise Le Fèvre's course was almost too popular, he told Thomas Radcliffe:

> at the opening whereoff, was present our noble Friend Sir Kenelm Digby, and most of the Curiosos of Paris; yet I thinke we shall not make the Philosophers stone this processe, because our worke was so publique: pray that we come home with our witts, and our monye, and that at last it dos not end in an Egg and pindust, as in the Comedy.

Society chemistry was not for Evelyn (or Ben Johnson), and alchemical exploration was more fittingly done behind closed doors lest it attract derision, but he enjoyed seeing Digby, 'with whom I had much discourse of chymical matters' and exchanged recipes for oils, solvents and powders.[68]

Digby straddled the worlds of the Catholic courtier and the early seventeenth-century virtuoso. He had been tutored at Oxford by Thomas Allen, a leading figure in the circle around John Dee and himself an adept in both alchemy and astrology. A cousin of John Digby, 1st earl of Bristol, Sir Kenelm had been knighted by James I and, on Allen's death in 1632, inherited his great library. When Evelyn first encountered him, he was a leading figure at Henrietta Maria's court in exile, moving between Paris and Rome, where he was negotiating with the pope on her behalf. Afterwards based in Paris from 1648 until 1654, he lived quietly and learnedly, 'like an Anchorite in a long gray coat accompanied by a great English masty [mastiff] and his beard down to his middle'.[69]

At the king's court, the jostling for favour continued. Nicholas wrote apprehensively to Hatton from The Hague: 'I very much fear that those counsels which have ruined the father and brought this good and hopeful King into this sad condition . . . will never do better. You are most right in your judgment that those kingdoms are rarely happy or long-lived whose kings govern by favourites more than by well-composed councils.'[70] Once news reached Paris of the disastrous Battle of Worcester, in late September 1651, the exiles felt utter despair, unaware that Charles had escaped with his life. By late October the latter was safely back in Paris, but when Evelyn visited Dr Steward, the royal chaplain, he found him lying dead. The pressures of penury and bad health were taking their toll even at court. Hyde now headed the government in exile, Nicholas being in The Hague. Until 1654 Browne's confidant, supporter and 'master' bore the full weight of responsibility for all aspects of the monarchy. In the straitened circumstances Evelyn reduced his own requirements. He told Jane he had no need of a third *valet de chambre*, but 'having bred your old servant Dick H[unt] so well to my hand we cannot easily part with one another'. He sent his sister some oranges, 'stolen' last winter and, following Mary's instructions, kept in boxes for two or three months until black and smooth, so that they might be polished up to be worn as bracelets. He was happy to hear that his nephew Will had recovered from illness. 'Surely he is the very life of your heart,' he wrote with a new sensitivity – Mary's miscarriage had introduced him to the emotions of parenthood.[71]

In December 1651 William Prettyman added his voice to those, which even included Jane Glanville, who felt it was high time he returned. Evelyn revealed an ambivalent state of mind as he readied himself for life in republican England. He even wondered 'if (as you tell me) there be any overtures of encouragement; not that I am so fond as to imagine there can be any solid composure of matters in England, amongst such a head-lesse people', but he would take his friends' advice. Characteristically swerving away from the precipice, he then continued: 'I shall therefore bring over with me no ambitions at all to be a states-man, or meddle with the unlucky Interests of Kingdomes.' Although 'I might have one day hoped to have bin considerable in my Country. A Friend, a Booke, and a Garden shall for the future perfectly circumscribe my utmost designes.'[72] The phrase became his motto in the 1650s.

James Stephens, who had once hoped to join Evelyn in Paris, thought there was little to tempt him home. 'Yet since you understand your owne danger soe well, and come armed with soe good resolutions', Stephens and their mutual friends looked forward to 'those pleasant privacyes, which pasports, searches, unsafe & toedious journeyes, have heretofore debarred us of'.[73] Now Evelyn planned to 'weane my selfe, and other relations here from doating upon this sweete and delicious recesse' and hoped to be back for the birth of Jane's next child. In early January William Glanville wrote to tell him he was too late. The sister who had been 'so deare a Friend, so antient a companion, so greate a part ever of my better nature and inclynations' had died in childbirth.[74]

Her death exposed a family rift caused, no doubt, by Evelyn's refusal to return earlier to England. Now he urgently needed to mend bridges with Richard, and wrote him a feeling letter, 'Though you are too prudent to provoke my impertinent letters unlesse expresse affaires require it; yet at this tyme I presume you will not refuse me the addresse of the inclosed ... Brother we have lost a deare Sister, and the losse is in earnest so greate, that the sorrows of it are not to be easily supported.' They must grieve together, by 'cutting the channell, and dividing the flood'. Evelyn's relationship with his sister had been special: 'a propensity betweene us, not the neerenesse of our Relation, education, humor, and particular engagements; but infinite other, which rendererd her most deare unto me.' Now he had been cheated of their 'deare Saint' (a favourite epithet) just as he returned. Those family members that remain, he said, must 'supply that losse by more strong and mutual affections'.[75] It was time to heal disagreements and for Evelyn to begin to play his part in their depleted family.

CHAPTER 7

Wise Men Possessing Themselves in Patience

After 1652, Evelyn never crossed the Channel again. From that point on all his information about France came from others, filtered through the gauze of his own memories. Travellers set off armed with his directions, recommendations and introductions, and in return brought him reports on French gardens, buildings, literature, scientific investigations and even the foibles of fashion. His envoys bought him prints and books, begged seeds and roots, and looked out for anything that might interest him. He wolfed down every morsel. They kept him in touch with his friends and were his eyes and ears in France.

So long a stalwart of the Resident's circle, he would be missed in Paris. Dr Earle wrote a letter to 'H' (Henry Hammond), so taken up with 'making bookes that you have little time to spare for letters', which he asked Evelyn to deliver by hand. Evelyn wanted to meet Hammond, the leading royalist theologian, a man equally critical of Presbyterians, Independents and Catholics, 'of whom he has heard so much good'. Earle also vouched for Evelyn, 'if I have any judgement, you will find great satisfaction in him too . . . I am sorry for his going into England . . . with all my hart, having left so few like him behind him.' The letter never reached Hammond since the former chaplain to Charles I was now in Worcestershire, working on his thousand pages of commentary on the New Testament.[1]

Evelyn returned to England accompanied by Wase, as no more than unofficial secretary to his father-in-law with 'addresses, & Cyfers, to Correspond with his Majestie and Ministers abroad'.[2] Sir Richard's own role was now increasingly in question and to help him Evelyn was buying the lease and title to Browne's estate in Deptford, thus funding the Resident's establishment in Paris – a most unusual marriage settlement.

For the next eight years he was Browne's link to England, and *vice versa*. Sir Richard depended on his son-in-law for low-level intelligence and to

11 Title page of Thomas Hobbes's *Leviathan* (1651) engraved by Abraham Bosse. The image of a monarch made up of his subjects was one which appealed to Evelyn.

represent his interests in England. Their correspondence shows Evelyn at ease. These letters were not models of epistolary style but an easy conversation about shared interests and domestic affairs.

Evelyn's farewell (or rather, his clarion call soon after arriving back in England) was a little book. The dedication to *The State of France* by 'JE', dated Paris, 15 February 1652, was to 'your Honor'. The unnamed dedicatee, to whom he owed 'so many signall obligations', must be Browne, under whose roof he had lived for the last two and a half years.[3] During hours of conversation and reading in his adoptive home in Paris, Evelyn had formulated his ideas and listened carefully to exchanges between intelligent, worldly men. He had become as familiar with Francis Bacon's writings as if he had written them himself, was a thoughtful reader of Machiavelli, and must have talked to Waller and even Hobbes on the 'Mysteries of Government and Polity'.

In the book he expressed the opinion, with Bacon, that a young man's experiences of foreign travel should be to the eventual benefit and service of his country, a lesson his own father had imprinted strongly upon him and his brothers, by word and deed. Republican England was now ruled by a radical assembly, in contrast to France, 'where a Soveraigne Prince is able to maintain an absolute and unarbitrary jurisdiction over his subjects'. As Richard Browne's friend Sir Thomas Hanmer concluded in his well-informed account of France, the recent confusions in England had played into the hands of the French.[4] The Ottoman despots apart, Machiavelli had judged the powers of their leaders unequalled. Little had changed in the interim. Evelyn's metaphor – 'in anatomising the Kingdom of France, which consists of a Body Politick, I will commence with the Head, that is the King' – appears to be taken from the frontispiece of Hobbes's *Leviathan*, engraved by his friend Bosse, a colossus made up of tiny figures, a crowned sovereign bearing the collective 'person' of his subjects.[5]

Evelyn rehearsed recent French history, in particular the surprising birth of the boy-king.[6] Richelieu had secured the monarchy absolute and unopposed authority, the overall ownership of the land, the ability to wage war and seek peace, the power to make laws, impose taxes and control the church, though 'none of the Edicts to passe as authentick until the Court of Parliament (who is absolutely at his devotion) have first verified them'. Now, Evelyn observed, 'the Government of France doth at present rather totter than stand upon the late great Cardinals substruction'. Richelieu's successor, Mazarin, faced ruin, having overstepped the mark by playing 'so hazardous a game'. The English would be wise to keep a close eye on the situation across the Channel for 'this Body Politick is of so high concernment to the health, and good estate of our poor Nation . . . there can never be too often inspections into the State and Regiment of this Kingdom'.

In *The State of France* Evelyn also celebrated the physical beauty of Paris: 'every Metropolitan and Royal City is likely the best Map of the Country wherein it stands.' London's shops and taverns were more lively ('a perpetuall Wake or Wedding'), the streets cleaner (Paris was famously muddy) and the Thames less polluted, but in all other respects there was no contest between the two cities. He claimed 'incomparable' air for Paris, its inhabitants rarely suffering from the plague, in contrast to disease-ridden London with its 'putrified climate and accidentally suffocated City'. For light relief he added his views on the French: their women aged fast, their intellectuals, craftsmen and artisans were impressive, but he warned of charlatan teachers and poor translations, and was wary of their doctors. Their children do not improve with age, 'angels in the cradle . . . more like Divels in the Saddle'.

The book appeared in July 1652, by which time Louis XIV, who regarded the English monarchy, his relatives, as a lost cause, was inching towards accommodation with Lord General Cromwell. *The State of France* was to be the first volume in a loose trilogy, in each of which Evelyn drew political analogies between the two countries through their capitals. *The Character of England* (1659), written as if by a dyspeptic French visitor, excoriated republican England, Presbyterian observance and the state of London with its congested streets and chaotic housing, noise and coal smoke: 'Hell upon Earth' on a foggy day.[7] Finally, *Fumifugium* (1661) was a reforming tract, suggesting ways in which London's polluted atmosphere could be blown away by the fresh breezes of a restored monarchy. Paris was always Evelyn's benchmark against which to judge London.

In 1652 personal advancement was out of the question for Evelyn unless he turned coat. The preface to *The State of France* carries a distinct whiff of self-justification. He complained how 'mine owne little interest hath suffered in the judgement of your stayed and more Thriving Geniuses' – that is, those who had remained in England or returned earlier. He was open to criticism for staying abroad so long but 'neither he who stayes at home, nor he that goes abroad, is (in mine opinion) to be altogether censured and blamed'. Now he aimed to 'but rubb out of this, into a better world, without the least impeachment to my Religion and Loyalty'.

It was still unclear whether Mary would agree to come to England yet. Evelyn wrote that he understood her reluctance to leave 'your owne, (though unnatural, yet native) country' but reassured her that 'prudent men have all decent libertyes heere, Ladys most of all; there being not a spot in the world where they more shine & are esteemed'. Her independent spirit would chafe under unreasonable restrictions; but she had superior drawing skills to the English and he tempted her with musical prospects, Italian recitatives rather than predictable French songs. In fact, her music teacher, M. Robert, chapel master of Notre Dame, was already in England.[8] Above all, Evelyn, 'your dearest Husband', could offer safety now that France was deep in its own 'Callamities and troubles'.

At Deptford, things were grim too. The house had been occupied and its grounds overrun at the end of the civil wars. But if the family abandoned Sayes Court now, he worried that Mary's uncle William Prettyman would do nothing. Evelyn proposed taking a joint lease and estimated that they could live there on £400 per annum, sharing running costs with Prettyman. Although the conduct books and her husband's advice were available to guide her, for the moment she would be freed from the burden of housekeeping: at fifteen, a daunting prospect. A sensible idea in principle, Mary knew her uncle well enough to spot the problems inherent in such a loose arrangement.

Sayes Court, whether as their family home or as a source of income, offered 'a settled life, either in this place, or some other', Evelyn told Mary, as he outlined their future domestic arrangements. She would have her own coach (designed in Paris, built in England) as well as a pearl necklace.[9] Though he was not with her in person, Evelyn was constantly before Mary on the page and she replied, in a careful, childish hand. She knew his tastes and reassured him that when she ordered their cabinet she would avoid heavily decorated ones ('all sculpture'); she actually chose a plain ebony piece, embellished with flowers that might have come straight from Pierre Morin's flowerbeds – ranunculus, dianthus and tulip.* Behind its doors, the ivory ornament and veneered cherry and rosewood were reflected by slivers of mirror glass. There were numerous deep oak drawers of every size, for all kinds of treasures. It was probably made by the rising young cabinetmaker Pierre Golle, who, driven on by his mother, refused to accept less than eight hundred livres for it. The next year he became the king's ebonist at the Gobelins.[10]

Mary Evelyn was already showing an impressive practical streak. Why not add to their plate later, when they could afford it, she wrote to her husband and surely they could borrow a necklace for the time being? She passed on messages from Dean Cosin and Dr Earle, and enquired anxiously after the Wallers, now back in England. Since her brother Dick was now away at school, Lady Browne was coming with Mary to help her settle in at Deptford, although Sir Richard was expecting her back again in Paris.

Evelyn wasted no time before contacting Waller and Fanshawe, his literary mentors, both of whom immediately came to see him at Sayes Court. They were reacting very differently in the political climate; Waller was already trimming his sails towards the Commonwealth, altering the drift of his poetry

---

*The pomegranates on the side panels symbolised fertility, suitable for a newly married couple.

and investigating the lie of the land while Fanshawe had withdrawn to rustic privacy, a steadfastly loyal cavalier gentleman. Evelyn was also visited by his 'deare friend', the bookish doctor from Cambridge, Jasper (also known as Gaspar or Caspar) Needham, who planned to go to Paris imminently and was, no doubt, given instructions.[11] Evelyn may have revealed to him that he had begun to translate Lucretius' *De rerum natura*.

Nor had Evelyn forgotten his pursuit of perpetual motion. M. Bressieux, a lens maker who had worked for René Descartes, was said to have a promising patent which he planned to register in London – something 'pour l'elevation des eaux' – and Samuel Hartlib, the all-knowing 'intelligencer' of the Interregnum, heard of him 'cleansing Amsterdam and freeing it from all stinking waters'. Evelyn's informant assured him that the inventor's objectives were practical – 'travailler sur lutil avant que travailler au curieux' (to work on useful things before pursuing the curious) – which suggested a machine with potential.[12] But that is all we hear of it.

The first weeks at home offered Evelyn a breathing space in which to consider his future but at the same time he saw the past being shamelessly reshaped by the new regime. In London, Cromwell's son-in-law, the regicide Henry Ireton, dead from the plague in Ireland, was given a funeral with full royal trappings. In Deptford, Evelyn had a ringside view of activity in the former royal dockyard, virtually over his own garden wall, as two great frigates, the *Diamond* and the *Ruby*, were launched in the presence of Cromwell and his 'Grandees'. These were warships with a purpose, as the Rump led the country towards the first of a ruinous series of trade wars with the Dutch.

George came to Deptford bringing a copy of Cromwell's Act of Oblivion, a peace offering 'to all that would submit to the Government'. Everyone was required to sign. Those who did not declare their allegiance could only hope for decent obscurity. Soon after, somewhat portentously, an almost total eclipse of the moon was followed, with rare symmetry, by an eclipse of the sun. Evelyn wavered, wondering whether it was wise after all to bring Mary to England. He toyed with returning to Paris and she responded, with ill-disguised delight: 'I am very sorry you finde England agree no better with you since it is the place you so much desire to setle in or ells certainly you might finde case for body and purse France agreeing well with both.'[13]

The uncertainty, exacerbated by delays between letters, caused misunderstandings. Mary told him that she was 'passionatly desirous not only to bee with you speedyly butt allso to conforme my selfe to any course of life with you.' Mob violence had engulfed Paris, orchestrated by the disaffected prince of Condé and his supporters, and Jasper Needham had cancelled his journey accordingly. Paradoxically, of the two countries, England now seemed marginally more stable. Mary decided: finally she would join her husband there.

Evelyn was still unsure whether they should settle at Sayes Court. Suddenly he heard that Albury might be for sale and wrote to his lawyer, Edward Thurland: 'It being now in your power to fix a wanderer, oblige all my Relations, and by one integral Cause, render me yours forever. I suppose the place will invite many Candidates, but my Mony is good.'[14] To buy the late earl of Arundel's precious refuge would have been the fulfilment of a dream. Like Wotton, Albury was a Tudor mansion in a deep-cut landscape of woods and water, embellished by Italianate gardens added by the earl and countess in the 1630s. Arundel 'made this place his darling', even when the house had been 'but an humble structure'.[15] An etching by Wenceslaus Hollar shows well-planted terraces with an arcaded central feature, perhaps the entrance to the famous caves or grottos.[16] John Aubrey heard that Arundel and Oughtred were nearly suffocated when one collapsed as they sat inside, distracted by higher matters.

With Richard now at Baynards to the south, a sizeable slice of Surrey would be in Evelyn hands – one estate for each brother. But Albury was not to be his after all. Henry Howard decided to keep it and three years later began 'to build, and alter the Gardens much'. For work on the house he called on the architectural services of Captain George Evelyn, 'the Traveller', but it was to John Evelyn that he turned for his garden.[17]

Evelyn was thus thrown back on run-down Sayes Court, finally securing the lease in February 1653, at a cost of £3,500, '300 pounds more than I bargain'd for'. It could hardly have offered a greater contrast to Wotton. He told Mary he was going there with George, 'to sit in counsell theere about his Gardens which hee assures mee have not advanced in expectation of myne advice & arrival'. The little hermitage in which he had pondered his prospects long ago was to disappear along with the knots, the moat and the rest of the Tudor remnants. The brothers cheerfully embarked on heavy earthworks, cutting back the hill (the top of which George had already flattened) and using the spoil to fill the moat and provide a platform for the parterre and fountain that would now set off the south side of the house.[18] Evelyn's head was filled with the Renaissance and Baroque gardens of Italy, their terraces, walls, steps and balustrades providing an architectural framework within which gardens were delineated by evergreens and the pencil-like cypresses of the natural landscape. These magic gardens of the South took their life from the sound and sight of plumes and cascades of water, from statues reflected in still pools and even from the comic theatrical effects of automata and echoes, hidden in grottos studded with glittering stones and shells. The garden at Wotton would be constrained by its dimensions, climate and (particularly) a lack of funds, but it might still evoke something of this.

But at Deptford the setting was unremittingly bleak, a few venerable elms and a small orchard relieving a hundred-acre expanse of exposed meadow, hemmed in on one side by the dockyard and on another by the rapidly expanding town. Most arrivals from the Continent travelled by water to London via Gravesend, and passed unsylvan Deptford en route. One French visitor saw 'nothing but continued Villages till you come to London. There is scarce anything to be seen on each Side of the River but Ship Carpenters, and Multitudes of all Sorts of Person imploy'd in Building and Fitting out Vessels for Sea; you have them of all Ages and Sizes . . . a vast Number.'[19]

Evelyn did not dissemble: he would take the house, he told Mary, 'with the land about it, not for any greate inclinations I have to the place, but in order to those other conveniences, and interests annexed to it, which will occasion my expending more mony to make it a tollerable seate, then wise men will yet thinke I had cause for.'[20] Despite his father-in-law's deep attachment to Sayes Court, Evelyn remained ambivalent. It took time for him to realise its potential.

Meanwhile, that spring Evelyn distracted himself from his domestic worries and uncertainties by helping his eight-year-old nephew George – he always warmed to an educational challenge. He had realised at Wotton that the boy was lagging behind in his schooling. His distracted father and an indulgent housekeeper had left him 'totaly ruin'd and neglected' but Evelyn believed that a tutor could turn him round and offered to undertake the experiment at Sayes Court. Christopher Wase would be the boy's tutor, allowing Evelyn to perform two favours at a stroke: providing employment for his cousin and education for George. He was, after all, Evelyn pointed out to George senior, 'the Chiefe of our family' and therefore a joint responsibility, to be weaned off 'sweete remembrances of Wotton' and 'other fondnesses' and prepared for the rigours of adult life.[21]

Edmund Waller then suggested their two families join forces and in May George accompanied his son and Wase to Hall Barn, Waller's estate outside Beaconsfield. They were welcomed warmly although 'I could obtaine from your noble friend Mr Waller no certainty for him being there'.[22] By November, 'my Lord Herbert sonne to the lord Pembroke' had joined the schoolroom. By the following summer the arrangement had broken down. In his father's view, young George was not mature enough to keep up with an aristocrat three years his senior, or to spend prolonged spells in town ('London is not a place for young boys'), and the Wallers paid scant attention to religious observance, keeping 'no family Dutys & prayers not so much as going a Sunday to church'.[23] This salutary episode stayed with Evelyn, a reminder that those with greater wealth and a more elevated social status often inhabited a very different moral and material sphere.

As he still waited for Mary, Evelyn learned that he too was to be a father. Sir Richard told him that his wife would 'bringe you a Deposition . . . a young cavalier who hath within these five days unexpectedly discoursed his vivacity by motion'. The baby was expected in five months. Having suffered no early sickness Mary had been taken by surprise by her condition. 'This (though yet a great secret here) is so reall a certainty that I exceedingly joye to give you this first Notice therof. And if Grandfathers love more tenderly their remote offspring you will nott, I hope, envie me my share in the greater contentment.' Browne's letter was followed by Mary's own confirmation: 'I never was more surprised' since she had been treated for another condition with 'phisick and letting blood, which was enough to have destroyed it.' Evelyn was delighted to hear the news from her 'owne fayre hand' and was 'affected with a kind of natural tendernesse, such as I never perceived in my Selfe before'.[24] Mary too felt that the pregnancy had brought them closer and that the child would be a 'greater tie to our affections'. Evelyn was to write that he had made her his wife 'and found a pearl'.

On the eve of her departure for the coast on the Rouen coach Mary told her husband she was busy, 'what with visits, and busines, and very much grief to part from so good a father . . . but I hope you will believe that since I must quit my father for any man living, I should not do it for one that I love more then your selfe'.[25] Mary, who had lived in France for eleven of her fifteen years, would never return, but the woman with whom Evelyn would share the rest of his life was nonetheless a Frenchwoman in all but nationality.

On their arrival at Rye, Evelyn told Mary, 'a very greate person, my old bed and schoolefellow heere (who hath the totall comand of that Towne)' would take care of her party and alert port officials. Colonel Herbert Morley, from Southover Free School, was now a member of the Council of State. However, appalling weather at sea sent their ship back to port and a shipping embargo, issued ahead of the First Dutch War, resulted in their only being able to cross safely when they were mistaken for a fishing vessel.

With time at his disposal, Evelyn went to church to experience the 'new fangled service' for himself, up to then having 'kept my eares incontaminate'. After the sermon and, presumably, long hours of prayer, the congregation was summarily dismissed without even a blessing into a town that observed the Sabbath with iron resolve. No non-religious activity was allowed and the smallest infringements were punished with fines.[26] From now on, Anglican observance in his family, as in many others, would be a largely domestic affair, using 'the church's fasts, festivals, and sacraments as prompts for what went on in the privacy of the individual's chamber'.[27] The Church of

England depended on the conservatism of the gentry for its survival at this time.

Finally, late one June afternoon a boat appeared on the horizon. It was, 'to my no small joy', the vessel bearing Lady Browne and her daughter. After a three-day voyage, Mary, by now well advanced in her pregnancy and surely apprehensive at what lay ahead, was very unwell. Evelyn too must have been nervous, as he prepared himself to be the head of a household within the strict hierarchy of the time in which the man stood to his family as God to the Church and as the monarch to the nation.

Their house was as yet unready and so they went straight to Tunbridge Wells, where Mary discovered her husband to be a determined opponent of the benefits of spa bathing, whiling away his time instead by writing to Paris about bookbinding. Growing restless, Evelyn went ahead to Deptford 'to prepare for the reception of my little family'. He had already ordered silk fabric from a Huguenot weaver in Moorgate and equipment for his 'elaboratory' from Reeves, the leading craftsman for lenses and optical devices. Had not Francis Bacon specified that the 'philosopher' needed a library, a garden, a cabinet and 'a palace fit for a philosopher's stone' consisting, in Evelyn's case, of a still-room, with the essentials for heating and chilling conserves and distillations, and a laboratory, with its own furniture and equipment?[28] But on his way back to Deptford, he was set upon by a thief and left tied to a tree. Struggling free after two hours, he raised the alarm and the following day distributed handbills around Goldsmiths' Hall, an effective measure since the stolen items (an onyx ring bearing his arms, an emerald and diamond ring and a pair of earrings set with rubies and diamonds) were soon found. The miscreant was, despite Evelyn's plea for leniency, sentenced to death for that and other crimes. Evelyn added the date, 23 June, to anniversaries deserving a special prayer of thanks.[29]

He soon turned back to Tunbridge Wells, however, for smallpox had broken out in London and Sayes Court was still buried beneath 'rubish and disorder'. To pass the days, the couple took the air in style in Mary's new coach, riding along the deeply gouged lanes between orchards and hop gardens. They called on Philip Packer, nearby at Groombridge, a 'prety Melancholy seate, well wooded and watred' and went to Penshurst Place, where, by apparent coincidence, Dorothy Sidney, the 'Sacharissa' of Waller's famous poem, was marrying an Oxford friend of Evelyn's. Meandering through Kent together must have reminded husband and wife of their companionable outings in the Ile de France. When they finally arrived at Sayes Court, in mid-July, they were greeted by both of Evelyn's brothers, their wives and 'two Coach fulls of friends', for two days of housewarming. From the beginning, Mary was made entirely welcome by his family.

Once settled, Elizabeth Browne wrote to her husband, detailing her brother Prettyman's 'huge' demands, presumably in recompense for his trusteeship and nominal care of the Deptford estate. The arrangements with her son-in-law, by contrast, were entirely harmonious; 'you may purcheis all agayne of my sonn when you ar able. In the mene time he will sitt it for you not intending soe to spoyle the seat', she told him. They were immensely obliged to him. Sir Nicholas Crisp, their neighbour, had built a large ware-house on the river bank and now wanted to further develop the site, 'intending to builld streets up towards Redrif [Rotherhithe]' which would crowd in on Sayes Court. Evelyn's objective was that their estate should remain both pleasant and profitable.[30] William Prettyman and Evelyn now contracted a 'penal bond' of £1,500 with their cousin James Stephens, 'setting out Lands to pay him a debt Sir R: owed him, within 6 months'. Prettyman was about to marry; his bride, Lady Browne reported, had an estate of £2,000 plus £500 from her mother. But the repercussions of the deal with Prettyman would dog Evelyn into old age.

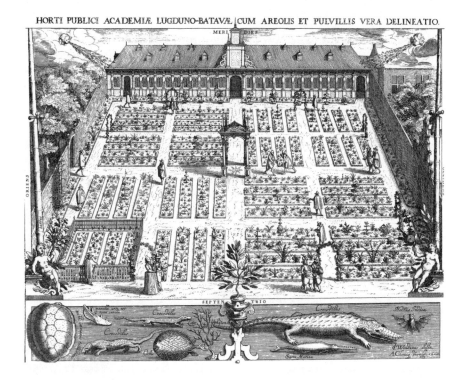

HORTI PUBLICI ACADEMIÆ LUGDUNO-BATAVÆ CUM AREOLIS ET PULVILLIS VERA DELINEATIO.

12 The Physic (Botanical) garden in Leiden (1610). Each quarter represents a continent while natural curiosities were displayed in the building to the north.

Mary had very little time left before the birth of their son. Hardly a month later his arrival marked the beginning of seventeen years of childbearing for her. Evelyn confessed to Mary's father that they had miscalculated the date by a month or even six weeks, which 'made us to be the less expectant but the more surprized'. He was born precisely at noon, the proud father told the grandfather, which 'I could calculate by a Ring or Universall Dial which I consulted very carefully at the very poynt and minute'. Even at such a moment, the two men were tempted to share their fascination with mechanical apparatus. With a wetnurse, and her mother's help, Mary could now rest. The christening took place at Sayes Court and Sir Richard, though absent, was named godfather. Only family members were invited to the service in the 'little drawing roome, next the Parlor'. Mr Owen, a 'cavalier parson', performed the Anglican service.[31] George Evelyn presented a silver basin worth £30 and the infant was named Richard.

The improvements at Sayes Court were already under way, starting with the essentials, a new stable and coach house. Lady Browne reported that Evelyn was 'making all veri fine' and prompted her husband: 'if you incoureg my sonn he will bestow 4 hundred pound to make the hous and all about it convenient to live in of which you shall heare more of hereafter.'[32] The specification and the contract with the carpenter Richard Skellman is signed by both Evelyn and Prettyman and dated 1 April 1652. Work on the house itself began the following February.

Sir Richard was as involved as he could be, from a distance. He remembered his 'father's fancy allways was to place the dwelling house at the other side of the mount soe to injoy the fresh prospect of the river and pleasure of the shipps' but he realised that Evelyn was in no position to embark on a complete rebuilding.[33] The most Evelyn could do was to give Sayes Court a bit of classical trim starting with a pedimented south-facing porch with 'Columns, cornish & architrave & other ornament with benches, Dorecases & doore framed with two leaves' estimated at almost £8. The doorcase, door and iron door furniture were modelled on those at 'Mr Bl.'s house at Chizelhurst'; in the absence of drawings, details were often borrowed from elsewhere. Above, there was a little room for Mary with a round window and ten openings, or 'lights'. Along the entire front elevation ran 'an Architrave & moulding' costing ten shillings, bringing a touch of modern Dutch elegance to the old house.

Evelyn's main object was to bring more light into the house. New or enlarged 'canted' or oriel windows, mostly of twelve lights, some double height, were added to the south, west and east – attractive additions which transformed the interior. Even the attics were improved and extended, with new garret windows and stairs 'made new & handsome'. A room called the 'presse chamber' – presumably the library – was to have a dormer as large as possible. The 'Great stayre', top-lit by 'a fayre skye light as large as the well or bigger if may be', rose out of the hall; the detailed specification suggests it was brand-new. The rooftop cupola ('the clockhouse') lit the hall and stairs but also stole a view of the river. The estimated cost was £55 15s.[34] Evelyn drew up a list of appropriate mottoes, eight for the principal doors and gates, which would be much admired by visitors. He also had considerable plans for the garden: Bacon had suggested that gardening surpassed architecture ('men come to build stately sooner than to garden finely, as if gardening were the greater perfection').[35]

Before Mary's mother left for Paris and the new household at Sayes Court settled into its domestic routine, albeit in the midst of the disruption that remodelling the house and garden would bring, the party decided to take a tour, visiting Lady Browne's sister Susan Hungerford at Cadenham, near Calne in Wiltshire, and Richard Evelyn in the house he had recently acquired on marriage, Woodcote in Epsom. As they prepared for the journey Mary's mother seemed unwell, then rallied. Once en route, however, she fell terminally ill with scarlet fever.

Evelyn now had to write the most difficult letter of his life, breaking the devastating news to Sir Richard. In the meantime Lady Browne's body was taken back to Deptford and the burial took place in the parish church of St Nicholas, close to the dockyard, following the established Church of England order of service. Mary's brother, Dick, arrived at the very moment the coffin was being taken into the church. Such a funeral had not been seen for seven years, Evelyn assured the distraught widower as if the splendour of her interment might offer him a tiny measure of comfort.[36]

Her mother's death affected Mary deeply. Just fifteen and with a new baby to look after, she was disconsolate, especially since she realised that her father mourned alone in Paris. Evelyn told Browne how proud he was of his resilience, an immovable rock 'against which all evills and misfortunes continually breake their selves'. As the Resident's private world collapsed, he had to deal with Charles and his retinue, back in Paris in extremely reduced circumstances, so much so that, according to Sir Edward Hyde the 'good man' (Browne) had even been briefly imprisoned for non-payment of rent.[37] In early November Browne was posted to Brittany, first to Brest and then to Nantes, to secure the prizes taken by royalist merchants at the ports to fund the wandering court.

Early in 1653, Evelyn conveyed to his father-in-law a message which offered another possibility for his future. It came, he told him, 'from your very reall freind Mr EW [Edmund Waller] who received comands from a Special Eminentissimo here to Sound, and treate with mee touching your

Inclynations, upon pretence of many good intentions towards you, in case that you would be brought to be made a Creature, I dare not say perverted'. The authorities were hoping to persuade Browne, after all his sufferings, to come over to Cromwell's side and represent the Commonwealth's interests in France, a man 'very considerable to be gained'. Evelyn had replied 'in such language & with that Caution as they could justly resent nothing'. But, he added, 'if you thinke good to give any answer, I pray it may be with that prudence, the vigilancy of neither part may construe amisse.'[38] These were highly sensitive matters and Evelyn asked Browne to burn the letter.*

The convoluted prose, always a sign of nervousness or uncertainty in Evelyn, showed his awkwardness when acting as an intermediary in such matters. Related to both Cromwell and John Hampden, the heroic parliamentarian who died in the civil war, Waller saw the Commonwealth as the future. No record survives of Browne's response (if the offer was even Waller's to make) but his probity prior to this date suggests he would never have compromised himself, to save either his skin or his fortune. He was too dutiful even to come to England as Evelyn asked, to 'comfort my often disconsolat poore Wife' whose mother's death 'hung long upon her'.[39]

Alone, Browne now embarked upon an internal exile of several years, carrying out tasks for which he appears to have been singularly unfitted. Evelyn kept Browne up to date on progress in Deptford. His apartment had been fitted out and the drawings would show the house 'infinitely changed and I hope much for the better'. As intended, Sir Richard took great comfort from the news:

> you will easily guess how agreeable the apartement you mention must needes bee unto mee when one never omitted clause of my daily prayers is, that God would soe dispose of my affaires that I may, with good grace, retire to that home and there end my dayes in peace and be layed in the grave of my ancestores and in the ashes of my deare wife.[40]

But it was the development of the garden which gave Browne greatest delight. Evelyn had started with an almost blank canvas, drawing up a scheme in which the artificial and the natural played off each other. At the centre was what he always called his 'Morin' or 'dial' garden, an immense oval parterre based upon the one he had so admired in Pierre Morin's Parisian garden. By autumn 1653 he told Browne he was transplanting 'my glorious nursery of neere 800 plantes' and refining the design for the oval-shaped garden 'whereof (together with our other environs) I purpose to send you coppied exactly from

---

*Fortunately he did not.

the plott which I have now finished and is the guide of all our designes'. Exquisitely drawn up as if for an engraver, the plan, together with Evelyn and Browne's correspondence, provides an invaluable record of the gestation and creation of a mid-seventeenth-century garden.[41]

Evelyn was continually reporting progress to Browne and receiving suggestions in return. A long letter from St Malo thanked him for his first view of the great plan, so admirable that his father-in-law said he felt excluded from paradise. 'I will only take the boldnesse to putt you in minde that on this side the sea ... the grand mode is to plant the whole avenue ... with severall rowes of trees which perhaps you have allowed'. He wondered, too, about taking the 'Broad Walk' from the summer house over the island and the meadow to the Thames.[42]

When planted out the following spring, the Morin garden was to be an exact copy of the French model, for Evelyn had asked Browne to convert French measurements to English. The initial subdivisions at Sayes Court may also have owed something to the eighteen-acre royal Jardin des Plantes in Paris, as shown in Abraham Bosse's exquisite engravings, no doubt in Evelyn's print collection. Faced with a similarly awkward triangular site, the Sayes Court garden was bound to offer 'a very wilde Regularitie', in Sir Henry Wotton's phrase.

As Christopher Browne had found to his cost, the site was too exposed, being both dry and wind-blown. Evelyn initially lost almost half of the thousand plants in his 'Morin' parterre. From the beginning he was happy to use his garden experimentally to test the tolerance and habit of unusual species, to try different ways of planting and evoke other designs he admired. Over the coming years, like any gardener facing the realities of soil and site, everything would be continually subject to change. Sayes Court also came to mirror his circumstances and ideas: the early garden was an Epicurean retreat from the pressures and disruptions beyond its walls, but after the Restoration it reflected his increasingly public persona.

Although Sayes Court was 'all in morter' and the work on the garden was progressing, his brothers still thought that Evelyn might be tempted by the right house elsewhere. Squerryes in Westerham, Kent, had become available, 'very complete', recently repaired, with a wooded estate, well outside the town. The asking price was high but, George suggested, if he sold his scattered lands in Essex and Sussex, Evelyn could raise £6,000 and borrow the £500 difference; he and Richard would happily stand security for him. He advised him to let Deptford, 'now that you have made it so handsome & conveniant' for a good rent.[43] Instead Evelyn took Mary, pregnant again, on a modest journey into his past. They visited Wotton for the first time as a couple and heard a sermon from the rector who had baptised Evelyn.

In Guildford they admired the almshouses which his father had always supported. Then they called on Henry Howard and William Oughtred at Albury.

Evelyn had 'scarce had the leasure to reade a line of any booke since I left Paris' but was now brimming with ideas for publications. He was in regular correspondence with his French contacts; both Bosse and Nanteuil sent him their latest work; and he was considering translating Le Fèvre's chemistry course, encouraged by the author himself. Most French Protestants envisaged a more secure future overseas and in 1660 Le Fèvre became chemist and apothecary to Charles II – possibly through the good offices of his former students. But for the time being, Evelyn, Mary and he corresponded about Glauber's writings on minerals and especially on strange lights, as well as on paintwork for carriages, Venetian glass, fabric printing and recipes for oil of rose. Le Fèvre told Evelyn he had assured Du Clos of his probity ('on a tout donné a vostre vertu') – essential reassurance if he were to entrust him with his highly secret recipe for gold varnish.[44] Mary's enduring pleasure was her painting, and M. du Guernier came from Paris to join their household for a while.[45]

The building works at Sayes Court may have pointed to a more urgent need for printed guidance which Evelyn was well placed to supply. As he wrote, 'an accomplish'd Master-Builder should be furnish'd beyond the Vulgar' since it is his role to guide the 'commonly illiterate Mechanick' and the humble workmen 'who make use of their hands and tooles in the grosser materials'. The problem was twofold: the lack of an authoritative English architectural treatise on the classical orders; and the intractability of builders. As he wrote:

> Let one find never so just a fault with a Workman, be the same of what Mystery [Guild] soever, immediately he shall reply, Sir, I do not come hither to be taught my Trade, I have serv'd an Apprenticeship and have wrought ere now with Gentlemen that have been satisfied with my work, and sometimes not without language of reproach, or casting down his Tools and going away in wroth; for such I have frequently met withal.[46]

While Evelyn was considering these matters, cousin 'Captain' George wrote from Wotton asking for pattern books, in particular those showing general door and gable adornments, and reminding Evelyn that he had promised him 'another famous book of Architecture', the name of which he could not remember.[47] This further confirmed Evelyn in his opinion that an English treatise was urgently needed. Abraham Bosse might solve his problem, for only in Paris would he find plates of suitable quality since 'our whole Nation hardly affords us One engraver comparable'. Compared to their French and Dutch counterparts, English printmakers were 'shameless Bunglers', disgracing 'so noble and ingenious an Art'.[48]

Describing himself as living in retirement in a country with 'ni Eglise, ni Roy, ni Loy', Evelyn asked Bosse to kindly send his latest work on perspective and told him about his latest project, 'an attempt to correct the common ignorance of our workmen and to raise the awareness of a fine and necessary art among our nobility'.[49] In fact Evelyn had brought Roland Fréart de Chambray's *Parallèle de l'architecture antique et de la moderne* (1650) with him from Paris but a bad-tempered dispute between Bosse and the academician Charles Errard over the rightful ownership of the plates threatened to stymie Evelyn's plan to translate it.[50] The quality of the engravings was crucial to the enterprise and in the end it took more than a decade for Evelyn to secure a suitable set, through the efforts of Hugh May, the leading Restoration architect. Meanwhile Evelyn pressed on with other projects, including his translation of Lucretius' *De rerum natura*.

In stark contrast to Evelyn, so fulfilled at last, Browne was living in impoverished loneliness in Brittany, battling with fraudulent officials. He had little to cheer him except the continual news of the works in Deptford. In Paris, his landlord threatened to seize his goods to cover the unpaid rent but Hyde advised him to look after himself before paying off any debts. Eventually they were met from funds from Cardinal Mazarin's pension to Charles II topped up by money taken at the ports 'with such a letter for his encouragement that he [the landlord] may understande it to be his Majesty's money and sent by his order'. But in the meantime, Hyde reported that 'we are all here in the same beggarly condition you left us, which I think by long custom, will grow a second nature to us'. He and Ormonde had been reduced to walking around the city, 'no honourable custom in Paris'.[51]

In December 1653 Oliver Cromwell became 'lord protector' under a constitution framed by the Army Council. Order was returning. Evelyn took comfort that in Greenwich Park, where the trees had been marked for felling, Cromwell had intervened to stop the desecration. Life at Wotton had already returned to normal; it was looking splendid.

Early drawings of Wotton show the old house belted by, successively, a band of garden, a wide moat and woodland. By 1653, when Evelyn drew it from the vantage point of the mount, the moat had gone, to be replaced by a sunken parterre with a fountain and raised walks to east and west which gave a view over a knot garden. Sending John Aubrey material for his *Natural History and Antiquities of Surrey* (not published until 1718–19), Evelyn pointed out that it was designed 'after the Italian manner' and that the mount was fifty feet high.[52] Under the mount was a grotto encrusted with shells and corals, their colours enhanced by the play of the water, and soon to be fronted by cousin George's bold portico which Evelyn criticised for its classical illiteracy.

That summer Evelyn was unable to go to George's party, perhaps held to show off his new garden and celebrate the birth of another John Evelyn. He told Jasper Needham that he was keeping his pregnant wife company ('thus you see it is to be devoted to a Woman . . . for indeede it is my fondnesse onely which keepes me from a neerer participation of your good company'). But he hoped Needham would represent him, where 'so many persons of honour, and illustrious Ladys . . . make it now the Court of Wotton, and the evening circle there the onely sceane of ingenious divertisement, from whence some Boccatian witt might furnish a better Decameron'. He imagines the two of them wandering through the groves and the fountains, discussing 'that Tulip, or this Anemonie', as they enjoy the same view, 'philosophize in the same p[e]ristyle' and share intelligent conversation. A modern statue of Venus overlooked the scene.

George was 'of so hospitable a nature as no family in the whole County maintained that antient Custome of keeping (as it were) open house the whole yeare . . . there being sometime 20 persons more than his family, & some that stayed there all the summer to his no small expense'.[53] Indigent cousins and nephews, relatives like William Glanville and countless friends came to stay, sometimes for months at a time. This side of life at Wotton was not to Evelyn's taste: the gentry mindlessly at play. He asked Needham how George accommodated so many guests, 'where you do nothing but feast and enjoy the creature, day and night too (I had almost sayd) for it cannot else sinke into my comprehension, how my Brother should possibly lodg so jolly a troope, unlesse you lye like the family of Love'.[54]

Evelyn and Henshaw were now back in the same country, albeit far apart, Kensington being as far west as Deptford east of London. In 1654 they reversed roles when Henshaw was called to the bar and the Evelyn brothers consigned him their chambers. But Henshaw told Evelyn how he missed talking to him more often: 'I grieve to thinke how short the days are & how long the way is from me to you which though it defends you from the frequent trouble I should give you, yet deprives mee of the satisfaction content instruction & advantage I always get by your conversation.'[55] It must have been Henshaw who drew Samuel Hartlib's attention to Evelyn, causing him to note in mid-1653: 'Mr Evelin at Dedford [*sic*] a chymist hath studied and collected a great Worke of all Trades, and wants no more to it but the description of 3 trades. Mr Grettrick [Greatorex], who hath an insight in most of the Trades, hath holpen him very much in it.'[56] Evelyn, he said, reportedly knew French, Italian and Latin, had 'many furnaces a going and hath a wife that can in a manner performe miracles, so curious and exquisite she is in painting or limming and other Mechanical knacks'.

Evelyn's laboratory was indeed taking shape. In his 1653 plan of Sayes Court he described 'a Portico of 20 foot long upon Pillars, open towards the Private Garden'. His chemical notebooks show sketches of stoves and furnaces, specimen bottles and utensils, as suggested by Le Fèvre. There, his wife beside him in the stillroom, Evelyn could become a model chemist, who while 'understanding Contemplation as well as any of them' always concentrates on the practical, to 'find the true cause of so many effects as be in the nature of things'.[57]

Outside too, the landscape had been transformed. Evelyn told Browne that they were planting five hundred trees, grown in Essex, and another eight hundred were to follow, all underplanted by nuts and berries. In time, coppicing would provide their firewood. A rough plan showed limes and elms bordering the field beyond the entrance court, leading to an avenue. Like any sensible gardener, Evelyn was establishing a linear and three-dimensional framework, pathways and steps providing important emphases on a somewhat featureless site. The trees had come first, after which he could stitch in the remaining detail of the 'Morin' parterre (which included six hundred fruit trees) and organise his own botanical garden. The latter was centred on a mount (perhaps that remaining from the Tudor garden) and incorporated unusual medicinal plants from all around the world – the Garden of Eden as a garden of simples.[58] His grove, a homage to those he recalled seeing in France and Italy, was to become a dense plantation of evergreens (including his beloved alaternus or Italian buckthorn), thickets cut by paths and 'meanders' and leading to a central glade planted with bay and laurels. Evelyn was in no doubt about the desirability of achieving a congenial marriage of utility and beauty: 'Now in truth the labour & expense over, I find the pleasure of adorning, fitting and sprucifying the place render me some return.' From the 1653 plan and other later drawings, family letters and scattered clues in the manuscript of *Elysium Britannicum*, a partial picture of Evelyn's garden at Sayes Court emerges in the absence of any other surviving evidence.

Sir Henry Wotton believed a man's house and home to be 'The Theater of his Hospitality, the Seate of Selfe-fruition, the Comfortablest part of his owne Life, the Noblest of his Sonnes Inheritance, a kinde of priuate Princedome; Nay, to the Possessors thereof, an Epitomie of the whole World'.[59] That Evelyn should have turned desolate Sayes Court into the villa of his imagination, his 'Tusculanum', its gardens conjured out of the charmless landscape by the dockyard, was a considerable achievement.[60] Indoors, he laboured on his 'self-fruition', turning the Latin of Lucretius' *De rerum natura* into English verse, trying to celebrate Epicurean virtue in a way that could sit at ease with his own Christian beliefs.

But, as Mary had foreseen, her troublesome uncle William Prettyman was now laying claim to Sayes Court, due to the badly drafted lease.[61] Evelyn suggested to Browne that he should sort out the problem and, in a mournful afterword, revealed that their second son, John Stansfield, born late in 1653, had died. However, their prodigious first-born, Richard, was already enjoying books and pictures and knew many French words. Beyond Deptford Evelyn saw 'the church undone, the new ones flourishing, the Taxes increasing, and wise men possessing themselves in patience'. The Barebones Parliament, which had replaced the Rump, consisted of 140 hand-picked men but still proved unworkable. By December 1653 Lord Protector Cromwell ruled the country with his New Model Army.

Even ardent royalists were encouraged by the stability brought by the Protectorate: exiles began to come home from overseas in greater numbers and the Evelyns decided to make their long-postponed visit to Wiltshire, a stimulating change after 'my Turmoile & building &c'. In summer 1654 they set off in their smart coach and four of Parisian design. Their first stop was at the grave of 'our blessed Martyr King Charles' in the vault below the Chapel Royal at Windsor; their pilgrimage also included several royalist battlefields. Once settled with Susan Hungerford, Mary's aunt and closest relative in England, they took excursions to Bath and, far more to Evelyn's liking, to Bristol, rivalling London in its 'manner of building, shops, bridge: Traffique: Exchange, Marketplace &c', an impressive city that was 'wholy Mercantile'. At a sugar refinery they ate eggs fried in the heat of the furnace, which they washed down with Spanish wine, a Bristol import, before clambering down the Avon Gorge to enjoy the hot springs and forage for rock crystals.[62]

Their next destination was Oxford. Evelyn had not returned since his student days, fifteen years earlier. After meeting Seth Ward, the Savilian Professor of Astronomy, he basked in a warm welcome from Balliol, his *alma mater*. He was surprised that some rituals remained: doctorates were still conferred 'by the Cap, ring, Kisse &c.' Bringing home the serious nature of the current religious climate, and exorcising Laud's memory, the authorities made four new doctors of theology, but only three of medicine. At Wadham, Dr John Wilkins offered them 'magnificent Entertainement'. Evelyn found himself in the midst of a group of Anglican intellectuals who were skilfully keeping their reputations and positions intact under the Protectorate. It was a revelation for him. Wilkins, who became Cromwell's brother-in-law in 1656 and was in the chair at the inaugural meeting of what became the Royal Society, was the central figure, a pioneering mathematician and natural philosopher, skilfully drawing together different strands of experience. Robert

Hooke described him as 'a man born for the good of mankind; and for the honour of his Country. In the sweetness of whose behaviour, in the calmness of his mind, in the unbounded goodness of his heart, we have an evident Instance, what the true and the primitive unpassionate Religion was, before it was sowred by particular Factions.'[63]

Wilkins, like Hartlib in London, was eager to attract young men of promise into his circle. He was hoping to tempt Robert Boyle away from his isolated laboratory ('a kind of Elysium') in Dorset and wondered how to 'heighten those inclinations, which you intimate of coming to Oxford, into full resolutions'. In 1655 Boyle came, telling Hartlib of his surprise at finding 'a knot of such ingenious & free philosophers, who I can assure you do not only admit & entertain real learning but cherish & improve it, & have done & are like to do more toward the advancement of it than many of those pretenders that do more busy the press'. His prejudice against academic pedantry and the 'prattling of our book-philosophers', which had seemed so at odds with the aspirations of a virtuous scholarly gentleman, evaporated. By 1656 Boyle had moved permanently to Oxford.[64] For Wilkins, busy John Evelyn with his intriguing garden, laboratory and two books to his name, at the very least, represented a virtuoso with potential.

It was here that Evelyn first met Christopher Wren, 'that miracle of a Youth', as he described him in retrospect. Wren was already an 'addicted Client' of Wilkins's. Evelyn's junior by twelve years, he had attracted attention as a prodigy of extraordinary inventive powers. His masters were William Oughtred and the physician Charles Scarburgh (William Harvey's trusted assistant), to whom he owed 'any little skill I can boast in Mathematicks'.

Evelyn guided Mary around Oxford, much changed since the 1630s. Dr Thomas Barlow, a cleric of Calvinist tendency who was currently the librarian of the Bodleian, showed them his treasure house and pulled out items to interest them both: for Mary he chose 'the Proverbs of Solaman written in French, by a Lady'. The Bodleian's new west wing contained almost thirteen hundred manuscripts in eighteen languages presented by Archbishop Laud.[65] But many of the chapels had lost their stained glass and had been crudely adjusted for the new liturgy. At least the Physic Garden (the future Botanical Garden) was finally taking shape behind its handsome walls.

Before leaving they spent more time with Wilkins, who showed his guests an Aladdin's cave of 'many . . . artificial, mathematical, Magical curiosities' – perhaps reminiscent of Kircher's room in Rome – mostly his own or Wren's inventions. Above all Evelyn was impressed by the garden at Wadham College, with a mount at its centre, and was mesmerised by the glass-fronted beehives designed 'like Castles & Palaces' which revealed the mysterious processes within. In the diary Evelyn claimed that Wilkins gave him 'a

Philosophicall Apiarie' then and there but it appears that Evelyn ordered one two years later. In April 1656 John Wilkins wrote to tell him: 'I have here in readines[s] for you, one part of the Bee-hive you desire, according to the same model I have in Oxford. If you should desire to have two other like parts made to this, (which I should advise), they may be done here in London by the same man who made this'.[66] In the *Elysium Britannicum,* the encyclopaedic book about gardens on which Evelyn embarked soon after, he wrote 'I should fill a Volume, not a Chapter onely' to deal with the culture of bees for 'of all the Living creatures . . . The Bee is the wisest . . . & aproaching neerest to the understanding of men'. Both architects and builders, they preside over 'a Citty, King, Empire, Society', occupied on public business, peaceable, loyal and 'affected to Monarchy & . . . reading a Lecture of obedience to Rebells in every Garden'.[67]

Reeling from the hospitality and abundant food for thought in Oxford, they returned to Aunt Hungerford's. Their next destination, Wilton House, boasted the finest garden in England according to Evelyn. In the 1630s, Philip Herbert, 4th earl of Pembroke, employed Isaac de Caus, supervised by Inigo Jones, to classicise his house and to create a lavish Renaissance garden. De Caus's scheme was commemorated in a set of prints which Evelyn may well have known (or even owned). The groves, statuary, grottos and hydraulics had attracted connoisseurs from Charles I onwards, but young Lodewijk Huygens, visiting two years before Evelyn, found many of the fountains out of order although he was impressed by the splendid grotto and the twenty-foot-high cypress avenues. The Pembrokes were parliamentarians and so their estate may have fared better than many during the civil wars.

When they visited, Christopher Wase may have been at Wilton with his pupil William Herbert, whose father (another Philip) had succeeded to the estate in 1650. He was a member of the Council of State. Perhaps Evelyn's rather jaded comments on the waterworks (he thought the pressure could be increased by raising the river level) reflected this fact. But Evelyn's later work at Albury suggests his familiarity with De Caus's engraving of the amphitheatre at Wilton, a crescent carved out of a hillside, just as in Surrey.

On Salisbury Plain the close-cropped downland and 'innumerable flocks' offered a contrast with bosky Surrey, and at Stonehenge they managed to count ninety-five stones. On their journey Evelyn was as intrigued by novel mechanical devices as he was by new architecture, as delighted by landscape as by traditional customs and antiquarian relics.[68] He was no longer content simply to store his impressions in a cabinet of curiosities. He was corralling them mentally, becoming as ambitious as Kircher and as discursive as Digby.

Since they were far from home, he wanted to show Mary, 'who from her childhood had lived altogether in France', more of her native country. They travelled from Gloucester, via the Malvern Hills, to Worcester, Warwick and Coventry, following a melancholy trail of civil war destruction of great houses and ancient castles. At Doncaster the atmosphere changed; here was the buzz of trade, the manufacture of 'greate Wax-lights & good stockings'. At York they turned south, to Hull, Lincoln and Grantham. A month later they reached Cambridge, where they again made the obligatory round of college chapels and libraries (remembering that Dr Cosin, whose extensive library in Paris Evelyn had toyed with buying, had been Master of Peterhouse). Evelyn was happily confirmed in his preference for Oxford, 'the noblest Universitie now in the whole world'. Cambridge was the protector's province, as Oxford had been the king's. They passed palatial Audley End, built for the 1st earl of Suffolk, James I's lord high treasurer, its parapet 'a bordure of Capital letters', and a reminder of the transitory nature of court favour. Back in Deptford, Evelyn estimated that their tour had taken them some seven hundred miles.

Now Evelyn set to work on his translations, fired by the visit to Oxford and the broader horizons it had opened. He was becoming recognised for his learning and overseas contacts. When he visited London he was an habitué of the booksellers' shops and instrument makers huddled around St Paul's Cathedral, a magnet for enquiring minds. From these specialist shops the path led to Gresham College where lectures in English and Latin covered subjects of current scientific interest. When Wren was appointed Gresham Professor of Astronomy in 1657 he found in the capital 'so general a Relish of Mathematick and the *libera philosophia* in such a Measure, as is hardly to be found in the Academies themselves'.[69]

Peter Pett, a son of the master-shipwright at Deptford of the same name and a Fellow of All Souls since 1649, wrote to thank Evelyn for allowing him to 'pelt' him with visits to Sayes Court and congratulated him on his grasp of languages, highlighting his own limitations since he had been no further than 'the island where he was born'. The well-travelled Evelyn had obviously made his mark in Oxford and now doors were opening to him in London.[70]

CHAPTER 8

Planting Cabbages and Blotting Paper

By the summer of 1655 Samuel Hartlib, the elder statesman of natural philosophy and the founder of the so-called 'Office of Address', had learned a considerable amount about Evelyn, although they had still not met. 'Hee approoves of Du Bosse etching. A great lover of Husbandry and Planting. Likes much of Mr [Johann] Morian's Way of Bee-hiving under roofes.' At last, that November, Evelyn visited him at his house in Axe-yard Westminster, the 'quondam back-kitchen' (or laboratory) shared with his son-in-law, a somewhat dubious alchemist, Dr Frederick Clodius (or Clod). Evelyn found Hartlib a 'Master of innumerable Curiosities & very communicative', and so the first face-to-face meeting between republican experimenter and royalist virtuoso took place.

Hartlib was from the Baltic city of Elbing, the son of a rich German merchant and his English third wife. By the time Evelyn knew him, he was in bad health, and despite being voted a pension in 1649, was descending into penury. But he was an eager proselytiser. Even Sir Kenelm Digby, after his return to England in 1654 when he became an intermediary between Cromwell and Mazarin, was in regular contact with Hartlib. When Evelyn and he parted that autumn day Hartlib gave him a copy of his *Legacy of Husbandry*, into which, over the coming years, Evelyn pencilled a dense addendum of notes.[1]

Evelyn reported the encounter as a largely practical discussion about dealing with smoking chimneys and an ink that would provide a dozen copies on damp paper. Hartlib's memory of the occasion was quite different: Evelyn came 'desirous to see my Bee-hive. Hee professed to have made only a great Apparatus for a Universal Mechanical Work and that hee would contribute all his collections to one that would write the History of all Mechanical Arts.' Succinctly put, 'Hartlib remembered a co-operative pansophic enterprise of utilitarian benefit, Evelyn an afternoon's distraction with smoky stoves'.[2]

Evelyn's great 'Apparatus', from which he was apparently trying to extricate himself, was one of the most important objectives which Francis Bacon had set for a world of universal knowledge and enquiry, a comprehensive history of the trades. Hartlib considered it central to his own 'Invisible College' and in 1647 told Robert Boyle that he hoped the remarkable young William Petty might be the man to do it and by 1649 hoped that Petty could be 'set apart or encouraged for the advancement of experimental and mechanical knowledge in Gresham college'. But soon after Petty's prodigious talents were diverted to Brasenose College Oxford and a professorship in anatomy.[3] Hartlib had to look for another compiler for his trades project and he must have considered Evelyn the ideal candidate, if he could be persuaded to broaden his frame of reference.

Characteristically, Evelyn's approach was to immerse himself in a catalogue, and his undated commonplace book of 'Seacrets & Receipts Mechanical as they came casualy to hand' was little more than a list of categories. His headings were arranged according to function but also status. 'Frippery trades' included 'cobler, last & heele maker, tinker, pedler', while women's occupations were, unsurprisingly, 'Preserving, Midwife, Spinster, Semster, Laundresse, Bleaching'. Artisan craftsmen were included under the 'Polite Artes', while a long list of 'Liberal Arts' began with merchants, and included engineers and architects. Finally, he listed occupations 'in and about the country & belonging to the Seas &c'. The trades on which he was most expansive were, predictably enough, those with which he was familiar; shipwrights, stone masons and craftsmen (he included the ornament of grottos), lens and spectacle makers, and artisans in varnish, gilding and enamelling (those secretive trades to which he had gained privileged access in Paris).[4]

Evelyn now had a task which gave him status in the informal intellectual grouping over which Wilkins and Hartlib presided. In 1655 Dr Jasper Needham, Evelyn's bibliophile physician friend, finally left for France. For Evelyn it was almost as good as going to Paris himself for Needham could re-establish ties with his contacts and, where the history of trades was concerned, pursue elusive recipes for japanning, gilding, marbling and varnishing. In addition, at Evelyn's suggestion, Needham attended some of Niçaise Le Fèvre's lectures at the Jardin des Plantes. When Evelyn eventually compiled his notes on chemistry, apparently with publication in mind, he inscribed them to 'GN'.[5]

Well read, widely informed and intellectually generous, Needham was busy looking out for material that either he or Evelyn could translate or publish. He immediately sent him the Epicurean scholar Pierre Gassendi's epitaph, a perfect note on which to end *De rerum natura* which arrived just as Evelyn was 'concluding this Discourse'.[6]

Evelyn was increasingly confused by the irreconcilable contradictions he found within Lucretius's text between atomism, Epicurean ideas and his own Christianity. In 1655 he began a long and intense spiritual conversation, first in person and then on paper, with the cleric Dr Jeremy Taylor, 'my Ghostly Father' as he refers to him. Taylor, who had been a chaplain both to Laud and Charles I, and who spent most of the time in Wales, had just completed his major work, a study of conscience and ethics which offered a Protestant retort to Catholic manuals on casuistry. *Ductor dubitantium* or *The Rule of Conscience* was eventually published in 1660. Taylor was an ideal sounding board for Evelyn's worries, and his guidance, together with intensive reading of the scriptures, contemplative texts and sermons, proved reassuring. But the line dividing the profound and the primitive was blurred and never more so than where alchemy was concerned.

In his account of the Royal Society Thomas Sprat distinguished between *alchymia* and *chymia*. Chemists, he wrote, have 'onely the discreet and sober flame, and not the wild lightning of the others Brains'. Yet even that respected scholar and mathematician William Oughtred had, Elias Ashmole claimed, offered him the secret of the philosopher's stone, transforming base metal to gold, as a deathbed legacy in 1653. Two years later, visiting Wotton, Oughtred (who survived) assured Evelyn that water was 'the Philosophers first matter; & that he was well perswaded of the possibility of their Elixir'.[7] For the curious, the arcane was unavoidable.

Evelyn's main contact with the world of alchemy was his close friend Thomas Henshaw. Hartlib had first reported on him in 1650, 'a universal schollar and pretty communicative. Hee pretends to have the Altahest or a true dissolvent'.[8] With his laboratory in Kensington and the means to employ a technician, he and Dr Thomas Vaughan from Oxford 'lay their heads and hands together to see what they can produce'. Even Robert Boyle, for all his unwavering Christianity (Aubrey described him as almost a 'Lay-Bishop'), was immersed in alchemy for a time. His antipathy to obscure and potentially fraudulent procedures grew – conceits 'no where to be found but in Utopia' as Milton put it in *Paradise Lost* – and he began to write the *Sceptical Chymist* in 1654.[9] The meeting point of arcana and Christianity also greatly troubled Evelyn. His notes from the chemist Anibal Barlet's guide to searching for metals with a divining rod included suitable prayers and a suggestion that the hazel rod with which the seeker should 'goe where you thinke there is treasure hidden' be shaped into a cross. If the rod twitches, 'consult with divines whether this be not witchcraft'.[10]

In mainstream society, the Anglican Church, so central to those 'whose commitments were protestant yet ceremonial, whose devotion was to the unity and the traditional liturgical practices of the English church', was

increasingly under attack.[11] Evelyn explained his continued church attendance 'whilst these usurpers possess'd the Pulpet' by his need to ensure 'that
I might not be suspected for a Papist'. Although he exaggerated the extent
of religious extremism, by late 1654 restrictions on mainstream observance
were biting hard. 'I seldome went to Church upon solemn Feasts; but either
went to Lond: where privately some of the orthodox sequestred Divines did
use the Common Prayer, administer Sacraments &c: or else procured one to
officiate in my house'. Soon royalists were forbidden to give ejected clergy
positions as chaplains or school teachers. Evelyn's household followed a
strict routine of regular daily religious observance. But sometimes Evelyn
was exposed to the outside world; he heard a stranger preaching at Deptford
'in an Enthusiastic style: I heard since he was a Trooper, & I minded him
but little.'[12]

On the last day of 1654, Richard (now two years old) almost choked to
death on a bone. His nurse fainted but his parents fought a successful race
against time to clear his larynx. A fortnight later, his brother John was born
and Richard Owen, who frequently conducted services and gave the sacrament at Sayes Court, christened him. William Prettyman, with whom they
still uneasily shared the house, stood godfather, as did their cousin Sir John
Evelyn of Godstone. In April the Prettymans finally moved out and the
Evelyns could call their home their own.

A year later, in April 1656, they hosted a dinner at Sayes Court. As well as
Jeremy Taylor and John Wilkins, Robert Boyle was a guest. Evelyn had not
met him before. Afterwards he confided to Taylor that he might have tried
too hard to to impress his visitors ('so many curious persons, to whom I had
been greatly obliged, and for whom I have much value') with his accomplishments and his devices ('I presented Dr Wilkins with my rare Burning-glasse').
He feared he had shown himself in a vainglorious, unspiritual light. 'It were
fitting you did see how I live,' he said, but worried that Taylor might see him
as being too immersed in his pleasures and gratified by the praise and attention of his admiring visitors – 'my condition is too well'. Not only had Evelyn
transgressed Christian precepts of modesty but he had also abandoned the
notion of Epicurean withdrawal.

But, as the uncensorious guardian of Evelyn's conscience, Taylor was
enchanted by 'your Tusculanum' and the 'union of blessings' that he enjoyed.
He could see no harm in the pride that Evelyn took in the beauty of 'outward
things' – always transitory, he pointed out. He commended him for his seriousness and on remaining available for 'the service of God'.[13] Evelyn did not
share Pepys's ability to happily break his own rules ('my love of pleasure is
such, that my very soul is angry with itself') but, within the limits he set
himself, he found great enjoyment.[14]

Evelyn's first meeting with Boyle was a momentous occasion, he recalled almost fifty years after. They were 'cultivating the same studies and designs, especially in the search of natural and useful things; myself then intent on collections of notes in order to an History of Trades and other mechanical furniture, which he earnestly encouraged me to proceed with'.[15] As Boyle had written to Hartlib earlier, commenting on his 'Utopian' endeavours, the most flourishing and contented nations, the Dutch and the Venetians, were 'where ingenuity is courted with the greatest encouragements'.[16] Evelyn was in complete agreement.

Yet in reality nothing was so simple. The following year he wrote to Boyle about his worries. He did not want to publish technical information, 'lest by it I should also disoblige some, who made those professions their living'.[17] The keeping of trade secrets was something to which Evelyn, however inquisitive, was sensitive. But if kept within the walls of what he called Dr Wilkins' 'Mathematico-Chymico-Mechanical School' in Oxford they would be safe enough, he considered. He told him he had already separated out his materials on etching and engraving ('which . . . I was once minded to publish') as well as several fine-art techniques from the rest. But before long he was to admit defeat in his attempt to collate a complete history of trades, citing his unsuitability, the obstruction of 'mechanical capricious persons' and his own unhappy circumstances.[18]

Another of those now drawn into Boyle and Wilkins's orbit was Henry Oldenburg from Bremen, the future secretary of the Royal Society. He arrived in London in 1653 as an emissary to Cromwell from his home town and moved to Oxford in the spring of 1656, when he immediately visited Wilkins's garden at Wadham College. It set him to musing: gardens 'infuse true beauty into the mind; they drive away clouds from the spirit; and moreover they put a curb upon the most potent passions of our age'. In his poem 'The Garden' Andrew Marvell, Latin secretary to the Council of State, celebrated withdrawal into a paradise garden, a gentle place for 'a green thought in a green shade' in which the methodical and industrious bee laboured. In Oxford, just as Evelyn had, Oldenburg found 'men who bend their minds to solid studies . . . and, disgusted with Scholastic Theology and Nominalist Philosophy have begun to embrace both nature and truth'. These free spirits 'dare to leave the well-trodden path to the Aristotelians and the beaten road to the wranglers, following a sounder and more glorious way'.[19] Prominent among them was Boyle, with whom Oldenburg was already acquainted and whose nephew, Lady Ranelagh's son, became his pupil that summer.

Evelyn himself found in Boyle the qualities he most admired: the attributes of the Christian humanist and the investigative scientist finely balanced. His personal integrity made him a man of crystal, 'withal clear and candid; not a blemish or spot to tarnish his reputation'. Yet after a flurry of letters in the late 1650s the two men rarely corresponded or met outside the meetings at Gresham College. Boyle's acute vision and intellect were far above the level of Evelyn's discursive mind – their strongest bond was dedication to the objectives of the Royal Society. But the long years spent there brought familiarity and when William Wotton began to prepare his (abortive) life of Boyle in 1696, Evelyn offered a perceptive portrait of 'our hero', pallid and withdrawn, calm and abstemious, working from an inspiringly disordered room. 'Glasses, pots, chemical and mathematical instruments, books and bundles of papers, did so fill and crowd his bed-chamber . . . as his whole equipage was very philosophical without formality.'[20]

As he moved further into that philosophical world, Evelyn was readying himself to publish his version of the last great Latin text to evade translation into the vernacular, *De rerum natura* ('On the Nature of Things'). He had embarked on this extraordinarily ambitious undertaking by 1651. The abbé de Marolles's French prose translation had appeared in 1650 and the close similarity of Marolles' frontispiece to Evelyn's, engraved by Wenceslaus Hollar after Mary Evelyn's design, suggests he is acknowledging a debt.[21] Lucy Hutchinson, who had already translated the six books, although they were not published until the 1670s, noted that 'a masculine wit hath thought it worth printing his head in a laurel crown for the version of one of these books'.* She was not impressed with Evelyn's effort: 'those walks of wit which poor vainglorious scholars call the Muses' groves, are enchanted thickets'.[22] She chose her metaphor carefully.

Evelyn had turned the stubborn Latin verse of Lucretius' first book into heroic English couplets by 1653. Sir Richard Fanshawe congratulated him – it was 'the taming of the shrew' – and Evelyn included his letter and a Latin poem by Christopher Wase, the sometime tutor at Hall Barn and himself translator of Sophocles' *Electra* in 1649, doubtless in acknowledgement of both men's considerable help.[23] Gassendi's epitaph provided Evelyn with a perfect witness in his defence: here was an admired thinker and avowed Christian, yet a 'great . . . Assertor of Epicurus's Institution'.

After the years of intense and essentially private self-tutoring, Evelyn was now placing himself under the scrutiny of his intellectual peers. As he quizzed Taylor about the immortality of the soul and God's ability 'to make all things out of nothing', he was torn between unquestioning faith and experimental natural philosophy, as epitomised by atomism, in which nothing came from nothing. In his preamble to the translation, as in his own mind, Evelyn had to find a way of moving 'between religious orthodoxy, which assumes the

*She referred to the vignette.

world to be unique, and progress in science, which suggested to him that there was a multiplicity'.[24]

Evelyn began to fear he had chosen the wrong vehicle, with its message of 'qualified hedonism'. Taylor wondered if he had allowed his 'too kind friends to prevail with you', suggesting that he thought it an ill-advised project. Evelyn must provide 'a sufficient antidote', he said, and so the translator composed tangled editorial comments which 'will I hope provide against all the ill consequences, and totally acquit me either of glory or impiety' but which obscured rather than clarified the issues. Robert Boyle aimed to 'write rather in a philosophical than a rhetorical strain, as desiring, that my expressions should be rather clear and significant, than curiously adorned'.[25] But this was not Evelyn's way, especially when he was unsure of his ground.

The prefatory contributions of two distinguished literary figures, Fanshawe and Waller, gave the publication and its unknown translator added status. They both referred to his courage in tackling the knotty task. Fanshawe was tactful: 'we know Lucretius in your Book, though it retains neither his voyce, nor yet his hairynesse, since it hath both his Soule, and his lineaments.'*

Waller's introductory poem was a sparkling combination of panegyric and allusion. He began by extolling Evelyn's achievement:

> Lucretius like a Fort did stand
> Untoucht, till your Victorious hand
> Did from his head this garland bear,
> Which now upon your own You wear.

The garden of Epicurus was a place of freedom and nature:

> For his immortal boundless wit
> To nature does no bounds permit;
> But boldly has remov'd those bars
> Of Heaven, and Earth, and Seas and Stars,
> By which they were before suppos'd
> By narrow wits to be inclos'd,
> 'Till his free Muse threw down the Pale,
> And did at once dispark them all.**

---

*A reference to Jacob's disguise in front of Isaac.
**An early version of Horace Walpole's description of William Kent who 'leapt the fence, and found all nature was a garden'.

But it was with an overt political reference that Waller pointed to the topicality of Evelyn's verse:

> Lucretius with a Stork-like fate,
> Born and translated in a State,
> Comes to proclaim in English Verse
> No Monarch Rules the Universe;
> But chance and Atomes make this All
> In Order Democratical,
> Where Bodies freely run their course,
> Without design, or Fate, or Force.

Evelyn quickly dissociated himself from Lucretius's (or rather Waller's) message with a printed marginal comment: 'not that the Interpreter doth justifie this irreligion of the Poet, whose Arguments he afterwards refutes.' By now Waller and Evelyn's friendship was on shaky ground for agnosticism was not to Evelyn's taste, especially when it was laced with outspoken Epicureanism.

The Greek philosopher was obviously a man 'of super-excellent candor and integrity, as testified by his Countrey in general', but his ideas associated with 'luxurious and carnal appetites of the sensual and lower man' had, in Evelyn's view, tainted him. Some might consider Lucretius 'altogether Irreligious and Profane and therefore not fit (say they) to be so much as read or entertained amongst Christians'. But Plato was a 'leveller' and none of the ancients, Aristotle included, was exempt from 'gross and absurd Fictions, apparent Levities, and horrible Impieties'. If Lucretius includes passages 'any whit obnoxious to our Faith', he also 'persuades to a life the most exact and Moral; and no man, I hope, comes hither as a Spider, to swell up his bag with poyson onely, when with half that pains, he may with the industrious Bee, store and furnish his Hive with so much wholesome and delicious Honey'. Despite these confident words in his introductory matter, Evelyn's letters to Taylor suggest that he was far less sanguine.

Evelyn had struggled with his translation. Epicurus

> . . . did his courage elevate,
> Natures remotest doors to penetrate;
> Thus did he with his vigorous wit transpierce
> The flaming limits of the Universe.

In his astonishing effort at comprehension he had attempted to

> ... first inquire of things above,
> The Reasons how the Sun and Moon do move:
> By what force all things on the earth are sway'd
> With strict enquiry, first each reason weigh'd.

But, as Evelyn added, 'In Latin verse, 'tis hard I must confess/ The Greeks obscure conceptions to express' and he confronts the inevitable uncomfortably irreligious conclusion: 'unto us this principle doth frame,/ That Out of nothing, nothing ever came.'

Evelyn began to distribute copies. One went to Thomas Barlow at the Bodleian Library (whose assistant there, until 1659, was Dr Henry Stubbe, soon to be the Royal Society's most tenacious critic) and another to Dr Taylor, now living in Wales. In October 1656 he sent his father-in-law 'Lucretius Englished', as Browne had described it in his own hyperbolic introductory poem. Evelyn told him that the remaining five books would follow since *De rerum natura* had been a success despite its 'mischances' at the printer's owing to Dr Triplet's failure to check the pages efficiently. 'What I scruple at in the fourth booke is by the poet physically intended but as this age is now depraved I have much rather all the poems in the world should perish then that anything of mine should contribute and minister to vice,' he wrote, worrying that 'I might thereby confute, not illustrat, the irreligion of the poet'. He even sent a copy to Lady Mordaunt, Mary's newly married friend Elizabeth Carey, at the same time questioning why she might want 'to reade so abstruse, and rugged a Poet', since 'you alone of all the faire Sex possesse a Spirit capable of the most refined, and abstracted speculations'. Disowning the errors, he said: 'I find my selfe engaged to proceede upon the remainder [of the books], which as they are the more divertissant, so I hope may appeare more adorned, and more worthy your acceptation.'[26]

Uncertainly, he pressed on with the task. He turned to Fanshawe, who often served as a sounding board for his worries and who probably helped with the translation. Jasper Needham, his 'deare & learned friend', would help him with book three and his schoolmaster Edward Snatt urged him on to 'finish that which none yet durst effect'. Even Taylor joined the chorus: 'they who can receive hurt by the fourth book, understand the Latin of it; and I hope they who will be delighted with Your English, will also be secured by your learned and pious annotations.' He was still encouraging him in 1659.[27]

Atomism had been a recurrent topic for natural philosophers across Europe and the discussion took new life in England. Inevitably Evelyn was implicated in the message of his translation, however far he tried to distance

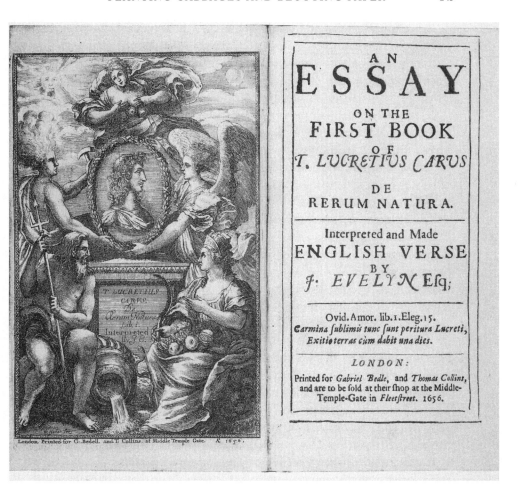

13 Frontispiece to Evelyn's translation of the first book of Lucretius' *De rerum natura*, etched by Wenceslaus Hollar in 1656 after a design by Mary Evelyn.

himself from it. Walter Charleton's *The Immortality of the Human Soul Demonstrated by the Light of Nature*, published in 1657, consisted of dialogues between 'Lucretius' (apparently Evelyn), 'Athanasius' (Charleton) and Isodicastes (his dedicatee Henry Pierrepoint, marquess of Dorchester).[28] It fell to 'Lucretius' to argue that atomism was a proof of God's existence. Evelyn never mentions Charleton's book, but the published discussion echoed ones elsewhere that tried to create a fragile alignment of Christianity with atomism.

But although he continued to work on a complete translation, Evelyn published no more of it and the first book was never reprinted or corrected.

He wrote to the scholar and divine Meric Casaubon, probably in 1670, that 'you may be sure I was very young & therefore very rash, or ambitious, when I adventured upon that knotty piece'. He had since 'repented of my folly' which 'still lies in the dust of my study where 'tis likely to be for ever buried'.[29]

Nevertheless, soon after publication, he was flattered and surprised to find himself the dedicatee of Dr William Rand's translation of Gassendi's life of Peiresc, a portrait of an exemplary intellectual. Rand, a physician who had studied in Louvain, was in Hartlib's circle. He and Benjamin Worsley had initially suggested the project which was published as *The Mirrour of True Nobility and Gentility* in 1657. When Rand was seeking a dedicatee – 'pertinency I have alwaies esteemed the Soul of a Dedication' – he was reminded of the only Englishman who epitomised the 'Peireskian Vertues', John Evelyn.[30] As so often, the web in which Evelyn found himself was of Hartlib's spinning.

Evelyn was described as 'a private Gentleman of real worth and suitable virtues', exhibiting that 'sprightly curiosity [that] left nothing unreacht into, in the vast all comprehending Dominions of Nature and Art', while having the ability, Janus-like, to look both forwards and backwards. There was even space for a tribute to Mary in the dedication. 'A Gentlewoman, in whom the English Gravity, being moderately allayed, sweetened and spirited, by the mettlesome Aire and Education of France has arrived so such a perfection, as to be no Hinderance, but a meet Help to her beloved Lord, in his most many Concernments.' In the face of such generous public praise, Evelyn worried that he might attract jealousy but Rand reassured him: 'I neither commended my Patron for Wealth or Power, nor his Consort for corporal Beautie. I should rather stir up a worthie emulation in the Virtuous, then Envie in such as are of a more brutish Temper.'

With this, letters flew between the two men. They even discovered that Rand's father had been the family doctor at Wotton, treating Evelyn's mother in her last illness. Rand admired Machiavelli, 'in whom the Censure of the Generalitie of Man has bin as much mistaken, as in the good Epicurus, the Master of your Lucretius'. Evelyn, it seemed, was now irrevocably linked to Gassendi, the man who had revived Epicureanism in the modern age. Rand nimbly dealt with his misgivings on the subject: 'a low popular & pusillanimous Spirit, prejudiced, frighted & shackled with the Superstition of vulgarly received maxims & tenets, could not allow of Lucretius any more than Sir Kenelme Digbie corrupted & awed by Roman Impressions, could duely handle the Nature of mans Soule, or rightly judge of the immortalitie or mortalitie thereof.' But even more difficult for Evelyn was the implied comparison to Peiresc, the most virtuous and admired of European scholars of his generation. Evelyn was being promoted far above his abilities, as even he realised.

Now Rand confessed that he had even not read his *De rerum natura* when he wrote the dedication (it may have been the inclusion of Gassendi's epitaph that had caught his eye) and Evelyn sent him a copy. They agreed on the deficiencies of printers and booksellers, 'disingenous Cormorants' unfit to serve educated writers. Rand confided to Evelyn that he and Hartlib had a plan, wondering

> whether learned and inventive men with others that love learning & art might not so combine, as that all new Bookes published by the Societie itselfe or any member thereof, might be upon such termes printed & published, as that the profit might redound to the said societie to make a stock for the Advancement of usefull Learning & assistance of learned Men.[31]

A cooperative self-publishing venture would be an ideal project for an academy or learned society.

Before this exchange, Evelyn had been looking for light relief after Lucretius and had asked Browne, finally back in Paris in the summer of 1656:

> If you encounter any pretty short piece in the French tongue, which is now excellent & not long be pleased to send it, my wife, who (Besides the greate progresse she has lately made in the Latine tongue on her own account) has a very good faculty in translating & her modesty may be well trusted with more than the ordinary erudition of her Sex whom Learning dos comonly but corrupt.

Evelyn's translations from the French owed much to Mary, at his elbow to correct and improve his text. He was extraordinarily proud of her and may have intended that she now publish something herself.

Browne was deputed to seek out wall-type fruit trees as listed in Nicolas de Bonnefons's *Le Jardinier françois* from Morin's nursery. He would be fully reimbursed. At the same time, others were still scouring Europe on Evelyn's behalf. Benjamin Maddocks (whom Jasper Needham had accompanied to Paris) apologised profusely for his ignorance but struggled to identify desirable Mediterranean plants at Montpellier, another early botanical garden. Others assumed his role as roving collector over the years. Meanwhile Needham returned from France in September with special acorns: despite his best efforts, they were rotten.

Evelyn began to realise that Sayes Court would be his true masterpiece. Compared to his trials at the hands of inept stationers and literary critics, the continually evolving garden gave him endless pleasure and provided a perfect theatre for his abilities. There he found a balance between a contemplative divine paradise, a Garden of Eden, and the delights of Nature's cabinet of curiosities, an Elysium. With the worries of *De rerum natura* largely behind him, he began his *Elysium Britannicum*. Rand's celebration of his breadth of knowledge and abilities may have given him new confidence. He heard, from Oxford, that Jasper Needham was now a doctor of physic and Abraham Cowley had been awarded an honorary doctorate. For Evelyn, toiling in Deptford on his rising pile of pamphlets, books and translations, no such academic affirmation was available. A major publication would varnish and elevate his reputation, however, and the *Elysium* was his chosen vehicle.

Staying at Wotton the previous summer, he visited Albury where he found Henry Howard beginning alterations to his house and garden. In these quiet green summers of the Interregnum, they may have first discussed the transformation of Arundel's legacy with Evelyn's memories of Wilton, Palestrina, St Germain-en-Laye and the Villa Aldobrandini before them. Howard's cousin Charles was also making a remarkable garden at Deepdene which Evelyn often visited.[32] The (lost) history chapter in *Elysium Britannicum* included Wotton and Albury as well as Wilton, Hatfield and Penshurst. Evelyn's admiration extended to the natural landscape and he walked from Box Hill to Norbury Park, where he remarked on the thick growth of box and yew, still a distinctive evergreen pelt on the North Downs.

In the spring of 1657 Evelyn was delighted to find his father-in-law's old friend from Angers Sir Thomas Hanmer living 'within a mile of us at Lewisham these 2 years & I never knew it till the other day, but we are since very Civill & often converse in matter of flowers wherein he excells: but he being now leaving us & returning into Wales that sweete Conversation will fade'. Hanmer, an expert florist who would imminently move far away to the Welsh borders, at Bettisfield, was to be a generous provider of material for the *Elysium*, sending Evelyn detailed entries on both tulips and daffodils.[33] At Deptford, a damp season had brought out the best in the dial garden, the tulips and ranunculuses were flourishing, but he was in need of orange trees and (as always) evergreens. Another of the *Elysium*'s appendices is a catalogue of evergreens, distinguished by their suitability to various situations, in the grove, the underwood or the thicket.[34]

It was at around this time that Evelyn began to curtail his collecting. He had begun a 'pretty collection of Insects, and butterflies' but a visit to John Tradescant's extraordinary, overburdened museum at Lambeth provided him with a warning.* Although not averse to gifts, he told his father-in-law soberly: 'Nor doe I suffer my curiosity to robb my purse, having already such a world of trifles.' He decided to cut back his print collecting; in 1695 he recalled that he had amassed quantities 'especialy, whilst I was at Rome and Abroad' but had hardly added to them in the last forty years. Many, he guessed, were an invaluable record of lost sites and antiquities. 'But as it tooke up a greate-deale of Time, and no little Mony; and that the Thirst of still Augmenting grew upon me; I at last gave it over.' Previously his choice of subject matter had known no limits, but now he drew the line and confined his new purchases to architectural subjects. He had also seen families brought down by the folly of unchecked collecting.

His own activities as an etcher were behind him, although he continued to draw. Printmakers still vied for his attention, perhaps hearing that he was preparing a book on the subject. A plate of 1656 by Wenceslaus Hollar is inscribed 'Titianus invent, J Evelyn Imitavit'; he began to write and compile *Sculptura* the next year.[35]

All of this provided a release from bewildering political realities. It was now rumoured that Lord Protector Cromwell was being pressed 'to take the Title on him', that is, to assume the kingship. But if Cromwell's England was driving others to their 'witts end', Evelyn was fulfillingly immersed in domestic life, 'building, planting, buying, felling etc in this madd & estranged country'. Where the education of his first-born was concerned, Evelyn's ambitions were limitless. His list of Richard's prodigious achievements at under five years of age was alarming. Though delighted to hear of his aptitude, his grandfather wrote: 'take heede of over charging his understandinge' for he is but a 'tabula rasa easily confounded'.[36] Was Evelyn forcing the child beyond his capacities and did Browne's worries stem from his own son Dick's unspecified problems?[37]

In June 1657 Evelyn and his wife had another son, George – their third surviving boy. A group of brothers could be a close and supportive unit, as he knew from the experience of his own family. Despite their earlier differences, he and Richard were described as a 'pair royal' and, with George, the three extending families gathered regularly.

In the mid-1650s, driven by his father-in-law's continuing financial difficulties and the needs of a growing family, Evelyn began to organise his finances and embarked on several new ventures. Since 1654 he had built some houses on the eastern boundary of Sayes Court along Butt Lane (which became Deptford High Street in 1825) which brought in useful rent. Now he

---

*This collection was taken to Oxford by Elias Ashmole after a prolonged legal wrangle with John Tradescant Jr's widow.

raised over £3,000 from the sale of some land, half of which he provided as a mortgage for his aristocratic friend from Paris, Lord Stanhope.[38] But the most promising investments were overseas. Evelyn was considering purchasing or leasing land in Ireland but of those settling there 'few [were] of greate fortune who love ease and England'. He told Browne that he planned to reconnoitre the situation the following summer with Prettyman, still bound to him in 'the dispatch and settlement' of his father-in-law's affairs, and would also 'endeavor to lay a foundation for my pretty children at least'.[39] He did not mention his plan to anyone else.

In October 1657 the East India Company was reconvened and Evelyn told Browne he was now a merchant adventurer. He hoped his youngest son George, 'of all the most beautiful & louvlie Child', might one day become a merchant.[40] After liquidation earlier that year, following serious mismanagement, the East India Company regained its charter as a joint-stock enterprise with 'new oathes, new orders a mixt committee & I thinke so reformed as that if Warrs with Holland (which we feare) doe not discompose us, it is likely to prove one of the most profitable secure & hopefull trades in Europe'. At its Leadenhall Street headquarters Evelyn paid his first contribution and took the oath required of new stockholders. He also offered his own prayer 'upon putting in a stock into the East-India Company', that his investment might return safely and profitably and 'be employ'd to the uses of Charity, the provisions for my Relatives, the Comfort of my Life & honnest subsistance of my family'.[41] The charter that Cromwell now granted was renewed without alteration at the Restoration. Evelyn's modest holding proved a good investment and allowed him to bolster the finances of the Royal Society some twenty-five years later.

Oddly, gardening was a topic on which Evelyn had still not published a word. Thomas Henshaw suggested he translate De Bonnefons's *Le Jardinier François* of 1651. 'I know no man in England that was able to doe it properly but your self.' The printer, John Crooke, would be equally happy to have it translated by Evelyn or Jasper Needham and would send an amanuensis to 'take it from your mouth as fast as you can speake it'. He suggested the 'piece' Needham was already translating could be added, probably *The Manner of Ordering Fruit-Trees* by the Sieur Le Gendre, published in French in 1653 and translated 'faithfully into English at the request of severall Persons of Honour' in 1660.[42] Henshaw must have noticed that the material for *Elysium Britannicum* was silting up and that this practical gardening manual might free the flow. Surprisingly, Henshaw himself had no desire for publication, telling Anthony à Wood years later that he 'never had learning nor ambition enough to raise my name by erecting myself to the title of an Authour'; in his view there were already too many and 'the multitude proved rather a hindrance than an advancement of learning'.[43]

Before Evelyn had fully completed his translation, his world shattered. After a swift fever, his oldest son, Richard, that paragon of learning and sweetness, died on 27 January 1658. Needham attended him and performed two key roles, that of trusted family doctor and consoling intimate. Later, at Evelyn's request, he also had the awful task of performing a postmortem.

It was several days before Evelyn could bear to write of his 'dearest, strangest miracle of a boy', as Jeremy Taylor described him later. The searing grief, the intense shock and sadness that united their circle, in an era supposedly inured to the sudden death of infants and children, reverberates in the letters of sympathy he received. Richard's special promise was known to all of their family and friends, largely through his father's testament. Thanks to him, Richard's had been a 'good' death, as Taylor had described in his *Holy Dying*. Then, hardly a week later, the infant George died too. Of their four children born since 1652, only one now survived, John; 'the cup of our afflictions is full and flowing over,' Evelyn wrote. He had no picture of Richard but his image was engraved on his memory, he told Browne. His impulse was to retreat to the countryside; to 'let my house, goe & sojourn in the country farther from envy & [?] & in some solitude where I [?] my losse & those sinne of mine which have bin the cause of it.'[44]

Evelyn told Sir Richard, desperately worried for his daughter but obliged to remain in France, that Mary wept continually and 'in every corner of this house she heares the voyce & sees the face of her deare companion that strangly cheerfull & beautifull child; but I begin to be transported, pardon my folly, it does molest both his and our repose, but I cannot helpe it, tis an extraordinary losse'. His signature is scarcely legible.

In his book of personal prayers Evelyn added one 'to be sometimes inserted ... when we perceive ourselves inclyn'd to take too much satisfaction in external things'. He prayed, in words perhaps written at a later date but indicative of his thoughts at that time: 'weane me daily from placing my happinesse upon any-thing but thee, that no worldly pomp, curiosity, superfluity & Abundance; the lust of the Eye or pride of life ... steal away my heart from thee.'[45] Browne, who had endured great unhappiness himself, was alarmed by his son-in-law's self-abasement and offered comfort, as Evelyn acknowledged: 'the short Truces which we sometymes have from the sad remembrances of our misfortunes, are chiefly due to the effects of your Letters, and the continued consolations of our Friends.' They must be careful 'not [to] suffer this griefe to triumph over our Reason, or our Religion'. Though 'a wound so deape and so deadly is not to be obduced without a scarr', Richard's bereft parents comforted one another; wisely enough, Evelyn

dealt with sorrow openly. Thanking Viscount Mordaunt, recently married to
his 'seraphic' Elizabeth Carey, for sparing them his thoughts at a moment of
such happiness for himself, he added: 'I have found that the Sharing Griefe is
like to the cutting of Rivers.'[46]

Evelyn remained prostrate for weeks. Peter Pett wrote from All Souls on
his own and Thomas Barlow's behalf to encourage him to return to work,
mentioning the translation of Naudé's 'directory for the ordering of a Library'
which had been a priority ever since his time in Paris – a far more appealing
task than completing the other books of Lucretius. But Evelyn confessed that
since the death of his child 'my mind has bin so discomposed, that I have
never so much as once touched those papers no indeed anything else with
satisfaction'. In fact he did complete the translation of Naudé; his dedicatory
letter to Barlow is dated 5 October 1658. In it he told him that he had
received this 'rare piece . . . from the Author himselfe'. But Barlow's printer
mislaid it, as he confesses contritely almost three years later.[47]

His only literary activity was a translation, from Greek, of *The Golden Book
of St John Chrysostom, concerning the Education of Children* – the saint on whose
feast day Richard had died. There was a long personal foreword to his own
brothers, an obituary of the little boy and an epitaph composed by
Christopher Wase which ran (in Latin) 'Marvellous as a child, what would he
have been when old'. Wase may well have helped with the translation for
Evelyn often referred to his poor grasp of Greek. The text compared a child's
mind to a 'city newly built and furnished' but, Evelyn added revealingly, 'some
have taken education for religion it selfe'.[48]

In the garden at Deptford, Evelyn's spirits revived, slowly restored by a
stoical approach to adversity, in which friendship, accord with God's creation
and a measure of self-sufficiency countered the pleasure principles of the
Epicurean view. As Seneca had suggested, and his admirers down to the
sixteenth century had proved, a garden could be 'a place of contemplation by
which the Stoic is led to right action, and, through wisdom, to subjection to
God. The freedom of the Stoics is found in submission to Reason, which is
the will of God.'[49] In Francis Bacon's words: 'God Almighty first planted a
Garden. And indeed it is the purest of human pleasures. It is the greatest
refreshment to the spirits of man.'[50] In the early weeks of bereavement the
Sayes Court garden helped to heal the Evelyns.

Routine tasks also eased the pain. Another harsh winter had brought its
ravages and Evelyn collected seed, especially cypress, for replacements, and
wrote to his father-in-law:

My Dial Garden is now as complete as it can be for 6 foote high at which
pitch I determine to hedge it some years the better to fortifie it, that the

expanse of poles may be spared; onely my Grove is yet a dwarfe. Pine & Fir & Laurel doe best of all other with me; but all the rest is now infinitely sweete & beautifull [except] . . . one plante the losse whereoff goes to my Soule, & that I must never forgett, because I shall never repaire it.

Browne was sufficiently knowledgable by now to collect seeds and plants from Morin's nursery. He was preparing a catalogue of evergreens but, he told Sir Edward Nicholas, his helper 'Mr Keipe' had returned to England. Browne was now a proselytiser: 'Alaternes beare a graine like that of privet, which beinge sowed comes upp and prospers without difficulty.' Whether he was contributing to the *Elysium* or pursuing an independent project, Browne, like his own father, was proving a horticulturist. Sadly, though, Pierre Morin was ill and bedridden, 'defunct to all purposes, wherin hee was formerly soe necessary'.[51]

By early July *The French Gardiner* was in the press and Evelyn dined with Henshaw, married the previous summer, and Elias Ashmole. Henshaw should consider it his own, Evelyn wrote, since 'as a Lover of Gardens you did promote it, as a Lover of you I have translated it'. In return, Henshaw thanked him for postponing his 'studies of a higher and nobler nature' to translate 'so knotty a peece, to make england emulous of the pleasure and profit france receives in its gardens'. He was flattered by the dedication, which told the world 'how much I honour you and how much I love gardens'. Mary Evelyn also had her own tribute in the text: three chapters on preserving fruit with sugar had been omitted since 'I am assured by a Lady (who is a person of quality, and curious in that Art) that there is nothing of extraordinary amongst them'.[52]

These moving exchanges between Henshaw and Evelyn celebrated a friendship that was to last throughout their long lives. They corresponded regularly from either side of London, exchanging gifts and loans of books (Maimonides and *Regy Phisica*), plants and rare seeds, such as 'scorza nera' or French pinks, while reporting the success or failure of cuttings such as alaternus and lime. When the book passed into its fourth edition in 1691 Evelyn again gave Henshaw his dues and commemorated 'our now ancient Friendship, which contracted first abroad, has continued both there, and since at home, through so many Vicissitudes and Changes, as we have seen and surmounted'.

Evelyn could add nothing to De Bonnefons's expertise on soil, situation and planting, or his knowledge of the orchard and kitchen garden. But he used the introduction to flag up his plan to add 'some other things of this nature from my own experience'. His next work would give advice on parterres, grottos, fountains, flowers and, above all, evergreens, 'especially the

Palisades and Contr-Espaliers of Alaternus, which most incomparable Verdure, together with the right culture of it, for beauty and sence, I might glory to have been the first propagator in England'.[53] He had already intended to publish his work on the 'garden of pleasure' had not 'some other things unexpectedly intervened'. Now Henshaw urged him to fulfil his promise, 'which hath raised a longing in many Curious persons who doe already question me when it will come out'. Crooke, the stationer, had asked to print it.

The French Gardiner ended on a pensive and compliant note. While

the Great ones are busied about Governing the World (which is but a wildernesse) let us call to minde the Rescript of Dioclesion to those who would perswade him to re-assume the Empire. For it is impossible that he who is a true Virtuoso, and has attain'd to the felicity of being a good Gardener, should give jealousie to the State where he lives.

Evelyn spoke for himself and Henshaw. Then, hardly a month later, in September 1658, a political event of great moment shook the country.

CHAPTER 9

Restoration

In the first week of June 1658, after a long harsh 'cold season as winter, wind northerly neere 6 moneths' came 'an extraordinary storme of haile & raine'. The next day a harpooned whale appeared on the shore near Sayes Court, spouting blood and water 'by two tunnells like Smoake from a chimny'. Beached, the leviathan gave 'an horrid grone' and died, drawing huge crowds. Evelyn was bemused by the immense corpse, 'nourished onely by slime', and even sketched it, one of very few drawings in the diary. Then, on 30 August, a ferocious south-westerly gale tore down his 'greatest trees' and did 'much mischiefe all England over' continuing well into the next afternoon. The entire fruit crop was destroyed.[1] To all who sought meaning in them, the violent portents that summer were suggestive. News of the lord protector's sudden death came just days later.[2]

Although he died on 3 September, Cromwell's state funeral did not take place until 23 November. The pageant to mark his passing was royal in every detail, appropriately so for a man who almost became king. Cromwell's effigy, decked out with crown, sceptre and orb, lay on a velvet bed of state drawn by six horses. Evelyn watched the procession from Somerset House to Westminster Abbey, 'the joyfullest funerall that ever I saw, for there was none that Cried, but dogs, which the souldiers hooted away with a barbarous noise; drinking, & taking Tabacco in the streetes as they went'.[3] An escaped pig ran among the chief mourners. Having assembled at eight in the morning, the long-delayed cortège finally arrived at Westminster Abbey as darkness fell. There were no candles and Cromwell was buried without funeral orations or further ceremony.

The protector's death had signalled frantic jostling for position. Literary figures trimmed their writings to the changing circumstances, aspirants to office in the likely new order began to shoulder one another out of the queue. But no one dissented from the view that Cromwell's successor, his son Richard, was a mere puppet, an inconsequential figure lacking his father's political skills and utterly unsuited to leading the faction-ridden army. By June 1659, he had abdicated and was in Paris, and the country was in the hands of the dwindling Rump.* Among Evelyn's circle of impeccably staunch royalist friends, it seemed as if change might be imminent. Samuel Tuke, who had recently been nominated by Henrietta Maria as the duke of York's secretary only to be rejected on religious grounds, hurried back to England and Richard Fanshawe left for France.[4] Clerics and bishops began to stir from their bookish retreats. For Evelyn, the likelihood of change shifted the prospect of patronage from the purely theoretical to the eminently practical.

The more realistic the prospect of a restored Stuart monarchy became, the more Evelyn made of the pleasures of 'a private and even life'. He told Browne that he had been interrupted by visitors in London; 'my studies suffer & the Hortulane diversions proceede but slowly & to redresse this, I steale now & then home to my Villa where I refresh my selfe a little & am out of the noise & confusion of a distracted Citty.'[5] When a friend of Sir Richard's, visited Sayes Court that July he found the Evelyn brothers, their wives and children enjoying a 'great feast' – only young John was absent – and 'The hous gardens and walks, her rich closett his library and all so curiously perfect that it did show the modell of what is more largely to be published in theory.' But he noticed that Evelyn's laboratory lay deserted; he was 'by his translation more taken up with the Epicurian then Hermeticall philosophy'. Evelyn's focus had shifted from chemical experiment to gardening, especially on the page.[6]

What also continued to intrigue Evelyn, as many others, was the possibility of founding a 'Solomon's House', a collegiate institution dedicated to learning and offering encouragement for 'ingenious persons . . . honour and reverence as well as large rewards to the Authors of all new and good Treatises, whether Divine or humane, of all artificial inventions, discoveries of new Countreys, Minerals, Earths, Waters, or whatsoever else is useful to mankind'. Translating the Platonic utopian dream from the pages of Francis Bacon's *New Atlantis* into reality was as compelling for royalist virtuosi as for those committed to radical political ends.

Evelyn may have heard from Hartlib that a man who had actually worked with Bacon, Thomas Bushell of Enstone, planned to set up 'my lord Verulam's New Atlantis', either in London or Wells. The young Robert Boyle wondered whether his 'Irish fortune' (which John Aubrey believed to be some £3,000 per annum) would allow him to 'trace such plans, and frame such models' while Kenelm Digby, William Petty and, long ago, Samuel Hartlib himself had toyed with variations, as had Henry Hammond who proposed a self-funded

---

*He returned to England eventually and died at Cheshunt in 1712.

college of 'godly men' in 1654.[7] Hardly had Thomas Henshaw returned from Paris in 1650, than he too was planning, as Hartlib reported, 'a Model of Christian Learned Society' with six friends, 'his owne familiars men of qualities and competencies, that will have all in common, dedicating themselves wholly to devotion and studies, and separating themselves from the World, by leading a severe life for diet apparel etc. . . . They can have Laboratories and strive to do all the good they can to their neighborhood.' Henshaw's 'college', was probably actually his own house in Kensington.[8]

Another of Evelyn's friends, Abraham Cowley, had drawn up plans for a purpose-built, self-sufficient free school, a series of courtyards and gardens, each with a designated function, above which rose a tower for observation of celestial bodies and below which were deep vaults for other experimental activities.[9] The scholars would contribute two-thirds of the profits of their inventions to the college. Cowley published it in 1661 as a *Proposition for the Advancement of Learning*. The year before someone hidden behind the initials 'RH' completed Bacon's *New Atlantis*.[10]

Evelyn's own scheme was little more than an expansion of his exploratory life at Sayes Court. He explained to Robert Boyle, the most likely source of both moral support and funds for such a project, 'if the modell be smale, it appears the more practicable, and . . . rightly conducted, it will be facile to enlarge' for 'we are not to hope for a Mathematical Coledge, much lesse a Salomans-house'. The site should be well outside London (about as far away as Wotton) in some forty acres of well-wooded grounds, and be a kind of academic Carthusian monastery which might, surprisingly, include women as well as men. By now Mary was essential to his life of ideas. Evelyn drew up a scheme but, he told Boyle, new buildings would not be needed if there was a suitable house for conversion.[11]

Nevertheless, Evelyn enjoyed thinking through his institution in architectural form, designing it in plan and elevation, all to scale. Each of the six 'cells' was set in an enclosed garden, with a stable behind, facing the 'cloyster'. A cell consisted of a large antechamber with a central chimney, with bedchamber and study beyond. The college house, to the south, was five bays wide, two and a half storeys high (the service areas being in the basement), with a front door reached by broad steps and protected by a classical porch. It closely resembled Sir John Harrison's Dutch-influenced house, Balls Park in Hertford, which Evelyn knew.[12] On the ground floor there was a library, refectory, archive and drawing room and, above, a gallery overlooking the quadrangle and fountain. The chapel, facing it on the north side, was surprisingly ornate, even Baroque, with full-height columns and a pediment (with clock) framed by scrolling volutes. Evelyn's most detailed surviving architectural proposal, and the only collegiate scheme of its kind with a delineated

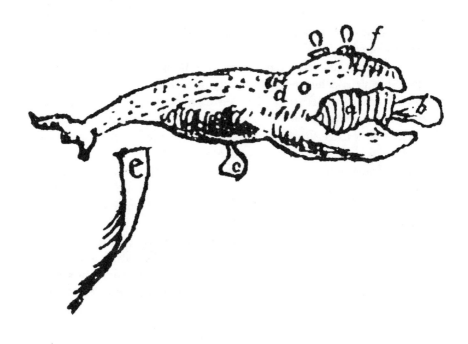

14 The whale which appeared on the shore at Deptford in late summer 1658, presaging Cromwell's death. This is one of very few drawings in the diary.

physical form, it shows how confident he had become of his standing within the Republic of Letters.

Like the industrious bee he celebrated in print, Hartlib continually brought those with complementary interests together. In 1658 he told Boyle about a prolific correspondent isolated in a country parish near Yeovil, Somerset. 'There is not the like man in the whole island, nor in the continent beyond the seas, so far as I know it; I mean that could be made more universally use of, to do good to all, as I in some measure know and could direct.'[13] Dr John Beale had been educated at Cambridge before travelling 'to learn to know Men and foreign manners' prior to the civil wars. He claimed connections to both Lord Chancellor Bacon and Sir Henry Wotton, but his early years remain tantalisingly obscure.

Although he did not crave fame or credit for himself, Beale continually pointed out how much effort was needed to keep alive the ideas of great men such as Bacon or Erasmus. He encouraged others to publish their work and ensure that their exchanges reached the widest possible audience, particularly through correspondence which, as he told Boyle (and no doubt Evelyn too), allows the writer to 'expunge and enlarge' upon the topics in question.[14] Hartlib and Beale's own letters were the material for *Herefordshire Orchards, A Pattern for all England* (1657). There, in the gentle climate of western England, every house was portrayed as being surrounded by fruit trees and gardens, the air sweetened and purified by blossom. Paradise was the walk from the orchard to the wood. But through its pages also ran important reformist ideals: efficient husbandry, English self-sufficiency and funds for the exchequer. Henry Oldenburg had been impressed by Beale's ability to combine Christianity and scientific knowledge, 'breathing in all he saith and doth on one side the exaltation of Christianity and the honor of God therein, and on the other for the improvement of usefull knowledge to the relife and advantage of man'.[15]

Hartlib began to forward Beale's letters to Evelyn who, since they 'concerne my designe so deeply', asked to see more. Soon he and Beale were sharing their adulation of 'our Verulam', Francis Bacon, and Evelyn had a colleague and helper for *Elysium Britannicum*. Beale told him of a hilly site in Herefordshire (Backbury Hill) which Evelyn described, establishing a notion of nature and art in utter harmony.[16] For almost thirty years, Beale became Evelyn's self-appointed mentor – his letters a continuous rambling conversation which frequently provided Evelyn with important ideas. Beale claimed to prefer anonymity and Evelyn believed him.

Hartlib saw in them an ideal partnership, ignoring the extent to which they intensified one another's failings. Evelyn's prolix tendencies were fed by Beale's illegible screeds of valuable, muddled information. As letters were forwarded or summarised to others, mistakes and misunderstandings were compounded. Soon Oldenburg joined in, at first from France. Beale told Hartlib he was careless: 'hee makes such haste to amasse wonders, that hee forgets solidity too often. I will suggest to Mr Old: mine owne errours That they may bee his instruction ... I meane only in relation to our hortulane affayres. (For in other points my errours were beyond accompt.)'[17] Oldenburg came to dread the avalanche of fat missives from Somerset (the recipient paid postal charges by weight) and eventually Beale's letters would be often minuted but left unread. As for his other correspondent, Beale confided nervously, 'for a world I will not take any Vegetable affayre out of Mr Evelyns hand. Doe not thinke I have soe much brasse about me.'[18] Beale was generous; Evelyn, he told Hartlib anxiously, 'overtakes & outruns me. I must nowe rebate his expectations.'

But Evelyn's long hours in his study were soon broken into by external events. That autumn General Monck, although a Presbyterian, began to offer solid promise as the military leader who might achieve the Restoration. His march on London raised expectations, since he had been courted assiduously by both the City and the Rump. As Evelyn put it to Browne, they were all 'corn between the mill-stones' of other men's ambitions. Samuel Tuke, still attached to the duke of York's court, headed back to Paris again; everything suggested that the royalists were readying themselves for action.

What Evelyn forgot to report to Browne until later was his failed attempt to persuade his old school fellow, the staunch parliamentarian Colonel Herbert Morley, to stage a royalist coup.[19] In October 1659, Viscount Mordaunt, who had known Evelyn since Italy, reported to the king that 'a person of fortune and interest . . . whose abilities have rendered him courted by all parties, and familiar with most of the intrigues since this unhappy warr', had applied 'to a neare friend of mine' to be of service to Charles's cause. Morley appears to be the former, Evelyn the latter.[20] Morley had sat in both the Long Parliament and the Rump, representing Sussex, and was now a commissioner for the army, a key player in the prolonged chess game of late Interregnum politics.

In an exchange of pamphlets they argued their respective cases – though both agreed on the necessity for a 'free' parliament. In Evelyn's repartee, *An Apologie for the Royal Party*, he described himself as 'neither Courtier, Soldier, or Church-man, but a plain Country Gentleman, engag'd on neither side' but nevertheless harangued Morley on the strengths of the royalist case.[21] Morley, essentially opportunistic, seemed fully persuaded. However, he was still seen as trustworthy enough to be appointed governor of the Tower of London in January and, convinced of his support, Evelyn and Mordaunt hatched a scheme for a coup, there on the City's doorstep.[22]

At the last moment Morley queried Monck's intentions and stalled. In fact, the General's opacity was masterly diplomacy. Mordaunt wrote to the king in mid January: 'He is a black Monck, and I cannot see through him.'[23] Morley was showing the political nous that both Evelyn and Mordaunt so signally lacked. Afterwards, Evelyn felt cheated of his part in what he considered could have been a dramatic putsch and peevishly complained that his school friend had been both disloyal and foolish. As often, Evelyn talked up the episode far beyond its rather lack-lustre reality. More forgiving than Evelyn, Mordaunt arranged for Morley's pardon after the Restoration, which cost him £1,000.[24]

Although the country was seeing 'stupendious changes' as Evelyn told Browne, Charles and his advisors were failing lamentably in their negotiations.

The K of Scotts . . . not declaring what hee would conceede . . . has bin an irreparable mistake whatever the politicians suggest . . . had he had any publiq Minister here his friend, how safely, honourably & successefully might he have transacted with the greate ones here & conciliated friends amongst them by Indulgences & other meanes whilst they were in this tottering posture; Believe it, Sir his affaires have bin manag'd ridiculously here by the Councill & the Sealed Knott as they tearme them, this under the Rose & to you only.

But the sun was nonetheless coming through the clouds, as he put it. The Rump was in a sweat; counties were rising everywhere, 'the whole nation is in a flame' and a free Parliament was the only answer.[25] Evelyn trusted George Monck and hoped that his advisors were equally honest.

But if the national picture seemed positive, pessimism reigned on the domestic front. Mary, in charge at Sayes Court while Evelyn convalesced at Wotton after a severe illness, reported that the dockyard workers were unpaid and no rents were coming in. 'I send and torment them butt to noe purpose for they have it not . . . there is a talke of a generall discharge sudenly in the yard however we must have patience.' Prettyman and Evelyn could no longer support Browne, 'for we are ruin'd expiring & not able to live so greate are the oppressions upon us, so beggard our tennants.' Evelyn chivvied his father-in-law to write to James Stephens, who had stepped into the financial breach, and send 'insignificant occurrances [to] entertaine him' in return for his support. But when he finally did so, Evelyn brusquely pointed out that had he contacted him earlier, '(as I often desired you) you had gained him eternally'.[26]

Mary happily attended to the garden in his absence and her near-monastic routine in Deptford reminded her, she wrote to her husband, of 'how we designed to live in our cells'. She was living 'as regularly and as pleasantly as I could propose it if I might add the contentment of visiting you in your solitude which is the only want I finde.' Her father had sent her an enamelled watch of her mother's, so that she could measure her 'well spent hours'.[27]

Whatever happened, Evelyn was sure that Browne would soon be recalled and so put in a heavy order with him for books, particularly titles on horticulture and waterworks, two volumes by Salomon de Caus on ornamental gardening and hydraulics, unless they were very expensive and 'by the very first opportunity' two books by 'Monsr de la Chesnée Montrevall' including a small book mostly about tulips – had he written anything else on the subject?[28] He also wanted to know the price of Ramelli's 'rare booke', *Le diverse et artificiose machine* (1588), which included fantastic apparatus for lifting water. After his fruitless investment in unworkable machinery, Evelyn's interest in engines was now confined to hydraulic garden devices, all grist to the mill of *Elysium Britannicum*. Browne was also deputed to measure out the pall malls, long alleys designed for a game of mallet and ball, which were a particular feature of the gardens of the Tuileries and Palais Royal. He pointed out that each foot was 'my ordinary single pace in my usuall walke, without constraint'.

The great book was now consuming much of Evelyn's energy. He sent outlines to Samuel Hartlib and John Beale, Sir Thomas Hanmer and Sir Thomas Browne in Norwich.[29] He explained to the latter that he aimed to counteract 'the many defects which I encounter'd in Bookes and in Gardens, wherein neither words nor cost had bin wanting, but judgement very much'. His object was to combine the 'noble, princely and universall Elysium' with something 'useful and significant to the least pretences and faculties', offering some distraction in 'our miserable yet dearest country' and taking the 'soule and spirits of man' to new heights.[30] Now he puzzled away at the title and turned to Jeremy Taylor, who suggested 'seeing you intend it to the purposes of piety as well as pleasure, why doe you not rather call it Paradisus rather than Elysium; since the word is used by the Hellenish Jews to signify any place of spiritual & immateriall pleasure, and excludes not the material & secular.'[31] Unusually, Evelyn ignored Taylor's advice – possibly to avoid confusion with John Parkinson's fully illustrated *Paradisi in Sole* (1629), the most admired volume on the subject of gardens in print, which Evelyn bought in 1650, only to cover the pages with marks and interjections.

But those close to Evelyn may have already detected his troubles in controlling his own ambitious project. In January 1660 Jasper Needham brought Evelyn a letter signed by a number of Oxford men urging him on to 'the Finishing of Elysium Britannicum'. It may have been a ruse to speed him on to completion. With Dr Philip Stephens, the physician and botanist who had recently revised the catalogue of the Oxford Physic Garden, Needham had rounded up a dozen signatories with particular horticultural expertise, including the Bobarts (father and son), who presided over the Oxford garden, and Robert Sharrock, author of an influential manual on vegetables. They pointed out that Evelyn's proposal was 'a theme altogether new to our writers as having not beene elaborated by any English pen that wee know' and his outline had already 'putt an edge and Keenenesse on our appetites to see the whole made publique'. Such a book required illustrations, 'figures and Cutts proportionable to the Noblenesse & State of the piece'. Not only was their missive designed to spur Evelyn forward but its signatories must have hoped that someone in Oxford, or even beyond, might proffer the resources needed for such an elaborate volume.[32]

Needham probably already knew what Evelyn now told Browne: he was planning to publish the *Elysium* to mark the Restoration.[33] He claimed his 'florid designe which has the ambition to [be] a Garland, to present to his Majestie as those who (for want of other abillities) brought . . . flowers to the Heroes of old' was nearly ready. He dreamed that his *magnum opus* would ornament Charles II's library, its hundreds of pages and numerous engraved plates a vivid testament to his abilities. Evelyn's spirits were rising and he began to wonder if he had been previously laid low by national calamity rather than illness.[34]

Looking further into the future, their family seemed well placed to secure patronage. Tuke was in Breda with Charles in early May and wrote, apparently at Evelyn's suggestion, a description of the king's character. He came back to England with dispatches and garrulously raised both Browne and Evelyn's hopes.[35] Sir Richard Fanshawe was now a master of requests, apparently at the very heart of the patronage network. But when Dr George Morley came over to negotiate with the Presbyterians he warned those at home that Charles was already scattering positions randomly, sometimes assigning them more than once. Meanwhile the discreet Fanshawe, so reserved that he 'never showed the thought of his heart in its greatest sense', prepared to travel back to England with Charles II, where he found neither patronage in his gift nor the post of secretary of state as promised.[36]

With the restoration of the monarchy just weeks away, Evelyn advised Browne to come home, assuming that he would be compensated for his suffering and long years of unpaid loyal service with a 'settled condition'. But he warned against complacency. Samuel Tuke 'thinkes you have so many Friends about his Majestie that it will be your owne fault if you miscarry in any thing that you shall desire'. Nevertheless, since the king is 'besett wth clyents, suitors & candidates for all places & offices of advantage, & remembring how often you have bin neglected by such as you esteem'd your fastest friends', he must come and present himself in person, 'tyme being so precious & all men so eagle-eyed upon every opportunity of the least advancement what appeares'.

If he came quickly, there would be 'Offices of the Clearkes, Treasurers of the Navie, Secretaries of State, a thousand other honourable & lucrative places'.[37]

Lord Jermyn had already been named ambassador to France: 'Can you thinke to thrive under that shadow, at so greate a distance from the sun?' wrote Evelyn, who was losing patience with his unworldly, passive father-in-law. Browne confided to Hyde that spring that he still hoped to stay in Paris, either in his former role or in a more 'eminent capacity', in reparation for his many 'indignities'. If not, he asked if he might attend the marquess of Ormonde in Ireland, 'and there . . . repaire the ruines of my decayd fortune!'[38]

Evelyn reminded Browne that everyone was out for themselves. But he seemed unaware that Sir Richard had hatched a plan for him, having already approached Hyde: 'I have no inclination at all to waite as Clerke of the Councill (for good reasons which I shall in due time impart unto you) my desire being to obtaine his Majesties consent to resigne that place (which I bought at a deare rate) to my sonne-in law, who is (if I mistake nott) in all respects very well qualified for it.'[39] Browne imagined that his political masters and friends would do as he asked, forgetting that they were jockeying for position themselves, faced with the rise of younger men. Browne underestimated the attraction of youth for the new regime, the sheer volume of favours being asked and the fact that those who had once enjoyed sinecures were eagerly reclaiming them. Later Evelyn explained Browne's failure: 'he is not, I confesse Calculated to the Meridian of Court; cannot importune.'[40]

For his part, Evelyn also overestimated the influence of their friends and relatives. Tuke, always so optimistic about his powers of patronage, was coming to 'refresh himself at our poor villa within a day or two', Evelyn reported to Browne. Mary had hurried to London to buy 'necessaries & ornaments' and Evelyn, though with 'ten thousand things more I have to say', had no time to write more. By the time he next took up his pen, it was against the 'horrid din' of drummers passing through Deptford on their way to Dover to meet Charles II.

As they marched, the frigate *Naseby*, renamed the *Royal Charles*, sailed across the North Sea. In the carpenter's cabin, an envoy, Samuel Pepys, dined with the three men who had looked after the exiled king's greatest needs – his exchequer, his religion and his health. Stephen Fox, overseas almost as long as Browne, had helped organise the itinerant court's finances and achieved the logistical miracle of moving it around Europe. Dr John Earle had 'followed him in all his exile with so clear a character, that the King could never see or hear of any one thing amiss in him', as Gilbert Burnet put it. The third man in the party, a formidable mathematician and bibliophile, was his personal physician Dr Charles Scarburgh.[41]

The king had not been in his own country for nine years. In the interim, the reserved youth had grown into a confident, polite man, schooled by his misfortunes to be forthcoming and socially assured. But Samuel Tuke described the physical toll events had taken on him: the 'very lovely' face of the twenty-year-old was, ten years later, drawn, solemn and thin, though his sallow complexion and sparkling eyes were set off by luxuriant black hair, 'not frizled' but worn as loose curls.

His character, as described by the sharp-eyed Florentine envoy Lorenzo Magalotti a few years later, was less reassuring. His 'fiercest enemies are diligence and business. He worships comforts, pleasures, and practical jokes, hates implacably all sorts of work, and loves with the greatest enthusiasm every kind of play and diversion. Serious men terrify him'. Magalotti found him relaxed towards religion, acute about politics but above all reluctant to say no: 'the more impudent the demand the more fortunate the supplicant.'[42] These characteristics did not bode well for the small army of the faithful who had served him, at immense personal cost, for so many years.

On 29 May 1660, the king's thirtieth birthday, 'after a sad, & long Exile, and Calamitous Suffering both of the King & Church: being 17 yeares', Charles arrived in Whitehall. General Monck had met him as he came ashore at Dover to the deafening sound of guns and cannon and from there he travelled via Canterbury and Rochester to Southwark. The restored king's short onward journey, over London Bridge, took four hours. Evelyn stood in the Strand and watched, listened and marvelled that 'all this [happened] without one drop of bloud'. Balconies and windows were spilling over with 'Ladys, Trumpets, Musick', the streets heaved with people and soldiers shouted and waved their weapons ('that very army, which rebell'd against him'). There were flowers in the king's path, tapestries hanging along the streets. Church bells pealed and fountains ran with wine. It was a feast day for the senses, an occasion for fine feathers; dignitaries of the City, aldermen and members of the Worshipful Companies flaunted their liveries, banners and chains of office, while the nobility wore 'Cloth of Silver, gold & vellvet'. Surely no day in the nation's history had been 'so joyfull . . . & so bright'. Evelyn, often cavalier with historical references, thought nothing had matched it since 'the returne of the Babylonian Captivity'.

After Charles II had been greeted by the lord mayor, fireworks and 'excesse of jubilee' were followed by religious rite. Evelyn plunged in. 'It is but one moment since I am returned from the publiq Eucharisticall offices solemnly performed . . . to the universall rejoicing . . . of all . . . good men', he wrote immediately afterwards. There was largesse for sailors and the entire fleet was due to set out the next day 'with all imaginable pomp & splendour'. Public hysteria led to Cromwell's corpse being disinterred and his head appearing on a pike, alongside those of other regicides, on London Bridge. Indoors at Whitehall, the king was overwhelmed by crowds, 'all sorts of people . . . from all parts of the Nation'. Evelyn had no compunction in adding to their number and, through the good offices of the duke of York (presumably engineered by Tuke), he was granted an audience 'when he was alone, & very few noble-men with him'. The easy charm and accessibility of the young king were his trump cards combined, where Evelyn was concerned, with a wide range of interests and a willingness to listen.[43]

Within days, Sir Richard Browne returned too, but unnoticed and empty-handed, greeted only by his family, his delight in being reunited with them and meeting his surviving grandson palpably undermined by the lack of recognition for his selfless service. Despite his efforts to pass the role to

Evelyn, Browne was reappointed a clerk to the Privy Council, the post he had bought for £1,500 almost twenty years before.[44] Yet the clerkship had the advantage of placing him at the heart of public affairs and government, the better to obtain preferment for his son-in-law and settle his own claims. After nineteen years abroad, he never crossed the Channel again.

For all his efforts to make himself visible, Evelyn remained no more than a spectator at the events marking the Stuart restoration. He added his signature to those of a hundred or so members of the Sussex gentry celebrating the 'miraculous and peaceable restauration' of the king and went to Whitehall again, now as just another country landowner, not the man of letters he saw himself as. Evelyn often recounted the risks he had run for the royalist cause: sending 'weekely Intelligence . . . abroad of transactions here, by a Cyfer', housing and hiding royalists 'when it had bin Treason to have but conversed with them', and writing various pamplets.[45] His cloak-and-dagger claims tended to be for the eyes and ears of succeeding generations. John Evelyn, royalist hero, was hardly more than a literary conceit.

Well down the queue of supplicants for favour, he watched the monarchy being re-established from afar. The king had begun to touch for evil and the sad cavalcade of thousands coming to be healed of scrofula by the royal laying on of hands was the surest proof that the divine right of the monarch had survived its nineteen-year hiatus.

In mourning after the death from smallpox of Henry, duke of Gloucester, the court was readying itself for the return of Henrietta Maria from France in November 1660. A month later, Mary, princess of Orange, died too.* Anne Hyde's dalliance with James, duke of York, was sealed by marriage and the birth of a son. Sir Edward Hyde, uncomfortable in his role as royal father-in-law but confirmed as Charles II's lord chancellor and the most powerful man in the land after the king, was installed at Worcester House on the Strand.[46] His daughter's translation to the ranks of royalty was, Evelyn commented, 'a strange change, can it succeed well!'

Anglican observance was quickly re-established but the king proved to be neither particularly religious nor sensitive to the resonances of ritual; to Evelyn, the addition of violins to the organ at the Chapel Royal seemed to smack of French church music, and thus Catholicism, so very unwelcome at court. The new dean of Westminster, the admirable Dr John Earle, preached in the Abbey on Christmas Day and Evelyn joined him to celebrate the end of a stupendous year. In retrospect in the diary Evelyn summed it up in a ringing phrase, 'annus mirabilis'. Soon after, Henrietta Maria and her

---

*The deaths were in September and December 1660 respectively, Mary's while visiting England.

daughter Princess Henrietta (Minette) set off back to France, to organise the latter's dynastic marriage to the French king's brother, Philippe d'Anjou, soon to be duc d'Orléans. By March the English princess was the first lady of France, immeasurably strengthening the ties between the two countries and in the process causing worry in many quarters.

Now forty years old, the sole official position Evelyn had yet secured was that of commissioner of sewers.[47] He rejected a commission in the army, with a fey admission that his tactical skills were limited to 'the disciplining of a few Flowers in my Garden, and ranging the Bookes in my studye'.[48] His hopes rested on the intellectual foundations he had so carefully laid and he even worried lest any new post would take up too much time 'from the nobler parts of life'. His self-chosen mission was to draw instructive comparisons between France and England that Charles II, the bilingual son of a French mother and who had spent so much time in Paris, would well appreciate. Evelyn had already prepared (at least) two translations from the French, one on books and bibliography, the other on classical architecture, both areas of generous state patronage in France.[49]

Yet he sought moral support as he left the protected world of his own study and circle of admiring friends to be exposed to superior and potentially critical intellects. In a letter drafted to Samuel Tuke he wrote: 'I have found when Speculatists would become pragmaticall, they stand in neede of all the collateral aydes to support their Title; and that the counsell of a steady Friend and his Example, is instructive above all the Bookes and fine discourses in the World.'[50] Currently Tuke was that friend. In the collegiate, collaborative atmosphere of 'our society', with its distinguished scientists, physicians and statesmen, he would learn to build on his strengths, his knowledge of engraving and the fine arts, architecture and, above all, horticulture and arboriculture.

The future Royal Society brought together those who were already meeting at Gresham College or informally in coffee shops or instrument-makers' premises in London. After the Restoration this group was given new purpose and energy by the return to London of Dr John Wilkins, Sir Robert Moray and Sir William Petty. The objective was to create a permanent learned academy, with premises, employees, a museum and library. But first they needed to be a legal entity and secure a royal charter. Moray, a valued courtier, had already conveyed the king's approval of their venture. He and Viscount Brouncker were sharing the office of president but Moray's ability to effortlessly combine statesmanship and science immensely impressed Samuel Sorbière who declared it a 'very edifying Thing, to find a Person imply'd in Matters of State, and of such Excellent Merit, and one who had been engaged a great Part of his Life in Warlike Commands, and the Affairs of the Cabinet, apply himself in making Machines in St James's Park and adjusting Telescopes'.[51]

Through his own contacts at court, Evelyn played a part in wooing the king, on the page and in person, claiming to have discussed 'severall particulars relating to our Society and the Planet Saturn etc.' Christopher Wren, professor of astronomy at Gresham College, was chosen to give the inaugural lecture in November 1660. Charles II's weakness for the instant gratification provided by optical instruments, mechanical devices and automata made Wren, a prolific inventor, ideal bait.[52] Evelyn was not present at Wren's talk (nor was the king) but a week later he was among those who agreed to attend weekly meetings 'to consult & debate, concerning the promoting of Experimental Learning' and to subscribe a shilling a week. Forty men were considered suitable candidates for fellowship and Evelyn was elected on 2 January 1661. He joined the executive of the society – the Council – in August 1662.[53]

The meetings took place in a comfortable panelled room at Gresham College, the society's home in the early years, around a large table surrounded by two rows of benches 'in form like an Amphitheatre'. The proceedings were, in the eyes of a French observer, conducted in exemplary fashion. The president sat with his back to the chimney in an armchair, controlling the discussion with a wooden gavel. The secretary, to his left, minuted the meeting. The Fellows leaned forward on their benches, listening quietly. There were no harangues and no interruptions. Proceedings were translated for overseas visitors.[54]

One of the earliest papers presented was Sir Kenelm Digby's 'discourse concerning the vegetation of plants', one of the seedlings that grew into the Royal Society's first official publication, Evelyn's *Sylva* (1664). If the world of Restoration science was personified for Evelyn by 'our Second Verulam, the Illustrious Boyle', Digby hailed from an older tradition, a melange of sense and nonsense. Though he often relied upon 'faulty observation and conclusions that went further than the facts allowed', getting caught up in alchemical distractions such as an attempt to reconstitute a bird from its ashes and his miraculous 'weapon salve', Digby also represented wider intellectual horizons, having disputed with Descartes, published widely and been immersed in natural-philosophical debates across continental Europe for decades.[55]

For all Evelyn's passion for the printed word, he quickly recognised the importance of close personal observation. He was to describe the Royal Society's aim as the extension of 'real knowledge' far beyond the pursuit of 'fantasms and fruitless speculations'. By attending the Wednesday meetings at Gresham College or going on the Fellows' field trips, Evelyn was gaining a new perspective on learning. Robert Boyle, he recalled almost forty years later, had learned 'more from Men, Real Experiments, & his Laboratory (which was ample and well-furnish'd), than from Books'.[56] Few of the leading Fellows were, according to John Aubrey, great readers. Hooke, Petty, Wilkins and Wren were essentially guided in their investigations by examination and firsthand experience.

Toiling on their own projects, virtuosi such as Evelyn or Henshaw were invaluable volunteers to the project, excited to see a Solomon's House finally taking shape. Evelyn looked into appropriate coats of arms and mottos for the Society, considering motifs such as a sailing ship, the sun, a globe and a tree. The Latin motto eventually chosen was *Nullius in verba*, 'on no man's word', suitably cautionary and empirical in tone. When wondering how the Royal Society had come to choose the patron saint of Scotland, William Petty offered John Aubrey an alternative to St Andrew. St Thomas might have been more suitable, he thought, 'for he would not beleeve till he had seen and put his fingers into the holes: according to the motto *Nullius in verba*.'[57] Evelyn's enjoyment in seeking out apt phrases from the ancients led him to suggest to his friend, Henry Slingsby, master of the Royal Mint, that '*decus et tutamen*' (ornament and protect) was an appropriate Virgilian sentiment for the milled edges of the coinage introduced in 1663, to foil the fraudulent practice of clipping. The words are there today.

In early 1661 Evelyn was invited to show the other Fellows his catalogue of trades and his work on the anatomy of trees, and to prepare oil of sulphur and a report on Tenerife for them. It was then that Evelyn realised that he had overstated his capabilities. His 'Circle of Mechanical Trades' was little more than a list of headings drawn up earlier and it was Jasper Needham who, that autumn, presented the Society with papers on china varnish, japanning (lacquering) and gilding, those techniques which he had pursued on Evelyn's behalf in Paris earlier. Evelyn confined himself to an account of marbling paper. In exoneration, Evelyn composed a letter to John Wilkins, asking him to intercede with the society on his behalf, 'knowing on what other subject I was engag'd . . ., [if] I may obtaine its indulgence, not to expect many other things from me, 'till it be accomplish'd'.[58]

The 'other subject' was probably his work on printmaking, the one trade with which Evelyn was fully familiar. He had published etchings after his own drawings, he knew many of the most skilled printmakers in Paris and London, and had long been an indefatigable collector of prints. He had already assembled his thoughts on the subject, planning to add a translation of Abraham Bosse's *Traité* (1645) to provide the technical information. Now the society encouraged him to publish 'what I had written of Chalcography'.[59] Due to the difficulties of securing Sayes Court from the Crown, *Sculptura* was delayed but when it was published in 1662 he prefaced it with Samuel Sorbière's biography of a Bolognese virtuoso who had attempted to compile a history of the trades, including samples and patterns, details of engines and machines, in short 'the Fabrick of all sorts of Works . . . for Use and for Magnificence'.[60] But even the resolute and upright Favi had been defeated by the secrecy surrounding 'the dark shops of Mechanicks' (as Robert Hooke wrote in *Micrographia*) as by the sheer enormity of his task. Evelyn was keen to make the point to the Fellows, in his own defence. Meanwhile the impossibility of publishing the *Elysium Britannicum* in time for the king's coronation must have become obvious to Evelyn.

In spring 1661 London prepared for the coronation. The succession of pageants and processions which preceded the event delighted Evelyn, the inveterate list maker. The Knights of the Bath were created in a ceremonial bathing in Westminster Hall, their crimson robes 'the noblest shew of the whole Cavalcade (his Majestie Excepted)'. He counted sixty-eight. 'I might have received this honour, but declined it', perhaps later regretting his decision.[61] As on the king's triumphant return almost a year earlier, London was a sea of colour, glitter and theatre for these days. Royal guards were dressed in white doublets and crowds of dignitaries shimmered in their bejewelled finery, crusted with gold and silver thread. The ranks of the nobility were swelled by new creations. Sir Edward Hyde became the earl of Clarendon and Arthur Capel, the earl of Essex. Everything was fantastic, closer to a masque than a state occasion. Oriental carpets disguised ramshackle houses, flowers (and gravel) covered filthy streets and temporary triumphal arches stood marking the monarch's route.

On 23 April 1661, St George's Day, Charles II travelled from Whitehall to Westminster by water. Unlike Pepys who enterprisingly found himself a perch inside the Abbey, Evelyn had to depend on the gazettes for his picture of what was happening inside. From his vantage point near Temple Bar he saw the long glittering procession pass, including Sir Richard Fanshawe, splendidly garbed to represent one of the two French duchies (Aquitaine and Normandy) claimed by England.[62] But Samuel Tuke was absent, having been sent to Paris to convey the sympathies of the English court to the French on Mazarin's death. He considered he ought to have had a role in the procession, 'if Loyaltie industrie & Success had anie signification in your state government'.[63]

Among the churchmen in the Abbey were Evelyn's old friends from Paris. Dr George Morley gave a sermon while to Dr John Earle fell the privilege of closing the king's waistcoat, before he was crowned Charles II. After the ceremony, the king walked on a blue carpet to Westminster Stairs and took a state barge back to Whitehall 'where was extraordinary feasting'.[64]

Pepys drank the king's health so enthusiastically that he gave himself a terrible hangover the next day, but Evelyn remained sober and purposeful.[65] He asked Viscount Mordaunt to present a panegyric he had written. Charles II, Mordaunt reported back, had asked if it was in Latin and hoped it was not too long, 'this I thought fit to intimate to you'.[66] The king knew Evelyn's tendencies on the page but in fact this verse pamphlet was short and euphorically to the point. 'Miraculous Reverse!' he shrilled, 'our redivive Phoenix' had come like Moses to deliver his people out of Egypt. The temporary arches must become marble, 'lasting as the Pyramids'. Next Evelyn recited the king's achievements to date: the act of clemency, the revival of institutions, settling matters for the church and in law, the army disbanded, the navy paid off, a council of trade established. Then came the turn of their society, and Evelyn was sure 'so Magnanimous a Prince' would encourage it, since 'the Augmentation of Science, and universal good of Man-kind . . . will consummate Your Fame and render it immortal'.

Evelyn was enjoying himself at the Royal Society. In these early months, as throughout his more than forty-year involvement, Evelyn confined himself to what he could best comprehend. Key experiments, such as those involving air pumps or blood transfusion, were little more than spectacles where he was concerned. However, he spent an anxious half-hour by the Deptford wet dock waiting for an employee to surface in a new diving bell (and was, two years later, instructed to sell the lead vessel for the 'best advantage of the society') and, another day, he crouched in Thomas Chiffinch's garden off St James's Park to observe how 'humble and sensible' plants reacted to stimuli, such as *aqua fortis* (nitric acid) or a glass to intensify the sun's rays. Those around the courtier's flowerbeds included Robert Hooke, soon to be the society's curator, Dr Wilkins, Viscount Brouncker, Sir Robert Moray and Thomas Henshaw.[67] The experiment was made at the king's request.

The inauguration of a state-funded institution for the liberal arts and sciences now seemed a distinct possibility, a version of Bacon's utopian project, 'which however lofty, and to appearance Romantic has yet in it nothing of Impossible to be effected'. The words came from Evelyn's translation of Gabriel Naudé's work, *Instructions Concerning the Erecting of a Library* (1661), which he had prepared some years earlier, encouraged by Barlow and Pett from Oxford, but now dedicated to Lord Chancellor Clarendon – the best man to promote the Royal Society, being, in effect, England's Mazarin. Naudé was a member of the so-called *libertins érudits*, a group of intellectual freethinkers, with Pierre Gassendi and François de la Mothe le Vayer – the latter called him a *bibliotheque vivante*, a 'living library' – and was librarian to both Richelieu and Mazarin, building up the latter's collection to some forty thousand volumes. He believed, as did Evelyn, that libraries should be open to borrowers.[68] A London worthy of the restored king should, Evelyn considered, build up its resources and nurture formal intellectual gatherings on the lines of Bacon's 'Amphitheatre of Wisdom'. He suggested to Chiffinch that he should prepare a catalogue of the treasures and curiosities in the royal collection, to put them on a par with the 'cabinets' with which foreign princes impressed their visitors.[69]

The intelligentsia in Paris, London and the Hague were acutely interested by each other's doings, continually fuelled and informed by visitors and correspondence, by turn covetous of one another's secrets and admiring of their achievements. In his guise as a Frenchman in *The Character of England* Evelyn had criticised London's lack of 'publique and honourable works, such as render our Paris and other Cities of France, renowned, and visited by all the World'. But, with its charter finally secured in July 1662, the Royal Society had suddenly stolen a march on the French. Sorbière asked Hobbes about the new 'London Academy of Physical Sciences' and to tell him 'what sort of thing it is, and on whose acuteness and theories we can set out hopes'.[70] The first meeting of the elite Académie des Sciences would only be held in Louis XIV's private library in December 1666.

But in the heady days of the Restoration, Evelyn addressed Clarendon to ask why 'the Chancellours of France . . . [should] bear away the Reputation of having rendred that Spot the envy of Europe'. Fine language was not enough, for 'Things are better than Words'. The Royal Society, as Evelyn named it there prematurely, was not a gathering of pedants or superficial persons but of 'Refined Spirits that are universally Learn'd, that are Read, Travell'd, Experience'd and Stout'. Clarendon had already encouraged their objectives, 'the Knowledge of Causes and the Nature of Things'. The lord chancellor was in effect the Royal Society's guarantor, named in both the first and second charters as the man who must, in the event of any wrongdoing or dispute, 'reconcile, compose, and adjust the same differences and abuses'.[71]

Later, struggling through the dense text of Evelyn's translation of Naudé, Pepys admitted it was 'above my reach' while greatly admiring the preamble to Clarendon.[72] His part in the Royal Society brought Evelyn altruistic ambitions: 'for my own part . . . I had rather be the Author of one good and beneficial Invention than to have been Julius Caesar or the great Alexander himself.' Yet he remained ambivalent about his own direction in life; power, possessions and wealth were not for him, he told Jeremy Taylor, 'not because I have no ambitions to serve: but because I have too many.'[73]

The Restoration, far from solving the Evelyns' family problems, exacerbated them. Sayes Court reverted to the Crown; re-establishing their title to it took three years' hard work. Now Mary began to represent the family's best chance to reverse their fortunes, for they remembered that the king had promised her a position as the future queen's 'Lady of the Jewels'. From Paris, Tuke wrote that he was glad to hear they were making progress on that score and offered to help on his return.

It was perhaps to show herself in person at court that Mary came to Whitehall to see Abraham Cowley's play *Cutter of Coleman-Street* which, she felt, did not live up to the author's promise. The court was out of mourning again and appeared very splendid. It was now Evelyn's turn to pursue her case, she told him, since her father 'hath dined with the Chancellor discoursed at large with him, the particulars I know not yet; only he tells me the king is sufficiently satisfied concerning me'. However, the ships had not yet left for Portugal to collect Charles's bride so it was too early to confirm her position.[74] Six months later, Philip Stanhope, now earl of Chesterfield and financially indebted to Evelyn, tipped them off that two ladies of the bedchamber were leaving to meet Catherine of Braganza and so, if Mary still wanted to enter the future queen's service, this was the moment to act. She must write, mentioning 'his Majesties promises at Breda, her fathers sufferings and her long being in suspence'. After he had shown her letter to the king, she should present herself at court.[75] But nothing came of it. Mary later learned enough about the queen's court through her friend, the second Lady Tuke, to realise that she had been fortunate not to be offered a position. It was, in the end, just one of a long string of broken promises that connected her family to the king.[76]

With Sir Henry de Vic (formerly Resident in Brussels) now installed as secretary for the French tongue and Sir Richard Fanshawe as his Latin counterpart, literary appointments at court were scarce.[77] But Evelyn may have been under consideration for the vacant post of historiographer royal when the king asked him to record 'the bloudy Encounter . . . betweene the French & Spanish Ambassador neere the Tower, at the reception of the Sweds Ambassador' on 30 September 1661. The commission proved a poisoned chalice, however, since everybody caught up in this tense, if trivial, diplomatic incident revised their stories by the hour, leaving Evelyn ill and 'harrass'd, with going about, & sitting up to write &c' – a salutary reminder of the difficulties of writing to order.[78]

Despite that, Evelyn worked to keep his conduits to the monarch open. In late 1661 he asked another contact from the old days in Paris, Sir Henry Bennet, keeper of the Privy Purse and a rising star, to pass on his pamphlet on French fashion, an uneasy mix of satire and arguments for home production entitled *Tyrannus or the Mode*. Behind the playful descriptions, his theme was trade and the desirability of self-sufficiency and sobriety.[79] He anxiously asked Bennet to 'take some lucky opportunity of reading it to [the king]: if he smile, mention your humble servant; if he frowne, conceale his name, and pardon the presumption'. If this appealed, he had other publications to offer. He reminded Bennet how cardinals Richelieu and Mazarin had 'a Bookish-Confident or two, who were wont from time to time, to informe them of all that was rare, and new both in the Sciences, and Bookes, on which, though their greate affaires permitted them not to looke so steadily; yet, were they (by this meanes) ignorant of nothing that pass'd in either'.[80] Perhaps Naudé's example had suggested such a role to Evelyn, an ideal combination of public service and literary life, fulfilling his father's hopes and his own ambitions while continuing to promote the infant Royal Society.

CHAPTER 10

City and Country

Casting around, Evelyn realised that the transformation of the capital to mark his return might be a good subject with which to capture the king's attention. Clear-headed and well informed, he positioned himself to play a part in the long-overdue improvements to London, a city that 'from Wood might be rendered Brick, and (like another Rome) from Brick made Stone and Marble'.[1] In print he continually reminded his countrymen of the example set elsewhere. In Paris the young king was surrounded by powerful, ambitious men, dedicated to the greater glory of their capital while in Rome, new piazzas and pilgrimage routes, palaces, fountains and churches were the legacy of a succession of powerful and moneyed papal dynasties. Alternatively, the orderly merchant cities of Holland epitomised moral and economic health, the physical embodiment of a well-governed and enlightened country.

Evelyn's *Fumifugium*, his tract on the dire state of London air published in September 1661, was formally addressed to the king and to the Parliament 'now Assembled'. The dedicatory letter to the king was surprisingly familiar in tone, perhaps reflecting Evelyn's claim that the short paper was written at Charles's 'special Command'. So long 'accustom'd to the excellent Aer of other Countries' the king must have been concerned to see smoke swirling indoors in his palace. Though ostensibly a diatribe about pollution from coal, the image of the corridors of Whitehall was all too emblematic.[2] The Restoration unleashed uplifting metaphor, pages laden with scenes of rebuilding, clearing skies and sweet-scented gardens, the end of what had been, for many around the king, a long and grim period of uncertainty. As Abraham Cowley wrote,

Who, that has reason, and his smell,
Would not among roses and jasmine dwell,
Rather than all his spirits choke
With exhalations of dirt and smoke?[3]

Evelyn began with a plea for a programme of 'Publick Works' to improve the image of the imperial capital, the power of which stretched to the farthest Indies. As Charles II regained his throne, Louis XIV reached his majority. Paris and the French monarchy would prove handy markers against which to judge the progress of London and the restored king. But currently London's parlous physical state, almost untouched for nearly twenty years, could be blamed on the upheavals of the civil wars and Interregnum, just as its crumbling churches mirrored the protracted miseries of the Church of England. Now its regeneration should be made to epitomise the restored kingdom.

London wraps 'her stately head in Clowds of Smoake and Sulphur, . . . Stink and Darknesse'.[4] Despite efforts to develop sulphur-free fuel, industry was powered by 'hellish' sea coal 'which darkens and eclipses all her other Attributes', belching from the lime kilns and premises of brewers, salt and soap boilers, chandlers and butchers, putting 'a sooty Crust or Fur upon all', inside and out. Pollution affected health, causing everything from mere inconvenience (Evelyn instanced a musician friend who had lost three notes in his vocal range) to death: as many as half those recorded in London were from consumption and lung disease.[5] Everywhere people gather, 'the Barking and the Spitting is uncessant'. Indoors pictures and hangings are yellowed, linen is laden with smuts, while outdoors, even the rain drops soot, bees and birds die and plants wither, their leaves choked, 'that can never be Aer fit for them to breath in, where not Fruits nor Flowers do ripen or come to a seasonable perfection'. He pictures how a canopy over London would catch the quantity of soot 'which now . . . comes down every Night in the Streets, on our Houses, and Waters and is taken into our Bodies'. Evelyn brought every weapon in his literary and scientific arsenal into play, ranging from ancient texts to notions about purifying the air with scented plants (John Beale's idea) as well as making use of John Graunt's groundbreaking statistics of mortality.[6]

What was to be done? Burning nothing but wood, as in Paris, 'were madnesse', yet improved husbandry of woodland could supply some of the need, especially in those northern counties where the timber 'seems inexhaustible'. If the polluting trades moved down river and down wind, they would give work to innumerable watermen, transporting and distributing goods to and from London.[7] A river fronted not by warehouses but by 'Tenements and . . . Noble Houses for use and pleasure, respecting the Thames to their no small advantage', would be attractive but also lessen the risk of fire. Surely, such public works were more urgent than draining the fens? Evelyn pleaded with those who (unlike himself) lived in London to argue his point.

Evelyn's other practical suggestion was for a prototype Green Belt, limiting the 'farther exorbitant encrease' of the capital. A perfumed *cordon sanitaire* would wrap itself around the east and south-west of the city, an area hedged by fragrant shrubs, trees and bushes, and bordered with scented flowering plants, with herbs underfoot. Evelyn suggested honeysuckles ('Woodbinds'), musk roses and Spanish broom, narcissi and pinks, and many more species. Within these 'Palisads, and Fences' would be paddocks for livestock and fields for marketable crops (but not smelly cabbages). Plantations of trees and nurseries would combine 'Ornament, Profit and Security'. The vast majority of park trees were still imported from Holland and so the proposal argued for self-sufficiency in this trade too. London's air and prevailing winds would be 'perpetually fann'd' by the hedges, trees, scented shrubs and flowers, the city bathed in 'sweet and ravishing' fragrances. Evelyn vividly remembered Genoese orange blossom on the air, even in winter.

On *Fumifugium*'s publication, Evelyn heard that the king was 'much pleased by it'. His dedication mentioned the forthcoming major work on gardens, which would include a full catalogue of native plants, and 'which I am preparing to present to Your Majesty, as God shall afford me Leisure to finish it'. In the meantime, the reputation of the experimental garden in Deptford spread; in early 1661 Hartlib received a letter from Dublin asking when Sayes Court would be 'open to publick view'.[8]

In everything he did at the Restoration Evelyn was eager to fit the part of a moral exemplar. In a word portrait, threaded through his essay against French fashion (and, thus, needless imports), he described himself dressed in a loose coat and breeches, rather than elaborate pantaloons, 'as if . . . supported with a pair of Ionic pillars'. Although he liked a measure of 'cheerfull Gaiety' and was not averse to displaying 'the shape of a goodly leg' his own tastes were for 'whatever is comely, and of use . . . choosing nothing that should be Capricious, nothing that were singular . . .'. His shoes were comfortable, neither exaggeratedly round nor long, and he was usually hatless – like the ancients, he adds. He derided courtiers, draped in so much ribbon 'as would have plundered six shops, and set up twenty Country Pedlers . . .' He had seen one, clattering like a fully rigged frigate or a maypole. He was no courtier in his dress but courtly language came naturally to him: 'we have a Prince whose shape is elegant and perfect to admiration . . . the most fit to give the Standard now to the Mode we next expect, and that not only to his own Nation, but to all the World besides.'[9]

That October he was an excited passenger on the royal pleasure yacht, the *Catherine,* as she raced the duke of York's *Anne* from Greenwich to Gravesend and back, and found himself discussing *Fumifugium* with Charles II, who asked him to prepare a parliamentary bill for the next session, 'being (as he said) resolved to have something don in it'. By keeping his vehicle brief and topical, Evelyn had caught the king's attention. In January 1662 he saw a draft of the Act.[10] 'A new Prince should make Everything New' had been Machiavelli's ringing phrase and this new king was showing promise.[11] A few weeks earlier Charles had regaled him with his plans for Greenwich, rebuilding the palace and 'quite demolishing the old'.[12] But nothing more was heard of the proposed law.

At the Restoration, Sir John Denham, poet, gambler and Knight of the Bath, became surveyor-general of the King's Works.[13] Evelyn had known him in Paris as a key courier in the royalist network, incessantly on the move. Denham, whose poem 'Cooper's Hill' (1642) famously celebrated the pastoral landscape of Egham (near Windsor Castle) while musing on the troubled monarchy, was, Evelyn thought, 'a better poet than architect', all too aware that his own knowledge of architecture was considerably greater than the surveyor's. Nevertheless Denham's services to the king had been sufficient to win him a handsome town house, although his deteriorating mental state forced him to sell it in 1667, unfinished, to Richard Boyle, eldest brother of the scientist. It was the original Burlington House.

In the early optimistic days of the Restoration Evelyn and Denham visited run-down Greenwich Palace together, coming to very different conclusions about what should replace it. Denham thought a new palace should sit on piles at the water's edge; Evelyn envisaged the building sited between the Queen's House and the river, 'so as a large Square Cutt, should have let in the Thames like a Baye' suggesting a memory of the artificial 'harbour' he had so admired at Maisons.

In May 1662 Evelyn's expertise was recognised when he joined Denham and Hugh May, since 1660 the paymaster of the works, as one of the commissioners to improve 'the buildings, wayes, streetes, & incumbrances, & regulating the Hackny-Coaches in the City of London'.[14] May, who claimed to have served the 2nd duke of Buckingham for twenty years, trading in works of art, had spent most of his exile in Holland.[15] Other commissioners well known to Evelyn by now included Stephen Fox, suitably rewarded as clerk of the green cloth and paymaster of the forces, as well as Sir William Petty, Henry Jermyn, the earl of St Albans and Edmund Waller. The moneys raised by licensing four hundred hackney cabs in the capital (at £5 each) would, in theory, fund the works. Perhaps London would finally come to resemble its fictional version in Thomas Moore's 'Amaurot', the city in his Utopia with its flat-fronted, terraced houses with gardens behind and broad streets in front. But like most independent advisory bodies, the commission did not endure long even though its membership should have guaranteed it the king's attention. Nor did the London streets see noticeable improvement; the preferred means of transport remained the river, where a flotilla of miscellaneous vessels and thousands of watermen were available to undertake quick ferry crossings

1 Wenceslaus Hollar's drawing of Amsterdam, 1634, showing the weigh-house.

2 Thames-side London, looking east towards St Paul's Cathedral from the roof of Arundel House. Etching after Wenceslaus Hollar.

3 Southover House (later Grange), Lewes, John Evelyn's home when living with his step-grandparents, a comfortable sixteenth-century gentry house.

4 Richard Evelyn's tomb in Wotton church showing his five children as mourners, amongst them John Evelyn, the middle son.

5 Portrait of Edmund Waller, drawn in Paris by Robert Nanteuil, *c.* 1650.

6 The Botanic Garden at Padua University, seen in winter. Founded 1545.

Pencil portraits by Robert Nanteuil showing John Evelyn and his new family in Paris, 1650.

7 Mary Browne.

8 Sir Richard Browne.

9 John Evelyn.

10 Lady Browne.

11 Portrait (studio of Van Dyck) of the young Lady Isabella Thynne (née Rich), later a key secret agent.

Honoratissima Domina,
Isabella Illust: Comitis Holland
filia: Hac ari incisa J. E.
devotissimus sua servus
dat dedicat, consecratq.
1649

12 John Evelyn's etched plate dedicated to Isabella Thynne, 1649.

13 Wenceslaus Hollar's 1645 etching of the gardens at Albury Park, with the classical structures erected in the earl of Arundel's lifetime.

14 The exedra, pool and entrance to the tunnel through the hill at Albury. These were part of Evelyn's redesign of the terraced gardens, executed in the 1660s.

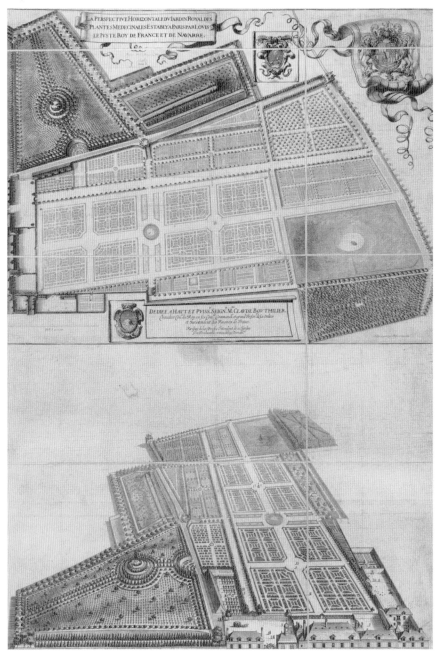

15 Abraham Bosse's paired engravings of the royal Jardin des Plantes, Paris (1641).

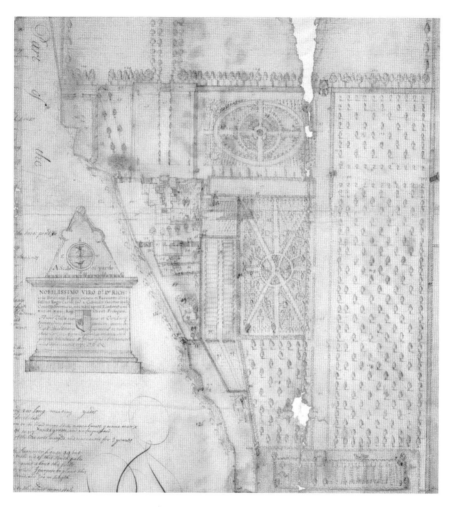

16 John Evelyn's 1653 drawing, its detail suggesting it was meant to be engraved, showing Sayes Court and the extensive new gardens.

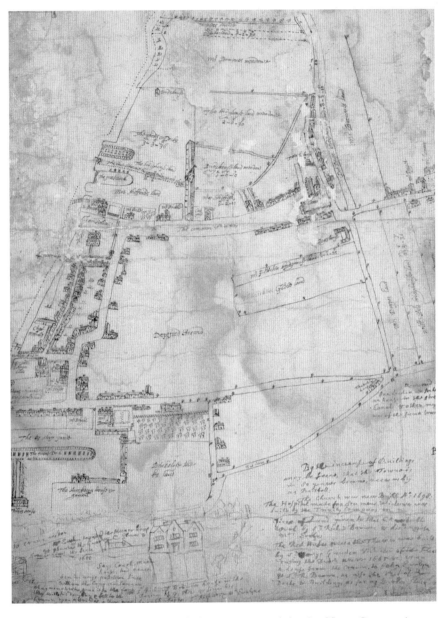

17 Plan of Deptford, 1623, with Evelyn's 1698 annotated sketch of Sayes Court at the very bottom.

18 Plate from Robert Hooke's *Micrographia* (1665) showing a spot of mould taken from a sheepskin book binding, which is described as 'a very pretty shap'd Vegetative body'.

19 Portrait of Thomas Henshaw FRS (by unknown artist), Evelyn's travelling companion and lifelong friend.

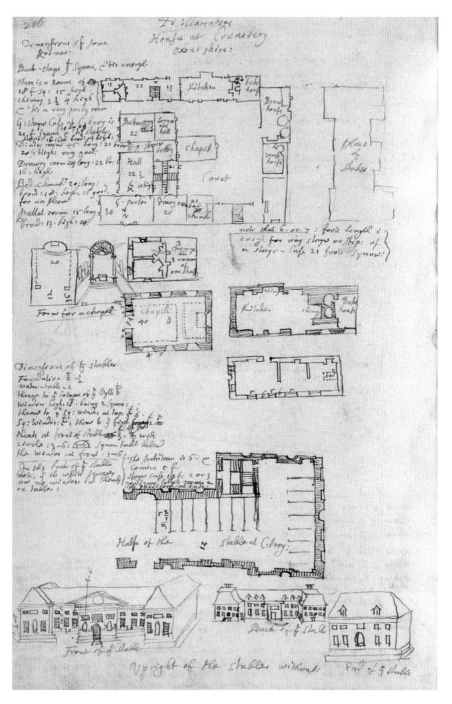

20 John Evelyn's 1664 annotated plans and elevations of Cornbury Park showing the house, chapel and stables, including unexecuted ideas of his own.

21 Eltham Lodge, 1664, by Hugh May, an exercise in Dutch classical architecture in Kent. Now the Royal Blackheath Golf Club.

22 Cornbury Park, 1665, as built by Hugh May, the new garden front added to an earlier house.

Some key people in Evelyn's life.

23 Charles II *c.*1675/80 (attributed to
Edward Luttrell, after Sir Peter Lely).

24 Margaret Blagge (engraving after
Matthew Dixon by W. Humphreys).

25 Samuel Pepys 1684 (after Sir Godfrey
Kneller).

26 Henry Howard, later the 6th duke of
Norfolk (engraving after Sir Peter Lely by
A. Blooteling, 1678).

27 The avenue leading to Euston Hall (showing the recently built church to the left) drawn by Edmund Prideaux, *c.* 1735, when Evelyn's landscape scheme had reached maturity.

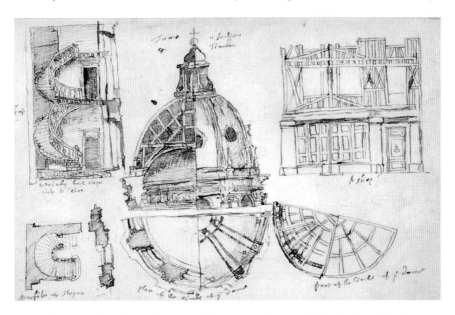

28 Evelyn's own drawing made in the 1690s, after a plate in d'Aviler's *Cours d'Architecture*.

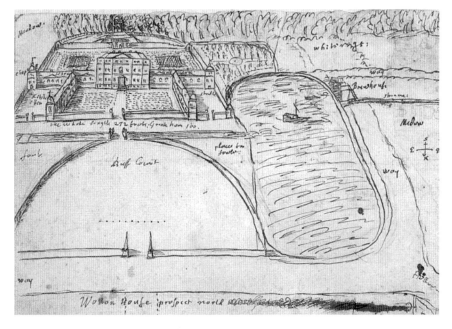

29 Evelyn's drawing of a classical Wotton, *c.* 1700, his 'Castle in the Air' that was never built. The terraced mount is shown behind the house.

30 The classical front to the grotto beneath the mount at Wotton, designed and built in the 1650s by cousin George Evelyn 'the traveller'.

from any of the innumerable landing stairs on both banks of the Thames, as well as longer journeys up and down river for both passengers and goods traffic.

Fumifugium showed Evelyn marshalling arguments and lobbying to the best of his ability. At the same time he was preparing *Sculptura* – a very personal overview of a subject, printmaking, in which he had considerable specialist knowledge. The continuing struggle to secure the title and tenure at Sayes Court from the Crown had delayed its completion but on 11 June 1662 Evelyn finally presented *Sculptura* to the Royal Society.[16] A muddled account of the history and practice of sculpture, medal-making and engraving, its strengths and weaknesses were those of its author, by turns well informed and perceptive, prolix and undiscerning.[17] The dedicatee was Robert Boyle, 'an accomplish'd Genius' personally committed to 'cultivating the Sciences, and advancing of useful knowledge, emancipated from the strong contentions, and little fruit of the former; Envy and imposture of the latter Ages'. He left out his translation of Bosse. Instead William Faithorne, the king's engraver who had worked with Bosse in Paris, published it as the *Art of Graveing and Etching* the same year.

Ironically given its subject, *Sculptura* had just three plates, including a crude frontispiece by Evelyn, engraved by Abraham Hertochs.[18] One, however, was a *coup* – the first mezzotint ever published in a book, Prince Rupert's copy of a portrait then thought to be by Ribera.[19] Unfortunately, when Sir Robert Moray arranged for him to see the plates being run off, the condition for this privilege was his continued secrecy about the process.[20] In 1668 John Beale, still urging Evelyn on from Somerset, encouraged him to reissue *Sculptura* in illustrated form, with engravings paid for by sponsors and in the hope that now Prince Rupert would allow him to reveal the mystery of the technique.[21] But by then Evelyn's mind was on other things and he admitted in 1689, 'Tis now more than Twenty-yeares, since I began indeede to make some Collections towards it, but other things intervening, I laied it by, and hardly can tell, what's become of them.'[22] Parts of *Numismata* (1697) had to serve as his second edition.

In early autumn 1662, the leading experimental scientist Christiaan Huygens wrote from The Hague thanking Moray for two books, one by Hobbes and the other by Evelyn, whom he remembered meeting several times in Sir Robert's rooms.[23] He was impressed by the sheer quantity of research in *Sculptura* and flattered to find his own work on the rings of Saturn mentioned. He was intrigued and delighted to see the mezzotint and thought he understood the basic principles of the process. Was this the same Evelyn who had promised 'un ample traité du Jardinage' (a full treatise on gardening)? If so, it would certainly be an important publication. When

15 Wenceslaus Hollar's 1667 frontispiece to Thomas Sprat's *History of the Royal Society*, showing the king (the central bust), Francis Bacon (right) and Lord Brouncker, the president of the society (left). Designed by Evelyn with John Beale's help.

Moray read out Huygens's letter at Gresham College he noticed that Evelyn blushed.[24] Public praise from such a distinguished overseas Fellow, soon to become a leading figure in the Parisian scientific world, was an accolade to treasure.

Perhaps encouraged by Huygens's high opinion of Evelyn's work to date, Moray suggested that he would be the ideal man to write the Royal Society's report on the state of the nation's timber, as requested by the commissioners of the navy. The task played to his strengths and interests as a self-proclaimed 'forester' and gave him, an industrious virtuoso, a clear role in the Royal Society. At their meeting on 15 October 1662 'Mr Evelyn reade his papers wherein he had put together the severall suggestions offered by others in distinct papers by way of Answer . . . together with his own Observations and apprehensions concerning the propagation of Timber trees'. He was thanked and asked to proceed.[25]

The resulting work, *Sylva,* was the publication by which Evelyn became best known, in his lifetime and long after, despite its genesis as a collaborative effort. His dedication to the king was dated 29 May 1663 and the Boscobel oak, where the king had sheltered after the Battle of Worcester, was given iconic importance, 'that Holy-Oak which you Consecrated with your Presence'. In fact the actual tree was soon stripped by souvenir-hunters, as if seeking relics of the True Cross. A second dedication was to the earl of Southampton, the lord high treasurer, who held the national purse strings.[26]

Prolonged consultation with the Royal Society's council delayed publication of their first official publication until February 1664.[27] Other Fellows provided material for *Sylva,* notably Christopher Merret's observations on France and Germany, John Winthrop the younger on the making of pitch and tar in New England, and Dr Jonathan Goddard on the physiology of trees. Another strand was the discussion of orchards, in a separate section titled *Pomona* in which John Beale's contribution on fruit trees was a major part. He crowned it with a rousing Latin poem, 'March on, you Cultivator, to be remembered by a future age'.[28] Beale was involved with *Sylva* every step of the way, as angry about printers' errors as if he were the author.

Sylva put the case for an enlightened transformation of the countryside that was no less ambitious than that advanced for the city in *Fumifugium.* Through its pages thread the utilitarian ideas of Samuel Hartlib, who had died in 1662, sick and disillusioned. As a pensioner of the Commonwealth, Hartlib's situation had become desperate at the Restoration, promises of help had failed to materialise and, alone amongst those who 'loved mee formerly' Evelyn lent him money. Hartlib and Beale still exchanged weekly letters but they often turned unpleasant, even becoming 'ugly arguments sometimes' – Hartlib does not reveal what their differences were.[29] Instead, Beale's attention turned to Evelyn; he used him as the outlet for his numerous ideas and concerns about the Royal Society.

With a second Dutch War likely, the nation's dependence on timber, the invaluable fossil fuel of its day, left the fleet desperately vulnerable to any interruption to supplies (from the Baltic or New England, especially) – hence the initial request from the naval commissioners to look into the national estate. Hartlib estimated that a plantation of a thousand acres of suitable trees 'would in forty years serve this Isle with Masts for ever'. Crown woodlands and forests had been successively pillaged to prop up Charles I's finances, provide perks to favourites and supply industry. They were then frequently laid waste during the Interregnum for symbolic reasons. According to Evelyn, the blame had to be divided between the 'late prodigious spoilers . . . unhappy

Usurpers and injurious Sequestrators' and the 'gallant and loyal gentry' who had added to this waste to 'preserve the poor remainder of their Fortunes'. By the Restoration there was believed to be a severe shortage of standing timber of any quality. In 1660 the official in charge of the Forest of Dean wrote miserably to the Admiralty: 'It eats my very heart and mind to see the barbarous dealings that are done in this forlorn, disowned piece of ground'. A ragbag of legislation was incompetently enforced and proved ineffective against endemic corruption.[30] Evelyn was confident that he could appeal to those who should act, above all the king himself. Carrying the imprimatur of the Royal Society, he directed his words to landowners. Instead of wasting their time on dogs, horses, racing or hunting why not consider the culture of woodland as a congenial pastime, bringing profit as well as national benefit? As Abraham Cowley had pointed out, 'old patrician trees' should stand above the 'plebeian under-wood'.

In the 1660s, just as in the 1650s, there was a need was for government action backed up, in Lindsay Sharp's words, with 'accurate information, equitable legislation and rational planning', as well as for improvements in technology and organisation. In this respect Evelyn's mixture of orotund phrases and sensible advice fell on fertile ground. The central argument was hardly new; Gervase Markham had written in *The English Husbandman* (1613) that 'there is nothing more profitable to the Husbandman, than the encreasing, and nourishing of wood'. Evelyn suggested that an orderly programme of timber management and conservation would put the economy to rights and ensure that the national defences, those 'wooden walls' that consumed such prodigious quantities of timber, were secure against imminent threat.

Some may have agreed with John Pell when he commented testily: 'I wish that some body, without any Embellishments & Flourishes, would give us the plaine precepts for planting & ordering of woods, hedge-rowes, Orchards & Gardens.' His criticism of the high-flown rhetoric and innumerable classical references in *Sylva* earned him Evelyn's unwavering enmity but others recognised that an ornate style would appeal to gentlemen and thus help it reach its target audience.[31] In fact, as Evelyn turned to the heart of the subject, the description, culture and uses of different tree species, both indigenous and imported, his tone and approach changed.

One section of *Sylva* was entirely practical. *Kalendarium Hortense* was 'but an imperfect limb' of the planned *Elysium Britannicum*, a practical monthly gardening guide, like that published by Pierre Morin (or one by Sir Thomas Hanmer which he may have read in manuscript). In 1666 the *Kalendarium* was printed separately and became Evelyn's most successful publication, running to ten editions.[32] In the words of another horticultural writer, books on gardening were rarely either small or practical, tending to be 'almost lost and smothered among Moral, Mystical and Philosophical Discourses, Quotations, and sometimes Whimsies, Crotchets, and Legendary Tales' but he considered it better to be understood by 'a Plow-man, than commended by a Scholar'.[33]

In Deptford, Mary Evelyn watched her husband transferring his experience and expertise to the page to produce 'the first learned piece published under the benigne influence of the Royall Society'. Never over-deferential, she mischievously told Samuel Tuke about her husband's 'new Almanack now under the presse foretelling the disasters of plants if not sett just in such a face and minute of the Moone, with rules and secrets how to governe plantation from the Tallest Tree to the meanest shrub'.

She also kept Tuke up to date with the alterations at Sayes Court:

> the grove is changed from a summer shade to ever greenes, the tall trees removed, arrived to some perfection, and that partly through your Industrie, the Cipresse hedge on the mount gone, and quite a new face of things, by which I observe there is noe end of improvment and that the various fancies of men have the reward of praise, when poore women are condemned for altering their dresse, or changing the patron of a gorget, and for this esteemed vain creatures.[34]

Tuke replied that he was looking forward to the new book but wondered why the trees in the grove needed to be rooted up; simply reading about it made his back ache.

Since the autumn of 1663 he had been stranded in provincial Norwich (England's largest city after London), in his supervisory role within the household of Henry Howard, the duke of Norfolk in waiting. He found the Norfolk gentry 'a nation as new to mee as the Americans'. He told Mary how much he was missing their discussions in the wooden parlour, 'even with a sea coal fire', since here 'I pass for a Witty Gentleman for such sayings as Jack would not indure'. Lucky Charles Howard was leaving his cousin's house to return to London and Gresham College, he told Evelyn.[35] Tuke was acting as an emissary for the Royal Society in Norwich, having been to visit the 'good-natured' philosopher Sir Thomas Browne (one of Evelyn's advisors on the *Elysium*), but he found him impenetrable, observing, 'we lay men cannot tell how to melt you Schollars'. Sir Thomas requested a favour of the Royal Society, a 'receipt for the preserving of the cases of birds with their feathers'.

Before his confinement in the subsiding Duke's Palace in Norwich, Tuke had his own moment of literary fame in London. His adaptation of a Spanish piece thought to be by Calderon turned into the runaway success of the play-going season.[36] Though Pepys admired it, for his part Evelyn thought the plot of *The Adventures of Five Hours* 'incomparable but the language stiffe & formall'. Nonetheless when Tuke's text was published it was garnished with verses by his friends and relations, including both John and Mary Evelyn.[37] He dedicated it to Howard and described it 'bred upon the Terrace Walks in your Garden at Aldbury; and, if I mistake not, it resembles the Place where it was Brought up: the Plot is Delightful, the Elevations Natural, the Ascents Easie, without any great Embellishments of Art'.

In the summer of 1662, while considering whether his son should join the Howard household at Arundel House (he did), John Evelyn had spent almost a fortnight at Albury, even swallowing his dislike of field sports and following a stag hunt in the park.[38] It was probably then that Evelyn seriously embarked on the redesign of the Albury gardens for Henry Howard. Then, from Norwich eighteen months later, Tuke reported that Howard wanted Evelyn's advice on 'a spring garden' in which to entertain 'the good company in the Towne'.[39] Work on the riverside public garden began during the winter of 1663/4 when Sir Thomas Browne's son reported that Howard intended 'a place for walking and recreations' and had already laid out paths 'round and crosse it, forty foot in breadth. If the quadrangle left bee spatious enough hee intends the first of them for a fishpond, the second for a bowling green, the third for a wildernesse, and the forth for a Garden.'[40] In 1681, when it must have matured well, Thomas Baskerville arrived at the duke's 'fair garden' by water and, climbing the 'handsome stairs' from the river, admired the bowling green and 'many fine walks'. Visitors were offered 'good liquors and fruits' by the gardener.[41] The long vanished garden on the Wensum was Evelyn's achievement.

In London, the Fellows of the Royal Society were taken up in their new enterprise, preparing their first authorised publications and readying themselves for a royal visit.[42] The difficulties of adequately presenting their case to the world beyond Gresham College were epitomised when Wren told Lord Brouncker that they had 'nothing proper, nothing remarkable enough' to show Charles II. They must beware of demonstrating 'onely things to raise wonder such as Keicher [Kircher] Schottus & even juglers abound with will scarce become the gravety of the Occasion', and yet must choose something 'whose use & advantage is obvious without a Lecture'. Potentially useful machines were unintelligible without explanations or demonstration: 'the key that opens treasures is often plain & rusty but unless it be gilt the key alone will make no shew at Court.' But they need not have worried, the king never came or provided them with any financial support. Evelyn's own doubts about the regime around the restored monarchy were growing, though only confided to trusted intimates such as Tuke who had asked for more of his 'politiq reflexions upon the Cabalists at Whitehall especially in that masculine stile which you are wont to treat matters of that nature'.[43]

Even before *Sylva* was printed, John Beale was pressing for an enlarged second edition. Evelyn eagerly complied, throwing his net widely, gathering information 'viva voce'. He asked Walter Pope, travelling with the trying young George Evelyn, to look out for 'any thing of new and rare which concernes Agriculture in general, and Gardning in particular' and 'enquire how the best husbands in Italy, and the Places you travell through, manage their woods and plantations, how they fell, season employ and convert these materials; and what improvements may be derivd to our Country'.[44] Almost a thousand copies of *Sylva*, nearly the entire print run, had been sold by autumn 1665. Such wide distribution of a publication brought international attention to the endeavours of the Royal Society and made public the 'conversation' between Fellows, so different from the closed world of the specialist trades, jealously guarding their secrets.

Sylva, the first book to bear the imprimatur of the Royal Society, was the work of a virtuoso Fellow and the second, *Micrographia*, was the achievement of its prodigious curator, the 'mechanick' Robert Hooke. Spectacular engraved plates recorded the minutiae of phenomena, ranging from the tip of a needle, a drop of urine and a snowflake to mould, fleas and fish scales but always noting their divine provenance. As Hooke wrote: 'the Wisdom and Providence of the All-wise Creator, is not less shewn in these small despicable creatures.' These pages were not filled with arcane speculation but with observations of the natural and man-made world, become visible through the finest available microscopic lenses.

Hooke used his preface, as Evelyn had in *Sylva*, to defend and promote the Royal Society which could already point to 'more fruits of their first three years ... then any other Society in Europe can for a much larger space of time'. When it appeared, early in 1665, *Micrographia* was a publishing sensation – word of which ran like fire through the academies of continental Europe. Like many a proud owner of a microscope, Samuel Pepys immediately bought a copy and marvelled at what he saw. Evelyn's credited contributions were his notes on the strange habits of the Italian hunting spider and a description of charcoal taken from *Sylva*.

But Evelyn may also have been instrumental in a more crucial way. The number and quality of the plates were the features which put *Micrographia* in a class of its own, yet there is no clear proof of who engraved and etched them or who paid. In 1663 Hooke told Robert Boyle that he was ordering plates, after his own drawings, hoping they would be 'very well done'. The immensely wealthy Boyle was the only man in Royal Society circles who had the surplus means to finance such a costly venture, and Robert Hooke had been his valued laboratory assistant until recently. When considering who might make the prints for the volume they doubtless turned to Evelyn, author of *Sculptura* and notable collector, for advice. The plates in *Micrographia* are evidently by various hands and in various techniques. Although Wenceslaus Hollar etched the dull image which Evelyn and Beale designed for the title page of Thomas Sprat's *History of the Royal Society* (1667) and David Loggan engraved the plates of Robert Boyle's *New Experiments and Observations Touching Cold* (1665) it seems more likely that young but excellently trained printmakers, pupils of someone like William Faithorne (who was himself, very slowly, engraving a portrait of Boyle at this date), were responsible for the illustrations to *Micrographia*, many of which are of exceptional quality.[45]

In Evelyn's mind, symmetry and order were equally desirable in architecture and in government. Henry Wotton had wisely remarked that 'plain compilements, and tractable Materials' were effective counter-balances to the 'Laberynthes and Mysteries of Courts and States'. By 1664 Evelyn felt that London 'begins to have the face of a Citie' although he wished that the king could demolish the 'ungovernable enormities' of the suburbs. Favourites at court were quick to take advantage of the situation. In 1662 the earl of St Albans had secured a Crown lease close to St James's Palace (the king's preferred seat in the capital) and converted it into a freehold. His ambitious speculative development, St James's Square, consisted of handsome town houses, with a church (on axis, to the north) and a market nearby. The earl of Southampton followed, laying out another more modest formal scheme further east, which was Southampton (later Bloomsbury) Square.

Hugh May was the architect of choice in Restoration court circles, eventually working for the king at Windsor. Evelyn followed his work closely and critically. Over the years May's clients numbered two of the newly created earls, Clarendon and Essex, the courtier Lord Berkeley of Stratton (whose London 'palace' Evelyn believed to have cost some £30,000) and more modest villas for the two men who had, respectively, overseen and supplied Charles II's financial needs while he was in exile, Sir Stephen Fox and Sir John Shaw. Samuel Pepys had frequent official dealings with May and learned that he was, like Evelyn, an advocate of simplicity in the garden. Walking up and down together at Whitehall, he told him: 'we have the best walks of Gravell in the world – France having none, not Italy; and our green of our bowling-alleys is better then any they have.'[46]

For Shaw, an English merchant based in Antwerp during the Interregnum and a close confidant of Clarendon, May designed Eltham Lodge, pleasantly sited on the rim of a saucer overlooking the Thames estuary, bearing a similar relationship to the capital as St Germain-en-Laye does to Paris.[47] Square and neat, it was in essence a Dutch classical town house translated to the leafy hills above the distant dockyards of Woolwich and Deptford. The entrance was marked by giant pilasters and an ornamented pediment, the brickwork punctuated by wafer-thin sash windows and shallow blind arches, wrapped by a heavy stone cornice under the eaves. (The core of the house was probably top-lit, with a balustraded platform above the hipped roof.)[48]

When he visited in the summer of 1664, Evelyn pronounced favourably on the well-wooded site but thought the house 'not well contrived, especialy the roofe, & roomes too low pitch'd, & Kitchins where the Cellars should be'. The first-floor rooms exploited the generous views but were dominated by their weighty compartmented ceilings. A handsome stair, ornamented by freely carved foliage and putti, took a sizeable bite out of the *piano nobile*. Eltham Lodge survives, the very image of the country seat of a Restoration magnate but not the orangery or the 'cabinet garden' and aviary upon which Shaw sought Evelyn's advice.[49] May, as Evelyn knew very well, was steeped in Dutch classical architecture and hardly bothered to adapt his designs to their English situation.[50] Evelyn may, justifiably, have felt that his own expertise deserved to be given more weight. Twenty years later, May built Sir Stephen Fox an almost identical villa in Chiswick, later known as Moreton Hall. Again Evelyn advised on the layout of the garden, despite its unsuitable site. When Lady Fox showed him the house, Evelyn was critical: 'somewhat heavy & thick; & not so well understood.'[51]

Evelyn's knowledge of the major classical treatises allowed him to spot architectural illiteracy and solecisms such as those evident in his cousin George's work at Wotton. In late 1664 his own important contribution to the available printed sources, his translation of Paul Fréart de Chambray's *Parallèle*, had finally been published, graced by excellent Dutch copies of the French engraved plates. Hugh May had secured them and persuaded Evelyn to publish it, 'to oblige the Publick, and in Commiseration of the few Assistances which our Workmen have of this Nature (compared to what are extant in other Countries)'. For that reason, Evelyn owed May a great deal. In his pages, Evelyn told readers that some material was new and 'mine own' but 'it is withal the Marrow and very Substance of no less than Ten judicious authors.'

The *Parallel* gave Evelyn architectural authority, even if, as Henry Wotton had said of himself, he was 'but a gatherer and disposer of other mens stuffe'.[52] In the dedication he equated Charles II with Augustus, patron of Vitruvius. Denham, as surveyor-general, was also a dedicatee. A treatise on building was a natural companion to one on trees: they were, Evelyn reminisced later, 'my sweet diversions during the days of destruction and devastation both of woods and buildings, whilst the rebellion lasted'.[53] Sir Richard Browne sent the earl of St Albans a copy, proudly pointing out his relationship to the translator.

The *Parallel* was ideal for a man like Roger North, a lawyer and virtuoso, who turned to architecture after a fire in the Temple in 1679. He was self taught, drawing from a model, working to scale by following 'the little practical geometry I had learnt before and . . . found the joys of designing and executing known only to such as practise or have practised it'. He owned continental architectural treatises, such as those by Palladio, Scamozzi and, later, Desgodetz, preferring the French edition of Vitruvius to the Italian one by Barbaro 'because of the great curiosity of the cuts.' But 'I found that the *Parallel* translated by Mr Evelyn gave me most clear instruction, for there were collated several designs accommodated to ocular inspection, with critical notes upon them. Hence I had a clear notion of the five orders, with their appendices.'[54] When he retired to the family seat, Rougham, in Suffolk, and began to build for himself, he had the *Parallel* beside him as well as *Sylva*.

Hugh May might have expected the plum private job of the Restoration to be his, but Clarendon House, the mansion for the king's first minister, the former Sir Edward Hyde, 1st earl of Clarendon, fell to a less prominent figure, Roger Pratt. Evelyn, who shared lodgings with him in Rome, was exceptionally intrigued by this commission. Pratt had unrivalled, first-hand knowledge of classical architecture, both *all'antica* and modern, gained over almost seven years abroad.[55] When he was appointed one of the commissioners for rebuilding London after the Fire, Pratt's cousin remarked that May and Wren 'will get more secrets of your art brought from Rome, & so from Athens, then you from them'.[56] Neither May nor Wren had immersed himself in the sites of classical antiquity as Pratt (and Evelyn) had.

Pratt's movements on his return to England are largely unknown.[57] During the Commonwealth he amassed an impressive library, particularly of architectural treatises, but he also paid three shillings to hire a coach for Lord Protector Cromwell's funeral, suggesting that he had been less of a recluse than Evelyn. Clarendon House was the *magnum opus* in a brief country house career before, as gentleman amateurs often did, Pratt retired to his own estate, Ryston in Norfolk, on marriage.[58]

If Clarendon proved no Richelieu or Mazarin in terms of state patronage, as a private client he was exceptionally involved, worrying about the expense, the weather, the phasing and myriad other details. Spending his winters indoors with punishing gout, 'it should not be unreasonable to make myselfe as much ease and pleasure ther as is possible' despite the immense financial risk ('not havinge wherewithall to finish half I goe about').[59] He had been granted the land in August 1664 and two months later Evelyn went with the Clarendons to see their 'Palace', the work of his 'old friend and fellow traveller', and 'project the Garden'. He and the lord chancellor talked far into the night and Evelyn presented him with a copy of the *Parallel*, just printed.

16 Clarendon House, seen in an early twentieth-century woodcut.

Rather more than a year later Evelyn went again, examining carefully what Clarendon was to call his 'house in the fields'.[60] Writing to Clarendon's eldest son, his friend Henry Hyde, Lord Cornbury, Evelyn even owned up to initial 'prejudice, and a critical spirit', telling him he 'had no design . . . to gratify the architect' but now admitted his unequivocal admiration for Pratt's work. Clarendon House, though still a shell, was 'without hyperbolies, the best contriv'd, the most usefull, gracefull, and magnificent house in England'. He had been into every room, from the basement cellars to the 'plat-forme on the roofe', and seeing it in its unadorned state, could vouch for the quality of the construction, testament to Pratt's professionalism, his familiarity with 'Artificers, Materyals, the places, prises, tymes where & when they are to be had'.[60] But later, in the diary, he remarked on the many defects as to the Architecture'.[61] Perhaps he had revised his opinions after Clarendon's fall.[62]

Evelyn's apparent approbation counted for much in the Hyde family. Lord Cornbury (the former Henry Hyde, currently the queen's private secretary) wrote: 'I am extremely glad you are so well pleased with our new house, your letter hath hugely satisfyed my father, he meanes very shortly to call upon you for your advice about his Garden.'[63] Their personal friendship led to Evelyn's close involvement with the remodelling of the family's country seat,

Cornbury, just outside Charlbury in Oxfordshire. They travelled there together in the autumn of 1664 with Hugh May, who would be the architect. In the only such surviving drawing in his hand, Evelyn drew a partial plan and elevations of the new stables and an annotated plan of the narrow south range of the existing house, as built by Nicholas Stone in 1632/3. He also showed the chapel with an apse and rectangular side windows, not as built (a simple rectangular box with round-headed windows).[64]

Twenty years later Evelyn recommended his son John visit the eccentric grotto and waterworks at Enstone, constructed by Bacon's secretary, Thomas Bushell, 'now repair'd' but 'above all Cornbery, at the planting of which park and fitting-out I had some hand, and fancy tis as well worth seeing as any place near Oxford'.[65] He may have hoped for even closer involvement at the time but Lord Cornbury crisply reminded him that May was in charge. All the same he had the upper hand on tree-planting – he and Cornbury shared a liking for evergreens, in the latter's opinion 'the greatest beauty that can be'. The next year, Cornbury told him, only Evelyn's responsibility as a commissioner for the sick and wounded saved him from being 'dragg'd ere this by importunity to Cornbury to finish the worke you have begunn'. Almost two thousand trees had been planted and 'I wish I could contrive some busines though never soe inconvenient to bring you hither'. They were 'very comode both in Towne & Countrey' though Cornbury wrote, seeing the political atmosphere as it turned against his father, 'perhaps too much envyed'.[66]

The visit to Cornbury gave Evelyn an excuse to go back to Oxford; he had not been there since 1654. A party led by the son of the chancellor of the University was bound to be 'handsomly entertaind', but Evelyn now came as a distinguished visitor in his own right, a Fellow of the Royal Society and benefactor of the Bodleian Library – his most recent gift was a copy of the *Parallel*, just sent to Thomas Barlow.

The most interesting and prominent new building was the Sheldonian Theatre, beginning to rise 'at an exceeding & royal Expense'. Evelyn had seen the model and claimed to have offered Wren advice.[67] The horseshoe-shaped hall, paid for by the archbishop, was intended for university ceremonial; meantime, below the dignitaries' feet the university presses would roll. Ralph Bohun, Ralph Bathurst's nephew who became John's tutor on Wren's recommendation, supervised the construction briefly and thought the 'ayry' ornament quite strange.[68] Though taken from Roman antecedents, the theatre was a surprising combination of a conventional model in novel dress. Evelyn went back to Oxford for the opening in 1669 and received an honorary degree within its walls.[69]

Satisfyingly, the empty walled enclosure of the Oxford Physic Garden of Evelyn's student days was filling with intriguing plants. Evelyn kept his eye on the gardens, and the following year, when his father-in-law was at court in Oxford during the plague, sent messages to the curator, 'old Bobart', welcoming 'any curiosity' he might care to send him for Sayes Court where the plane trees were already flourishing. Did any of the botanists he met enquire about the progress of the *Elysium Britannicum* which they had urged on so enthusiastically just a few years before? Now Evelyn's plans were for a display of exotic trees and shrubs in his new Deptford plantation, with plentiful evergreen planting. A double white syringa, more plane and lotus-tree saplings and roses would also be useful in his 'grand design'. At the end of the decade, Robert Morison, the Scot who had been in charge of the duc d'Orléans's remarkable garden (so admired by Evelyn) at Blois, was appointed professor of botany at Oxford. From then on, Morison helped the eccentric-looking Bobarts to turn the Oxford Physic Garden into one of the great botanic gardens of Europe and developed a system of accurate plant classification in parallel with John Ray in Cambridge.[70]

During his tour, Evelyn met Robert Boyle, closeted with the mathematician John Wallis and Wren 'in the Tower at the Scholes, with an inverted Tube or Telescope observing the Discus of the Sunn for the passing of [Mercury] that day before the Sunn'. They gazed upwards without success.

Evelyn and Cornbury's party returned from Oxford via Beaconsfield, perhaps stopping at Hall Barn where Waller had by now rebuilt his house and laid out a fine park, with avenues, wilderness, evergreen planting and water features.[71] Their journey culminated, the next day, in a handsome feast at the lord chancellor's house. Soon after, Evelyn casually encountered the king in the Privy Gallery at Whitehall. Charles thanked him for the copies of *Sylva* and the *Parallel*, both so useful, admiring the quality of the plates in the latter, 'the best that he had seene'. Then, asking Evelyn if he carried chalk and paper with him, the king sketched out a scheme for rebuilding Whitehall and presented him with the result.[72] He seemed to have gained, at last, both recognition and acknowledgement from Charles II, so very approachable and apparently open to new ideas.

CHAPTER 11

The Active Life

In the autumn of 1664, with *Sylva* now published, Evelyn composed a letter to Clarendon, suggesting that he might be suitable for a post that he knew to be in the offing and hoping that the lord chancellor might intercede with the king and the duke of York (the lord high admiral) on his behalf. He had a clear advantage: 'my dwelling is neere the Towne, and the ordinary station of the Navy.'[1] That October Evelyn became one of four commissioners for the sick and wounded and prisoners of war, the others being Sir Thomas Clifford, Colonel Bullen Reymes and Sir William Doyley. Captain George Cocke was the treasurer. Each was to receive an annual salary of £300.

For all his relief at finally gaining a foothold in public service, where he now envisaged his future to lie, Evelyn had grave misgivings about the wars with the Dutch, a nation he particularly admired. As usual at times of stress, he composed a prayer. 'Lord I have long desired of thee that thou wouldest choose my Employment, furnish out my person and render me use-full in something that might please thee.' He asked for divine blessing with his responsibilities in 'this unhappy war with our neighbour' and hoped to carry out his duties 'with integrity, as to his Majesties trust, and with Charity, and Tenderness as to thine; that having obtain'd the grace to be any-wayes help-full to those who are in distresse, I may be accepted, and remember'd for good'. Finally, he prayed for the victims and their relatives and, above all, for an end to the war.[2]

The commission had been appointed as a second Anglo-Dutch War seemed inevitable, following naval engagements around trading posts in West Africa and continuing hostilities between the two greatest mercantile powers. Each of the commissioners was consigned a coastal region: Clifford had Devon and Cornwall, Reymes was responsible for Hampshire and Dorset, and Doyley covered the eastern counties. Evelyn's patch was Kent and Sussex, those counties that, with Doyley's, were most likely to be overwhelmed with the injured, the sick, their dependants and prisoners of war. Engagements would be in the North Sea or the Channel: the well-used avenues of friendly trade had suddenly become the deadly field of battle. The Dutch declared war in January 1665 and the English reciprocated a month later. Hostilities began, in Evelyn's penetrating opinion, 'because the Hollander exceeded us in Industrie, & all things else but envy'.[3]

The commission met to prepare accommodation, appoint staff in each town and design administrative systems to provide medical assistance and humanitarian relief on a huge scale. Many beds in civil hospitals were requisitioned and the option of hospital ships was discussed – to little effect, only one being available at the outbreak of war. Evelyn's attitude towards Dutch prisoners of war was coloured by his sense of moral justice and the proper rules of engagement during war, but also by his admiration (shared by many others) for their nation and its achievements. Samuel Tuke pointed out from Paris that they were 'your Christian brethren though now the publick enemy. . . . The commun people in England are too apt to despise & insult our strangers and I believe the animosities are very greate.' Yet Tuke envied Evelyn's involvement – 'to have both the will & the meanes in some measure to redress the miseries of the effects'. He dreaded the aftermath: 'I believe this warr will make many Cripples & it will be a dishonour to the nation to see them hopping & begging about the streets.' This led him to enquire, he hoped not impertinently, if the London hospitals were properly run.[4] Reassured by Evelyn's reply, he added a further query: he was worried about English prisoners of war under the Dutch and hoped that teams of observers could go to inspect – 'one divine, one surgeon & a layman'.[5]

The commissioners were expected to be superhuman. Evelyn had, he told Mary, a hundred letters to write, a thousand things to do. With the simultaneous spread of plague, the nightmare worsened. In June the court left London for Oxford, the duke of York for York. Fears that sick seamen might bring disease with them ensured that doors that were previously open were suddenly shut; few would offer lodgings in such circumstances if payment was not assured. Men found themselves cast out, or simply living on the street, sometimes without even clothing. The fighting season was relatively short, but the repercussions of the hostilities were long term.

In January 1665 Mary gave birth to her fourth son, another Richard. William Glanville sent congratulations, while hoping that their next child would be a daughter, to inherit her qualities. His gifts included Rhine wine, dried lemon, some 'Lima oranges' and two canaries for Mary's room. Richard seemed absoluely healthy but only lived two months. His parents suspected 'the Nurse had over-layne him'. Once again, the family was reduced to three in number. The baby was buried with his brothers, 'my deare children', Evelyn wrote.[6]

In August Mary was well advanced in pregnancy again and she left Deptford for Wotton with young John. Evelyn longed to be with her but his movements changed by the day: 'the contagion being sadly broaken in amongst my sick-men I must settle pest ships before I stirr and allay some disorders at Chelsey.'[7] He frequently fainted under the strain. By late September, almost a year into his work with the commission, he told Mary he was 'entring upon [the] impossibilities of my Charge, which is to keepe and maintaine 3000 prisoners with nothing'. He was 'oppressd with buisinesse (the trouble & danger wheroff you can hardly imagine) but carry my life hourly in my hand'. Without his faith in God and her affection 'my heart would plainely breake'. Mary must bear up, be a comfort to her father, look after Jack and see that his tutor 'doesn't trifle with him'. Evelyn asks her not to let anyone else see his papers or the contents of his trunk – she must take some money for herself, he thinks it holds about £50 and sends her the key: 'you are my selfe, & I trust you with all, for there are some things there, I would never else have expos'd.' The letter was signed 'your most inviolably loving husband . . .'.[8]

A month later he received news of the safe and easy delivery of their latest child: a first, 'long'd for' daughter, Mary. His wife would never believe the state he was in, he wrote, 'so extreamely miserable is my condition, being thus unhappily plung'd into a Servitude, neither honorable nor safe, according to the manner we are usd'. In London the plague had brought 'nothing but desolation'. But he urged her not to delay the christening, blessing his 'full moon daughter' and hoping that the midwife and nurses 'modell her nose betimes that she do not want a handle'. At one moment he told her he had reached the end of his tether and planned to go to Oxford to confront the Privy Council – he was 'resolv'd to lay down my Comission & for reason you will approve if you wish me to live' – but then changed his mind, realising that he could not turn his back on his responsibilities, and asked instead for his black shoes and beaver hat from the secret trunk – repeating the tantalising injunction 'let none peruse my papers & privacy there'.[9]

By late October Leeds Castle, outside Maidstone in Kent, had been hired for prisoners of war, which meant that their situation was at last 'in some tollerable manner settled'. The lack of arrangements for the Dutch prisoners had jeopardised the treatment of English prisoners of war. Now the Dutch ambassador agreed to take responsibility for his own countrymen, and the English reciprocated. This agreement would help Evelyn enormously. Meanwhile 'our greate neighboure', presumably Sir George Carteret, the treasurer of the navy, had diverted £2,000 assigned for Evelyn's use at

Gravesend and Chatham, incurring the anger of the duke of Albemarle, still 'my onely fast friend'. Evelyn had no chance to petition the king before he prorogued Parliament and headed for the relative safety of Windsor or Hampton Court.[10]

Evelyn was a political innocent by comparison with those who determined national expenditure. Until now he had been no closer to government than sitting on various independent and toothless commissions, but suddenly he found himself lobbying secretaries of state for supply, while staving off the desperate demands of thousands of individuals whose collective voice he represented. This period put his personal and religious convictions to the sternest test and confronted him with harsh reality; he saw social, economic and institutional failure on all sides.

Evelyn now had little time or energy for his private pleasures and was separated from his family for long stretches. Even Wotton was now menaced as the plague crept on to Reigate and even Albury. Mary wrote tenderly:

> lett me prevaile with you as well as entreat you to take some advice . . . to your distemper, I am perswaded it proceeds partly from the spleene moved by your too great concernment for the publick, and in part by your sitting up late a nights, . . . you cannot oblige me more than by endevouring your owne preservation for what have I to value if you faile, or indeed to trust to, that can be more deare to me.

By the winter he was exhausted and unwell, telling her of his dizzy spells and fainting. He was 'so us'd to motion now that I can hardly stand still; though I desire nothing more.'[11] Yet, for all the difficulties he faced, he was, finally, an official of government. The frequent contact with officers of state, the problems that he confronted and hoped to solve, held his attention and compelled his interest.* The organisation of commission activities, from the local to the international, concentrated his mind as never before, and even under the weight of his exhausting responsibilities he revealed himself to be a first-class public servant.[12]

His daily duties involved carrying out many roles simultaneously – chasing for payment and, if successful, dispensing it, securing billets and treating the sick and wounded, as well as handling the sensitive issues surrounding foreign prisoners of war with diplomacy. In everything, the commissioners found themselves the single point of referral, administrators and intermediaries who were also required to take executive, disciplinary and even political decisions.

---

*Typically Evelyn found time to design a seal for the commission. It showed the Good Samaritan.

Physicians and surgeons, town officials, landladies and nurses, all had to be instructed in their duties and responsibilities, and then handled with tact, in view of the desperate shortage of funds. There was nothing with which to pay the men, let alone widows, orphans or dependent parents. The healthy had to be restored to the fleet, the dead buried and those who defrauded the system (including its own officers) or malingered dealt with. From locations 'scattered, in the nasty Corners of the Townes' seamen found it easy to desert after their recovery. At the same time came the plague, no longer held at bay by quarantine or the sea.

Before the war had even begun, Evelyn saw the hideously burned survivors of the *London*, shocking victims of an accident that killed hundreds and maimed many more. Throughout the two and a half years of hostilities, the human cost escalated inexorably, especially after the major engagements each summer: the Battle of Lowestoft in 1665 and the confrontation off the Downs in Kent in 1666, to which Evelyn was alerted when he heard the guns from his own garden. The former was a victory for the English, the latter a defeat. But casualty levels took little account of winners or losers. Evelyn reported 'exceeding shattring of both fleetes, so as both being obstinate, both parted rather for want of ammunition & tackle than Courage'.[13] Throughout, the commissioners exchanged terrifying anecdotes and compared horror stories, sometimes even finding humour in the situation. When Colonel Reymes ran out of brandy (the only available anaesthetic) he found himself under siege by irate nurses ('terrible scolds') who believed he had misappropriated the king's supply. Hunger affected all – English seamen and captives alike. At Winchester the sufferers were 'strangers . . . prisoners' while those at Portsmouth were 'most pitifull because sick, because natives.'[14] Reymes's reports were the most vivid; he was, like Evelyn himself, desperately moved by the human plight he witnessed.

Everything seemed to be spinning out of control. The commissioners wrote jointly from Whitehall to 'our very good friend' the mayor of Rochester about Tobias Battle, who had

not only refused to entertain any sick man in his house, but in a very vyolent manner forced them out of Doors and sett his Mastiff upon our Deputy, which has sorely Bitten him to the great hurt of the said Mr Stephens and prejudice of his Majesties Service as it concernes the sick, and the discouragement of our said officer who is expressly impower'd by order of his Majesties Privy Councill to Quarter the sick in all Convenient places.[15]

Nonetheless, Evelyn, ever the note-taker, proved remarkably efficient, an example to his colleagues. Samuel Pepys, the chief administrator at the Navy Office, in his role as clerk of the acts, reported to Sir William Coventry (secretary to the Admiralty) that he had just been to visit him: 'I find that if the rest of his companions take the same course he doth, they will save the King a very considerable sum in the remedy.' Evelyn showed him the accounts for Gravesend, 'where for every penny he demands allowance for, and for every sick man he hath had under his care, he shews you all you can wish for in columns'. Pepys enclosed an example. 'I dare say you will say with me he deserves great thanks.' A few days before, at Sayes Court, the two men had discussed 'our confounded business of prisoners and sick and wounded seamen, where he and we are so much put out of order'.[16] Pepys had already visited Sayes Court twice, and admired Evelyn's glass beehive, but the two men's paths now crossed at the Royal Society, where Pepys became a Fellow in February 1665. That autumn the plague drove Pepys's office down river and he lodged for a while in Greenwich with Captain Cocke's friend William Glanville, Evelyn's brother-in-law. (A mistress, Mrs Bagwell, whose husband was a ship's carpenter, was another attraction for Pepys at the Deptford docks.) The dealings between the two diarists were initially a blend of business and pleasure but soon matured into a lifelong friendship built on shared interests.

In his efforts as a commissioner, Evelyn could count on the wholehearted support of George Monck, the earl of Albemarle. He found presentation volumes had their uses, offering a pretext for an audience and usually leading to a face-to-face meeting. However, Albemarle was too busy to receive his copy of *Sylva* personally. Evelyn sent a note; he did not presume to 'instruct your Grace, who is already so greate a Master in this laudable and princely Industry' but hoped his tactful efforts to turn the English gentry to 'solid improvements' would receive his support. Since Albemarle was so close to the throne, Evelyn carefully distanced himself from any taint of radicalism, asserting defensively: 'I have nothing to answer for the Cider-part beyond a Praeface, they being Papers I was orderd to Insert.'[17] 'Pomona' was largely Beale's work and Evelyn perhaps felt it promoted the old reformist agenda of Hartlib and others.

That November, in Oxford, where the court had moved to avoid the plague, Albemarle pleaded his case to the new Lord Arlington with all the force at his command.

Mr Evelyn being come to Oxford to attend your Lordships about a supply of monies for the sick seamen & soldiers & Dutch prisoners (who are in very great necessity) I desire your Lordship will give him all possible expedition in his business . . . and the sooner he has his Dispatch for more Monies it will be the better. But I cannot see any way how hee can be sooner supplyed unlesse the Lords Commissioners will help him out of the prisoners.[18]

In 1666, Prince Rupert and Albemarle replaced James, duke of York, and the earl of Sandwich (now ambassador in Madrid) as joint commanders of the fleet. With the entry of the French into the war alongside their Dutch allies, a second front opened, splitting the English navy in two (with disastrous consequences) and adding a second wave of prisoners of war – and another round of negotiations about their treatment.

As the commissioners struggled to convert any sizeable empty building into makeshift hospital accommodation, it became clear that nothing was more essential (or economical) than purpose-built lodgings for the suffering men. Doyley had improvised hospitals in existing buildings at Ipswich and Harwich, as had Reymes at Porchester Castle. Evelyn squeezed thirty beds into a barn at Gravesend, and added space at Chelsea Hospital and Leeds Castle. At the first intimation of the major battle in June 1665, Evelyn petitioned for the use of the Savoy Hospital. But even with extra provision in London's civilian hospitals, the available accommodation was woefully inadequate.

It was obvious that a dedicated naval hospital was essential. In the absence of any evidence of any government action, and under mounting pressure, Evelyn took it upon his own shoulders to look for a site at Chatham and began to consider possible plan forms, plumping for the collegiate or almshouse pattern of an enclosed quadrangle. It was an opportunity to pull together his considerable knowledge of continental public buildings and to test his own growing architectural expertise. Of all the models he had in mind, the Soldaatenhuise in Amsterdam, with its wards reputedly built by Queen Elizabeth I for injured English soldiers, was 'for state order & accommodations one of the worthiest things that I thinke the world can show of that nature'.[19] Travelling with Pepys in late January 1666, Evelyn 'intertained me with discourse of an Infirmery which he hath projected for the sick and wounded seamen against the next year, which I mightily approve of – and will endeavour to promote, it being a worthy thing – and of use and will save money'. By the time Pepys was hearing about them, Evelyn's plans were well developed.

Philip Packer of Groombridge was a strongly royalist friend, a contemporary from Oxford and a colleague at the Royal Society. In 1668, having been his deputy, he assumed Hugh May's position as paymaster of the works. At New Year 1666 he invited Evelyn to Henrietta Maria's former palace, Nonsuch at Epsom, which had housed the exchequer since the previous

summer's plague, and where he and his brother currently shared the position of usher. Although much damaged and with its garden laid to ruin, a
handsome avenue survived, 'a[n] Elme and a Walnutt set one after
another in order', as Pepys described it. Packer showed Evelyn round the
exotic old house, ornately decorated with a Renaissance theme of 'heathen
gods' and glittering with expensive materials, lead and gilt.[20] Admiring this
damaged folly, they began to work out the form and organisation of the naval
hospital.

After that, Evelyn (and perhaps Packer too, as a friend of the family) went
to join his brothers, their wives, children and friends for a well-deserved
break. They spent several days together with 'extraordinary mirth & cheere.
. . . after much sorrow & trouble during this Contagion, which separated
our families'.[21] The conversation about the Chatham hospital continued.
Afterwards, Richard congratulated his brother:

> I perceive . . . [the] proiect of the Infermary design'd at Woodcott hath so
> . . . pleased his Majestie that he hath ordered the finishing . . . with speede,
> Mr Packer indeede wrote me word of meeting you at Chatham, & I now
> understand the occasion, I [doubt?] not, but his Invention, ioyned with
> your Direction will advance the Designe to be no lesse Profitable to the
> abatement of . . . than Charitable for the Relief of the Distressed.[22]

Sir Richard Browne advised Evelyn to hurry to present 'your infirmary' to the
king but sounded a warning: 'The King borrows money of all his servants.
Lord Arlington hath brought in 2000, Mr. Williamson 500, Mr Chiffing
500.'[23] Meanwhile Evelyn's deputy from Gravesend wondered if he had yet
been to Hampton Court, where the king now was, to show him 'the proposals
we discussed'. Four days later, at the end of January 1666, he went and was
invited to return, presumably to present the scheme in greater detail. There
was no time to lose: money was disappearing before everyone's eyes and the
fighting season was coming.

To date, the only institution that Evelyn had designed was the paper
college he discussed with Robert Boyle in 1659. Evelyn's keen eye, sharpened
during his travels and informed by his continuously expanding print collection, as well as his recent translation of Fréart's *Parallèle* and the building
works at Sayes Court, enabled him to hold his own with the architects in his
circle, Pratt, May and Wren in particular. But when it came to design he was,
as he often admitted, deficient in geometry. His hospital design was a rudi-
mentary ground plan for a vast quadrangle, for which he apologised when he
sent it to Pepys.[24] But he had an expert grasp of the arrangements and the
finances. If it housed five hundred inmates, the king's initial outlay of £1,400

would be reimbursed within fifteen weeks, based on the savings made by cancelling alternative accommodation. He expanded upon the practical and moral advantages, including the treatment of the sick under one roof, the ease of administration and the encouragement of temperance. In peacetime, the building could revert to a workhouse. Meanwhile 'the clamours of landladys etc. to the reproch of the service will be taken away', and a proper record could be kept of those who entered and who were discharged as healthy, fit to return to active service at sea. The building would be an engine of national and economic efficiency.

The duke of York promised to pass the detailed scheme on to the king and, clearly impressed, suggested a second hospital be built at Harwich. On 17 February Browne reported that 'Lord Arlington much desires to be fully informed of all the whole concerning the Hospital which he says shall be speedily put in hand; whatever shift is made for money'. But when Evelyn met the commissioners to the navy they gave him a different message, despite their strong support for his scheme. They were realists and 'saw no money'. Evelyn dined with Pepys afterwards, who no doubt reinforced that message.

From the Palace of Whitehall, where the court was now reinstalled after six months in Salisbury and Oxford, Browne encouraged Evelyn to hurry to Chatham 'to set out the ground & to proceed with all diligence'. The search for a location was complicated but Commissioner Pett helped and 'we at last pitch'd on a Field call'd the Warren', facing north, at a suitable distance from the town, with fresh water and good chalk foundations. Evelyn gave Pepys detailed estimates: brick could be produced on site and timber bought at a good rate.[25] Even with the project scaled down from five to four hundred occupants, the savings would be enormous. Somebody must have advised him on the costs and quantities, perhaps a fellow member of the 1662 Commission or that skilled mathematician and surveyor, the curator of the Royal Society Robert Hooke?

Evelyn's hospital would transform the wretched men's lives, providing 'honorable, Charitable, and frugal Provision; Effectual, full of Encouragement, and very practicable'. He hoped that a decision would be taken by the autumn, since the facilities at Chatham and Rochester alone had cost the king £13,000 in 'cures and quarters' over eighteen months.

With a touch of justifiable pride, Evelyn apologised to Dr Wilkins for his continued absence from the Royal Society, 'particularly that I cannot be there of Wednesday; his Majestie having enjoyn'd me to repaire to morrow to Chatham, for the taking order about erecting an Infirmary capable to enter-taine 500 sick Persons and all to be finishd against the next occasion'. If the king dropped the project Evelyn would be 'an intollerable looser, by being so long diverted from a Conversation so profitable, and so desirable'.

Occasionally, he told Wilkins (for even 'Warrs ... will have a period'), he had a moment for 'Philosophy; but it is so little and jejune, as I despaire of satisfaction 'till I am againe restored to the Society'.[26]

Spring 1666 signalled renewed hostilities and heavy demands for supply. Nothing more was said of the Chatham project – Evelyn's passionately conceived scheme was buried beneath an avalanche of weightier documents and more pressing problems. But, despite the disappointment, it was an invaluable exercise for the future. In the short term, the most visible outcome of his campaign was the appointment of an extra commissioner, Sir George Downing, with specific responsibility for the inspection of hospitals. Evelyn distrusted him personally, noting that Downing, once penniless, was now suspiciously rich; but the addition of another well-connected official to their team was welcome.[27] By the autumn of 1666, two years into the war, the commissioners were responsible for a permanent army of invalids, as well as the exchange and repatriation of prisoners and the increasingly pressing need to settle accounts. On many occasions they had to dip into their own pockets to prevent catastrophe. The satisfaction Evelyn had felt on becoming, finally, a servant of the restored monarch had evaporated. Tuke tried to stiffen his resolve. 'Cousin faint not in your undertaking, nor proiect your retirement to your house of pleasure, there is greate need of such men as you are in the publike charges of our Contrie and by the example of our glorious cheefe wee are assur'd that the active life is to be preferd to the contemplatife.'[28]

The end of the war the following summer was brought about by an act of extraordinary bravado, which took place almost under Evelyn's nose. In June 1667 the Dutch attacked the fleet as it lay at anchor at Chatham, 'by a most audacious enterprise entering the very river . . . doing us not onely disgrace, but incredible mischiefe in burning severall of our best Men of Warr'.[29] Led by the great admiral Michael de Ruyter, the man who had led the Dutch fleet in confrontation with the English off the coast of West Africa not long before, they had broken the chain across the Medway and slipped through the barricade intended to prevent any such incursion. Once there, they set fire to several English vessels, capturing and hauling home the *Royal Charles*, the frigate which had brought the king triumphantly back from exile. The flagship of the fleet was flauntingly displayed before being scrapped but its counter, bearing the royal arms, was preserved – and can be seen at the Rijksmuseum to this day. The Dutch States General presented their fearless admiral with a souvenir, a gilded goblet ornamented with scenes of the Medway, the towns and forts on the river's banks acting as a backdrop to the blazing hulls and wrecked ships in the water. Had it been built, Evelyn's hospital might have been a feature of the panorama.

Since the Dutch had managed to sail unchallenged into the Medway and devastate the English fleet, it was feared that they might extend their adventure further up the Thames. Evelyn thus organised the dispersal of his most important possessions; hardly had he returned to Deptford than the dockyard went up in flames. At Sayes Court, as in Deptford itself, there was panic. Inevitably the finger of suspicion was pointed at the Dutch, but the fire quickly proved to be an accident. Afterwards Evelyn went to Chatham, 'to view not onely what Mischiefe the Dutch had don, but how triumphantly their whole Fleete, lay within the very mouth of the Thames . . . a Dreadfull Spectacle as ever any English men saw, & a dishonour never to be wiped off'. Evelyn, as did everyone, blamed those who had persuaded the king to leave the fleet at anchor that spring, especially Clarendon.

He made a sketch of the engagement for Pepys, which he said had been 'taken on place', above Gillingham, over 10, 11 and 12 June: 'Such a sight I wish no Englishman may ever see againe.' Pepys took his share of the blame for laying up the navy for economic reasons and joked that Evelyn's drawing should replace the tapestries commemorating the Armada in the House of Lords, to mortify everyone concerned.[30]

Although the *Royal Charles* was now a trophy in the Netherlands, Admiral de Ruyter's success had been more symbolic than practical. The nation was shocked by the impudence of the act, disturbing proof of Dutch supremacy on the water. The relationship between the two premier trading nations, competitors for the merchandise of much of the known world, was now both placatory and mutually suspicious. In London, the attentions of the mob fell on the lord chancellor's sparkling new palace, Clarendon House, reducing its gleaming sash windows to shards of broken glass and its newly planted trees to stumps. The king apart, no man was more closely associated with the disaster than the first minister; the blame was laid firmly at Clarendon's door.

Though a peace was signed at Breda that summer, Evelyn's cares and responsibilities dragged on. From May 1667 all accounts had to be authorised by the Treasury, slowing the process further still; two years later he was called upon to explain the Commission figures, despite his reputation as a skilled bookkeeper. It emerged that the commissioners' own treasurer, Captain Cocke, had his hand deep in the till. He was tried at the Guildhall in 1670.[31] The books were not finally closed until 1675. The single certainty that Evelyn held to throughout these painful tests of his probity and competence was the importance of creating an institution that could house and care for the human casualties of war: a national naval hospital.

Evelyn had won his spurs and now other offices fell his way. He was one of a number of virtuosi who were judged suitable for office, being versatile, discriminating and widely informed in matters both artistic and intellectual.[32]

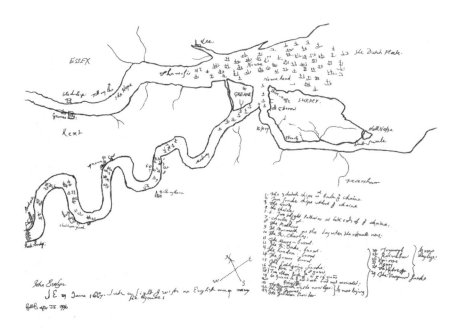

17 Evelyn's drawing, sent to Pepys in early 1668, showing the Dutch incursion into the Medway at Chatham in June 1667 'as it appear'd to me from the Hill above Gillingham'.

Later he was appointed, successively, a commissioner for trade and plantations, for the sick and wounded during the Third Dutch War, and for the Privy Seal. Even an old petition dating back to 1662 – for a place on the 'Commission set on foot for making saltpetre, to prevent fraud and ease grievances' on the grounds that his great-grandfather and grandfather were pioneers in the manufacture which 'continued in the family till the decease of the late King' – was finally granted in the summer of 1666.[33] He joined colleagues from the ordnance (several of whom he knew well), as well as Jonas Moore, in 'regulating the farming & making of Salt-peter through the whole Kingdome'.[34]

But the termination of the Second Dutch War allowed Evelyn to withdraw from public life for some time and revert to more congenial tasks. John Beale was glad that *Elysium Britannicum* 'draws to a conclusion' and that Evelyn was pressing on with a new edition of *Sylva*. He urged him to finish with naval matters so that he might 'unlock the best cabinets'; for he saw Evelyn as an excellent communicator of their shared interests – 'cabinets' containing many different topics.[35] Praise for *Sylva* had come from many directions. Joseph Glanville heard that thousands of trees had been planted: 'a very hopefull, & incouraging success of your generous Labours; And I doubt not but this will

tend very much to the advantage of the Nation, as well as to your glory &
reputation.'[36]

Evelyn's garden at Sayes Court had started to become a kind of outdoor
salon, an extension of London's literary and intellectual life. Sayes Court was
neither city (now so tainted by the court) nor country, often the graveyard of
intelligent life – as the gaggle of increasingly sottish nephews and cousins at
Wotton proved. His old friend from Paris, Abraham Cowley knew nobody
who 'possesses more private happiness than you do in your garden; and, yet
no man, who makes his happiness more public, by a free communication of
the art and knowledge of it to others'.[37]

Visitors poured into Sayes Court, so convenient to royal Greenwich.
Queen Henrietta Maria, the earl of St Albans (Henry Jermyn), Clarendon,
finally even the king himself came in spring 1663, 'viewing the Gardens &
even every roome of the house'. (His visit was probably in connection with the
restitution of the Sayes Court leases to Browne and Evelyn that summer.)[38]
From abroad came old Constantijn Huygens (father of Christiaan) while
Samuel Pepys even visited in Evelyn's absence, so impatient was he to see the
results of his naval colleague's passion for horticulture.[39] Everything visitors
saw bore the marks of Evelyn's gradual fulfilment of his ambitious overall
scheme. The 1653 plan had shown a kind of idealised perfection whereas the
reality was inevitably more the result of trial and error, of unpredictable
weather and continual experiment, of financial limitations and the variable
competence of gardeners. In autumn 1664 at least forty of the elms he had
planted that spring were stolen (he implied by the same nurserymen who
supplied them), reappearing in Greenwich Park: 'it is a base and dishonest
thing . . . selling to you the last year 5L worth of Trees and stealing of them
the next.' If it happened again, Evelyn said he would complain to the king.[40]

Evelyn's friendship with Abraham Cowley was reinforced by the exchange
of plants and verses, and reciprocal garden visits. Henry Jermyn's secretary at
the court of Queen Henrietta Maria in Paris, by 1654 Cowley had returned
to study botany and medicine at Oxford, where he became a friend of Dr
William Harvey. Now the man celebrated by Thomas Sprat as the 'English
Ovid' moved from Barn Elms, in Barnes on the Thames, south-west of
London, down river to Chertsey in Surrey. Evelyn celebrated, in his own
awkward poem, Cowley's withdrawal, musing that if he were, like Cowley,
master of his own life, he would not be envious of the poet,

> Under the Chertsean Platane, free
> From Noysie Worldes, ambitious Care
> And empty Shew.[41]

Cowley owed his life of literary rusticity to the continued patronage of Jermyn and George Villiers, the 2nd duke of Buckingham.[42] Though he had been in 'daily sight of greatness', nothing altered his views about 'the paint of that kind of life', the poison of adulterated beauty. Cowley's essay and poem *The Garden* (1666) was dedicated to Evelyn and celebrated both him and Mary. Evelyn returned the favour in his *Kalendarium Hortense*. Cowley's only ambition was to be 'master at last of a small house and large garden, with very moderate conveniences', but he found himself confined to a rented house and garden 'among weeds and rubbish: and without that pleasantest work of human industry, the improvement of something which we call . . . our own'. But he was honoured to have his name attached to 'the epistle you are pleased to prefix to the most useful book that has been written in that kind, and which is to last as long as months and years'. Evelyn also intended that Cowley's words should be included in his 'other Worke on this Argument', *Elysium Britannicum*. Freed from his punishing schedule as a commissioner, he was, once again busy with the great project.

From late 1667 onwards, he reestablished contact with Sir Thomas Hanmer (the prince of florists as Evelyn referred to him) and sent him the latest outline, including the chapter on flowers. Hanmer recommends John Rea's *Flora, seu De florum cultura* but comments that the author's ignorance of languages is a limitation. He promises to send him various notes of his own on flowers such as 'Tulips, Anemones, Narcissi, Beares Eares [Auricula]'. How long, he asks, is Evelyn's book to be and how will he illustrate it?[43]

But Evelyn's next venture in print *Publick Employment and an Active Life Prefer'd to Solitude . . . In Reply to a Late Ingenious Essay of a Contrary Title* (1667), was a contribution, in Cowley's words, to 'one of the noblest controversies both modern and ancient'. Sir Robert Moray had suggested that Evelyn reply to the anonymous *A Moral Essay, Preferring Solitude to Publick Employment, and All it's Appanages; such as Fame, Command, Riches, Pleasures, Conversation &c.* (1665, reissued under George Mackenzie's name in 1666).[44] Evelyn's friends, and Cowley in particular, were initially surprised to find him arguing for the active life. 'You had reason to be astonish'd at the presumption . . . that I, who have so highly celebrated Recesse, and envied it in others, should become an Advocate for the Enemie, which of all others it abhors and flies from.' Evelyn reassured Cowley that his views were unchanged and his admiration for his friend, who had never 'given hostages to fortune, nor obliged your selfe to the formes and impertinences of my manner of life', was undimmed. 'But as those who prays'd dirt, a flea, and the gowte, so have I Publiq Employment.'[45]

Evelyn dedicated *Publick Employment* to Sir Richard Browne, an exemplary public servant who retained his probity, remaining faithful to his monarch and nation despite personal hardship and privation. Browne had always had 'infinite contempt of Vanity and gilded appearances'. He was a model, an example to fellow office-holders, 'and if that have been the chief design of this little Piece to declare it to the World, I attain my Purpose'.

The exchange between Mackenzie, a rising young Scottish lawyer, and the middle-aged English virtuoso and public servant was no more than a bit of rhetorical duelling backed up by ancient authorities – a light-hearted literary joust.[46] They even chose the same man to argue their respective cases. For Mackenzie, Robert Boyle showed how 'there is such a kind of difference betwixt virtue, shaded by a private, and shining in a publick life, as there is betwixt a candle carryed aloft in the open air, and inclosed in a lantern'. The former gives more light but is bound to be extinguished. In response, Evelyn argued 'there lives not a Person in the World, whose moments are more employ'd then Mr Boyles, and that more confirms his contemplations by his actions and experience'.[47]

Evelyn and Mackenzie exchanged admiring letters, although they did not actually meet until 1689. Most copies of Mackenzie's pamphlet had been destroyed in the Great Fire and now Evelyn hoped that Royston would reprint it, since readers needed both sides of the argument. Mackenzie, later lord advocate of Scotland, was flattered. He found it strange to face such a kindly opponent but, he wondered a little pointedly if Evelyn's flattery was like the Romans dressing their prisoners in fine clothes 'that therby they might adorn so much the more these ther triumphs'.[48]

Against a background of loss and suffering in the Dutch Wars, and a foreground of a decadent court (described by George Evelyn as 'very gay & splendid, wholy diverted to Mascarading minding no business which means a prospect of sad consequences; the nation untimely ruined'), it was a good time, as Moray had intimated, to discuss serious matters.[49]

Evelyn argued that ''tis a grand mistake to conceive, that none are employ'd, but such as are all day on horse-back, fighting battels, or sitting in Tribunals: What think you of Plow-men and Artificers? nay the labours of the Brain that excogitates new Arts and produce so many useful things for human society.' As usual, he argued the Royal Society's case. For instance, if anyone dared to criticise that model Fellow, Robert Boyle: 'I can assure him, there is nothing more publick, than the good he's always doing.'[50]

Evelyn conceded that those who used their office for gain undermined his argument. But God did not sit still, as Mackenzie implied, but was constantly 'Creating, Preserving, and Governing'. In the same way no nation could be passive; 'the Commonwealth is an assembly regulated by active Laws, maintain'd by Commerce, disciplin'd by Vertue, cultivated by Arts', without which it would fall into 'universal confusion and solitude'. Calm waters are stagnant.

Money must circulate: when great men build they employ lesser men. Set against those who shoulder responsibility in Evelyn's vision is the country gentleman, pleasing himself with tobacco and good food, sitting on a cushion picking his teeth. The detached contemplative man is no more than a ghost in a churchyard, so deep in his books that he ignores his starving family.

His son's tutor Ralph Bohun received a copy of *Publick Employment* in March and was very complimentary, despite balking at 'two or 3 adopted words which nevertheless are so few that I shall not bee implacable' (Evelyn was much given to inventing words, oddities such as 'apodemick' or 'indenizon'). He liked the 'spirit & heat' of the argument, which suggested Evelyn was 'more confirm'd to the former method then your own, but thats easily excusable in answering bookes'. Bohun wrote that some considered Evelyn had been

> too kind to so neare a kinsman, but it seems to me not so much a pane-
> gyrick to Sir Richard, as a soft vindication of his fidelity to the church, for
> I know many courtiers that represent him as no enemy to the reformed
> church of France which I supose was occasion'd by the ungratefull clergy
> which he kept from starving at Paris. And I thinke you have rescued his
> honour in a most handsome & cleanly manner.[51]

At the time of its publication, Sir Robert Moray (an equally exemplary public servant) was in Scotland, sent to contact the Presbyterian rebels and offer a pardon. He teased Evelyn that his words had stirred up his passions: 'Therefore in stead of flying out like lightning upon the wanton & tempting language by which you assault my humility, my sobreity, my ingenuity & my unconcernednesse, exciting me to pride, vanity, ambition & affectation, I do but smile upon the liberty of your pen, and commend the pretty texture of your ingenious words.' By way of antidote, he would happily 'confine my self to that little world that goes under the name of Says Court, and there not court the most courted glories of our Terrestial planet' but instead take pleasure in joining 'the two luminaries that keep up a perpetuall spring in that rich place'.[52]

As Moray and others detected, the tract was subtly critical of the political regime: 'to conserve ones self in a Court, is to become an absolute Hero.' One morning in April 1667, Evelyn and Samuel Pepys met in Westminster Hall and walked about together for two hours, discussing, not for the first time, the 'badness of the Government, where nothing but wickedness, and wicked men and women command the King. That it is not in his nature to gainsay anything that relates to his pleasures.' Like Pepys, Evelyn was repelled by the remorseless rise of favourites, male and female, and the king's restless, easily distracted character. For a monarch who paid such close attention to choosing birds for his aviary, frivolity was all. Evelyn told Pepys that even the king of France was said to mock Charles's weakness in the face of his mistresses's greedy claims, both for themselves and their children.

By the time of the Treaty of Dover, signed secretly by the king and his French sister in 1670, the country seemed in terminal decline, the court sliding towards Catholicism. Even Thomas Clifford, under Arlington's patronage, and by 1667 at the Treasury, was said to be tending that way, as was Anne Hyde, duchess of York.[53] However worrying the march of Catholicism, if there was political patronage to be had, Evelyn needed to stay in view.

For Evelyn and Pepys, business meetings regarding naval matters were liable to slide into congenial conversations about books, prints, gardening, architecture and music. Evelyn knew he could be off-putting. 'They say'd I had a forbidding Countenance, and were in earnest a fraide of me; Some take me for a Schole Master.'[54] But Pepys, who in January 1666 had suggested both Evelyn and Moray as potential new members of the navy board, impressed by the former's conscientious performance as a commissioner, realised that beneath Evelyn's apparent self-satisfaction was a man both more entertaining and less conceited than might at first be thought, even if his poetry and plays left much to be desired. Soon he was 'desirous of keeping my acquaintance with him'. After walking around the garden at Sayes Court with Evelyn 'with mighty pleasure' on a spring day, Pepys (never tolerant of bores) decided 'the more I know him the more I love him'.[55]

Browne's position at Whitehall meant that Evelyn was well informed about goings on there. The monarch's principal advisors, Albemarle, Clarendon and Southampton, were sick, older men who were being superseded by 'young rogues' while the bishops were held at arm's length. The follies at court, the ups, downs and astonishing extravagances of royal mistresses, and all the gossip besides were known in Deptford. The fastest-rising star was Arlington (the former Henry Bennet), 'much more to be made one's patron then my Lord Chancellor, who never did nor will do anything but for money'. This unusually negative judgement was offered by Evelyn in his disappointment at the continued failure to settle his father-in-law's claims. In Whitehall there was not even enough money to supply paper for Privy Council meetings.[56] By contrast, Evelyn believed Louis XIV to be the very model of a king, telling Pepys 'how great a prince he is'. On the subject of the French monarchy Samuel Tuke's regular letters, 'setting aside frailties, Speculative Disputes, and some different apprehensions of things', were a useful source.[57]

Although Evelyn's continual barbs about Tuke's Catholicism sometimes threatened to poison their exchanges, they were always frank with one another. 'I understand not your vision of the Jesuits but you are so unfriendly to that Order that suggestions pass with you for adumbrations,' Tuke wrote. Even Evelyn's translation of a couple of French anti-Jesuit pamphlets (apparently done at Clarendon's request), which included an attack upon the 'wild fanatics of the Romish fashion' had not jeopardised their friendship.[58] Evelyn allowed himself to be intrigued by the Catholic baptism of Tuke's son Charles at Somerset House, attended by 'many odd Ceremonies, Spittle & anointings' – like the Jewish ceremonies he had observed in Venice and Amsterdam, utterly remote from his own experience but of arcane interest. When Tuke remarried the links between their families grew stronger. His second wife, Mary (Sheldon), who lived with them for some months in 1668 and was in 'every way worthy of him', became Mary Evelyn's closest friend. She told Ralph Bohun, who was far more anti-Catholic than her husband, that Lady Tuke had spent seven years as a canoness (a kind of nun, without the vow, she explained) but was the best of company: 'I am apt I confesse to enlarge the Characters of those I esteeme, but to be just to the merit of this person I aught to say much more.'[59]

George Evelyn wrote to his brother in the summer of 1667, remarking on the 'changes & vicissitudes of things & persons'. News of Clarendon's difficulties was spreading:

the Storme that is unexpectedly fallen upon the great man your noble freind, makes us at this distance & so great a stranger to the intrigues of Court to stand amaz'd & wonder; wee heard his seale was taken from him, but by a later intelligence tis assured us tis yet continued to him – however being upon the Question & heaved att, I feare he wilbee hardly able to weather this out.

George appealed to his brother to 'unriddle this mystery of state'.[60] The clues were all there in Andrew Marvell's *The Last Instructions to a Painter*, dated 4 September 1667.[61] In this verse satire Marvell laid about the court, 'this race of drunkards, pimps and fools', opening his devastating group portrait with the earl of St Albans, 'full of soup and gold,/ The new court's pattern, stallion of the old'. The king's mistress Lady Castlemaine, Arlington, Buckingham, even Clarendon's sons, Henry and Laurence Hyde (respectively Lords Cornbury and Rochester), all come in for ridicule but it is Clarendon himself, and the events of that disastrous summer, culminating in his dismissal by Charles ('The wondrous night the pensive King revolves,/ And rising straight on Hyde's disgrace resolves') that are the subject of the poem.

Evelyn had known Clarendon during both the best and the worst of times. He owed him a great deal for his discreet but crucial support for the Royal Society's charter and for his own appointment as a commissioner. In return

Clarendon had taken advice from Evelyn, who was eleven years younger than he, on the architecture and landscaping of his family seats, his portrait collection and his library. Evelyn was a close friend of Lord Cornbury and his wife and, though aware of the growing feeling against Clarendon at court, was shocked by his peremptory removal from office and the ease with which the king abandoned him after twenty years of loyal service.

Clarendon's downfall had begun with his daughter's marriage to the duke of York. Now, the queen being childless, the likelihood was that the York children would succeed to the throne. In 1667, his troubles escalated. A few months after the Clarendons moved into their sumptuous house, the countess died and Clarendon was facing impeachment by parliament. A combination of specific charges, including the blame for the Dutch invasion at Chatham, as well as growing distrust for a man who had held power too long, and appeared to be amassing great wealth, allowed his enemies, especially the so-called 'Cabal', to prevail with the king. Clarendon's loyal supporters, such as his son-in-law the duke of York and the duke of Ormonde, could not influence events. By the end of August, Clarendon found himself utterly bereft, having lost his wife, his office and his king. When Evelyn visited him in these days he found him 'in his bed Chamber very Sad' – a broken man.

In the diary, written later, Evelyn commented that Clarendon's end was hastened since 'he made few friends during his grandure among the royal Sufferers; but advanced the old rebells, that had money enough to buy places' – inferring that he had not favoured loyal cavaliers but sold favours to turncoats. Nevertheless he admired Clarendon's old-fashioned virtues, believing in 'the forme & substance of things in the nation' unlike the court, 'the boufonnes & Ladys of Pleasure'.[62]

To Evelyn, Clarendon was 'my particular kind friend on all occasions' and dining with him the next day, he was shocked to find how quickly 'many of his friends & Sycophants abandon'd him'.[63] Now stripped of rank and means, Clarendon's debts mounted, an immense burden for the next generation.

Always examining his soul in preparedness for the next life, Evelyn found his worries exacerbated by Clarendon's fall:

> O Lord, I have Built and Repair'd my House, being thereto engaged by little & little, partly out of necessity & decency, and so by degrees too much for pomp, ostentation, seacret vanity and profusion beyond my quality, even to the wronging of my fortune and much disabling thy Servant from performing other more necessary duties, incumbent on me.[64]

There was a fine line between the style proper to a leading servant of the state and the grandiose ostentation that came with power. Evelyn's education had taught him that 'a brave and generous soule [with] the advantages of Birth or Laudable Acquisition' could be a force for good.[65] He would give the same advice to his own son, ensuring that he served his country: 'I designe him not for a Gallant, but an usefull and honest man.'[66]

Yet not all of Evelyn's acquaintances met his clear criteria concerning what constituted that 'useful and honest' life. No one confused the picture more than Margaret Cavendish, since 1666 the duchess of Newcastle. Having known the Cavendishes well in Paris, Evelyn was eager to re-establish the connection when they returned from the north to their Clerkenwell mansion, Newcastle House. He became a regular visitor, and twice took Mary. Everywhere the eccentric Margaret went her demeanour and dress ensured that she turned heads. In fact she had to be seen to be believed, Sir Charles Lyttelton wrote, 'dressd in a vest, and, insteed of courtesies, [she] made leggs and bows to the ground with her hand and head'.[67] The duke of Buckingham wrote that the Newcastles 'are Persons of fine Parts/And have peculiar ways of gaining Hearts'.[68]

Samuel Sorbière had formed his impression of 'English books, by the learned collection he carried over with him of the works of that thrice noble Marchioness', Evelyn pointed out witheringly in 1664.[69] But now his sarcasm had somersaulted into sycophancy. The duchess was the first woman guest of the Royal Society, inviting herself despite being a critic of Boyle and Hooke.[70] Evelyn had never encountered such an assertive woman and decided she was another Zenobia, the warrior queen of Palmyra. Mary, on the other hand, found her farcical and insincere. As the tree-felling and lavish entertainments had continued at their northern estate, Welbeck, no word came of the £1,000 promised to Elizabeth Browne after the Newcastles' wedding in Paris, which would have been such a fitting (and welcome) tribute to her mother's good offices. Yet William Cavendish had accepted a dukedom and absolved the king of Crown debts owed since 1639.* Adding insult to injury, Margaret now called Mary 'daughter' – she said, in acknowledgement of Lady Browne's kindness.

Seething, Mary wrote to Ralph Bohun, and copied the missive into her letterbook: 'I hope as she is an Originall she may never have a Copie.' Though she was critical of Margaret's 'fantasticall' garb, Mary's scorn was reserved for her intellectual pretensions. 'She swore if the scooles did not banish Aristotle and read Margaret Duchesse of Newcastle they did her wrong . . . my part was not to speake but admire' as she rambled on, 'Magnifying her owne generous actions statly buildings noble fortune her Lords prodigious losses'. For Mary her example merely served to emphasise the accomplishments of the modest poet Katherine Philips.[71]

---

*In total, £3,500 plus interest.

All was far from well at the Royal Society. Thomas Sprat's vindication of its activities, the so-called *History of the Royal Society*, took an age to appear. Evelyn designed a frontispiece as suggested by Beale. Wenceslaus Hollar's engraving showed a bust of Charles II on a pedestal, with the president, Lord Brouncker, and Bacon as his supporters. In 1667 Evelyn had asked Cowley for an introductory poem. 'There be who aske, What have they don? Where their Colledge?' Cowley could describe 'the Arts, the Inventions and Phænomenas already absolved, improvd or opened', for all that, he added with a touch of desperation, 'we are sometimes the Subject of Satyr, and the Songs of Drunkards; Have a King to our Founder and yet want a Mecænas, and above all a Spirit like Yours, to raise us up Benefactors, and to compell them to thinke the Designe of the Royal Society as worthy their regaurds'.

A few months later Abraham Cowley was dead. He was buried in Westminster Abbey next to Chaucer. In 1657 he had been best man at the duke of Buckingham's wedding to Mary Fairfax, and now his body was taken to Poets' Corner from his patron's town house, Wallingford House, in a hearse with six horses, followed by 'neere an hundred Coaches of noble men & persons of qualitie following, among these all the Witts of the Towne, Divers Bishops & Cleargy men &c'. The splendour of what was virtually a state funeral was at odds with Cowley's recent seclusion, which Evelyn had so admired: 'there is no Person alive,' he had assured him, 'who dos more honor and breath-after the life and repose you so happily cultivate and adorne [than myself].'[72]

When it finally emerged Sprat's *History* drew the ire of Henry Stubbe, polemicist and pamphleteer who plagued the Royal Society with a torrent of printed denunciations which culminated in his declaration that the new science was a papist plot. Joseph Glanville, supported by Boyle, continued to argue elegantly that the ideological demands of science and religion could be accommodated. Evelyn thought the case was self-evident and wondered why members still worried about 'the empty, and malicious cavells of these delators ... let the Moon-dogs bark on, 'till their throats are drie; the Society every day emerges.'[73] The controversy echoed those debates into which Evelyn had been plunged with his translation of *De rerum natura*.

Mary Evelyn shared her admiration of Sprat's work with Bohun, since, as she put it, she could judge and censure authors as well as anyone else in the 'wooden room' their comfortable panelled little parlour; 'though it needs not my suffrage to make it passe for an admirable peece both for witt and eloquence, force of Judgement, and evennesse of style, yet suffer me to do my selfe the right to acknowledge I never liked any thing more'. It defended 'worthy and learned men [and] a cause which promises so many future advantages'. She liked its style, 'in knowne and yet not vulgar english', but offered some trivial corrections: 'one is against making rendesvous plurall, since the word imports it in french without the addition of the last syllable rendesvouses, which hurts the care as much as if for friendships, you should say friendshipses, and is alltogether as unessessary.'[74] Mary was pregnant again, and William Glanville wrote in his customary flirtatious tone: 'Since there are very few of your sexe that come neere you, there cannot bee too many Coppyes of so unparalel'd an Originall, especially when done by so good a hand as my Brothers.'[75] Now he would be allowed to meet her without Evelyn 'looking yellow', since even the 'severest ladies' are free to socialise without their husbands during lying-in. In September Mary gave birth to her second daughter, Elizabeth.

With more time on his hands, Evelyn turned to his son's education. John had been tutored first by Milton's nephew Edward Phillips, who 'though brought up by him' was not 'tainted' by the revolutionary puritan poet, and then by Ralph Bohun.[76] Now Bohun was recalled to New College and proposed that the twelve-year-old should go to Oxford too. His advice was followed and John matriculated in 1668. He stayed with Bohun's uncle's family, the Bathursts, at Trinity. Evelyn thanked them and hoped that his son did not inconvenience them: having his legs in irons. The crookedness of John's legs, sometimes referred to in childhood, was still pronounced and must have made him acutely self-conscious, especially with his roistering relatives at Wotton. At Oxford John, who wore long coats to cover his disability, would need the help of a maid. Mary Evelyn was delighted that the Bathursts would be looking after him. She had strong feelings about raising children: 'rules and precepts do well if fitted to the occasion; but example still has the stronger influence, and fixes best.' However, 'my custome being not to impose', she left the arrangements to her husband.[77]

Bohun and Evelyn enjoyed setting John's educational programme: 'the Atomicall Hypothesis is illustrated by chymistry & experiment every day', but Bohun was not dispensing with Aristotle entirely. 'I confesse that prodigious witt Lucretius has given us almost a compleat system of Epicurus', but neither Platonists nor Stoics had fully explained their thinking. Aristotle, despite his shortcomings, had 'insensibly crept into all modern writers by the use of his terms, it's almost impossible, as things stand, to be either divine, physician, or lawyer without him . . . how then can it be expected that we should understand the new philosophies without him.' John must be taught to argue against Aristotle from conviction, not because he was 'censured in the last coffeehouse, or think it out of vogue in the Royal Society'.[78] Evelyn's son was being handed the torch in a demanding intellectual race, one which he was already showing signs of reluctance and incapacity to enter.

CHAPTER 12

Paris and London

In spring 1665 Evelyn heard from the surveyor-general, Sir John Denham, that his deputy, Christopher Wren, was to visit Paris. Busy as he was dealing with the sick and wounded, Evelyn found time to send Wren 'addresses of Friends of mine there, that shall exceedingly cherish you' and entrusted the non-French-speaker to Samuel Tuke, now living in Paris as companion to Henry Howard's sons. Evelyn also gave Wren a copy of his *Parallel*, 'not . . . in the least assistant to you (who are your selfe a Master) but as a toaken of my respect', proof of 'the affection I beare to an art which you so hapily Cultivate'.[1] Wren's official mission was to observe the works at the Louvre, since Charles II was considering ambitious improvements to Whitehall Palace (the scheme he had sketched out previously in front of Evelyn) but Evelyn recognised that this was a perfect opportunity to update himself on Parisian architecture through expert eyes. Since the queen mother was preparing to return to France with her courtiers, the earl of St Albans and Lord Berkeley of Stratton, for what was expected to be a lengthy stay, Wren was to travel with them. He told a friend in late June that he expected to see the architects Mansart and Bernini 'within this fortnight'.[2] The latter had just arrived from Rome.

But Wren did not meet Bernini until August and it was to be a frustrating encounter. 'Bernini's Design of the Louvre I would have given my Skin for, but the old reserv'd Italian gave me but a few Minutes View; it was five little Designs in Paper, for which he hath receiv'd as many thousand Pistoles; I had only Time to copy it in my Fancy and Memory.'[3] Tuke had already told Evelyn that having been sent inaccurate plans Bernini now thought that he could not rectify the problems at the Louvre without 'pulling downe the greatest part of the building which sure would be a greater error than anything.' Bernini's studio at the Palais Mazarin was cluttered with visitors, most of whom came to see him working on his bust of Louis XIV, and Wren was just another English interloper who spoke neither French nor Italian.

Tuke told Evelyn: 'Your schollars heere Dr Wren, Dr Smith Dr Croone etc are noe more understood as if they had spoken in Irish nor doe they understand another nation.' Henry Justel, the Royal Society's French correspondent since 1664, acted as their interpreter on important occasions.[4]

By the time Tuke returned to Paris from Bourbon, where he had been with Henrietta Maria, Bernini had gone back to Rome, leaving his designs for the Louvre: he 'returned with greate rewards & has left great fame'. Since Wren was still in Paris, Tuke would leave it to him to report back on recent architecture. In fact, Wren had already done so. His letter to a 'friend' (it has only survived as an incomplete later transcript) covered architecture and gardens, engraving, the trades and arts, academies and libraries – everything points to that friend being Evelyn. He wrote that it was only intended as a foretaste of conversations to come and that he would enlarge on Bernini's designs for the Louvre 'by Discourse, and a Crayon', but to keep his memory fresh he had already bought 'a great deal of Taille-douce' (prints) at considerable expense. 'I shall bring you almost all France in Paper.'[5] Evelyn had not been in Paris for almost fifteen years. The images of the idealised city assiduously promoted by Louis XIV and Colbert must have confused him. What had been built, what merely projected? Now, with Wren's help, he could clarify his impressions and bring his knowledge of Paris up to date.

By early 1666 the English were no longer welcome in France, as the countries prepared for war. Mary Evelyn had now lost her chance to take up the Tukes's repeated invitations to her and young John to visit them in their house near her old home, while Evelyn remained 'bound to his charitable imployment' and thus rarely at home.[6] Wren and his friends left Paris in February. However Sir Samuel and the pregnant Lady Tuke were obliged to wait for Howard's return; by May Tuke was 'the onely housekeeper of an English man in Paris'.[7]

In London, Evelyn's expertise in architectural as well as horticultural matters had become widely acknowledged and in August 1666 Clarendon appointed him a surveyor for 'repaires of Paules, & to consider of a model for the new building, or (if it might be) repairing of the Steeple, which was most decayd'. A sense of urgency had at last entered the interminable discussions, the Gothic cathedral being now so dilapidated that Wenceslaus Hollar inscribed his view of the nave with the words 'quotidie casum expectantis' (daily expecting collapse).[8] The other two surveyors were John Webb and Roger Pratt for John Denham was no longer competent, his insanity seemingly hastened by his wife's flagrant behaviour as the mistress of the duke of York: 'bitchering' as Evelyn had described it so graphically to Pepys.[9]

Behind Inigo Jones's classical western portico, an 'intire and excellent Piece', St Paul's Cathedral sat listing and decaying, bearing the scars of vandalism, desecration and misuse during the civil wars and Interregnum. The commission appointed in 1663 had wide powers to appoint advisors, 'persons of known ability and integrity'. By the summer of 1665 large sums of money had been spent but no major decisions taken, despite three reports, one recommending the complete demolition of the tower (then scaffolded) and crossing piers. The south transept had collapsed long ago. Now, on 27 August 1666, Evelyn and several other lay observers joined Wren, May and Pratt for a meeting, 'to survey the generall decays of that antient & venerable Church' and to present a final report, including cost estimates.[10]

Pratt argued eccentrically that the current outward tilt of the walls was a perspectival device. Evelyn followed Wren in being 'quite of another judge-ment'. Wren believed St Paul's should neither be made too grandiose nor simply patched up, 'a further Object of Charity'. Evelyn agreed, hoping that it might be topped by 'a noble Cupola, a forme of church building, not as yet knowne in England, but of wonderfull grace'. A new dome, here atop an Anglican cathedral, would 'become an Ornament to his Majesty's most excel-lent Reign, to the Church of England and to this great City, which it is a pity, in the Opinion of our Neighbours, should longer continue the most unadorn'd of her Bigness in the World'. Wren's dome was based upon Bramante's for St Peter's, although the Englishman chose a double-shell construction following Lemercier's Sorbonne Chapel and Mansart's Val-de-Grâce, the latter still under construction while he was in Paris.[11]

Evelyn's contribution gives a measure of his architectural expertise – he had an excellent eye and could add to the discussion, but was no match for either Pratt, so impressively self-schooled in antiquity, or Wren, a mathematical genius and of great inventive powers. His own mission was to turn London into a handsome modern capital rather than a city assembled from shored-up fragments of the past. St Paul's Cathedral was, in every sense, the keystone of the Restoration.

On 31 August he dined, as so often, with his old friend Thomas Henshaw. Hardly thirty-six hours later, at 2 a.m. on Sunday, 2 September, a small fire in a bakery in Pudding Lane, fanned by strong east winds and benefiting from an exceptional summer drought, turned in a matter of hours into a terrifying all-consuming blaze of the sort that Evelyn had foreseen in *Fumifugium*. (Sending Pepys a copy of 'the old smoky Pamphlet you desir'd', he commented that 'had it taken Effect, [it] might have sav'd the burning of a Greate Citty'.)[12] Most of the houses in the City of London were of medieval timber construction, with gimcrack extensions and additions, jettied out until they almost met across the street. Once alight, the materials were as kindling, the intense heat they generated soon engulfing the few buildings made of stone or brick in the area. Evelyn hurried across the Thames with his wife and

18 Engraving of old St Paul's Cathedral on fire, in early September 1666, after Wenceslaus Hollar.

son, where with thousands of others they watched the stupefying destruction on the other side of the water, 'the whole Citty in dreadfull flames'.[13]

After passing an eerie night, 'as light as day for 10 miles round about', he wrote that the fire was still raging on: people had 'hardly stirr'd to quench it, so as there was nothing heard or seene but crying out & lamentation, & running about like distracted creatures'. Pepys reported that some had moved their possessions several times, each time being caught by the spreading fire. Helplessly they now watched the flames 'leaping after a prodigious manner from house to house & streete to streete' and consuming in 'incredible manner, houses, furniture & everything'. Those who could, threw their goods onto any passing vessel on the Thames or onto carts leaving the city. The outlying fields 'for many miles were strewed with moveables of all sorts, & Tents erecting to shelter both people & what goods they could get away'. Londoners flocked south to St George's Fields, or north to Moorfields and the higher ground of Highgate and neighbouring villages. Over these ghastly premonitions of modern refugee camps, the sky appeared lit up 'like the top of a burning Oven'.

Evelyn resorted to biblical language to describe the horror. 'God grant mine eyes may never behold the like, who now saw above ten thousand houses all in one flame, the noise & crakling & thunder of the impetuous flames, the shreeking of Women & children, the hurry of people, the fall of towers, houses & churches was like an hideous storme'. He compared what he saw with Sodom and Troy. This was no longer London. Dozens of churches, virtually all the City livery halls, the customs house and the Royal Exchange had been destroyed, the remaining fragments standing erect like rotten tooth stumps in a diseased jaw. Clouds of smoke and even ash reached Oxford, fifty miles west.

By Tuesday evening, after the City had been ablaze two entire days, the fire was licking at the western boundaries, heading for the Temple and Fleet Street, while pieces of stonework catapulted off St Paul's Cathedral like missiles, its lead 'mealting downe the streetes in a streame'. With roads like a fakir's bed of coals, mountains of rubble and charred timbers blocking thoroughfares, it was impossible to get help into the area. The continuous east wind even threatened Whitehall. The Exchequer moved quickly to Surrey, to Nonsuch Palace, where it had sat out the plague. Fire breaks were knocked through Scotland Yard. Earlier that Tuesday afternoon Sir Richard Browne had dashed off a note to his daughter.

> The Fire is in Fleetestreete. The wind . . . violent . . . We doubt Whitehall will notte escape. I pray send me two or three Deptford wherries by this night or at farthest by tomorrow's tyd after dinner. And Henry Couper John Butter or some other hands to helpe putt my goods into the Boates; If we can afford a small lighter it would be best of all, for I can oblige friends with what I employ nott myselfe. God have us all in his blessed keeping (4 o'clock).[14]

Evelyn joined a firefighting party in Holborn as the flames moved towards Smithfield, close to where many sick and wounded seamen lay in St Bartholomew's Hospital. But during Tuesday night the wind suddenly dropped and the fire halted in its progress east of Holborn Bridge. Unnervingly, it broke out again in the Temple but by then tactical demolition had opened up fire breaks. Only the wharves, containing inflammable materials, continued to belch fire. Deep below the warehouses, foul-smelling clouds of smoke billowed out of basements. Some cellars would still be alight four months later.

Throughout, Evelyn was mindful of his official duties: a rumour that French or Dutch incendiaries had started the fire made him request extra vigilance towards those in his commission's care.* The king and his brother had been exemplary, 'even labouring in person, & being present, to command, order, reward, and encourage Workemen; by which he shewed his affection to his people, and gained theirs'.

---

*The finger of suspicion then shifted to English Catholics.

Five days after the outbreak, Evelyn clambered 'over mountaines of yet smoking rubbish', the ground singeing the soles of his shoes, to get to St Paul's Cathedral. Just a few days earlier, he had been discussing plans for its redevelopment. He found Inigo Jones's west front and Corinthian portico remarkably unscathed; it did not fall until it was demolished in the 1680s. The immense masonry blocks were proof against the fierce heat and, although the ornament was shattered, 'the Inscription in the Architrave ... shewing by whom it was built had not one letter of it defac'd'. The survival of the executed king's name seemed an augury. The rest of the cathedral had been reduced to a skeletal state, while virtually the entire stock of the London book trade smouldered in its carapace of molten lead in the crypt below.*

The scene looked like the aftermath of a gigantic, misconceived chemical experiment. Metalwork had liquefied and reformed as hideous amorphous lumps, finely carved stonework had been pulverised or, at best, whitened into a calcified imitation of itself. Sources of water were now dry or boiling. Timber ash powdered every surface. Although surprisingly few had been killed, 'the people who now walked about the ruines, appeard like men in some dismal desart, or rather in some great Citty, lay'd wast by an impetuous & cruel Enemy'. The modern reader is inevitably reminded of Manhattan one sunny morning in September 2001.

Evelyn claimed to have presented his post-Fire plan and report to the king just a week after the fire, but it was not the first. In the queen's bedchamber they had carefully 'examind each particular', discussing it for almost an hour, 'extreamly pleasd with what I had so early thought on'.[15] Evelyn had pulled together all the ideas about cities that he had assembled over the years. *Londinium Redivivum* (London Revived) as the report is called, is a model of practicality and careful good sense. In modern terms, Evelyn proposed a combination of planning guidelines and building regulations. London would become 'far superior to any other city in the habitable world for beauty, commodiousness, and magnificence'.[16]

The king and Parliament were eager to start rebuilding, Evelyn told Tuke in Paris: 'I believe it will universaly be the employment of the next Spring. They are now buisid with adjusting the claimes of each proprietor, that so they may dispose things for the building after the noblest Model.' He reported on his contribution, the second plan submitted.

But Dr. Wren had got the start of me: both of us did coincidere so frequently, that his Majestie was not displeased with it; and it causd divers alterations and truely, there was never a more glorious Phoenix upon Earth,

---

*The Stationers' church of St Faith was housed there.

if it do at last emerge out of those cinders, and as the designe is layd, with the present fervour of the undertakers.[17]

Both Wren and Evelyn drew up rectilinear, schematic plans bearing little relation to what had stood before the fire, with piazzas and circuses superimposed at intervals. Though Evelyn's was more diagrammatic, and relocated the Royal Exchange on the riverside, there were few major differences between the two schemes.

There was a big difference between the commentaries, however. Wren's concentrated on key points, particularly those relating to means of construction. Evelyn's ranged widely, closely based on *Fumifugium* – now he could apply his theories to reality. He began with strictly practical concerns: first, the city must be mapped and surveyed (by Jonas Moore, he suggested), both above and below ground, the latter an ancient mesh of vaults, cellars and tunnels. Once crucial details of land ownership were clarified, a plan could be drawn up, on the advice of 'the ablest men, Merchants, Architects, and Workmen, in consort', those best fitted to determine the form of a modern capital – among whom, presumably, Evelyn counted himself. With all the information to hand and clearance complete, site preparation and levelling should begin, including 'some of the deepest valleys, holes, and more sudden declivities', both for ease of movement around the city but also 'for the more handsome ranging of the buildings'.

It was an invaluable opportunity. If the Crown or the City authorities allowed piecemeal building before the establishment of a plan or royal ordinance, then 'it may possibly become a new indeed, but a very ugly city, when all is done'. But, carefully prepared, 'such a city [will] emerge out of these sad and ruinous heaps, as may dispute it with all the cities of the World; fitter for commerce, apter for government, sweeter for health, more glorious for beauty; and in sum for whatsoever indeed could be desired to render it consummately perfect'.

Evelyn's vision blended Sixtus X's Rome, in which obelisks, fountains and churches acted as eye-catchers, with Parisian urbanism. City gates 'might be ... triumphal arches, adorned with Statues, Relievos, and apposite Inscriptions, as Prefaces to the rest within'. New churches would reflect demographic need, with parish boundaries being redrawn according to John Graunt's remarkably accurate statistics. Thoroughfares of varying widths 'for commerce and intercourse, cheerfulness and state' would be scored through the fabric, diagrammatically linking key buildings such as livery halls and the Guildhall, while visual breathing spaces would allow for 'breakings, and enlargements into piazzas'. Here would stand the architectural high notes in the city. Hospitals, workhouses and prisons would be located conveniently,

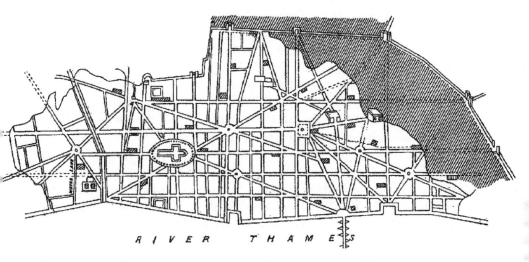

R I V E R   T H A M E S

19 Evelyn's 1666 scheme for the rebuilding of the City after the Great Fire, redrawn in the late nineteenth-century.

with taverns 'sprinkled' about. All must 'respect uniformity'. Markets and 'the better sort of shopkeepers' would be allotted 'the sweetest, and most eminent streets and piazzas' while craftsmen and artisans would be tucked away in the streets and passages behind. In this revised city, commerce and trade would take their proper place.

At the very hub would stand St Paul's Cathedral on 'the only spot in the whole city, where I would plat that ancient and venerable cathedral again' (Wren had also done the same) with grammar school, library, deanery and stationers' shops gathered around it. Another focal point would be the College of Physicians. Evelyn warmed to his subject; leading down to the river new houses 'would peep over one another successively, with a far better grace than those do at Genoa' where the streets were too steep. Regularity was Evelyn's watchword, an unbroken street front his ideal, with 'ample Courts, Yards and Gardens' tucked behind, and the shacks, sheds and 'ugly shops' removed from city walls, gateways and even London Bridge. The uniform residential areas of his new city would be laced with wide paved streets made of stone or brick, in the Dutch fashion, dry both underfoot and overhead, the present gushing waterspouts replaced by downpipes. Heavy carts would be banned from the streets and sleds introduced, as in Bristol.

The Thames, 'the goodliest river in the world', would be given due prominence with the Exchange on its bank and a 'new and ample quay . . . parallel from the very Tower to the Temple at least' reducing the need for 'ugly stairs, bridges and causeways . . . dirty and nasty . . . at every ebb'. He envisaged a broadened River Fleet, channelled from Holborn to the Thames, the wharves used for 'considerable vessels', and bridged over, with streets raised accordingly. Where the Fleet met the Thames its waters would be filtered and 'preserved sweet . . . through flood-gates'. Ideally another bridge, with iron balustrades and statues, and plenty of space for pedestrian ways – like the Pont Neuf in Paris – would cross the Thames.

On Bankside, on the south bank, the existing 'wretched houses' could be demolished in favour of 'wharfs before, and yards behind made large enough for the placing and working of cranes, the laying of deal, timber, clap-board, pipestaves, millstones, faggots, wood and coals, and other gross commodities'. Warehouses in the City should face the street, not the river, 'because of the dull and heavy aspect of those kind of erections'. As for the industries, those already identified in *Fumifugium* as fire hazards, he hoped that the king would disperse them – to the riverside at Bow or Wandsworth, or inland, to Islington or Spitalfields.

Evelyn's London was clean, sanitary and uniformly handsome. Every element in it was reformed – water, transport, waste, commerce, as well as the citizens and their institutions, ecclesiastical and civic. He suggested cladding fresh water pipes in plaster of Paris to prevent contamination and encouraged burials well away from churches. In the event, it was another fifty years before a burial ground was established in fields beyond the northern limits of the town.[18]

The week after the Great Fire, the Royal Society met in Dr Walter Pope's rooms. The City Corporation moved into Gresham College, sharing it with the Royal Exchange; among the Fellows, only Robert Hooke lingered on there – presumably having nowhere else to go. The Royal Society's ambitions had been set back by its removal from London during the plague the previous summer, and now it had to find alternative premises. Recent issues of the *Philosophical Transactions* were on the smoking pyre of paper below St Paul's and Oldenburg saw 'smaller hopes, than ever, of Benefactors to the Society . . . but charges to encrease'. Nevertheless, he also quickly perceived that it could make itself useful at a time when there was such pressure for rebuilding 'and that in such a manner (with Bricks, and large Streets, leaving great Intervalls and partitions in severall places) that for the future they may not be so easily subject to the like destruction. I hope that some of our Society will signalize themselves in this Survey and Dessein.'[19]

At a meeting a week later held, at Henry Howard's invitation, at Arundel House, Viscount Brouncker encouraged the Royal Society to take action. Robert Hooke showed the Fellows his own plan for the reconstruction of London while Oldenburg was irritated that Wren had already submitted his to the king without their concurrence. Wren's scheme 'contrived by him, and reviewed and approved by the R Society . . . would have given the Society a name, and made it popular, and availed not a litle to silence those, who aske continually, What have they done?' Wren's defence was that it had to be presented quickly 'before other Desseins came in' and assured him that he would describe himself as a Fellow of the Royal Society to Parliament. Evelyn's contribution was not even mentioned.[20] The rash of rebuilding schemes was grist to satirical playwright Thomas Shadwell's mill. In *The Sullen Lovers* Sir Positive At-all claimed 'seventeen models of the city of London of my own making'.[21]

Yet, as Evelyn reported to Tuke in Paris, resilient Londoners were already back at work outside the affected area, 'the same noyse, buisinesse and commerce'. The merchants had 'complyd with their forraine Correspondence as punctually, as if no disaster at all had happned; nor do we heare of so much as one that has fail'd'. Only the booksellers had been ruined, so 'ill treated by Vulcan', their losses estimated to run into hundreds of thousands of pounds, 'an extraordinary detriment to the whole Republique of Learning'.[22] Despite that, Oldenburg managed to get the latest *Philosophical Transactions* into print, albeit 'with some difficulty' and sent a copy to Boyle in Oxford. A month after the fire, after noting the death of François Mansart, 'who vyed with the Cavalier Bernini', he reported that the rebuilding 'is still very perplext', with three different approaches favoured by the House of Commons. 'Some are for a quite new Model, according to Dr Wren's draught: some, for the old, yet to build with bricks; others, for a midle way, by building a Key [quay], and larging some streets, but keeping the old foundations and vaults.' Prompt action was essential lest Londoners decide to 'scatter into other parts.'[23] Wren and Hooke were appointed to carry out 'the Survey and admeasurement of all such Foundations'.[24]

In November Hugh May, unusual in not producing a plan of his own, was telling Pepys: 'the design of building the City doth go on apace . . . it will be mighty handsome, and to the satisfaction of people. But I pray God it come not out too late.'[25] The estimated costs stood at £1.8 million. These were the last weeks of grand dreams, before the disputes over legal ownership, boundaries, law and custom began. Thirteen thousand dwellings had been lost. The ownership of every foot of an entire medieval city centre now had to be determined. John Beale (who had briefly visited London on business) joined in the debate: 'I see many platforms for the rebuilding of London . . . then let Fumifugium banish all the brewing houses up & down the Thames', he told Evelyn.[26] Even the king added his opinions (some of which echoed Evelyn's) on improvements, suggesting that markets be relocated off main thoroughfares, that streets be widened and the approach to London Bridge raised.[27]

By December an initial survey had been carried out by John Leake and his colleagues at the behest of the City authorities. Wenceslaus Hollar then made an authoritative record of the extent of the devastation, an exquisite map of London with a great hole at its heart. Evelyn turned to the surveys to adjust his own plan for reconstruction, altering 'what I had so crudely done, though for the most part I still persist in my former discourse'.[28] Soon after, Hollar asked Evelyn to help him secure the king's financial support to complete his great map of London, begun before the Fire and now 'in danger of being unfinished, and the ancient record of the city irrecoverably lost'.[29]

In whatever form London was to be rebuilt, enormous supplies of building materials would be required. In *Londinium Redivivum* Evelyn suggested that the good-quality brick and stone should be cleaned and stored, 'because all seasons are not fit for it', while the rest of the rubble might be put to use for 'building, coving, filling up, and to be sifted for the mortar'. Timber was no problem. Astutely, Dutch merchants used the relaxation of the Navigation Act to supply Scandinavian wood.[30] By late September, Pepys was hatching a plan with Sir William Penn to bring in timber from Scotland, 'which while London is building, will yield good money'.[31] Hooke and Sir William Petty worked out construction methods that used less wood and offered considerable savings.*

Supplies of new brick and tile were the most pressing problem. The City authorities quickly encouraged the setting up of brickyards and made sure that the products were standardised and that prices were reasonable, to encourage builders. Despite previous stipulations that new buildings be constructed of brick or stone, the regulations had never been enforced. Now the Royal Society had found itself a project. 'It was moved, that the materials for building, and the several sorts of earth for making brick and tile, might be now considered of'.[32] They compared clays and discussed 'klinkers', Dutch vitreous brick, before commanding the desperately stretched Hooke to carry out trials. By April he had come up with a machine that could produce brick at speed but by then their attention had moved on.[33]

But Evelyn and Sir Robert Moray, firm admirers of Dutch construction, continued to take the subject seriously. Moray had restarted his history of masonry and had 'whet my self into an humor' to write about brickmaking,

---

*Evelyn referred to them in later editions of *Sylva*.

'for that is my next chapter'.[34] A patent would fund the Royal Society and answer its critics, who would now see the Fellows applying themselves to trade and useful commerce.

In early December 1666 the former burgomaster of Rotterdam, Jan Kievit (or Kiviet), currently in exile because of his links to the prince of Orange, visited Sayes Court with Sir Gabriel Sylvius and Joseph Williamson, 'to examine whither the soile about the river of Thames would be proper to make Clinkar brick with & to treate with me about some accommodations in order to it'.[35] Experienced brickmakers tested clay in their mouths, the taste and feel offering clues to its quality – perhaps an unpleasant task for someone in their party.[36] Brickmaking was seasonal, the clay being dug in the autumn and left to weather over the winter, manufacture taking place from April onwards; if the riverside clay proved suitable, the kilns needed to be set up immediately. Sylvius, who had previously been involved in exporting wool from Ireland, seems to have been the prime mover in this attempt to burn special extra-hard brick, on the Dutch model, while the presence of the secretary of state's right-hand man, Williamson, suggests that the proposal was being taken seriously.[37]

The Act for the Rebuilding of the City of London was passed in February 1667 and specified brick construction. If kilns at Deptford could produce Dutch-type tough bricks, then Evelyn might actually be able to play a practical role. Mary Evelyn reported conversations on lime and clinker, 'the advantage being in prospect, the expence certain'.[38] Letters (in French) flew between Kievit, Sylvius and Evelyn. Four Dutch workmen were brought over especially but the planned demonstration was delayed or even cancelled, although discussion of prices and means of transport (to London Bridge) continued.[39] In May 1667 Evelyn and Sylvius petitioned 'for the sole licence for 14 years of their invention of a new sort of kilns and furnaces for burning bricks tiles and plaster of Taris [Paris]'.[40] Presumably it was this part of the trial that cost Evelyn £500;* as Mary guessed, there would be no return on his investment. Evelyn was chastened: 'the clay is not excellent; as by sad experience I found, attempting to make Clinquer.'[41]

The 1667 Act also set up the Fire Court to expedite settlement of property disputes. Meanwhile the new legislation also introduced a range of house-types, of a kind which became standard in the eighteenth century. There would be flat-fronted brick terraced housing instead of the old melee, paved streets and symmetrical squares instead of muddy lanes and filthy courtyards. The Rebuilding Acts (a second followed in 1671) required standardised construction and materials, houses of defined height, thickness of wall and

*Almost £60,000 in modern currency.

street elevation, allowing for accurate cost estimates. They provided a useful guide for the builders who were flooding in from the countryside – the trade was not short of hands for long.[42] But Paris did not rise immediately from London's ashes. A city rebuilt on a strict new plan, with bold axes emphasising fine public buildings, was to prove impracticable – financially, legally and organisationally.

Henry Howard who had provided 'asylum' for the Royal Society now offered to given them some land adjoining Arundel House 'to establish her on for ever, and fix her at your very Threshold'. Howard, Hooke and Wren all drew up plans and Evelyn donated fifty thousand bricks but the response from the Fellows was disappointing – not enough to build a shed. In 1670 John Beale proposed an alternative plan. 'Wee sustain'd a great losse by Mr Hooks employment [as Surveyor]. But nothing could Secure the RS more for the future than if a good plot of ground were purchased for them & Leases graunted to the Builders.' Since the Royal Society was not to be funded through excise from home-brewed spirits (another of Beale's pipe dreams) then it might earn itself much needed income by carrying out some post-Fire redevelopment – he had heard Covent Garden had proved very profitable for the dukes of Bedford.[43] But the only permanent headquarters offered to the Royal Society was part of crumbling Chelsea College, a waterside site with sufficient ground for a physic garden, which was a grant from the king. He first intimated its availability as early as 1664, but the fruitless negotiations continued for many years.[44] Eventually it proved too distant for meetings and too derelict to be practical. It was Charles II's sole gesture of support to the body to which he had given his charter.

In contrast, Henry Howard (still waiting on his dukedom but already assuming the style) was unfailingly generous to the Royal Society. At Evelyn's suggestion he donated the major part of his grandfather Arundel's library to them which, since he had 'little inclination to bookes', ensured its preservation. The gift consisted of some four thousand volumes and many hundreds of manuscripts and, as the Royal Society was currently under his roof, it was also a practical arrangement.[45] Later that year, Evelyn and he organised the transfer of the much damaged Arundel marbles, many of them inscriptions and bas reliefs built into the garden walls of the house on the Strand, to Oxford University (where they were reinserted in the boundary walls between the Sheldonian Theatre and the Ashmolean Museum, opened in 1683). Howard had taken no more care of the marbles than he did of the books, and it was entirely due to Evelyn's efforts that a good part of the collection was secured for Oxford, where it could be displayed, like the statuary on the Capitol in Rome he had so admired long ago, for the benefit of the public and 'preserv'd for the honor of the Place'.[46] Statuary from the

Arundel collection was displayed off the Old Schools Quadrangle at the Bodleian, moving much later to the classical galleries at the Ashmolean Museum.

The following year Evelyn dedicated another translation of Fréart, *An Idea of the Perfection of Painting Demonstrated* (1668), to Howard. He wrote that he was now done with the 'drudgery of Translating of Books', immediately qualifying his words, for 'it were a far beter, and more profitable Work to be still digging in that Mine, than to multiply the number of ill Ones, by productions of my Own'. The volume, coming after *Sculptura* and the *Parallel*, completed his trilogy on the visual arts. He wrote that Howard's gift of his grandfather's marbles was an act of 'never-to-be-forgotten' generosity (not omitting to point out his own role in the donation, however). Evelyn's introduction also celebrated the wide-ranging abilities of artists such as Poussin, Bernini and Wren. He contrasted them with the narrow achievements of genre painters such as Bassano who was 'ever bringing in his wife, children and servants, his dog and his cat and very kitchin-stuff' into his work. Evelyn had little patience for those without intellectual ambition; in fact, men like Howard.

Also implicit in his choice of dedicatee was Evelyn's pride in Howard's patronage. Henry Howard had by then invited him to design two gardens: the riverside pleasure garden in Norwich and Albury Park. There the vestiges of Arundel's design from the 1630s combined with Evelyn's mastery of an Italianate garden vocabulary resulted in a masterpiece – which, remarkably, has survived. Evelyn subtly anglicised his memories of the great Renaissance gardens of Italy and France. By 1670 he was delighted to find that the new work at Albury was being 'exactly don according to the Designe & plot I had made', the tunnel punched through the hill ('such a Pausilippe is no where in England besides'), the vineyards planted and the canal being dug.[47]

In 1673 Evelyn drew a detailed plan of Albury (with scale), perhaps an idealised version of his eventual intentions, much as the 1653 Sayes Court plan had been. He included a cascade below a hilltop tower, two viewing pavilions at either end of the topmost terrace, an octagonal pool on the lower terrace and embrasures at intervals along the two long upper walls. The trees look like cypresses rather than yews. Aubrey's description includes a mention of a 'handsome banqueting House' on the hill, suggesting that one at least of the structures actually existed.[48] He returned to Albury in 1677, the year in which Howard finally became duke of Norfolk, noting in the diary that he had 'first design'd' the garden and devised the 'Crypta through the mountaine'. Yet when he lovingly described Albury to the editor and translator of the new edition of Camden's *Britannia* in the 1690s, he omitted to mention his own part in it; by then he was deeply disillusioned with the 6th duke of Norfolk and 'those base, & vicious Courses he of late had taken'.[49]

There is no better description of Albury Park than William Cobbett's in the early 1820s, when the garden was over 150 years old. At the back 'goes a yew hedge, or, rather, a row of small yew trees, the trunks of which are bare for about eight or ten feet high, and the tops of which form one solid head of about ten feet high'. Behind it 'is a wall probably ten feet high, which forms the breastwork of a terrace; and it is this terrace which is the most beautiful thing that I ever saw in the gardening way. It is a quarter of a mile long, and, I believe, between thirty and forty feet wide; of the finest green sward, and as level as a die'. The yews protect the fruit trees on the terrace from wind, but without shading them.

> In the middle of the wall, at the back of the terrace, there is a recess, about thirty feet in front and twenty feet deep, and here is a basin, into which rises a spring coming out of the hill. The overflowings of this basin go under the terrace and down across the garden into the rivulet below. So that here is water at the top, across the middle, and along at the bottom of this garden. Take it altogether, this, certainly, is the prettiest garden that I ever beheld . . . Every where utility and convenience is combined with beauty.[50]

The only elements missed by Cobbett lay out of sight. There was a 'Roman' bath beneath the terrace, perhaps a survivor from Arundel's time since he had installed one in his London garden. But as Evelyn told Edmund Gibson, 'above all singular and remarkable . . . [was] an Hypogaeum or Perforation made through a mighty hill', similar to the grotto of Posilippo near Naples. The Albury tunnel, bored through the friable sandy stone and still intact, offered a seductive, key-hole glimpse of what lay beyond. As the grotto at Pozzuoli, close to the putative site of Virgil's tomb, had opened onto the Elysian Fields, so this secret passage led inwards to the Elysium – the garden that Evelyn had designed for Howard, and his own memorial to Arundel.[51]

After the failure of progress on his Chatham hospital scheme and the inertia which seemed to have cost the Royal Society its new headquarters, Evelyn lost faith in ambitious architectural projects on paper. Even the Monument, built in the early 1670s, disappointed him, so inopportunely sited at the point where the Great Fire began rather than 'plac'd where the devouring Flames ceas'd and were overcome . . . where a plain Lugubrous Marble with some apposite Inscription had perhaps more properly become the Occasion'. His objections may have been overruled, yet 'I question not but I have the Architect himself on my side'.[52]

One building stood to gain a great deal from its almost total destruction –
St Paul's Cathedral. The 'contamination' of its recent past, and the fire
damage, drove a burst of fundraising.[53] From now on Wren and his team at
the office of works were the sole arbiters of the design of the new cathedral.
Evelyn was no longer directly involved, although he watched it rise with
intense interest and occasional criticism. As he did so, his aspirations for an
imperial capital were fading away.

The more London failed to answer his expectations, the more intently
Evelyn's eye fell on Paris – where they seemed to order everything better. In
early 1667 Samuel Tuke, recently doubly bereaved having lost both wife and
baby, promised to return with prints of the 'most famous gardens in and about
Paris' as well as seeds and plants. Next William Glanville and his son arrived
in Paris in autumn 1668. With typical irony, he told Mary Evelyn that he was
only acting as the French did, saying 'what I doe not thinke', and she must not
expect his comments on the place or the people; he had not even climbed
Notre Dame for the view over Paris. Their manservant, obviously a stolid
'rosbif', refused to let them speak French, even to ask for 'vin'.[54] But for all
that, Glanville had errands, instructions and introductions aplenty from his
brother-in-law.

He complained that he was unfit to carry out Evelyn's commissions – 'the
art of Horticulture, I understand it no more then I doe the language of China'
– but he promised to track down M. de Quintinye and ask about growing
melons, to call on Nanteuil and Bosse, and to look out for anything else of
interest, though he was 'so little a Judge either in [archi]tecture or Gardening'.
Despite that, he noticed 'the Tuileries I meane the Garden to the Louvre is
now under the pick axe spade and whee[l]-barrow, it beeing to bee alter'd in
order to the designe and Modell for perfecting all that is intended to bee built
for the Kings Court'. Glanville's ear was well attuned to gossip and politics.
'Heere are discontended as well as in other parts of [the] world, they wish a
warre but doe not very well know with whom they should fall out.' Louis XIV
was growing formidable, but Holland was rumoured to be about to declare
war. His young William, 'uppon whome France can make no impressions for
the better', seemed set to be another recruit to the regiment of unpromising
young men in the Evelyn family. Their commanding officer was George
Evelyn the younger, of whom Tuke had said on meeting him in Paris, 'if I
mistake not he will make Wooton smoake'.[55]

Hospitable Robert Nanteuil showed Glanville 'what pictures of his owne
doing hee had in his house, hee hath since you left Paris much alterd his way
of working and the King of France I am informed hath made him a chevalier', and asked fondly after the Evelyns. The elderly Bosse had been equally
kind: 'I asked him particularly whether the booke your letter spoke of were

finishd hee told mee No.' He was working on a herbal and told him that engraving the plants was very time-consuming. De Quintinye, who had welcomed Wren two years before, 'received mee very civilly [and] hath since communicated to mee as much as I am capable off, in relation to the pruning and ordering Melons'. But young William Glanville fell ill, so, frustratingly for Evelyn, 'of this and my voyage to Fountainbleau, Veau, Essone, Versailles, Maison St Germain St Cloud Ruel etc I am not in a condition to give you a present account'.[56]

The next visitors to Paris bearing introductions from Evelyn were Samuel Pepys and his French-born wife, altogether more receptive than desultory, sarcastic Glanville. Evelyn longed to share the city with them. He sat up late, writing 'snatches and night-work', somewhat disconnected since they were being kept awake by building work at the dockyard (he was teasing, since it was Pepys's province). He tried to remember everything but 'it is from you I shall expect to be pay'd with fresh and more material Observations. I could have set you down Catalogues of the many rare Pictures and Collections to be seen in that City, but you will every day meet with fresher intelligence. It is now many years since I was there, *et mutantur tempora, et mores, et homines.*' This generous letter is one of the most attractive he ever wrote, mixing nostalgia and enthusiasm, distant memories and more recent information.[57]

He sent Pepys just three introductory letters; any more, to 'Persons of great Quality', would involve 'making and repaying but impertinent Visites, in which I believe you would not willingly engage'. His Parisian contacts, though 'of the lower Rank', were impeccable. 'Monsieur Du Bosse's Books of Architecture and Perspective are worthy your Collections. And if you stayd so long to have your Lady's and your own Pictures engraven by le Chevalier de Nanteuille you would bring home Jewels . . . He is the greater Man that ever handl'd the Graver, and besides, he is a Scholar and a well-bred Person.' As for Bosse, he was 'a plain, honest, worthy, and intelligent good man', and both were 'my Singular Friends and Correspondents for those Matters'. The third introduction was possibly to a chemist, for Evelyn tells Pepys on no account to miss 'the King's medicinal Garden and Laboratory with all the Apparatus . . . so well furnish'd and so rarely fitted for the Design'. If they had more time he should take a course, 'there and in several private Places shew'd to the Curious to their wonderful satisfaction and Benefit of Philosophic Spirits'.

They would travel across 'a Frontier and miserable Country', badly treated by a 'Tyrannical Government, and the Effects of a continual War' – Evelyn remembered it as it had been in his day. On arrival, an Irish friend of Tuke's would help find them furnished accommodation and once settled in, they must immediately climb the Tour St Jacques, 'to take a synoptical Prospect of the monstrous City, to consider the Situation, extent, and Approaches; so as to be the better able to make Comparisons with our London'. The tower was a seventeenth-century Eiffel Tower from which to survey the city and suburbs.

The Faubourg St Germain, Evelyn continued, is where 'Persons of Quality' live and the hospital of La Charité is so impressively run, so clean and so devout 'as must needs affect you'. Among the great houses, the Palais d'Orléans (the Luxembourg) is pre-eminent, though now 'much neglected since the Decease of the best Gardiner in the World, the Duke': for architecture, setting and landscape, it is 'almost as fine as Clarendon House, whose situation somewhat resembles it'. Pepys must try to visit the gallery and library, assuming that 'these Curiosities remain still in the Lustre they did at my Sojourn there'. At the Louvre 'ten thousand Particulars will take you up a good time' and he recommends an audience with the king and queen, to 'Observe his Table, his Guard, Council'. The palace is reached across the Pont Neuf, with its handsome statue of Henri IV, such a contrast to the jumbled houses on 'ours of London'. Below is the Samaritaine, 'in my time such a curious and rich Piece of Artifical Rock-Work, as was hardly to be seen in Europ'. The proprietor is dead and it may now be 'demolish'd and sold . . . However one would see the Machine.' Mazarin's Collège des Quatre Nations was unfinished (but worth investigating) and Pepys must report back whether the Parisian virtuosi, 'our Emulators', had formed their college yet.*

He pointed him to the great libraries, though not sure what had become of Mazarin's, and to 'the King's Manufactures', all to be visited 'studiously'. The Parisian administration at the Hôtel de Ville, the Palais de Justice and Parlement was to be observed. To attend Mass would make him 'love your own Religion the better'. The list (like all of Evelyn's lists) is long, and included the Bastille and Arsenal, the Huguenot chapel at Charenton and entertainments, 'none more Divertissant than the Mountebanks and prodigious Concourse of Mankind' who perform on the Pont Neuf, 'a lively Image of that Mercurial Nation'.

Beyond the city, he pointed them to St Germain-en-Laye, which he believed had 'run exceedingly to decay' but they must view François Mansart's Maisons, which was, in his opinion, 'for the Architecture, Situation, cutt into the River, Forest, Gardens, Stables, etc, one of the most accomplish'd and sweet Abodes that ever I saw'. Vaux-le-Vicomte, like Versailles, will 'amaze you for the infinite Cost both in Building and Gardens', though Fouquet's palace was now ruined, as was Fouquet.

---

*He was out of date: Colbert had funded the setting up of the Académie des Sciences in 1666.

But one building stands out from all the others by the intensity of Evelyn's description. Having seen Mansart's Val-de-Grâce, 'your Eyes will never desire to behold a more accomplished Piece. There it is you will see the utmost effects of good Architecture and Painting, and heartily wish such another stood where once St Pauls was.' Evelyn had only seen it in engravings; surely he was reporting someone else's impression – Wren's? He exhorted Pepys to buy prints of everything they saw: 'they will greatly refresh you in your Study and by the fire side, when you are many years return'd.'

On their way home through Flanders, Elizabeth Pepys was taken ill. Her husband's thanks to Evelyn, 'to whom singly I owe the much great part of the satisfaction I have met with in my late voyage', were brief and distracted. Elizabeth died a week later.[58] Evelyn attended her funeral, held at night at St Olave's, then as now entered beneath an archway lugubriously decorated with skulls and crossbones. Her widower wrote an epitaph and commissioned a memorial bust.[59] Any conversations Pepys and Evelyn subsequently had about Paris were, sadly for us, conducted in person, not on paper. But near the end of his life Pepys told Evelyn that this, too short, journey had given him a 'degree of satisfaction and solid usefullnesse that has stuck by mee through the whole Cours of my Life and Businesse since'.[60]

CHAPTER 13

Perpetual Motion

Exhausted after his demanding term as a commissioner, Evelyn took advantage of a lull. Mary described, in luminous prose, Sayes Court at dead of winter. 'You will not expect,' she told Samuel Tuke, 'an account in this season of the yeare, how the flowers, and greens, prosper in the garden since they are candying in snow to be preserved for the spring and our delights, confined to the litle wooden Roome.' But, could her cousin look in, he would see by the fire

> a philosopher, a woman, and a child, heapes of bookes, our food and enter-
> tainment silence our law, soe strictly observed that neither Dog nor Cat
> dares transgresse it. The crackling of the Ice, and whistling winds are our
> Musica, which if continued long in the same quarter may possibly freeze
> our witts as well as our penns, though Apollo were himselfe amongst us.

She felt like a hibernating tortoise, 'whilst it is for you to have the honour of approaching the splendor of Courts, and the society of our earthly Gods . . .'.[1]

Her husband had a new retreat, a 'little Cell & Cabinet which I built below towards the South Court, at East end of the Parlor'. A scholarly and godly man needed privacy and absolute quiet, hard to find in a house of growing girls and frequent visitors. He grew used to working at dead of night. Writing Pepys a particularly long letter, Evelyn broke off, ''tis now neere Three in the morning, I will sleepe a little', and continued it the next day, 'now I am up againe'.[2] Mary saw little of her hermit husband. In addition, her father was unwell and anxious since, she told Bohun, 'my Uncle torments him more and more, what conclusion will be made cannot yet be forseene'. She had not even been able to use her own retreat, her kitchen, since alterations to the house meant it had been out of bounds for much of the last year.[3] In May 1669, Mary gave birth to her third daughter and last child, Susanna.

When the second edition of *Sylva* appeared in 1670 it was twice as long as the first. John Beale found it 'totally chang'd in style in substance in importance; so elegant, so philosophical, so acute, so profound, so obligingly useful'.[4] But it had stirred up that one-man hornet's nest Henry Stubbe, physician and tireless pamphleteer, whose hot-headed mission had become the destruction of the Royal Society. He unleashed a flurry of publications in 1670 attacking the society, considering its scientific ambitions a threat to Protestantism and established humanist education. Oldenburg warned Evelyn that he considered it a greater menace 'than the Dutch Warr, the Plague and the Fire . . . he threatens you . . . and saith that he will handle you as he hath done Henshaw' (whose report on saltpetre he had savaged). Evelyn must parry his blows at *Sylva*; 'you will be amazed, to see the vileness of this 4th book and of the soule of its Author.'[5]

Evelyn was distracted; his brother Richard had died, in agony, of kidney stones in March 1670 having failed to heed Pepys's advice to have the operation. Then Evelyn heard that the office of Latin secretary might fall vacant. The incumbent, Nicholas Oudart, was gravely ill and Evelyn wrote to Joseph Williamson that, though he did not wish Oudart dead, he would like his post as it offered a chance to re-enter the king's service. He added: 'If this succeed not, be kind to me, and burn this paper.'[6] Evelyn was not successful (nor did Williamson destroy the evidence) but the scent of the Latin secretaryship perhaps helped put Stubbe's arrant nonsense into perspective. Oudart, secretary to the princess royal during the 1650s and the man who brought old Constantijn Huygens to Sayes Court in 1664, did not die until 1681.

Now both father and son were seeking patronage. John junior was admitted to the Middle Temple in May 1672 and Mary believed he was settling down, planning to 'bid faire for the Lord Chancellorship by setling in good earnest to the study of the Law', as she put it to Bohun, although Evelyn had reason to worry about his son. In September 1671 John wrote provokingly from Wotton, boasting that he, together with his cousins and four friends, had drunk nearly two dozen bottles of his uncle's claret after dinner. While his sister in Deptford 'doubtless is much improv'd in her intellectualls by Mr Bohuns conversation' he appeared to be taunting his father with the empty hedonism of his life in Surrey. Prior to his first communion, Bishop Gunning gave young John instruction and Evelyn provided a short theological reading list, including works by Grotius, Hammond and Patrick. He was, as his father phrased it rather alarmingly, on stage and God was watching him. 'Resolve to be Religious, if you will have me your friend.' He hoped they would go together to the Passion Week services at Whitehall, 'which you know we have not in the country so solemn'.[7] Evelyn remorselessly probed his own behaviour for flaws and misdemeanours, in the hope of winning God's forgiveness and in order to 'make my calling & election sure', as he wrote later.[8] He marked important birthdays or moments of extreme happiness or misery with special prayers and even periods of spiritual withdrawal. It was all part of his continuous programme of self-examination. There was little sign that John was similarly inclined.

Evelyn reminded Lord Clifford at the Treasury that, once Browne's debts were settled, John could finish his education and would be 'fit to serve you and his Countrie'. Clifford was Evelyn's model, having risen at court 'without the little Arts and the less prostitutions', and was 'ever more than ordinarily kind to me, even to intimacy & friendship'. He counted on both him and Lord Arlington but 'I cultivated neither of their friendships with any meane submissions'.[9] When John's translation from Nicholas Rapin's Latin poem, *Of Gardens*, appeared the following year, it was dedicated to Arlington. Coyly, John wrote that he 'presumes not to intrude into your Cabinet, but to wait upon you in your Gardens at Euston', where Arlington might enjoy 'the first Blossoms of my Youth'. With its long sections on timber it was almost *Sylva* in verse.[10] The choice of topic, if not the pen, were familiar: a gardener, 'fly[ing] the smoak and clamour of the Town' for the pleasures of country and his 'Villa', was clearly a sympathetic figure to his father.

Sir Richard Browne was considering resigning his clerkship on grounds of age and failing health. But when it emerged that Arlington had offered first refusal of the post to his own secretary, Williamson, 'preferrable to all others whatsoever', Browne changed his mind and remained in his post until January 1672. He blamed himself, however, for the fact that Evelyn would not inherit his position, having, in his son-in-law's words, 'waited to the brink of his grave' to help him. Browne's reluctance to jostle for favour had, not for the first time, left Evelyn without a 'good Angell'. But Arlington had a far more lucrative and interesting post in mind for him anyway, a seat on the Council for Foreign Plantations, which Evelyn took up in early 1671 at £500 per annum – double the clerk's salary. Lord Sandwich was its president and the terms of the appointment were broad, exhorting members to inform themselves on the state of overseas trade and the means by which to encourage it.[11] Evelyn, the merchant adventurer, was in his element.

As Arlington's protégé, Evelyn now found himself on the fringes of the court and in 1671 was swept east in the annual autumn royal progress, beginning with racing at Newmarket – a particular passion of the king's. At Arlington's country seat, Euston Hall, he joined a lavish house party lasting a fortnight. Virtually the entire court was there, the house 'fill'd from one end to the other . . . for 15 dayes there were entertain'd at Least 200 people, & halfe as many horses, besids Servants, Guards, at Infinite expense'.[12]

Euston had a continental air, reflecting the former Henry Bennet's many years of overseas service, in France first with George Digby, the earl of Bristol, and then with the duke of York, and after the Restoration as ambassador in Madrid. Bearing his prominent scar on his nose as a royalist badge of honour, he further increased his European credentials by marrying Isabella van Nassau-Beverweerd of the House of Orange in 1666. Behind the ceaseless hospitality at the comfortable mansion, the diplomatic business continued.

One of Evelyn's fellow guests was Charles Colbert, marquis de Croissy. He had been French ambassador since 1668 and was the architect of the infamous 1670 Treaty of Dover which had secured a pension for Charles II in exchange for (secret) undertakings, both religious and military, favouring the French interest. Previously Colbert had been at Mazarin's side, and his brother Jean-Baptiste, now superintendent of the royal works, was Louis XIV's aide.* Suddenly Evelyn's stay was changed from being an awkward obligation into a stimulating immersion in Parisian news. He engineered regular conversations with Colbert (a relief from tedious games of cards and dice), which no doubt touched on the transformation of the French capital, in particular the ambitious military hospital and chapel now under construction.

Also in the party was Louise de Kéroüalle, 'now comeing to be in great favour with the K–'. Charles's paramour was so relaxed in her new role that she spent days in dishabille. Evelyn's mouth must have been pursed tightly as he remembered (writing up the scene in his diary later) how the king lost no opportunity to fondle the woman he called 'my dearest dearest fubs'. There, at the accommodating Suffolk home of his first minister, Charles took his wife's pert maid of honour as his mistress – an event marked by the ceremonial flinging of her stocking 'after the manner of a married Bride'. Did Evelyn remember that her aristocratic Breton parents had befriended Sir Richard Browne almost twenty years before? The duchess of Portsmouth, as she became, was one of a group that Evelyn referred to collectively as 'concubines', but her influence, as a politically astute Frenchwoman with the ear of the king, was not to be underestimated.[13]

Evelyn found Arlington himself 'hospitably easy to be withall', a testimony that Lorenzo Magalotti corroborated when he described him as impatient and arrogant but always 'generous to his friends and very affable to deal with'. Arlington had some congenial tasks in mind for Evelyn and in his 'prety apartment, where I was quite out of all this hurry', the new councillor first prepared guidance on tree planting and 'other laudable Rusticities', and then, since his host 'has a comprehension & a genius which are not allways borne

*Charles Colbert became the French minister of state for foreign affairs in 1680.

with Titles', a library catalogue for him, for in his view the only thing still wanting in the magnificent establishment at Euston was 'intellectual furniture'.[14] Arlington was a linguist and well read, 'absolutely the best bred & Courtly person his Majestie has about him'. For his part Magalotti judged his intelligence to be 'mediocre'.

Euston Hall was in remote Breckland on the Suffolk–Norfolk border. Samuel Pepys heard that Arlington had been advised against purchasing it in 1667 but, recently married, had been in no mood to change his mind.[15] Evelyn now advised him to bring the park closer to the house and suggested long avenues of elms and limes, as well as knots of firs which would flourish in the poor sandy soil. Arlington approved his proposals and Evelyn had the satisfaction of seeing the results a few years later.[16]

During the house party Henry Howard took Evelyn to the Duke's Palace in Norwich, confiding that he hoped his son might marry one of the king's daughters. In fact, it was Arlington's daughter who was to marry royalty. In 1672 his five-year-old Isabella was betrothed to Henry Fitzroy, duke of Grafton, the king's son by the duchess of Cleveland. Evelyn, who was present at the time, reported that he 'tooke no greate joy at the thing for many reasons'.[17]

Howard also confessed to a dalliance with Jane Bickerton, a woman of whom even the king disapproved. The Duke's Palace was still decked out after the recent visit of the court but Evelyn thought it a 'wretched building, & that part of it, newly built of brick, is very ill understood . . . it had ben much better to have demolish'd all'. He suggested an entirely new site near the castle but Howard already had plans for another wing, a 'pavilion' in the garden and stables on the site of the bowling alley. Inside, the palace was filled with the earl of Arundel's most valuable possessions, which seemed little more than a burden to his grandson.[18]

At close quarters, Evelyn began to see Tuke's patron more clearly, a charming man of 'so eminent birth . . . & smoth a tongue' but without judgement and utterly inconsistent, having 'fits of good resolutions, greate generositie &c, & then of things quite contrary'. The evening they arrived at the house Evelyn was shocked to witness a furious argument between Howard and his carpenter which lasted for hours. It was nothing more than a disagreement about measurements, 'so much beneath his dignitie, & for so wretched a trifle'. Howard was thinking of converting to Protestantism (thereby regaining his grandfather's title of earl marshal of England) and putting his elder son into the church.[19] Evelyn was unsure how much to believe of what he said.

But his Norwich visit also introduced him at last to Sir Thomas Browne, physician, polymath and celebrated author of *Religio Medici* (1642). Sir Thomas had earlier been a recipient of the outline of *Elysium Britannicum* and had contributed material. So independent a thinker that he had at different times been attacked with equal vigour by both Sir Kenelm Digby and Alexander Ross, he now showed Evelyn round his house and garden, 'a Paradise & Cabinet of rarities'. He also guided him about the great city, godly and prosperous with dozens of flint-walled churches, 'exquisitely headed & Squared', an art, Sir Thomas told him, the builders had now forgotten. Norwich, its wealth built upon textiles, was also a town of florists, specialists in bulb cultivation who were now arriving in increasing numbers from Europe as Protestant exiles. Did Browne perhaps take Evelyn along the Wensum to see the riverside pleasure garden he had helped Howard lay out eight years earlier but had never seen? Evelyn had missed gardening of late, telling Sir Thomas Hanmer that he had 'for some yeares wholy addicted my selfe to the propagation of Foresters, and rusticities of that nature' and, as a result, had neglected his 'little flower garden'.[20] Meeting Sir Thomas Browne, the stimulating provincial philosopher with whom he shared so many interests, after his disillusion with Howard, so philistine and decadent, gave Evelyn further pause about the state of the court.

Nevertheless, despite the 'luxurious & abandon'd rout' he witnessed on his way back through Newmarket, he realised that his daughters' futures might lie at court, where, suitably prepared, it was possible to live a godly life and emerge unscathed. Evelyn and Mary's young friend Margaret Blagge was a good example, a 'Miracle of a young Lady in a licentious Court & so deprav'd an Age'. Her royalist family, originally Suffolk gentry related to Henry Jermyn, had been attached to Henrietta Maria's court in exile. On their return from Paris, after the death of the father and with mounting debts, one daughter became a maid of honour in the duchess of York's household. Then, after the worst of the plague was over, the youngest of the four girls, fourteen-year-old Margaret, joined her.

Samuel Pepys had met them at the Treasurer's House in Deptford and quaffed ('more than I have drank at once these seven years') with Dorothy Howard, Margaret Blagge and other maids of honour, before joining the duke and duchess of York, Lady Castlemaine (Barbara Villiers, the king's mistress at the Restoration) and others to sitting on the floor in an unfurnished room upstairs and playing party games. His impression was of a cheerful 'gang'.[21] The two girls were often at church in Deptford but at that time Evelyn was suspicious of the court, disinclined to believe 'there were many Saints in that Country'.[22]

Margaret had seen the former Anne Hyde, both of whose sons had died, gaining weight and losing her looks as her husband's attention moved elsewhere. On the duchess's death in 1671, by which time she had converted to

Catholicism as had her husband, the maids of honour were shuttled over to Whitehall, into the gloomy establishment around the childless Queen Catherine. But Margaret had formed an attachment to a young courtier in the king's household, Sidney Godolphin, and her future seemed secure. That autumn Evelyn, Margaret and Sidney, as well as Evelyn's future close friends, the earl and countess of Sunderland, had all been at Euston.

When Godolphin went to Spain, then Paris, with Sunderland, Margaret now twenty, had asked Evelyn for fatherly guidance in her financial affairs. He decided to help, partly as a way of reassuring himself about the moral climate at court. Evelyn found her to be someone who, like himself, had an intense spirituality. The Church of England, he wrote, is 'as well adapted, for the Courtier, as for the most resign'd Christian'.[23] His own religious impulses, left dissatisfied by the ritual of daily prayers and contemplation at Sayes Court and regular church services, required a more personal outlet. Evelyn and Margaret's platonic friendship, learning 'to love on earth as they love in heaven', was, in their eyes, a step towards salvation, the kind of friendship treasured by the early saints of the church.[24]

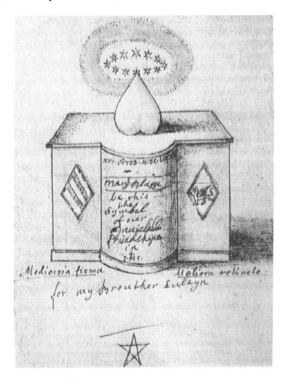

20 The 'altar of friendship': Evelyn's drawing of the symbol of his platonic friendship with his 'seraphic' Margaret Blagge, later Godolphin.

As the weeks passed the leaves of his diary became progressively more thickly speckled with the pentacle, a symbol of both divinity and stoicism, which he used to mark meetings with his 'seraphic'. The intense relationship, in Frances Harris's phrase 'a kind of spiritual betrothal', was sealed on 16 October 1672 with his drawing of their altar of inviolable friendship.[25] As he desperately attempted to contain this new relationship Evelyn put everyone around him under strain. Seraphic love, as set out by the celibate Robert Boyle, or spiritual kinship, as it was called by his religious mentor Jeremy Taylor, was easier to define on the page than to test against the reality of sympathetic emotions or even sublimated sexual attraction.[26]

Mary Evelyn was patently uncomfortable with the situation. At Christmas she wrote to persuade Evelyn to come home from 'glorious court', where he was communing with those 'whose ideas are of a higher nature, whose minds are pure and actions innocent'. Her own claims, she said, stood 'upon no other account, but as I have a little interest in you, and possibly am kindly thought of by you'.[27] By New Year Margaret had left court, apparently only just in time, for the atmosphere there was now so decadent that just to be a maid of honour meant a girl was guilty by association. Dorothy Howard commented, 'God keep us inocent.'[28] Margaret went to live with Sidney's cousins Lord and Lady Berkeley, envisaging her stay at the palatial Berkeley House as a retreat. But the demanding Christian Berkeley wanted a companion.

However, Evelyn's meetings at the Council for Foreign Plantations were usually held on Tuesdays, so this now became his day for Margaret. Evelyn's earnest and self-serving attentions became increasingly overwhelming as he bombarded her with devotional guidance and religious instruction, eliciting a weary request from her that he should put his 'method into blake and whit and I will obey you'. Her own concern was learning to 'know herself' and considering whether her spiritual and temporal future included marriage to Godolphin. Evelyn's views on that topic were ambivalent; years before he told (the unmarried) Robert Boyle, author of *Seraphic Love*, that both the Ark and Paradise itself were populated by couples, and 'every creature was in love'. His own marriage had lasted almost twenty-five years and he was led to the diffi-cult conclusion that Margaret should marry or risk becoming 'singular and fantastic'.

Frances Harris has deftly described the background to their tortuous rela-tionship, as Evelyn blithely elevated their spiritual friendship above his own marriage, let alone Margaret's engagement. Mary, far worldlier and more perceptive than he, saw her husband in the grip of a fevered, if ostensibly reli-gious, relationship – which Evelyn, with matchless self-delusion, claimed she had instigated. Disingenuously, even cruelly, he told Mary that the innocent Margaret, 'my Friend and your child (for so I pray you now esteeme her with me)', had asked him 'why I would have a friend, who have so good a wife'.[29] She was still destined to be Godolphin's wife and considered Evelyn as, above all, Mary's husband. Yet her vacillation in the face of Evelyn's spiritual tutorials had much to do with her nervousness about the long-postponed marriage, which she was now weighing against a life of religious retreat. After an intense period of self-examination, during which she often did not eat or drink, she decided that Evelyn was responsible for her elevated state. 'I love you for God and some times I thinke I love God for you,' she told him.[30]

In 1669 Evelyn was approached by the king to write a history of the (apparently) concluded Dutch Wars that would refute French and Dutch accounts. Instead he proposed Christopher Wase for the task, nudging him towards the job of historiographer royal, vacant since 1666.[31] But his scholarly cousin, now a country schoolmaster, did not strike the right note with Charles, nor was he reliable. His English translation of Vitruvius, steered by Evelyn, did not go beyond an announcement, preface and first chapter. Both the king and Arlington were clear that Evelyn was the best and only candidate. When Pepys was later preparing his own history of the navy, the memory of the unhappy period came back to Evelyn. The history was a task for which he had little taste or aptitude. 'I cannot think of it without emotion.' He remembered the 'ocean of papers, treaties, declarations, relations, letters, and other pieces, that I have ben faine to saile through, reade over, note, and digest, before I set pen to paper; I confesse to you the fatigue was unsufferable . . . so much trash there was to sift and lay by.' Nor did he have the judgement to 'elect and dispose the materials that were apt for use'. In August 1672, by which time the country was deep in the Third Dutch War, Evelyn sent the lord high treasurer, Baron Clifford of Chudleigh a two-sheet outline for comment, perhaps hoping to stall the project, since the full account would run to a thousand pages by his estimate.[32]

By then Evelyn must have had intimations of another approaching Dutch War when incidents on remote seas were reported at the Council for Foreign Plantations. This time the French and the English were allies and seemed invincible. Faced with the 'goodly, yet tirrible sight' of the fleet sailing through the Dover–Calais straits, the Dutch initially withdrew. Evelyn found himself reappointed as a commissioner for the sick and wounded and prisoners of war along with two of his former colleagues, Doyley and Reymes, and under the patronage of another Thomas Clifford. Soon after, Clifford, a Catholic convert, lost his position under the terms of the Test Act, which bound all office-holders to be communicants of the Church of England. By autumn 1673 Clifford was dead, Evelyn believed by his own hand. He mourned 'a valiant, uncorrupt gent: ambitious not Covetous, generous, Passionate, and a most constant sincere friend to me in particular'.[33]

The commissioners were better prepared and more experienced this time. Their systems were both rigorous and flexible and they were urged to deal with everything 'in as husbandly and thrifty manner as you can'. But the Stop of Exchequer, caused by the Crown's mounting debt and which suspended all cash payment for the following year, was a disaster. Within a year Evelyn's district (enlarged since the previous commission) was £9,000 in arrears.

He returned to a peripatetic life. The day-to-day horror was no less disturbing for being familiar. Witnessing an operation on a seaman with severe gangrene, Evelyn mused: 'Lord, what miseries . . . & what confusion & mischiefe dos the avarice, anger, and ambition of Princes cause in the world, who might be happier with halfe they possesse: This stoute man, was but a common sailer.' Returning from Rochester, he took comfort in the beauty and order of the Kentish landscape 'after the sad & afflicting specctacles & objects I was come from'.[34]

The system still proved utterly inadequate. Even in Deptford, Evelyn discovered that sick seamen were sent to lodgings 'destitute and wretched', only to be turned away. To abandon them without so much as shifts 'is not only very unchristian but plainly barbaric', he reported to the Admiralty. Those left behind in the hospitals were often seen as naval detritus: 'Captains are glad to have that excuse to be rid of them being most ploughmen and labourers, Taylors, Cobblers tinkers and such like, more fit to be at home or at Plough or in their chimney corners than to serve His Majesty.'[35]

The Dutch fleet, still under Admiral de Ruyter's command, met the duke of York's fleet off the Suffolk coast in the devastating Battle of Sole Bay on 28 May 1672. Among those who died was Pepys's patron the earl of Sandwich, incarcerated with hundreds inside the burning hull of the new frigate the *Royal James*. Evelyn observed that Sandwich had been 'utterly against the War from the beginning' and 'was for deliberation, & reason'. Albemarle and others were 'for action & slaughter without either'. Brave to the end, Sandwich had 'perish'd to gratifie the pride & envy, of some I named'. At his state funeral the catafalque was taken along the river from Deptford to Westminster Abbey. Only the previous month, Evelyn and Reymes had been pallbearers at the funeral of a French admiral, another victim of the same battle, in Rochester Cathedral. Evelyn thanked Reymes for coming to support him, for 'the stresse of both these Warrs, lay more on me, by far, than on any of my breatheren'. By the time Evelyn met the king in July at Sheerness, on the wrecked *Charles*, he was incandescent with rage at the waste of 'so many good men' as well as at the destruction of the fleet.[36]

Some individuals came to Evelyn's aid, giving money or gifts in kind. Lord Ossory, Ormonde's son and Evelyn's friend, donated £40, while Samuel Tuke personally provided beds and provisions for sick and destitute seamen and visited them in St Thomas's Hospital. Back at court and living at Somerset House where Catherine of Braganza spent much of her time, Tuke had asked the queen to arrange for a thousand clean shirts to be sent to the ports, but the king objected. 'Of this take noe further notice but my deere wyfe & I resolved wee would do somthing in this matter', Tuke told Evelyn. With their friends, 'wee will make up 100 & dispatch them to you, wee hope wee are not mistaken in the application of our Charity. My wyfe sayes you must have them washed before they wear them.' They had no objection to some being given to Dutch prisoners. The energetic, humane couple cut through the lethargy and indifference around them.[37] Later Tuke told Evelyn that the Dutch ambassador was offering a peace but the king was unable to accept it without French agreement.

Like Clifford, Tuke did not live to see the peace treaty signed in February 1674. But for the commissioners the end of war was merely the beginning of another argument about the accounts. Over the coming years the Navy Office unpicked the figures: in 1681 the commissioners learned that a staggering £50,866 remained unpaid and would remain so until the accounts were signed off as correct.[38] The obvious moral rectitude of Evelyn, who had never accepted a bribe, colluded or connived (and who personally lost at least £500 in office), was persuasive but the case dragged on until 1688. The Admiralty even had the effrontery to accuse the author of *Sylva* of felling trees without permission.

Answering now to Danby, who took on Clifford's role as lord treasurer, Evelyn completed the first part of his history, entitled *Navigation and Commerce*, in 1674. Immediately, the stationer Benjamin Tooke received a warrant to stop the presses. 'There were things in it of State which you had not to doe with derogatory to His Majesty's Allys, the complaint I am informed comes from the Dutch Ambassador,' Tooke said. He asked Evelyn to confirm that they were not putting themselves in danger.[39] So used to prostrating himself in print in front of the king, Evelyn now faced a royal injunction on the sale or printing of his book, said to contain 'expressions derogatory to the amity and good understanding between us and some of our allies' and, more cruelly to Evelyn, 'wherein [the author] also intermeddles with certain matters of state beyond what becomes him or belongs to him'.[40] Notwithstanding the king's subsequent reassurances that he was merely pacifying the Dutch ambassador, Evelyn was out of his depth; he had been asked the impossible, to write a history of the conflict that offended none of the parties. That summer the siege of Maastricht was re-enacted below the castle walls at Windsor, showing the Dutch being humiliated at the hands of the French. Yet at the same time preparations were beginning for the marriage of

Charles's niece Mary (Clarendon's granddaughter) to William, Prince of Orange.

Tuke's death, in January 1674, upset Mary Evelyn greatly. 'I believe it almost impossible to meet with a person so worthy in himself, and so disposed to esteem me again.'[41] His widow, left with small children to look after, had to find support. Through her family, the Sheldons, she had connections at court and Evelyn pleaded her case with Arlington. As a Catholic she was at an advantage where Queen Catherine was concerned, but as a widow wearing a veil she could not attend court, unless as a lady of the bedchamber.[42] That spring she became a dresser to the queen, a full-time role usually held by women in the upper ranks of the gentry, beginning a miserable existence tossed to and fro by the vicissitudes of her sombre mistress's life.

In the summer of 1674, eight-year-old Mary Evelyn spent several weeks with Lady Tuke and her daughters at Windsor Castle. She returned home steeped in details about fashion and gossip; she could recognise the finest lace and ribbon, 'point de Venice and Rubans, [and] knows the Names of every one in their Court and their concerns'.[43] The duke of York's young Italian second wife, Mary of Modena, was a breath of fresh air at court compared to the lugubrious Portuguese queen. Mary Tuke reported that she

> sups abrode two or three times in a weeke and comes home by Torch light. She does not love to come the ordinary way downe staires, as every body els dos, but she creps out of her windos and runs downe the steepest hill that ever you saw. Some times she tumbles and makes those that follow her doe the same. The truth is I did never think the Italine [breeding?] could have aforded such a romp as she proves.[44]

Meanwhile the Evelyns' financial affairs had taken a turn for the worse. William Prettyman, who had been dragged down by his fraudulent brother, went to Chancery to recover the money he claimed Richard Browne still owed him. The case ran for many years, resulting in immense legal fees and not finally reaching a settlement until 1690, by which time a Pandora's box of family disputes about entail was open. Evelyn – like Dickens – came to loathe the Chancery court, seeing it as venal and merciless, as it proved to be in his experience. The Evelyn girls might yet become as impoverished as the Tuke girls who lived with them for some time in Deptford.

But, for all the black clouds, life at Sayes Court charmed visitors. Rather as the teenage duchess lightened the atmosphere at court, Mary Evelyn brought a touch of France to Deptford. Bohun, who had never 'breath'd the soft aire of the continent', felt going there was almost like travelling. He realised that Mary missed Paris and guessed: 'you look upon your selfe as sent home by the

malice of fortune, & banish'd into your native country by the Angry gods.'[45]
She had revealed her feelings to William Glanville when he went to Paris in
1669. The Faubourg St Germain is 'so pleasant a part of the towne I admire
you can live out of it', she told him, saying he should look out for their house
when he passes the Charité. He must forgive her reminiscences: 'I feare you
will judge I mention Paris with that affection persons in Age remember the
satisfactions of their youth.'[46]

Mary was cheerfully both mistress of her house and superintendent of the
garden during her husband's frequent absences. Life went on as usual except
they played more 'ombre', a popular three-handed Spanish card game. With
the return of smallpox, there could be no social life. And there were small
annoyances, as she told Bohun, writing in her father's room, where he is
unwell. 'I do not write 3 lines without the interuption of the girls, the noise
of the hammer in the next roome, and my Fathers complaints which I hope
will excuse all omissions'. But she stuck to house rules, apologetically refusing
Bohun's offer of some Spanish pigs since 'I cannot entertaine them so kindly
as I wish for Mr Evelyn you know is an Enemy to those creatures in generall
for making of gaps and rooting up the turff, which are crimes he scarce
pardons the proffitable sow'. Another gift from a neighbour 'was removed to
Wooton on the same account'.[47]

Her life was surprisingly independent, centred on a circle of devoted
friends, both men and women, who were appreciative of her sharp intelligence and emotional honesty. Mary Evelyn had no patience with social or
intellectual posturing but she deployed gentle irony to great effect. She told
Ralph Bohun (who left Deptford in 1671): 'I have lived under the roofe of the
learned, and in the neighbourhood of science, it has had no other effect on
such a temper as mine is, but that of admiration and that too, but where it is
reduced to practice.' She told him not to expect her to have 'extraordinary
notions of things wholy out of my way', for, she continued: 'Women were not
borne to read Authors and censure the learned, to compare lives and judge of
virtues, to give rules of morality and sacrifice to the muses.' They have other
duties, 'the care of Children's education, observing a Husbands commands,
assisting the sick, relieving the poore, and being serviceable to our friends',
and if 'one of a thousand aspires a litle higher, her fate commonly ixposes her
to wonder, but adds litle of esteeme'. Her benchmark of absurdity was
Margaret Cavendish. If she disliked someone her pen could be wickedly
sharp.[48]

When Glanville set off for France, she compared their situations: 'I cannot
reach much beyond Westminster, I somtimes get as farr as the Play House,
where the moderne humors are brought upon the stage, whether excelling the
Ancient I pretend not to Judge but they divert, and the more, the Originalls

being extant . . . Epitomies of the folly of life.' Commenting on John Dryden's *The Conquest of Granada*, she called it,

> a play so full of Ideas that the most refined Romance I ever read, is not to compare with it. Love is made so pure, and valor so nice, that would imagine it designed for an Utopia rather than our stage. I do not quarrell with the Poet but admire one borne in the decline of morality should be able to feigne such exact virtue.

She was something of a moralist, but used a light touch: 'though it be an Erring, it is a dicerning Age we live in which does not a litle add to our condemnation, that we faile by consent.' She hoped he would not laugh at her reflections and hoped she was fair to Dryden: it 'is as much as you can expect from the leisure of one who has the care of a Nursery'.[49] When their second gardener Richard married a wealthy woman and went to Barbados it struck her as being like Spenser's *Faerie Queene*.

Mary and her daughters were the bachelor Bohun's closest female friends. Aware of Evelyn's entanglement with Margaret Blagge, he allowed his letters to take on an almost flirtatious tone. How strange that someone admired in two courts and praised by famous wits, he observed, 'should now wholly be abandon'd to the conduct of her domestic affairs' in the nursery or kitchen, rather than 'philosophizing'. Glanville, more red-blooded than the tutor, continually assured Mary of his affection – 'were I in love with you, I could not love you better than I doe' – but, he told her, he could not have 'trusted' himself to be her platonic admirer twenty years before. 'At Wotton I am merry, at Deptford happy.' He would be delighted if she would hang his portrait in her closet – when he wrote this, he must have known that Evelyn had commissioned Margaret's portrait from Matthew Dixon, to show her (at her own request, he claimed) looking withdrawn in a mournful setting.[50]

Sidney Godolphin was still wooing Margaret. He argued that it was better to deal with temptations at court rather than to retreat. 'I desire your kind-nesse as much as ever & to bee with you as long as I am to bee in this world,' he reassured her.[51] After months in which her virtue (expressed by her various charitable activities) and Sidney's vice (he was an inveterate gambler) seemed to be at odds, they became increasingly committed to one another. Evelyn's London meetings were fewer and she asked him to return her letters. She spent the summer with the Berkeleys in Twickenham but returned to take part in an ambitious Christmas masque at court. Now the tenacious Christian Berkeley proposed that Margaret accompany her to Paris. The invitation proved a catalyst and on 16 May 1675 she and Godolphin were finally married in the Temple church, in utter secrecy.

Evelyn did not discover the union for a year. When he did, he drew up a hundred-page document of guidance. Shorter, and more to the point, were Mary's housekeeping instructions for Margaret. The latter, 'being from a Child, bred in Courts, may be thought (without reproch) not much to have buisied her head about Oeconomique matters', as Evelyn told Pepys when loaning him the manual as a guide for his own housekeeper.[52] Evelyn always saw his relationship with 'that concealed Saint, and incomparable Creature, so well known to me, and my Wife in particular' as one of blameless innocence.[53]

He continued to sit on the Council for Foreign Plantations where Benjamin Worsley, a stalwart of Hartlib's circle, was secretary. Cold exchanges about slaves, human 'commodities', as they were termed, traded by the Africa Company like cocoa beans, were minuted dispassionately alongside mundane discussions of premises, duties and appointments and the reports from Jamaica, New England or Surinam, the latter where English planters were in contention with the Dutch. In the handsome room on Queen Street, its atlases and globes opening a window on a wider world, the focus was sometimes on topics closer to Evelyn's competence, such as whether Asian plants could be transplanted to temperate climes.[54]

After he became a commissioner for the sick and wounded, as well as taking on the secretaryship of the Royal Society while Thomas Henshaw was in Copenhagen, Evelyn rarely had time to attend meetings at the reconstituted and renamed Council of Trade and Plantations. John Locke had become secretary, the philosopher replacing the dissenter Worsley, who had been forced to resign under the harsh terms of the first Test Act. But the financial sclerosis which affected all public bodies soon furred the council's veins and George Evelyn's New Year letter to his brother ended with commiserations that the council had been 'declared void'. He hoped he had received all his arrears.[55]

Councils were dissolved; powerful men lost their positions; nothing lasted. In 1674 Arlington was demoted to lord chamberlain.[56] Prodigal hospitality and a love of 'fine things' had plunged the family into serious debt but Evelyn remained extremely proud of his own contribution to the Euston landscape. 'My Lord himselfe is given to no expensive vise but building & to have all things rich, polite & Princely' and 'knows not how to retrench'.[57]

As Arlington left the political stage on one side, John Berkeley re-entered it on the other, just back from a spell as lord lieutenant of Ireland. Berkeley House, west of Clarendon House, may have cost £30,000 but Evelyn thought it unwieldy and poorly planned, 'there are no Clossets, all are roomes of State'. It had the architectural defects he had come to expect from Hugh May, who had not chosen wisely from Palladio, the portico being 'the very worst of his booke'.[58] The gardens, however, drew no cavils. The gleaming holly hedges on the terrace were Evelyn's idea.

In 1675 Berkeley was sent to Paris as ambassador and invited young John to join his household, which included Margaret Blagge, by then married to Godolphin, though still unknown to anyone.[59] John had been living in London with young William Glanville and one of his uncle George's two sons, 'Wotton Jack' since, as his mother put it, 'young Men will have their way'. The group of young men who had first become friends at Wotton had been reduced by one member since their cousin, Daniel Parke, was now back in Virginia. In Paris, lovingly supervised by Margaret, John would be in trustworthy hands, her responsibility for the education, moral and spiritual guidance of Evelyn's increasingly errant son serving as a continuing close link between them. As a *quid pro quo* Berkeley put all his business affairs in John's father's hands: 'I know not how to avoyd or refuse it', wrote Evelyn. For the next three years during his missions to France and then Holland, Berkeley brusquely, even rudely, treated Evelyn as his steward, without payment or thanks for his trouble, as Evelyn told Lady Sylvius, the former Anne Howard, later.[60]

On arrival in Paris, John found himself left to his own devices in a garret since Lady Berkeley was 'mighty busy in buying Clothes and furniture'. He carried out tasks for the Royal Society, delivering Oldenburg's letter to Henri Justel, who asked if *Sylva* had yet appeared in Latin and suggested that John try translating *Kalendarium Hortense* and the as yet unpublished *Terra* into French under his supervision.[61] Christiaan Huygens had heard from Oldenburg too, who suggested that he should contact John so that the young man might 'profit from your learning & virtue' and be introduced to 'persons of honour & learning' around the Académie des Sciences. He would bring copies of the latest *Philosophical Transactions* and Robert Hooke's 'contentious treatise on helioscopes' with him.[62] Meanwhile Lord Berkeley grumbled that Evelyn had not written or sent him the gazettes, the news-sheets which reported current events. His lordship also wanted his spectacles sent to Paris, together with six bamboo canes with round heads.[63]

To start with, Evelyn assumed the worst of John, left to roam in Paris alone. A particularly sore point was his horse ('Beast'), which John had insisted on taking, despite the fact that it was almost blind, lame and unrideable. He had even failed to write to his mother, who was 'not of a temper you know, to take exceptions; but therefore should you give her no occasion,' his father warned him. Where were his reports on the ceremonies at Versailles? 'You are very frugal in leting us know any-thing of what you see and observe, and we hope it is, because you are better Employ'd.'[64] But there were good reasons for John's silence, as the Berkeleys' chaplain wrote in his defence. John was never taken to audiences at court or invited when the family entertained, which the 'incomperable Madam Blagge' could corroborate.[65] Mary realised her son's miserable situation; surely Lord Berkeley was not too grand 'to treat people levelly according to their quality'? She sympathised with Margaret, who, Jack reported, was out of favour too: 'her life must needs be uneasy since she chiefly went in complaisance to my Lady and the unsteadeness of my ladyes temper proove a griefe to her who is so sincere and so good.'[66]

Having stayed on after her family left Paris at the Restoration, Margaret was a Francophile and she encouraged John to follow her example. He was learning conversational French and developing a taste for the literature. He was also proposing to move out of Paris, ostensibly to avoid the English, but really to escape the monstrous Berkeleys.

Evelyn was particularly insistent that John learn mathematics. With a solid grounding, 'handsomely season'd with other ingenuous Learning', he could join the ranks of lawyers, bishops, men of science and medicine who had benefited from a grasp of the subject – none more so than 'that prodigie of all usefull and ingenious arts Sir Christopher Wren, his Majesties Surveyor General'. With mathematics, 'I should not despaire of any Employment; such Security and Confidence it gives upon all occasions', but he will not impose anything on his son, 'whilst yet I wish you would once determine your Choice for your owne repose, as well as for my satisfaction'.[67]

Later Evelyn wrote in distress to Anne Sylvius, hearing that Christian Berkeley thought him ungrateful for their hospitality to his son. He quoted Margaret as his witness when he complained that they had 'so little distinguish'd him from the Domestic servants; that a Deare friend of your Ladyships and mine there . . . Advis'd me to give him leave to Remove, and shortly after he came quite away . . . Let my Lady then say no more of Ingratitude upon this account.'[68] Anger rarely surfaces in Evelyn's letters but the Berkeleys stretched his accommodating nature to breaking point.

In December 1675, Evelyn received a tactful letter from Dr Thomas Good of Balliol, surprised that he had forgotten his old college, not even sending presentation volumes of his publications to the library, decimated by the civil wars and depleted of new stock after 'the dreadful fire in London'. Good hit a nerve. Evelyn was mortified, pleading in exoneration that he was currently owed almost £2,000 ('most of it for rent') though 'it is not to every one that I would discover this infirmity'. As for his books, he disingenuously claimed that he only presented copies if asked and 'did not think them considerable enough to make any public present of'. In March Good wrote again, thanking him for his £20 gift and hoping that he would still consider adding to the library.[69] The distractions of his life in the mid-1670s, both personal and financial, had made Evelyn forgetful of old obligations and even lax in the promotion of his own work.

Nonetheless he was considering publishing an extract from *Elysium Britannicum* – the 'Treatise of Acetaria'. But how could it be extracted without 'some blemish to the rest', he asked Beale. For more than twenty years he had struggled to organise and digest the material for his great book but now he doubted 'I shall ever have strength and leasure to bring it to Maturity'. Even his most successful venture *Sylva* had failed in one important respect. 'We are not yet Oeconomists' Evelyn told Beale, pointing out that the Royal Society's printer had made almost £500 from the book but not a penny had reached the society's coffers.

Financially imprudent, the Fellows were also easy figures of fun, as Thomas Shadwell's play *The Virtuoso* (1676) made clear. The central figure in this comedy is Sir Nicholas Gimcrack, who quotes virtually verbatim from *Micrographia*.

> Then for the Blue upon Plumbs [*sic*] it is nothing but many living Creatures. I have observ'd upon a Wall-Plum (with my most exquisite Glasses, which cost me several thousands of pounds) at first beginning to turn blue, it comes first to Fluidity, then to Orbiculation, then Fixation, so to Angulization, then Christallization, from thence to Germination or Ebullition, then Vegetation, then Plantanimation, perfect Animation, Sensation, Local Motion, and the like.[70]

After this disquisition, Gimcrack's servant brings him back to reality: 'Sir there are a great number of sick men waiting in the Hall for your Worship.' Evelyn could recognise aspects of himself caricatured in Sir Formal Trifle, a stuffy figure prone to long-winded explanations, since his account of the habits of the hunting spider appeared in virtually the same words he had given Hooke for *Micrographia*.[71] The cruel thrust of Shadwell's message was delivered by one of his characters: 'Knowledge is like virtue, its own reward.'

The Fellows were further mortified to learn that the king had attended a performance of the play, evidence that the Royal Society was a laughing stock at court. Charles's behaviour seemed to bear out Magalotti's portrait of him: 'he seems to take great delight in every noble curiosity, not excluding the next experiments and natural science; but even if he manages to have some taste for these things, he is not capable of having any esteem for them, nor for those who practise them.' He referred to the Fellows as 'my fools' and the mention of serious men weighing the air guaranteed mirth at court.[72]

Hooke saw *The Virtuoso* with Thomas Tompion the clock-maker. 'Damned Doggs. *Vindica me deus*. People almost pointed', he wrote in his diary.[73]

Evelyn, already shocked by mockery of the church in fashionable circles, now found himself in the satirist's stocks and, like Hooke, took the jibes personally. If Evelyn's beloved Margaret Blagge had fallen for Shadwell's foolishness, what could he expect of scoffing courtiers? He wrote Margaret an agonised letter, attacking the 'Trade of Mocking and Jeasting & disguising the Person' as unchristian and improper.[74]

The Royal Society was in urgent need of new blood and strong leadership. Attendance was dropping, year by year, and subscription income had fallen. In November 1677, Sir Joseph Williamson – by then secretary of state – was chosen (not without opposition) to succeed Viscount Brouncker, president since 1662.[75] Hooke was stretched beyond endurance by his extramural activities as an architect and surveyor, designing the new Royal College of Physicians as well as Bethlehem (Bedlam) Hospital, which Evelyn compared admiringly to the Tuileries. In the late 1670s Evelyn, though by no means a natural denizen of the new world of the coffee house, found himself periodically in Man's on Chancery Lane or Garaway's on Cornhill discussing the increasingly desperate finances of the Royal Society with Hooke and other Fellows such as Wren, the treasurer Abraham Hill and Sir John Hoskins (another future president). He and Hooke were also composing the argument with which to preface the third edition of *Sylva*.

When Williamson stood aside in 1681, Wren took his place as president. From time to time Evelyn, once again at the heart of the Royal Society, took the chair. Occasionally he still presented papers; he and Henshaw jointly offered their recipes for perfumes to the Fellows in March 1681 but Hooke's own minutes of a meeting the previous month state that 'Mr Evelyn gave an account' after which came a blank.[76] The diary offers no clues. By now the Royal Society had returned to its interest in useful trades and the spread of practical information. In late 1679 Joseph Moxon began to issue his *Mechanical Exercises*, a monthly part work (the first ever in English), and became the first tradesman elected as a Fellow. Moxon, hydrographer royal since 1662 and aspirant to the position of the Royal Society's printer, cited Bacon's insistence 'that Philosophy would be improv'd by having the Secrets of all Trades lye open . . . I find that one Trade may borrow many Eminent Helps in Work of another Trade.'[77] Evelyn helped move the Arundel library to Gresham College and regularly attended meetings, at one of which topics ranged from the study of embryos and the effects of freezing to the habits of the Greenland whale. Sometimes the Royal Society effortlessly mimicked Shadwell's satire.

In Deptford, Mary Evelyn was still dogged by Margaret's needs as interpreted by Evelyn. In 1677 she told Bohun that she had been finishing a picture for him: 'he would not let me breath after any thing till it was don and presented to his seraphick who deserves that and any thing a thousand times better.'[78] Mary's dry wit allowed her to deal with it all gracefully.

Evelyn had accepted a diminished role in Margaret's life, becoming trustee for her marriage settlement, and observing of the couple, 'never were Two so fram'd for one-anothers Dispositions; Never liv'd paire, in more peace & harmony'. By early 1678 she was pregnant and a gossipy letter to her husband ended happily: 'I love you as my life.'[79] Evelyn's diary still marked most Tuesdays with a pentacle. On her third wedding anniversary, Evelyn invited Margaret, the recently married Anne Howard (now Sylvius) and her sister Dorothy (now Graham) to dine and, two months later, took both his wife and his 'Seraphic' to see John Tradescant's 'Ark' in Lambeth. It was now owned by 'Industrious' Elias Ashmole, a man of whom Evelyn was always mistrustful, describing him as addicted to astrology, 'though I believe not learned'.[80]

One evening that autumn he went to dine with Margaret, only to find her in labour. Sidney was in Windsor, at court, and so Evelyn stayed on. All went well. She gave birth to a boy and Mary joined them for the christening of the infant, Francis, in the Whitehall apartment Evelyn had helped to furnish.[81] Hardly returned home, however, the Evelyns heard that Margaret had fallen desperately ill with fever and went back by boat to Whitehall. On 9 September, aged twenty-six, she died. Evelyn lost 'the most excellent, & most estimable Friend, that ever liv'd', believing 'my very Soule was united to hers' in a 'virtuous, & inviolable friendship'. He was inconsolable but was obliged to cede the post of principal mourner to her distraught husband, who on hearing the news 'fell downe flat like a dead man'.[82]

Mary wrote to Bohun that Margaret had died in the prime of life and at the height of her happiness. And, 'tho not in the first rank of her friends', Evelyn's wife allowed that she combined the grace of a lady of the court with the sincerity and innocence of a primitive Christian.[83] The letter is at odds with Evelyn's careful image of Margaret as his wife's intimate friend. Now he tried to transfer his friendship to Margaret's widower, but his pressing need for a patron in his campaign to settle Sir Richard's debts complicated their dealings. Godolphin's son was brought up by his aunt, Godolphin's sister and Evelyn's friend Jael Boscawen, and it was through her that he continued his close relationship with the family.

Evelyn was now counting on Lord Danby to resolve his father-in-law's financial affairs. In Paris some twenty-five years earlier, Thomas Osborne, as Danby then was, had known both Evelyn and Browne well, 'on which account I was too Confident of succeeding in his favour, as I had don in his Predecessors'.[84] Evelyn reminded him of his obligations to Sir Richard when he had been 'in those daies almost domestique with us at Paris, and a witnesse of his Sufferings', hoping he might 'do him now a real kindenesse', although 'favour is deceitfull, and stations sliperie, and daily changes render all things uncertaine'.[85] Danby could well appreciate the force of his words, for though 'his Lordship does yet keep the King's ear' impeachment proceedings against him had begun and Lady Sunderland reckoned him 'a wounded deer'. Since her husband was now secretary of state, Evelyn was unusually well informed.[86]

With the two Houses at loggerheads, the monarch (seen as in the grip of the French) was once again at odds with Parliament. The nation was fired by rabid anti-Catholic feeling, whipped up by the Popish Plot and Titus Oates's outrageous allegations. The Test Acts were, in Evelyn's view, 'a mighty blow' which caught many 'good Protestants' in the net as well as being punitive for Catholics. Evelyn was horrified by the growing religious extremism and by Oates's ludicrous accusations that the queen, so 'pious & vertuous', had planned to poison the king.[87]

In early January 1679 the skies darkened unnaturally one Sunday morning. Evelyn was a past master in finding a concordance between climatic and cosmic extremes and current affairs. A fortnight later the Cavalier Parliament, which had sat since the Restoration, fell. Dr Pierce, dean of Salisbury, laid the blame for the current turmoil on 'the pernicious doctrines of Mr Hobbs'.[88]

In the elections of February, George Evelyn was returned as a Whig member for Surrey along with his neighbour and friend Arthur Onslow. The next month, Tory Sidney Godolphin became a commissioner at the Treasury, in Danby's place. He assured Evelyn that he might now be able to do him 'some little service' but at the appropriate moment. Evelyn invited him to Sayes Court and pressed a copy of the handsome new folio edition of *Sylva* on him, hoping that 'sated with the Splendor & Pomp of courts' he could now 'Contemplate these Rusticities with more solid delight'.[89]

CHAPTER 14

Endeavour to Submit

In 1679 Evelyn summarised his life over recent years in 'these dismal times' for old John Beale in Somerset. Who but the unworldly Dr Beale, he teased '(that stands upon the Toure, lookes down unconcern'dly on all those Tempests), can think of Gardens, and Fishponds, and the Delices and Ornaments of Peace and Tranquility?' Until recently he had been 'in perpetual motion, and hardly two moneths in a yeare at my owne habitation, or conversant with my Family' and battered by 'the publique Confusions in Church and Kingdome (never to be sufficiently deplor'd) and which cannot but most sensibly touch every sober and honest man'.[1]

The Exclusion Crisis led to public hysteria, the explosive anti-Catholic feeling exacerbated by the new grouping around the earl of Shaftesbury, the nascent Whig party. The duke and duchess of York, on whom fears about a Roman Catholic succession and unnatural alliances with France and Spain centred, were driven out of England by pamphleteers, the press having been freed by the rescinding of the 1662 Licensing Act. Religion was politics, politics religion. Parliament spoke (once again) against the king's prerogative to choose his successor.

In July Sir George Wakeman, the Catholic royal doctor, 'a worthy gent', was tried at the Old Bailey on charges of trying to poison the king and 'subvert the Government & introduce Poperie'.[2] Evelyn went to 'informe my self, and regulate my opinion of a Cause that had so alarm'd the whole Nation'. Blameless Catholic peers such as Lord Petre and Viscount Stafford were incarcerated in the Tower but walked free once the Wakeman case was revealed to be a travesty. Loyal to the duke of York, Samuel Pepys, member of Parliament for Castle Rising in Norfolk and since 1673 first secretary to the Admiralty, was accused of papist leanings. On evidence orchestrated by Shaftesbury, determined to dislodge James from the succession, he was arraigned by the Commons and committed to the Tower for his part in crimes of 'Piracy, Popery and Treachery'.

Few were safe when random accusations, rumour and perjury could bring any prominent man down overnight, a sour reminder of the early 1650s. At the Tower and then in the Marshalsea in Southwark, Evelyn visited Pepys regularly and they enjoyed congenial venison dinners together, discussing books and the current concerns of the reinvigorated Royal Society. Pepys was released, at first on bail, until the witnesses fell away and the case was dropped altogether.[3]

Mounting disillusion left Evelyn unguarded, and in an angry preface to the latest edition of *Sylva*, he lashed out at those who denigrated the Royal Society as well as at Charles II's failure to provide support for it. 'Princes have been more Renowned for their Civility to Arts and Letters, than to all their Sanguine Victories.' The French rewarded their thinkers with 'sumptuous Buildings, well furnish'd Observatories, ample Appointments, Salaries and Accommodations . . . whilst we live Precariously, and spin the Web out of our own bowels'. He might also have added that Louis XIV ensured that he was portrayed with the great institutions he founded, including the Académie des Sciences.[4] Robert Hooke, who read Evelyn's 'vindication' of the Royal Society as he prepared it and may have also been helping him with the *Elysium*, added his own comments.[5]

But Evelyn continued to hope that one of his prodigiously wealthy merchant contacts, perhaps Sir Stephen Fox or Sir Robert Clayton, the former scrivener soon to be lord mayor, who had just bought the much depleted Evelyn estate at Godstone, might rescue the Royal Society. In an indirect way, Fox was soon to help to do just that, as was Evelyn himself. In April 1681 Abraham Hill, currently the society's treasurer, advised Evelyn to sell his East India stock. Instead he delayed until December 1682, by which time his £250 investment had trebled in value.[6] He transferred it to the Royal Society and wrote to Daniel Colwall, the previous treasurer, about the transaction.[7]

In 1681 Sir Stephen and Lady Fox were considering buying the countess of Chelsea's seat, once Sir Thomas More's. The Thames-side situation answered Fox's brief for 'something neere the River, and within sight of White-Hall' while being 'as it were alltogether in the Country'. Evelyn was brokering the deal, delighted that two friends would benefit from the sale, the vendor and the purchaser.[8] However, the asking price (touching £6,000) was prohibitive and for all Evelyn's efforts, having 'never in my life eaten better fruit of all sorts, then I did there this summer and could not imagine there had ben such abundant variety, especialy of Figgs, Grapes, Peaches, Nectarine and Peares of the choycest kinds', Fox's offer fell £500 short of what was wanted. (Fortunately, the eventual buyer was equally appreciative of such a horticultural cornucopia, for the future duke of Beaufort's wife, Mary Somerset, was the great gardener of Badminton House.)[9] Instead, Fox asked

Hugh May to build him a new house, a calm haven where Evelyn became a frequent visitor. After that Evelyn found himself caught up in Lady Sunderland's unsuccessful siege of Sir Stephen Fox's daughter Jane as a match for her son Robert, stalling heroically since he had seen warning signs of a wastrel.

In spring 1680, the earl of Essex invited Evelyn to Cassiobury to admire his 'plaine' new house, yet another by Hugh May, again with ornament by Gibbons and Verrio, the reigning artists at court.[10] Evelyn always took great pride in the rise of his protégé, the Dutchman Grinling Gibbons whom he found working as a wood carver in the Deptford dockyard some ten years earlier. Gibbons's latest patron, the former Arthur Capel, was a man after Evelyn's heart, well read, 'a sober, wise, judicious & pondering person'.[11] As usual, Evelyn was critical of May's work. As Wotton and Pratt warned, retaining an existing house at all costs (as was the case here) compromised the result. Evelyn may have been regretting that he had done so at Sayes Court.

The planting at Cassiobury was bold: the immense park dissected by avenues and focused upon effects such as Spanish firs planted three deep in an oval, closing a vista. Near the house, were splendid gardens – they 'cannot be otherwise, having so skillfull an Artist to governe them as Mr Cooke, who is as to the Mechanic part not ignorant in Mathematics, & pretends to Astrologie'. Evelyn had quoted Moses Cook, a skilled arboriculturist, in the recent edition of *Sylva*.[12] While there, he and Essex spent the mornings 'Walking or riding about the Grounds & Contriving', the afternoons in the library. Essex was redundant on the political stage, and (like Arlington) had happily retreated to his estate.

The new generation of gardeners were educated men, on an equal footing with architects, and also commercially astute. Cook was George London's partner at the Brompton Park nursery.[13] Evelyn's links with plantsmen and their clients, connoisseurs such as Essex and Henry Compton, the bishop of London, brought him into a circle of expert botanists and further expanded his knowledge of species and the beginnings of modern nomenclature.

But these were pleasant distractions; and Evelyn's increasingly desperate mission was to resolve his family financial problems before his three daughters reached marriageable age. Arlington had advised Mary to request an audience with the king, a prospect 'which has neither permitted her to hope or dispaire'. Her claim, the 'ruine of her Fathers Estate', was no exaggeration.[14] Meanwhile Godolphin had not forgotten them. He intimated that a new Council of Trade might be established, since the members of the Privy Council were too few to deal with the enormous task involved and their 'presence is requird for the affaires of England alone'. Shaftesbury was prepared to help but wished, he told Mary, 'I had ben a parliament man'.[15] Perhaps, in view of what was to follow, it was as well he was not.

Evelyn wrote to Mary with rare exasperation. If she thought he could solve Sir Richard's problems through 'my owne score of acquaintance (as you seeme to do) farther than I have told you, you lay a thing on me which I cannot promise you to succeede in'. Since he could not gain employment himself, 'I cannot force great men to what we wish'. Godolphin was even unable to help his own brother. Many positions had been axed to save money. The next day Evelyn was in court again about (her) cousin George Tuke's affairs, and would have to pay another £20 to 'cursed lawyers'. He told Beale that three executorships and the continual family lawsuits were enough 'to distract a more steady, and composed Genius then is mine'.

But periodically optimism broke through. Both Godolphin and Fox were commissioners to the Treasury, and suggested that they could at least secure the lease of Sayes Court. Yet, despite Fox's assurance of his 'cherefull Concurrence' in August 1680, they lost their petition by one vote, that cast by Laurence Hyde, earl of Rochester, whose own father had personally persuaded Browne to stay on at the French court, 'at the expense of his patrimonie, when every-body deserted his Majestie and his Cause' and then drew up the king's (worthless) 'solemn Promise'. In voting against, Rochester invoked the dangers of precedent – the case was one of many.

Now Evelyn, perhaps egged on by Mary, turned his eloquence once more on Godolphin. In a remarkable letter which he may never have sent in this outspoken form, he detailed their sacrifices, which, in the name of friendship and justice, as he put it, were long overdue for repayment. Browne had stayed in post, having lost his own estate and his wife's jointure, while Evelyn bought the leases 'out of my owne fortune', enabling his father-in-law to 'continue in his Majesties Service, to keepe-up the House, the Chapell, and the Service of the Church of England'. Browne's expensive clerkship had been a waste and he was still owed almost £12,000. He had received £200 for twenty years' service – was that not enough to make 'a Friend Concern'd and perhaps a passionate Greate man angrie'?[16]

Godolphin queried why the claim had only just arisen. Evelyn replied that Browne had not pursued it while he was in France, lest he expose Evelyn's remaining assets to the authorities. Mild-mannered and credulous as Browne was, he had imagined that at the Restoration 'Honors, and Estates, and Offices etc would have rain'd from heaven on him'.[17] Now in 1682 if, as Evelyn had heard, all requests for recompence were being deferred, they would be exposed to 'slippery' changes and the whim of 'the next Favourite that shall succeed you; and how soone, who can tell?' He was desperate 'for want of some more lucrative office than any I yet have prospect of', as he told his son, whose debts were yet another burden on his estate.

Although driven by necessity, Evelyn's hunger for office could be mistaken for ambition. He told Pepys, who nominated him for the navy board, that he was hurt to hear it was said that 'I aym'd at high matters, and things that I understand not'. He had confided, back in 1680, that 'I am now a Candidate for some such thing in this Shuffling of the Cards', but only through the kind efforts of his friends.[18] Whatever it was, it did not materialise.

John was preparing to marry Martha Spencer. Before the wedding Evelyn chose to write to him 'because Words are transient sounds, & little minded, and the reading these few lines may perhaps give you occasion of fixing your Meditations the better on what I suggest'. John was not well but 'God Almighty never sends any Affliction but for our good', and his father suggested he read the scriptures for an hour and a half a day.[19] John appears to have suffered from depression, as had his uncle Richard Evelyn, perhaps a legacy from their morose grandmother. His physician had been Dr Jasper Needham, one of Evelyn's 'dearest remaining sincere friends', who had died in 1679.

John had dropped his law studies, 'the Calamity of the times interrupting', but, wrote his father, he had also wasted his time and 'deceiv'd both me and your selfe'. Now, until he found 'decent employment' he must settle at Sayes Court and help look after the demesne. When John protested, Evelyn asked him if he had thought about the expense of living in town: rent, furniture, servants, parish duties and city temptations. Now that everything was settled on him 'except one poor farm in Sussex', he must repay his debts. While he could not force John to stay under his roof against his inclinations, if he lived 'in a mean way' in London, people would think they had had a family breach. Evelyn was adamant that the family must stay together – should they all come to London? 'Speake boldly, without reserves or pretences,' he instructed his son.

John's short attention span was 'a disposition that a saint now with God [Margaret Blagge] was wont to tel me she had observ'd in you'. Evelyn lambasted him: he was getting fat and drinking too much, nor did he 'pray nor reade nor meditate', appearing to find neither books, arts nor 'ingenuous industry' worthwhile. In mounting desperation Evelyn made a confession to John. 'I advise you of that which in my owne selfe I find would have the same effect did I not labour to prevent it.' His busy life had been, he seemed to hint, a displacement activity for a similar tendency. While he had been obliged to set out in life without the guidance of his own father, John had always benefited from his father's close attention to his education and wellbeing.[20]

Perhaps taking refuge from this barrage of chastisement, John was now at Wotton with George, 'the young master', and his cousins, 'Wotton Jack' and William Glanville. The letters continued; he was in his late twenties, it was time to leave his 'insignificant & unsteady life' since he was not one of those 'raw & more giddy heires of opulent families, who consume their best yeares among their dogs' just as their own parents had done. John had wider interests and 'time & domestic concernes calls you to a steadier course'.

John had claimed he wanted to study languages and serve overseas but his father knew he would hate the boredom of court life, the endless ceremonial and elaborate dress, 'what you were wont to despise'. A courtier needs 'a particular politenesse & greate addresse' and must 'most infallibly make havoc of his Conscience & his vertue as the place is now depraved'. Of course, some emerged unscathed: 'I have seene of both sexes, without reproach, but they were persons extraordinary.' Evelyn warned that, like their friend Sir Gabriel Sylvius, 'weary of running abroad to no purpose' he would probably end up 'exceedingly out of purse', for 'either abroad or at home you will be payd at great Leasure'. How could he succeed as 'a meere Courtier'?

Instead, why not use his father's influential contacts and 'the credite which I have (without vanity I mention it)'? Although John had a prejudice against the law, 'for feare of not succeeding', he would travel the country on circuit and have time for 'other polite studies'. By the age of thirty he could have a considerable practice 'and by 40 what may you not promise yourself of prefer-ment'. Evelyn asks him not to burn his letter or put it aside 'but sit downe & seriously ponder what I have suggested', and signs himself 'your most loving Father'.[21]

Having dealt with his morality and future employment, on the eve of his wedding (on Shrove Tuesday 1680) Evelyn offered his son advice on all aspects of marriage, pointing out the seriousness of a couple's vows. Martha had two examples to follow: those of her mother-in-law and that 'incomparable saint Mrs Godolphin'. Nevertheless, in 'an Age when people do not so much reguard the Person, as the Possessions', he was pleased with the marriage, as was his wife, who told Mary Tuke that, though partial, 'I never saw Bride and Bridegroom behave themselves better'. She added: 'They continue pleased with one an other and are now with us where the pretty little woman seems well enough contented and much delighted with her appartment.'[22]

Mary Tuke wrote back from Brussels, where she had gone to avoid the anti-Catholic feeling in England. She knew both bride and bridegroom and felt that closer acquaintance would 'increase fond love into a really and constant friendship', the essence of marriage. She hoped Martha enjoyed living at Deptford as much as she had. Meanwhile her late husband's patron, the duke of Norfolk, had refused her any financial help.[23] She did not return to England until 1682, admitting she had not hurried back to court since those in royal service are 'like tir'd horses willing to rest'.

Within eighteen months of the wedding, £3,000 of Martha's settlement had gone to meet interest payments and the costs of the Chancery suit with Prettyman. Evelyn again pressed Godolphin. With his hold on the exchequer, the customs and tax collection services, and the navy, his position at court 'and a thousand more that streame from the Ocean of the Lord Tressurers', could he not find anything to alleviate their difficulties? Evelyn's three daughters 'grow upon me apace'. *In extremis*, Evelyn realised that the Test Acts could work to his family's advantage: might positions not fall available, their incumbents 'not conforming' to the church? Godolphin was the only man to whom 'I display my Infirmities freely, and without reserve'. Consider, said Evelyn, Sir Richard Browne 'growing old in sorrows' compared to Sir George Downing, rewarded for a career of 'continuous disloyalty' at some £10,000 a year. He apologised to his correspondent for 'this tedious Paper; I think it shall be the very last, I will ever entertain my Friend so long, upon an account which lookes so like selfe-Interest; I dare say, 'tis uneasy to you and what you did not expect'.[24]

Evelyn was buckling under the strain and opened 1682 with a bout of bad health, including fits, which he dealt with by sitting in a 'deepe Churn or Vessell' and drinking an infusion of thistle before going to bed, heavily swaddled. Much weakened by 'this Warning & admonition', he decided to put his papers in order, inventory the house and make a new will. With intimations of mortality, he embarked on a mental spring-cleaning exercise, going back to his diary and working it into a continuous narrative based upon his library, his correspondence and notebooks, and his (usually) accurate memory. From the beginning of 1684 the diary, increasingly laden with his sermon notes, becomes more of a contemporary account rather than a memoir.[25]

Yet he had another quarter-century ahead of him, and, as if a happy augury, at sunrise on 1 March 1682 his second grandson was born, another John Evelyn, the boy who would fulfil all his grandfather's hopes. John and Martha's first son had not survived infancy; now a 'hopeful' boy had arrived during his (maternal) great-grandfather's lifetime. Lady Tuke was glad to hear that the 'pretty little silent woman', so good at bearing pain without fuss, had had an easy labour. That summer Sayes Court was unusually calm; Mary, back from taking the waters at Tunbridge Wells, told Bohun that 'we live much more quietly then wee have done a great while. All the litle designes are finished at present' and it was time to look around for new projects. John was busy with a translation from Plutarch's *Lives* but 'you are to take no notice till you see him in print among the witts who have sett upon translating the whole, every one taking a part'; 'as for Mr Evelyn he lives most part of the night in his hole according to custome.' Probably as yet unknown to Mary, he was preparing a life of Margaret Blagge.[26] The only potential disruption of their calm came from Wotton where George, William Glanville had reported to his nephew, was 'very difficult & unsettled in his resolutions which proceeds from the influence my Cozen Mary has on him who disswades him from securing any of his mony in land it being her interest to have it otherwise'.

At this opportune moment, something concrete emerged to engage Evelyn's energies. Since he was a council member of the Royal Society, Sir Stephen Fox asked him to persuade the Fellows to sell their interest in Chelsea College in September 1681. The king wanted to build a barracks – despite fierce parliamentary opposition to a standing army – and a home for elderly ex-combatants. It was not Charles, however, who would pay for the site. Fox, a man for whom Evelyn had unlimited respect, paid the £1,300 the Royal Society asked. Some thought the arrangement fair since his fortune had come from the army.[27] In the end Fox's total personal contribution to the hospital was over £13,000. His generosity was ascribed to humanitarian motives, being prompted by his shame at seeing honourable men who had given themselves for their nation reduced to begging on the street. Thus, he did 'what he could to remove such a scandal to the Kingdom'.[28] The building at Chelsea merely intensified the urgent need for a similar institution for seamen.

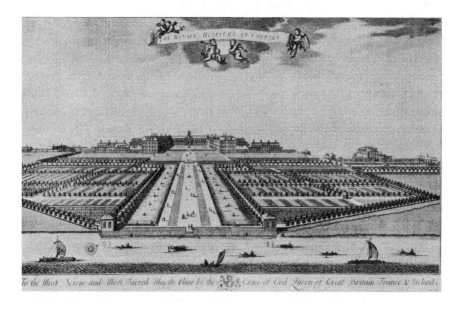

21 Wren's hospital in Chelsea, seen from the river. Evelyn was much involved in planning London's first military hospital.

Since Evelyn's fruitless efforts at Chatham, two military hospitals had been built overseas. One, the Invalides, founded in 1670 by Louis XIV, was almost complete, and its plans and elevations were widely published. John had sent his father prints of the king's new buildings in Paris. In Dublin, Kilmainham had been recently founded by the duke of Ormonde on the king's behalf.

Now Fox asked Evelyn to help him draw up the 'Government' for Chelsea, which he did promptly, proposing that four hundred men be housed in thirty-two dormitories with 'laws & orders as strict as in any religious convent'. As well as a chapel, Evelyn was eager that there should be a library 'since some souldiers might possibly be studious, when they were at this leasure to recolect'.[29] The surveyor-general, Sir Christopher Wren, went with Evelyn and Fox to present Archbishop Sancroft with the 'plot & design' in May 1681. Although there is disappointingly little anecdotal evidence of Evelyn's dealings with Wren, the two men met regularly at the Royal Society and Evelyn had stood godfather to Wren's son William in June 1679.[30]

By summer 1682 the foundations were laid. As the building rose, Wren's elegant riverside military hospital of brick and stone arcaded courts and colonnades began to appear more palace than almshouse.[31] Located well back from the Thames but linked to it by regal gardens and canals cut down to the riverside, the setting owed much to that of Maisons on the Seine, to which Evelyn had directed Wren many years before.

In Deptford Mary Evelyn was tired out. Old age and poor health, including persistent gout and dropsy, had made her father querulous. While she and her older daughters went to Tunbridge Wells for a month, her husband held the fort with his youngest daughter, Susanna. Bohun, as ever veering between the sanctimonious and the concerned, implied that Evelyn might offer her more support and fewer philosophical homilies. Seneca 'said many fine things in prays of resignation and poverty, when he was most at ease in his fortune of any man in his time; In such a case a magnificent morall sentence is a pretty diversion, but will serve us in small stead in reall afflictions.' He recalled their discussions 'under the Holly hedg at Deptford'.[32]

Sir Richard Browne's sudden death in late February 1683 came as a relief. Nearing eighty, his kindliness had hardened into peevishness. Mary was understanding. 'Compare the state of health with that of sicknesse despondency Age,' she wrote to Bohun, considering his 'last salleys of displeassure as attendants of paine'. Family friends were sympathetic. Lady Sylvius wrote from The Hague: 'the partting with an old frind must be a grate affliction to those who kno so well that charicter and have lived so long togeather.' Mary was fortunate, Mary Tuke reminded her, to have had 'so good a father' and to have still 'so kind a husband and the prospect of children that my proove daily greater comforte yet', but it was nonetheless difficult to lose someone 'one esteems and cherrishes'.[33]

Always modest, Sir Richard had asked that the burial be 'with as little pomp and Vanity as Decency and his qualitie permitts'.[34] In exile in the 1650s it had seemed impossible that he would die an old man, in the house in which he was born, with his family around him. He was buried at St Nicholas, Deptford, in the churchyard, much preferable to 'the novel Costome of burying every body within the body of the Church & chancel' – a privilege that Evelyn considered should be restricted to martyrs and royalty.[35]

But Browne's death did nothing to resolve their financial problems. William Prettyman struck a sour note by shifting his interminable litigation onto Evelyn's shoulders. Evelyn reminded him crisply of the Latin motto 'the suit dies with the person'. He was upset that 'the long Animositie' between the brothers-in-law should be transferred to those 'who have never (knowingly) ben the least occasion of either beginning or promoting it'. Further, Prettyman had misled him over the lease of Sayes Court. 'I dearely reimbours'd what you purchas'd here from an ill Title, by which you induc'd me to fling-away above £3000, when, sure I am, none else would have touch'd it.' Sir Richard's last words had been that he believed he owed Prettyman nothing. Evelyn levelly suggested 'a faire, and just Accommodation' mediated by 'Friends (prudent and worthy Persons, indifferently chosen to examine all pretences)' rather than a return to Chancery 'at the expense of so much Charge, Time and the Anxiety of mind'. Prettyman was in no mood to listen.[36]

Lady Tuke, diverting Mary from her 'sad thoughts', tried to obtain a place for John from the duke of York – but the position apparently did not exist. He was now studying law again. It would take two or three years and, Mary wrote to Bohun, might end up like the story about Indians weighing themselves down to lighten their burden. 'I really feare instead of lessning his debt he will considerably improve it and then imagine how uneasy he will be'.[37] But she was relieved when Evelyn told her he had 'taken my son by the hand & forgoten all that's past'. Little Jack and his nurse stayed with them in Deptford while John was at the Middle Temple.

It was time to introduce their daughters to society, building on contacts made the previous summer at Tunbridge Wells. Evelyn agreed that Mary and the girls could spend the winter in London. They prepared themselves at Deptford. Elizabeth told Bohun: 'on Thursday we had young Foubert Mr Isak with two more gentlemen and Sir Charles Tuke and Mis Tuke a dansing till three of the clock in the morning.'[38] Mary had already rejected a proposal. John Hussey's only fault – according to her father – was 'a small defect in his speech'. Reminding her that she must be guided by them, he told her tenderly: 'yet will I never make use of this Authority to impose upon your aversion.' But it was difficult to find husbands and wives 'without defect in this wicked and perverted age' and she must not 'looke for perfection, and all things agreable to the Idias you reade of in Romances' for 'there is no such thing'.[39] The balance between paternal authority and parental understanding was a fine one.

The family stayed in Villiers Street, in York Buildings – Bohun remembered how badly the chimneys smoked – and enjoyed the excitement of London. Deptford was as remote from city life, with its theatres and gatherings, as deepest Surrey. Presenting her daughters at court must remind Mary of her own appearances at the Louvre, suggested Bohun, and she could 'phansey [her] self as happy as then'. Each of her daughters had a share of her qualities: Mary had 'Learned notions' and her mother's talent for writing and singing, while Elizabeth showed promise in 'the more beneficial part of good-huswifry'. That still left some accomplishments for Susanna.[40]

The court, seen through Mary Tuke's eyes, was a viper's nest of petty disputes. New favourites were in the ascendant. Lady Clarendon and Lady Churchill had quarrelled: 'I pitty my Lord Clarendon and his familie . . . goeing downe faster then ever they got up.' Lady Tuke, her salary five years in arrears, was on sick leave. She had sacrificed herself to duty, subjected herself to an exigent mistress and was particularly disillusioned by Godolphin, so 'backward to shew his [kindness] to Mr Evelin, when there was a thousand reasons, besides his obligations to move him to serve him'. He might have shown 'hee has other maxims then ordinary courtiers who only seeke there owne interest, but I doubt hee is as sensible on that side as those that does not pretend to be soe Learned'. Though he claimed to have Evelyn in mind, 'no effects follow'.[41]

Clarendon House was demolished that summer. It had stood for hardly twenty years; Evelyn averted his gaze as he passed. The country was back in the grip of conspiracy. The Papist Plot, utterly discredited, gave way to, in Evelyn's phrase, the 'Protestant-Plot'. Orchestrated initially by Shaftesbury (who died in January 1683), this came to be known as the Rye House Plot, but could with equal justification have been called the Cassiobury Plot. Key meetings were held on the earl of Essex's congenial estate. By midsummer it had been revealed and by 13 July Essex was dead, apparently murdered (though Evelyn believed, despite the evidence to the contrary, that he had taken his own life).[42] If the double assassination of Charles and James had indeed been averted, the throne was nonetheless tottering. It was no time to expect any favours from court.

The winter of 1683–4 was the harshest in living memory, bringing prolonged cold, frost, snow and thick smog. The frozen Thames turned into a busy street. A year or two earlier, the lord keeper, Lord Guilford, had enjoyed a 'philosophical meal' at Sayes Court observing the exquisite garden which was 'most boscaresque and, as it were, an exemplar of his book of Forest Trees'.[43] But when Mary went down to see the damage she reported that it was 'strangely desolate' and the garden 'mortified'. The Royal Society, keen to observe the effects of extreme cold, asked Evelyn to present a paper on the state of the Deptford garden. Many Fellows knew Sayes Court in its glory but, as Evelyn told them, 'the past winter has played the French King in my territories'. The losses included the rosemary hedges, most of the cypresses (especially those 'kept short in pyramids') and even well-protected 'exotics' such as sedum and aloe. Evelyn feared for the cork trees and cedars but the ilex and scarlet oak had survived; it was hardly surprising that the indigenous species had fared best. Among his treasured bulbs, most tulips and narcissi had been lost, the majority of his anemones had rotted and only the tuberoses, 'kept in the chimney corner, where was continual fire', had been saved. His tortoise was 'quite dead after having for many years escaped the severest winter'.[44]

The previous summer Evelyn heard of John Beale's death, but their correspondence had faded out some years before. He agreed to compose a Latin epitaph but pointed out that he could not write about his family. In all the hundreds of letters sent between Yeovil and Deptford, Beale's wife and children were scarcely ever mentioned. It had been an impersonal, didactic relationship. Ironically, as Beale's letters ceased, the Royal Society began to realise its potential as an institution. As Boyle wrote: 'the arguement is become much more pleasant, more hopefull, & the season to revive it is perfectly ripe.'[45] Worldly men such as Sir Joseph Williamson, Sir Christopher Wren and Samuel Pepys, all so experienced in government, provided much-needed professionalism. Scientists of the calibre of Isaac Newton, John Flamsteed, Edmund Halley and Hans Sloane swelled the ranks of the Fellows. There were even modest funds available, though not enough to pay for the publication of Newton's *Principia*.

Evelyn's defunct history of the Dutch Wars was proving an invaluable quarry for Pepys's own work on the navy, supposedly a critical history of its administration between 1679 and 1684 which caused him almost as much grief as the earlier project had done Evelyn.[46] Evelyn, currently 'calme from publique buisinesse', urged Pepys on. From the shelves of his library and the depth of his experience, 'joyn'd to an Industrie and Capacity (beyond any Mortal man that I know)', would come a 'Treasure' for 'your Prince, your Country and your Friends'.[47] He bombarded him with material for what he hoped to coax into becoming an encyclopaedic voyage from ancient to modern ('the greate and usefull part will be the Mathematical and mechanical'), as ambitious as his own overview of gardening. Like the *Elysium*,

Pepys's history progressed in fits and starts, interrupted by his official mission to Tangier in the summer of 1683, while the following year he regained his position as secretary of the Admiralty. *Memoires Relating to the State of the Royal Navy* was finally published in 1690.

Evelyn's own writing took second place to his 'tedious Chancery suit'. The return of Sidney Godolphin to the Treasury in 1685 (his appointment the previous year resulted in a breakdown) was good news, despite a growing coolness between the men.[48] Mary was convinced of his obligations: 'if he has that good will to serve him hee pretends, now will be the time to shew it, for I daire say hee will have the same power my Lord Rochester had.' Finally, there was movement on their claim for £11,846.

The Lords of the Treasury now admitted the justice of Evelyn's claim 'that Mr Pretiman, receiver of first fruits and tenths and indebted to his Majesty in very considerable sums', had maliciously pursued Browne (and now his heirs) for £4,181.17s. 'with thirty years' interest'. Since the costs were ruinous, the Evelyns asked to be paid on account, from Prettyman's debt to the Crown through his own office.[49] Later, Evelyn referred to the 'Tyrannous and unjust persecution' that had exploited his own inexperience and 'Sir Richards Forgetfullnesse, greate Age, Impotence Infirmitie to defend himselfe'. That winter Evelyn worked his contacts hard, dining with Lord Newport, treasurer of the royal household, Lord Falkland, treasurer of the navy and a Deptford neighbour, and the earl of Sunderland.[50]

In Deptford, Mary was, as so often in recent years, left in charge of the garden. She desperately tried to reverse the last winter's damage. She must keep a close eye on the workmen, only open the greenhouse from ten till three and plant the new trees in November, Evelyn told her.[51] It may have been while delegating his duties to his wife, as well as instructing their new apprentice gardener, Jonathan Mosse, that Evelyn set out his 'Directions for the Gardiner at Says-Court But Which May Be of Use for Other Gardens' which depicts the garden in the mid-1680s. Sadly the plan Evelyn included is lost.

Every suitable wall was smothered with fruit trees: apricot, peach and nectarine. In the great court, fountain garden and greenhouse garden were more fruit and nut trees: pear, cherry, quince, walnut and medlar. Even the island was planted productively, with melons, artichokes, cucumbers, cabbages and beets. Fruit trees were espaliered around the walls of the bowling green (the old Morin garden) and the various sections filled by dwarf pears and standard apples, damsons and cherries. Violets grew below, the trees interspersed with gooseberries, the borders with strawberries. Lettuces were being forced on under bell glasses and the vegetable garden was edged by chervil, the 'coronary' or flower garden by clipped cotton lavender. Evelyn provided long lists of annuals and perennials, shrubs and trees, and of course evergreens.[52]

Apart from Christmas, Evelyn himself spent all winter in London – as did his eldest daughter Mary. Lady Falkland had taken a liking to her and she lived with the family, taking lessons from an Italian music teacher. The Falklands wanted to take her to Oxfordshire in the spring, but by that time Mary was tired of 'the vaine & empty Conversation of the Towne, the Theaters, the Court, & trifling visites which consum'd so many precious moments, and made her sometimes (unavoidably) misse of that regular Course of piety, which gave her the greatest satisfaction'.[53] Evelyn's (posthumous) portrait placed Mary in the thin air of his spiritual pantheon alongside Margaret Blagge and his son Richard. She was, quite probably, also homesick.

As he grew older Evelyn's female friends were a mixture of the flighty girls of the 1660s, now influential matrons such as Lady Sylvius, and the relicts of the great, dowagers and widows. One day he dined at Somerset House with Lady Arlington and 'in all 11 Ladys of qualitie, no man but my-selfe', as he noted smugly. With his wide interests, his skittishness in female company and his admiration for accomplished women, which became more pronounced (and discerning) with age and Mary's influence, he was rather a favourite in female society.[54] The prolonged stay in London also gave him more time for the Royal Society. He was still thirsty for new experiences, such as getting a glimpse of a young rhinoceros, the first in England, a mouse-coloured creature with the skin of an elephant, as he noted. The unwieldy beast had tiny, closely spaced eyes, hefty legs almost the size of a man's waist and 'dreadful' teeth, all emerging from a vast bag of skin, apparently in two layers. In the past Evelyn's observations would have been drawn from engravings but this vivid image, taken from reality, is as evocative as his description of the production of phosphorus, apparently bringing light out of chaos.[55]

London was seething with gossip, such as the news that the king 'lay with [the] Queene the night he arived from Newmarket'. But nothing had really changed. One Sunday evening in late January Evelyn witnessed 'a sceane of uttmost vanity': the king holding court with his three mistresses or 'concubines', 'Portsmouth, Cleaveland, & Mazarine', serenaded by a French boy singing love songs. Nearby some twenty courtiers were gaming at a large table, with a huge mound of coins – 'at least 2000 in Gold' – in front of them. No wonder Evelyn had warned John off the court. After years spent pursuing the tangled finances of his family, the result of the king's failure to honour his promises to Browne, this – on a holy day – appeared to Evelyn to be a scene from Sodom and Gomorrah.

On Monday, 2 February 1685, little more than a week afterwards, Charles II, in his mid-fifties, was seized by fits – a symptom mysterious enough to feed a variety of conspiracy theories. Four days later the king was dead. Evelyn tried to balance his 'many Virtues & many great Imperfections', having heard that

he had received the Roman Catholic last rites ('I hope is it not true'). The duke
of York was at his bedside and Charles's children had been entrusted to his
care, with the exception of the Protestant James, duke of Monmouth, who had
been living, well pensioned, in Holland since his involvement in the Rye
House Plot. The king had died without showing any concern for 'the Church
or of his people' and, in Evelyn's view, the country was now in the hands of a
'Prince suspected for his Religion, after about 100 yeares the Church & Nation
had ben departed from Rome'. Charles was buried modestly, 'soone forgotten
after all this vainity'.[56]

James's strategy on his accession was to offer reassurance. He told the
nation that he would eschew arbitrary powers and 'endeavour to maintaine
the Government both in Church and state as by Law establish'd'. On oath,
the new king assured office-holders that their posts were safe. James II was
not profane and did not act the buffoon, his court was more seemly than his
brother's had been. Lord Arlington was reinstated while Godolphin became
chamberlain to the queen. The earl of Clarendon (Henry Hyde, Lord
Cornbury, had succeeded his father in 1674) became Lord Privy Seal. Despite
the fact that 'Papists now swarmed at Court', a 'popish oratory' had been
installed at Whitehall and the Catholic Mass was being said in public, all
seemed surprisingly well for the moment.[57]

The only challenge to the new order appeared that summer when the duke
of Monmouth landed in the West Country, bidding for his uncle's throne
with a volunteer force and offering the country revolutionary measures
including the calling of regular parliaments, religious toleration for dissenters
and the dissolution of the standing army. But the so-called Monmouth's
Rebellion proved a damp squib and merely consolidated the growing power
of James and his 'Tory-Anglicans'.[58]

In Evelyn's family, national convulsions were overtaken by domestic catastrophe. Evelyn's beloved eldest daughter, Mary, fell ill in March and quickly
died of smallpox. It was her mother who conveyed their desolation, writing to
Bohun that the sun still shone, the plants still grew, but she had lost her
favourite daughter. 'I loved them all yet some distinction might reasonably be
allowed the eldest, as first and for many reasons somthing to be preffered?'
Although they carried on, 'I cannot finde wherin the felicity of life consists'.
But, she added, as if to remind herself, 'there are those yet remaining that
chalenge my care and for their sakes I endeavour to submitt all I can'.[59]

Among these were her two surviving daughters. Elizabeth's aunt had taken
her to Oxford, where she saw 'the theatre, the repositary, the elabatory, the
anatomie school, library, physic garden' but, she flattered Bohun, she liked
New College Chapel best because of its associations with him. At home, 'my
mother continues still as sorowfull as at first so that our house is full of sorow'.

Susanna wrote to him in a childish hand, thanking him for his kindness to Mary, 'whose memory is very fresh amongst us and whose virtues I must never hope to reach yet I will do my best to imitate her', and she described James II's coronation: 'I saw it with advantage both the procession and the two extraordinary Dukes of Aquitane and Normandy whose drese and mine [mien] were very charming but indeed the Queene and Ladyes were very fine.'[60]

As the dowager queen mourned Charles II in a taper-lit room at Whitehall hung entirely with black, to which foreign envoys and grandees came to pay their respects, the Evelyns' close friends conveyed their sympathy for Mary's loss by letter or in person at Deptford. For Elizabeth, almost eighteen, devastated by the loss of her sibling and yet excluded from her parents' grief, this became a time of crisis. Her release came in the shape of the attentions of a young man at the naval dockyard.

Her father's escape was the replanting of his garden. 'Mr E endeavours to divert his thoughts with the alterations of the Garden which would at any time but this have been very fine and seemes much improved, but all delights are more and lesse so, Mary Evelyn wrote.' Sayes Court was, again, 'his businesse and Delight. It now grows towards finishing and does answer expectation very well being finer than ever. For the future I hope it will be lesse expensive which will be very convenient.'[61]

But just as the revived garden began to lift the family's spirits, Elizabeth eloped. Evelyn enlisted Pepy's help to track down the seducer, but less than three weeks later she too went down with smallpox. Her mother went to visit her immediately, and remained at her bedside throughout. Her father stayed away and cut her out of his will but as the gravity of her illness became clear he relented, bringing Dr Holden, the rector at Deptford, to give her a blessing and the sacrament. The previous year Evelyn had told his daughter Mary, when she refused John Hussey's hand, 'I impose no Comands upon you, or (like other Parents) deprive you of my Blessing and Prayers', but now he found it difficult to forgive his errant dying daughter, remaining implacable towards her lover who had stolen Elizabeth from under his very nose and married her. In contrast, Mary Evelyn forgave him.[62] The following year Evelyn's coachman died after an agonising illness and he hurried home to take the sacrament with him and grieve, 'a very honest, faithfull servant'. Evelyn judged other men and women by their actions and their words, but where his own family was concerned, he was the ultimate authority and he expected his children to respect his wishes above their own.

John and Martha ('a good soule') rallied to Mary's aid. John had supported his sister 'in her trouble' and they were both 'very sensible of the calamity'. They invited Mary and Susanna to spend the winter with them in London and she replied: 'I can be no where very easy, yet for Sues sake am allmost prevailed on to pass some part of the dull season with them . . . from a toller-able womans courage I am now becom a perfect coward every accident makes me tremble.'[63] She tried to immerse herself in 'brushing up' Susanna. Although she was 'the same sincere rough girl, she grows tall and rather better in her person' and was becoming an accomplished draughtswoman. Mary told Bohun: 'You will find the same method in the family but lesse happinesse.' John was a changed man, newly mature and understanding, and Jack 'a pretty good-natured child . . . you know I love all children very well.'[64]

In the midst of all their sorrow the lord treasurer, Laurence Hyde, now Lord Rochester, informed them that their petition was under consideration again. A year later Evelyn wrote jubilantly to tell Anne Sylvius that their suit was settled: '(. . . Good Lord! Just as long a servitude as Jacobs was to Rebecah) . . . I am now as it were a new man, have got a new suite, bespoken a new Vehicle and Equipage.' Giving Rochester his heartfelt thanks he reminded him that the sum granted by Privy Seal did not fully cover Prettyman's claim.[65] He recouped the remainder (the interest) in 1690, by which time they were embroiled in a new lawsuit over Baynards Park, where Richard Evelyn's widow and her son-in-law William Montagu had used 'fraude & unworthy dealing' to break the existing entail to old George Evelyn.[66] A jovial dinner with the lord chancellor was soured for Evelyn when the three senior barristers present began to joke about the tricks of the trade such as 'how long they had detained their clients in tedious processes'. It was, he thought, like a meeting of highwaymen, not at all amusing to someone engaged in prolonged litigation.[67]

Soon after Elizabeth's death, Evelyn became a commissioner of the Privy Seal, one of three appointed to take the earl of Clarendon's place while he went to Ireland as lord lieutenant. Lady Tuke hoped the new appointment would help 'a little [to] suspend sorrow', especially since 'my Lord had obtained it of his Majesty before he acquainted Mr Evelyn with his intention'.[68] William Glanville wrote to Mary that he was 'extreamly pleasd with that marque of the Kings favor and good opinion' while being brutally frank about Elizabeth: 'I should not bee sincere should I tell you, that I am sorry you have lost my cosine Betty, because I think she would have been more Lost, and much Less happy than now she is, had shee Lived.' She was, in his eyes at least, a girl with self-destructive tendencies who had disgraced and 'undon her self by a disobedient and dishonorable marriage'.[69]

Ralph Bohun, passionately anti-Catholic and therefore strongly averse to James's accession offered Evelyn some typically tactless advice, since 'wise and good men can not easily apply to themselves what advice they could readily give to others'. Congratulating him on his 'honourable employment', he pondered, 'as you now need it not, so I should hardly have engag'd afresh in public bysnes, were I in your circumstances'.[70] Bohun's concern may also have been for Mary, so distraught and lonely.

Undeterred, Evelyn went to Windsor where Clarendon presented him to the king, announcing his appointment to courtiers who 'us'd never so much as to take the least notice of me'. His friends Rochester, Godolphin and Falkland congratulated him. Then he attended a service in St George's Chapel and admired Verrio's 'stupendious' *Triumph of the Black Prince* in St George's Hall. The North brothers, Roger and Dudley, were there, returning the Great Seal after the death of their brother Francis, Lord Keeper Guilford, an event that led to feverish speculation as to his successor. (It was to be Judge Jeffreys, whom Evelyn later recorded as being 'of nature cruell & a slave of this Court'.)[71] Clarendon instructed Evelyn on what was expected of him. 'I find it is not to be by deputation from my Lord as his deputies, but by a commission from his Majestie under the Broade Seale, which is (they say) more honorable.' The salary was £500, paid quarterly, for no more than half a morning's work a week.[72]

The post took Evelyn on a royal progress, not to the gaming tables and race-tracks, but to the newly built fortifications at Portsmouth and the Isle of Wight where he and Pepys were to meet the king. They travelled via Winchester, which he had first visited more than forty years ago with his brother Richard. Now he could steal a glimpse of Wren's unfinished Winchester Palace, Charles II's extravagant folly on which work had been suspended – to the advantage of Whitehall, where James planned an extensive remodelling.[73]

On closer acquaintance Evelyn found the king to be a very different character from his brother: 'I find that infinite industry, sedulity, gravity, and greate understanding & experience of affaires in his Majestie, that I cannot but predict much happinesse to the Nation, as to its political Government.' In fact, 'there could nothing be more desired, to accomplish our prosperity, but that he were of the national Religion'. Although a conversation turning on miracles and sacred relics illustrated their differences, Evelyn believed that with God's help James might even 'open his Eyes, & turne his heart'.[74]

But the early months of James II's reign were a false honeymoon. In France the revocation of the Edict of Nantes made Evelyn fear for his French Protestant contacts still in the country, but he convinced himself that this was the work of Jesuits, not Roman Catholics of good will. James offered to protect the Huguenots in England and Evelyn came to know the leading members of the French Protestant community, whose chapel and school were in Greenwich. In early October, Pepys summoned Evelyn and his old friend James Houblon to his house to show them documents that proved that, like Arlington (who died that year), Charles II had died a Catholic. Shocked by this confirmation of the rumour, Evelyn welcomed the present king's sincerity and honesty, his 'free & ingenuous profession, of what his owne Religion is, beyond all Concealements upon any politique accounts what so ever'.

Understandably enough, James forbade bonfires and anti-papist rejoicing on 5 November. Gradually Catholic pamphlets and images began to appear and a papal nuncio arrived at court, the first since the Reformation. But tolerance was strictly limited. The king's attempts to exempt Catholic army officers from the Test Acts upset both Houses, 'a greate surprize to a Parliament, which people believed would have complied in all things'. At the turn of the year the more intractable among the Anglican clergy began to fall foul of the new regime.

On Christmas Eve 1685 the commissioners of the Privy Seal were sworn in and signed their first pardons. In late January they passed seals for £276,000 'upon severall accounts, Pensions, Guards, Wardrobes, Privie purse'. Evelyn fitted out his official apartment in Whitehall and moved there in mid-February. Meetings were generally held once a week, but business was varied and their length unpredictable. In practical respects the part-time but highly lucrative position allowed him to 'cultivate such other Inclinations of mine, as I trust, are Innocent, and to some, usefull', but Evelyn was increasingly worried by the moral dilemmas it posed, telling Godolphin that 'perhaps I make more Scruple that I neede'. It was a difficult test of his faith; years ago he had told Samuel Tuke that he belonged to the Church of England by conviction, and was always ready and willing to 'earnestly contend for the Truth' with him.

He seemed taken aback that his duties might sometimes conflict with his stern Protestant principles. Evelyn had, for example, arranged to be absent when the secretary to the English ambassador to Rome was appointed, since the Commission was still quorate without him. Sometimes he argued his case for dissent. Ever the casuist, he asked Godolphin if when he and his colleagues felt unable to pass 'indulgences as concerne Religious matters etc. inconsistent with our Oathes' could they be dealt with through some kind of automatic warrant?[75] Religious tolerance was starting to strain at the seams.

Evelyn was also made uncomfortable by the emergence of political parties, town and country interests, 'whig' and 'tory' allegiances. His brother was a whig and Godolphin, his patron, a tory. Later he warned his grandson not to take political office for reasons of vanity, popularity or 'the being caryed away by a faction or to serve a party'. A suitor for Susanna was rejected out of hand, his father being 'obnoxious, & in some suspicion & displeasure of the King', an active whig.[76] But it was the rapid ascendancy of Catholics over Protestants on every front that caused him greatest concern despite his personal loyalty to the Catholics in his circle. Of nineteen appointments to the bench and Privy Council in Ireland, only three were Protestants. Churchmen lost their livings 'for preaching against popery'. In Deptford, the tensions spread to the household itself since it included both Mary's Catholic cousin Lady Tuke and the zealously protestant Ralph Bohun. The latter, deliciously described by one young friend as 'that quintessence of snuff and spleen', was deputising for the Deptford vicar: a typical sermon attacked the 'idolatrie & other errors of the Roman Church'.[77]

At Whitehall, the new Chapel Royal, its statues by Grinling Gibbons and painted decoration by Antonio Verrio, dedicated to the glory of Catholicism in England, distressed Evelyn. He could not believe 'I should ever have lived to see such things in the K of Englands palace'.[78]

When Clarendon returned from Ireland, the king reconsidered his Privy Seal arrangements and decided the office should henceforth be held by 'a single hand', assuring the dismissed commissioners that their excellent service would be fully recompensed. Evelyn's quandaries were at an end, as was his invaluable salary of £500. It soon emerged that Clarendon had been replaced by Lord Arundell of Wardour, a 'zealous' Catholic.

The Declaration of Indulgence was issued in April 1688 suspending both civil and ecclesiastical laws, including the Test Acts. Sunderland, first minister and the king's closest advisor, lost no time adjusting his position, making a fair-weather conversion to Catholicism in June. But most of those whom Evelyn respected, above all Dr Thomas Tenison, rector of St Martin-in-the-Fields, were actively opposed to it. Even Pepys, that stalwart supporter of James II, opposed the high-handedness of this move. Archbishop Sancroft had been ejected and, with six bishops, sent to the Tower as punishment for drawing up a petition of opposition that was read from the pulpit in many churches. Evelyn visited the seven incarcerated churchmen and watched their trial (and subsequent acquittal) with close interest.[79]

The church began to seem under siege, as it had during the Interregnum, even if the battle lines were drawn differently on this occasion. Evelyn knew and admired Dr Thomas Ken, a former chaplain to Charles II and now bishop of Bath and Wells, as he did William Lloyd, the bishop of St Asaph, both of whom were of the party in the Tower. But his particular personal ties were with leading low churchmen, essentially moderate and tolerant men – John Tillotson, the dean of St Paul's and, above all, his friend Tenison who became bishop of Lincoln and then followed Tillotson at the see of Canterbury. Evelyn kept his own bearings within Church of England by reading the writings of Simon Patrick – and encouraging all around him to do the same – and by following the sermons of Edward Stillingfleet.[80] It began to seem that the Catholic convert James II was leading the country towards a precipice.

In the midst of the growing turmoil, the queen gave birth to her first son, James. Suspicion of the legitimacy of the infant was rife, fanned by the rumour that it had been secreted into the palace in a warming pan, but James countered, hoping that 'none would presume to think him so barbarous as to impose a child upon the Nation.' Princess Mary was now displaced from the succession, as was her husband, and the new heir to the throne was Catholic. Pepys, whose loyalty to James was in direct confrontation with his support of the dissenting bishops, provided momentary distraction for the Evelyns, inviting John and Mary to watch the fireworks celebrating the 'Queenes up-sitting' – her recovery after childbirth – a spectacular pyrotechnic garden of pyramids and statues, which cost 'some thousands of pounds' and was all gone in no time. In quiet moments throughout these months, Evelyn tried to write a history of religion.[81]

He remained in constant contact with Lady Sunderland, an unswervingly Protestant daughter of a Catholic father. Evelyn asked her if she could help find employment for John just as her own son Robert, another Catholic convert, died in Paris. He wrote again to offer his sympathy, painting a portrait of the dangerous modern world that had ensnared their sons – 'the White-Halls, the Windsors, the Versailles, the Noisy Den, and Crowds of Ambitious Men, Corrupted with Vice, and immers'd in sensuall pleasures, that consume their precious Moments, in pursuite of Vanity and the Shadow of a dreame'.[82] Soon after, he and John were invited to Althorp. He warned his hostess that she would find him an 'old Morose Creature, who every day looses the Tast of this World' but, once there, he was delighted by Lady Sunderland's household, in which even the 'meanest servant [is] lodged so neate & cleanely'. Anne Sunderland and her mother, the countess of Digby, set an example in a nation 'dissaffected & in apprehensions'. Although Lord Sunderland had 'made himselfe unworthy', Evelyn was confident that his wife would remedy his failings.[83]

Evelyn sensed, as he told Pepys, an 'impendent Revolution'. William of Orange was invited to come over to England by a group of politicians, both Whigs and Tories. By September the court was convinced that the Dutch prince had arrived, but James II recalled Parliament and began to readjust or dissolve his recent orders. The eclipse of the sun on the king's birthday spoke volumes to Evelyn. John reported from court that James was preparing to defend his Crown, and his son's legitimacy, and had convened peers, bishops and men of state to support his case. Witnesses, including Lady Sunderland, were called to Whitehall which was seething with agitated crowds, to attest to the birth.[84] But over the autumn James's support leached away.

William of Orange's arrival, no invasion but an orderly handover to a man who was after all James's brother-in-law, still looked like a revolution and the events of late 1688 made it an *annus mirabilis tertius*, as Evelyn put it, a year to put beside 1588 and 1660.[85] Disillusioned by successive Stuarts, he had revised his views on the hereditary succession, differing from friends such as Samuel Pepys who remained steadfast Jacobites and non-jurors. After all, now it could be argued that James had abdicated. In an odd letter in his copybook, addressed to 'my Lord', presumably Sunderland, he drew up a wide-ranging agenda for change which included electoral reform yet retained the monarchy since a prince 'neede not to feare Parliaments, the dread of our late greate Monarchs, the Peoples sovraine Remedy, and the best of Constitutions'.

The elderly Evelyn had come to believe that the retrieval of national self-esteem was through the reform and proper use of its governing institutions, above all Parliament. His profound pessimism of recent years was turning to moderate optimism: 'if it were possible, Holland and England were made one people inseparably to be United' and their king 'the Head and Defender of all Protestants in Europe'.[86] A free Parliament was possible with peace. His experience of the vicissitudes of power led Evelyn to dream of a body that applied itself 'with moderation justice & piety & for the publique good'.[87] It was now that he confided to Lady Sunderland: 'I have the vanity sometimes to think what I would do if I were a great man.'[88]

John met the prince of Orange in Abingdon, where he was with his father-in-law, having been one of Lord Lovelace's 'Gentlemen Volunteers on horse-back and townsmen on foot'. As James II's army approached Oxford, 'the Passive Obedience men trembled for their Plate and librarys' and his father should be proud, said John, to know that he had defended 'our English Athens'. Now they had disbanded, ending 'my 5 days Rebellion in very good company, if being in Arms for the Nassorian Hero, the Primitive Religion and the liberty of my country deserves not a more honorable Title'. He described the future king: 'grave and deliberate in his speech and motion, and even while he eats, not unthoughtfull. Tranquility, order and silence reign among his Attendants.'[89] John expected a 'small share of temporall, as well as spiri-tuall advantages that will attend Protestants in this Revolution' and asked his father to suggest what he should do next. But for all the royal Dutchman's own dour probity, he had unleashed an 'ungovernable Rabble' who were unjustifiably seizing Catholic 'Reliques and Altar Baubles all of which if of any value the Prince has strictly commanded to be restored'.[90]

As James II fled, Lord Sunderland left for Rotterdam. His wife now suggested he compose a pamphlet to justify himself and asked her friends Evelyn and Dr Tenison to advise him. Sunderland's contradictory recanta-tion, *Letter to a Friend*, was printed and translated into High and Low Dutch and French and distributed in early 1689. Lady Sunderland believed her husband a 'new creature', telling Evelyn that 'he had too much sense to be a papist, and, thank God, I am more and more convinced of it, and that he thinks it as foolish a religion as I do'.[91] Evelyn's friend Tenison, who 'deeply influenced his moral compass', spoke of Christ as a 'mediator' and it was in that guise that they had guided Sunderland.[92]

Sunderland was a man of exceptional suggestibility and expensive habits, his demeanour typified by 'his Court Tune', a languid drawl caught, happily, by Roger North in his satirical 'Whaat, said he, if his Maajesty taarn out faarty of us, may not he have faarty athors to saarve him as well?'[93] His wife, on the other hand, was a woman of crystalline sincerity and strong religious convictions, leavened by considerable charm and beauty; of the two she was Evelyn's friend. Despite clear intimations that the earl was an amoral political trimmer, Evelyn lobbied on his behalf, spending more time and effort than was wise for his own sake, but always aware of his obligations to the Sunderlands. Once Lady Sunderland joined her husband in Holland they lived as a prosperous Protestant family, supported by their domestic establishment imported from Althorp. From there, Sunderland demonstrated his flexible loyalties when he wrote to William of Orange, regretting he was unable to 'give my vote for placing your Majesty on the throne, as I would have done with as much joy and zeal as any man alive'.[94]

In the early weeks of 1689 the future of the Crown was debated furiously in both Houses of Parliament. In the Lords, some, such as Archbishop Sancroft, believed that James II was still king, solely on the grounds of hereditary succession. Most wanted to establish a regency, allowing William and Mary to rule but leaving James as nominal monarch. But in the Commons, members tussled with the undeniable fact that no one currently occupied the throne: James had, to all intents and purposes, abdicated. On 6 February, William and Mary were recognised as king and queen of England, 'but [with] the executive Authority to be vested in the Prince'. A week later, despite their apparent misgivings, they were officially proclaimed. John reported everything to his father, including William's chilly reserve, not the best manner with which to win 'us English-men, who are sooner vanquish'd with kind Words and good lookes, than with Armies, and at cheaper rate'. However 'the Prince has been told of his stiffness and begins to correct it, at eleven in the morning and eight at night he is seen with most freedom'.[95] Meanwhile, in Ireland French troops were landing in support of James, who arrived there in person in March along with German reinforcements. Evelyn observed: 'this is likely to be one of the most remarkable summers for action, as has happed for many Ages.'[96] William was destined to spend most of his reign overseas with his troops.

The Declaration of Rights, which was drafted at this time, ruled out any repetition of the recent troubles. It insured against abuse of power, by either monarch or Parliament. It pointed to a revolution on the Dutch model, guided by a regularly elected Parliament rather than a disposable puppet body. After the bizarre turn of events that had seen James II's Protestant daughter (and Clarendon's granddaughter) take her father's throne, William and Mary promised a return to enlightened rule and the end of Catholic ambitions.

Once again 'innumerable ... Crowds' gathered around the court in the hope of catching crumbs of office. Lord Danby emerged from the melee as president of the Privy Council, 'exhumed from the graveyard of discarded politicians', as one historian puts it.[97] The coronation took place in mid-April. Though his attributes and allegiances might suggest that Evelyn belonged to the 'country' party, a natural Tory set against corruption at court, he found himself torn as he watched the drift of affairs, anxious for John's sake as much as for his own.[98]

In early 1690 the Privy Seal was put into the hand of commissioners once again. Evelyn imagined he might have been reappointed 'had I thought it seasonable, & would have ingaged my friends'.[99] But the hopes of 1689 were fading: Whigs, Tories and Dutchmen were at one another's throats, 'the government so loose and neglected ... that we are likely to fall into greate Confusion, Partys, Interests of private persons, animosities, & vice in aboundance'. William was currently in Ireland, with the queen acting as his regent. Evelyn could not advise Lady Sunderland, still in exile in Holland: she must consult her friends 'as are neerer the Resorts and Springs of Buisinesse than I am, or pretend to be'.

Of his friends among churchmen, the 'moderate (and I think) wiser' seemed to favour William and Mary, while elsewhere 'those of the higher straine, are expecting their Turne, whilst the morose and discontented party, are not unactive, but labour to come in Senators againe: how the Balance at last will fall, Time will discover'.[100]

By now old and wordly wise, Evelyn had seen statesmen, close personal acquaintances such as Clarendon, Arlington, Clifford and latterly Sunderland and Godolphin, rise and fall – and rise again, like Danby. When the Sunderlands greeted William III on his return from Holland in 1691, Evelyn was lost for words – the earl was jockeying for power once more. 'This is a Mysterie.' Within three years the royal entertainments at Althorp were as lavish as Arlington's had been at Euston. He now described Sunderland, in the privacy of his diary, as 'the greate favorite, & underhand politician'. Almost as surprising was Sidney Godolphin's return to the Treasury in 1690.[101]

In refusing the oath of allegiance and becoming a non-juror, Pepys joined a large number of churchmen and statesmen. On most matters, though not on this, Pepys and Evelyn were as one and Evelyn often used him as a sounding board, someone with whom to exchange information or to rehearse ideas. In one spectacularly long letter, Evelyn mused on an English dictionary that might give the meanings and derivations of words, including technical terms ('glean'd from Shops, not from Books') and those used in medicine and philosophy, as well as foreign phrases, and vernacular idioms and dialects. He shared his dreams for public libraries, such as Dr Tenison's charitable library, now being set up in his parish of St Martin-in-the-Fields. Evelyn fondly recalled Clarendon's love of books, his 'ample Library', his elegant writing style and his support for and promotion of the Royal Society. He had dedicated his translation of Naudé to a cultured man who had used his position to achieve commendable ends. As to Clarendon's innocence or guilt in matters of state, he told Pepys he was undecided.

Evelyn thought the political changes, as seen in the summer of 1689, positive. Looking back over the most turbulent decades of their country's history both he and Pepys had been touched by almost every convulsion in Whitehall or Oxford. Yet, allowing for the fact that 'both their late Majesties fell into as pernicious Counsels, as ever Princes did', the major officials of state and judiciary were honourable, upright men. There was a sense of 'Gravity and Forme . . . more agreable to the Genius of this Nation, than the open and avowed Luxurie and prophanes which succeeded a la Mode de France'.[102] Yet only two years later, Evelyn saw the government 'very loose & as it were on floates', and his friend in prison once again, 'on suspicion of being affected to K James'.[103]

CHAPTER 15

An Absolute Philosopher

John Evelyn attributed his longevity to careful diet and regular activity, as well as constitution. He believed his brother to be the oldest surviving member of the House of Commons. Duly appreciative, he wrote to his old friend Jael Boscawen: 'what has an old-man to Complaine of, whome God has bless'd with so many Yeares of extraordinary health?'[1] Evelyn subscribed to the view of the Renaissance scholar Luigi Cornaro that it was important in old age to grasp 'any thing that may either teach or delight me'. In his eighties, Cornaro, whose Paduan music room Evelyn had visited fifty years before with the earl of Arundel, penned a celebration of his temperate busy life (before living on to a hundred). As charmingly translated by George Herbert, he had said: 'the life which I live at this age, is not a dead, dumpish and sowre life; but cheerfull, lively and pleasant.'[2]

Evelyn faced the future with extraordinary equanimity, built upon the rock of his Christian faith and the hope of his spiritual redemption after a godly life. On his birthday, 31 October 1690, 'now full 70 yeares of Age' he thanked God 'for the continuance of my health, & of all his mercies' and prayed for the blessings to increase, 'with the yeares of my life, 'til in compassion thou bring me to the consummation of Glory in the life to come'. The next day he took communion at St Martin-in-the-Fields and listened to his friend Dr Tenison's excellent sermon (or 'moral discourse') recommending 'Sobreity, comity [courtesy], Charity, Industry &c as most christian vertues'. But when he was nominated ('by 21 voices') to be president of the Royal Society on St Andrew's Day 1690, he sensed it was likely to be a politically exposed post and refused the honour 'in this ill Conjuncture of publique affairs'. He would turn down the post again in 1693.[3]

Robert Boyle had died on the last day of 1691 and his will included a bequest for an annual Boyle lecturer who would defend Christianity from atheism (as from 'Libertins, jewes &c.'). Evelyn was a trustee. He admired Boyle intensely for his life-long promotion of the essential compatibility between religion and the new science, having 'made God & Religion the object and scope of all his excellent Tallents in the knowledge of Nature' and he arranged for the scholarly Richard Bentley to deliver the first lecture in 1692.

Earlier Evelyn had been engrossed in John Locke's *Essay concerning Human Understanding* (1690): 'so rare and excellent a piece, that "twas not possible for me to dismisse him at one Reading,' he told Pepys who lent him his copy.* For Evelyn, Locke's philosophy successfully 'vindicated, and Asserted the Existence of God Almighty', unlike those of Hobbes and Descartes (although Hooke had encouraged even the pious Boyle to consider the ideas of the Frenchman). Locke challenged the authority of the ancients by celebrating 'the stupendious operations of Algebra, Mechanical Arts, and Experimental Philosophy', and dealt with 'simple Ideas . . . able to produce infinite variety of Complex ones' but without prejudicing spirituality. Finally, he explained the metaphysical 'strip't of the Jargon and Gibbrish of the Cloister'. Evelyn had been waiting for a philosopher like Locke, so clear in his exploration of new ideas, so steadfast in his beliefs. While they might have been forgiven for withdrawing from the cut and thrust of intellectual life, both he and Pepys remained fully engaged. When the Evelyns considered letting Sayes Court in 1691, Mary Evelyn told her husband that she wished his friend 'had occasion for a countrie house' for he would be the ideal tenant, 'prefferred to any other for his Neatnesse and friendship'. Although she does not name Pepys, he is the most likely candidate.[4]

One night, after reading Aristotle on dreams, 'me-thought Mr Pepys and I were . . . discoursing in his Library'. Evelyn was taken aback. 'I was never in my Life subject to Night-Visions 'til of late.' St Peter had said: 'your Old-men shall dreame dreames.' Mary also dreamt but, unlike his own, hers 'hung as orderly together, as if they had ben studied Narratives, some of which I had formerly made her write downe for the prettynesse of them', which proved Aristotle's theory that dreams were a reflection of character.[5]

Evelyn had long argued that portraits, more than being mere likenesses, served as reminders of wisdom and virtue for succeeding generations. William Rand had prompted him to consider his children as 'statues' to himself.[6] Now he stood proudly behind his grandson John (Jack), starting his education at a Huguenot school in Greenwich. Evelyn was always aware of the limitations of his own schooling and now accepted that he had overloaded John, who was grateful that his own son's education (entirely in Evelyn's hands) was not being 'so hastily crowded into him because when we grasp at quick, and early

---

*Evelyn knew Locke from their time together at the Council for Trade and Foreign Plantations.

perfection and knowledge of every thing, we are most in danger of falling short, and losing of all'.[7]

By the time Jack matriculated at Oxford he had already been head of Eton's sixth form and had mastered 'useful' mathematics and algebra, though his grandfather thought he should 'unlearn' philosophy. His only 'fault', Evelyn crowed to Bohun, was his 'inordinate love of a Library'. According to her son, Mary was spoiling Jack and was 'pretty well advanced in it . . . for she had ever a good stroke that way in my sisters'. Much rested on the boy's shoulders as his grandfather's 'onely remaining solace'. But when he proposed leaving university early, just as his grandfather had done, he argued his case so well that he won.[8]

Although he remained committed to the idea of inheritance within families, particularly in view of his own grandson's obvious probity, his experience of the effects of profligacy on later generations in families such as the Howards, Clarendons or Arlingtons had made Evelyn clear-headed. Possessions lose their value 'where the next Heire is not a consummat Virtuoso', he told Pepys.[9]

When George's last surviving son, John ('Wotton Jack'), died in 1692, the estate passed by entail to Evelyn's family. He was chief mourner at the funeral, although he was convinced that his nephew was dead from drink.[10] Financial complications followed when George's middle-aged daughter Mary unexpectedly married Sir Cyril Wyche, the distinguished public servant and stalwart of the Royal Society (he was president in 1683–4) necessitating a dowry of £6,300 which the Wotton estate could ill afford.

Her old father was faltering, asking to be excused the office of sheriff since he could no longer attend the judges at the assizes or carry out official business. Now George offered Evelyn and Mary an apartment at Wotton, 'a Retreate (with my sole companion) in the place that gave me Birth, & most shortly Burial'. Evelyn warmed to the idea of living under the same roof as his brother. The year before he had written a valedictory letter to George: 'your Advancement in Yeares, my treading so very neere after you, and the Vicissitudes of Secular and worldly things (of which we have both had so much Experience) calls upon us both, to make-up our Packetts, and be prepard for the Call.' Since they had both exceeded 'the ordinary limites of humane-life' they must consider 'how we may leave the World as becomes us, and the greate Obligations we lie under, for having ben hitherto conducted through such difficult Times and extraordinary Revolutions'.[11] The survival of the older generation to such a great age made it all the more important that their successors should be aware of their history.

John was sanguine; he thought his parents sensible to leave Sayes Court, which 'you have bred, nurs'd and brought to a great degree of commodiousnesse and pleasure', and hoped they would be cheered with 'the consideration of Wotton as the place where all interests must center and will require all assistance to support'. The cost of maintaining the Sayes Court gardens properly and the expansion of Deptford, further encouraged by the discovery of medicinal waters, which brought crowds pouring into neighbouring fields and gardens at the first sign of fine weather, were two good reasons for his ageing parents' move.

In June 1689 both John Evelyn and William Glanville junior had bought positions as clerks at the Treasury. William Glanville was still in his post at his death in 1718 but John was dismissed in June 1691. Evelyn doesn't mention the appointment or the dismissal in the diary. In his late thirties, John finally secured a decent post as a commissioner of customs and excise in Dublin through the good offices of Godolphin and Fox. John, Martha and seven-year-old Elizabeth left England in August 1692, entrusting Jack to the care of his grandparents. That autumn they began a new and more independent life far from their relations in England, and regularly rode out early in the park for the good of John's health.[12]

Evelyn reassured George that he had no ambitions for Wotton except 'the care & supervisal of your Gardens, and the Culture & Adornment of the place of our worthy Fore-fathers'. The gardens had become run down in the last forty years and could do with being freshened up but advanced age ruled out that Evelyn '(unlesse in Models, & Castles in the Aer) [should] think of building palaces & Habitations here'. He sent his brother a customarily late-night note, with a sketch 'representing my thoughts in order to a Grove of Evergreens'. He also suggested they build a conservatory, a 'temporary shead of boards and thatch', for his orange and myrthe trees.[13]

This last idea must have been inspired by his latest translation, Jean De La Quintinye's *The Compleat Gard'ner* (1693), a book, he told George, 'for use not for show & parade'. It was not entirely his own work: 'the toile of meere translating would have been very ungrateful to one who had not so much time to spend thrashing; but as a considerable part of it was, and the rest under my care, the publishers & printers will have it go under my name.' It was dedicated to Baron Capel of Tewkesbury, a Privy Councillor, and ran to seven editions in twenty years. He hoped that George would let his 'skilful' gardener Abraham peruse the best publication on fruit-growing that existed.[14] De La Quintinye (whom Glanville had visited in 1669) was a lawyer-turned-gardener who had been in charge of the prince de Condé's gardens at Chantilly and, until his death in 1688, of the king's *potager* at Versailles. Charles II had tried, and failed, to obtain his services. His travels in Italy and England had even taken him to Sayes Court and he was a regular correspondent of the Royal Society. Evelyn's opening remarks 'to the Nobility and

Gentry' explained that the original was 'so prolix and interwoven, that the Reader was rather tired than informed'; as a result he had reorganised the text. The folio edition included a puff for the Brompton Park nursery, in which George London and Henry Wise had 'not made Gain the only mark of their Pains', unlike other nurserymen who pretend to horticultural expertise. Geoffrey Keynes suggested that London may have been Evelyn's helper with the translation: hence the advertisement.

In case George forgot to show the book to him, Evelyn wrote separately to 'Honest Abraham', apologising for the mistakes. He would bring with him the best plants Mr London '(chiefe Gardner to the King) & his partner Mr Wise', could provide. They

> think themselves obliged to furnish me with whatever they have of choice, for some kindnesse I have don them; and would have come with me to Wotton to direct me for the setting up a Greenehouse, which with very little expense of Loame, boards & thatch and other warme Clothing, would have served the Orange Lemon Myrtil & other pretious shrubbs which I also thought to send.

Evelyn would be no more than 'an under Gardner with you' at Wotton signed himself 'Your assured Friend.[15] But once in Surrey, Evelyn found himself living in an intellectual desert. For all the 'wood and water, meadows and mountaines, the Dryads and Hamadryads; but here's no Mr Pepys, no Dr Gale ... all's insipid, and all will be so to me 'til I see and injoy you againe,' he wrote.[16] He had been desperate for conversation until he met the young tutor (to the Finch children at Albury), William Wotton, 'an unexpected blessing ... in the wildernes', and then realised that he must sound as 'famish'd and half-sterved men are said to eate when they come to plenty of provisions'. His new friend was up to date with Locke's writings. He remained in touch with Dr Tenison enthusiastically discussing the phenomena in the skies, comets and meteors, sharing a scientific passion for extraordinary events in the heavens.[17]

But the stay at Wotton was becoming uncomfortable. George was charging rent and John heard that they were being faced by 'inconveniences and impediments'. Lady Wyche had not followed her husband to Ireland, where he was chief secretary. He did not return until 1695, when he appeared in considerable state, filling the house and stables. In the meantime she was being influenced by 'false friends' who exacerbated and fed 'her aversion to her father's relations'. The entail was in question again. To begin with, William Glanville had been a helpful intermediary but the financial crises of the mid 1690s, 'like another plague', said Evelyn, made everyone desperate. George, although at his daughter's mercy, remained well disposed towards his brother and grandson and told Evelyn it was no time to be suspicious of one another.[18]

Evelyn admitted the disagreements to Abraham sadly. 'I would have none to thinke, I come to take possession without being Wellcome.' He was happy to reimburse him for any work he had done on his behalf and promised to send seed. He saw no objection to mixing different fruit trees on the same wall (the only one bare now was in the kitchen garden) and was planning to change the planting, which he would supervise himself; he envisaged a resolution to the current difficulties too.

John's heavy debts were at the root of the problem. They now fell on the estate under the entailment. The family at Wotton demanded that he pay the interest himself but William Glanville stepped in and played the part of a 'Guardian Angel'. Banking was in turmoil, speculation was rife and the going was difficult. John felt it unjust that his uncle George should continue to 'persecute' his father for his own misdeeds, especially since, as he was soon able to point out, he was earning praise from the Treasury for improving revenue in Dublin beyond all expectation.[19] Nevertheless, the atmosphere was poisoned and Evelyn and Mary quietly withdrew to John's house on Dover Street.

Susanna Evelyn's marriage prospects were under active discussion. Like her late sisters, she had her own views about suitors and rejected more than one candidate, amusing her tolerant mother: 'it would make a little novell all her adventures are so various.'[20] Evelyn had his ideas too: why not consider his old friend Hendrick van der Borcht's son? He planned to ask Jael Boscawen if she knew anything of him. 'I have heard there was a very handsome Estate in the Family . . . I need not say to you let this be yet a seacret betweene us'. But he was long dead.[21]

Fortunately William Draper soon proved an ideal candidate, acceptable to all. John was pleased for his sister and relieved financially – Draper had two rich childless uncles, Sir Thomas Draper and Sir Purbeck Temple of Addiscombe in Surrey. Although Evelyn had difficulty raising his daughter's settlement, John saw light at the end of the tunnel and envisioned a future 'out of the reach of care, and anxiety, which I have bin too well acquainted with these many years'.[22] Ralph Bohun, for so many years part of their family, was delighted to hear that Susanna had found a man of such integrity, prudence and good estate, as he put it. Mary reported that 'Sue is very well pleased and wee have reason to be so for her sake'. Evelyn was equally delighted, inviting Anne Sylvius to the celebrations with heavy irony: 'an unusual Buisines, that you are desird to honour a paire of silly Young People, that have Adventurd honestly to Marry, before they Lie together; which (since you and I remember the World) grows now every day a rare thing in this Libertine Age'.[23]

The wedding, in April 1693, was held in the chapel at Ely Place in Holborn and conducted by Dr Thomas Tenison, now bishop of Lincoln. It was a modest occasion for close friends and family only. Francis Godolphin and Jack Evelyn were pages; young Mary Tuke (although a Catholic) and Jael Boscawen attended the bride. Once married, Susanna had her own coach, two footmen and two maids, as well as a chamber in her mother-in-law's house in Surrey Street, elegantly furnished with a 'damask bed and hangings, her dressing roome filled with Japan cabinet china tea table cups tea pot chamber plate in the best manner'. Her mother liked Draper, who was so well travelled and knowledgeable, 'yet no bookish man rather for conversation and is very good company loves the towne which agrees very well with Sue seems to like her upon all accounts they are very well pleased on both sides so that I have no more to wish but the continuance of it'. Although the bridegroom's family had contributed £1,000 to the union, 'wee streched our uttmost to compasse this match and must shrink for it'. They had spent £4,000 on the settlement and more to meet the expenses of 'a decent wedding'. Mary had no regrets; however, 'When our great work now in hand is over we pretend to return to Deptford and reduce ourselves to as narrow a compasse as possible'.[24]

To Bohun, the marriage appeared to solve Evelyn's worldly worries. 'It's a very happy condition, when our affairs are so settled that we can steal out of this troublesome life, without being at least interrupted by the disquieting anxieties which most persons have for the families they leave behind.' His belief that Evelyn would wind down in his seventies suggests that he did not understand him particularly well. Nor did the former tutor show any sensitivity when he wrote to Mary after the wedding to criticise her son-in-law.[25] She defended him fiercely: William Draper did not resort to 'dice cards or tavene', 'is not so ignorant of books as I find you aprehend' and seemed to like his wife 'better and better'.

But Bohun's real concern was their friendship with their Catholic cousins, the Tukes. Mary retorted that 'they are both young and do not engage in controversio nor our converse about Religion' and it was hardly hospitable 'to torment a guest with conversion if one finds no disposition to hearken'.[26] When Lady Tuke asked Evelyn about the wisdom of returning to England from Portugal, for her daughters' sake, he reassured her (or, rather, himself) that English Catholic observance was moderate: 'here be no Inquisition; fewer Monasteries, lesse mumbling of Beades' nor had Catholics ever 'been more at ease, and lesse disturb'd in all my observation, than here at present'. Nor were they so far apart in their faiths: 'I most heartily pray for your Ladyships happinesse, and that you'l Remember me in yours; For (what ever you are made believe) we serve the same Merciful God and Saviour.'[27]

Susanna's marriage seemed a kind of consummation of the Evelyns' long life together and it moved Mary to write a touching testimony to her husband. She remembered his 'tender care of my education to improve both mind and person, by love unwearied patience bearing with my faillings and the unhappy circumstances of my relations'; thinking over 'the early uncomon obligations I have had to you as a friend as well as husband I can never make any returns equall to them'.[28] Evelyn, cheerfully improving the fishing at Sayes Court, restocking the waters for his son-in-law's benefit, shared her delight in the happy state of affairs.[29] In July, the newlyweds and Mrs Draper came to visit for five days – all too few, he told Pepys, 'for they are the most obliging, worthy, usefull, and ingeniously dispos'd Conversation I could ever have desir'd to place my Daughter among I think in England: I assure you, both the Mother and Son are perfect Virtuosi, and know and (which is more) effect, a world of Ingenious things without Vanity'.[30]

After so much unhappiness, so many losses, these simple family pleasures were intensely felt. John benefited from his father's bonhomie, glad that Sayes Court was 'in so smiling a condition'. He thanked Evelyn for offering it to him as a retreat if his own circumstances changed; meanwhile in Susanna's room a little library was organised for Jack. Evelyn urged Pepys and his close friend (and cousin) Dr Thomas Gale when next on the river to 'divert for a Moment to the young House-keepers' at Deptford. 'They are I heare a family of 21: Mrs Tuke is Library-Keeper: The Rest Painters, Embroiderers, Carvers, Gard'ner.'[31] He was happy to report that marriage had not changed his daughter; she remembered her friends, was a good wife and was working on her accomplishments, particularly painting.

For his part, young Draper was touched by Evelyn and Pepys's friendship: 'I know it is a frequent pleasure to you to be at Mr Pepys.' He fed his father-in-law's enthusiasms, looking out for items of antiquarian interest to tell him about, and visiting Sir Kenelm Digby's old home near Oxford, now in ruins. In the garden at Sayes Court he followed Evelyn's instructions, keeping the woods, hedges and groves under 'tolerable control'. There was not enough work now for two men and he discharged the under-gardener.[32] Their first child, Thomas, was born in September 1694; he survived six months. A daughter, Mary, was born the following autumn and more children followed at regular intervals.

In 1694 George enticed his brother and sister-in-law back to Wotton. Much as Mary preferred to be 'fixed at Deptford a place that has ben agreable to friends', she told Bohun 'wee are going this summer to passe the greatest part of it att Wotton being kindly pressed to it by my Brother who declines very much yet is heart whole and very kind to his friends. Deptford will be filled with my daughter Drapers family.'[33] They still planned to let Sayes

Court 'to one who will preserve the Gardens as well as give rent', for they were living beyond their means: 'taxes are so high repairs and accidents so frequent that we cannot reckon upon ease but are in the way towards it, as farr as is yet in our power.' One potential tenant was a relative of Henry Wise, the newest partner in the Brompton Park nursery, who promised to keep it 'as neat as any man in England', that is, except Evelyn himself or, it now seemed, his son-in-law.

In 1694 George was nearly eighty, stone deaf and with failing sight. He was pathetically pleased to have their company and conversation, perhaps particularly Mary's kindness. Mary Wyche 'pretends great concerne . . . but her way of shewing her love and respect is not in the usuall way for she keeps close in her Chamber 2–3 dayes at a time, unseene of any one'. At least now they found themselves 'upon easy terms' with her father.[34] Evelyn's health was mostly good, although he had lost his teeth. In his eighties he was persuaded to spend three weeks at Bath, as Mary told her daughter-in-law Martha, and felt much better, though still 'not willing to impute any good to the waters'.[35]

William Glanville was also glad that Evelyn and Mary were apparently settled back at Wotton, 'Which may an Evelyn inherit . . . long as sun and moon endure; and in this wish heaven knowes I am sincere whatever conveniencyes you have parted with at Sayes court I hope you will find where you now are'. He is sure that they will make what remains of old George's life as easy and cheerful as possible and wonders which of them, George, Evelyn or himself, would be the first to go – 'but I should bee glad that wee might once more come together before wee part'.[36]

Mary Evelyn began to transfer some possessions from Deptford to furnish their apartment at Wotton ('books, Pictures, Hangings, bedding &c.') while leaving Sayes Court sufficiently furnished for the Drapers. As before, John supported his parents' move, knowing how resilient they both were still and hoping it would bring peace and 'a long healthy and more affluent old Age'. He added: 'if I live to come into England again, shall think my self very happy and easy to be there in any condition.' He was sorry that they had not been given the rooms 'by the Bird-Cage', the aviary, 'for it is much more convenient than the other'. He guessed that 'the lady', despite her generous settlement, was still supported by her father and that even more trees would have to be axed.

If the Great Elms before the house, and Chapman's Grove over the mount be spared, there will be some shelter and shade enough to read, and meditate in, with which and a good kitchen Garden (and Orchard yet wanting) one may live there very contentedly. As for the magnificence and perfection of a seat which require many thousand pounds to accomplish, I look

on them to be very different to those who have long since sett their hearts
on better things.

He was not greatly concerned by the prospect of 'a Totall destruction of the
woods', believing that it would help the air circulate and break up 'unwhole-
some fogs' in the valleys and above the house. He had been looking at Irish
gardens.[37]

In the 1670s Evelyn had told John Aubrey proudly: 'Surrey is the Country
of my Birth and my delight.'[38] In 1691 he contributed notes for a revised
edition of his late friend's county history, regretting, as he told Anthony à
Wood, that he had not compiled them earlier, 'soon after my Perambulation,
whilst the Idea of them was fresh and lively; I should then have given it more
Spirit'. Now he found himself liable to 'set things down tumultuarily as if
tumbled out of a Sack, as they come to my Hand, mixing Antiquities and
Natural Things together'.[39] He also wrote to offer his help to Edmund
Gibson, who was translating Camden's *Britannia* from Latin and revising the
material on each county; Evelyn's additions on Surrey ran to almost half the
length of the original entry.[40] Palaces such as Oatlands and Nonsuch had
almost disappeared; the latter where 'one would think, that the whole art of
Architecture were crowded into this single work' was all gone, 'scarce one
stone being left upon another'. He described the Howard brothers' gardens,
Deepdene and Albury, including a detailed, if confusing, evocation of the
Albury tunnel: 'large enough at one end for a coach to pass, being about a
furlong or more in length, and so leads o'er into an agreeable and pleasant
valley. It was at first intended for a way up to the house, but a rock at the
south-end hinder'd that design.'* Finally, he described Wotton, 'the severall
streames gliding thro the meadows, gentle rising and venerable woods
flanking & invironing them', while fountains and 'other hortulan decorations'
were evidence of its former glories.[41] He wrote with the glowing pride of
possession.

Unable to travel during a seven-week cold spell over the winter of 1695/6,
a reminder of the great freeze of 1683/4, he told Pepys they were comfortable,
with 'Luculent Fires in most of the Roomes', but were obliged to suffer 'very
sorry Conversation among the Bumkins'. The following December, despite
pouring rain, he recounted: 'I take a walke in the gardens and a little grove I
am planting . . . and when I am confind, reade and scribble, or build castles in
the aer.' He had time for contemplation and pondered how rarely kings and
princes took advice from 'honest, wise, and worthy persons' – men such as
themselves, he implied.[42]

---

*As it survives, the tunnel could certainly not accommodate a carriage.

The castle in the air was Wotton as redesigned by Evelyn himself, a symmetrical Palladian villa, the spring, ponds and streams now feeding a lake. He was immersed in architectural treatises, expanding his essay for the forthcoming edition of the *Parallel*, and was presumably well informed about new developments thanks to his old friend Wren. Among the handful of architectural drawings that survive in Evelyn's hand, one shows a selection of carpentry details, from a double-skinned dome to domestic timberwork, taken directly from a plate in D'Aviler's *Cours d'Architecture*.[43] The recent crop of sophisticated publications allowed him to dream but Evelyn also kept himself abreast of the new. In August 1697, when for several months there are no entries in the diary, the keen gardener Charles Hatton reported that he had been recently to look at flower paintings in Montagu House with 'old Mr Evelyn'.[44] Hooke's house had burned in 1686 but was now restored, the most Parisian town house in London.

Mary was distracted by another crisis in John's condition and wished they were settled: 'we have many things before us not very pleasing my sonne gives me many melancoly hours I pray God he may find a right cure and get out of this dangerous way he is now.' Later, a friend who had lived with the family in the past, Elizabeth Packer from Groombridge, the daughter of Evelyn's late friend Philip, was struck by the sad contrast between the generations, the brothers' longevity and John, so 'early gone to decay'.[45] Even George was solicitous about his nephew and felt he should not yet return to Ireland. John was conscious of the contrast between himself and his uncle, the latter apparently well enough to 'look over into the next Century at least'. Once again Mary put her faith in Godolphin, hoping that 'our good friend' will stay in power and either keep John's post open or find him another 'on this side, which would be better'. Jack was 'as bookish as his Grandfather can wish', and Susanna, John told Bohun, was 'very well married and I think the only one of us yet at ease'.[46]

Having 'retrenched all superfluous things', they decided after all to keep Sayes Court in the family. As Mary wrote:

We had thought of parting with Deptford upon good terms and were courted to it, but it being a commodious retreat for my daughter Draper and her family they being at the expence of the Garden wee chuse rather to oblige my sonne and daughter, then let it yet, since wee know not how to dispose of our goods and to leave them to strangers is not any way advantagious.[47]

John's letters from Dublin were growing increasingly gloomy. Lord Capel 'looks like a Ghost, pinch'd in his face, appetite lost, leggs extremely swell'd

mr Strickland

22 John Strickland's waterfront house, Greenwich, 1703. Evelyn's steward helped him with his work as treasurer of the Royal Naval Hospital.

and the Dropsy fairly mounting to his stomach'. In his circle in Ireland, only Mary's husband, the elderly Sir Cyril Wyche, seemed in good form. But though depressed, John had become a committed bibliophile ('you will easily conjecture from whom I derive this laudable infirmity, if it be one'). He told his father he planned to sell some duplicate volumes but none of the French ones. He admired the language 'and loved to read good sense clothed in it', although 'I have as all Englishmen ought, an aversion to the People'. He had also begun to buy pictures at auction. Such a bookish man should, his father felt, have been a lawyer, but John still defended his decision. 'I could never find my head turn that way, allways wanted memory, without which that study is not to be succeeded in and for many reasons was never fitt for so bustling a Profession.'[48]

Wyche and John were involved in the Dublin Philosophical Society, the 'colony' meeting regularly on Wednesdays 'as you do there'.[49] John seemed to be becoming the son Evelyn had wanted, erudite and public-spirited, even if Thomas Keightley's son, 'very Active', had risen to be a Privy Councillor.[50] Sadly, John's renaissance was brief. He returned from Ireland in spring 1696 and Sir Hans Sloane diagnosed him as deeply depressed, which made him 'believe his distempers to be much worse than really they are'. As the months passed without improvement, his father suggested he take practical steps, 'some daily exercise of body, as ball, bowle, walking, riding, & thus to free your thoughts from all . . . difficultys'.[51]

But as John's term in public office faltered, his father's began again. Through Godolphin's intervention, in February 1695 he was appointed treasurer to the projected Royal Naval Hospital at Greenwich.[52] The salary was a modest £300. As usual at such moments, he went on an architectural tour, visiting Morden College in Blackheath, the Turkey Company almshouse still under construction, possibly designed by Wren who was to be the architect for the new hospital. John wrote to his father, that though the post was

> neither equall to your merit, nor answerable to your occasions, yet I cannot forbear congratulating you upon it, as it may be a means to oblige you to enjoy the secret abode again of Sayes Court, now it is in so flourishing a condition and of being likewise so near my sister and her family, which must needs be a very great comfort and satisfaction to you and my Mother.

Evelyn set to the task immediately; their Deptford steward John Strickland (previously Sir Richard Browne's man) became his trusted emissary. As Evelyn assured William Draper, he had entrusted him with 'things of Consequence, and many Thousands of publique Mony' for almost twenty years. He had even been authorised to sign Evelyn's name when collecting his fee as commissioner for the privy seal.[53]

Meanwhile life at Wotton suited Mary Evelyn well. Gratifyingly, George was responding, feeling able to ask for things 'more freely than of late' and even climbing the mount once more. Ignored by his daughter for so long, he had become cowed and inactive; Mary's kindness restored his energy. By the following year even he had plans. He wanted to ask the surveyor-general, his brother's friend, a favour: 'I hope you will not forget to speake to Sr Xtopher Wren about ordering (by his advise) . . . how to make a mortar to keep in the water in the piscina, which you know now will not hold, as also an abiding Mortar for the wall & pillars in the grotta.' The defects in the water garden had to be sorted out before winter and the wall built while it was still dry: 'if you cannot come in very reasonable tyme, you must send down the directions how you will have it built & . . . I will looke after it . . . in your absense'.[54]

As their most prized possessions made their way to Surrey, Mary was relieved to find nothing broken. Odd things had been left behind – a drawer of the 'triangle table' was either at Deptford or with the joiners. She reported that the hay was almost all in the barn but the grove overrun with weeds, 'a neglect the gardner cannot well answer'. No one did any more than necessary.[55] A few weeks later she wrote again. The pictures were hung and made a 'great show' and the clocks were in order; her own closet was so full that 'I know not where to stick a picture more'. Their cabinet suited the house very well and was set out with china 'to the great liking of all'.

Their gardener from Deptford, Tom, had even walked to Wotton from Deptford, some thirty miles, Mary told her husband. He had mown the grass walks and employed a man to clear the weed-infested flower beds but needed a new spade and roller and had difficulty finding a scythe. She was unsure whether he was being obstructed or if there really were no tools. Wotton was run down, and some of the workforce had been taking advantage of their old master. Now a nursery of cuttings was flourishing, ready to freshen up the grove and give substance to the threadbare garden with Evelyn's favourite evergreens. Mary, now in her sixties, and Evelyn in his mid-seventies, were applying the enthusiasm of people half their age to their project, bringing Wotton back to life.

Mary had powers of observation akin to her husband's. When she and Susanna had stopped at Hampton Court, on their way back from taking the waters at Bath in the summer of 1691, she reported that although building work at the palace was not yet finished, 'it will be very fine one front to the gardens the other to the water'. The gardens, with 'noble walks' and a canal, were densely patterned with fountains, knots of box and statues. She particularly admired Tijou's iron gates, 'in as curious feullage and as hollow work as Mr Gibons carving, they are not cast but wraught by hand'. But her eye was caught, above all, by the greenhouse, 'filled with the most rare plants of the Indies things wonderfull in the kind some with leaves 3/4 of a yard long and a quarter broad others of different forms not to be described easily the name I know not . . . I wish you there a day with all my heart and hope you will go the gardners are holanders.'[56]

In contrast, the long abandoned palace at Greenwich had been earmarked for a naval hospital since 1687; yet another Dutch War (the fourth, 1680–4) intensified the need for this. In 1691 Queen Mary gave her consent for the palace site to be used and after the devastating Battle of La Hogue, offered further help.[57] Pepys wrote to Evelyn that he was 'recollecting his old thoughts on the matter' but was confused by the many plans, ranging from basic conversion to 'an Invalides for the sea' which would offer accommodation for widows and orphans as well as the aged and incapacitated. But 'the work is too near akin to me, and to the Commands I have heretofore had concerning it, to let it want any degree of furtherance I can give it'. Pepys was adamant that the money must be voted by a Parliament which was 'as little disposed to deny as any I sat in'. The queen's death on 28 December 1694 and her husband's great sorrow (Draper reported that 'everybody agrees the king to be a very melancholy widdow') did not delay the project unduly.[58]

The treasurer was faced with a busy building site and negligible funding, despite the £10,000 which had been subscribed, but not handed over: 'one way or other mony mealts away' he told Mary. She told John more of his father's immediate difficulties:

the Estimat Sr Chris Wren has given in to fitt the building already erected, will come to neere 8 thousand p. to compleat the whole designe and provide for two thousand persons will amount to 2 hundred thousand which will be a great while a collecting by subscriptions, it is feared, tho the designe is so reasonable and proper for the honour of the nation and encouragment of seamen there are so many wages for mony so few expedients to raise summs and people uneasy at the excessive rates of provisions of all sorts, that the new parlament will finde many difficulties to place what will be expected from them.[59]

As at Chelsea, Evelyn assumed responsibility for the 'government' and pointed Samuel Travers, the surveyor, to the example of France where they might follow the regulations of the Invalides or those of 'the French Kings late Colledge at Brest (erected about 10 Yeares since, upon a Designe in part like what is intended at Greenewich)'. Alternatively the great London hospitals were suitable examples ('by long experience found sufficient'), as was Chelsea, while the constitution of the little almshouse, the College, at Dulwich was exemplary.[60]

At New Year 1696 Evelyn wrote to William Vanbrugh, secretary to the hospital commissioners and cousin of the architect and playwright Sir John, that he would come up to London when the building works had 'absolute neede of present Mony', since he had already spent the last three months in the capital 'to no purpose'.[61] He deputed William Draper to appear on his behalf. He could see danger signs: waning enthusiasm and difficulties in extracting the king's promised contribution, an annual £2,000, from the Treasury. On 21 April 1696 the grand committee (which included Draper, Evelyn's nephew William Glanville and Pepys) met and perused the plans and on 30 June, at precisely five o'clock, 'Mr Flamsted the Kings Astronomical Professor observing the punctual time by Instruments', Wren and Evelyn laid the foundation stone. Godolphin was the first to pay his share – £200 – but other subscribers reneged and meetings were seldom quorate. The Treasurer was reduced to begging. When he approached 'Greate persons' for money, he told Godolphin: 'My Lord, The[y] seeme to looke on and avoyd me, as one Carying the Pest about me.'[62]

Mary wrote solicitously to her husband. While not belittling his worries after his first year as treasurer she reminded him: 'you are generally aprhensive of the worst, when all is don, wee must submit and acquiesce in what Almighty God determines for us.' Now that he was with such kind friends (his daughter and her family), he must make life easier for himself. 'Time wears out many troubles your uneasiness proceeds from the generall misfortunes you cannot impute any part to late imprudence therefore wait with

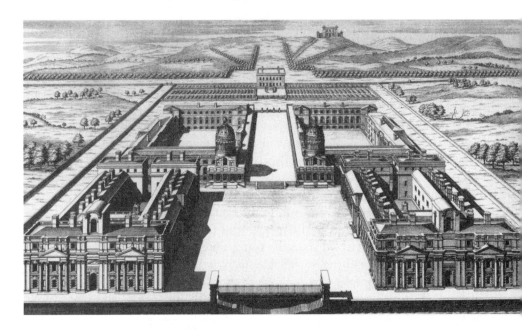

23 Perspective of the completed Royal Naval Hospital, Greenwich from Colen Campbell's *Vitruvius Britannicus* (1725).

patience & hope the best.'[63] Evelyn told her he was trying to follow her advice 'as far as I am able amidst so many perplexities in this my great Age . . . who entirely loves you'.

With £5,000 already disbursed, by September 1696 just £800 had been received. Wren had suggested diverting some of the coal duties voted for City church building, now finished, to this 'Charity'.[64] Draper, again deputising for Evelyn, turned to Sir Stephen Fox since Godolphin was no longer at the Treasury. Now the old Chelsea team, Evelyn, Wren and Fox, was reunited. When not in Surrey, Evelyn was often on site in Greenwich and in April 1700 he and Wren presented William III with a model and engraved plans. Three years later, aged eighty-three, Evelyn resigned and handed his appointment to Draper. Expenditure stood at £88,305, receipts £89,879. The hospital was in sound financial health. Fox, once it appeared that the subscriptions were failing to come in, had suggested that substitute funding be provided by levies on seamen's wages. Surreptitiously, it had been arranged that the pensioners of the future should pay for their own charitable foundation.[65]

Evelyn still had tantalising access to patronage. His cousin, Daniel Parke, who was rather less admirable than Evelyn realised, was hoping for a seat on the Virginia Privy Council. He gave him a glowing reference: 'he has one of the fairest, and most considerable Plantations and Estates in the Country, is as understanding, sober, Industrious, and fortunate young Gentleman as any I know; Having had his Education here in England; he has since applied himselfe to such Improvements where he resides.' Evelyn did not reveal that Parke had recently lost his ship, the *Loyall Evelyn*, in the West Indies and so was unable to return to England as he had planned.[66] Parke obtained his goal and, in thanks, put Evelyn in touch with a most compatible Virginian.

From an address at 'the head of Mautopony river' John Walker wrote to Evelyn about local plants, unfamiliar in Europe. The problem was the sheer extent of the vegetation, making it almost 'imposible to say what here is'. He sent a drawing of some 'drye plants', but he felt himself swimming against the tide for 'this is a place wheire few or none doe delight in aneything but a present proffit which is a ruine to a Cuntry and espeatially to him that his inclination is that way inclineable'. In his next letter, Walker apologised for just missing a boat on which he could have sent some trees, but a bottle of sassafras oil was on its way and dried specimens would follow in the spring. He listed the plants he knew by name. Walker knew Evelyn's reputation from *Pomona*, and was keen to help; he was a fellow spirit who found Virginia no place to study chemistry or herbalism for 'want of gentlemen and mony'.[67]

In his reply, Evelyn suggested Walker send back anything interesting with George London's contact, who was there 'to Make, and Plant the Garden, design'd for the College, newly built in your Country [William and Mary College in Williamsburg]; and likewise to enquire out, what Plants, rare in this Kingdome, may be transported hither'. Although some of the plants Walker had named were familiar, Evelyn encouraged him to send more information: everything was valuable. He had been delighted by Walker's description of the possum, for although he had seen the strange animal which carried its young in a sack below its stomach, Walker provided much more detail. He hoped that he would continue to be in touch: 'I thinke (if God continue an old mans life so long) to spend part of the next Winter in London.' This contact with the new territories, through such a sympathetic intermediary, provided yet another avenue for Evelyn's still insatiable appetite for the new, to be fully shared with the Fellows at the Royal Society. Encouraged during his days on the Council of Trade, Evelyn's eye was continually drawn overseas to wider, stranger worlds – intrigued as much by William Penn's map of Pennsylvania as by spices from the East Indies or fossils from the Americas.[68]

Evelyn was still collecting information on many different fronts. *Numismata. A Discourse of Medals* (1697), a rambling, unfocused volume, was little more than an illustrated list of lists although it had topicality, appearing just after the recoinage of 1696 which had been masterminded by Isaac

Newton.[69] Evelyn dedicated the volume to Francis Godolphin, Margaret Blagge's son, for he had high hopes of the new generation. A portrait gallery of virtuous men was an essential ingredient of most utopian schemes, present in every thinking household from Francis Bacon's to Clarendon's and Pepys's – ideally, it should be installed in and around the library.[70] But Evelyn's own hall of portraits was this book, with the sitters accorded marks for their achievements and failures. He was a great believer in the truths of physiognomy, even on the faces of royal dogs. Only look at Cromwell, he wrote, the 'Falls and Lines of his ambiguous and double Face ... to read in it ... Dissimulation, Boldness, Cruelty, Ambition'. (He did not compare it with another lined, saturnine face, that of Charles II.) Predictably enough, Francis Bacon had 'a spacious Fore-head and piercing eye, always (as I have been told by one who knew him well) looking upward' as befitted one 'who by standing up against Dogmatists was to emancipate and set free the long and miserably captivated Philosophia'. Abraham Cowley's 'candid, ingenuous, and agreeable Nature' was easy to read, compared to Thomas Hobbes's expression of 'supercilious Saturnine Opiniatrety'. William Oughtred's calm face reminded Evelyn of other personal heroes: Harvey, Wilkins and Moray.

Like Pepys, Evelyn was again active as the Royal Society was re-energised by the rise of new men. Hans Sloane became secretary in 1693 and remained in the post for twenty years. When Evelyn sought corrections to *Numismata* he turned to Sloane as well as to two promising younger scholars, William Wotton and Richard Bentley, the royal librarian and divine.

Evelyn resumed his campaign to find the Royal Society a permanent home, so that it might continue its 'investigation of causes, principles, energies, powers, and effects of bodies, and things visible; and to improve them for the good and benefit of mankind'. Wren drew up plans while Richard Waller wrote of Hooke's 'great Project ... to build an handsome Fabrick for the Societies use'.[71] In the end no such philosophical college was built despite their tenacious construction of so many Solomon's Temples. Evelyn continued to attend Royal Society meetings into extreme old age. He missed the informal gatherings of 'The Saturday Academists' at York Buildings, which were no longer possible, with Pepys living outside London and Dr Gale now dean of York; they had been 'the most advantagious and gainefull, as well as the most diverting to me of the Weekely Circles'.[72]

Pepys had settled in his clerk William Hewer's country house in Clapham, which Evelyn found 'wonderfully well furnished' with an exceptional collection of 'all the Indys & Chineze Curiositys'. Between their irregular meetings Pepys and Evelyn carried on conversations on paper, discussing their impressions of Clarendon's long-awaited *History of the Rebellion*, newly published (though the author had died in 1674) and presented, volume by volume, to

Evelyn by his friend, Clarendon's son Henry Hyde. Both he and Pepys were engrossed by what they read. Evelyn commented on the unexpectedly elegant style and his apparent lack of desire for revenge. Clarendon was, wrote Pepys, the only man who could tell the whole story. Recent history had greater reality for them than troubling current events; as Pepys put it: "Twere endlesse to talke at this Time of Publique matters, and not to much more purpose to thinke of them, if one could help it.'[73] Memory, the perfection of which had long engrossed the Fellows of the Royal Society, seemed an increasingly precious faculty.

Evelyn read Roger Bacon's *Cure of Old Age* and *Preservation of Youth*, brought the insights of age to bear on his writing and acted as if an important part of his life still lay before him. Unlike Pepys who had experienced depression in the early 1690s, he was living proof of the prophet Isaiah's observation, 'Planters are often blessed with Health and Old Age'.[74] Out of the near-thousand pages of the stillborn *Elysium Britannicum* he extracted the material for *Acetaria* (1699), a platform, as ever, for the Royal Society. The little book on salads included a lengthy discourse on eating habits, both ancient and modern, as well as information on plants and recipes. Despite his enjoyment of venison, Evelyn wrote that he was rather tempted by vegetarianism, the 'herby-diet'.

Of all his publications, Evelyn remained proudest of *Sylva*.[75] In Kneller's portrait, commissioned by Pepys in 1689, Evelyn stands against an exotic landscape, holding a copy in his hand. It may be the first book ever reviewed in an English newspaper. But the pages of *Sylva* were always open for new material. Pepys summarised a letter from Boston for Evelyn's benefit, dealing with plane trees and the possibility of transporting them across the Atlantic.[76] Younger friends such as William Wotton urged him to press on with a fourth edition, which appeared in 1706. The *Parallel* too was well advanced towards a second edition, finally published in 1707.[77]

Yet by the time *Sylva* appeared, he was mourning the desolate scene that his own woods now presented. They had been decimated by the gales of 1703, both those trees 'left for Ornament' and those which were 'Valuable materiall', and by the continual felling which had been essential to meet debts and marriage settlements and keep the estate solvent. The timber trees that Evelyn saw from the windows of Wotton House and identified as his grandson's best hope of profit and pleasure were also the family's cash cow.[78]

Eventually Sayes Court was let, to those with business at the dockyard. One tenant was more colourful than careful. 'There was a ball last night at St James's House, where the Czar was incognito. He intends to remove out of Norfolk Buildings, and has hired Mr Evelyn's house at Deptford, as being more private and nearer the shipping which he most delights in.'[79] Peter the

Great obtained his lease from Evelyn's current tenant, Admiral Benbow. Evelyn heard about the goings on from one of his servants; the house was full, and the people 'right nasty'. He told Bohun about it. 'I suppose you heard that Says Court is of late erected into an Imperial Palace, where the Muscovian Czar is my poore tenant. He lies in Sr Richards chamber Dines in the parlor next my little Closset, Entertaines the King in the other parlor next the Bird-Cage.'[80] A servant reported he was seldom there since he was usually at the King's Yard (in the dockyard, since the purpose of the visit was to observe shipbuilding) or on the water, 'dressed in several dresses'. That day the king was expected: 'the best parlour is pretty clean for him to be entertained in.'[81]

The famous story about the tsar being pushed in a wheelbarrow through Evelyn's glorious holly hedges, whose growth he updated in each successive edition of *Sylva*, may be apocryphal but the state of Sayes Court after the Russians left in late April suggests it was not so far from the truth. Wren and George London went in early May to survey the damage and estimate the sums due from the Treasury. Evelyn received £107.7s for the house and £55 for the garden, and Benbow, whose lease was shortly to expire, got £133.2s.6d. for his damaged furnishings. Evelyn finally plucked up courage in June 'to view how miserably the Tzar of Moscovy had left my house after 3 moneths making it his Court', but cheered himself up afterwards by going on to Greenwich, where the foundations of the hall and chapel were being laid.[82]

Now, yet again, things were going wrong in Surrey. Elizabeth Packer, writing to Mary about the 'unkindnesse from Wotton' had 'wondred indeed at your being so much at London'.[83] George's granddaughter Catherine (one of George junior's daughters) had married, apparently against the wishes of her family, a Dr George Fulham, rector of Compton, Surrey. When he preached at Wotton on Christmas Day 1697 all seemed well to Evelyn, except that his 'elegant and trim discourse' seemed more suitable for court than a modest country parish.[84] What began as a wrong note turned into yet another towering row about inheritance.

Fulham, 'a Crafty & intriguing person', began to unpick the Wotton entailment and six months later had so fouled the waters, confusing old George even further, that the Evelyns were forced to retreat back to Dover Street and were still there throughout the summer of 1699. By then the case and petitions had been to both Houses, where Evelyn marshalled his forces. At the Commons 'they durst not proceede, I have so very greate an Interest among them in favour of my right' while at the Lords 'I had not onely almost all the Bishops, & so very many of the secular Lords . . . they had no hope to prevaile there.' His goal was to prevent the 'Patrimony of my Ancestors' being lost. In his branch of the family the two Sir Johns, of Godstone and West Dean, and

Sir Edward at Long Ditton had left nothing, their estates being broken up or passing down the female line, 'dissipated, sold or scattered, among strangers . . . & our name & family extinguished'.

George agreed to let Evelyn and his male heirs retain their right to the estate 'if I would alowe him 6500 pounds, to inable him to discharge his owne debts, & give legacys to his Gr:Children' after which he would become a life tenant, unable 'to make any further wast of the woods & other spoile he had begunn'.[85] Elizabeth Packer was shocked by these developments: surely at George's age the settlement should have been irrevocable and she 'regretted the honest good gentleman should be faln into such hands now at his last & they have much to answer for who have thus wrought upon him'. One of Fulham's supporters was old William Glanville, which surprised her, it being so 'contrary to his former judgement & friendship to you'. She presumed 'mercenary' motives had changed his mind. In 1692 Glanville had persuaded George to settle the estate on his brother, 'making it irrevocable', but in recent years Evelyn and he had had religious disagreements, the freethinking Glanville tending to Socinianism (a radical and religiously tolerant sect, which disputed the Trinity) and 'he who till of late had much obliged me, on a suddaine withdrew his kindnesse to my greate prejudice.'[86]

Elizabeth Packer remembered the dramas over Richard Evelyn's estate, where the entailment was broken at the instigation of his widow Elizabeth on behalf of her daughter Anne and son-in-law William Montagu. By 1692 when both women were dead, Montagu 'who had lived dissolutly & Scandalously with another woman' found himself heir to Baynards – much as Fulham had hoped to obtain Wotton for himself.[87] She pitied them both and wished she lived near enough to visit, 'how many causless injuries have you receiv'd & what work have two undeserving husbands made'. She now hoped that their grandson might take on Wotton in Evelyn's lifetime 'that no further wrongs may reach him'. Through it all, Jack remained 'the stay and hope of a Family which some are endeavouring to discompose & ruin'. Evelyn's love for this 'deare, deare good child' was boundless.[88]

In the spring of 1699, aged forty-four, Evelyn's 'onely remaining son', John, died after a long illness. As so often, a suitable omen marked the event: another whale was washed up the Thames two days after the death. John's had been a sad, unfulfilled life and his depression had grown worse since his return from Ireland. He was buried quietly in the family mausoleum a week later, but neither his father nor son attended. Evelyn was avoiding Wotton while the arguments ran on, and was in any case unwell. In October, George died, aged eighty-three. Despite his frailties, he was 'in perfect memory & under-standing'. Evelyn reminisced how he had kept open house in the old way; people came to visit and stayed all summer. His funeral, befitting his status in the county, was 'in great state' and attracted more than two thousand mourners.[89] Although he still did not feel comfortable at Wotton, 'sending onely a servant thither to looke after my Concerns', Evelyn hoped that, after almost sixty years of 'conversation', he and Glanville, could salvage their friendship – which they did.[90] When Glanville himself died, aged eighty-four, in 1702 he requested burial off the Goodwin Sands in a lead coffin – a whim, according to his brother-in-law, since he had 'no relation at all to the Sea'.[91] His humour transcended death: his epitaph ended with the pun 'Memento Mare'.[92]

George's death, Elizabeth Packer hoped, might finally secure Jack's inheritance but though 'Wotton is a fine seat I know & so esteem'd & you'l have reason to keep it in repair' she personally preferred Sayes Court with its many happy memories and 'the pretty Philosophical order of the place'. She wondered if their grandson would use the house, for ''tis pitty but the gardens should be look'd to & enjoy'd by some that value them'. It had something special, 'pleasing to my fancy beyond the stateliness of Wotton or Woodcott I remember your pretty Grandson too in those days of his childhood had a strange fondness for it'. She wished that Lady Wyche might recover her hearing, which would make her 'more capable of society', and thought it strange that she and William Glanville junior were executors of the estate.[93] As she suspected, yet again the entail was in dispute and another round of expensive legal jousting began. Evelyn heard that they planned to drain the ponds and sell the fish as well as 'removing severall other things' and he hoped that Glanville realised that the woodland could not be touched following George's death; nor, legally, could any other fixtures and fittings, not even the fish or the doves.[94]

Inheriting Wotton, even with all the continuing difficulties, gave Evelyn a new lease of life. A last load of possessions went from Deptford to Surrey – a great barge took one hundred bales to Kingston, from where they went on by road. Once it all arrived the house looked more like a 'merchant's storehouse', Mary remarked. Now Evelyn wrote to Pepys in May 1700: 'Vetruvius has said nothing of repaires, nor hardly remember I of any who repented not of an expense commonly greater than new-building, but at Wotton necessity compells me for the present, whilst I please my selfe with a Castle in the Aire which I have built in paper.'[95] It was probably then that Evelyn drew his lakeside villa, to one side of a small lake, symmetrical within an irregular landscape, just as Henry Wotton had advised. The actual changes were modest. Evelyn told Pepys he had given himself time to stand back and admire the improvements, 'partly in the dwelling-house, and without doores, for Conveniences suitable to our Oeconomy . . . My Tast for things superfluous, being extreamely alter'd, from what it was.'

An inventory drawn up by Evelyn in 1702 gives a snapshot of his family home – while his memoire put together for his grandson's benefit a couple of years later added further details, inside and out.[96] The entrance hall was hung with the trappings of a traditional country house – heavy armour, muskets and stags' heads as well as portraits of royalty and nobility – but interpolated with Evelyn's possessions such as a 'a large & excellent Map of Rome'. On the 'Great Staircase' hung battle and crowd scenes, a landscape of Wotton 'before the alterations done by my bro.' as well as Hondius' map of the world and another of Paris. Family portraits hung in the dining room; in his will he instructed the Trustees not to sell or dispose of them.

In the great parlour, the public room, stood a walnut table with a lime frame 'incomparably carved with 4 angels, flowers, & frutages by that famous Artist Gibbons & presented me in acknowledgement of my first Recomending him to K Charles the second before which he was scarce known'. There were sconces and mirrors, china ranged over the fireplace and two 'Egyptian marble pyramids' – perhaps obelisks. The paintings there were the cream of the collection, with fine gilded and carved frames, some of ebony and pearwood. There were family portraits by Riley and Closterman and flower paintings by Susanna as well as trophies from Rome such as Maratti's 'the church and reason submitting to faith', a painting by Rosso Fiorentino and an 'enigmatical figure by M Angelo'.

The chamber alongside was hung with tapestries depicting fruit and flowers, while the little parlour was fresh with white calico curtains. The pictures there included a 'representation of London's Conflagration' by Wenceslaus Hollar and there was a 'closset of curiositys' that was full of china. Evelyn told his grandson that such collections were for the entertainment of 'virtuoso ladies'. Over the fireplace in their own bedchamber was a copy, perhaps of Van Dyck's painting, showing Charles I on horseback, portraits of Evelyn's father and mother, two paintings by Evelyn himself and a number of miniatures, some possibly Mary's own work. A portrait of Louis XIV, engraved by Nanteuil, was in the 'Gray cloth chamber at the top of the great stair'.[97] Wotton now epitomised Evelyn and Mary's long life together, set against the backdrop of his ancestry.

With the death of his uncle Temple in 1700, William Draper inherited Addiscombe. In a long letter, Draper thanked him for all he had done for him; 'you gave me happiness at first, when you admitted me into your family & you have taken care to encrease it ever since.'[98] Eighteen months later, Mary told Bohun that the Drapers were 'resolved to build notwithstanding the prospects of great taxes' and had turned to the team at Greenwich, including Nicholas Hawksmoor, the clerk of works, and Edward Strong, master mason. In the summer of 1703 the Evelyns went to see the new house, built of brick and Portland stone but still unfinished. Evelyn pronounced it had 'all the points of good & solid Architecture'.[99] Later, a young James Thornhill decorated it, his first domestic commission.

Although everything they now did was for future generations, the delight that the elderly couple took in their venture at Wotton is tangible. On his eightieth birthday Evelyn counted his blessings: a return to health, good sight and hearing, 'other senses & facultys tollerable'; if he were to live longer, he might be even better prepared for his end. For all that he told his friends that he expected every day to be his last, to follow 'a Wiser Monitor, who is gon before to provide better places, and more lasting habitations', he and Mary lived enthusiastically in the present.[100] In February 1702 Evelyn had a small triumph at the Royal Society, when an account of his tables of arteries and veins, acquired long ago in Padua, was read to the meeting and the tables were confirmed as being more accurate even than Vesalius's. Soon afterwards they were published in the *Philosophical Transactions* with two magnificent plates by Van der Gucht (one dated 1667).[101] When James Yonge visited Gresham College that spring to accept a fellowship, he was impressed by the lack of ceremony and was pleased to see 'the famous Mr Evlyn among them'.[102] The next year after his adversary Robert Hooke's death, Isaac Newton became president, ushering in an efficient and active era for the Royal Society. Evelyn witnessed two of his experiments with the burning glass.

The future looked promising. Jack had fought off smallpox at Oxford in 1700, an episode that had provided a raw reminder of their earlier sorrows. He was making the very best of his talents, as his grandfather told Pepys, but there could be no question of him going abroad – the sole male heir, his life was too precious. Evelyn found himself arguing with Pepys, ironically enough since Pepys's passionate views on the benefits of travel were formed by Evelyn, who had mapped out that European journey for him and his wife, long ago.

Mary, the chatelaine of Wotton, was flourishing, often busy until ten at night. Evelyn had made a new will and was attempting farming. His first efforts were blessed by good weather but, he told Pepys proudly, 'never was any matron more buisy than my wife, disposing of our plaine country furniture for a naked old extravagant house, suitable to our imployments' and becoming 'a very Sabine' in her dairy. She delayed her return to London in their first winter, staying behind in Surrey to see the pig slaughtered and to show the cook, Margret, how to make the famous Wotton pork puddings. Evelyn wrote that his friend must think he had forgotten 'Philosophy, Gresham College, and the example of Mr Pepys and agreable conversation of Yorke buildings', but 'Know I have ben ranging of no fewer than 30 large cases of books, destined for a competent standing library'. Pepys replied he had 'no herds to mind, nor will my Doctor allow me any books here', because of his eyes, but was happy just thinking. 'And thinking, I take it, is working', although nothing compared to what the Evelyns were up to. But, he fondly chided, take care and 'pray remember what a clock it is with you and me'.[103]

From time to time they met. Pepys's nephew, John Jackson, now on his own protracted travels, had visited Lady Tuke, still in the household of the dowager queen Catherine in Portugal. He was to tell her, said Pepys, that their good friends the Evelyns had recently visited, from Wotton, 'with their whole family of children, children in law, and grandchildren, and dined with me'.[104] Pepys was fond of Jack Evelyn and invited him to Clapham to stay overnight and share the results of his optical experiments – but only on a sunny day.[105]

In March 1703 Evelyn broke his shinbone in Brompton Park nursery, but was sufficiently mobile again to visit Pepys in May, less than a fortnight before he died. Their friendship was one of the greatest delights of Evelyn's life. Here was a man he did not need to impress, and who did not try to blind him with his own superiority, either social or intellectual, and whom he admired unreservedly for his 'greate Integrity' in public office and steadfast principles towards the monarchs he had served. 'Hospitable, Generous, Learned in many things, skill'd in Musick, a very great Cherisher of Learned men, of whom he had the conversation.' Together they had batted their enthusiasms to and fro, with Mary Evelyn and Mrs Skinner, 'Mr Pepps' inclination' as Evelyn put it, close by.[106] Pepys's funeral, like his wife Elizabeth's long before, was at St Olave's. 'Mr: Pepys had ben for neere 40 years, so my particular Friend, that he now send me Compleat Mourning.' He and Jack had mourning rings and he was asked to be a pallbearer, but his age and recent injury prevented him.[107]

Evelyn still continued to visit Deptford occasionally, either on his way to Greenwich or in an emergency, such as after the hurricane of November 1703 which had wreaked such havoc at Wotton. William Draper reported that his family had left their beds to huddle in the kitchen at Addiscombe, while John Strickland, his steward, told him that Sayes Court was 'very much shattered'. The roofs were badly damaged, the elm in the backyard was down as were many other trees, while ships had blown out to the Isle of Dogs.[108]

The living at Wotton was now Ralph Bohun's, largely thanks to Mary who had interceded with the bishop of Salisbury, Dr Gilbert Burnet. Evelyn told Bohun early in 1701 that the living was worth 'seven score pounds' but guessing he would not want 'the care & toil of husbandry' he planned to leave the tithes as they were. The glebe was in good order, the parsonage house dilapidated and he was unsure who was legally responsible for its repair. He emphasised the worst aspects, Evelyn told him, so there would be no nasty surprises. Many others had solicited for the living but he had told them all it was 'long since engaged'.[109]

When Bohun arrived in May 1701 Mary apologised, from Greenwich, for not greeting him in person and not fitting out his apartment but they were very pleased for the chance 'to shew our esteeme of you'. Their steward Thomas Bedingfield and Margret, the cook, would help him settle in. Soon Bohun was so much part of the household again that Mary asked him to remind her to feed up the turkeys, bantams and partridges in the weeks before Christmas.[110] In the garden, his responsibilities were largely in the new green-house. Bohun's sermons were generally acceptable to Evelyn although he thanked him for one particularly which dwelt on the 'terrour of Judgement to the vicious & Impenitent, with pertinent Inferences, to prepare us for death & a futur state' and told the humourless cleric: 'I tooke it kindly, as my Funerall Sermon.'[111]

One May evening in 1703, after a punishing seven-hour journey from London to Wotton, Mary arrived back, unable to resist walking in the garden until dusk. She found the borders under the wall enlarged and replanted neatly and the new trees flourishing. Stone paving now led to the 'best parlour' door. Indoor repairs had been carried out, though it was still too damp to lay the new floors in the 'Deale chamber'. The wainscot panels and windows of the great chamber were being made up and other floors relaid. Only her painful corns stopped her walking further to the upper kitchen garden. The pleasures of Wotton had banished all thoughts of Sayes Court.[112]

The marriage, in September 1705, between their grandson, Jack, and Anne Boscawen, Jael's daughter, completed their happiness, while also contributing helpfully to their finances. Once again, Tenison, now archbishop of Canterbury, performed the ceremony, this time in the chapel at Lambeth Palace.[113] Another possible match, between Pepys's nephew John Jackson and Susanna's daughter Elizabeth, was rejected – Evelyn could not raise a large enough settlement for the 'satisfaction of Relations'; two weddings in a matter of months would be beyond his resources.[114] That summer, Evelyn and Mary, Jack, his future bride and her mother had gone down to admire the Royal Hospital at Greenwich. The first seamen were being admitted and 'the Building [was] now going on very magnificent'.[115] The many disparate elements in his life, his aims and dreams, had suddenly come together in a highly satisfactory fashion.

When William III died and James's Protestant daughter Anne ascended the throne in 1702, she became the fifth monarch to rule in Evelyn's lifetime. Bohun welcomed an 'English Queene with an English heart that the mony will be spent at home'. Despite that, 'where the Carcasse is there are the

Eagles, for St James is so thronged with Numbers and Coaches it is a difficult thing to find a passage to the park'. One such eagle, Lord Godolphin, was
now perched back as lord treasurer and had obtained a post as receiver of
stamp duties, at a salary of £300, for Jack Evelyn. Jael Boscawen helped
remind her brother of his moral obligations towards the Evelyns, still struggling to find the interest on £9,000; their grandson's easy move into a well-
remunerated office was an immense relief. 'We hope to acquitt all loose debts
at present and by degrees as far as the portion mony will go.'[116] The Evelyn
and Godolphin families were now united, for Jack's wife was Lord
Godolphin's niece. In addition Evelyn had a personal link to England's
newest hero, the duke of Marlborough, for Francis Godolphin had married
Lady Henrietta Churchill, the duke's eldest daughter in 1698. When Evelyn
met him again, introduced by Godolphin, the victorious commander took the
old man's hand 'with extraordinary familiarity & Civility . . . without any
alteration of his good nature'.[117]

Jack's wedding brought together 'aboundance of Relations on both sides'
and a few days later a great dinner was held for eighteen guests. Ralph Bohun
was not among them and, characteristically splenetic, was affronted at being
invited neither to officiate nor to dine. Mary explained: 'It was neither want
of kindnesse or respect that wee did not envite you to be a witnesse of what
passes' and, in a conciliatory aside, added they thought 'that wee might be free
with so good a friend'.[118]

At New Year 1706, staying in London in the Dover Street house as they
usually did at this season, Evelyn did his annual accounts, paid wages, distributed gifts and 'Tho much Indisposed, & in so advanced an Age I went to our
Chapell to give God publique Thanks'. If he was allowed to 'Continue my
Pilgrimage here' he asked protection for himself and his family.[119] He felt
increasingly unwell in the next days, with pain in his kidneys and shaking.
The final entry in his diary is dated 3 February, where he notes a sermon by
'a Scotchman . . . Let every one that names the L Jesus depart from Evill, &
increase in love of that profession.'[120]

On 27 February Evelyn died, and he was buried at Wotton on 4 March.
He had wanted to be buried in the garden with Mary, 'under the oral circle
of the laurel grove by me planted . . . with a plain marble stone and on it a
pedestal of black marble bearing an urn of white marble'. If that was
impractical, then in the 'dormitory of my ancestors'. He was buried, not in
the garden, but near his mother and father. His epitaph described him as
having lived through 'extraordinary events, & revolutions' and 'serv'd ye
Publick in several employments . . . & perpetuated his fame by far more
lasting Monuments than those of Stone, or Brass, his Learned & usefull
works'. Mary Evelyn wrote to Ralph Bohun.

I wish I were as capable of putting in practice so good councell as I aught but it is not possible to be insensible of so great a losses. 58 years experience of the goodnesse kindnesse worth and virtue of such a friend, is not easily effaced ... all is his due, I only comfort myselfe that having lived so long together wee may not be long parted, I cannot wish a happyer state then to be where he is ... I have obligation to him from my first being put into his hands, his way was tender fatherly and friendly and the continuance of his kindnesse held to the last moment, his memory must be precious to me.[121]

In return she received a pious letter of condolence, followed by another hoping that she would not 'act the same part as you did for your beloved daughter; you could not fetch her out of the grave, but you had very near sunk your self into it by your sorrow for her death'. Bohun, ever the sanctimonious cuckoo in his nest, reiterated that Evelyn had been a good man, innocent, devout and charitable.[122]

Mary lived until February 1709, dying in her seventy-fifth year, and her daughter lived until at least 1755, when she was eighty-seven. Susanna's later life was blighted by debt (by sad irony, brought upon them through her husband's duties at Greenwich) as well as disappointments with, and losses of, children.[123] But Sir John Evelyn Bt, as Jack became in 1713, prospered and became the heir his grandfather had always hoped for. Ten years after inheriting Wotton he built a new library. He took good care of the gardens and husbanded the woods, adapting the landscape according to the new taste for naturalism. Before long Alexander Pope requested a chance to visit Wotton, the beauties of which he had heard about from the Harcourts, Elizabeth Draper, Susanna and William's daughter, having married Simon Harcourt of Nuneham Courtenay. In Jack's long life – he died in 1763 – he managed to be both an engaged virtuoso, a Fellow of both the Royal Society and the Society of Antiquaries, and a conscientious member of the upper gentry, holding public office, for more than forty years a customs commissioner, and highly regarded in his county. He never went abroad.[124]

Two generations later, Evelyn's books remained untouched on the Wotton library shelves, his sheaves of papers mouldering and depleted by their use as drawer-liners and dress patterns. Then, in 1813, came William Upcott. With the arrival of Lady Evelyn's attentive if light-fingered visitor, John Evelyn's long journey into historical prominence began – almost as if he had planned it that way.[125]

Abbreviations

BL: British Library.

Boyle Correspondence: *The Correspondence of Robert Boyle* ed. Michael Hunter, et al. (2001).

Bray: *Diary and Correspondence of John Evelyn* ed. William Bray (4 vols, 1852).

CSP Dom: Calendar of State Papers, Domestic.

CSP Treasury: Calendar of State Papers, Treasury.

Diary i–vi: *The Diary of John Evelyn* ed. E. S. de Beer (1955).

Elysium: Elysium Britannicum or The Royal Gardens ed. John E. Ingram (2001).

HP: Hartlib Papers (Sheffield University).

LB: Letterbooks.

Milieu: John Evelyn and his Milieu ed. Frances Harris and Michael Hunter (2003).

NRA: National Register of Archives.

ODNB: *The Oxford Dictionary of National Biography*.

Oldenburg Correspondence: *The Correspondence of Henry Oldenburg* ed. and trans. Rupert A. Hall and Marie Boas Hall (1965–86).

Particular Friends: Particular Friends. The Correspondence of Samuel Pepys and John Evelyn ed. Guy de la Bedoyere (1997).

RS: Royal Society.

SP i–xi: *The Diary of Samuel Pepys* ed. R. Latham and W. Matthews (1971–95).

Transformations: Frances Harris, *Transformations of Love; The Friendship of John Evelyn and Margaret Godolphin* (2002).

Writings: The Writings of John Evelyn ed. Guy de la Bédoyère (1995).

Notes

Introduction

1. Virginia Woolf, 'Rambling around John Evelyn' in *The Common Reader* (1925).
2. *SP* vi, 220; BL Add Ms 78431, JE to ME, 29 Jan. 1665/6.
3. *John Evelyn in the British Library* (1995) 12, quoting David Piper.
4. And mountain it is: Evelyn's own material amounts to 227 volumes and a considerable proportion of the 525-volume total is relevant. See introduction to *Milieu*.
5. Substantially revised editions of *Sylva* and the *Parallel*.
6. Stephen Switzer, *Ichnographia Rustica* ii (1715).
7. John Evelyn, *Numismata* (1697), 323. The ingredients for his recipe for the seventeenth-century English were 'Britains, Romans, Saxons, Danes, Normans, Belgians, &c'.
8. See Steve Shapin, *A Social History of Truth* (1994), 177–8, as even the eminent Sir Thomas Browne or William Harvey did.
9. In the early volumes of the Royal Society's *Philosophical Transactions*.
10. Horace Walpole, *Catalogue of Engravers* (1763).
11. *Particular Friends* [C12] JE to SP, 28 April 1682.

Chapter 1: Early Years

1. *Particular Friends* [E5] JE to SP, Wotton, 22 July 1700.
2. Isabel Sullivan, 'Their "own Sweet Country": The Evelyns in Surrey' in *Milieu*. Her account of the complicated strands of the Evelyn family is the clearest yet.
3. BL Add Ms 78301, f. 53, JE jr to JE, 26 March 1694.
4. BL Add Ms 78333, ff. 6–7.
5. BL Add Ms 78386 (advice to Mrs Blagge).
6. John Evelyn, *Sylva* (1664), 110.
7. Charles I issued a proclamation limiting digging to two hours a day, to minimise disruption, since pigeons were a valuable source of fresh protein for the winter months.
8. John Aubrey, *Natural History and Antiquities of Surrey* (1718–19), v, Evelyn's letter as unfoliated preface in which he told Aubrey that the streams and ponds around Wotton had been long 'since fill'd up and drain'd'.
9. Confusingly another Sir John Evelyn, their cousin from West Dean, Wiltshire, was a political radical. His Surrey namesake, knighted in 1641, was a moderate Parliamentarian who sat for Bletchingley from 1628.

10. *Diary* ii 2.
11. Jenny West, *Gunpowder, Government and War in the Mid-18ᵗʰ Century* (1991); Glenys Crocker, *Gunpowder Mills Gazetteer,* Occasional publication 2, Wind and Watermill Section, Society for the Protection of Ancient Buildings (1988). Only the East India Company, operating mills at Chilworth, also on the Tillingbourne, was licensed to produce powder for its own use.
12. Mary Hervey, *The Life, Correspondence and Collection of Thomas Howard, Earl of Arundel* (1921), 378.
13. John Morrill, *Stuart Britain: A Very Short Introduction* (2000).
14. *Diary* i 1–2, ii 1–2 n. 2.
15. *Ibid.* ii 563, iii 276, 428 n. 6. He refers to getting 'most dextrously off' the proffered knighthood.
16. I am following Dr Johnson's *Dictionary* in which 'well timber'd' (the term Evelyn uses) is defined as 'well built'.
17. *Diary* ii 6.
18. Colin Brent, *Pre-Georgian Lewes: c 890–1714* (2004), 270–1.
19. BL Add Ms 78290, 'Nestor's Panygyric: The Praise of Old Age' (1624). Sampson graduated BA in 1625, MA in 1628, and was appointed the vicar of Blewbury, Berkshire in 1629.
20. BL Add Ms 78315, f. 2, Jane Newton to JE, 31 May 1637.
21. The brothers retained it until April 1648, when they sold the living for £1,836 and the tithes. East Sussex Record Office Lewes; AMS 5763/97, 20 April 1648.
22. Stansfield left Richard and Eleanor Evelyn the manor of Denton and, after his widow's death, the reversion of land and properties in Cliffe, Eckington and Ripe.
23. BL Add Ms 78305, f. 4, Jane Evelyn to JE, from Lewes, 27 June 1642.
24. Victoria County History, *Surrey* (1911), ii 413–14. Not vested in the local priory but in independent feoffees, it survived the Dissolution of the Monasteries. In the early 1700s the school moved to a site on the main street, where it remained the town grammar school until the 1950s.
25. *ODNB.* Morley was elected to Parliament for Lewes in 1640 and saw service in the first civil war, earning himself enmity from the royalists of Sussex.
26. It was also very typical of its sort; John Bramston, the future lord chief justice, and the brothers North, including Francis, who became Lord Keeper Guilford, and Dudley, a successful merchant, received similar educations at their local schools.
27. George Evelyn secured him a living at Denton in 1672 and in 1674 that of Cliffe and 'those lesser things', All Saints' and St Michael's in Lewes. William Snatt enthusiastically pursued the oppression of Quakers and became canon of Chichester. See Brent, *Pre-Georgian Lewes,* 380.
28. John Evelyn, *Memoires for my Grand-son* ed. Geoffrey Keynes (1926). See also *Bray* iii 347, JE to William Wotton, 30 March 1696.
29. The early years of his 'diary' were substantially revised and then rewritten (see below, p. 000). See *Diary* i 75–7 for pages from a 1636 almanac with the entries typographically distinguished.
30. *Diary* ii 10–12.
31. *Ibid.* ii 13.
32. Anthony Fletcher, *A County Community in Peace and War: Sussex 1600–1660* (1975) 142–3.
33. Quoted in Michael Hunter, *Science and the Shape of Orthodoxy* (1995), 69.
34. BL Add Ms 15948, f. 2, GE to RE sr, 30 June 1634; ff. 2v–3, RE sr to GE, 10 July 1634; BL Add Ms 78274, f. 32, GE to RE sr, 29 Feb. 1635/6.
35. *Ibid.* f. 30, GE to RE sr, 2 [or 1?] Feb. 1635/6.
36. BL Add Ms 78302, f. 4, RE sr to JE, 3 May 1636.
37. BL Add Ms 78291, f. 81.

38. *Diary* v 358.
39. BL Add Ms 78442, JE to JE jr, 17 March 1680/1.
40. *John Evelyn in the British Library*, 32.
41. *Transformations*, 152–3.
42. BL Add Ms 78282, f. 53, 15 Nov. 1636, sending Newton £5 for their board and a sum for their schoolmaster 'to take what paynes he cann with them to make them schollars'; *ibid.*, f. 57, 14 Nov. 1637.
43. H. Evelyn, *The Evelyn Family* (1915), 40–4; the plays alone cost £843, excluding that at St John's, for which Laud paid: see Nicholas Tyacke, *The History of the University of Oxford* (1997), iv 645 n. 17.
44. George Bathurst was killed in royalist service in 1645. BL Add Ms 78274, f. 44, GE to RE sr, 22 Feb. 1636/7.
45. Walter Pope, *The Life of . . . Seth, Lord Bishop of Salisbury* (1697), 92.
46. Roger North, *Notes of Me: The Autobiography of Roger North* ed. Peter Millard (2000), 92.
47. *Lorenzo Magalotti at the Court of Charles II*, ed. and trans. W.E. Knowles Middleton (1980), to Cardinal Leopold from Paris, 29 June 1668, 62 n. 86.
48. [LB] BL Add Ms 78298, f. 136v, JE to C. Wren, 4 April 1665 (asking for a tutor for John).
49. *Diary* ii 17. Bradshaw, who was to become master of Balliol himself, was distracted by his disputes with Laud's nominee, Thomas Laurence. Evelyn suspected, rightly, that Bradshaw was suggested by a family friend who knew his father. [LB] BL Add Ms 78299, f. 9, JE to Robert Plot, 16 March 1682/3.
50. *Diary* ii 16 n. 2; he was soon replaced by Laurence, then in 1648 by Bradshaw himself.
51. See Lindsay Sharp, 'Walter Charleton's Early Life, 1620–1659 and Relationship to Natural Philosophy in Mid-Seventeenth Century England', *Annals of Science* 30, 311–40, re Charleton's *Immortality* (1657) in which 'there is nothing of Fiction, beside that of Names'. In a modern Platonic dialogue JE appears in the character of Lucretius and refers to 'Fellow-Collegiates'. His Oxford contemporaries included Jonathan Goddard (Magdalen Hall), George Joyliffe (Wadham), Thomas Willis (Christ Church), Christopher Merrett (Gloucester Hall) and William Brouncker (college unknown). See Robert G. Frank, *Harvey and the Oxford Physiologists* (1980).
52. *Diary* ii 17–18. BL Add Ms 78311, f. 3, JT to JE, Oxford, 1640 (in Latin, to 'Charissime'). A note on the reverse, apparently in the same hand, refers to Bradshaw. 'Alas who would thincke this snake Envy should lurke in flowers, who would expect in good words so much falsity.' He apologises for his vehemence but would explain the circumstances. Thicknesse became a Fellow of Balliol in 1641.
53. Alan Bray, *The Friend* (2003), ch. 4.
54. John Earle, *Microcosmographie* (1628).
55. Tyacke, *The History of the University of Oxford*, 301.
56. *Diary* ii 20.
57. BL Add Ms 78329, inscribed at the opening of Evelyn's second volume of commonplaces.
58. BL Add Ms 78315, f. 3, William Newton to JE, 5 Feb. 1637/8; f. 2, Jane Newton to JE, 31 May 1637.
59. *Diary* i 15.
60. See John Spurr, '"A Sublime and Noble Service": Evelyn and the Church of England' in *Milieu*, 145; [LB] BL Add Ms 78298, f. 44, JE to TK, 25 March 1651.
61. BL Add Ms 78274, f. 100, GB to RE sr, 25 Oct. 1637.
62. *Ibid.*, f. 108, GB to RE, n.d.
63. *Diary* i 16; in summer 1639, with John Crayford, a family friend, he went west to the 'Summerset-shire Bathes, Bristoll, Cirencester, Malmesbury, Abington and divers other townes of lesser note; cursorily view'd'. See *Diary* ii 23.

64. Bradshaw told him that his son had spent, and accounted for, £20 by March and needed more. Richard Evelyn agreed to add a further £15 for John's use and £30 for the tutor, an indication of how heavily he had subsidised him. BL Add Ms 78302, f. 7, RE sr to JE, 22 May 1639.

65. *Ibid.*, f. 10, 29 June [?1639, JE has scored out '1640']; BL Add Ms 78303, f. 6, GE to JE, 20 Jan. 1639/40.

66. A. Jessopp, et al. eds, *The Lives of the Norths* (1890), iii 14. Roger North's scholarly brother John was virtually his tutor at Cambridge.

67. BL Add Ms 78302, f. 9, RE sr to JE, 4 Feb. 1639/40. He mentions the Sussex estates and cousin Hatton, who became Evelyn's legal guardian.

68. BL Add Ms 78303, f. 7, GE to JE, 17 Feb. 1639/40.

69. It cost £4,468. See J. B. Williamson, *History of the Temple* (1924), 376–7.

70. BL Add Ms 78303, f. 10, GE to JE, 26 Oct. 1640.

71. BL Add Ms 78302, f. 12, RE sr to JE at Middle Temple, 1 Dec. 1640.

72. Vanessa Harding, *The Dead and the Living in Paris and London 1500-1670* (2002), 196, 227–8.

73. *Diary* ii 26.

74. BL Add Ms 78311, f. 1. JT to JE, Oct. 1640. *SP* vi 289. He may have seen *Thersander* (1663), a play set in Byzantium. See BL Add Ms 78358. At much the same age, Pepys tried fiction, though his *Love a Cheate* has not survived. See Claire Tomalin, *Samuel Pepys: The Unequalled Self* (2002), 40. *The Originals* is BL Add Ms 78359.

75. BL Add Ms 78303, f. 14, GE to JE, 5 March 1640/1.

76. *Diary* ii 78 n. 1.

77. BL Add Ms 78305, f. 2, Jane to JE, 17 Feb. 1641/2.

78. BL Add Ms 78442, JE to JE jr, 17 March 1680/1.

Chapter 2: The Fruits of Travel

1. *Diary* ii 28.

2. *Bray* iii 106–7, JE to Thurland, 8 Nov. 1658, referring to Lord Percy, son of the duke of Northumberland; [LB] BL Add Ms 78298, f. 121, JE to GE jr, 5 Aug. 1663.

3. *Diary* i 22.

4. John Evelyn, *The State of France* (1652).

5. Francis Bacon, *The Essays* ed. John Pitcher (1985), 18, 113–14.

6. See A.N. Wilson, *The Life of John Milton* (1983). He was struck by the enlightened republicanism of the Italian city-states set against their lack of essential freedoms, epitomised by the hold of the Jesuits over the Catholic Church.

7. [LB] BL Add Ms 78299, f. 51v, JE to Flower Hyde, Lady Clarendon, 12 Oct. 1688.

8. [LB] BL Add Ms 78298, f. 186, JE to Thomas Clifford, 14 July 1671.

9. John Stoye, *English Travellers Abroad 1604–1667* (1989), chs 7 and 8; Bacon, *The Essays* 'Of Travel', 113–14, in which he advocates both the keeping of a diary and maintaining correspondence afterwards.

10. Preface to Evelyn, *The State of France*.

11. Arundel's bill for hospitality to the court of the House of Orange included £14 for washing 240 pairs of sheets at twelve pence a pair. See Hervey, *The Life, Correspondence and Collection of Thomas Howard, Earl of Arundel*, 432.

12. Ryl. English Ms 883, f. 36. I am grateful to Anne Young at the John Rylands Library, Manchester for her help. The sketchbook may have been put together at a later date; the Amsterdam and Leiden drawings are dated 1634.

13. CSP Dom 1667, Aug. [?] 1667, Hollar to Evelyn, 431–2.

14. In his *Numismata,* 50, Evelyn remembered how the earl of Arundel 'incited others to build with stone and brick after the present Gusto and which Inego Jones since pursued' while 'neglecting his own Palace'.

15. *Diary* ii 28 n. 5. Apparently Evelyn had spent the night after Strafford's execution at Caryll's home, Great Tangley Manor near Guildford, and left his name etched on a pane of glass there. Perhaps it was then that they resolved to travel. He is not to be confused with the Roman Catholic poet and politician of the same name.

16. *Diary* i 23.

17. *Ibid.* ii 568–71 (bibliographical notes).

18. Evelyn owned a letter in her hand reporting on the situation at The Hague to George Goring, entirely conveyed in a pictorial code of rebuses and hieroglyphics.

19. Andrew Saunders, *Fortress Builder: Bernard de Gomme, Charles II's Military Engineer* (2004), 14, 49 and 53, showing the siege map of Ginnep dated 1641 (BL King's Top Coll cii 21, f. 37).

20. BL Add Ms 78386, JE's advice to Margaret Blagge.

21. *Diary* ii 39. This account has been questioned.

22. Without Henrietta Maria, who had planned to accompany her mother and sell her jewellery to fund the royal cause, which she did some months later.

23. Contrary to all biographical accounts, including the *ODNB,* the Arundels did not part at this date. Letters from the earl to Sir Richard Browne, Evelyn's future father-in-law, dated 1643 and 1644 request passes into France from Antwerp for the entire family: see Add Ms 78193 and p. 000 below. He travelled on to Brussels and Rheims later in 1644, with at least two of his children, bound for Italy. The family remained in regular contact.

24. BL Add Ms 78303, GE to JE, f. 17, 7 Aug. 1641; f. 19, 29 Aug. 1641.

25. *Diary* ii 42–3. Jacob Ruisdael drew the Jewish cemetery in 1655 and painted an imaginary romantic landscape around it. In December 1655 Cromwell's Whitehall Conference prompted Evelyn to note 'now were the Jewes admitted'; *Diary* iii 163. See *Jewish Quarterly,* summer/winter 2006, nos 202 and 203.

26. *Ibid.* ii 33.

27. *Ibid.* ii 52.

28. Tim Huisman, *A Theatre for Anatomy,* Boerhaave Museum, Leiden (2002). Petrus Pauw, the first professor of anatomy, set up the collection which was expanded into an ambitious visual encyclopaedia by his successor Otto Heurnius.

29. See John Evelyn, *Navigation and Commerce* (1674).

30. *Diary* ii 68.

31. *Ibid.* i 74.

32. See Williamson, *History of the Temple.*

33. Junius, a Dutchman, was Arundel's librarian and author of *De Pictura Veterum* (1637), translated into English the following year and dedicated to the countess of Arundel.

34. BL Add Ms 78442, JE to JE jr, 1680.

35. BL Add Ms 78315, f. 11, R. Poole to JE, 28 April 1642.

36. *Diary* ii 78.

37. His next contribution to the royalist cause, the following summer, was to send his fine black horse 'and furniture' to the king in Oxford.

38. For example, Thomas Henshaw fought with the king's forces at York before going overseas to join the prince of Orange's troops and then embarking on several years of travel: see *ODNB* entry below, and p. 00.

39. *Diary* ii 80 n. 3.

40. BL Add Ms 78315, f. 13, Van der Borcht to JE, 15 Dec. 1642. See R. Harding, 'John Evelyn, Hendrick van der Borcht the Younger and Wenceslaus Hollar', *Apollo* 144 (Aug. 1996), 39–44.

41. Alison Plowden, *Henrietta Maria* (2001), 178–9; having marshalled men and ammunition and agreed strategy, she eventually marched south from York with William

Cavendish, the earl of Newcastle, and an impressive royalist phalanx, and met her husband at Kineton, close to Edgehill, on 13 July.

42. *Diary* i 55.
43. This and other drawings are in BL Add Ms 78610.
44. Bodleian MS Aubrey 10, 'Notes on Education of Young Gentlemen', f. 145.
45. See *Calendar for Committee for Advance of Money* (1642–56) ed. M.A.E. Green (1888), i, preface.
46. There were two Covenants put forward in 1643, one in June and another on 11 September.
47. Harding, 'John Evelyn, Hendrick van der Borcht the Younger and Wenceslaus Hollar', includes a letter dated 1 April 1648 from Van der Borcht in Alkmaar to Evelyn, telling him that the Hollar prints he had sent, including the Van Dyck, had gone astray.

Chapter 3: 'Out of the garden into Paradice'

1. BL Add Ms 78311, f. 6, JT to JE, from Balliol, 6 April 1642.
2. Evelyn, *The State of France*.
3. *Diary* ii 94, see also general bibliographical notes, 571–7. Most of Evelyn's itinerary was provided by the 1643 edition of Claude de Varennes's *Le Voyage de France*.
4. G. E. Aylmer, *The King's Servants* (1974), 25–6 discusses the inexact role of overseas representatives or agents before the existence of a diplomatic service. Resident ambassadors were sent to Spain, France, the emperor and German Diet, the States-General and Stadtholder of the United Provinces as well as to the sultan of Turkey.
5. His grandfather refers to '"little Dick", so refined, *à la mode* and a stout horseman'. BL Add Ms 15857, f. 44, Christopher Browne to RB, London, 17 Feb. 1641; BL Add Ms 78220, CB to RB, 6 Nov. 1644, refers to him travelling south.
6. Browne also served his successor, Lord Scudamore. For the masque 'Cupids Banishment' held at the Ladies Hall, Deptford, see Pierpont Morgan Library, MA 1296.
7. Stoye, *English Travellers Abroad*, 9–10.
8. *Diary* ii 90–1. George Goring, created first earl of Norwich in 1644, held the appointment briefly before being replaced by Henry Jermyn, the earl of St Albans and favourite of Queen Henrietta Maria. Goring's daughter Lady Catherine Scott became a family friend. This was the second consecutive regency; Marie de Médicis acted for her son Louis XIII. He later banished her to the Spanish Netherlands, where she died in 1642.
9. Peter Burke, *The Fabrication of Louis XIV* (1992), 39–40.
10. *Diary* ii 637–9, Appendix B from Evelyn's *The State of France*.
11. Henri IV's Place de France, the last open ground within the walls on the Right Bank, never materialised, and his scheme for the Collège de France died with him. See Hilary Ballon, *The Paris of Henri IV: Architecture and Urbanism* (1991), 211.
12. *Ibid.*, 6–13. Writing of domestic architecture Thomas Hanmer distinguished between buildings of 'whyte free-stone, or whyte rough stone, covered with plaister of Paris'.
13. See Antony Griffiths, 'John Evelyn and the Print' in *Milieu*. He bought a set of engraved cartouches after Stefano della Bella. The date of the purchase makes him one of the earliest recorded British print collectors, though the break-up and sale of his collection in the 1970s dispersed the clues to his youthful interest. For Nandé see below, p. 000.
14. *Diary* ii 133.
15. BL Add Ms 78305, f. 5, 28 Jan. Jane Evelyn to JE, 1643/4.
16. BL Add Ms 78315, William Ducie 'from your chamber at the Mid Temp' to JE, 22 Feb. 1643/4.

17. *Diary* ii 107 n. 3, 108 n. 4 *et passim*.
18. The terraces that exist there today were added in the mid-1660s by André le Nôtre. In *Elysium Britannicum* Evelyn described St Germain as 'rather a *Series of Cascads* then to be at all esteem'd a Garden' (see *Elysium*, 132). The old château survives, the new one has gone.
19. John Dixon Hunt, *The Garden and the Grove: the Italian Renaissance Garden and the English Imagination 1600–1750* (1986), 145 *et passim* emphasises, e.g., the similarities of St Germain-en-Laye to the Villa Lante, near Viterbo.
20. His son Henry (b. 1628) may have been of the party too.
21. BL Add Ms 78193, TH to RB, 19 and 26 Feb. 1643/4 (referring to Browne as 'my very good friend'). Health and money problems (no rents were being remitted from his estates in England) kept the family in the Spanish Netherlands. Browne obtained the passes for him but Arundel continued to hesitate between France and Germany. By autumn 1644 he had reached Rheims, though his wife remained in Antwerp.
22. *Ibid.*, Padua, 10 July 1646.
23. The Hôtel de Liancourt was built by Soloman de Brosse in 1613 and, after the duke bought it in 1623, was greatly extended by Lemercier.
24. *Diary* ii 112–15.
25. Harding, 'John Evelyn, Hendrick van der Borcht the Younger and Wenceslaus Hollar', 39–44 (letter from Antwerp, 17 Dec. 1645).
26. Prudence Leith-Ross, 'A Seventeenth-Century Paris Garden', *Garden History* 21:2 (Winter 1995), 50–7. In his copy of Parkinson's *Paradisus* (1629) Tradescant noted recent additions to the Parisian nursery stock, including two kinds of single white ranunculus and one named '*Drape de Argent*', and various white anemones including one described as 'Duble Greene with a littill leafe'. In 1631, Morin's older brother René, also a nurseryman, supplied bulbs, including narcissi and scented geranium; see R. T. Gunther, *Early British Botanists and their Gardens* (1922). Sir Thomas Hanmer and the duc d'Orléans agreed that Morin overpriced his plants.
27. Leith-Ross, 'A Seventeenth-Century Paris Garden', fig. 1, shows Morin's garden in 1649; in the original the miniature hedges are painted in green.
28. BL Add Ms 78352, A & B.
29. *Diary* ii 167–71. See Zytaruk, 'Occasional Specimens, 189–91.
30. Richard Lassels, *Voyage of Italy* (1670). Griffiths, 'John Evelyn and the Print', 109, publishes a transcript of Evelyn's 1687 library catalogue (BL Add Ms 78632) including Rubens's volume.
31. [HP] *Ephemerides* (1650): 'His Father is dead a great chymist, and so is his Mother who is yet alive.'
32. Possibly introduced by the alchemist and antiquarian William Backhouse, whose wife Flower was related to the Henshaws and who was a 'renowned chymist and Rosicrucian and great encourager of those that studied chymistry and astrology'. Elias Ashmole was his neighbour in Berkshire. Hartlib (*Ephemerides* iv) mentions that 'Hinshaw and his friends have at last prevailed with Oughtred to publish all his Mathematical Tracts of which hee hath very many made ready and some are yet to bee perfected'.
33. Bacon, *The Essays*, 'Advising the Study of Philosophy', 263.
34. See Anthony Radcliffe and Peter Thornton, 'Evelyn's Cabinet', *Connoisseur* 197 (April 1978), 256–61. The plaques of animals and Orpheus by Fanelli (a protégé of the earl of Arundel) were probably made later in Paris. His second ebony cabinet, now in the Geffrye Museum in London, was made up in Paris, under the supervision of Mary Evelyn.
35. BL Add Ms 78302, f. 14, RE to JE, [9?] Dec. 1644.
36. BL Add Ms 78305, f. 13, Jane to JE, 9 Dec. 1644.
37. BL Add Ms 78302, f. 18, RE to JE, n.d. [late 1644].
38. BL Add Ms 78305, f. 8, Jane to JE, 14 Dec. [actually Nov.] 1644.

39. His financial support came from his iron-willed sister-in-law Olimpia Maidalchini Pamphili. See Anthony Majanlahti, *The Families Who Made Rome* (2005), 276–88.

40. [LB] BL Add Ms 78298, f. 124v, JE to Walter Pope, 30 March 1664.

41. BL Add Ms 78311, JT to JE, 16 Nov. 1644. 'My better part, For so is my Freind.'

42. [LB] BL Add Ms 78298, f. 23, 26 Nov. 1644, JE to a Signor Borgi, who was packing up some statues and other curiosities for him.

43. *Ibid.*, f. 196, JE to JE jr, 31 Jan. 1675/6.

44. Now in the Naples Archaeological Museum. See de Beer's careful notes on these pages, *Diary* ii 216 *et seq.*

45. Pratt is recorded as having matriculated at the school of law in Padua on 13 January 1645, so their cohabitation may have been irregular. His notebooks were published in the 1920s. See R. J. Gunther, ed., *The Architecture of Sir Roger Pratt* (1928).

46. Jake Morrissey, *The Genius in the Design* (2005), 105, 144–55.

47. *Diary* ii 230.

48. Paula Findlen, *Athanasius Kircher: The Last Man Who Knew Everything* (2004), 13–19. Kircher arrived in southern France in 1632 claiming he had a heliotropic clock; it proved to be worked by a magnet.

49. Lassels, *Voyage of Italy*.

50. See the exhibition catalogues *The Ecstatic Journey* (University of Chicago Library, 2000) and *Il Museo del Mondo* (Palazzo Venezia, Rome, 2001).

51. Cassiano dal Pozzo (1588–1657); see *Diary* ii 277–8; Ian Jenkins, 'Ideas of Antiquity' in *Enlightenment: Discovering the World in the Eighteenth Century* ed. Kim Sloan with Andrew Barnett (British Museum 2003).

52. BL Add Ms 78403, inventory of Wotton 1702. A painting of St Catherine and St Sebastian is described as being by 'the pope's chief painter copyed for me by him at Rome, from the original by Corregio, which I borrow'd of Cardinal Fr. Barberini 1646'.

53. *Diary* ii 253–4, 404.

54. *Ibid.* 270.

55. *Ibid.* 228 n. 6, 281–2.

56. *Ibid.* 290.

57. *Robert Boyle by Himself and his Friends* ed. Michael Hunter (1994), p. 19 *et passim*, Document 1, *An Account of Philarctus* written by Boyle, 1648–9.

58. *Bray* iii, JE to Thomas Tenison, 29 May 1694.

59. *Diary* ii 292–3. Circumcision is usually carried out on eight-day-old infants.

60. *Diary* ii 332.

61. *Diary* ii 298. De Beer notes that few travellers remarked on the ceiling.

62. Returning home from Malta in 1637–8, he witnessed the eruption of Etna, saw Stromboli and Vesuvius active and experienced an earthquake in Calabria. The book was *Mundus Subterraneus* (1665).

63. Griffiths, 'John Evelyn and the Print', 102–3, figs 6 and 7.

64. *Diary* ii 386.

65. [LB] BL Add Ms 78298, f.44, JE to TK, 25 [23] March 1651.

66. Henshaw reported to the Royal Society on 9 April 1690; see RS, JBO 8 299.

67. *Diary* ii 393–7.

68. *Ibid.* 421–2.

Chapter 4: 'Sweete Mrs Eveling'

1. It was the last time the current doge, Francesco Erizzo, would perform the ceremony. He died early in 1646.

2. *Diary* ii 431.

3. In his edition of the *Discourses* Bernard Crick highlights Machiavelli's belief that republics preserve states to better effect than principalities, the difficulty being to spread power equitably.

4. BL Add Ms 78311, f. 35, TH to JE, 29 July 1645; [LB] BL Add Ms 78298, f. 38v, JE to John Crafford (Crayford), from Venice, 31 [*sic*] June 1645.

5. See Stoye, *English Travellers Abroad*. Aylesbury was already indebted to Richard Browne to the tune of almost a thousand French livres, spent during Buckingham's stay in Paris.

6. Those who matriculated were the Villiers brothers, Lord Stafford (Henry Howard's uncle), Thomas Radcliffe and the Digbys, John and Kenelm. The latter was listed again in April 1648.

7. In volume two of Kircher's *Oedipus Aegyptiacus* (1655) Henshaw (as Henschau) alone was given credit, both for the drawing and its discovery (pp. 456–7). See *Diary* ii 469 n. 4, iii 171.

8. BL Add Ms 78311, f. 32, TH to JE, 10 June 1645.

9. *Ibid.*, from Padua, 29 Jan. 1645/6.

10. [LB] BL Add Ms 78298, f. 38, JE to John Crafford, from Venice, 2 June 1645.

11. See Harding, 'John Evelyn, Hendrick van der Borcht the Younger and Wenceslaus Hollar'.

12. *Diary* ii 463.

13. J.M. Robinson, *The Dukes of Norfolk* (1995). Arundel's son Henry Frederick, Lord Mowbray, died in 1652. His sons Thomas and Henry became the 5th and 6th dukes.

14. *Diary* ii 466–7.

15. *Ibid.* iii 31–2.

16. [LB] BL Add Ms 78298, f. 24, JE to Bartholino, from Padua, 23 Sept. 1645.

17. Bray, *The Friend*, 166.

18. [LB] BL Add Ms 78298, f. 25, JE to Bartholino, 4 Oct. 1645.

19. Morley was chaplain first to Lady Ormonde in Caen and then to Sir Edward Hyde's household. He seems to have been a secret agent.

20. In conversation (and MS draft) Waller's biographer, John Safford, makes a convincing case for Waller's innocence, arguing that he was set up by Pym in order to remove an able royalist from the vicinity.

21. *ODNB* entry.

22. Thomas Hobbes, *The Correspondence* ed. Noel Malcolm (1994), i, letter 39, Hobbes in Rouen to Waller in Calais, 29 July/8 Aug. 1645.

23. Christine Phipps, ed., *Buckingham: Public and Private Man* (1985), Commonplace book, 15.

24. John Aubrey, *Brief Lives* ed. John Buchanan-Brown (2000), 323.

25. *Diary* ii 473–5.

26. Evelyn described Rogers as 'Consul then at Padoa for the students of our Nation'. He may have met Joyliffe at Oxford.

27. Therese O'Malley, introduction to *John Evelyn's 'Elysium Britannicum' and European Gardening* (1998) 31.

28. BL Add Ms 78315, f. 135, GJ to JE, May 1649. In 1650 Joyliffe went to Cambridge to complete his medical studies.

29. *SP* vi 289: 'leaves laid up in a book of several plants, kept dry, which preserve Colour however, and look very finely, better than any herball.'

30. Wellcome Institute, autograph letter collection, JE to William Cowper, Dover Street, 21 Jan. 1702. He had offered 150 scudi and requested a fourth panel, showing the 'Liver, Gastric nerves & other vesseles'. See Richard K. Aspin, 'John Evelyn's Tables of Veins and Arteries: A Rediscovered Letter', *Medical History* 39 (1995), 493–9.

31. *Exercitationes de Generatione Animalium* (1651), Dr George Ent's dedicatory epistle quoting Harvey. See G. Keynes, *Harvey* (1966), 330–1.
32. The surgeon William Cowper (see above, note 30) read a paper to the Royal Society where they had been displayed since 1674, which was published, illustrated by Van der Gucht's engravings, in *Philosophical Transactions* 23 (1702–3), 1177–201.
33. *Diary* ii 479; David Howarth, *Lord Arundel and his Circle* (1985), 216.
34. BL Add Ms 78315, f. 81, JA to JE, 24 Aug. 1646. That summer Abdy was elected the *syndicus artistarum* of the English students at Padua, an honorary post (with attendant expenses) that Evelyn claimed to have turned down the year before.
35. Hunter, *Science and the Shape of Orthodoxy*, 74.
36. Scamozzi was far less well known than Palladio at this date – several of the buildings Arundel identified as being by Palladio were his. See Edward Chaney, 'Evelyn, Inigo Jones, and the Collector Earl of Arundel', in *Milieu*, 52–3. For Arundel's instructions see *Remembrances of Things Worth Seeing in Italy*, ed. J.M. Robinson (1987).
37. BL Add Ms 78311, f. 17, JT to JE, from London, 27 May 1646.
38. See facsimile of letter from Arundel to JE, 9 Aug. 1646, plate 8 in *Catalogue of the Collection of Autograph Letters and Historical Documents, formed between 1865 and 1882 by A. Morrison*, ed. A.W. Thibaudeau, vol. 1 (1883).
39. Robinson, *The Dukes of Norfolk*, 118–19.
40. Howarth, *Lord Arundel and his Circle*, 210. The will was drawn up in 1641 as he left Dover.
41. BL Add Ms 78311, f. 21, JT to JE, 6 Oct. [1646].
42. *Diary* ii 534. His studies were confined to 'learning of the high-dutch & Spanish tongues, & now & then refreshing my Dauncing'.
43. Hobbes, *The Correspondence*, 155–9, Hobbes to Sorbière, 12/22 March 1647. It was published in Latin; the translation was *Philosophicall Rudiments concerning Government and Society* (1651).
44. BL Add Ms 78311, f. 17, JT to JE, from London, 27 May 1646.
45. BL Add Ms 78315, f. 105, EW to JE, from Rouen, 5 Sept. 1647.
46. *Ibid.,* f. 86, EW to JE, from Rouen, 6 Oct. 1646.
47. *Ibid.,* f. 91, EW to JE, from Dieppe, 18 Oct. 1646.
48. Bodleian MS Montague d 1, f. 47, from Rouen, 1646. The short poem begins 'Que la belle chantante encore/ Rend incurable nostre amour'.
49. BL Add Ms 78315, f. 71, EW to JE from Rouen, 3 Aug. 1646; f. 77, 22 Aug. 1646 (with JE's reply drafted on the reverse, 23 Aug.); f. 91, from Dieppe, 18 Oct. 1646. Waller was busy on his behalf. He offered him financial advice, believing that Evelyn could make 8 or 9 per cent if he wanted to bring his money overseas but suggesting he waits for his brother's answer.
50. Aubrey, *Brief Lives*, 322.
51. Hobbes, *The Correspondence* i 124–5 and note 7, Hobbes to Waller, 29 July/8 Aug. 1645.
52. He taught Philippe d'Orléans, having been rejected (by the queen) as tutor to Louis XIV. Lynn Sumida Joy, *Gassendi the Atomist* (1987), 43–5, 62–5.
53. Evelyn, *The State of France*, 99.
54. BL Add Ms 78335, f. 6.
55. *ODNB* (*c.* 1610–69). Le Fèvre came to England at the Restoration, becoming chemist to the king and apothecary-in-ordinary to the royal household in December 1660, in charge of the laboratory at St James's Palace.
56. Glauber (1603/4–1668/70), born in Karlstadt, lived in Vienna and Cologne and eventually settled in Amsterdam in 1648. Evelyn claimed familiarity with his work as 'an ocular witness of all his operations'. His work was first published in English in 1651. Barlet's course was published as *Vray et Méthodique Course de la Physique* (1653 and 1657).

57. BL Add Ms 78311, f. 38, TH to JE, from Venice, 1 Sept. 1646.

58. *Ibid.* f. 40, TH to JE, 20 April, 1647.

59. Denham joined Henrietta Maria's court only to be sent back to attend Charles I in captivity on her behalf the following spring.

60. CSP Dom 6/16 Aug. 1644.

61. Scudamore was sidelined by the appointment of the earl of Leicester as extraordinary ambassador – much as Goring was by Jermyn. Quoted *ODNB*.

62. Gilbert Burnet, *History of My Own Time* (1724), vol. 1, 225.

63. BL Add Ms. 78392, f. 36, 'The Legend of Philaretes & the Pearl'. For Mary's age, see drafts of her will, BL Add Ms 78412, 9 Feb. 1708, in which she refers to having been left a widow 'in the 71 year of my Age', four years earlier.

64. BL Add Ms 78315, f. 98, TK to JE, from Paris, 5 Feb. 1646/7; BL Add Ms 78198, EP to RB, from Brussels, 14 Dec. 1647.

65. BL Add Ms 78303, f. 30, GE to JE, 14 July 1647.

66. BL Add Ms 78392, f. 36, 'The Legend of Philaretes & the Pearl'.

67. BL Add Ms 32497, ff. 145v–6.

68. See *ODNB*. Ralph Hopton (1596–1652), created Baron Hopton in 1643, was nephew of Sir Arthur Hopton (1588–1650), the king's ambassador to Spain see above, p. 67.

69. BL Add Ms 15858, f. 114, Endymion Porter to RB, from Brussels, 29 Nov. 1647; BL Add Ms 78198, EP to RB, 7 Dec. 1647.

70. BL Add Ms 78303, f. 37, GE to JE, 25 Aug. 1649.

71. BL Add Ms 78311, f. 23, JT to JE, from London, Aug. 1647; f. 22, 11 Sept. 1647.

72. BL Add Ms 78223, WP to RB, from Deptford, 21 July 1647.

73. HP 50H 28/2 f. 7r. 'Greattrick [Greatorex] the Mathematical-Instrum[ent] Maker of a most piercing and profound witt' was intimately acquainted with Mr Wyld [Wild] a rich Parliament man of £3,000 per annum who buys 'all man[n]er of Invent[ions] but . . . makes no Use of them'.

74. William Frizell was Charles I's postmaster for foreign affairs as well as an art agent. He re-entered royal service again for Charles II in the late 1650s. See Brian Reade, 'William Frizell and the Royal Collection', *Burlington Magazine* 89 (1947), 70–5. [LB] BL Add Ms 78299, f. 75, 10 Nov. 1691, JE to Alderman Charles Chamberlain, in which he refers to exchanging paintings with Frizell long ago.

75. BL Add Ms 78405 (B), list of debts owing to Evelyn carefully written out by his amanuensis Richard Hoare. Against the two entries for Frizell is marked 'doubt'. There is no indication that Evelyn was ever repaid.

76. HP, Letter 13/180A, 18 Jan. 1647.

77. BL Add Ms 78315, f. 104, WF to JE, from Rotterdam, 22 Aug. 1647.

Chapter 5: 'A very great Alarme'

1. *Aplanos* was Greek for 'steadfastly'; Peters was the steward at Sayes Court, Kibble was probably a fictitious name, although Browne later prepared a catalogue of evergreens with 'Mr Keibel' in Paris. See Kenny et al., *John Evelyn at the British Library*, 17.

2. BL Add Ms 15857, f. 62, RB to JE, 13 Nov. 1647.

3. BL Add Ms 78221, f. 3, JE to RB 25 Oct. 1647. Anne Fanshawe, *Memoirs of Anne Lady Fanshawe* ed. Herbert C. Fanshawe (1907), 46–7, records the Fanshawes' visit to Hampton Court that month when Sir Richard was given his credentials for Spain. There must have been a semblance of normality.

4. *Bray* iii 5–7, 6 Dec. 1647.

5. D. Brunton and D. H. Pennington, *Members of the Long Parliament* (1954).

6. *Calendar for Committee for Advance of Money* i 349–50.

7. Basil Duke Henning ed. *The History of Parliament: The House of Commons 1660–1690*, vol. 2, members C–L (1983), 278–80.

8. Debts of £200 were 'still hanging upon our hands' Christopher Browne to Richard Browne, BL Add Ms 15857, f. 46, 16 March 1642. Browne was born around 1577; his father, also Richard Browne, had been an MP and member of the earl of Leicester's household.

9. *Diary* ii 537 n. 6, 538 n. 1. Prettyman (or Pretyman) proved incompetent, even dishonest, in financial affairs. He was also the legal guardian of his nephew Dick.

10. BL Add Ms 78221, f. 1, JE to RB, 20 Oct. 1647.

11. BL Add Ms 15857, ff. 46 and 47, CB to RB, 16 March and 16 June 1642.

12. BL Add Ms 78221, f. 30, JE to RB, 1 Jan. 1648/9; *Transformations*, 18–19.

13. *Ibid.*, 20 Oct. 1647.

14. BL Add Ms 15857, f. 61, RB to JE, 9 Nov. 1647.

15. HP *Ephemerides* 28/1/26, 1649 part 3, July/Aug.–Dec. Later Hartlib observed that Calthoff's contacts at court and with important figures were so advantageous that 'if [he] and Petty might bee joined together they might doe wonders, as well for their owne benefits privatly as otherwise. I meane for the Priviledge of it in Fraunce and other Countries.' 'Mr Robinson' was Henry Robinson (*c*. 1605–73), a utopian economist with responsibility for trade under the Commonwealth government and Hartlib's patron both for the proposed 'office of address' and for a college of inventions in Vauxhall. See *ODNB*.

16. The marquess of Worcester (1601–67), wrote A *Century of Inventions* in 1655; it was published in 1663.

17. G. Doorman, *Patents for Inventions in Netherlands* 144 G 432 patents of the States-General, f. 467v, granted in March 1649. It was one of thirty-seven variants on perpetual motion machines listed there up to 1691. The patent (for the model) was granted to 'Caspar Cathoff, Johannes Digges and Willem Cordery'.

18. See R.G. Howarth, ed., *Letters of Samuel Pepys* 42, Balthasar de S. Michel (his son) to SP, from Deal, *and the Second Diary* 8 Feb. 1673.

19. North, *Notes of Me*, 100–1.

20. BL Add Ms 78221, f. 1, JE to RB, 2 Oct. 1647: 'there is one picture case which any man may open . . . as for the rest of the trunkes and boxes, if you thinke there is any reallity in the person, you may deliver them as you see occasion and other security for my mony.'

21. He sold Hurcott, in Worcestershire, for £3,400 (a profit of £100 since the summer), and provided a £1,000 mortgage to Lord Montague. Mr Christmas (the steward at Wotton) agreed to hold £5,000 for him.

22. BL Add Ms 78221, f. 26, JE to RB, 30 Nov. 1648.

23. *Ibid.*, f. 30, 1 Jan. 1648/9. *Bray* iii published twenty-four letters signed by 'Aplanos'.

24. The engraver was Richard Gaywood, the sculptor Edward Marshall. Marshall's bust was later set up in St Andrew's church, Hempstead, Essex.

25. Evelyn, *The State of France*, 100–1.

26. *Diary* ii 539–40. He visited Clipsby Crew (whom he had met in Tours) in Isleworth to see a collection of miniatures by Peter Oliver and a garden with 'curious flowers'. See 539 n. 5 for the theatre.

27. *Camden's Britannia* (1695, edited by Edmund Gibson) from Evelyn's additions to the material on Surrey.

28. *Diary* v 496–7.

29. BL Add Ms 78221, f. 5, JE to RB, 13 Jan. 1647/8.

30. G. D. Scull, *The Evelyns in America* (1881). George Evelyn, eldest son of Robert of Godstone, arrived at Kent Island, Maryland, in December 1636 and gained title to the island. 'He seemed to have visited it only to sow discord, to impoverish the people, to waste and neglect the property of his principals' (p. 42).

31. BL Add Ms 78221, ff. 9 and 10, JE to RB, 24 and 27 April 1648.

32. *Ibid.*, f. 14, 20 July 1648.

33. *Ibid.*, f. 26, 30 Nov. 1648.

34. Michael Hunter, *Establishing the New Science* (1989), 67 n. 2. The Seneca was *Epistolae Morales*. See BL Add Ms 78431, 27 June 1648, in which Evelyn ('vostre Inviolable Calianthe') explained the symbolism to Mary ('chere Meliora').

35. BL Add Ms 78430. Compiled 1649.

36. [LB] BL Add Ms 78298, f. 40, JE to KE, from Paris, 7 Feb. 1650.

37. BL Add Ms 78315, f. 113, A du G to JE, from Paris, 13 Jan. 1648.

38. BL Add Ms 78221, f. 16, JE to RB, 'from your villa', 28 July; f. 18, 'from your villa', 1 Sept.; f. 20, from London, 4 Sept. 1648.

39. *Ibid.*, f. 24, from London, 20 Nov. 1648.

40. Fanshawe, *Memoirs*, 79–80.

41. Thomas Carte, *Life of James, Duke of Ormonde* (1851), letter 571, Oct. 1648.

42. BL Add Ms 78198, Hanmer to RB, 29 Dec. 1648.

43. BL Add Ms 15948, ff. 24–5, JE to RB, from London, 18 Dec. 1648.

44. BL Add Ms 78221, f. 30, JE to RB, from London, 1 Jan. 1648/9.

45. *Ibid.*, f. 31, 11 Jan. 1648/9.

46. *Ibid.*, f. 32, 'from your villa', 29 Jan. 1648/9.

47. BL Add Ms 78303, f. 34, GE to JE, 30 Jan. 1648/9.

48. Eva Scott, *The King in Exile* (1904), 76. She was offered 40,000 French livres.

49. He wrote that his brother's 'reall merits, and known Integrity so justly challenge a part in the management of those important affaires of this Kingdome'.

50. See Adrian Johns, *The Nature of the Book* (1998). Ross debated with Dr John Wilkins, arguing an orthodox theological view against the latter's support for Copernicus and heliocentric astronomy. This dispute, referred to by Milton in *Paradise Lost*, epitomised the collision course on which the new science and fundamentalist theology were set. Ross saw Evelyn off to France in 1649 and they continued to correspond. Ross opposed Hobbes in *Leviathan Drawn Out by a Hook* (1653).

51. *Diary* ii 547; Geoffrey Keynes, *John Evelyn: A Study in Bibliography* (1968), 34–6.

52. BL Add Ms 78221, f. 34, 29 Jan. 1648/9.

53. *Ibid.*, f. 36, 1 Feb. 1648/9.

54. BL Add Ms 15858, f. 58, 9 March 1648/9.

55. BL Add Ms 78221, f. 38, JE to RB, 12 March 1648/9.

56. *Diary* ii 475 n. 5, 553 and 555.

57. BL Add Ms 78684, f. 93 GN to JE from Covent Garden, 5 April 1649.

58. *SP* i 132–3. Pepys admired a petition 'finely writ by Mr Whore' from the king's embroiderer to the king in Breda. *Ibid.* vi 339, where Pepys sees an example of 'fine writing-work and Flourishing of Mr Hore' whom he had known long ago. After the Restoration, Evelyn secured Hoare the post of clerk to the registrar to the Prerogative Court of Canterbury, in which he drew up deeds of probate in his exquisite hand; *Bray* iii 44–5, 5 April 1649; BL Add Ms 78221 f. 45, JE to RB, 14 June 1649.

59. *Diary* ii 557. He got his pass from 'the Rebell Bradshaw then in great power'.

Chapter 6: 'I am exceedingly happy heere'

1. They are the earliest non-topographical landscape prints made in England: see Griffiths, 'John Evelyn and the Print', 100–1. In Griffiths' estimation, Rowlett was 'the most remarkable print publisher in London during the entire seventeenth century' and he wonders whether Evelyn backed him financially. He was only active from 1645 until 1649.

2. Cal. Clarendon Papers ii 50; on 18 March 1650 Hyde wrote to Morley from Madrid: 'Poore Lady Isabella, it is a horrid thing that no friends in England should have charity enough to provide for her.'

3. On Edward Nicholas's list her cypher appears with those of Dr Morley, Col. Whitley and Mr Aiton. Her code name was 'profligantes'. BL Ms Eg. 2550, f. 49, n.d.

4. BL Add Ms 78442 (1679). Proper respect for religion indicated that a couple should have no sexual relations before the monthly sacrament or weekly devotions. However, abstention from Friday to Monday and throughout Lent was, Evelyn thought, excessively harsh. Although he became very fond of his daughter-in-law, he had been shocked to discover that she was not a communicant.

5. BL Add Ms 78296, JE to JG, from Paris, 27 Nov. 1649.

6. *Ibid.*, JE to JG, 17 Nov. 1650.

7. See Harris, 'The Letter-books of Mary Evelyn', *English Manuscript Studies* (1998) 204–13., for her skill as a letter writer.

8. BL Add Ms 15948, f. 38 onwards.

9. *Nicholas Papers*, i, Camden Society (NS) 1886; Lord Hatton to EN, 26 May/5 June 1649.

10. *Ibid.*, RB to EN, 2/12 June 1649.

11. BL Add Ms 78315, f. 139, JS to JE, 'from my hermitage', 20 Sept. 1649.

12. Quoted in Scott, *The King in Exile*, 103.

13. BL Add Ms 78296, JE to JG, 27 Nov. 1649.

14. *Nicholas Papers*, Lord Hatton to EN, from Paris, 24 Dec. 1649.

15. *Diary* ii 566.

16. *Nicholas Papers*, Lord Hatton (calling himself CP or Charles Parker) to EN, 11/21 May 1650.

17. BL Add Ms 78311, f. 60, from 'Philanax' to JE, 3/13 Jan. 1649/50; f. 64, 'mid term', 20 Sept. 1649; f. 66, from 'Philobafileus', 7 Oct. 1649; f. 67, from 'Philalethes' to 'Dearest Amico', 15 Nov. 1649. The references to Lady Gardiner and Mary Evelyn confirm that Packer had been in Paris quite recently.

18. See [LB] BL Add Ms. 78298, ff. 40 and 41v, JE to KE, 7 Feb. 1649/50 and 26 March 1650. *Diary* ii 558 n. 4.

19. BL Add Ms 78303, f. 46, GE to JE, 26 Feb. 1649/50.

20. BL Add Ms 78302, f. 20, RE to JE, 1649; f. 26, from London, 21 Nov. 1649. Surprisingly, Browne was still able to build up a library, having the volumes finely bound. Before Evelyn left England, he asked him to send a copy of *Mercurius Rusticans* (BL Add Ms 34720, f. 47, 10 April 1649).

21. *Diary* iii 25.

22. BL Add Ms 78311, f. 41, TH to JE, 3 April 1650.

23. BL Add Ms 78306, f. 90, ST to JE, 9 Oct. 1650.

24. BL Add Ms 78685, f. 75, EW to RB, 3 July 1649.

25. Fanshawe, *Memoirs*, 44–5.

26. *Diary* i 66–7, ii 102. See *ODNB* for Davisson (*c.* 1593–1669). See *Diary* ii 565. He and Anibal Barlet were probably the (unnamed since still living) pretentious pedlars of 'chymical philosophies' referred to by Robert Boyle in the *Sceptical Chemist* (1661): see Antonio Clerizio, 'Carneades and the Chemists: a study of the Sceptical Chymist and its impact on seventeenth-century chemistry' in *Robert Boyle Reconsidered*, ed. M. Hunter (1994). William Petty, a polymath – economist, inventor and administrator – was an early and stalwart supporter of Harvey's doctrine of the circulation of the blood. He left Paris in 1646, when Evelyn may have first met him, and went to Oxford, becoming professor of anatomy there in 1651; see Frank, *Harvey and the Oxford Physiologists*, 101–3.

27. BL Add Ms 78315, f. 137, JS to JE, 31 Aug. 1649.

28. BL Add Ms 78316, f. 4, GJ to JE, 6 Feb. 1649/50.

29. Gunther, *Early British Botanists*, 284, 286, refers to Howe's *Phytologia Britannica* (1650) in which Joyliffe had identified two additions for a new edition, 'daucus proliferus' and 'sambucus laciniatis foliis', the latter seen near Winchester.

30. BL Add Ms 78316, f. 4, GJ to JE, 6 Feb. 1650/1. Joyliffe gained his MD at Cambridge in 1652 and then practised in London while continuing a programme of experimental medicine. In 1656 he assisted Robert Boyle in taking a spleen out of a live dog, which survived.

31. *Diary* iii 4–7. The episode occurred at Vanves, 'a place famous for the butter', just south-west of Paris. Philip Stanhope became earl of Chesterfield and later married Elizabeth Butler, sister of their companions.

32. BL Add Ms 78392, ff. 20–3, anniversary prayers, 7 May 1650 and various dates.

33. *Diary* iii 8.

34. [LB] BL Add Ms 78298, f. 4, JE to Cosin, 28 July 1651.

35. Evelyn, *The State of France*, 9.

36. *Diary* ii 128–31 and notes.

37. See Mirjam Foot, 'John Evelyn's Bookbindings' in *Milieu*. Browne's prize volumes eventually became Evelyn's and were bound in fine calfskin, tooled in gold, with his own monogram, 'RB', or one combining his wife's initial, 'RBE'.

38. Gassendi, helped by Peiresc, had published a commentary in 1647. His three-volume work *Animadversiones in Decimum Librum Diogenis Laertii* appeared in 1649 and the final, posthumous version, *Syntagma Philosophicum*, included his life by Samuel Sorbière.

39. C.A. Gordon, *A Bibliography of Lucretius* (1985), item 301. The exiled Christopher Wase, a cousin of Lady Browne's, had been ejected from King's College, Cambridge.

40. *Bray* iii 57, AR to JE, from London, 21 July 1651.

41. *ODNB*.

42. Evelyn, *Acetaria*, 8.

43. He was pleased that 'you did accept of the demonstration of my affection by the Dedication of Sr Anthony van dycks Pictur unto you'. Evelyn owed him 'for 6 pictures 9 pistolls' which he would appreciate at his convenience. From Amsterdam, 24 Nov./ 14 Dec. 1648 (*sic*); see Harding, 'John Evelyn, Hendrick van der Borcht the Younger and Wenceslaus Hollar'.

44. *Ibid.*: 'shee hath another houwse at Amersfordt but is seldom there.' After her death in 1654, Van der Borcht returned home to Frankenthal, in the Palatinate, where he was still living in late 1665.

45. In 1651 Samuel Tuke asked for some costume prints for Princess Louise, the artist daughter of the Winter Queen, very probably the Hollar engravings. Evelyn replied that if she wanted to be repaid, he would happily accept 'her owne picture drawne by her Selfe, that so I might be in a capacity to send her back the reflection of it from the hand of our famous Nanteuille, the same who by performing so well with me, was (by your meanes) so much honoured with her Majesties approbation'.

46. BL Add Ms 78316, f. 10, RH to JE, from Paris, July 1650. His 'Greate Booke' would no longer hold all the points he had collected.

47. Griffiths, *The Print in Stuart Britain*, 125–8.

48. BL Add Ms 15948, ff. 53–4, RH to JE, 9 July 1650; the fifth state included a swag emblazoned with 'Meliora Retinete'. His monogram is on a book to his right, a truncated pentacle on one to his left. Nanteuil may have employed Bosse to add the lettering: Griffiths, *The Print in Stuart Britain*, 131.

49. BL Add Ms 78316, f. 2, Catherine Scott to JE, 13 Jan 1649/50; *Diary* iii 15.

50. BL Add Ms 78303, ff. 49 and 50, GE to JE, 12 Dec. 1650 and 12 Jan. 1650/1.

51. *Diary* iii 24.

52. BL Add Ms 78303, ff. 57, 58 and 52, GE to JE, 29 Sept., 1 [Nov?] and 5 Feb. 1650/1.

53. *Diary* iii 17, 20, 37–9.
54. BL Add Ms 78306, f. 89, ST to JE, from The Hague, 25 Oct. 1650.
55. *Elysium*, 131, 181.
56. *Diary* iii 18 (5 Sept. 1650), also ii 563. At Maisons-Lafitte, as it has been known since the nineteenth century, traces of the 'harbour' remain close to a ruined water mill.
57. For Evelyn's intellectual programme see Hunter, *Science and the Shape of Orthodoxy*, 71–4.
58. BL Add Ms 78302, f. 30, RE to JE, 20 Dec. 1650.
59. [LB] BL Add Ms 78298, JE to TK, 25 March 1651, recounts Evelyn's actual – as opposed to his claimed – religious experience in the 1650s. See Spurr, '"A Sublime and Noble Service"'. Until 1655 it was not as difficult as Evelyn suggests to hear the Anglican service in church.
60. BL Add Ms 78311, f. 70, PP to JE, 3 March 1651/2.
61. [LB] BL Add Ms 78298, f. 185v, JE to James Hamilton, a nephew of the duke of Ormonde, 27 April 1671.
62. John and Mary Evelyn went out to St Germain with the Wallers, to comfort them in their loss. See *Diary* iii 40.
63. *Ibid.* iii 41–3.
64. *Diary* iii 163. See introduction to Thomas Hobbes, *De Cive* ed. Howard Warrender (1983).
65. He specified Raphael's 'gallerie', François Perrier's Roman bas-reliefs, the Escorial 'at large', the Fontane di Roma, the new front of St Peter's and the baldacchino. He had a good crucifixion by Van Dyck already.
66. BL Add Ms 78311, f. 41, TH to JE, 3 April 1650. See Griffiths, *The Print in Stuart Britain*, 129–31, figs 80e and 80f. The pencil preparatory drawing is in the British Museum. This was Evelyn's second set of etchings. An earlier set was published in London in 1649, and was far less personal.
67. See F. Sherwood Taylor, 'The Chemical Studies of John Evelyn', *Annals of Science* 8:4 (Dec. 1952), 286–92.
68. *Diary* iii 48–9; [LB] BL Add Ms 78298, JE to Radcliffe, late Dec. 1651, referring to Ben Jonson's *The Alchemist*.
69. Hobbes, *The Correspondence* ii 831.
70. *Nicholas Papers*, EN to CH, from The Hague, 1 Feb. 1651.
71. BL Add Ms 78296, JE to JG, from Paris, 17 June and 21 Oct. 1651.
72. [LB] BL Add Ms 78298, f. 48, JE to WP, 2 Dec. 1651.
73. BL Add Ms 78316, f. 25, Cousin Stephens to JE, 28 Feb. 1651/2.
74. BL Add Ms 78296, JE to WG, from Paris, 10 Jan. 1651/2.
75. [LB] BL Add Ms 78298, f. 52, JE to RE, 10 Jan. 1651/2.

Chapter 7: Wise Men Possessing Themselves in Patience

1. BL Add Ms 78316, f. 24, Dr. Earle to 'H', by hand of Evelyn, from Paris, 29 Jan. 1651/2.
2. On the way home Evelyn was entrusted with a mission to the governor of Dunkirk on behalf of George Goring, Earl of Norwich, but something went amiss. [LB] BL Add Ms 78298, f. 34, 12 March 1651/2.
3. 'The late subject of our discourse' was printed by 'TM' for Gabriel Bedell and T. Collins. He had intended a wider account but decided all other nations and governments 'deferr to the present Grandezza of the French Empire'. Although Browne must be his dedicatee, he implies that the individual is in England, perhaps to disguise his identity.

4. See appendix, 'Sir Thomas Hanmer's Account of France', in Sir Henry Bunbury (ed.), *The Correspondence of Sir Thomas Hanmer* (1838), 245–319. Hanmer's account of 1648 was intended for publication. His analysis of Richelieu's diplomatic skills was very acute.

5. Noel Malcolm, *Aspects of Hobbes* (2002). Although *Leviathan* appeared in England, the plate was engraved earlier in France. In his translation of Guarini's *Il Pastor Fido*, dedicated to Prince Charles in 1647, Sir Richard Fanshawe refers to the 'body politic' and a portrait of de Séguier, the French chancellor, consisting of a 'multitude of little faces'.

6. Key members of his family were his brother Philippe, duke of Anjou ('Monsieur'), his uncle Gaston, duke of Orléans, and Gaston's daughter, Anne Marie d'Orléans, ('Mademoiselle'). In the wings, but at a tangent, stood the two Princes Condé, sworn enemies of Cardinal Mazarin.

7. See *Writings*, 69–90. It was printed by John Crooke, brother of Hobbes's publisher and man of business, and brother-in-law of Benjamin Tooke.

8. Lodewijk Huygens hoped to hear 'the famous Paris singer' perform: see A. G. H. Bachrach and R. G. Collmer, *Lodewjck Huygens: The English Journal 1651–1652* (1982) 185. Her new teacher was the 'petit Lambert, maister of the french king's musique'.

9. Evelyn asked Mary to consult her mother about the advisability of the arrangements with Prettyman – he had not revealed the plan to anyone. But Deptford has 'so few persons of quality' that he wonders if it is suitable. BL Add Ms 78431, JE to 'my dearest Browne', from London, 8 Feb. 1651/2. See her reply, BL Add Ms 78300, f.3, 1 March 1652.

10. The cabinet is in the Geffrye Museum, London. Pierre Golle was born near Amsterdam, working in Paris from 1643 where he was apprenticed to Jean Mace the royal cabinetmaker. He was Daniel Marot's uncle. (Information in the museum archive.)

11. Jasper Needham was accompanying young Benjamin Maddocks. Evelyn provided them with introductory letters to Bosse and others. Needham was, he wrote in French, knowledgeable and 'extrémement ingenieux' and his charge a 'personne de qualité, qu'est aussy fort curieux'. (In the end, their journey was postponed until 1655.)

12. BL Add Ms 15948, f. 55, Rousselle (on Le Fèvre's behalf) to JE, 20 April 1652; ff. 75–6v, 22 Nov. 1652 or 1653. See also BL Add Ms 78316, 7 Jan. 1652/3. Rousselle was a protégé of Sir Kenelm Digby – his name is spelt in many different ways.

13. BL Add Ms 78300, f. 4, ME to JE, 'about' 30 March 1652.

14. [LB] BL Add Ms 78298, f. 55v, JE to ET, 25 April 1652.

15. Bodleian MS Eng b 2043, f. 331, Evelyn's notes on Surrey for Edmund Gibson, who was revising Camden's *Britannia* in 1694.

16. Douglas Chambers 'The Tomb in the Landscape: John Evelyn's Garden at Albury', *Journal of Garden-History*, i., 1981, 38–9, fig. 3. Several commentators described the building as ruined.

17. *Diary* iii 154–5. For George Evelyn's Maryland exploits see p. 000.

18. *Ibid.*, iii 60–1.

19. Samuel Sorbière, *A Journey to England*, 12.

20. [LB] BL Add Ms 78298, f. 56, JE to ME, 28 April 1652.

21. *Ibid.*, f. 55, JE to GE, 3 April 1652; f. 55, JE to EW, 13 April 1652. It was to be a temporary position for Wase (a cousin of Mary Evelyn's) ''til he should find some better Condition, for he was worthy of it, both for his exceeding greate Erudition & no lesse modesty'. *Diary* iii 55.

22. BL Add Ms 78303, f. 60, GE to JE, 9 May 1652; f. 63, GE to JE, 17 Oct. 1652. Waller may have begun rebuilding Hall Barn at this date, which may account for their removal to London.

23. BL Add Ms 78221, f. 59, JE to RB, 13 Nov. 1652; BL Add Ms 78303, f. 64, GE to JE, 3 June 1653.

24. BL Add Ms 78306, f. 7, RB to JE, 11 May 1652; BL Add Ms 78300, f. 8, ME to JE, from Paris, 25 May 1652; [LB] BL Add Ms 78298, f. 56v, JE to ME, 10 May 1652.

25. BL Add Ms 78300, f. 10, ME to JE, 7 June 1652.

26. Fletcher, *A County Community in Peace and War,* 112–13.

27. Spurr, 'A Sublime and Noble Service', 149.

28. Bacon, *The Essays,* 262–3. See *Transformations,* 67, for a detailed list of still-room equipment.

29. BL Add Ms 78392.

30. BL Add Ms 78220, EB to RB (the last letter she wrote to him), 4 July 1652.

31. BL Add Ms 78221, f. 53, JE to RB, 25 Aug. 1652; *Diary* iii 75.

32. See n. 30 above.

33. BL Add Ms 34702, ff. 73–4, RB to JE, from St Malo, 10 Jan. 1653/4.

34. BL Add Ms 78613. It was to have balusters, rails and strings, 'together with foure posts, whereoffe one of them to be opened on 3 sides & all the rest according to order. The standards to be six inches knobbs.' In December 1653 another agreement was drawn up with William Staples (bricklayer) to build new chimneys for the brew house and wash house, and to set up, fit and erect two 'furnaces or coppers'. Staples was also responsible for finding the materials.

35. Bacon, *The Essays,* 46, 197.

36. BL Add Ms 78221, f. 57, JE to RB, 11 Oct. 1652; *Diary* iii 76–7.

37. Clarendon SP iii 126. Charles remained in France, in the vicinity of Paris, until 1654 when Cardinal Mazarin offered him a pension of £6,000 to leave; [LB] BL Add Ms 78298, f. 58, JE to EH, 1 Nov. 1652, thanking him for his condolences; BL Add Ms 78316, f. 49, EH to JE, 2 Nov. 1652, Hyde promises to support Browne in his difficulties. Sir Richard's removal from Paris suited the queen mother's court which preferred the Scottish solution, since he was allied to the king's Anglican courtiers, Hyde, Nicholas and Ormonde who opposed it.

38. BL Add Ms 78221, f. 60, JE to RB, 25 Feb. 1652/3.

39. Quoted in *Transformations,* 67.

40. BL Add Ms 15857, f. 136, RB to JE (scrap of letter), [7?] April 1653.

41. Prudence Leith-Ross, 'The Garden of John Evelyn at Deptford', *Garden History* 25:2 (Winter 1997) 138–52; Mark Laird, 'Parterre, Grove and Flower Garden: European Horticulture and Planting Design in John Evelyn's Time' in O'Malley and Wolschke-Bulmahn, eds, *John Evelyn's Elysium Britannicum',* 171–219.

42. See note 33, above.

43. *Diary* iii 219. On 5 August 1658 he visited Squerryes which had been bought by William Leech, Sir John Evelyn's son-in-law, in 1654 and observed a 'pretty finely wooded & watred seate: The stables good, the house old but convenient', but made no mention of his own previous interest as a potential purchaser.

44. See various letters to JE from Paris in BL Add Ms 78316 during 1652–3, including from Le Fèvre (in French) f. 27, 23 March 1652, and f. 40, 25 May 1652. His other correspondents were Rousselle, Bosse, Nanteuil, Du Guernier and Du Clos.

45. He seems to have been Alexandre, the son of the distinguished miniaturist of the same name and brother of the better-known Louis, who became professor at the Académie Royale de Peinture and painted a portrait of James, Duke of York, in 1656.

46. Evelyn, trans. *Parallel,* (1664), from 'the interpreter to the Reader'.

47. In one later very damaged letter (BL Add Ms 78316, f. 112, GE to JE, 28 July 1656) Scamozzi's name can be discerned.

48. Eileen Harris with Nicholas Savage, *British Architectural Books and Writers 1556–1785* (1990), 62; quote from the 1707 edition of the *Parallel.*

49. BL Add Ms 78298, ff. 26v–7, JE to AB, 26 Jan. 1653/54; BL Add Ms 78316, f. 58, AB to JE, from Paris, 26 Oct. 1653, refers to his *Moyen Universel de Pratiquer la Perspective sur les Tableaux ou Surfaces Irregulières* (1653).

50. For the dispute between Charles Errard and Bosse, see Marianne Le Blanc, *D'Acide et d'Encre: Abraham Bosse* (2004), 48 esp. n. 78; also BL Add Ms 78316, ff. 59–60, Du Guernier to JE, 26 Oct. 1653. Bosse eventually published *Traité des Manières de Dessiner les Ordres* (1664) but in later editions Errard's name is on the title-page.

51. Scott, *The King in Exile*, 435; Clarendon SP iii 174–5.

52. Bodleian MS Aubrey 4, f. 28r, 8 Feb. 1675/6.

53. *Diary* v 358.

54. [LB] BL Add Ms 78298, f. 58v, JE to JN, 16 June 1653. The reference is to a free-thinking religious community.

55. BL Add Ms 78311, f. 43, TH to JE, 27 Sept. 1652. Henshaw and Evelyn discussed gilding and prices of microscopes and telescopes. Henshaw could buy him one of each for £12.

56. Hartlib notes that Greatorex's work on the system of trades is divided into a number of volumes, including Oughtred's treatise on clockmaking. The project is not recorded anywhere else.

57. Taylor, 'The Chemical Studies of John Evelyn'; BL Add Ms 78345, f. 24 *et seq.* in which he emulated Lord Hatton's laboratory furnishings and Du Clos's arrangement of alcoves and long tables; BL Add Ms 78335, f. 10.

58. John Prest, *The Garden of Eden* (1981), 47–8. In the expanded catalogue of the Oxford physic garden (1658) a poem by 'RI' (probably Richard Inglett) refers to Adam 'the great Simpler'.

59. Henry Wotton, *The Elements of Architecture* (1624), ii 82.

60. Dr Jeremy Taylor first named it, alluding to Pliny's country villa. See below, p. 000.

61. Prettyman's financial affairs were spinning out of control. His staunch royalist brother, Sir John Prettyman, Bt, was either corrupt or incompetent in his office of receiver of first fruits and tenths and died an insolvent debtor in the King's Bench prison. William Prettyman's own tenure as remembrancer in the same office ended in debt and his suspension. See G. E. Aylmer, *The Crown's Servants* (2002), 90, 113–14.

62. *Diary* iii 102.

63. Quoted from *Micrographia* in Lisa Jardine, *The Curious Life of Robert Hooke* (2003), 75–6.

64. Boyle Correspondence, i 81, JW to RB, 6 Sept. 1653; i 85, RB to SH, 14 Sept. 1655; Shapin, *A Social History of Truth*, 170–75.

65. *Diary* iii 107 n. 5.

66. Yale Beinicke Library Osb. 19484, Wilkins, from Oxford, to unnamed correspondent but docketed in JE's hand; 2 April 1656.

67. *Elysium*, 274, 276.

68. Evelyn noted an intricate lock, made by a country blacksmith, and an eccentric house, more like a barn, built by a local dignitary with no windows on the side facing the view.

69. Christopher Wren, *Parentalia* (1750), 206; J. A. Bennett, *The Mathematical Science of Christopher Wren* (1982).

70. BL Add MS 78316, f. 73, PP to JE, from All Souls, Oxford, Dec. 1654. Pett was ejected from his fellowship at the Restoration but became an early (though inactive) Fellow of the Royal Society (see *ODNB*).

Chapter 8: Planting Cabbages and Blotting Paper

1. HP *Ephemerides* 1655, iv, Aug.–Dec.; *ibid.*, i, Jan.–Feb. 'Mr Evelin in Broomfield neare Dedord green much about Society of Arts.' BL Eve. a. 78, the third edition.

Inscribed as a gift from 'S Hartlibi Authoris', 1655. See Giles Mandelbrote, 'John Evelyn and his Books' in *Milieu*.

2. *Diary* iii 162–3; Mark Greengrass et al., *Samuel Hartlib and Universal Reformation*, (1994), 12–13.

3. Boyle Correspondence i 63–4, Hartlib to RB, 16 Nov. 1647. He refers to Petty as a linguist ('a perfect Frenchman' since he had been educated by French Jesuits), anatomist, and 'excelling in mathematic and mechanical learning'. But later, 78–9, SH to RB, 24 July 1649, he wants him 'set apart or encouraged for the advancement of experimental and mechanical knowledge at London'. See *ODNB*.

4. For a detailed account, see Hunter, *Science and the Shape of Orthodoxy*, 74–82. See also BL Add Ms 78339, n.d., except 1652 (varnishes) and 1656 (wood-monger).

5. *Diary* iii 175 n. 1; BL Add Ms 78345, preface 'to my honour'd & Learned friend Mr G[aspar] N[eedham]'. A translation in English appeared in 1664 by 'PDC'.

6. Carola and Alaistair Small, 'John Evelyn and the Garden of Epicurus', *Journal of the Warburg and Courtauld Fustitutis* 60 (1997). The transcription was 'made by 4 of his scholars'. Gassendi was in the same circle as François de la Mothe le Vayer and Gabriel Naudé, works by both of whom Evelyn translated.

7. Aubrey, *Brief Lives*, 229; *Diary* iii 87–8; Ashmole and his wife moved to Albury, living at Weston-in-Shere, opposite Oughtred's rectory.

8. HP *Ephemerides*, 1650. He also observed that he 'brought over an excellent Historie of China in Italian wherin are the Annual Letters of the Jesuits which is worthy to bee translated. Hee is to bee ranked in the number of Experimental Philosophers. Hee hath a good Optical Glasses and knows one that hath one wherin you use both your eys.'

9. The debate at the heart of the book aimed to establish the difference between 'vulgar' and learned chemists, between men such as Davisson and Barlet (the former) and Van Helmont (the latter). See A. Clericuzio, 'Carneades and the Chemists': A Study of the "The Sceptical Chymist" and its Impact on Seventeenth-Century Chemistry' in *Robert Boyle Reconsidered*, ed. M. Hunter (1994), ch. 5.

10. BL Add Ms 78335, f. 126.

11. Margot Todd, *Christian Humanism and the Puritan Social Order* (1987), 14–15.

12. *Diary* iii 163 n. 1, 150. Evelyn refers to 'Anabaptists & other Inthusiasts' who believed themselves to be speaking in tongues: *Diary* iv 550.

13. *Bray* iii 71–3, JT to JE, 16 April 1656; JE to JT 27 April 1656.

14. Tomalin, *Samuel Pepys*, 191.

15. *Bray* iii 392, 396, JE to William Wotton, 12 Sept. 1703. Evelyn claims there that the Boyles and the Brownes are related.

16. Boyle Correspondence i, 58–9, RB to SH, 8 May 1647.

17. *Ibid.* i 212–13 and nn., JE to RB, 9 May 1657. He lists 'Painting in Oil, in Miniatiure, Anealing in Glass, Enamelling, and Marble Paper' as well as details on 'brass &c' which 'properly belong to etching and engraving'.

18. Hunter, *Science and the Shape of Orthodoxy* 79–81; Boyle Correspondence i 212–13, 9 May 1657, 362–4, 497n., 9 Aug. 1659, 362–4: 'in the History of Trades, I am not advanced a step.'

19. Oldenburg Correspondence i 94, HO to Edward Lawrence, April 1656.

20. Shapin, *A Social History of Truth*, 176, 191. Boyle's published work in its various editions between 1659 and 1700 ran to more than eighty volumes in English, and many more in Latin. *Bray* iii 346–52, JE to WW, 30 March 1696.

21. Hunter, *Science and the Shape of Orthodoxy*, 88 and fig. 14. The four elements were personified, overlooked by a Venus or Great Mother figure, with a vignette of the author in the middle.

22. Keynes, *John Evelyn*, 43 n. 2. See also H. Jones, *The Epicurean Tradition* (1989), 196. Thomas Creech published the first full English translation of Lucretius in 1682 and John Dryden reworked it in 1685.

23. Bodleian, MS Add. B. 5, f. 39v, 1654: 'Johannem Evelynum Lucreti jnterpretem.' At the end of a tiny notebook containing Latin poems and letters Wase adds: 'Des grands hommes les moindres choses sont précieuses' (of great men, the smallest things are valuable), suggesting he shared Evelyn's inclusive view of information. Wase's *Electra* was dedicated Charles I's sister, Princess Elizabeth, exiled in The Hague. It includes two poems in the Epilogue showing the author's devotion to the Stuarts. (Thanks to Robert Harding for his notes on *Electra*.)

24. *Bray* iii 98–100, JT to JE, 29 Aug. 1657; Michael M. Repetzki, *John Evelyn's Translation of Titus Lucretius Carus De Rerum Natura* (2000), xvi.

25. Robert Boyle, *Certain Physiological Essays* (1661), quoted by J. T. Harwood in M. Hunter, ed., *Robert Boyle Reconsidered* (1994), 45.

26. [LB] BL Add Ms 78298, f. 73v, JE to EM, 16 Jan. 1656/7.

27. *Bray* iii 77, JT to JE, 15 Nov 1656, 109, JT to JE, 9 April 1659.

28. See *ODNB* for Walter Charleton (1620–1707). Pierrepont was a friend of Charleton's and a patient of William Harvey, a virtuoso with his own physic garden and laboratory. See Frank, *Harvey and the Oxford Physiologists*, 29.

29. *Bray* iii 246, JE to MC, misdated 15 July 1674 (he died in 1671); H. Jones, *The Epicurean Tradition* (1989), 205.

30. Rand's dedication was dated 30 Jan. 1656, 'to the ingenious and learned Gentleman, the worshipful John Evelyn Esquire'. Nicolas-Claude Fabri de Peiresc (1580–1637) was a distinguished scholar and Epicurean philosopher, based, like Pierre Gassendi (1592–1655), in Aix-en-Provence.

31. BL Add Ms 78316, f. 126, WR to JE, 12 Feb. 1656/7; *ibid.*, ff. 130–1, WR to JE, 13 March 1656/7; ff. 136–7, WR to JE, 10 May 1657.

32. *Diary* iii 154. He later described an 'Amphitheater Garden, or Solitarie recesse, being 15 Ackers, invirond by an hill: he shew'd us divers rare plants: Caves, an Elaboratory', not the garden he saw then.

33. *Elysium*, Appendices 7 (tulips), 445-8; and 9 (daffodils), 453–4.

34. *Ibid.*, Appendix 5, 441–2. This may have been Sir Richard Browne's contribution.

35. Griffiths, *The Print in Stuart Britain*, 129.

36. BL Add Ms 34702, f. 150, RB to JE, 31 March 1657.

37. Among much else, the child would be subjected to a novel system of learning grammar invented by Christopher Wase, who now had a school in Dedham, Essex.

38. In 1655 he raised £500 by selling a Sussex property to Herbert Morley, and raised £2,600 from the sale of Warley, a profit of £100 in six years. He claimed he was selling because of punitive new taxes, perhaps 'decimation', a 10 per cent tax levied on royalist land holdings.

39. BL Add Ms 78211, JE to RB, 25 Nov. 1657.

40. *Diary* iii 201 n. 5, 202, 203 n. 1. He paid an eighth of his £500 subscription, which entitled him to a vote. The aim was to raise £800,000.

41. BL Add Ms 78392, devotional papers inc. f. 13.

42. Hartlib had already recommended it to Boyle: Boyle Correspondence i 169–79, 8 or 9 May 1654. See BL Add Ms 78311, f. 53, TH to JE, 11 Jan. 1657/8. De Bonnefons dealt with the culture (and culinary preservation) of fruit, vegetables and herbs, their grafting, pruning and diseases, their pests and predators – including moles. On seeing their hills 'fling them dextrously out with the spade', as Evelyn put it, and then, if they survive, use them as bait. He also included a gardening calendar. Since *The Manner of Ordering Fruit-Trees*, which Geoffrey Keynes tentatively ascribed to Evelyn has no dedication or prefatory material. Needham is a more likely candidate.

43. Stephen Pasmore, 'Thomas Henshaw FRS (1618-1700)', 36 (1981-2) *Notes and Records of the Royal Society* 177–88.

44. BL Add Ms 78221, ff. 75–6, JE to RB, 6 Feb. 1657/8; f. 77, 15 Feb.1657/8.

45. BL Add Ms 78392, ff. 33–4.

46. [LB] BL Add Ms. 78298, f. 85, JE to JM, 20 March 1657/8.
47. BL Add MS 78316, f. 153v, PP to JE, 29 March 1658, with draft reply from JE. See Hunter, *Science and the Shape of Orthodoxy*, 93 n. 108. Queen's College MS 231 includes a manuscript letter from Evelyn to Barlow, 5 Oct. 1658. *Bray* iii 132-3, TB to JE, from Queen's College, Oxford, 10 June 1661.
48. *Writings* 35, 37–68.
49. Mark Morford, 'The Stoic Garden', *Journal of Garden History* 7:2 (1987) referring to Langius's garden, described by Lipsius.
50. Bacon, *The Essays*, 'Of Gardens', 197.
51. Gunther, *Early British Botanists*, 270, 355, quoting from letter from Browne to Edward Nicholas, 5 July 1658: see *Nicholas Papers* Camden Society 31 (1920), 65. See BL Add Ms 34702, f. 147, RB to JE, 19/29 Dec. [1657?]. Browne had been so distracted about his house that he had not attended fully to Evelyn's gardening commissions. However, he recalled that his father considered autumn best for planting in that soil. BL Add Ms 34702, f. 160, RB to JE, 23 July 1658.
52. BL Add Ms 78311, f. 56, TH to JE, 28 Feb. 1658/9. Evelyn claimed it had already run through six French editions and one Dutch. He refers to a cookbook by the same author. This was De Bonnefons's *Les Délices de la Campagne*, from which Evelyn read the section on breadmaking to the Royal Society in 1666, which he also published as an essay, 'Panificium'. Evelyn did not credit the author. See the texts compared in William Rubel, 'Parisian Bread *circa* 1654', *Petits Propos Culinaires* 77 (2004), 9–33. (Information from Tom Jaine.)
53. As well as 'Walks, Perspectives, Rocks, Aviaries, Vivaries, Apiaries, Pots, Conservatories, Piscina's, Groves, Cyrpta's, Cabinets, Eccho's, Statues'.

Chapter 9: Restoration

1. *Diary* iii 214–15; Edmund Waller linked the August winds to Cromwell's death in a poem: *ibid.* iii 220 and n. 2.
2. John Dryden refers to 'That Giant-Prince of all her Watry Herd' in *A Poem upon the Death of His Late Highness, Oliver Lord Protector* (1659): see Mark Laird, 'Sayes Court Revisited' in *Milieu*.
3. *Diary* iii 224 and n. 4.
4. In 1661 the Catholic Tuke appealed to the first session of the House of Lords to 'relieve his co-religionists': see Ronald Hutton, *Charles the Second, King of England, Scotland and Ireland* (1989), 176.
5. BL Add Ms 78221, f.90, JE to RB, 28 Nov. 1659.
6. BL Add Ms 78678, f. 129, Lord Galloway to RB, 22 July 1659.
7. Boyle Correspondence i 178, Hartlib to Boyle, 15 May 1654; *ibid.*, 89, Boyle to Hartlib, 1 May 1650; for a detailed account of these proliferating ventures, at home and abroad, see Charles Webster, *The Great Instauration: Sciences, Medicine and Reform 1626–1660* (1975). Bacon envisaged that Solomon's House would utilise knowledge for the benefit of the state.
8. HP, *Ephemerides*, 1650 part 3 (May–Oct.). Henshaw's scheme also echoed the earl of Arundel's bequest for an establishment at Albury housing six men, with plenty of books and 'convenient rooms to make all Distillations, physics and Surgery'.
9. Cowley's version was a systematic miniature university, two hundred boys taught by twenty professors, of whom four would be travelling at any time. It was to be free from interference from 'any parties in State or Religion' and organised along new principles of learning. There would be lectures, meetings and publications (in Latin), reading lists and personal tuition for scholars.

10. See Johns, *The Nature of the Book*, 478–80, 510, arguing that the importance accorded to the inventor makes Robert Hooke a possible candidate. There is no circumstantial evidence for his authorship. It was printed in 1660.

11. Boyle Correspondence i 365–9, nn. 497–8, JE to Boyle, 3 Sept. 1659. This records the significant changes between the original letter as sent (BL Add Ms 4293, ff. 69–70) and Evelyn's letterbook copy which was published by Bray.

12. *Diary* ii 81, his visit in April 1643. Howard Colvin, *A Biographical Dictionary of British Architects 1600–1840* (1995) 931 dates it to 1638–40 and suggests it was built by Nicholas Stone. Lady Anne Fanshawe was Harrison's daughter. See fig. 2 in Gillian Darley, '"Action to the Purpose": Evelyn, Greenwich and the Sick and Wounded Seamen' in *Milieu*.

13. Michael Leslie, The Spiritual Husbandry of John Beale' in M. Leslie and T. Raylor, eds, *Culture and Cultivation in Early Modern England* (1992).

14. John Harwood, 'Science Writing and Writing Science' in M. Hunter, ed., *Robert Boyle Reconsidered*, 45.

15. Oldenburg Correspondence, i, letter 154, HO to Hartlib, 13 Aug. 1659.

16. [LB] BL Add Ms 78298, f. 94, JE to SH, 8 Aug. 1659. For Backbury Hill, see *Elysium*, 96–9 and Peter Goodchild, '"No Phantasticall Utopia, But a Reall Place". John Evelyn, John Beale and Backbury Hill, Herefordshire', *Garden History* 19 ii (1911) 105–27.

17. HP 62/25/1A–4B, 15 Nov. 1659.

18. Oldenburg Correspondence ii, letter 256, Beale to HO, 21 Jan. 1662/3.

19. Although Morley was appointed a commissioner at the trial of Charles I, he conspicuously failed to attend or to sign the death warrant. See *ODNB*.

20. Camden Society, ser. 3 (1946), LXIX 64, letter 93, Mordaunt to the king, 9/19 Oct. 1659.

21. See *Writings*, 91–109; 'to gratifie a few mean and desperate persons, you cancell your duty to your Prince, and disband your Religion, dishonour your name, and bring ruine and infamy on your posterity.' The clue to Morley's identity as his addressee lay in the words 'I . . . knew your education'.

22. Esmond De Beer, 'Evelyn and Colonel Harbert Morley in 1659 and 1660', *Sussex Archaeological Collections* 77 (1937), 177–83.

23. Quoted in Austin Woolrych, *Britain in Revolution 1625–1660* (2002), 751

24. BL Add Ms 78221, f. 91, JE to RB, 22 Dec. 1659; see Fletcher, *A County Community in Peace and War*, 317–20. Morley returned to the obscure ranks of the middling Sussex gentry, serving as member of Parliament for Rye until he died in 1667.

25. BL Add Ms 78221, f. 93, JE to RB, 5 Jan. 1659/60; ff. 97–9, 13 Feb. 1659/60.

26. BL Add Ms 78300, f. 12, ME to JE, 27 April 1660; BL Add Ms 78221, f. 90, JE to RB, 28 Nov. 1659, f. 95, JE to RB, 12 Jan. 1659/60.

27. She wrote: 'the seeds are in the ground . . . the garden is weeded . . . John [their gardener] tells me he has sowed some gillyflower seed, and that the litle garden does not require any, being full of other sorts. The great garden has enough . . . the wall fruit and the small trees are very well taken.' BL Add Ms 78300, f. 12, ME to JE, from Deptford, 27 April 1660; BL Add Ms 34702, f. 186, RB to ME, 6 Jan. 1659/60.

28. The titles by de Caus were *Les Forêts mouventes, aux diverse machines utiles et plaisantes et plusieurs desseins de Grotts et Fontaines* (1615) and *Hortus Palatinus* (1620) but the latter only if it is cheap since he has not seen it and it may not be worthwhile. In his next letter Evelyn told him not to worry about the *Hortus Palatinus* or the '20 crown' books.

29. [LB] BL Add Ms 78298, f. 94, JE to Hartlib, 8 Aug. 1659: 'I am bold to add this farther account of my owne as they seeme to hold some proportion with the thoughts of Mr. Beale . . . (to which myne desires the honour onely of being a handmayd).'

30. See extract from letter of JE to TB, 28 Jan. 1659/60 (not 1657) in J. Dixon Hunt and P. Willis, eds, *The Genius of the Place: The English Landscape Garden 1620–1820* (1975) 57–8.

31. *Bray* iii 127–8, JT to JE, 10 Feb. 1659/60.
32. *Elysium,* Appendix 11, 460–1. It is dated 20 January 1659 but the distribution of the outline and the finalising of the title suggest it was 1660. Tellingly, the signatories specified that the information upon the gardens of St Germain-en-Laye and those in Italy would be 'most acceptable to our english nobility and gentry'.
33. BL Add Ms 15959, f. 146 (in RB's hand, pencil inscription by JE), 1660. Browne continued to send last-minute additions for the text.
34. BL Add Ms 78221, f. 103, JE to RB, 10 May 1660.
35. Charles Lyttelton to Lord Hatton, from Breda, 6 May 1660: 'What are his pretences and buisnesse I know nothing. I heare he writt the King's charrectker.' *Hatton Correspondence*, Camden Society, n.s., 22 (1878), i 20.
36. But instead Sir Edward Nicholas 'to his great vexation . . . engrossed all the petitions which really . . . belonged to the Masters of the Requests': Fanshawe, *Memoirs*, 96. The post of secretary of state was given to William Morrice, a protégé of Monck; see Antonia Fraser, *King Charles II* (1979), 243–4.
37. BL Add Ms 78221, f. 105, JE to RB, 14 May 1660, f. 107, 17 May 1660. One possibility was the treasurership of the navy, the role 'your ancestor Mr Gonson has served heretofore'. Tuke would lobby the duke of York and Admiral Montagu on his behalf.
38. Bodleian Ms. Carte 214, f. 194, RB to Ormonde from Paris, 14 May 1660. He realises that to benefit from 'the glorious sun' he must first approach 'benefic planets', the greatest of which is Ormonde.
39. BL Add Ms 78221, f. 105 JE to RB, 14 May 1660; BL Add Ms 78192, f. 99, RB to EH, 14 May 1660.
40. BL RP 5460, JE to Clifford, 23 Nov. 1670.
41. Walter Pope, *Life of Seth Ward* . . . (1699), 19–20. Scarburgh was generous, 'always accessible to all learned Men but more particularly to the distressed Royalists & . . . the Scholars ejected out of either of the Universities'.
42. *Lorenzo Magalotti at the Court of Charles II*, 27–9.
43. *Diary* iii 246–7, iv, 409; see Hutton, *Charles II.*
44. BL Add Ms 78192, f. 99, RB to EH, from Paris, 14 May 1660.
45. BL Add Ms 78614, JE petition to Sir Philip Warwick, 18 July 1662, an addendum to another for his father-in-law. Evelyn's pamphlets included *The Late News or Message from Bruxels Unmasked*, a retort to Marchmont Needham's *News from Brussels*, 'a wicked forged paper . . . to defame his Majesties person, Virtues, & render him odious'. See *Diary* iii 243; *Writings*, 111–23.
46. *Diary* iii 264. Sir Richard Browne had known Anne Hyde well, when she was a lady-in-waiting to the king's sister, Mary, in Paris in 1656.
47. He had turned it down previously, being unprepared to swear the oath of allegiance to the Commonwealth.
48. [LB] BL Add Ms 78298, f. 106, JE to Robert Spencer, 25 Aug. 1660.
49. Gabriel Naudé, author of the French original of *Instructions for Erecting of a Library*, was a protégé of both Richelieu and Mazarin, while Paul Fréart de Chambray, whose *Parallèle de l'Architecture* Evelyn was preparing for publication, was close to the court.
50. [LB] BL Add Ms 78298, f. 109, JE to ST, 8 April 1661; Tuke's commonplace book (with dates in 1656 and 1659) shows his interests paralleled Evelyn's with extracts from Bacon, Descartes, Hobbes's *Leviathan* and Montaigne: see BL Add Ms 78423.
51. Sorbière, *A Journey to England.*
52. Jardine, *On a Grander Scale: The Outstanding Career of Sir Christopher Wren* (2002), 176.
53. *Diary* iii 266–7 n. 6. He paid the full £7.4s to cover the period until September 1663, and continued to be a scrupulous contributor. See also *ibid.* 332 and n. 1.
54. *Journal des Voyages de M de Monconys* (1666) and his description is echoed by Sorbière's.

55. See *ODNB* and above p. xxx.
56. Evelyn, *Acetaria*, dedication; *Bray* iii 346–52, JE to William Wotton, 30 March 1696.
57. *Diary* iii 336. The crest was a golden eagle holding the royal coat of arms which also ornamented the society's own armorial shield, supported by 'two Talbots, argent'. See Aubrey, *Brief Lives*, 402.
58. RS Cl.P/3i/1; i, 104–5; [LB] BL Add Ms 78298, f. 108, JE to Dr John Wilkins, 17 Feb. 1660/1.
59. See Griffiths, 'John Evelyn and the Print'. The title of Bosse's work was *Traité des manières de graver en taille douce sur l'airain*.
60. Favi arrived in Paris in 1645, a close friend of the inventor, Petit. He 'neglected nothing' and continuously sent immense volumes of his discoveries back to Italy. His efforts promised an *encyclopédie* – a century before Diderot's – and must have seemed a sympathetic endeavour to Evelyn.
61. *Diary* iii 276 n. 6, 279.
62. Soon after, Fanshawe was sent to Portugal and Spain on diplomatic missions. He died in Madrid in 1665.
63. BL Add Ms 78435, ST to ME from the Palais Royal, Paris, 16 April 1661.
64. *Diary* iii 284.
65. *SP* ii 87–8, 'which I am very sorry for'.
66. *A Panegyric to Charles the Second Presented to His Majestie the XXIII of April, being the Day of his Coronation MDCLX1*. See BL Add Ms 78679, f. 35, Mordaunt to JE, 23 April 1661.
67. RS Copybook of Council Minutes, 1663–82, f. 23, 20 July 1663; *Diary* iii 293 n.1.
68. Naudé's volume was first published in 1626 and reissued in 1644. Evelyn put his translation aside when Richard died. See the earl of Crawford and Balcarres, 'Gabriel Naudé and John Evelyn: with some Notes on the Mazarinades', *Library* S4-XII (1932), 383–408.
69. *Bray* iii 135–6, undated petition.
70. *Hobbes; The Correspondence* ii 519, translation of letter 142, 2/12 May 1661; Hobbes, who never became a Fellow, sent him information on the experiments at Gresham College: see *ibid.*, 526, translation of letter 146.
71. The first royal charter was given on 15 July 1662, followed by a second on 22 April 1663. *Royal Society Record* (1940), 236, 262. Clarendon was made an Honorary Fellow in 1665.
72. *SP* vi 252.
73. [LB] BL Add Ms 78298, f.110 JE to JT, 9 July 1661.
74. The play was an adaptation of Cowley's *The Guardian* (1641), the hero a less than perfect royalist colonel. BL Add Ms 78300, f. 13, ME to JE, 27 Dec. [also marked Sept.] 1661.
75. BL Add Ms 78678, f. 37, Chesterfield to JE, 19 July 1662.
76. *Diary* iii 275 nn. 5, 6. Evelyn claimed Lady Scroope had obtained the post of second dresser to the queen irregularly, believing that the king had promised Mary a position in the queen's household.
77. *Ibid.* iii 294 n. 3.
78. *Ibid.* iii 297–300; 297 n. 4.
79. See *Writings*, 157–72. In *Tyrannus* Evelyn argues that the use of home-produced cloth, not 'Silk, foreign Stuffs, or Cloth', would 'many thousand hands imploy! How glorious be to our Prince, when he should behold all his Subjects clad with the Production of his own Country.'
80. [LB] BL Add Ms 78298, f. 114, JE to HB, 7 Oct. 1661; f. 115, 4 Dec. 1661.

Chapter 10: City and Country

1. Evelyn, *Fumifugium* (reprinted by the National Society for Clean Air 1972); see also *Writings*, 125–6. The words are those of the Emperor Augustus, *ibid.*, 131, n. 10.

2. See Mark Jenner, 'The Politics of London Air'; John Evelyn's *Fumigugium* and the Restoration', *Historical Review* 38:3 (1995): 'it would be extraordinary if a text published in 1661 and dedicated to Charles II had been entirely devoid of political significance.' Jenner also points out that Robert Boyle had examined air in his *New Experiments Physico-Mechanical, Touching the Spring of the Air* (1660).

3. *The Garden* quoted Keith Thomas, *Man and the Natural World: Changing Attitude in England 1500–1800* (1983), 246.

4. The commercial possibilities of sulphur-free fuel intrigued Evelyn; he visited the ironmonger Sir John Winter's novel coking works in Greenwich in 1656 (Winter patented the coking process in 1661). In *Sylva* he described a concoction of charcoal dust and loam from Maastricht. See *Diary* iii 180–1. The king called on his knowledge when fuel was in short supply after the Great Fire; *ibid.* 486–7.

5. Samuel Hartlib, *Legacy of Husbandry* (1655 edition), 136–7, mentioning lung disease and consumption caused by coal smoke, which even rotted iron casements.

6. Jenner, 'The Politics of London Air'; John Graunt's study of the *Bills of Mortality* was published in 1662, dedicated to Sir Robert Moray, and written with help from Sir William Petty (in his capacity as a physician). Evelyn may have learned about Graunt's hove demographic work ahead of publication from Moray or Petty.

7. He identified a site near Greenwich and Plumstead marshes, where prevailing westerly winds would spare the royal palace – and incidentally Deptford too. He also pointed out that burial outside the city walls would help improve the air.

8. [HP] 33/1/73A–74B, Robert Wood to SH, from Dublin, 23 March 1661.

9. See *Tyrannus*, in *Writings*, 163–72. Evelyn claimed he had 'once intended' to collect a volume of essays, no doubt treading in the footsteps of Bacon. Editors have found several quotations from Montaigne in *Tyrannus*.

10. *Diary* iii 296–7, 310. De Beer could find no such bill.

11. Machiavelli, *Discourses* ed. Bernard Crick (1986), Book 1, discourse 26. Sir Nicholas Crisp was claiming land from Browne and Evelyn to provide an extra dock, but ultimately decided against it.

12. *Diary* iii 300–1, 313. The eventual design was Webb's but only one block was built, in the mid-1660s, the central part of the surviving King Charles block.

13. Brendan O'Hehir, *Harmony from Discords: A Life of Sir John Denham* (1968), 154–5. Denham claimed the king's promise dated from September 1649. He had 'some knowledge in the Theory of Architecture; but nothing of the practique' according to John Webb, Inigo Jones's able assistant who hoped for the post.

14. *Diary* iii 288.

15. Colvin, *History of the King's Works*, 457. Hugh May's elder brother Adrian became the nominal surveyor of the royal gardens, on a salary of £200 and a house in the new St James's Park, its chimneys adjusted to provide nesting places for the king's storks. They were cousins of the royal favourite Babs (Baptist) May.

16. [LB] BL Add Ms 78298, f. 107v, JE to Tuke, 3 Feb 1660/1, refers to 'some accidents (new, and on this period unexpected) [that] have their little Paroxysmes upon me; which to a Spirit unaccustom'd, immerg'd in the world, and giving hostages to fortune, passe not without their effects.' See *Diary* iii 262 n. 4, 356. The matter was not resolved until May 1663.

17. *Diary* iii 268. It was subtitled 'The History and Art of Chalcography and Engraving in Copper with an Ample Enumeration of the Most Renowned Masters and their Works'. Among several digressions was one about the recent degradation of 'kings and heros', their heads being used as signs on 'every Tavern and Tippling-house'.

18. The same man, 'A' [Abraham] Hertochs, engraved the plates for the *French Gardiner*.

19. See Griffiths, *The Print in Stuart Britain*, 211–12. The painting is no longer believed to be by Ribera. Prince Rupert seems to have only perfected the tools, the invention being that of Ludwig von Siegen whom he met in the household of Elector William of Hesse-Cassel.

20. BL Eve a.19, 145. The demonstration also showed a drawback to mezzotint: 'the plates last not so long under the rolling press.'

21. BL Add Ms 78312, JB to JE, 21 Oct. 1668.

22. [LB] BL Add Ms 78299, f. 59, JE to John Harwood, 1 Aug. 1689.

23. The Hobbes title was *Problemata Physica*. He also wrote 'dans le Reys-Verhael il est souvent question de John Evelyn' which can be paraphrased as 'abroad people are often asking about John Evelyn'.

24. 'Celluy de Monsieur Evelyin est docte et de grandissime recherche et j'ay eu beaucoup de saitisfaction en le lisant, sans compter celle là de m'y avoir inséré si honorablement. And: 'Il me semble que je comprens assez la méthode nouuelle du Prince Rupert quand je considère cette teste de sa façon et le peu d'ouuerture que Monsieur Evelin nous a donné. C'est un merveilleux abbrégé en des choses ou il y a beaucoup d'ombres et fait un très bel effect.' Constantjyn Huygens, *Oeuvres Complètes* iv 200 (letter 1046) CH to RM, 18 Aug. 1662; 216 (letter 1055) RM to CH, 1 Sept. 1662.

25. BL Add Ms 78344, part 4, f. 116, 15 Oct. 1662.

26. Evelyn described him as 'a builder'. As Thomas Wriothesley he had embarked on the leasehold development of Bloomsbury Square, close to his mansion Southampton (later Bedford) House. Evelyn called it 'a little town'; *Diary* iii 398.

27. *Writings*, 173–4. Printing was ordered in March 1663.

28. Mayling Stubbs, 'John Beale, Philosophic Gardener of Herefordshire, Part II: The Improvement of Agriculture and Trade in the Royal Society 1663–1683', *Annals of Science* 46 (1989), 323–63; see also *Writings*, 195 n. 38.

29. BL Add Ms 78317, ff. 1–2, SH to JE, 14 April 1660; ff. 8–9, 14/4 Oct 1660; ff. 12–13, 26 Nov. 1660. He asked if he could help him unfreeze payment of his pension and arrears, knowing 'you have many worthy and special Friends [in the Council of State] as well as in the Royal Court'. For Beale's correspondence passing through Axe Yard, see Upcott, *Miscellaneous Writings*, item 28.

30. CSP Dom 413, quoted in R. G. Albion, *Forests and Sea Power: The Timber Problem of the Royal Navy 1652–1862* (1926); Kevin Sharpe, 'Restoration and Reconstitution' in C. MacLeod and J. M. Alexander eds, *Painted Ladies: Women at the Court of Charles II* (2001), 10–23.

31. Hunter, *Science and the Shape of Orthodoxy* 95.

32. *Writings*, 347–408 (after the 1706 edition). Pierre Morin, *Remarques Nécéssaires pour la Culture des Fleurs, Diligemment Observées par P Morin avec un Catalogue des Plantes Rares Qui Se Trouvent à Present dans son Jardin* (1658, posthumous publication).

33. BL Add Ms 78318, f. 6, Richard Chiswell (printer) to JE, 20 Jan. 1680/1, telling him that a T. Langford hoped he would write a prefatory letter to his *Plain and Full Instructions to Raise All Sort of Fruit-trees That Prosper in England* (1681). Evelyn did so.

34. Harris, 'The Letter-books of Mary Evelyn', 209.

35. BL Add Ms 78435, ST to ME from Norwich, 21 Sept. [1663]; 28 Oct. [1663]; BL Add Ms 78306, f. 116, ST to JE, from Norwich, 30 Nov. 1663.

36. *SP* iv 8 n. 2, 16. Samuel and Elizabeth Pepys saw the first performance at the Duke of York's Theatre in early January 1663. He pronounced it 'the best, for the variety and the most excellent continuance of the plot to the very end, that ever I saw or think ever shall': nor, to his relief, did it have a trace of ribaldry. He was back, with a colleague, a fortnight later. He saw it when it returned to the repertory at the Duke of York's theatre in late January 1669 and again at Whitehall in February; *SP* ix 429, 450.

37. *Diary* iii 350. Evelyn went to see 'my kindsman's' comedy at the Duke's Theatre, 'so universally tooke as it was acted for some weekes every day'. The printed text included many complimentary verses. Evelyn's included the lines 'Your Head has brush'd the Sphears,/Then 'tis no wonder if you Charm our Ears'. Others were provided by Abraham Cowley, Jasper (Gaspar) Needham and Christopher Wase. The postscript by 'MEIpomene' may have been by Mary Evelyn. It concluded: 'Good writers (like good Christians) never have/ Their state of Glory till th'are in the Grave.'

38. *Diary* iii 326, 355. John was removed from the Howards after many months: ''til for feare of their perverting him, in the popish religion, I was forc'd to take him home.' Pepys believed Howard was 'no rigid papist', having said (of a servant) 'that he had rather have an honest protestant then a knavish catholique': *SP* ix 28.

39. BL Add Ms 78435, ST to ME, 28 Oct. 1663, 'about the contrivance of his garden.' BL Add Ms 78306, f. 109, ST to JT, from Norwich, 28 Sept. 1663; f. 111, 7 Oct. 1663.

40. BL Ms Sloane 1906, 2 and 16 Jan. 1664. Edward Browne visited 'Mr Howard's garden in Cunsford' on the latter date.

41. See Ernest A. Kent, 'The Houses of the Dukes of Norfolk in Norwich', *Journal of the Norfolk and Norwich Archaeological Society* xxiv (1931), 73–87.

42. BL Sloan Ms 2903, ff. 104–5, 30 July 1663; *Diary* iii 357, 364.

43. BL Add Ms 78306, f. 115, ST to JE, 23 Oct. 1663; Sharpe, *Restoration and Reconstitution.*

44. [LB] BL Add Ms 78298, f. 124v, JE to WP, 30 March 1664.

45. I am indebted to Robert Harding and Antony Griffiths for examining *Micrographia* with me. They both noticed that a number of the plates combine etching with engraving but gently quashed my hope that Wenceslaus Hollar might have been a contributor.

46. *SP* vii, 213, 22 July 1666. Ornament should be 'a little mixture of Statues or pots' and flowers set 'in a little plat by themselfs'. Orchards should have 'Walls built Circularly, one within another, to the South, on purpose for fruit, and leave the walking-garden only for that use'.

47. In 1663 Shaw was granted the lease of the crown manor of Eltham, where remnants of a palace, largely demolished during the Commonwealth, served as farm buildings.

48. A print of the interior, still in the house, now the Royal Blackheath Golf Club, shows it with a top light.

49. *Diary* iii 375–6; B. Cherry and N. Pevsner, eds, *Buildings of England: South London* (1983), 302–4; *ODNB.* Shaw fell from his immensely profitable position as customs farmer soon after Clarendon's disgrace. The family retained Eltham Lodge into the nineteenth century. See also BL Add Ms 15948, f. 121, Thomas Povey to JE, about his advice on a 'cabinet garden', [1665] and f. 123, John Shaw to JE, 18 Feb. 1666, about an aviary.

50. In 1672 Evelyn visited Berkeley House 'or rather palace', also by May, and again pointed to its inconvenience, although it is 'very well built' and 'has many noble rooms'. Pratt admired Eltham Lodge, noting how the thickness of the brickwork was graded from three stretchers in the basement to two on the first floor. He also took detailed notes on the construction of the chimney stacks; Gunther, *The Architecture of Sir Roger Pratt*, 130, 232, 234.

51. Sally Jeffery, '"The Flower of all the private gentlemens palaces in england": Sir Stephen Fox's "Extraordinarily fine" Garden at Chiswick', *Garden History* 32:1 (Spring 2004), 2005, 1–19.

52. Wotton, *The Elements of Architecture*, Preface.

53. *Bray* iii 365, JE to Dr Richard Bentley (royal librarian at St James's), 20 Jan. 1697. Harris and Savage, *British Architectural Books*, 499.

54. *Notes of Me*, 129–30.

55. Gunther, *The Architecture of Sir Roger Pratt*, 157. Pratt may have come to Clarendon's notice through his brother-in-law Sir Charles Cotterell, Charles I's master of ceremonies, or they may have met abroad. May played a part, signing off Richard Cleere's bills for carved 'Bunches of Leaves & berryes' and 'double Golosse' (guilloche) at Clarendon House.
56. *Ibid.*, 11, Edward Pratt to RP, 29 Oct. 1666.
57. Colvin, *A Biographical Dictionary*, 560, 778 with his work at Coleshill. Sally Jeffery believes that Pratt, as a novice, received considerable assistance and suggests that it was provided by Inigo Jones, who died at Somerset House in 1652 (personal communication). The house was burned and then demolished in 1952.
58. Ryston Hall, Norfolk. Notebook C, f. 9 'coach to ye Ptrs funeral' (omitted from Gunther's transcription).
59. Richard Ollard, *Clarendon and his Friends* (1988), 253–6.
60. Clarendon described it as such in his will. For Evelyn's visit, see *Diary* iii 379–80.
61. *Bray* iii 177–8, JE to Viscount Cornbury, 20 Jan. 1665/6.
62. See Gunther, *The Architecture of Sir Roger Pratt*; *Diary* iii 470.
63. BL Add Ms 78678, f. 44, HH to JE, from Oxford, 24 Jan. 1665/6.
64. John Newman, 'Hugh May, Clarendon and Cornbury' in J. Bold and E. Chaney, eds, *English Architecture Public and Private, Essays for Kerry Downes* (1993).
65. BL Add Ms 78431, JE to JE jr, 23 June 1681.
66. BL Add Ms 78678, f. 45, HH to JE, from Oxford, 17 Jan. 1665/6; Ollard, *Clarendon and his Friends*, 250–1; BL Add Ms 78678, f. 44, HH to JE, from Oxford, 24 Jan. 1665/6.
67. *Diary* iii 385. He claimed his advice was accepted, without revealing what it was.
68. BL Add Ms 78431, f. 22, 19 May 1668.
69. *Diary* iii 531–6. Evelyn was dismayed that vandals had already desecrated the Arundel marbles, set into the walls near the theatre, and suggested that holly be planted to protect them – a very modern horticultural ploy. See Mavis Batey, *Oxford Gardens* (1982), 49.
70. BL Add Ms 78221, f. 124 and f. 129, 9 Dec. 1665 and 20 Jan. 1665/6; see Batey, *Oxford Gardens* 52–9.
71. In the early eighteenth century the park trees at Hall Barn were mature, suggesting that it must have been laid out well before. Edmund Waller, who celebrated the planting of St James's Park in verse, must have discussed his project with Evelyn, whom he continued to meet over the years.
72. *Diary* iii 386–7.

Chapter 11: The Active Life

1. [LB] BL Add Ms 78298, f. 130, JE to Edward Hyde, 1 Nov. 1664. See *Diary* iii 386–8, where he neatly conflates his talk with the king and his appointment to the commission. For a fuller account of this episode see Gillian Darley, '"Action to the Purpose": Evelyn, Greenwich and the Sick and Wounded Seamen' in *Milieu*.
2. BL Add Ms 78392, f. 14, 1664.
3. *Diary* iii 630. No doubt a comment added later.
4. BL Add Ms 78306, ff. 121–2, ST to JE from Paris, 14 March 1664/5.
5. *Ibid.*, ff. 123–4, 13 May 1665.
6. *Diary* iii 371.
7. BL Add Ms 78431, JE to ME, 8 Sept. 1665.
8. *Ibid.*, 22 Sept. 1665.
9. *Ibid.*, 20 Oct. 1665.
10. *Ibid.*, 28 Oct. 1665.

11. BL Add Ms 78300, ff. 15–16, ME to JE, from Wotton, 2 Sept. 1665; BL Add Ms 78431, JE to ME, 4 Dec. 1665.
12. J. J. Keevil, *Medicine and the Navy 1200–1900,* ii, 1649–1714 (1958). See also Darley, '"Action to the Purpose"'.
13. *Diary* iii 439.
14. BL Add Ms 78320, BR to JE, from Portsmouth, 4 May 1665.
15. Library of the Society of Antiquaries,199/ter/22, 25 Oct. 1666.
16. *The Letters of Samuel Pepys* ed. Guy de la Bedoyere (2006), letter 41, SP to WC, 14 Oct. 1665; SP iv 253.
17. [LB] BL Add Ms 78298, f. 146, 24 Sept. 1665.
18. BL Add Ms 78320, Lord Albemarle to Lord Arlington, 4 Nov. 1665.
19. *Diary* ii 43 n. 2, 45 n. 6.
20. *SP* vi 235; *Diary* iii 427.
21. *Diary* iii 428.
22. BL Add Ms 78302, RE to JE, from Wotton, n.d. (pencil note 'early 1666').
23. BL Add Ms 78306, RB to JE, [illeg.] Jan. 1665/6.
24. *Particular Friends* [A 19] JE to SP, 31 Jan. 1665/6.
25. *Ibid.* [A 25] 26 March 1666.
26. [LB] BL Add Ms 78298, f. 109, JE to John Wilkins, Dean of Ripon, 12 March 1665/6.
27. Keevil, *Medicine and the Navy,* 106.
28. BL Add Ms 78306, ff. 145–6, ST to JE, from Paris, 2 March 1666/7.
29. *Diary* iii 484–7.
30. *Particular Friends* [A27] SP to JE, 8 Feb. 1667/8; also fig. 4.
31. Keevil, *Medicine and the Navy,* 109.
32. Aylmer, *The Crown's Servants,* 213.
33. CSP Dom 1662, 622, para. 110.
34. *Diary* iii 442–3. Lord Berkeley of Stratton, Sir John Duncombe, Thomas Chicheley, Col. William Legge and Edward Sherburne were the other commissioners. George Wharton was secretary.
35. BL Add Ms 78312, JB to JE, 24 May 1666; 23 July 1666.
36. BL Add Ms 78684, f. 10, JG to JE, from Frome, 15 Jan. 1666/7.
37. Abraham Cowley, *Several Discourses by Way of Essays in Verse and Prose* ed. H. C. Minchin (1904) 60 *et passim.*
38. *Diary* iii 330–1, 354, 356.
39. *Ibid.* iii 377–8, 582. He came twice in the summer of 1664 and again in 1671.
40. Leith-Ross, 'The Garden of John Evelyn at Deptford'.
41. [LB] BL Add Ms 78299, ff. 66–7v, JE to Flower Hyde, Lady Clarendon, undated but April–June 1690. He added the 'Chertsean Platane' to a poem originally drafted for Cowley himself: see [LB] BL Add Ms 78298, f. 157v, 24 Aug. 1666. He uses it as a conscious anachronism, since the 'London Plane' was only introduced a year or two before Cowley died.
42. See Cowley, *Several Discourses.*
43. BL Add Ms 78316, f. 90, TH to JE, 30 May 1668; Jenny Robinson, 'New Light on Sir Thomas Hanmer, *Garden History* 16:1 (Spring 1988), 1–70.
44. Brian Vickers, ed., *Public and Private Life in the Seventeenth Century: the Mackenzie–Evelyn Debate* (1986),.
45. [LB] BL Add Ms 78298, f. 157v, JE to AC, 24 Aug. 1666; f. 164, 12 March 1666/7.
46. Joseph Levine, *Between the Ancients and the Moderns* (1999), 8–10.
47. Quoted by Shapin, *A Social History of Truth,* 189.
48. BL Add Ms 78317, f. 69, GM to JE, 5 March 1666/7. Draft answer from JE, f. 70v, 15 March 1666/7.
49. BL Add Ms 78304, f. 60, GE to JE, 'at Mr Carters house', 31 Jan. 1670/1.
50. Vickers, *Public and Private Life,* 118.

51. BL Add Ms 78314, ff. 10–11, Bohun to JE, 13 March 1666/7.

52. BL Add Ms 15858, f. 81, RM to JE, from Yester, 14 Jan. 1667/8.

53. *SP* viii, 26 April 1667.

54. BL Add Ms. 78392, f. 36 'The Legend of Philaretes & the Pearl'.

55. *SP* vii 49, 112.

56. *SP* viii 181–6.

57. [LB] BL Add Ms 78298, f. 168, JE to ST, 26 Sept. 1667.

58. See *Writings*, 16; BL Add Ms 78306, f. 115, ST to JE, from Norwich, 23 Oct. 1663; *Bray* iii 143, Thomas Barlow to JE, 21 June 1664 congratulated him on his task.

59. BL Add Ms 78539, ME to Bohun, 17 July 1668; *Diary* iii 585. One godparent was the Countess of Huntingdon, avowedly Anglican.

60. BL Add Ms 78304, f. 52, GE to JE, from Wotton, 30 Aug. 1667.

61. This genre of poems possibly began with Edmund Waller's *Instructions to a Painter* (1666) which was addressed to the king. See Andrew Marvell, *The Complete Poems* ed. Elizabeth Story Donno (1996), 279–81.

62. *Diary* iii 493–4.

63. *Ibid.* 502.

64. BL Add Ms 78329, f. 79.

65. *Bray* iii 431–4, to the countess of Sunderland, 23 Dec. 1688.

66. [LB] BL Add Ms 78298, f. 186, JE to Thomas Clifford, 14 July 1671.

67. *Hatton Correspondence*, Camden Society n.s. 22 (1878), i 47, CL to Hatton, 7 Aug. 1665.

68. *Buckingham: Public and Private Man*, ed. Christine Phipps (1985), p?

69. *Bray* iii 146, JE to Sprat, 31 Oct. 1664. He is playing on one of her own titles: *Playes Written by the Thrice Noble, Illustrious and Excellent Princess, the Lady Marchioness of Newcastle* (1662).

70. For an entertaining full account of the visit, see Kate Whitaker, *Mad Madge: Margaret Cavendish, Duchess of Newcaste, Royalist, Writer & Romantic* (2004), 302–4.

71. BL Add Ms 78539, ME to Bohun, n.d. [1667] also see F. Harris, 'The Letter-books of Mary Evelyn', quoting a letter from ME to Bohun: if 'one of a thousand [women] aspires a little higher, her fate commonly exposes her to wonder, but adds little of esteem'.

72. [LB] BL Add Ms 78298, f. 164, JE to AC, 12 March 1666/7.

73. [LB] BL Add Ms 78298, f. 170, JE to Joseph Glanville, 24 June 1668.

74. BL Add Ms 78539, ME to Bohun, 3 Feb. [1667/8].

75. BL Add Ms 78434, WG to ME, 6 Aug. 1667.

76. *Diary* iii 364–5. Philips was at Sayes Court from October 1663 to February 1665.

77. BL Add Ms 78539, ME to Bohun, 3 Feb. [1667/8]; *Diary* iii 474. Before leaving for Oxford, John was presented to the chancellor of the university, the earl of Clarendon.

78. BL Add Ms 78314, f. 20, Ralph Bohun to JE, n.d. [1668?].

Chapter 12: Paris and London

1. [LB] BL Add Ms 78298, f. 136v, 4 April 1665. Although Evelyn felt obliged to dedicate his translation to the current surveyor-general, Denham, the 1707 edition carried a fulsome tribute to Wren, dated ten years earlier.

2. Wren to Ralph Bathurst in Oxford: Lydia M. Soo, *Wren's 'Tracts' on Architecture and Other Writings* (1998), 93–4. The queen mother's party left England on 29 June 1665.

3. 'Mons Abbe Charles introduc'd me to the Acquaintance of Bernini, who shew'd me his Designs of the Louvre, and of the King's Statue', *ibid.*, 103.

4. BL Add Ms 78306, ff. 123–4, ST to JE, from Paris, 13 May 1665; f. 134, 13 Jan. 1665/6. For a fuller account, see Jardine, *On a Grander Scale* 244–5.
5. See Soo, *Wren's 'Tracts'*, 103–6.
6. BL Add Ms 78435, Mary Tuke to ME, 16 July 1665.
7. BL Add Ms 78306, ff. 129–30, ST to JE, 23 [?28] Oct. 1665; BL Add Ms 78435, MT to ME, from Paris, 10 Jan. 1665/6; BL Add Ms 78306, f. 134, ST to JE, from Paris, 13 Jan. 1665/6; f. 139, 10 May 1666.
8. See Gillian Tindall, *The Man Who Drew London: Wenceslaus Hollar in Reality and Imagination* (2002), 128.
9. *SP* vii 297.
10. *Diary* iii 448–9 and nn.; Gordon Higgott, 'The Fabric to 1670', in D. Keene et al., eds, *St Paul's: The Cathedral Church of London* (2004), 183–6; Soo, *Wren's 'Tracts'*, 34–5. The committee included two churchmen, Humphrey Henchman, Bishop of London, and William Sancroft, Dean of St Paul's as well as two public officials, Thomas Chichely and Henry Slingsby, respectively commissioner of the ordnance and master of the mint.
11. Both Pratt and Wren had submitted written reports. Wren's was dated 7 May 1666; see Soo, *Wren's 'Tracts'*, 48–55; Higgott, 'The Fabric to 1670', 184–5 and plates 105 and 106.
12. *Particular Friends* [C41] JE to SP, 31 July 1688.
13. *Diary* iii 450 *et passim*. De Beer corrects his facts. Later, when teasing Mary Evelyn about living far from the city, Ralph Bohun wrote: 'had you not seen the flames you had believ'd the city still standing.'
14. BL Add Ms 78431, RB to ME, 4 Sept. 1666 at '4 a clock'.
15. *Diary* iii 463. The queen, dressed in her riding outfit, with 'hat & feather & horse-mans Coate' soon left them to take the air.
16. *Writings* 333–45; see *Londinium Redivivum*. There were two versions (the second was drawn up for the Royal Society) but neither survives. It is known from a published version of 1756.
17. [LB] BL Add Ms 78298, f. 159v, JE to ST, 27 Sept. 1666.
18. Evelyn, as often, was floating ideas ahead of his time. St George's burial ground in Holborn, the first Anglican burial ground to be detached from a place of worship, was not founded until 1713.
19. Oldenburg Correspondence iii 226–7 (566), HO to Robert Boyle, 10 Sept. 1666.
20. *Ibid.* iii 230–1 (568), HO to Robert Boyle, 18 Sept. 1666.
21. Thomas Birch, *History of the Royal Society* (1756–7) ii 115, 19 Sept. 1666 quoted by Adrian Tinniswood, *His Invention So Fertile* (2003), 199–200. Robert Hooke's plan was presented to the Royal Society. Peter Mills prepared his for City officials, while two more came from mapmaker Richard Newcourt and a Captain Valentine.
22. [LB] BL Add Ms 78298, f.159v, JE to ST, 27 Sept. 1666.
23. Oldenburg Correspondence iii 238–9 (572 and 575), 2 and 16 Oct. 1666.
24. Jardine, *The Curious Life of Robert Hooke*, 140–1. By March Hooke, still the Royal Society's Curator, was officially designated surveyor for the City of London.
25. *SP* vii 384–5.
26. BL Add Ms 78312, JB to JE, 16 Feb. 1666/7.
27. Michael Cooper *'A More Beautiful City': Rober Hooke and the Rebuilding of London after the Great Fire* (2003), 132.
28. Oldenburg Correspondence iii 299–300 (590), JE to HO, 22 Dec. 1666.
29. CSP Dom 109, Aug. 1667, 431. Hollar asked Evelyn to intercede with Joseph Williamson, since he believed himself appointed ichnographer to the king, had paid his fees, but 'received no benefit nor salary to encourage him to finish his great work of the city' and now his great map was 'in danger of being unfinished'.
30. T. F. Reddaway, *Rebuilding of London* (1940), 73 n. 1.

31. *SP* vii 300–1.
32. Birch, *History* ii 117, 24 Oct. 1666.
33. Stephen Inwood, *The Man Who Knew Too Much* (2002), 98.
34. Sir Robert Moray's (lost) history of masonry was written while he was with the court in Salisbury during the plague. See Oldenburg Correspondence ii 507 (410), RM to HO, 16 Sept. 1665.
35. Kiviet was Van Tromp's brother-in-law and was knighted by Charles II in 1667. *Diary* iii 471.
36. Alan Cox, 'Bricks to Build a Capital' in Hermione Hobhouse and Ann Saunders, eds, *Good and Proper Materials* (1989).
37. Bodleian Ms Carte 42, f. 711, the king to the duke of Ormonde, 8 Sept. 1662; CSP Dom 1673, 337.
38. BL Add Ms 78539, ME to Bohun, 19 April 166[?7].
39. BL Add Ms 78317 (all letters to JE), f. 79, from Kiviet, 22/2 Nov. 1667; f. 80, from Gabriel Sylvius, from Whitehall, Dec. 1667; f. 81, n.d., '6 in the evening'; f. 82, from Kiviet, 1 Jan. 1667/8; f. 84, n.d., illegible, with a reference to 'M Moorlandt' (Samuel Morland).
40. CSP Dom, 1 May 1667, 67.
41. BL Add Ms 78435, Bohun to ME, 17 June 1668, commiserating on the extravagant failure; Tinniswood, *His Invention So Fertile,* 248; BL Add Ms. 78341, ff. 88–9. Kiviet was back in Rotterdam by 1673.
42. Reddaway, *Rebuilding of London*, 129.
43. BL Add Ms 78313, JB to JE, 13 Aug. 1670. If someone bought a suitable piece of ground for the Royal Society to develop it might be as profitable as Covent Garden, 'which I believe is by this time a faire Jewel in the E of Bedford's coronet'.
44. Hunter, *Establishing the New Science*, 158–9, quoting from Thomas Sprat[t]'s *History of the Royal Society* (1667) where he suggested that Chelsea was ancillary accommodation to provide space for gardening and agriculture as well as all experiments 'that belong to the Water'.
45. *Diary* iii 472–3 n. 3; *SP* viii 6–7 n. 1; *Diary* iv 140–4 for the eventual transfer of the library to Gresham College.
46. Some of the Arundel Marbles were dispersed, including some to Hall Barn, although apparently after Evelyn's contemporary Edmund Waller's day.
47. *Diary* iii 495–6, 561–2; iv 111. The exact chronology for Evelyn's redesign of Albury is unclear, the dates in the diary are often inaccurate.
48. Michael Charlesworth, 'A Plan by John Evelyn for Henry Howard's Garden at Albury Park, Surrey', in T. O'Malley and J. Wolschke-Bulmahn, eds, *John Evelyn's 'Elysium Britannicum' and European Gardening* (1998), Appendix, 289–93; Aubrey, *Natural History and Antiquities of Surrey* iv 69.
49. Bodleian MS Eng. Lett. c 196, f. 182, JE to Edmund Gibson, 10 July 1694; *Diary* iv 558; iii 593. Nothing angered Evelyn more than Howard's marriage to his mistress, Jane Bickerton.
50. There was a lower hedge 'running along from east to west. From this hedge there go up the hill, at right angles, several other hedges, which divide the land here into distinct gardens, or orchards.' They sound like the 'palisades' in *Fumifugium*. The canal had already shrunk to a stream but the pool and water courses were still fed by the spring. See William Cobbett, *Rural Rides* ed. George Woodcock (1967), 98–100.
51. Charles Howard, at nearby Deepdene, cut a similar passage under a hill. John Aubrey drew it in plan in 1673. See Small, 'John Evelyn and the Garden of Epicurus', which suggests that the (pin-hole) view was designed to be viewed from the outside in, rather than *vice versa* as argued by Chambers, 'The Tomb in the Landscape'.

52. Evelyn, *Numismata*, 162. Evelyn's description of 'what he is still about, and advancing under his Direction, will speak and perpetuate his Memory as long as one Stone remains upon another in this Nation' tends to suggest that Wren was the executive architect, however much Hooke was also involved.

53. David J. Crankshaw, 'Community, City and Nation, 1540–1714', in Keene et al., *St Pauls*, 60–8.

54. BL Add Ms 78434, WG to ME, 17 Nov. 1668.

55. BL Add Ms 78306, ff. 121–2, ST to JE, from Paris, 14 March 1665.

56. BL Add Ms 78305, f. 45, WG to JE, from Paris, 10 April 1669; f. 49, 14 June 1669.

57. *Particular Friends* [A28] JE to SP, 21 Aug. 1669.

58. *Ibid.* [A29] SP to JE, 2 Nov. 1669.

59. Tomalin, *Samuel Pepys*, 283–4.

60. *Particular Friends* [E14] SP to JE, 24 Dec. 1701.

Chapter 13: Perpetual Motion

1. *Bray* iv 31–2; see Harris, *The Letter-books of Mary Evelyn*, 209–10.

2. *Diary* iv 37; see BL Add Ms 78539, ME to Bohun, 21 May [1668?] where she tells him she had been continually entertaining 'persons of different humor, Age and sence, not only at meales, and affternoone, or the time of a civill visit, but from morning till night'; *Particular Friends* [C 7] JE to SP, 'Wednesday-night after the Musique', 7 and 8 July 1680.

3. BL Add Ms 78539, ME to Bohun, 12 April 1668.

4. JB ?to HO? re 1670 edn Sylva, so obliging . . .

5. The book is *Campanella Revived* (1670), subtitled 'Whether the Virtuosi There Do Not Pursue the Projects of Campanella for the Reducing England into Popery'. See Oldenburg Correspondence vii [1482], 8 July 1670, nn. 2 and 3, 57–8.

6. CSP Dom 28, Addenda 1660–85; 28 Feb. 1670, 92 JE to JW from Sayes Court; 30 May 1670, 242 ex Whitehall. It brought a salary of £80.

7. BL Add Ms 78301, ff. 9–10, JE jr to JE, from Wotton, 18 Sept. 1671; Gunning's marking of Christmas had led to the Evelyns' alarming encounter with the military at the Exeter House chapel in 1657. *Diary* iii 203–4; BL Add Ms 78442, JE to JE jr, 16 March 1672/3.

8. *Diary* iv 223 (his sixtieth birthday).

9. *Ibid.* iii 571. He had, however, dedicated his own *The History of the Three Late Famous Impostors* (1669) to Arlington; see *ibid.*, 522 n. 2, 523.

10. As in:

    The other parts of woods I now must sing
    With Beech, and Oke, let Elm, and Linden spring.
    Nor may your Grove the Alder-tree disdain
    Or Maple of a double-colour'd grain.

11. CSP Dom 24 April 1671; BL RP 5460, JE to TC, 23 Nov. 1670 (misdated in his letterbook as 28 Jan. 1672). CSP Dom 24 Jan. 1672, 198–200, JE to JW, referring to his father-in-law's health, 'you shall dispose of him and me as you have kindly designed it'. Williamson was the intermediary.

12. *Diary* iii 590.

13. *Ibid.* iv 413, see MacLeod and Alexander, *Painted Ladies*, 136.

14. BL Add Ms 78317, ff. 116–19, draft in JE's hand, 16 Oct. 1671. It begins: 'You have commanded me to set downe in Writing somethings which you are pleas'd to call directions for the planting of Trees and other laudable Rusticities about your Seate.'

15. *SP* viii 288–9.
16. *Diary* iii 591, describing the estate as Evelyn saw it in 1677; see also *ibid.* iv 117–19.
17. *Ibid.* iii 622.
18. BL Ms Sloane 1906, 2 Jan. 1663/4. Edward Browne described the pictures, prints and drawings, jewels, rings and seals, 'all manner of stones and limnings beyond compare' bought by Arundel's agents, especially in Italy and Greece.
19. *Diary* iii 596.
20. [LB] BL Add Ms 78298, JE to TH, 'Knight and Baronet Prince of Florister', 13 Dec. 1670.
21. *SP* ix 469.
22. *Transformations*, 84.
23. [LB] BL Add Ms 78298, f. 185v, JE to James Hamilton, the duke of Ormonde's nephew, 27 April 1671.
24. *Transformations*, 155, referring to the probable influence of Francis de Sales's writings on Evelyn's ideal of 'passionate, spiritualized' friendship.
25. *Ibid.*, 152–3 for the source of the five-pointed star symbol, apparently borrowed from Sir Robert Moray in this context. *Diary* iii 628 (and facing illustration).
26. *Bray* iii 121–6, JE to Boyle, 29 Sept. 1659.
27. See Harris, *The Letter-books of Mary Evelyn*.
28. BL Add Ms 78317, f. 127, Dorothy Howard to JE, 24 [Aug.?] 1673.
29. BL Add Ms 78431, JE to ME, 7 July 1675.
30. *Transformations*, 182, where Margaret is also quoted as longing for Evelyn's company 'and what is all one with you [and] your wife'.
31. Samuel Tuke's mother was a Wase and he may have encouraged Evelyn to support their cousin. Evelyn and William Prettyman joined forces with the stationer Benjamin Tooke to fund the project. See Harris and Savage, *British Architectural Books*, 462; also Robert Hooke, *Diary 1672–80* ed. H. W. Robinson and W. Adams (1935), 143, 250.
32. For the chronology see *Diary* iii 523 n. 1. [LB] BL Add Ms 78298, f. 186v, 31 Aug. 1671.
33. *Diary* iv 18–23.
34. *Ibid.* iii 611–12.
35. PRO 106/283, 284, 16 July, 25 Aug. 1673.
36. *Diary* iii 618–20.
37. BL Add Ms 78306, ff. 155–6, ST to JE, from Somerset House, 10 June 1672.
38. CSP Treasury vii, 23 April 1681.
39. BL Add Ms 78314, f. 85, Benjamin Tooke to JE, 15 Aug. 1674.
40. CSP Dom. Charles II 16 1673–5, 12 Aug. 1674, from Hampton Court, 'The King to the Master & Wardens of the Stationers' Company.'
41. *Bray* iv, wrongly dated 1670/1; see Harris, *The Letter-books of Mary Evelyn*, ME to Bohun, 29 Jan. 1673/4.
42. MacLeod and Alexander, *Painted Ladies*, 40–1.
43. BL Add Ms 78539, ME to Bohun, 27 Sept. '1674' JE inscription.
44. BL Add Ms 78435, MT to ME, 12 Aug. [no year].
45. *Ibid.*, Bohun to ME, 13 Feb. 1667.
46. BL Add Ms 78438, f. 7, ME to WG. Harris, *The Letter-books of Mary Evelyn*.
47. BL Add Ms 78539, ME to Bohun, 20 Sept. 1675.
48. *Ibid.*, [?May] 1668. John Donne fell short of her expectations: 'had he not bin really a learned man, a libertine in witt, and a courtier, might have bin allowed to write well, but I confesse in my opinion with those qualifications, he falls short in his letters of the praises some give him.'
49. *Ibid.*, 27 Feb. [1670/1]; it was first published in 1672.

50. BL Add Ms 78434, WG to ME, 23 Oct. 1671 and 21 Aug. 1673. He hinted at his inside knowledge by naming Dixon, an obscure painter. Evelyn's own portrait by Walker, for Mary, had the same characteristics.
51. *Transformations*, 195.
52. BL Add Ms 78386, 'Oeconomics'; see *Transformations*, 247–57.
53. *Particular Friends* [C27] JE to SP, 3 Oct. 1685. See also *ibid.*, 160 n.5.
54. See Phillipps Ms 8539, 'Journall of the Council for Plantations', Library of Congress, Washington DC. I am indebted to Frances Harris for the loan of her notes.
55. BL Add Ms 78304 f. 65, GE to JE, 13 Jan. 1674/5.
56. Violet Barbour, *Henry Bennet, Earl of Arlington* (1914), 253: 'my Lord Arlington . . . hurls himself at all doors in the effort to re-enter affairs'. He had manoeuvred against Clarendon, been outflanked by his close friend Clifford, was no favourite of the duke of York and felt apprehensive at the duke of Buckingham's return to power. He was a nervous negotiator of the triple alliance.
57. *Diary* iv 113–20.
58. *Ibid.* iii 624–46. Evelyn always tended to be critical of May's domestic work, see below, pp. 00–0.
59. Fifteen years earlier Berkeley had suggested that Evelyn accompany him to Breda to meet the king prior to his restoration. Wisely, he used his recent ill health as an excuse to decline.
60. [LB] BL Add Ms 78299, f. 52, JE to Lady Sylvius, 4 Nov. 1688.
61. BL Add Ms 78317, f. 133, [illeg.] Frasier to JE, 5/15 Feb. 1676, offered to introduce young John to Abbé Marolles, 'the curiousest gentleman', who translated Lucretius into French. He also had the largest collection of prints in Europe. In London, Evelyn read his *Terra*, alternatively titled *A Philosophical Discourse of Earth*, to the Royal Society on 29 April and 13 May 1675 and the council ordered it to be published. See *Diary* iv 62 n. 3.
62. Oldenburg Correspondence xii (2762), 12 Oct. 1675, 15; (2772), 8 Nov. 1675, 40; (2799), 13 Dec. 1675, 90, in which he expects that Evelyn 'has made you his bow'.
63. BL Add Ms 78443, Lord Berkeley to JE, from Paris, 10 Dec. 1675.
64. [LB] BL Add Ms 78299, f. 196, JE to JE jr, 31 Jan.1675/6.
65. BL Add Ms 78317, f. 132, Samuel Benson to JE, from Paris, 4 Jan. 1675/6.
66. BL Add Ms 78300, f. 21, ME to JE, 31 Jan. 1675/6.
67. [LB] BL Add Ms 78298 f. 196, JE to JE jr, 31 Jan. 1675/6.
68. [LB] BL Add Ms 78299, f. 52, JE to Lady Sylvius, 4 Nov. 1688.
69. *Bray* iii 246–9, TG to JE, 13 Dec. 1675; JE to TG, n.d.; TG to JE, 2 March 1675/6.
70. Compare with Hooke's original words, *Micrographia*, 127.
71. Albert Borgman, *Thomas Shadwell: His Life and Comedies* (1969), 171–3.
72. *Lorenzo Magalotti at the Court of Charles II*, 27–9.
73. Hooke, *Diary*, 235.
74. Quoted in *Transformations*, 259–60.
75. *Diary* iv 123, 125 n. 3; Brouncker had held the post for sixteen years.
76. RS, Hooke Folio (manuscript uncatalogued at present, acquired 2006), entries for 30 March and 2 February 1681.
77. CSP Dom 1678 (Addenda 1674–9), JE to Joseph Williamson, 13 July 1678. 'The bearer, Mr Moxon, having begun a laudable work, and having already published specimens, has desired me to bespeak your favourable encouragement by not only permitting the notice of his undertaking to be inserted in the *Weekly Gazette* but that you, as President of the Royal Society, will give him your *imprimatur*.' But the envied (and profitable) situation of printer was already Richard Chiswell's.
78. BL Add Ms 78539, ME to Bohun, 19 Nov. 1677 [misdated 1676].
79. Quoted in *Transformations*, 263, 266.
80. *Diary* iv 134–5, 138–9.

81. Evelyn 'undertook to Contrive, & Survey, & employ workmen' for the Godolphins' Whitehall apartment. With Margaret he went to a Dutch marble workshop in Lambeth to choose chimney-pieces and looked at mirrors at the duke of Buckingham's Vauxhall glassworks.

82. *Diary* iv 147–9. So distraught was her family that Evelyn attended to the practical business of paying the doctors and arranging the funeral; *ibid*. 151.

83. BL Add Ms 78435, ME to Bohun, 10 Sept. 1678.

84. *Diary* iv 14, 18–23.

85. [LB] BL Add Ms 78298, f. 201v, JE to Charles Bertie, secretary to Lord Danby, 15 Feb. 1678/9.

86. *Bray* iii, 252–3, Anne, Countess of Sunderland, to JE, 25 Dec. 1678.

87. *Diary* iv 158–9.

88. *Ibid.* 164.

89. Quoted in *Transformations*, 291.

Chapter 14: Endeavour to Submit

1. [LB] BL Add Ms 78299, f. 2v, JE to JB, 11 July 1679.

2. Charges were laid by Oates and Bedloe against Wakeman and three monks.

3. Tomalin, *Samuel Pepys*, 318–20, 321–5.

4. Burke, *The Fabrication of Louis XIV*, 53–4 and fig. 18 showing Sébastien Le Clerc's frontispiece to Claude Perrault's *Mémoires pour l'Histoire Naturelle des Animaux* (1671).

5. Hooke, *Diary*, 394; 'Added to Mr Evelyns praeface', 24 Jan. 1678/9.

6. BL Add Ms 78431, JE to ME, 7 April 1681.

7. *Diary* iv 298, in which he refers to having 'sold' the stock to the Royal Society. See also India Office Library L/AG/1/10/2.

8. [LB] BL Add Ms 78299, f. 2, JE to SF, 12 June 1679. The countess was Lady Sunderland's mother.

9. *Diary* iv 185 n. 2; [LB] BL Add Ms 78299, ff. 2v–3, JE to SF, 14 Nov. 1679.

10. David Esterly, *Grinling Gibbons and the Art of Carving* (1998), ch. 1.

11. He had a fine library; a top-lit oval hall was planned which 'together with the other wing . . . will be a very noble Palace'. For his visit to Cassiobury see *Diary* iv 199–202. His sister, Mary Somerset, Duchess of Beaufort, was also a great gardener at Badminton House, Gloucestershire.

12. Moses Cook, *The Manner of Raising, Ordering, and Improving Forrest-Trees* (1676).

13. It had been founded in 1681 but Henry Wise did not replace Cook until 1687.

14. [LB] BL Add Ms 78299, f. 4v, JE to Arlington, 12 March 1679/80.

15. BL Add Ms 78431, JE to ME, 29 April 1679.

16. He told Godolphin that he had purchased his father-in-law's estate for £3,500, 'under hand and seale . . . to take off a mortgage from other Lands of Sir Richard, without which he could not have subsisted in his Majestie's Service', arguing that it was only the reassurance of eventual repayment that allowed him to spend the money and compound with soldiers and sequestrators 'when I had the wide world before me and opportunities of much more advantagious bargains'. [LB] BL Add Ms 78299, f. 5v, JE to SG, 13 Aug. 1680; *Diary* iv 217–19, iii 394 n.3. The exact figure was £11,846.

17. [LB] BL Add Ms 78299, f. 13v, JE to SG, 23 March 1681/2. He compares Browne's difficulties with the rise, at the time, of Sir Robert Long, Sir Edward Nicholas (courtier), Sir George Carteret (treasurer), Sir John Shaw (merchant), Lord Jermyn and Sir Edward Hyde himself.

18. *Particular Friends* [C1] JE to SP Whitehall 'after Supper' 30 Jan. [1680].

19. BL Add Ms 78442, JE to JE jr [1679].

20. *Ibid.*, undated letters, [1680].
21. *Ibid.*, 17 March 1680/81.
22. BL Add Ms 78435, ME to MT, 5 March 1679/80. John and Martha, whose mother was Lady Stonehouse, were living in the part of the house that Lady Tuke had occupied.
23. *Ibid.*, MT to ME, 6 May 1680.
24. [LB] BL Add Ms 78299, f. 11v, JE to SG, 19 Dec. 1681.
25. *Diary* i, introduction, 73.
26. BL Add Ms 78539, ME to Bohun, 22 Aug. 1682; *Transformations*, 297. Although he had been planning it for some time, he wrote it in early 1684 and presented it to Lady Sylvius that August. *The Life of Mrs Godolphin* was edited by Samuel Wilberforce, bishop of Oxford, and published in 1847; BL Add Ms 78301, f. 26, JE jr to JE, Wotton, 25 April 1682.
27. [LB] BL Add Ms 78298, f. 195, JE to Lady Berkeley, 13 April 1675. When Fox lost his office of military paymaster, Evelyn was unable to imagine 'from what malevolent Influence the clowd has covered Sir Stephen, who could never fall into his Majesties displeasure, if somebody were not very ambitious, and full of envy'.
28. The words of the Rev. Richard Eyre at his funeral in 1716: 'his Motive to it I know from his own Words, he said "he could not bear to see the Common Soldiers who had spent their Strength in our Service to beg at our Doors" and therefore did what he could to remove such a Scandal to the Kingdom'. See C.G.T. Dean, *The Royal Chelsea Hospital* (1950), 28.
29. *Diary* iv 257, 269 *et passim*.
30. *Ibid.* iv 169–70. 'Poor Billy' was mentally handicapped (see Tinniswood, *His Invention So Fertile*, 239–40).
31. Evelyn visited, for comparative purposes, Boone's almshouses in Lee, Kent, a modest quadrangle of school, chapel and accommodation. See *Diary* iv 288–9.
32. BL Add Ms 78435, Bohun to ME, 30 June 1682.
33. BL Add Ms 78539, ME to Bohun, 6 March 1682/3; BL Add Ms 78309, f. 40, Lady Sylvius to ME, from The Hague, 10 or 16 Feb. 1682/3; BL Add Ms 78435, MT to ME, 1 Oct. 1684.
34. [LB] BL Add Ms 78299, f. 18, JE to MT, 13 Feb. 1682/3.
35. *Diary* iv 304 and n. 4.
36. [LB] BL Add Ms 78299, f. 18, JE to 'William Pretyman Esq. Master of the First-fruits Office', 3 March 1682/3. He had already been dismissed, see n. 49 below.
37. BL Add Ms 78539, ME to Bohun, 25 March 1684; BL Add Ms 78431, JE to ME, Nov. 1684.
38. BL Add Ms 78539, Bohun from Elizabeth Evelyn, 6 Oct. 1683.
39. [LB] BL Add Ms 78299, f. 14v, JE to ME jr, 31 May 1682. Hussey succumbed to smallpox that July, 'for which I was extreamly sorry; because it is apparent, he never enjoy'd himselfe after my daughters death'; see *Diary* iv 455.
40. BL Add Ms 78435, Bohun to ME, 29 Oct. 1683. As evidence of his daughter's writing abilities, Evelyn published *Mary's Mundus Muliebris: or the Ladies Dressing-Room Unlock'd* posthumously in 1690.
41. *Ibid.*, MT to ME, from Barton 10 Oct. 1684.
42. See *ODNB*; *Diary* iv 326–9.
43. Jessop, *The Lives of the Norths* ii 181. He also wrote: 'The house was low, but elegantly set off with ornaments and quaint mottoes at most turns.'
44. BL Add Ms 78318, f. 24, JE from Francis Aston at Gresham College, 10 April 1684. JE's draft reply on reverse. In *Philosophical Transactions* xiv (1684) 766–79, Robert Plot and Jacob Bobart reported on the wider 'effects of the Great Frost'.
45. *The Works of Robert Boyle* (2002) ed. Michael Hunter and Edward B. Davis, v 302.
46. Tomalin, *Samuel Pepys*, 357–8. Pepys's loyalty to the Stuarts meant that his *Memoires Relating to the State of the Royal Navy* was surprisingly uncritical of Charles II.

47. *Particular Friends* [C1] JE to SP, from Whitehall, 30 Jan. [1680].
48. For Godolphin's dealings with the Evelyn family's expectations, see *Transformations*, 287–95.
49. Prettyman had been suspended lately as remembrancer of the first fruits and tenths, 16 May 1682 in *Calendar of Treasury Books, 1681–85*, 471; in December 1690 Evelyn was repaid from the First Fruits office with interest. *Ibid., 1689–92*, 434.
50. [LB] BL Add Ms 78299, f. 31v, JE to SG, 22 May 1685.
51. BL Add Ms 78431, JE to ME, Nov. 1684, telling her he had heard nothing from Mr London in Fulham. This was George London, the king's gardener and the future owner of the Brompton Park nursery.
52. See John Evelyn, *Directions for the Gardener at Sayes Court*, ed. Geoffrey Keynes (1932).
53. *Diary* iv 427–8.
54. In *Numismata* he gives considerable space to the achievements of women painters, poets and even the handful who had entered academic life.
55. *Diary* iv 389–90, 491.
56. *Ibid.* 405 *et passim*.
57. *Ibid.* 418–19.
58. Morrill, *Stuart Britain*, 70.
59. BL Add Ms 78539, ME to Bohun, 20 May, 3 June 1685.
60. *Ibid.*, EE to Bohun, 2 June 1685, SE to Bohun, n.d.
61. *Ibid.*, ME to Bohun, 20 May, 3 June 1685.
62. The tragedy unfolded in Mary's letters to Bohun. *Ibid.*, 30 July, 19 Aug., 27 Aug., 31 Aug. 1685.
63. *Ibid.*, 14[?] Sept. 1685.
64. For Susanna, see Carol Gibson-Wood, 'Susanna and her Elders: John Evelyn's Artistic Daughter' in *Milieu*; BL Add Ms 78539, 7 Nov. and 9 Nov. 1685.
65. *Calendar of Treasury Books* viii, 14 June 1687 (1404–5).
66. CSP Dom Charles II, iii, 1684–5, 6 Nov. 1684, 198; *Diary* iv 582–3. Anne Montague died in 1688 at Woodcote.
67. *Diary* iv 530.
68. He enjoyed refusing the duke of Norfolk's invitation to dine, since he was also invited by the earls of Sunderland and Clarendon, to whom he was indebted for the appointment. BL Add Ms 78431, JE to ME, 8 Sept. 1685.
69. BL Add Ms 78434, WG to ME, 4 Aug., 15 Sept. 1685.
70. BL Add Ms 78314, f. 31, Bohun to JE, from Oxford, 19 Sept. 1685.
71. *Diary* iv 484 (de Beer notes 'added later'). Jeffreys was the scourge of the Rye House Plotters; see *ibid.* 466 and n. 6.
72. BL Add Ms 78431, JE to ME from Chiswick, 8 Sept. 1685.
73. *Diary* iv 480. The work caused the court to decamp to St James's Palace for some time.
74. *Ibid.* 468 *et seq.* See his account of much of what follows.
75. *Diary* iv 493; [LB] BL Add Ms 78299, f. 37v, JE to Godolphin, 23 May (Whitmonday) 1686. His fellow commissioners were Robert Spencer, created Viscount Teviot in 1685, and Col. Robert Phelips – their patent was delivered in late December 1685.
76. *Diary* iv 502–3 n. 5.
77. Quoted in *Transformations*, 84; *Diary* iv 520.
78. *Diary* iv 534–5.
79. *Ibid.* 585. All opposed agreed 'the Injunction came so crudely from the Secretary's office, that it was neither sealed nor sign'd'; *ibid.*, 587–8 and notes.
80. For discussion of his links to the various figures, see Stephen Pincus, 'John Evelyn: Revolutionary' in *Milieu*, 202–7.
81. *Diary* iv 591; 568 n. 1.
82. [LB] BL Add Ms 78299, f. 49, JE to Lady Sunderland, 23 July 1688.

83. *Diary* iv 594, 597.
84. BL Add Ms 78301, f. 29, JE jr to JE n.d. [Oct. 1688].
85. *Diary* iv 566.
86. [LB] BL Add Ms 78299, ff. 52v–53v, JE to 'Robert Spencer', n.d., [Nov. 1688]. See Spurr '"A Sublime and Noble Service"'.
87. *Diary* iv 606.
88. See Spurr, '"A Sublime and Noble Service"', 155, copy of letter of 7 Dec. 1688.
89. Those eating with him included Prince George and Lord Mordaunt to his right, on his left Sidney, Bentinck and Zulesteyn. Dr Burnet said grace.
90. BL Add Ms 78301, f. 31, JE jr to JE, from Radley, 15 Dec. 1688.
91. See Kenyon, *Robert Spencer, Earl of Sunderland 1641–1702* (1958), 228–9.
92. See Pincus, 'John Evelyn: Revolutionary', 206; *Diary* v 1.
93. North, *Notes of Me*, 14.
94. See Kenyon, *Robert Spencer, Earl of Sunderland*, 231.
95. BL Add Ms 78301, f. 35, JE jr to JE, from London, 9 Feb. 1688/9. The *rapprochement* between father and son continued; he sent his father some books – Dr Burnet's sermon to the Commons, a (cleaner) copy of Cicero, Spenser's *Faerie Queene*, Corneille's plays, some modern operas, Sir Philip Sidney's *Arcadia* and the answers to Jovian which he was returning.
96. *Diary* iv 621–2.
97. Mark Kishlansky, *A Monarchy Transformed: Britain 1603–1714* (1996), 291.
98. Pincus, 'John Evelyn: Revolutionary', considers that Evelyn's friends in government from the 1670s onwards show him to be independent and surprisingly radical. His advice to his grandson suggests that he held a more non-partisan stance, see above, p. 000.
99. *Diary* v 7 n. 5.
100. [LB] BL Add Ms 78299, f. 64v, JE to Lady Sunderland, from London, 12 Jan. 1689/90.
101. *Diary* v 49, 39, 432.
102. *Particular Friends* [C 47] JE to SP, 26 Aug. 1689.
103. *Diary* v 60.

Chapter 15: An Absolute Philosopher

1. Although Evelyn claimed George had sat since 1641, he is not recorded entering the Long Parliament until 1645. [LB] BL Add Ms 78299, ff.63–4, JE to Jael Boscawen, 1 Oct. 1689.
2. Luigi Cornaro, *A Treatise of Temperance and Sobrietie*, translated by George Herbert (1634).
3. *Diary* v 38–9, 160. On the second occasion Sir Robert Southwell, King William's emissary in Ireland, was persuaded to continue. He corresponded with Evelyn about his garden at Kingsweston near Bristol; see BL Add Ms 15858, ff. 156 to 161, 3 Nov. 1684 and 8 Jan. 1684/5. He asked him for advice, especially on growing yew and the practicality of clipping it into a 'canopy'.
4. BL Add Ms 78300, ff. 36 and 38, ME to JE, from Bath, 21 July and 3 Aug. 1691. She refers to 'your M . . . [illegible]': no one else in their close circle seems to fit. Claire Tomalin (personal communication) believes that Pepys's circumstances at that date (before he moved to Hewer's house in Clapham) might point to him.
5. *Particular Friends* [C 49] JE to SP, 4 Oct. 1689.
6. In the dedication to his translation of Gassendi's life of Peiresc, Rand wished the Evelyns 'many faire, wise and well-bred Children, that may tread in their Parents steps, and as living and speaking Statues, effectually present your names and vertues to succeeding Generations'.

7. For his grandson John's (Jack's) education see Edward Gregg, 'Sir John Evelyn, his Grandfather's Heir' in *Milieu*.
8. BL Add Ms 78539, JE to Bohun, from Berkeley Street, 16 Feb. 1698/9; JE jr to Bohun, 27 Oct. 1687; ME to Bohun, Dec. 1701.
9. *Particular Friends* [C 47] JE to SP, 26 Aug. 1689.
10. *Diary* v 54–5.
11. BL Add Ms 78291, JE to GE, 22 Feb. 1690/1; also [LB] BL Add Ms 78299, f. 71, JE to GE, 23 Feb. 1690/1.
12. *Office Holders in Modern Britain, volume 1. Treasury Officials 1660–1870* (1972) 34–5. BL Add Ms 78301, f. 41, JE jr to JE, from Dublin, 19 Sept. 1692.
13. BL Add Ms 78291, JE to GE, 21 Nov. 1692; *ibid.*, 13 July 1696.
14. *Ibid.*, JE to GE, from Dover Street, 24 March 1692/3.
15. BL Add Ms 78318, f. 64, JE to 'Honest Abraham', 24 March 1693/4; f. 82, HW to JE, from Brompton Park, 9 Dec. 1693, promising to rectify a mistake with tulip bulbs; Evelyn asked him to parcel them up with other 'roots' in time for the spring.
16. *Particular Friends* [D15] JE to SP, 29 Aug. 1692.
17. For example *Bray* iii 339, Tenison, Bishop of Lincoln to JE, 5 April 1694. Other, later letters on the subject are in Lambeth Palace Library.
18. BL Add Ms 78301, f. 41, JE jr to JE, from Dublin, 19 Sept. 1692; BL Add Ms 78304, GE to JE, 3 Oct. 1693.
19. BL Add Ms 78301, f. 45, JE jr to JE, from Dublin, 25 Feb. 1692/3; f. 59, 26 Feb. 1694/5.
20. BL Add Ms 78539, ME to Bohun, from Dover Street, 2 Feb. 1691/2.
21. [LB] BL Add Ms 78299, ff. 63–4, JE to Jael Boscawen. Evelyn was misinformed; the son had died in 1676.
22. BL Add Ms 78301, f. 46, JE jr to JE, from Dublin, 27 March 1693. He had heard that William's uncle Sir Thomas Draper had £6,000 per annum and 'other prospects'.
23. BL Add Ms 78299, f. 83, JE to Lady Sylvius, 26 April 1693.
24. BL Add Ms 78539, ME to Bohun, 15 April 1693.
25. BL Add Ms 78314, ff. 34–5, Bohun to JE, from New College, Oxford, 17 May 1693. Bohun often pointed the finger at the religious inclinations of the Evelyns' friends and family; see BL Add Ms 78539, JE to Bohun, 12 Dec. 1673: 'Mrs Howard of whose stability in Religion you have no more reason to doubt than of her kindnesse to you in particular'.
26. BL Add Ms 78539, ME to Bohun, 24 May 1693. The Tuke girls, Mary and Teresa, stayed regularly at Sayes Court. Their brother Sir Charles (1670–90), whose Catholic christening Evelyn attended, was killed at the Battle of the Boyne.
27. [LB] BL Add Ms 78299, f. 84, JE to Lady Tuke, 10 June 1693.
28. BL Add Ms 78300, f. 43, ME to JE, 1 June 1693.
29. BL Add Ms 78442, JE to WD, from Sayes Court, 4 Aug. 1693. They had already taken about forty carp and several pike, which were either given to their neighbours at King's Yard or put back into the water.
30. *Particular Friends* [D18] JE to SP, 6 July 1693; *Diary* v 146.
31. *Particular Friends* [D21] JE to SP, 30 May 1694.
32. BL Add Ms 78300, ff. 91, 104, 98, WD to JE, 22 Aug., 23 Sept. 1693, 21 May 1694.
33. BL Add Ms 78539, ME to Bohun, 2 April 1694.
34. *Ibid.*, ME to Bohun, 7 April 1695.
35. BL Add Ms 78442, ME to Martha Evelyn, 3 Sept. 1704.
36. BL Add Ms 78305, ff. 80–1, WG to JE, from London, 12 June 1694.
37. BL Add Ms 78301, f. 53, JE jr to JE, from Dublin, 26 March 1694; f. 56, 10 July 1694.
38. Bodleian MS Aubrey 4, f. 28r, 8 Feb. 1675/6.
39. Quoted in Aubrey, *Natural History and Antiquities of Surrey*, i.
40. *Diary* v 206. Samuel Pepys helped update entries on various naval dockyards and arsenals, while the botanist John Ray had catalogued plants in the various counties.

41. Bodleian MS Eng b 2043, ff. 329–40, Evelyn's notes on Surrey addressed to Edmund Gibson, the future bishop of London.

42. *Particular Friends* [D30] JE to SP, 3 Dec. 1696.

43. D'Aviler's *Cours d'Architecture* was published in 1691 and reissued in 1696; plate facing page 189.

44. Hatton Correspondence ii 228 (1878), CH to Christopher Hatton, his brother, 7 Aug. [16]97. They were the sons of Lord Hatton who had been in Paris in Evelyn's day.

45. BL Add Ms 78300, f. 60, ME to JE, June 1696; BL Add Ms 78436, EP to ME, 7 Jan. 1696/7.

46. *Ibid.*, f. 58, ME to JE, 19 April 1696; BL Add Ms 78300, JE jr to Bohun, from Berkeley Street, 25 Feb. 1696/7.

47. *Ibid.*, ME to Bohun, 7 April 1695.

48. BL Add Ms 78301, f. 46, JE jr to JE, from Dublin, 27 March 1693.

49. BL Add Ms 78318, f. 77, Cyril Wyche to JE, from Dublin Castle, 7 Sept. 1693; BL Add Ms 78301, f. 54, JE jr to JE, 5 May 1694. John gave credit to a Dr Ashe – an exemplary and well-read man.

50. BL Add Ms 78291, JE to GE, from Deptford, 21 Nov. 1692.

51. BL Add Ms 78301, f. 89, JE to JE jr, 20 March 1698/9.

52. BL Add Ms 78305, f. 83 WG jr to JE, 12 Feb. 1694/5: telling him he had already 'put your Papers into my Ld G's [Godolphin's] hands desiring him to lay them before the King'. Yesterday, having talked to the king, he could confirm that Evelyn would be appointed treasurer at Greenwich, 'which by reason of your vicinity [to] that town . . . would be very fit for you especially since it would be a place of no manner'.

53. [LB] BL Add Ms 78299, f.109, JE to WD, 10 Jan. 1696/7. Receipt of £388 on 20 Oct. 1686 is signed for in Evelyn's name but in Strickland's hand as Evelyn's assignee.

54. BL Add Ms 78304, GE to JE, 4 June 1697.

55. BL Add Ms 78300, f. 61, ME to JE, 10 July 1696.

56. *Ibid.*, f. 40, 14 Aug. 1691.

57. John Bold, *Greenwich: An Architectural History of the Royal Hospital for Seamen and the Queen's House* (2000).

58. BL Add Ms 78300, f. 106, WD to JE, 7 Feb. 1695/6.

59. BL Add Ms 78431, JE to ME, from Surrey Street, 11 Nov. 1695; BL Add Ms 78442, ME to JE jr, 2 Nov. 1695.

60. [LB] BL Add Ms 78299, f. 97, JE to Travers, 29 Dec. 1695.

61. John Vanbrugh joined the board of directors at Greenwich in 1703, as did Evelyn after handing over the treasurership to his son-in-law.

62. [LB] BL Add Ms 78299, f. 105, JE to SG, 3 Aug. 1696. He named 'the Duke of Shrewsbery, Earles of Dorset, Pembroc, Lord Keeper, Lord Montague' and other 'noble men, knights and Gentlemen of the first Rank'.

63. BL Add Ms 78300, f. 61, ME to JE, 16 July 1696; BL Add Ms 78341.

64. BL Add Ms 78300, f. 107, WD to JE, 21 Jan. 1695/6.

65. The contribution from merchant seamen was £26,457 and from those on the royal ships £43,444. See Bold, *Greenwich*, 121.

66. [LB] BL Add Ms 78299, f. 86, JE to William Blathwayte, 4 April 1694.

67. BL Add Ms 78318, ff. 71 and 83, JE from John Walker, 20 and 26 Dec. 1693.

68. RS Hooke Folio, 9 Nov. 1681, when Penn's map was received. At the same meeting Evelyn was appointed one of three Fellows advising a Mr Hedges who was going to live on the Ganges. BL Add Ms 78683, f. 100, Dr John Woodward to JE, 5 Oct. 1697, an encouraging report for the Royal Society including the receipt of fossils from America, proving it to have been 'under water as well as Asia, Africa & Europe at the Deluge'.

69. *Diary* v 245–6, for Evelyn's analysis of the causes of the crisis of coinage and his fear that scarcity would lead to 'tumults'.

70. The full title was: *Numismata. A discourse of medals, antient and modern. Together with some account of heads and effigies of illustrious, and famous persons, in sculps, and taille-douce, of whom we have no medals extant; and of the use to be derived from them. To which is added a digression concerning physiognomy.* See K. Sloan et al., ed *Enlightenment: Discovering the World in the Eighteenth Century* (2003) 126.

71. See RS RBC.9.143 (n.d. but *c.* 1702): 'Proposals for building a house for the R S by Sir Christopher Wren.' For the earlier schemes in 1667–8, including Wren's, see Hunter, *Establishing the New Science*, 158–77.

72. *Particular Friends* [E13] JE to SP, from Dover Street, 10 Dec. 1701.

73. *Ibid.* [E15] JE to SP, 20 Jan. 1702/3; for Pepys's reaction, see 295 n. 4; [E12] SP to JE, Clapham, 19 Nov. 1701.

74. *Sylva* (1706 edition), Pepys's black summer, 1692, may have encouraged him to consider preparing the diaries for publication. Had Evelyn's example also been a prompt?

75. In Thompson's *Domestick Intelligence* (one of three publications bearing the same name) on 31 October 1679 it was reported that *Sylva* and *Pomona* had 'come forth in a 3rd edition, very much improved, and with considerable Additions . . . 'Tis esteemed by the Judicious, the most accomplished Volume that ever was published in any Language.'

76. BL Add Ms 78318, f. 38, E. Randolph to [?] Pepys, from Boston, New England, sending wishes to JE, 27 March 1688.

77. *Particular Friends* [D8] JE to SP, 26 Sept. 1690.

78. *Diary* v 550. Wotton is now a conference centre and the restored gardens open to the public on occasion. Evelyns still own the estate which continues to grow timber commercially.

79. CSP Dom William III ix, 8 Feb. 1698 Whitehall, J. Ellis to Lord Ambr. Williamson.

80. BL Add Ms 78539, JE to Bohun, from Wotton, 16 Feb. 1697/8.

81. *Diary* v 284 n. 5.

82. *Ibid.* 290–1 n. 6.

83. BL Add Ms 78436, EP to ME, 2 Sept. 1699.

84. *Diary* v 282–3 n. 2.

85. *Ibid.* 336–9 for full details.

86. *Ibid.* 103, 497–8.

87. *Ibid.* iv 582–3, v 86.

88. BL Add Ms 78539 JE to Bohun, from Berkeley Street, 16 Feb. 1698/9.

89. *Ibid.* v 359–60.

90. BL Add Ms 78296, JE to WG sr, 5 Oct. 1699.

91. *Diary* v 497 n. 3, 108.

92. BL Add Ms 78539, JE to Bohun, 3 April 1702.

93. BL Add Ms 78436, EP to ME, 15 Nov. 1699.

94. He lists 'brew-house vats etc, furnaces, cisterns & other fixed matters, either to house or soil. Chariot & dung-cart, timber & planks'.

95. *Particular Friends* [E4] JE to SP, from Dover Street, 18 May 1700.

96. See Evelyn, *Memoire for my Grand-son.*

97. See BL Add Ms 78403, Wotton inventory of 1702; see also BL Add Ms 78404, Mary Evelyn's inventories, 1706.

98. BL Add Ms 78300, f. 124, WD to JE, 9 Nov. 1701. Evelyn's reply (13 Nov.) is drafted on the letter, apologising for the shortcomings of great age and thanking him for his company.

99. BL Add Ms 78539, ME to Bohun, 8 Jan. 1701/2. For Addiscombe see Colvin, *A Biographical Dictionary;* also Kerry Downes, *English Baroque Architecture* (1966), plate 163, photographed before its demolition in the 1860s, showing an eccentric giant order. *Diary* v 425, 541.

100. *Particular Friends* [E15] JE to SP, from London, 20 Jan. 1703.

101. See *Philosophical Transactions* 23:280 (July/Aug. 1702), 1177–201; *Diary* v 487 n. 1. R. Aspin, 'John Evelyn's Tables of Veins and Arteries: A Rediscovered Letter', *Medical History* 1995 (39) 493–9.

102. *The Journal of James Yonge (1647–1721): Plymouth Surgeon* ed. F.N.L. Poynter (1963), 214.

103. *Diary* v 422; BL Add Ms 78300, f. 79, ME to JE, 10 Dec. 1701; *Particular Friends* [E5 and E6] JE to SP, 22 July, and SP to JE, 7 Aug. 1700.

104. Howarth, *Letters and the Second Diary of Samuel Pepys*, 312–14, John Jackson to SP, 8 Oct. 1700.

105. *Particular Friends* [E9]: Jack's poem about Pepys's nephew bringing home prints of Rome, since he had never been there, JE to SP, from Wotton, 25 Aug. 1700. Translated 280 n. 3.

106. BL Add Ms 78431, JE to ME, 11 Nov. 1695. Mrs Skinner was buying a cabinet for £50 but had been prepared to pay £60.

107. *Diary* v 537–8 and notes.

108. BL Add Ms 78300, f. 127, WD to JE, 27 Nov. 1703.

109. BL Add Ms 78539, JE to Bohun, Dover Street, 13 Feb. 1700/1. Mary Evelyn had approached Burnet's wife, the widow of gardening friend, Robert Berkeley of Spetchley.

110. *Ibid.*, ME to Bohun, 21 May 1701.

111. *Diary* v 550.

112. BL Add Ms 78539, ME to Bohun, from Wotton, May 1703.

113. *Diary* v 609.

114. Quoted in *Particular Friends*, 296, JE to Will Hewer.

115. *Diary* v 600. Eighty-one rooms were occupied and there were two hundred residents. By the time of Evelyn's death, three hundred pensioners were in residence.

116. BL Add Ms 78539, ME to Bohun, 29 Sept. 1705.

117. *Diary* v 584.

118. BL Add Ms 78539, ME to Bohun, 29 Sept. 1705.

119. *Diary* v 620.

120. *Ibid.* 622.

121. BL Add Ms 78539, ME to Bohun, 8 March 1705/6.

122. BL Add Ms 78435, Bohun to ME, 4 March 1705/6. 'I lament the death of my Honord patron, my constant benefactor, my dear and most valuable friend with the utmost degree of tenderness and concern: They must have no esteem for Religion & vertue & good nature and learning and ingenuity, who did not admire and love Mr Evelyn but a long acquaintance, innumerable obligations and the gratefull remembrance of his benificience towards me for forty years past affect me so powerfully that never any thing made such deep impressions on my mind.' For his will see BL Add Ms 78412, codicils, 29 Feb. 1703/4 (re. the garden burial) and 26 Feb. 1702/3.

123. Gibson-Wood, 'Susanna and Her Elders'.

124. Gregg, 'Sir John Evelyn, his Grandfather's Heir'. Also Peter Brandon in (forthcoming) *A Celebration of John Evelyn*, publication of April 2006 conference papers.

125. For an overview, see Kenny et al., *John Evelyn in the British Library*.

Select Bibliography

See also John Evelyn's Works (p. ix) and Abbreviations (p. 307).

Primary printed sources

Aubrey, John, *Brief Lives* ed. John Buchanan-Brown (2000).
———— *Natural History and Antiquities of Surrey* (1718–19).
Bacon, Francis, *The Essays* ed. John Pitcher (1985).
Birch, Thomas, *History of the Royal Society*, 4 vols (1756–7).
Bunbury, Sir Henry, ed., *The Correspondence of Sir Thomas Hanmer* (1838).
Burnet, Gilbert, *History of my own Time* (2 vols, 1897, 1900).
Camden's Britannia ed. and trans. Edmund Gibson (1695).
Cowley, Abraham, *Several Discourses by Way of Essays in Verse and Prose* ed. H.C. Minchin (1904).
Dixon Hunt, John and Willis, Peter, *The Genius of the Place: The English Landscape Garden 1620–1820* (1975).
Evelyn, John, *Memoires for my Grand-son* ed. Geoffrey Keynes (1926).
———— *Notes to the Gardener at Sayes Court* ed. Geoffrey Keynes (1932).
———— *London Revived: Considerations for its Rebuilding in 1666* ed. E.S. De Beer (1938).
———— *Acetaria: A Discourse of Sallets* ed. Christopher Driver (1996).
———— *John Evelyn, Cook* ed. Christopher Driver (1997).
———— *John Evelyn in the British Library* (2nd edn 1995).
———— *John Evelyn's Translation of Titus Lucretius Carus De Rerum Natura*, ed. Michael M. Repetzki (2000).
Fanshawe, Anne, *Memoirs of Anne Lady Fanshawe* ed. Herbert C. Fanshawe (1907).
Fréart de Chantelou, Paul, *Diary of the Cavaliere Bernini's Visit to France*, trans. Margery Corbett, ed. Anthony Blunt and George Bauer (1985).
Sir Thomas Hanmer's Garden Book ed. E.S. Rohde (1933).
Hatton Correspondence, Camden Society (third series), vols xxii, xxiii (1878).
Thomas Hobbes; the Correspondence ed. Noel Malcolm (1994).
Hobbes, Thomas, *De Cive* ed. Howard Warrender (1983).
Hooke, Robert, *Diary 1672–80* ed. H.W. Robinson and W. Adams (1935).
Huygens, Christian, *Oeuvres Complètes*, 22 vols (1888–1950).
Huygens Lodewijk The English Journal 1651–1652, ed and trans A.G.H. Bachrach and R.G. Collmer (1982).
The Correspondence of Henry Hyde, Earl of Clarendon and his Brother Laurence Hyde, Earl of Rochester ed. S.W. Singer (2 vols 1828).
Machiavelli, *Discourses*, ed. Bernard Crick (1986).
Lorenzo Magalotti at the Court of Charles II, ed. and trans. W.E. Knowles Middleton (1980).

Marvell, Andrew, *The Complete Poems* ed. Elizabeth Story Donno (1996).

Nicholas Papers, Camden Society (third series) vols xl, l, lvii, xxxi, (1886, 1892, 1897, 1920).

North, Roger, *Notes of Me: The Autobiography of Roger North* ed. Peter Millard (2000).

The Letters of Samuel Pepys ed. Guy de la Bédoyère (2006).

Howarth, R.G., Ed. *Letters and the Second Diary of Samuel Pepys* (1932).

The Architecture of Sir Roger Pratt ed. R.T. Gunther (1928).

Sorbière, Samuel, *Journal d'un Voyage en Angleterre* (1664) translated as *A Journey to England* (1709).

Sprat[t], Thomas, *The History of the Royal Society* (1667).

Taylor, Jeremy, *The Whole Works* (9 vols, 1847).

Upcott, William, *Miscellaneous Writings* (1825).

Wotton, Henry, *The Elements of Architecture* (1624).

The Poems of Edmund Waller ed. G. Thorn Drury (2 vols 1901).

Wren, Christopher, *Parentalia* (1750).

Secondary sources

Albion, R.G., *Forests and Sea Power: The Timber Problem of the Royal Navy 1652–1862* (1926).

Ashley, Maurice, *General Monck* (1977).

Aspin, Richard K., 'John Evelyn's Tables of Veins and Arteries: A Rediscovered Letter', *Medical History* 1995 (39) 493–9.

Aylmer, G.E., *The King's Servants* (1974).

———— *The Crown's Servants* (2002).

Ballon, Hilary, *The Paris of Henri IV: Architecture and Urbanism* (1991).

Barbour, Violet, *Henry Bennet, Earl of Arlington* (1914).

Beal, Peter et al., *Index of English Literary Manuscripts*, vol. 2, 165–1700.

Bennett, J.A., *The Mathematical Science of Christopher Wren* (1982).

———— and Mandelbrote, Scott, *The Garden, the Ark, the Tower, the Temple: Biblical Metaphors of Knowledge in Early Modern Europe* (1998).

Bold, John, *Greenwich: An Architectural History of the Royal Hospital for Seamen and the Queen's House* (2000).

Bray, Alan, *The Friend* (2003).

Brent, Colin, *Pre-Georgian Lewes: c 890–1714* (2004).

Brunton, D. and Pennington, D.H., *Members of the Long Parliament* (1954).

Burke, Peter, *The Fabrication of Louis XIV* (1992).

Campbell-Culver, Maggie, *A Passion for Trees: The Legacy of John Evelyn* (2006).

Carte, Thomas, *The Life of James, Duke of Ormonde*, 6 vols (1851).

Chambers, Douglas C., 'The Tomb in the Landscape: John Evelyn's Garden at Albury', *Journal of Garden History* 1:1 (Jan.–March 1981), 37–54.

———— *The Planters of the English Landscape* (1993).

———— '"Excuse these Impertinences": Evelyn in his Letterbooks' in *Milieu*.

Chaney, Edward, *The Evolution of the Grand Tour* (1998).

———— 'Evelyn, Inigo Jones, and the Collector Earl of Arundel' in *Milieu*.

Charlesworth, Michael, 'A Plan by John Evelyn for Henry Howard's Garden at Albury Park, Surrey' in O'Malley and Wolschke-Bulmahn.

Clay, Christopher, *Public Finance and Private Wealth; The Career of Sir Stephen Fox 1627–1716* (1978).

Colvin, Howard, *A Biographical Dictionary of British Architects 1600–1840* (third edition, 1995).

———— *History of the King's Works*, vol. 5, *1660–1782* (1977).

Colvin, Howard and Newman, John, *Of Building; Roger North's Writings on Architecture* (1981).

Cooper, Michael, *'A More Beautiful City' : Robert Hooke and the Rebuilding of London after the Great Fire* (2003).

Darley, Gillian, "'Action to the Purpose": Evelyn, Greenwich and the Sick and Wounded Seamen' in *Milieu*.

De Beer, Esmond, 'Evelyn and Colonel Harbert Morley in 1659 and 1660', *Sussex Archaeological Collections* 77 (1937), 177–83.

Dixon Hunt, John, *The Garden and the Grove: The Italian Renaissance Garden and the English Imagination 1600–1750* (1986).

Downes, Kerry, *English Baroque Architecture* (1966).

Esterly, David, *Grinling Gibbons and the Art of Carving* (1998).

Evelyn, Helen, *The Evelyn Family* (1915).

The Evelyn Library (Christies sale catalogue), 4 vols (1977–8).

Findlen, Paula, *Athanasius Kircher: The Last Man Who Knew Everything* (2004).

Fisk, Deborah Payne, ed., *Cambridge Companion to English Restoration Theatre* (2000).

Fletcher, Anthony, *A County Community in Peace and War: Sussex 1600–1660* (1975).

————— *Gender, Sex and Subordination in England 1500–1800* (1995).

Foot, Mirjam, 'John Evelyn's Bindings' in *Milieu*.

Frank, Robert G., *Harvey and the Oxford Physiologists* (1980).

Fraser, Antonia, *King Charles II* (1979).

Gibson-Wood, Carol, 'Susanna and her Elders: John Evelyn's Artistic Daughter' in *Milieu*.

Godfrey, Richard T., *Wenceslaus Hollar: A Bohemian Artist in London* (1995).

Goodchild, Peter, '"No Phantasticall Utopia, But a Reall Place". John Evelyn, John Beale and Backbury Hill, Herefordshire', *Garden History* 19 ii (1991) 105–27.

Gordon, C.A., *A Bibliography of Lucretius* (1985).

Greengrass, Mark, Leslie, Michael and Raylor, Timothy, eds, *Samuel Hartlib and Universal Reformation* (1994).

Gregg, Edward, 'Sir John Evelyn, His Grandfather's Heir' in *Milieu*.

Griffiths, Antony, *The Print in Stuart Britain 1603–1689* (1998).

————— 'John Evelyn and the Print' in *Milieu*.

Guillery, Peter, *The Small House in Eighteenth-Century London* (2004).

Gunther, R.T., *Early British Botanists and their Gardens* (1922).

————— *The Architecture of Sir Roger Pratt* (1928).

Harding, Robert, 'John Evelyn, Hendrick van der Borcht the Younger and Wenceslaus Hollar', *Apollo* 144 (Aug. 1996), 39–44.

Harris, Eileen, with Savage, Nicholas, *British Architectural Books and Writers 1556–1785* (1990).

Harris, Frances, 'The Letter-books of Mary Evelyn' in *English Manuscript Studies* (1998) 204–13.

Harwood, John T., 'Rhetoric and Graphics in *Micrographia*' in *Robert Hooke: New Studies* ed. Michael Hunter and Simon Schaffer (1989).

————— 'Science Writing and Writing Science' in M. Hunter, ed., *Robert Boyle Reconsidered* (1994).

Henning, Basil Duke, ed., *The History of Parliament; The House of Commons 1660–1690*, vol. 2, members C-L (1983).

Henrey, Blanche, *British Botanical and Horticultural Literature before 1800* (1975).

Hervey, Mary, completed Catherine Phillimore, ed. G.C. Williamson *The Life, Correspondence and Collection of Thomas Howard, Earl of Arundel* (1921).

Higgott, Gordon, 'The Fabric to 1670' in Keene *et al. St Pauls.*

Hiscock, W.G. *John Evelyn and His Family Circle* (1955).

Houlbrook, Ralph, *Death, Religion and the Family in England 1480–1750* (1998).

Howarth, David, *Lord Arundel and his Circle* (1985).

Hunter, Michael, *The Royal Society and its Fellows 1600–1700* (1982).
———— *Establishing the New Science* (1989).
———— *Science and the Shape of Orthodoxy: Intellectual Change in Late Seventeenth-Century Britain* (1995).
Hutton, Ronald, *Charles the Second, King of England, Scotland and Ireland* (1989).
Inwood, Stephen, *The Man Who Knew Too Much* (2002).
Jardine, Lisa, *Ingenious Pursuits: Building the Scientific Revolution* (1999).
———— *On a Grander Scale: The Outstanding Career of Sir Christopher Wren* (2002).
———— *The Curious Life of Robert Hooke* (2003).
Jenkins, Ian, 'Ideas of Antiquity' in *Enlightenment: Discovering the World in the Eighteenth Century* ed. Kim Sloan with Andrew Burnett (British Museum 2003).
Jenner, Mark, 'The Politics of London Air; John Evelyn's *Fumifugium* and the Restoration', *The Historical Journal* 38:3 (1995), 535–51.
Jessop, P.A., et al., ed. *The Lives of the Norths* (1890).
Johns, Adrian, *The Nature of the Book* (1998).
Jones, Howard, *The Epicurean Tradition* (1989).
Jones, John, *Balliol College: A History* (1997).
Josten, J.H., *Elias Ashmole* (1966).
Joy, Lynn Sumida, *Gassendi the Atomist* (1987).
Keay, John, *The Honourable Company* (1991).
Keene, Derek, Burns, Arthur and Saint, Andrew, eds, *St Paul's: The Cathedral Church of London* (2004).
Keevil, J.J., *Medicine and the Navy 1200–1900*, ii, *1649–1714* (1958).
Kenyon, J.P., *Robert Spencer, Earl of Sunderland 1641–1702* (1958).
Keynes, Geoffrey, *John Evelyn: A Study in Bibliography* (1968).
Kishlansky, Mark, *A Monarchy Transformed: Britain 1603–1714* (1996).
Laird, Mark, 'Parterre, Grove and Flower Garden: European Horticulture and Planting Design in John Evelyn's Time' in O'Malley and Wolschke-Bulmahn, eds, *John Evelyn's 'Elysium Britannicum'*, 171–219.
———— 'Sayes Court Revisited' in *Milieu*.
Leith-Ross, Prudence, 'A Seventeenth-Century Paris Garden', *Garden History* 21:2 (Winter 1995), 150–7.
———— 'The Garden of John Evelyn at Deptford', *Garden History* 25:2 (Winter 1997), 138–52.
Leslie, Michael, 'The Spiritual Husbandry of John Beale', in M. Leslie and T. Raylor, eds, *Culture and Cultivation in Early Modern England* (1992), 151–72.
Levine, Joseph, *Between the Ancients and the Moderns* (1999).
Lynch, William T., *Solomon's Child* (2001).
MacLeod, Catherine and Julia Marciari Alexander, *Painted Ladies: Women at the Court of Charles II* (2001).
McKellar, Elizabeth, *The Birth of Modern London* (1999).
Malcolm, Noel, *Aspects of Hobbes* (2002).
Mandelbrote, Giles, 'John Evelyn and his Books' in *Milieu*.
Marshall, Alan, *Intelligence and Espionage in the Reign of Charles II, 1660–1685* (2003).
de Montclos, Claude, *La Mémoire des Ruines: Anthologie des Monuments Disparus en France* (1992).
Morrill, John, *Stuart Britain: A Very Short Introduction* (2000).
del Negro, Piero, ed., *The University of Padua: Eight Centuries of History* (2003).
Newman, John, 'Hugh May, Clarendon and Cornbury', in *English Architecture Public and Private, Essays for Kerry Downes*, eds. John Bold and Edward Chaney (1993).
Ochs, Kathleen, 'History of Trades', *Notes and Records of the Royal Society* 39 (1984–5), 129–58.
O'Hehir, Brendan, *Harmony from Discords, a Life of Sir John Denham* (1968).

O'Malley, Therese and Wolschke-Bulmahn, Joachim, eds, *John Evelyn's 'Elysium Britannicum' and European Gardening* (1998).

Ollard, Richard, *Clarendon and His Friends* (1988).

Pasmore, Stephen, 'Thomas Henshaw FRS (1618–1700)', *Notes and Records of the Royal Society* 36 (1981–2), 177–88.

Picard, Liza, *Restoration London* (1997).

Pincus, Steven, 'John Evelyn: Revolutionary' in *Milieu*.

Prest, John, *The Garden of Eden: The Botanic Garden and the Re-creation of Paradise* (1981).

Reddaway, T.F., *Rebuilding of London* (1940).

Robertson, Alexander, *The Life of Sir Robert Moray* (1922).

Robinson, John Martin, *The Dukes of Norfolk* (1995).

Rowland, Ingrid D., *The Ecstatic Journey: Athanasius Kircher in Baroque Rome* (2000).

Rubel, William, 'Parisian Bread *circa* 1654', *Petits Propos Culinaires* 77 (2004), 9–33.

Scott, Eva, *The King in Exile* (1904).

———— *The Travels of the King* (1907).

Scull, G.D., *The Evelyns in America* (1881).

Shapin, Steve, *A Social History of Truth* (1994).

———— and Schaffer, Simon, *Leviathan and the Air-Pump* (1985).

Sharp, Lindsay, 'Timber, Science, and Economic Reform in the Seventeenth Century', *Forestry* 48:1 (1975), 55–86.

Sharpe, Kevin, 'Restoration and Reconstitution' in MacLeod and Alexander, *Painted Ladies*.

Small, Carola and Alastair, 'John Evelyn and the Garden of Epicurus', *Journal of the Warburg and Courtauld Institutes* 60 (1997), 194–214.

Soo, Lydia M., *Wrens 'Tracts' on Architecture and Other Writings* (1998).

Spurr, John, *The Restoration Church of England* (1991).

———— '"A Sublime and Noble Service": Evelyn and the Church of England' in *Milieu*.

Stevenson, Christine, *Medicine and Magnificence: British Hospital and Asylum Architecture, 1660–1815* (2000).

Stoye, John, *English Travellers Abroad 1604–1667* (1989).

Strong, Roy, *The Renaissance Garden in England* (1979).

Sullivan, Isabel, 'Their "own Sweet Country": The Evelyns in Surrey' in *Milieu*.

Taylor, F. Sherwood, 'The Chemical Studies of John Evelyn', *Annals of Science* 8:4 (Dec. 1952), 286–92.

Thomas, Keith, *Religion and the Decline of Magic: Studies in Popular Beliefs in Sixteenth- and Seventeenth-Century England* (1971).

———— *Man and the Natural World: Changing Attitude in England 1500–1800* (1983).

Thurley, Simon, *The Whitehall Palace Plan of 1670* (1998).

Tindall, Gillian, *The Man Who Drew London: Wenceslaus Hollar in Reality and Imagination* (2002).

Tinniswood, Adrian, *His Invention So Fertile* (2003).

Todd, Margot, *Christian Humanism and the Puritan Social Order* (1987).

Tomalin, Claire, *Samuel Pepys: The Unequalled Self* (2002).

Tyacke, Nicholas, *The History of the University of Oxford* iv (1997).

Vickers, Brian, ed., *Public and Private Life in the Seventeenth Century: The Mackenzie–Evelyn Debate* (1986).

Victoria County History, *Surrey* iii (1911).

Webster, Charles, *The Great Instauration: Science, Medicine and Reform 1626–1660* (1975).

Weinberger, Jerry, *Science, Faith and Politics; Francis Bacon and the Utopian Roots of the Modern Age* (1985).

Whitaker, Kate, *Mad Madge: Margaret Cavendish, Duchess of Newcastle, Royalist, Writer & Romantic* (2004).

Whitney, Charles, *Francis Bacon and Modernity* (1986).

Williamson, J.B., *History of the Temple* (1924).

Woolrych, Austin, *Britain in Revolution 1625–1660* (2002).

Zytaruk, Maria, '"Occasional Specimens, not Compleate Systemes": John Evelyn's Culture of Collecting', *Bodleian Library Record* 17 (April–Oct. 2001), 185–212.

Index

Abdy, John, 64
Abraham (George's gardener), 282–4
Académie des Sciences, Paris, 172, 231n
Act for the Rebuilding of the City of London (1667), 225
Adam, James, 49
Addiscombe, Surrey: William Draper and plans to rebuild, 301, 303
Admiralty: accuses JE of unlawfully felling trees, 243
Albani, Cardinal Alessandro, 49
Albemarle, George Monck, 1st duke of: and prospective Restoration, 160–1; meets Charles II on return to England, 165; anger at Carteret's diverting relief money from JE, 195; JE presents *Sylva* to, 197; supports JE as commissioner for sick and wounded, 197–8; takes over command of fleet (1666), 198; decline, 208; and Third Dutch War, 242
Albury: Arundel at, 4, 16, 31; George and Mary Evelyn at, 16; JE designs gardens, 34–5, 119, 184; Oughtred at, 44; and Arundel's absence in Italy, 64, 66; JE attempts to buy, 119; JE visits with Mary, 128; Henry Howard alters, 148; JE revisits, 148; threatened by plague, 195; Cobbett describes, 228; tunnel, 228, 288
alchemy and alchemists, 49, 57, 109, 110, 136, 138
Allen, Thomas, 110
Alps: JE travels in, 65
Althorp, 274, 277
Ammanati, Bartolommeo, 59
Amsterdam, 27–9, 31
Anglo-Dutch Wars *see* Dutch Wars

Anne of Austria, Queen regent of France, 38, 70, 109
Anne, Queen, 38, 304
Anne (yacht), 177
Antwerp, 30, 34
Apsley, Captain Peter, 25
Aristotle, and Aristotelianism 8, 12, 103, 143, 213, 280
Arlington, Isabella, countess of (*née* van Nassau-Beverweerd), 236, 267
Arlington, Sir Henry Bennet, 1st earl of: as secretary of state, 164; JE asks to read *Tyrannus* to Charles II, 173–4; JE requests aid for Chatham hospital, 197, 199–200; rise at court, 208; criticised, 209; at Euston Hall, 235–6; JE's relations with, 235–7; qualities, 236–7; retires to Euston, 256; reinstated by James II on accession, 268, 277; Catholicism at death, 271
Arundel, Alathea, countess of, 26, 59, 64, 67, 103
Arundel House, London, 22, 184, 223
Arundel, Thomas, 2nd earl of: at Albury, 4, 16, 119; escorts Marie de Médicis to Low Countries, 21, 26, 29–31; as art patron, 22, 31; friendship with JE, 31, 62, 64; escorts Queen Henrietta Maria to Holland, 32; exile in Antwerp, 34; provides introductions for JE on travels, 46; ill health, 54, 59; in Italy, 58–9, 64–5, 279; death, 66; correspondence with JE, 67; and Waller's proposed trip to Spain, 67–8; supports Charles I, 68; collecting, 75, 149; marbles transferred to Oxford, 227; library moved to Gresham College, 251
Arundell of Wardour, Henry Arundell, 3rd

baron, 273

Ashburnham, John, 78

Ashmole, Elias: on Oughtred's alchemical interests, 138; takes Tradescant's collection to Oxford, 149n; JE dines with, 153; JE mistrusts, 252; owns Tradescant's 'Ark', 252

atomism, 102, 138, 141, 143–5, 213

Aubrey, John: on rustic wits, 35; on Waller, 62, 68; on Albury, 119; on Boyle, 138, 156; on Royal Society members, 169; and JE's pride in Surrey, 288; *Natural History and Antiquities of Surrey*, 129, 291

Audley End, Essex 135

Augustus, Roman Emperor, 187

Avignon, France, 42, 48

Aviler, Augustin Charles d': *Cours d'Architecture*, 289

Backhouse, William, 49

Bacon, Francis: influence on JE, 14, 19, 21, 32, 37, 44, 64, 100, 115, 122, 159; on gardens and gardening, 125, 152; and universal knowledge, 137; and John Beale, 158; and proposed learned institution, 158–9, 172; advocates openness of trade secrets, 251; library, 296; *New Atlantis*, 156–7

Bacon, Roger: *Cure of Old Age*, 297; *Preservation of Youth*, 297

Bagwell, Mrs (Pepys's mistress), 197

Balliol College, Oxford: JE attends, 11–15; JE presents books to, 249–50

Balls Park, Hertford, 35, 157

Barberini, Cardinal Francesco, 49, 53, 58

Barlet, Anibal, 69, 138

Barlow, Thomas: in Oxford, 133; JE sends Lucretius translation to, 144; and JE's French translations, 152, 171; JE presents copy of *Parallel* to, 191

Baskerville, Thomas, 184

Bathurst family, 213

Bathurst, George, 12

Bathurst, Ralph, 12, 191

Battle, Tobias, 196

Baynards Park, near Ewhurst, 18, 45, 119, 270, 299

Beale, John: correspondence with JE, 158–9; Hartlib recommends to Boyle, 158; JE sends outline of *Elysium Britannicum* to, 161; advocates scented plants, 176; encourages JE to reissue

Sculptura, 179; contributes fruit trees section to JE's *Sylva*, 181, 197; correspondence with Hartlib, 181; in Royal Society, 181; presses for enlarged second edition of *Sylva*, 185; co-designs title page for Sprat's *History of the Royal Society*, 186, 212; and completion of *Elysium Britannicum*, 203–4; on London after Great Fire, 223; plan for Royal Society building, 226; on second edition of JE's *Sylva*, 234; and JE's printing extract from *Elysium Britannicum*, 250; JE summarises situation for, 254; death, 265

Bedell, Gabriel, 90, 92

Bedingfield, Thomas, 304

bee-hives, 133–4, 136

Benbow, Admiral John, 298

Bennet, Sir Henry *see* Arlington, 1st earl of

Bentley, Richard, 280, 296

Berkeley House, London, 247

Berkeley, Christian, 240, 246, 248–9

Berkeley, John, 1st baron, 78, 186, 214, 240, 246, 248–9

Berkeley, Robert (of Spetchley), 303

Bernini, Gianlorenzo: sculptures, 50, 97; Wren meets in Paris, 214–15

Bethlehem (Bedlam) Hospital, 251

Bickerton, Jane, 237

Blagge, Margaret (*later* Godolphin), 238–41, 246–9, 251–2, 261, 267

Blaeu, Joan, 29

Bobart, Jacob, 14, 162, 191

Bobart, Jacob, the Younger, 162

Bohun, Ralph: tutors John Evelyn Jr at Oxford, 190; supervises construction of Sheldonian Theatre, 191; reads JE's *Publick Employment*, 207; Protestant zeal and anti-Catholicism, 209, 270, 273; friendship and correspondence with Mary, 211–12, 233–4, 246, 251, 260, 263–4, 271; admires Sprat's *History of the Royal Society*, 212; and John Jr's law studies, 234; and death of Margaret Blagge, 252; and Mary's exhaustion, 262; on Mary's Villiers Street lodgings, 264; and Elizabeth Evelyn in Oxford, 268; congratulates JE on appointment to Privy Seal commission, 270; and JE's grandson John, 281; on Susanna Evelyn's marriage, 284–5, 289; and Peter the

Bohun, Ralph (*cont.*)

Great's occupation of Sayes Court, 298;
and Draper's building plans, 301; gains
living at Wotton, 303–4; welcomes
Queen Anne's accession, 304; absent
from Jack Evelyn's wedding, 305; and
JE's death, 305–6
Bologna, Italy, 55
Bonnefons, Nicolas de: *Le Jardinier françois*
(*The French Gardiner*), 147, 150, 153–4
Borcht, Hendrick van der, 21–2, 33, 35,
41, 59
Borromini, Carlo, 47
Boscawen, Jael (*née* Godolphin), 252, 279,
285, 305
Bosse, Abraham, 86, 100, 103, 115, 127–9,
229–30; *Art of Graveing and Etching*
(*Traité*), 169, 179
Boyle lecturer (annual), 279
Boyle, Richard (*later* 1st earl of
Burlington), 178
Boyle, Robert: dislikes Jesuits, 49, 51; and
Kircher's hydraulic organ, 49; and
Worcester's water-raising machine, 81;
Wilkins invites to Oxford, 133; and
Hartlib's hopes for Petty's cooperation
in trades project, 137; and alchemy, 138;
Christianity, 138; JE meets at Sayes
Court, 139–40; qualities, 140–1; on JE's
Lucretius translation, 142; finances,
156; and JE's plans to expand scientific
work at Sayes Court, 157; and Beale's
proposals for exchange of knowledge,
159; scientific supremacy, 168; JE
dedicates *Sculptura* to, 179; and plates of
Hooke's *Micrographia*, 185; JE meets in
Oxford, 191; and JE's design for college,
199; on exchange between JE and
Mackenzie, 206; duchess of Newcastle
criticises, 211; on compatibility of
religion and science, 212, 279–80;
receives copy of *Philsophical Transactions*
from Oldenburg, 223; on seraphic love,
240; on revival of Royal Society, 265;
death, 279; *New Experiments and
Observations Touching Cold*, 186;
Seraphic Love, 240
Bradshaw, George, 12
Bramston, Francis, 60, 64, 69
Breda, peace of (1667), 202
Breda, Treaty of (1650), 98
Brentford, Battle of, 33
Bressieux, M. (lens maker), 118
Bristol, George Digby, 2nd earl of, 236

Brompton Park nursery, 256, 283
Brosse, Salomon de, 102
Brouncker, William, 2nd viscount: and
founding of Royal Society, 167, 171;
and Royal Society publications, 184;
depicted on frontispiece of Sprat's
History of Royal Society, 212; and Royal
Society's search for new premises, 223;
Williamson succeeds as president of
Royal Society, 251
Browne, Christopher (father of Sir
Richard), 79, 127
Browne, Elizabeth, Lady (*née* Prettyman):
in Paris, 38, 74, 92; gifts from Verney,
71; JE praises, 75; pride in daughter
Mary's talents, 86; injured in Paris
affray, 101; portrait, 103; accompanies
daughter Mary to England, 117, 122–3;
on improvements to Sayes Court, 124;
death and burial, 125; Newcastles
promise money to, 211
Browne, Sir Richard (JE's father-in-law):
in Paris, 37–8, 41, 67, 70–2, 89;
friendship with JE, 72–3; financial
difficulties, 73, 82–3, 92, 125, 129, 149,
161, 235, 252–3, 256–7, 260; and JE's
marriage to daughter Mary, 73–4;
correspondence with JE in England,
77–85, 87, 91, 115, 156, 160; botanical
interests, 88, 153; and JE's proposed
return to Paris, 90–2; accompanies JE to
audience with Louis XIV, 97; letters
from Robert Long, 98; receives money
from Richard Evelyn, 99; party attacked
in Paris, 101; and JE's Lucretius
translation, 103, 118, 144; portrait, 103;
JE acquires Sayes Court from, 113, 115;
and JE's 1652 return to England, 113,
115; JE dedicates *The State of France* to,
115; on Mary's pregnancy, 121; and
improvements to Sayes Court, 123–4,
126–7, 131; as godfather to grandson
Richard, 124; declines invitation to
represent Commonwealth in Paris,
125–6; sent to Brittany, 125, 129; and
wife's death, 125; and William
Prettyman's claiming Sayes Court, 132;
collects plants and seeds for JE, 147,
153; JE requests French works for
translation, 147; on John Evelyn Jr's
upbringing, 149; and death of
JE/Mary's sons, 151; and preparations
for Restoration, 160, 163–4; JE orders

for Restoration, 160, 163–4; JE orders books from, 161; and publication of JE's *Elysium Britannicum*, 161–2; remains in Paris, 163, 257; reappointed clerk to Privy Council on return to England, 165–6, 235; sends copy of *Parallel* to St Albans, 187–8; in Oxford, 191; supports JE's proposals for naval hospital, 199–200; JE dedicates *Publick Employment* to, 205, 207; informs JE of court affairs, 208; describes Great Fire of London, 218; ill-health, 233, 245; Prettyman claims money from, 244; decline and death, 262–3; Prettyman loses case against, 266

Browne, Richard, the Younger (Dick) 125; childhood in Paris, 38, 92; schooling, 117

Browne, Sir Thomas: and JE's observations on French gardens, 40; JE sends outline of *Elysium Britannicum* to, 162, 183, 238; Tuke visits in Norwich, 183; JE meets, 237–8; *Religio medici*, 237

Bruggen, Louis van der, 40

Buckingham, George Villiers, 1st duke of, 9

Buckingham, George Villiers, 2nd duke of: in Italy, 57; on Waller, 62; as advisor to Charles II, 98; Hugh May serves, 178; as Cowley's patron, 205; criticised, 209; on Newcastles, 211

Buckingham, Mary, duchess of (*née* Fairfax), 212

Burlington House, London, 178

Burnet, Gilbert, later bishop of Salisbury, 60, 71, 164, 273, 303

Bushell, Thomas, 156, 190

Butler, Lord Richard, 101

Calthoff (Kalthof), Caspar, 76, 81

Cambridge: JE visits with Mary, 135

Camden, William: *Britannia*, 11, 227, 288

Campen, Jacob van, 25

Capel, Sir Henry, baron Capel of Tewkesbury, 282, 289

Carisbrooke Castle, Isle of Wight, 78, 84

Carteret, Sir George, 95, 194

Cary, Lucius *see* Falkland

Cary, Patrick, 46

Caryll, John: travels with JE to Low Countries, 22–3, 25–6, 28, 31

Casaubon, Meric, 146

Cassiobury Park, Herts, 256, 264

Castlemaine, countess of *see* Cleveland, duchess of

Catherine of Braganza, Queen of Charles II, 173, 239, 244, 267, 269

Catherine (royal yacht), 177

Catholicism *see* Roman Catholicism

Caus, Isaac de, 134

Caus, Salomon de, 161

Cavendish, Charles, 100

Cavendish, Margaret *see* Newcastle, Margaret Cavendish, marchioness of

Charenton, France, 70–1, 97

Charles I, King: visits Oxford University, 11; relations with Parliament, 12, 17; and beginnings of Civil War, 19; extravagance, 23; receives Nineteen Propositions from Parliament, 32; retires to Oxford in Civil War, 33; negotiates with Parliament in Civil War, 45; defeat at Naseby, 58; and Frizell, 75; JE's audience with, 77–8; under arrest, 77–8; rumoured escape from Carisbrooke, 84; removed from Isle of Wight, 87–8; trial and execution, 88–9; JE visits grave, 132; JE owns equestrian portrait of, 301; *Eikon Basilike*, 100

Charles II, King (*earlier* Prince of Wales): as fugitive in Civil War, 58; in Paris, 67, 71, 85, 95–7, 125; escapes to Holland, 84, 87; pleads for father's life, 89; seeks support in Scotland, 97–9; bans Book of Common Prayer in Paris, 102; escape from Battle of Worcester, 111; and preparations for Restoration, 160, 163; and publication of JE's *Elysium Britannicum*, 162–3; appearance and character, 164–5, 296; return to England, 164–5; touches for king's evil, 166; and founding of Royal Society, 168, 171; coronation, 170–1; JE dedicates *Fumifugium* to, 175, 177; JE dedicates *Sylva* to, 181; JE's disillusion with regime, 184, 207; scheme for rebuilding Whitehall Palace, 191, 214; thanks JE for copies of *Sylva* and *Parallel*, 191–4; and JE's plans for naval hospital, 199–200; visits Sayes Court, 204; love of pleasure, 207–8; court's inclination to Catholicism, 208; and Treaty of Dover, 208, 236; court attacked, 209; depicted in Sprat's

Charles II, King (*cont.*)
   History of the Royal Society, 212; in
   Great Fire of London, 218; and
   rebuilding of London after Great Fire,
   219, 224; offers land for Royal Society
   headquarters, 226; racing at
   Newmarket, 235; mistresses, 236, 267;
   asks JE to write history of Dutch wars,
   241; and Stop of Exchequer, 242;
   attends Shadwell's *Virtuoso*, 250;
   attitude to Royal Society, 251, 255;
   differences with Parliament, 253;
   supposed assassination attempt on, 264;
   death, 267–9; marriage relations, 267;
   Catholicism at death, 271; attempts to
   recruit De La Quintinye as gardener,
   282
Charles (ship), 242
Charleton, Walter, 13; *The Immortality of
   the Human Soul Demonstrated by the
   Light of Nature*, 145
Chatham: JE proposes seamen's hospital
   in, 198–201, 228, 262; Dutch attack
   fleet at, 201–3
Chelsea: Royal Hospital, 261–2, 293
Chelsea College, 226, 261
chemistry, 9, 44, 69, 100, 102, 110, 128,
   131, 137, 138, 156, 295
Chesterfield, Philip Stanhope, 2nd earl of,
   101, 106, 150, 173
Chiffinch, Thomas, 171–2, 199
Church of England: JE's adherence to, 14,
   107–8, 122; Parliament's measures
   against, 82; and Charles II's court in
   exile, 97; upheld at Oxford University,
   132; under attack, 138–9; re-established
   under Restoration, 166; and rise of
   Catholicism under James II, 273
Churchill, Sarah, Lady, 264
Citolin, M. (French tutor), 7
civil wars (1642–8): outbreak, 33, 40;
   conduct of, 58, 85; Clarendon's history
   of, 297
Clarendon, Edward Hyde, 1st earl of:
   warns against teaching mathematics to
   son, 12; separated from family, 80; in
   Paris, 95–6, 125; on Henrietta Maria's
   influence, 97; moves to Madrid, 97;
   heads government in exile, 111; and
   Browne's situation in France, 129,
   163–4; as lord chancellor, 166; earldom,
   170; JE dedicates Naudé translation to,
   171; supports Royal Society, 172; Hugh

   May designs for, 186; Pratt designs
   house for, 188–9; JE dines at house,
   191; blamed for naval humiliation at
   Chatham, 202, 210; visits Sayes Court,
   204; decline and downfall, 208–10, 277;
   relations with JE, 209–10; wife's death,
   210; love of books, 278, 296; *History of
   the Rebellion*, 297
Clarendon, Flower, countess of, 264
Clarendon, Henry Hyde, 2nd earl of
   (*earlier* viscount Cornbury): education,
   12; works with father abroad, 80; and
   building of Cornbury, 189; and design
   of Clarendon House, 189–90; as
   Queen's private secretary, 190; visits
   Oxford with JE, 190–1; Marvell
   satirises, 209; and father's downfall, 210;
   as lord privy seal, 268; succeeds to
   earldom, 268; as lord lieutenant of
   Ireland, 270; presents JE to James II,
   271; presents father's *History of the
   Rebellion* to JE, 297
Clarendon House, London, 188–9, 202;
   demolished, 264
Clayton, Sir Robert, 255
Cleveland, Barbara Villiers, duchess of
   (*earlier* countess of Castlemaine), 209,
   238
Clifford, Sir Thomas, 1st baron, 192, 208,
   235, 241–2, 277
Clodius (or Clod; Hartlib's son-in-law),
   Frederick, 136
Cobbett, William, 228
Cocke, Captain George, 192, 202
Colbert, Charles *see* Croissy
Colbert, Jean-Baptiste, 215, 231n, 236
Colchester, siege of (1848), 85
commission for sick and wounded and
   prisoners of war, 192–8, 201, 202–3,
   241–3, 247
commissioners for saltpetre and
   gunpowder, 3, 203
Committee for Advance of Money, 35,
   78
Commons, House of: Waller in the, 60
   George returned to, 253; George as
   oldest member of 279; JE plea to, 298
Commonwealth (English): proclaimed
   (1650), 104; Waller idealises, 126
Compton, Henry, Bishop of London, 256
Condé, Louis II de Bourbon, prince of,
   119
Cook, Moses, 256

Corderoy, William, 76
Cornaro, Luigi Alvise, 59, 279
Cornbury, Henry Hyde, viscount *see* Clarendon, 2nd earl of
Cornbury House, Oxfordshire, 190
Cosin, John, Bishop of Durham: in Paris, 71, 73, 97, 102; sends greetings to JE in England, 117; at Cambridge, 135
Cosin, John, Jr, 107
Coster, Laurence, 29
Cottington, Francis, Baron 95, 97
Council of Trade and Plantations (formerly Council for Foreign Plantations): JE serves on, 2, 203, 235, 240–1, 247
Coventry, Sir William, 197
Cowley, Abraham: in Paris, 70, 99, 204; honorary doctorate, 148; plans for free school, 157; on urban smoke, 175; on timber resources, 182; friendship with JE, 204; moves to Chertsey, 204; and JE's *Publick Employment*, 205; under patronage of Jermyn and Buckingham, 205; death, 212; JE requests poem for Sprat's *History of Royal Society*, 212; appearance, 296; *Cutter of Coleman-Street* (play), 173; *The Garden*, 205; *Proposition for the Advancement of Learning*, 157
Cowper, William, 91
Craven, William, earl of, 72
Crisp, Sir Nicholas, 123
Croissy, Charles Colbert, marquis de, 236
Cromwell, Oliver: military command in Civil War, 58; related to Waller, 62, 126; negotiates for end of war, 72; Charles I meets, 77; campaigns on Welsh borders, 85; and prospective trial of Charles I, 87; in power, 104, 132; Waller supports, 108; at launch of warships, 118; as Lord Protector, 129; negotiates with Mazarin, 136; death and funeral, 155; corpse disinterred and beheaded, 165; physiognomy, 296
Cromwell, Richard, 156–7
Crooke, John, 150, 154
Culpeper, Sir Cheney, 76

Danby, Henry Danvers, earl of, 14
Danby, Thomas Osborne, 1st earl of (*later* duke of Leeds), 243, 252–3, 277
Darcy, Elizabeth (*née* Evelyn; JE's sister), 5, 9

Davenant, Sir William, 70
Davisson, William, 100
de Beer, Esmond, 23
De Caus *see* Caus
Dee, John, 110
Deepdene, 148, 288
Denham, Sir John: in Paris, 70, 99; in Poland, 93; as Surveyor-General of King's Works, 178, 187; JE dedicates translation of Fréart's *Parallèle* to, 187; on Wren's visit to Pais, 214; mental decline, 215; 'Cooper's Hill', 178
Denham, Margaret, Lady, 215
Deptford: dockyard burnt, 202; *see also* Sayes Court
Descartes, René, 25, 100, 168, 280
de Vic, Sir Henry, 173
Diamond (warship), 118
Digby, Anne, countess of, 274
Digby, John, 67
Digby, Sir Kenelm: in Italy, 57–8; in Calais, 87; interest in chemistry, 100, 110; in Jardin des Plantes, Paris, 100; background, 110; discursiveness, 134; relations with Hartlib, 136; Rand on, 146; and proposed founding of learned society, 156; presents paper to Royal Society, 168; dispute with Thomas Browne, 238; William Draper visits home, 286
Dixon, Matthew, 246
Donatello, 15
Dorchester, Henry Pierrepont, 1st marquess of, 145
Dover Street, London, 284, 298, 305
Dover, Treaty of (1670), 208, 236
Downe, George (servant), 45
Downing, Sir George, 201, 260
Downs (Kent): naval battle (1666), 196
Doyley, Sir William, 192, 198, 241
Draper, Elizabeth (JE's granddaughter) *see* Harcourt, Elizabeth
Draper, Mary (JE's granddaughter), 286
Draper, Susanna (*née* Evelyn; JE's daughter): birth, 233; at Sayes Court with father, 262; mother introduces to society, 264; with mother after sisters' deaths, 269–70; writes to Bohun, 269; suitor rejected, 272; marriage and children, 284–5, 289; later life and death, 306
Draper, Sir Thomas, 284
Draper, Thomas (JE's grandson), 286

Draper, William (JE's son-in-law), 284–7, 291, 293–4, 301, 303
Dryden, John: *The Conquest of Granada*, 246
Duarte family, 30
Dublin Philosophical Society, 290
Ducie, Sir William, 40
Du Clos, Samuel, 69, 128
Duncomb, Sir Sanders, 9
Dutch: JE opposes wars with, 192
Dutch Wars: First (1652–4), 118, 121; Second (1665–7), 28, 181, 192–8, 201–3; Third (1672–4), 203, 229, 241–2; Fourth (1680–4), 292

Earle, John (*later* Bishop of Salisbury): caricatures university students, 14; in Paris, 71, 73, 95–6, 105; marriage relations, 80; sends letter to Hammond via JE, 113; sends greetings to JE in England, 117; and Charles II's return to England, 164; as Dean of Westminster, 166; at Charles II's coronation, 170
East India Company, 150
Eaton *see* Eyton
Edgehill, Battle of (1642), 33
Elizabeth, Princess (Charles I's daughter), 89
Elizabeth, Princess (Queen of Bohemia's daughter), 25
Elizabeth, Queen of Bohemia ('the Winter Queen'), 25
Elsevier's printing works, Leiden, 29
Eltham Lodge, Kent, 186–7
Enstone, Oxon, 190
Epicurus and Epicureanism, 102–3, 132, 137–9, 141–4, 146, 152, 213
Erasmus, Desiderius, 24, 159
Errard, Charles, 129
Essex, Arthur Capel, earl of, 170, 186, 256, 264
Eton College, 8, 281
Ettenhard, Signor, 67
Euston Hall, Suffolk, 235–7, 247
Evelyn family: gunpowder manufacturing, 2–3
Evelyn, Anne (*née* Boscawen; Jack's wife), 304
Evelyn, Sir Edward (of Long Ditton), 299
Evelyn, Eleanor (or Ellen; *née* Stansfield; JE's mother), 5, 9
Evelyn, Elizabeth (JE's daughter): birth,

213; mother introduces to society, 263–4; in Oxford with aunt, 268; elopement and death, 269
Evelyn, Elizabeth (John Jr's daughter), 282
Evelyn, Elizabeth (*née* Mynne; Richard's wife), 83, 299
Evelyn, George (JE's brother): birth, 5; education, 9–13; studies law, 10, 16; clothing expenses, 11; marriage, 16; at Wotton on father's death, 17; corresponds with JE in Low Countries, 26; art purchases, 33; widowed, 42; closes up Wotton in Civil War, 45; marriage to Mary Cotton, 72; as Member of Parliament, 78, 83, 87, 253; public offices, 79; helps Richard Browne with financial difficulties, 82, 92; describes Charles's execution, 89; JE dedicates *Of Liberty and Servitude* to, 90; counsels caution on JE in France, 98; children, 104; seeks JE's help in developing Wotton, 104–5; gives christening present to JE's son Richard, 124; hospitality at Wotton, 130, 259; improves Wotton, 130; on decadent court, 206; writes to JE on troubled times, 209; on winding up of Council of Trade and Plantations, 247; difficulties and legal disputes at Wotton, 261, 298–9; and Baynards Park entail, 270; offers JE and Mary apartment at Wotton, 281; and JE's improvements of Wotton garden, 282; charges rent to JE, 283–4; in old age, 287, 291; on John Jr's health decline, 289; death and funeral, 299–300
Evelyn, Captain George (JE's cousin): returns from Maryland, 84; proposes developing Wotton gardens, 104; improves Albury, 119; asks for pattern books, 128
Evelyn, George (JE's grandfather): at Wotton, 1; gunpowder manufacture, 3–4
Evelyn, George (JE's nephew): survives boyhood illness, 42; JE helps tutor, 120; travels with Walter Pope, 185
Evelyn, George (JE's son): birth, 149; JE's hopes for career as merchant, 150; death, 151
Evelyn, Jane (JE's sister) *see* Glanville, Jane

Evelyn, John
    ACTIVITIES AND INTERESTS: as
    art patron, 5; painting and drawing,
    15, 52, 91, 149; architectural interests
    and expertise, 24–5, 178, 187–90,
    199, 215, 288–9; art purchases and
    collection, 26, 33, 46, 91, 104; garden
    designs at Wotton, 34–5, 119–20,
    184, 282–4, 292; observations on
    French gardens, 40–2; book
    collection, 46, 57, 92, 106; visits
    Italian gardens, 54; studies human
    anatomy in Padua and Paris, 62, 101;
    acquires anatomical tables, 63–4, 87,
    91; herbarium, 63; chemistry, 69, 100,
    110, 131; involvement in Royal
    Society, 69, 150, 156, 167–9, 171–2,
    251, 267, 295–6, 302; print
    collection, 69, 103, 169; and
    patenting of water-raising wheel,
    76–8, 80–1, 118; sends art objects to
    France, 82; literary interests, 92;
    etchings, 93, 109–10; culinary
    interests, 94; hunger for knowledge,
    103; helps improve Wotton, 104–5;
    improvements to Sayes Court house
    and garden, 123–7, 131, 148, 153–4,
    183, 204–5, 265, 269; laboratory and
    experiments, 130–1; bee-hives,
    133–4, 136; and Hartlib's trades
    project, 137; collects plants and trees,
    147–8, 153; collects insects and
    butterflies, 148; restricts print
    collection to architectural subjects,
    149; builds houses alongside Sayes
    Court, 150; concentrates on
    gardening, 156; supported by Beale,
    159; and printmaking, 169, 179, 186;
    suggests motto for coinage (decus et
    tutamen), 169; proposed
    improvements to London, 175–8;
    writes Royal Society report on
    nation's timber (Sylva), 180, 182–3;
    redesigns Howard's Albury garden,
    184; advises on gardens for Hugh
    May's houses, 187; and survey of old
    St Paul's cathedral, 216; designs
    gardens for Howard at Albury and
    Norwich, 227–8; botanical interests,
    256; visits Addiscombe, 301–2
    BELIEFS AND IDEAS: religious
    views and practices, 14–15, 53, 58,
    93–4, 107–8, 121, 138–9, 141–3, 151,
    240, 272, 280; refuses to sign Solemn
    League and Covenant, 35; royalist
    sympathies, 36; attitude to Roman
    Catholicism, 272; on party politics,
    272; on political reform, 275; inclined
    to vegetarianism, 297
    CAREER: serves on Council of Trade
    and Plantations, 2, 203, 235, 240,
    247; early education, 7–8; enters
    Middle Temple, 10, 16, 31–2; at
    Oxford (Balliol), 11–16; matriculates
    at Leiden University, 28; activities in
    Civil War, 33; matriculates at Padua,
    60; as commissioner for sick and
    wounded and prisoners of war,
    192–8, 203, 241–3, 247; as
    commissioner of Privy Seal, 203,
    270–2; Pepys suggests for navy board,
    208, 257; applies unsuccessfully for
    post of Latin Secretary, 234; acts as
    Berkeley's steward, 248; denies
    ambition, 258
    FINANCES: inheritance from parents,
    18; investments, 150; reduced
    through unpaid rents, 161; and
    Prettyman's lawsuits, 263; wins case
    against Prettyman and recoups losses,
    266, 270; salary as commissioner of
    Privy Seal, 271; legal wrangles over
    property, 283–5, 298–300; salary at
    Greenwich, 290
    HEALTH: smallpox, 66; recovers from
    illness at Wotton, 161; fits, 260;
    longevity, 279; in old age, 287; breaks
    shin, 303; final illness, 306
    PERSONAL: birth and infancy, 4–6;
    appearance, 5; upbringing by step-
    grandparents, 7–9; motto (omnia
    explorate, meliora retinete: look into
    everything, keep the best), 11, 40; on
    parents' death, 17–18; portraits, 21–2,
    40, 85, 103–4, 297; betrothal and
    marriage to Mary Browne, 72–5,
    93–5; correspondence with Eyton
    ('Thomas White'), 98; and death of
    sister Jane, 112; settles in England
    (1652), 113; fatherhood, 121, 124,
    149–50; attacked and robbed, 122;
    Rand dedicates translation of
    Gassendi's life of Peiresc to, 146; and
    death of sons, 151–3; dress, 177;
    marriage relations, 194, 240; dispute
    with Mackenzie, 205–7; manner, 208;

Evelyn, John (*cont.*)
  PERSONAL (*cont.*)
    in Great Fire of London, 216–19;
    self-examination, 234–5; relations
    with Margaret Blagge, 239–41,
    246–7, 252; visits Pepys in prison,
    255; involved in family lawsuits, 257;
    advice to son John, 259; female
    friends, 267; dreams, 280; moves back
    to Wotton House, 281–2, 287, 292;
    and daughter Susanna's marriage,
    284–6; moves from Wotton to son's
    house in Dover Street, 284; removes
    again from Wotton to Dover Street,
    298; misses son John's funeral, 299;
    inherits and improves Wotton, 300–2;
    eightieth birthday, 302; will, 302;
    death and burial at Wotton, 305–6
  PUBLIC LIFE: military experience in
    Low Countries, 25–6; meets Charles
    II on return from exile, 165–6; seeks
    position at court, 173–4; drafts bill
    for London improvements, 177–8;
    Oxford honorary degree, 190;
    proposes building naval hospital,
    198–201, 203, 262; presents plan and
    report for rebuilding London after
    Great Fire, 219–22, 224; and
    brickmaking for London rebuilding,
    224–5; opposition to Third Dutch
    War, 242; temporary secretaryship of
    Royal Society, 247; declines
    presidency of Royal Society, 279; as
    treasurer to Greenwich Royal Naval
    Hospital, 291–4
  TRAVELS: tours of southern England,
    15; journeys and observations in Low
    Countries (1641), 19–31; wartime
    stay in France and Italy, 34, 37,
    39–69, 71; returns to England (1647),
    75–6, 77, 83, 88; considers exile, 90;
    returns to Paris exile, 93, 95–6, 102,
    111; revisits England (1650), 103–4;
    to Oxford, west country and north
    with Mary, 132–5; to Newmarket and
    Norwich, 235–8
  WRITINGS: diary, 9, 23, 47, 260;
    plays, 17; poetry, 58; translations from
    French, 68, 90, 128, 147, 150, 153–4,
    167, 187–8, 226, 235, 282; translation
    of Lucretius, 102–3, 118, 129, 131,
    137–8, 141–7, 212; on history of
    trades, 140, 169; translates St John

Chrysostom, 152; panegyric on
    Charles II's coronation, 170–1; verses
    printed in Tuke's *Adventures of Five
    Hours*, 184; Charles II requests to
    write history of Dutch wars, 241,
    243, 265; prepares life of Margaret
    Blagge, 260; begins history of
    religion, 274; considers dictionary
    giving derivations, 278; contributes
    notes for revised edition of Aubrey's
    Surrey, 288; papers rediscovered, 306;
    Acetaria, 297; *An Apologie for the
    Royal Party*, 160; *The Character of
    England*, 116, 172; *Elysium
    Britannicum*, 106, 131, 134, 148–9,
    151, 153, 159, 161–2, 170, 182, 191,
    203, 205, 250, 255, 297; *Fumifugium*,
    116, 175, 177, 179, 181, 216, 220,
    222; *Kalendarium Hortense*, 182, 205,
    248; *Londinium Redivivum*, 219, 224;
    Memoire, 301; *Navigation and
    Commerce*, 243; *Numismata*, 179,
    295–6; *The Originals* (unpublished
    play), 17; *Publick Employment and an
    Active Life Prefer'd to Solitude*, 205–7;
    Sculptura, 31, 149, 169, 179, 227, 297;
    The State of France, 115–16; *Sylva*,
    168, 181–2, 185, 192, 107, 203, 234,
    251, 253, 295, 297; *Terra*, 248;
    Tyrannus or the Mode, 173
Evelyn, Sir John, Bt (JE's grandson; Jack):
    education, 8, 280; birth, 260; at Sayes
    Court, 263; stays with grandparents
    during parents' absence in Dublin, 282;
    acts as page at Susanna's wedding, 285;
    library at Sayes Court, 286;
    bookishness, 289; JE's love and hopes
    for, 299; inheritance, 300, 306; career
    and accomplishments, 302, 306;
    recovers from smallpox, 302; marriage,
    304–5; as receiver of stamp duties, 305
Evelyn, John (JE's son): at Wotton, 1;
    letters of advice from JE, 32; birth, 139;
    JE recommends to visit Enstone, 190;
    Bohun tutors at Oxford, 191, 213;
    crooked legs, 213; education, 213, 280;
    misbehaviour, 234; studies law, 234,
    258, 263; accompanies Berkeley to
    Paris, 248–9; depressions, 258, 290, 300;
    marriage to Martha, 258–9; unsettled
    state, 258–9; translates Plutarch's *Lives*,
    260; children, 260; JE warns against
    court, 267; supports mother after death

of sisters, 269; position at Treasury, 274; visits Lady Sunderland with father, 274; supports William of Orange, 275; favours JE's move from Sayes Court to Wotton, 281; short tenure as junior treasury official, 282; as commissioner of customs and excise in Dublin, 282, 289; debts, 284; and father's relaxed state, 286; and parents' life at Wotton, 287; decline, 289–90; develops love of books and picture collecting, 289–90; death, 299–300

Evelyn, Sir John (of Godstone), 3–4, 139, 299

Evelyn, Sir John (of West Dean), 299

Evelyn, John Stansfield (JE's son): birth and death, 132

Evelyn, John ('Wotton Jack'; JE's nephew), 130, 248, 259, 281

Evelyn, Martha (née Spencer; John Jr's wife): marriage and children, 258–60; supports Mary Evelyn after death of daughters, 269; moves to Dublin with husband, 282; and JE's health in old age, 287

Evelyn, Mary (née Caldwell; George's first wife): marriage, 16–17; death 42; friendship with Mary Tuke, 209

Evelyn, Mary (earlier Lady Cotton, née Offley; George's second wife) marriage, 72; at Wotton 78; birth of daughter 83; birth of son

Evelyn, Mary (George's daughter) see Wyche, Mary, Lady

Evelyn, Mary (JE's daughter): birth, 194; accomplishments, 264; in London, 264, 267; death, 268

Evelyn, Mary (née Browne; JE's wife): in Paris, 38, 71; betrothal and marriage to JE, 71–5, 93–5; artistic and musical accomplishments, 86, 95, 116–17, 128, 131; JE compiles book for ('Instructions Oeconomique'), 86; portraits, 86, 103; and JE's return to Paris, 91, 93; Tuke admires, 99–100; miscarriage, 106; Henshaw sends greetings to, 109–10; delays following JE to England, 116–19, 121; domestic management, 117; orders cabinet for Sayes Court, 117; pregnancies and children, 121–4, 149, 193–4, 213, 233; arrival in England, 122–4; and mother's death, 125; on uncle William Prettyman's claim to

Sayes Court, 132; visits Oxford, west country and north with JE, 132–5; designs frontispiece to JE's translation of Lucretius, 141; in Rand's dedication of Gassendi translation, 146; helps JE with French translations, 147; and JE's translation of Bonnefons, 153; supports JE's plans for learned institution, 157; manages Sayes Court in JE's absence, 161, 245, 266; on unpaid rents by dockyard workers, 161; prepares for Restoration, 164; fails to win position at court, 172–3; on JE's writing for Royal Society, 183; verses printed in Tuke's Adventures of Five Hours, 184; and JE's duties as commissioner for sick and wounded, 193; marriage relations, 194, 285–6; visits duchess of Newcastle, 211; admires Sprat's History of the Royal Society, 212; on brickmaking for London rebuilding, 225; and Glanville's visit to Paris, 229; describes Sayes Court in winter, 233; and JE's relationship with Margaret Blagge, 240, 246, 251, 261; entertaining at Sayes Court, 244–5; mourns Tuke's death, 244; independence of mind, 245–6; misses Paris, 245; son John fails to write to from Paris, 248; claims support against father's ruined estate, 257; on son John's marriage, 259; takes waters at Tunbridge Wells, 260, 262; and father's decline and death, 262; introduces daughters to society, 263–4; and frost damage to Sayes Court garden, 265; on Godolphin's obligation to help JE, 266; mourns death of daughter Mary, 268–9; on JE's gardening, 269; favours Pepys as tenant, 280; and grandson Jack's upbringing, 281; lives at Wotton with JE, 281–2, 287, 291–2, 302–4; on daughter Susanna's marriage, 284–5; moves from Wotton to Dover Street, 284; observations on Hampton Court, 292; and JE's anxieties as treasurer of Royal Naval Hospital, Greenwich, 293; removes again from Wotton to Dover Street, 298; returns to Wotton, 300; on Drapers' building plans, 302; and Bohun's living at Wotton, 303; on JE's death, 305–6; death (1709), 306

Evelyn, Richard (JE's brother): birth, 5; in Lewes with JE, 9; attends Oxford University, 15–16; writes to JE in

Evelyn, Richard (JE's brother) (*cont.*)
  Rome, 45; meets JE on return from
  France, 78; acquires Woodcote, Epsom,
  83, 125; marriage, 83; at Deptford, 87;
  considers joining JE in France, 98–9; on
  JE's enjoyment of Paris, 106; and JE's
  return to England, 112; at Baynards,
  119; congratulates JE on Chatham
  hospital conversion, 199; death from
  kidney stones, 234
Evelyn, Richard (JE's father): inherits
  Wotton, 1; property, 4, 7; public and
  charitable activities, 4–5, 9; appearance,
  5; on family's upbringing and careers,
  9–11, 16; decline and death, 16–18;
  will, 18; and dispute over Wotton, 299
Evelyn, Richard (JE's fourth son): birth
  and death, 193
Evelyn, Richard (JE's son): birth, 124;
  childhood and upbringing, 132, 150;
  nearly chokes as child, 139; childish
  achievements, 149; death, 151–2; JE
  idealises, 267
Evelyn, Robert (JE's uncle), 4
Evelyn, Susanna (JE's daughter) *see*
  Draper, Susanna
Evelyn, Thomas (JE's uncle), 4
Exclusion Crisis (1679), 254
Eyton, Sir Kenrick ('Thomas White'), 86,
  95, 98

Fairfax, Thomas, 1st baron, 85
Faithorne, William, 179, 186
Falkland, Anthony Cary, 5th viscount,
  266, 271
Falkland, Lucius Cary, 2nd viscount, 46
Falkland, Rebecca, viscountess, 267
Fanshawe, Ann, Lady, 80, 87
Fanshawe, Sir Richard: at The Hague, 87;
  travels to Paris with Waller, 100; and
  JE's Lucretius translation, 103, 118,
  141–2, 144; JE's relations with, 106;
  visits JE at Sayes Court, 117; and
  preparations for Restoration, 163; at
  Charles II's coronation, 170; as Latin
  secretary at court, 173, 234
Favi, Giacomo Maria, 170
Figliola, la (musician), 60
Finch, Sir John, 25
Fire Court: established (1667), 225
Fisher, Mr (prospective travelling
  companion), 67
Flamsteed, John, 265

Fleet, river, 222
Florence, Italy, 44, 55
Fontainebleau, 41
Forest of Dean, 182
Fox, Jane, 256
Fox, Sir Stephen: support for Royal
  Society, 27; and Charles II's return to
  England, 164; on commission to
  improve London, 178; Hugh May
  designs for, 186–7; fails to secure Sayes
  Court lease for JE, 257; advises Royal
  Society Fellows to sell interest in
  Chelsea College, 261; and building of
  Royal Hospital, Chelsea, 262; finds post
  for John Evelyn Jr in Dublin, 282; and
  funding of Greenwich naval hospital, 294
France: JE's wartime stay in, 34, 36–43,
  67; absolutist monarchy, 39; gardens,
  41–2; and Fronde conflict, 89, 101–2;
  JE's second visit and exile in, 93, 95–9;
  political/religious upheavals, 107; JE's
  continuing interest in from England,
  113; enters Second Dutch War against
  England, 198; prepares for war with
  England, 215; alliance with England in
  Third Dutch War, 241; repression of
  Protestants, 271
Frascati, Italy, 54
Fréart de Chambray, Roland: *An Idea of
  the Perfection of Painting Demonstrated*,
  227; *Parallel of Architecture*: translated
  by JE, 129, 189–90, 192–3, 202, 217,
  230, 292, 300
Frederick, Elector Palatine (*earlier* King of
  Bohemia), 25
Frederick Henry, Elector Palatine, 11
Frederick Henry, Prince of Orange, 25
Frizell, William, 75, 81
Fronde (France), 84, 87, 89, 101, 118
Fulham, Catherine (*née* Evelyn; George's
  daughter), 298
Fulham, George, 298–9

Gale, Thomas, Dean of York, 286, 296
Galileo Galilei, 49
Galloway, James Stewart, 2nd earl of, 156
Gassendi, Pierre, 90, 100, 102, 137, 141,
  146, 171
Geneva, 66
Genoa, 43
George III, King of Great Britain, 49
Gibbons, Grinling, 256, 273, 301
Gibson, Edmund, 228, 288

Glanville, Jane (*née* Evelyn; JE's sister): birth, 5; inheritance, 18; requests portrait of JE, 40; in wartime Wotton, 42; as royalist housekeeper in Civil War, 44; marriage, 83; pregnancies and children, 94, 111; and JE's economising in Paris, 111; death in childbirth, 112

Glanville, Joseph, 204, 212

Glanville, William: marriage to JE's sister, 83; Mary recommends to visit Maisons, 94; on wife's death, 111–12; stays at Wotton, 130; congratulates Mary on pregnancies and children, 193, 213; Pepys lodges with during plague, 197; in Paris, 229–30, 245; on George Evelyn at Wotton, 259, 261; congratulates JE on appointment to commission of Privy Seal, 270; visits De La Quintinye, 282; and JE's difficulties at Wotton, 283; financial support for John Evelyn Jr, 284; supports Fulham in dispute over Wotton, 299; reconciliation with JE, 300; death, 300

Glanville, William, Jr, 104, 230, 259, 282, 300

Glauber, Johann Rudolf, 69, 128

Gloucester, Henry, duke of, 87, 89, 166

Goddard, Jonathan, 181

Godolphin, Francis (Margaret and Sidney's son), 285, 296, 305

Godolphin, Lady Henrietta (*née* Churchill; Francis's wife), 305

Godolphin, Sidney (*later* 1st earl): courtship and marriage to Margaret Blagge, 239–41, 246; and wife's death, 252; appointed commissioner at Treasury, 253; JE seeks support from for Browne, 256–7, 260; Mary Tuke's disillusionment with, 264; appointed chamberlain to Mary of Modena, 268; and JE's appointment to Privy Seal commission, 271–2; returns to Treasury (1685), 269; (1690), 277; and John Evelyn Jr's post in Dublin, 282, 289; and JE's plea for money for Greenwich hospital, 293; as lord treasurer under Queen Anne, 305

Golle, Pierre, 117

Gomme, Bernard de, 26

Good, Thomas, 249

Goring, George (*later* earl of Norwich), 32, 38–9, 93

Grafton, Henry Fitzroy, duke of, 237

Grafton, Isabella, duchess of (*née* Bennet), 237

Graham, Dorothy (*née* Howard), 238, 240

Graunt, John, 176

Gravesande, Arend van 's, 28

Greatorex, Ralph, 130

Greenwich: Charles II plans rebuilding of palace, 178; Royal Naval Hospital, 291–4, 304

Greenwich Park: trees, 129, 204

Gresham College, London: JE attends scientific lectures, 135; Royal Society meets at, 167–8; City Corporation occupies after Great Fire, 222; Arundel library moved to, 251

Grotius, Hugo, 65, 100

Guernier, Alexandre II du, 86, 128

Guilford, Francis North, 1st baron, 265, 271

Gunning, Peter, Bishop of Ely, 234

gunpowder: manufacture, 2–4

Hague, The: JE visits, 24–5, 29

Hall Barn, Beaconsfield, 108, 120, 191

Halley, Edmund, 265

Hamilton, William, 2nd duke of, 98

Hammond, Henry, 113

Hampden, John, 62, 126

Hampton Court, 77, 292

Hanmer, Susan, Lady, 80

Hanmer, Sir Thomas, 87–8, 115, 148, 162, 182, 205, 238

Harcourt, Elizabeth (*née* Draper; Susanna's daughter), 304, 306

Harcourt, Simon, 306

Harris, Frances, 240

Harrison, Sir John, 35, 157

Hartlib, Samuel: and patenting of water-raising wheel, 76, 81, 118; on JE at Deptford, 130; circle, 133, 146; JE visits, 136; and 'Invisible College', 137; and trades project, 137, 140; on Henshaw, 138; and founding of learned society, 156, 158; and John Beale, 158–9, 181; JE sends outline of *Elysium Britannicum* to, 162; asked about opening Sayes Court to public, 177; death, 181; *Herefordshire Orchards, A Pattern of All England* (with Beale), 159; *Legacy of Husbandry*, 136

Harvey, William: studies at Padua, 62; anatomical specimens, 64; portrait, 83;

Harvey, William (*cont.*)
  friendship with Cowley, 204;
  appearance, 296
Hatfield House, Hertfordshire, 35, 148
Hatton, Charles, 289
Hatton, Christopher, 1st baron, 95, 97;
  Nicholas writes to from The Hague,
  110
Hatton, Robert, 18, 20, 31
Hawksmoor, Nicholas, 301
Heath, Robert: friendship with JE, 8;
  sends information on France to JE, 42
Henrietta Maria, Queen of Charles I:
  visits Holland, 32; returns to England,
  34; Digby acts as papal envoy for, 57;
  exile and court in Paris, 70–1, 89, 93,
  97, 110, 204; pleads for Charles's life,
  89; and Charles's ban on use of Book of
  Common Prayer in Paris, 102; proposes
  Tuke as duke of York's secretary, 156;
  attends daughter's marriage in France,
  166; return from exile, 166; Nonsuch
  Palace, 198; visits Sayes Court, 204;
  returns to Paris, 214–15
Henry, Prince *see* Gloucester, duke of
Henshaw, Thomas: travels in Italy, 43–4,
  49, 51–4, 56–8, 60, 109–10; JE gives
  pastoral poem to, 58; illness, 69; plans
  return to England, 69–70, 83; and JE's
  second stay in France, 99; JE dedicates
  etchings to, 109; studies in England,
  109; called to bar, 130; in Kensington,
  130; and alchemy, 138; and JE's *Elysium
  Britannicum*, 150; suggests JE translate
  Bonnefons, 150, 153; friendship with
  JE, 153, 216; marriage 153; and plans
  for learned society, 157; returns to
  England, 157; in Royal Society, 169,
  171, 251; in Copenhagen, 247
Herbert, George, 279
Herbert, William, Lord (*later* 6th earl of
  Pembroke), 120
Hertochs, Abraham, 179
Hewer, William, 296
Hill, Abraham, 251, 255
Hill, Richard, 3–4
Hoare, Richard, 52, 86, 92–3, 104, 106,
  109
Hobbes, Thomas: tutors Waller's son and
  nephew, 61; as tutor to Charles II, 67,
  71; Waller introduces JE to, 68; in
  France, 96, 100; Samuel Tuke
  recommends writings, 105; JE's

relations with, 108–9, 115; reputation,
  108; Sorbière asks about Royal Society,
  172; blamed for political turmoil, 253;
  philosophical ideas, 280; appearance,
  296; *De Cive* (translated as *Philosophical
  Rudiments concerning Government and
  Society*), 67–8, 108; *Leviathan*, 109,
  114–15
Hogue, La, Battle of (1692), 292
Holden, Revd Dr Richard, 269
Holland *see* Dutch Wars; United Provinces
Holland, Henry Rich, 1st earl of, 93
Hollar, Wenceslaus: as neighbour of Van
  der Borcht, 22; engraves Van Dyck's
  self-portrait, 35; makes prints for Van
  der Borcht, 41; etchings of Albury, 119;
  engraves frontispiece to JE's Lucretius
  translation, 141; engraves Titian/JE
  picture, 149; etches frontispiece for
  Sprat's *History of the Royal Society*, 186,
  212; view of St Paul's, 215; great map of
  London after fire, 224; JE owns print of
  Great Fire, 301
Hondius, Abraham, 29
Honthorst, Gerard, 25
Honywood, Captain Benedict, 26
Hooke, Robert: on Worcester's water-
  raising machine, 81; describes Wilkins,
  132; in Royal Society, 169, 171; and
  costing of JE's proposed seamen's
  hospital, 200; duchess of Newcastle
  criticises, 211; remains at Gresham
  College after Great Fire, 222; plan for
  rebuilding London, 223; survey of
  London after Great Fire, 223; and brick
  production after Great Fire, 224; plans
  for Royal Society building, 226; treatise
  on helioscopes, 248; architectural
  designs, 251, 289; sees Shadwell's
  Virtuoso, 250–1; and JE's defence of
  Royal Society, 255; recommends
  Descartes to Boyle, 280; death, 302;
  Micrographia, 170, 185–6, 250
Hopton, Sir Arthur, 67
Hopton, Ralph, 1st baron, 67, 74
Hoskins, Sir John, 251
Hotham, Sir John, 32
Houblon, James, 271
Howard, Charles, 148, 183
Howard, Dorothy *see* Graham, Dorothy
Howard, Henry (*later* 6th duke of
  Norfolk): in Italy, 56, 58; keeps Albury,
  119, 128; alters Albury house and

garden, 148; Tuke serves, 183; invites JE to redesign Albury garden, 184; Tuke dedicates *The Adventures of Five Hours* to, 184; offers Arundel House for Royal Society meetings, 223; JE dedicates Fréart translation to, 226–7; offers land to Royal Society building, 226; presents grandfather's marbles to Oxford, 226–7; JE designs gardens for, 227, 237; succeeds to dukedom, 227; JE's disillusion with, 228; qualities, 237–8; takes JE to duke's palace in Norwich, 237–8; refuses help to Mary Tuke, 259

Howard, Philip (Cardinal of Norfolk), 58, 64

Howard, Thomas *see* Arundel, Thomas, 2nd earl of

Howard, Thomas (*later* 5th duke of Norfolk), 59

Howard, William *see* Stafford, 10

Huguenots, 70–1, 271

Hungerford, Susan (*née* Prettyman), 125, 132, 134

Hunt, Dick (servant), 10, 45, 111

Hunter, Michael, 106

Hussey, John, 263, 269

Hutchinson, Lucy, 141

Huygens, Christiaan, 100, 179, 248

Huygens, Constantijn, 25, 204, 234

Huygens, Lodewijk, 134

Hyde, Anne *see* York, Anne, duchess of

Hyde, Edward *see* Clarendon, 1st earl of

Hyde, Henry *see* Clarendon, 2nd earl of

Hyde, Laurence *see* Rochester, 1st earl of

Indulgence, Declaration of (1688), 273

Innocent X, Pope, 46, 50, 53

Invisible College, 137

Ireland: massacre and rebellion in (1641), 32; Cromwell in, 97; French troops in to support James II, 276

Ireton, Henry, 118

Italy: JE visits, 43–65; gardens, 54

Jackson, John, 303–4

James II, King (*earlier* duke of York): in exile in Paris with mother, 89, 99; hears Earle's sermon in Paris, 105; and JE's audience with Charles II at Restoration, 165; marriage to Anne Hyde, 166, 210; leaves London in plague, 193; replaced as commander of fleet, 198; and JE's plans for naval hospital, 200; supports Clarendon, 210; liaison with Denham's wife, 215; in Great Fire of London, 218; Arlington serves in France, 236; Pepys meets, 238; commands fleet at Battle of Sole Bay, 242; driven from England, 254; supposed assassination attempt on, 264; accession following Charles II's death, 268; Catholicism, 268, 271–4; coronation, 269; plans remodelling of Whitehall, 271, 273; birth of son James, 273; deposed, 275; proposes naval hospital at Greenwich, 292

James Francis Edward Stuart, Prince ('the Old Pretender'): birth, 273

Jeffreys, George, 1st baron, 271

Jermyn, Lord Henry *see* St Albans, 1st earl of

Jesuits: JE's attitude to, 30, 51, 209; in Rome, 48, 51; JE studies theology of, 57

Jews: JE encounters in United Provinces, 27; in Rome, 51

John Chrysostom, St, 152

Jones, Inigo, 59, 134, 215

Joyliffe, George: studies anatomy at Padua, 63; scientific interests, 83; JE requests skeleton and plants from, 101

Junius, Franciscus, 32

Justel, Henri, 215, 248

Keightley, Thomas: conversion to Catholicism, 15, 53, 107–8; in Paris, 42, 108; interest in Mary Browne, 72

Keightley, Thomas, Jr, 290

Keightley, William: permitted to leave for France, 34; in Paris, 42; marriage, 87; converts to Catholicism, 108

Ken, Thomas, Bishop of Bath and Wells, 273

Kent, William, 143n

Kérouaille, Louise de (*later* duchess of Portsmouth), 236, 267

Keynes, Geoffrey, 283

Keyser, Hendrik de, 24, 35

'Kibble, Robert', 77

Kievit (or Kiviet), Jan, 225

Kilmainham, Dublin, Ireland, 262

Kircher, Father Athanasius, 48–9, 52, 57, 134; *Lingua Aegyptiaca Restituta*, 50

Kneller, Sir Godfrey: portrait of JE, 297

La Mothe le Vayer, François, 171; *Of Liberty and Servitude*, 68, 90

Lassels, Richard, 49

Laud, William, Archbishop of
  Canterbury: as Chancellor of Oxford
  University, 11, 13, 132; Arminianism,
  15; executed, 51; gifts to Bodleian
  Library, 133
Leake, John, 224
Leeds Castle, Kent, 194
Le Fèvre, Niçaise, 69, 110, 128, 137
Le Gendre, Sieur: *The Manner of Ordering
  Fruit-Trees*, 150
Legge, Colonel William, 78
Leiden: JE visits, 28–9; JE matriculates at, 28
Leoni, Giovanni, 63
Lewes, Sussex: Stansfield family in, 6–7;
  JE's early life in, 7–9, 11; JE revisits, 15,
  33
Licensing Act (1662), 254
Lilburne, John, 77
Livorno, Italy, 55
Lloyd, William, Bishop of St Asaph,
  273
Locke, John: criticises academic
  conservatism, 12; as secretary of
  Council of Trade and Plantations, 247;
  Essay concerning Human Understanding,
  280
Loggan, David, 186
London: smallpox epidemic, 26;
  Parliamentary forces in, 84; JE proposes
  improvements, 175–7, 186, 216;
  pollution, 176; town planning and
  development, 186; Great Plague (1665),
  193–7; Great Fire (1666), 216–19, 221;
  post-Fire rebuilding plans, 219–23,
  225–6; brickmaking after Great Fire,
  224–5
London, George, 256, 283, 295, 298
London (ship), 196
Long Ditton, Surrey, 4
Long, Sir Robert, 98
Longueil, Madeleine, 94
Longueil, René de, 94
Lords, House of: abolished, 88; JE plea to,
  298
Louis XIII, King of France, 37
Louis XIV, King of France: minority
  under regency, 38–9; succeeds under
  regency, 39; performs in ballet, 59;
  popular concessions, 87; ordered to stay
  in Paris, 92; JE's audience with, 97;
  returns to Paris from Compiègne, 97;
  progress in Paris, 108–9; accession on
  reaching majority, 109, 176;

accommodation with Cromwell, 116;
  court, 175; JE admires, 208; Bernini's
  bust of, 214; and planning of Paris, 215;
  supports learned institutions, 255;
  builds Invalides, 262; JR owns portrait
  of, 301
Louise, Princess (Elizabeth of Bohemia's
  daughter), 25
Low Countries: JE travels in (1641),
  20–31
Lowestoft, Battle of (1665), 196
Loyall Evelyn (ship), 295
Lucas, Sir Charles, 85
Lucretius: *De Rerum Natura*: JE translates,
  102–3, 118, 129, 131, 137–8, 141–7,
  212
Lyons, France, 43
Lyttelton, Sir Charles, 211

Maastricht, siege of (1674), 243
Machiavelli, Niccolò, 56, 90, 115, 146
Mackenzie, George: *A Moral Essay,
  Preferring Solitude to Publick
  Employment*, 205–6
Maddocks, Benjamin, 147
Magalotti, Lorenzo, 12, 164, 236, 250
Maisons (château), France, 94, 105–6,
  262
Mansart, François, 94, 214, 223, 231
Maratti, Carlo, 49, 57
Margret (Wotton cook), 302, 304
Marie de Médicis, Queen regent of
  France, 21, 26, 29–30, 102
Markham, Gervase: *The English
  Husbandman*, 182
Marlborough, John Churchill, 1st duke of,
  305
Marolles, Michel, abbé de, 103, 141
Marvell, Andrew: in Italy, 57; 'The
  Garden', 14; *The Last Instructions to a
  Painter*, 209
Mary of Modena, Queen of James II
  (*earlier* duchess of York), 244, 254, 274
Mary, Princess of Orange, 166
Mary (Stuart), Queen (*earlier* Princess):
  betrothal to William of Orange, 21, 32;
  favours Anne Hyde, 78; marriage, 244;
  displaced from succession by birth of
  James, 273; reign, 276–7; death, 292;
  supports building of hospital at
  Greenwich, 292
May, Hugh: helps JE find engravings of
  Fréart's *Parallèle*, 129; on commission to

improve London, 178; architectural practice, 186–8; designs Cornbury, 190; Packer succeeds as paymaster, 198; and survey of old St Paul's cathedral, 216; and designs for London after Great Fire, 223; designs Berkeley House, 247; builds house for Stephen Fox, 256; designs earl of Essex's Cassiobury house, 256

Mazarin, Cardinal Giulio: as minister of state in France, 39, 115; book collection and library, 68, 171, 174; taxation proposals, 89; la Mothe le Vayer addresses, 90; exiled, 107; negotiates with Cromwell, 136; death, 170

Mazarin, Hortense Mancini, duchess of, 267

Medway, river: Dutch penetrate, 201–3

Merret, Christopher, 181

mezzotints, 179

Middle Temple: JE enters, 10, 16–17, 32

Milan, 65

Milton, John: in Naples, 19; and Patrick Cary, 46; *Paradise Lost*, 138

Monck, George *see* Albemarle, 1st duke of

Monmouth, James Scott, duke of: birth, 97; Rebellion (1685), 268

Montagu, Anne (*née* Evelyn; Richard and Elizabeth's daughter), 299

Montagu House, London, 289

Montagu, William, 270, 299

Montaigne, Michel Eyquem de, 90

Monteverdi, Claudio: *Coronation of Poppea*, 62

Monument (London), 228

Moore, Jonas, 203, 220

Moray, Sir Robert: in London, 167; in Royal Society, 171; and mezzotint process, 179; sends books to Huygens, 179; suggests JE write Royal Society report on nation's timber, 180; suggests JE reply to *A Moral Essay, Preferring Solitude to Publick Employment*, 205–7; mission to Scotland, 207; Pepys suggests for navy board, 208; and brick production for London rebuilding, 224; appearance, 296

Mordaunt, Elizabeth, viscountess (*née* Carey), 144, 152

Mordaunt, John, 1st viscount, 152, 160, 171

Morden College, Blackheath, 291

More, Sir Thomas: *Utopia*, 138, 178

Moreton Hall, Chiswick, 187

Morin, Pierre, 41–2, 88, 117, 126–7, 131, 136, 147, 153, 182

Morison, Robert, 102, 191

Morley, Agnes, 7

Morley, George, Bishop of Winchester, 60, 93, 96–7, 163, 170

Morley, Harbert (or Herbert): friendship with JE, 8; in Civil War, 33; as member of Council of State, 121; in Rye, 121; and preparations for Restoration, 160

Morley, Robert, 8

Mosse, Jonathan, 266

Mowbray, Henry Frederick Howard, baron (*later* 3rd earl of Arundel), 41, 66

Moxon, Joseph, 251; *Mechanical Exercises* (part work) 251

Nantes, Edict of (1598): revoked (1685), 70, 271

Nanteuil, Robert, 103, 128, 229, 230

Naples, 51–2

Naseby, Battle of (1645), 58

Naudé, Gabriel, 90, 152, 174; *Advis pour dresser une bibliothèque*, 68, 171–2

navy, the: hospital for, xi, 200; gunpowder for, 3; paid off by Charles II, 171; divided into two, 198; laid up, 202; Pepys prepares history of 241, 265–6

Navy Board: JE nominated for, 208, 258, 260

Navy Office, 197, 243

Needham, Jasper (Gaspar or Caspar): friendship with JE, 83; deals with booksellers for JE, 92; JE gives engraved portrait to, 104; cancels journey to Paris, 118; at George's party for new garden at Wotton, 130; corresponds with JE from France, 137; helps JE with Lucretius translation, 144; collects acorns for JE, 147–8; as doctor of physic, 148; and encouragement of JE's translation of Bonnefons, 150; as translator of Le Gendre 150; attends JE's dying son Richard, 151; encourages JE to finish *Elysium Britannicum*, 162; presents paper to Royal Society, 169; attends John Evelyn Jr, 258

New Model Army, 132

Newcastle, Margaret Cavendish, marchioness (*later* duchess) of (*née* Lucas), 30, 71, 74, 80, 100, 211, 245

Newcastle, William Cavendish, marquess (*later* 1st duke) of: in Antwerp, 30, 100; opposes Scottish army, 40; marriage, 71, 74; poem on JE's wedding, 74; as advisor to Charles II, 98; absolves Charles II of debts, 211
Newmarket, Suffolk, 235, 238
Newport, Francis, viscount, 266
Newton, Sir Isaac, 265, 296, 302
Newton, Jane (*earlier* Stansfield; *née* Michell*;* JE's step-grandmother), 6–7, 99
Newton, William (Jane's second husband), 7, 11, 14
Nicholas, Sir Edward, 69, 87, 95, 97–8, 153
non-jurors, 277
Nonsuch Palace, Epsom, 198, 218, 288
Norfolk, 6th duke of *see* Howard, Henry
North, Sir Dudley, 271
North, Francis, 81
North, Roger: opposes study of natural sciences, 12; on brothers at Oxford, 16; on perpetual motion machine, 81; takes up architecture, 188; at Windsor, 271; on Sunderland's drawl, 276
Norwich: JE designs garden for Howard at, 227, 237–8; JE visits, 237–8

Oates, Titus, 253
Oatlands (house), Surrey, 288
Office of Address, 136
Oldenburg, Henry: in Boyle–Wilkins circle, 140; on Beale's combining Christianity and scientific knowledge, 159; corresponds with Evelyn and Beale, 159; and Royal Society after Great Fire, 222–3; on Stubbe, 234; and John Evelyn Jr in Paris, 248
Oliver, Isaac, 85
Onslow, Sir Richard, 64
Orléans, Gaston, duc d', 39, 102
Orléans, Henrietta, duchesse d' (Minette), 167
Orléans, Philippe I, duc d', 167, 191
Ormonde, James Butler, 1st duke of, 87, 93, 97, 129, 163, 210, 242, 262
Ossory, Thomas Butler, earl of, 102, 242
Oudart, Nicholas, 234
Oughtred, William, 10, 16, 22, 44, 49, 119, 128, 133, 138, 296
Owen, Richard, 124, 139
Oxford (city): Charles I in, 33–4; burned

in Civil War, 46; life in during war, 66–7; Sheldonian Theatre, 190, 226; court removes to during plague, 197–8; Arundel marbles transferred to, 227; Ashmolean Museum, 227
Oxford University: JE attends (Balliol College), 11–15; educational principles, 12–14; Botanic Garden (*earlier* Physic Garden), 14, 133, 162, 190; Thicknesse describes, 67; JE revisits with Mary, 132–4; JE receives honorary degree, 190; JE visits from Cornbury, 190

Packer, Elizabeth, 289, 298–300
Packer, Philip, 98, 104, 107–8, 122, 198
Padua, Italy: JE visits, 58–60, 62–4, 279; anatomical studies, 62–3; botanical gardens, 63
Palladio, Andrea, 65, 248; *Quattro Libri*, 43, 47
Paris: JE in, 37–40, 67–9, 71, 93, 95–9, 102, 105–6; town planning, 39, 229; gardens, 40–1, 229; Henrietta Maria's expatriate court in, 70–1, 89, 93, 97, 110, 204; under siege, 89, 236; unrest in, 92, 101–2, 118; as cultural and intellectual centre, 100; Jardin des Plantes, 100, 127, 137; JE praises in *The State of France*, 116; Bernini's Louvre plans, 214; Wren visits, 214–15; English visitors to, 229–30; JE describes and recommends to Pepys, 230–2; Mary Evelyn misses, 245; John Evelyn Jr in, 248–9; Invalides built, 262
Parke, Daniel, 248, 294–5
Parkhurst, John, 13
Parkinson, John: *Paradisi in Sole*, 162
Parliament: relations with Charles I, 12, 17; divisions and factions, 78; George Evelyn serves in, 78; persecutes Church of England, 82; plans trial of Charles I, 87; Barebones, 132; Rump, 156; and preparations for Restoration, 160–1; differences with Charles II, 253; fall of Cavalier (1679), 253
Patrick, Simon, bishop of Ely, 273
Peiresc, Nicolas-Claude Fabri de, 48, 100, 146
Pell, John, 182
Pembroke, Philip Herbert, 4th earl of, 134
Pembroke, Philip Herbert, 5th earl of, 134
Penshurst Place, Kent, 151

Pepys, Elizabeth, 230, 232, 303

Pepys, Samuel: on JE's plays, 17; JE shows herbarium at Sayes Court, 63; JE gives engraved portrait to, 104; love of pleasure, 139–40; and Charles II's return to England, 164; observes Charles II's coronation, 170–1; struggles with JE's translation of Naudé, 172; buys Hooke's *Micrographia*, 185; dealings with Hugh May, 186; becomes Fellow of Royal Society, 197; visits JE as commissioner for sick and wounded, 197; and JE's plans for naval infirmary, 198–9; JE sketches Dutch attack on Chatham for, 202; visits Sayes Court, 204; discussions with JE, 207–8; friendship with JE, 208, 286, 296–7, 302; JE sends copy of *Fumifugium* to, 216; on Great Fire of London, 217; plans to import timber for London rebuilding, 224; visits Paris, 230–2; wife's death, 232; letter from JE at Sayes Court, 233; on Arlington's purchase of Euston Hall, 237; meets Blagge family, 238; borrows JE's housekeeping instructions, 247; accused of Catholic sympathies and committed to Tower, 254; nominates JE for Navy Board, 258; prepares history of navy, 241, 265–6; and revival of Royal Society, 265, 296; mission to Tangier, 266; reinstated as secretary of Admiralty, 266; and Elizabeth Evelyn's elopement, 269; on Charles II's dying a Catholic, 271; opposes Act of Indulgence, 273; invites JE and family to firework display, 274; supports James II, 274; Jacobitism, 275; as non-juror, 277; affected by political changes, 278; imprisoned again (1691), 278; lends Locke's *Human Understanding* to JE, 280; and JE's daughter Susanna's marriage, 286; and JE's life at Wotton, 288, 303; on naval hospital at Greenwich, 292; library, 296; retires to Clapham, 296; reads Clarendon's *History of the Rebellion*, 297; and JE's inheritance of Wotton, 300; and JE's redesigning Wotton house, 300; discusses foreign travel with JE, 302; death and funeral, 303; *Memoires Relating to the State of the Royal Navy*, 266

Peter I (the Great), Tsar of Russia, 298

Peters, William, 75, 77, 92

Petre, William, 4th baron, 254

Pett, Peter, 23, 152, 171, 200

Pett, Peter, Jr, 135

Petty, Sir William: in Paris, 100; Hartlib and, 137; and proposed founding of learned society, 156; returns to London, 167; in Royal Society, 169; on commission to improve London, 178; plans to import timber for London rebuilding, 224

Philips, Katherine, 211

Phillips, Edward, 213

Pierce, Thomas, Dean of Salisbury, 253

Piscopia, Elena, 60

plague (1665), 193–7, 199

Plantin's printing house, Antwerp, 29

Plato and Platonism, 143, 213

Plutarch: *Lives*, 260

Pope, Alexander, 306

Pope, Walter, 185, 222

Popish Plot (1678), 253, 264

Porter, Sir Endymion: and JE's marriage to Mary Browne, 72, 74; and patenting of perpetual motion machine, 81; death, 91

Portsmouth, 271; siege of (1642), 32

Post, Pieter, 25

Poussin, Nicholas, 49

Pozzo, Cassiano dal, 49

Pratt, Sir Roger, 47–8, 188–9, 199, 215–16, 256

Presbyterianism, 35, 121

Prettyman (or Pretyman), William: as executor of Sayes Court estate, 79; as courier between JE and Browne in Paris, 86; JE entrusts Sayes Court to on going abroad, 91; arranges Browne's finances with JE, 92, 123; urges JE to return from Paris, 111; JE proposes sharing Sayes Court running costs with, 117; marriage, 123; and improvements to Sayes Court, 124; legal disputes over Sayes Court, 132, 259, 263; moves out of Sayes Court, 139; stands godfather to JE's son John, 139; and JE's proposals to purchase land in Ireland, 150; and financial support for Sir Richard Browne, 161; differences with Browne, 233; claims money from Browne, 244; JE wins case against, 266, 270

Pride's Purge, 78

Privy Seal: JE appointed to commission, 270–2; commission reconstituted, 273; returned to commissioners, 277

Quintinye, Jean de la, 229–30; *The Compleat Gard'ner*, 282

Radcliffe, Thomas, 110
Ramelli, Agostino: *Le diverse et artificiose machine*, 161
Rand, William, 146, 280
Rapin, Nicholas: *Of Gardens*, 235
Ray, John, 191
Rea, John: *Flora, seu De florum cultura*, 205
Reeves, Richard, 122
Renzi, Anna, 62
Reymes, Colonel Bullen, 192, 196, 198, 241–2
Richelieu, Cardinal Armand Jean Duplessis, duc de, 39–40, 68, 90, 171, 174
Richmond, James Stuart, 1st duke of, 58
Rights, Declaration of (1688), 276
Robert, Pierre, 116
Robinson, Henry, 81
Rochester, Laurence Hyde, 1st earl of, 209, 257, 266, 270–1
Rogers, George, 63, 69
Roman Catholicism: hostility to in England, 254–5, 259; at James II's court, 268, 271–2; revival in England, 273; JE claims to be moderate in England, 285
Rome, 45, 46–50, 53–4; JE arrives at, 45; town plan, 220
Ross, Alexander, 90, 103, 238
Rougham Hall, Norfolk, 188
Rowlett, Thomas, 93
Royal Charles (ship; earlier *Naseby*), 164, 201–2
Royal College of Physicians, 251
Royal James (ship), 242
Royal Society: Wilkins chairs inaugural meeting, 132; Boyle's dedication to, 141; JE supports financially, 150, 255; founding, 167–8, 171–2; JE's involvement in, 167–9, 171–2, 251, 267, 295–6, 302; JE presents *Sculptura* to, 179; JE writes report on nation's timber (*Sylva*), 180–3; publications, 184–5; Sprat's history of, 186, 212; Pepys attends, 197; Charter, 209; controversy over, 212; entertains duchess of Newcastle, 211; Stubbe attacks, 212,

234; meets after Great Fire, 222; seeks new premises, 222, 296; sets standards for materials for rebuilding of London, 223–5; Howard presents Arundel's library to, 226; plans for after Great Fire, 226; JE's temporary secretaryship, 247; satirized, 250, 252; financial difficulties, 251, 255; JE defends against critics, 255; JE presents paper on Sayes Court garden to, 265; JE declines presidency, 279; 'Saturday Academists', 296; account of JE's anatomical tables presented to, 302; Isaac Newton's presidency, 302; *Philosophical Transactions*, 222–3, 248, 302
Royston, Richard, 206
Rubens, Peter Paul, 49; *Palazzi di Genova*, 43
Ruby (warship), 118
Rueil, France, 40
Rupert, Prince, Count Palatine of the Rhine: visits Oxford, 11; commands royalist cavalry, 25, 40; patronises de Gomme, 26; at Edgehill, 33; reported movements, 86; departs for Holland, 87, 89; and Lady Catherine Scott, 93; mezzotint portrait, 179; takes over command of fleet (1666), 198
Ruyter, Admiral Michael de, 201–2, 242
Rye House Plot (1683), 264, 268
Ryston Hall, Norfolk, 188

St Albans, Henry Jermyn, 1st earl of: in Paris, 70, 85; named as ambassador to France, 163; on commission to improve London, 178; develops part of London, 186; receives copy of JE's translation of Fréart's *Parallèle*, 188; and Cowley, 204–5; visits Sayes Court, 204; accompanies Henrietta Maria to Paris, 214
St Michel, Alexandre (Pepys' brother-in-law), 81
St Paul's Cathedral (old): dilapidation, 215–16; burnt in Great Fire of London, 217–19
St Paul's Cathedral (new): in post-Fire plans, 221; rebuilt, 229
Sampson, John, 6
Sancroft, William, Archbishop of Canterbury, 262, 273, 276
Sandwich, Edward Montague, 1st earl of, 198, 235, 242

Sayes Court, Deptford: Brownes granted Crown lease, 79; Christopher Browne's garden at, 79; JE manages for Browne, 79–80; Prettyman appointed executor, 79–80; JE entrusts to Prettyman on going abroad, 91; JE visits on 1650 visit from Paris, 104; JE acquires, 113, 117, 119; JE proposes sharing running costs with Prettyman, 117; condition and setting, 120, 123; JE and Mary arrive at, 123; improvements, 124–6, 128, 131, 148, 156; garden, 126–7, 148–9, 153, 177, 183, 204–5, 265–6, 269; Prettyman's claims over, 132, 259, 263, 266, 270; Prettymans move from, 139; JE builds houses along boundary, 149; reverts to Crown, 172; JE struggles to secure tenure, 179; fishing at, 187; visitors, 204, 244, 264; elms stolen from, 205; JE's cell in, 233; JE fails to secure lease, 257, 263; John Jr at, 258; JE and Mary leave for Wotton House, 281; William Draper manages garden, 286–7, 289; JE retains, 289; let, 298; Peter the Great occupies, 298; hurricane damage (1703), 303; JE visits in old age, 303

Scamozzi, Vincenzo, 24
Scarburgh, Charles, 91, 133, 164
Scott, Lady Catherine (née Goring), 93, 98
Scudamore, John, 1st viscount, 71
Seneca, 152
Shadwell, Thomas: The Sullen Lovers, 223; The Virtuoso, 250–1
Shaftesbury, Anthony Ashley Cooper, 1st earl of, 254, 256, 264
Sharp, Lindsay, 182
Sharrock, Robert, 162
Shaw, Sir John, 186–7
Sidney, Dorothy ('Sacharissa'), 122
Siena, Italy, 43, 46
Six Bishops: sent to Tower, 273
Sixtus V, Pope, 50
Sixtus X, Pope, 220
Skellman, Richard, 124
Skinner, Mrs, 303
slaves and slave trade, 247
Slingsby, Henry, 169
Sloane, Sir Hans, 265, 290, 296
Snatt, Revd Edward, 8, 10, 14, 82, 144
Snatt, William, 8
Sole Bay, Battle of (1672), 242
Solemn League and Covenant, 35, 78

Somerset, Mary (later duchess of Beaufort), 255
Sorbière, Samuel, 67, 100, 167, 169, 172, 211
South Malling, Lewes, Sussex, 6, 18
Southampton, Thomas Wriothesley, 4th earl of, 181, 186, 208
Southover Free School, 7, 9
Southover House (now Grange), Lewes, 7
Sovereign of the Seas (ship), 23, 25
Spain: JE plans visit to with Waller, 67
Spencer, Robert (son of 2nd earl of Sunderland), 256, 274
Spenser, Edmund: The Faerie Queene, 246
Sprat, Thomas: on alchemy and chemistry, 138; on Cowley, 204; History of the Royal Society, 186, 212
Squerryes (house), Westerham, Kent, 127
Stafford, Willam Howard, 1st viscount, 10, 254
Stanhope, Lord Philip see Chesterfield, 2nd earl of
Stansfield, Eleanor (née Comber; JE's maternal grandmother), 6–7
Stansfield, John (JE's maternal grandfather), 6–7, 82
Stephens, James, 74, 85, 96, 100, 111, 161
Stephens, Philip, 162
Steward, Richard (former, dean of St Paul's), 71, 105, 111
Stillingfleet, Edward, Bishop of Worcester, 273
Stoics, 152, 213
Stone, Nicholas, 35, 190
Stop of Exchequer, 242
Strafford, Thomas Wentworth, 1st earl of, 19, 21
Strickland, John, 291, 303
Strong, Edward, 301
Stubbe, Henry, 144, 212, 234
Sully, Maximilien de Béthune, duc de, 39
Sunderland, Anne, countess of, 253, 256, 274–7
Sunderland, Robert Spencer, 2nd earl of: travels to Spain with Godolphin, 239; JE dines with, 266; Catholicism, 272, 273, 274; and James II's departure, 275–6; exile in Holland, 276; recants, 276; greets William III on return from Holland, 277; Letter to a Friend, 275
Sylvius, Anne, Lady (née Howard), 248–9, 252, 262, 267, 270, 284
Sylvius, Sir Gabriel, 225, 259

Tangier: Pepys's mission to, 266

Taylor, Jeremy: attends Charles I during house arrest, 77; JE discusses and corresponds with on religion, 138; religious ideas, 138, 141; JE entertains at Sayes Court, 139; and JE's Lucretius translation, 142–5; on death of JE's son Richard, 151; and title of JE's *Elysium Britannicum*, 162; and JE's ambitions, 172; on spiritual kinship, 240; *Ductor dubitantium* (*The Rule of Consciousness*), 138; *Holy Dying*, 151

Temple, Sir Purbeck, 284, 301

Tenison, Thomas, Archbishop of Canterbury (*earlier* rector of St Martin in the Fields and Bishop of Lincoln), 273, 275–6, 278, 279, 284, 304

Test Acts, 241, 247, 253, 260, 272

Thames, river: transport on, 178–9; in post-Fire plans, 222; frozen (1684), 265

Theobalds Park, Hertfordshire, 35

Thicknesse, James: at Oxford, 13–14; and JE's literary endeavours, 17; and JE's leaving England, 19; accompanies JE abroad, 36–8, 40, 42; leaves JE for Siena, 43, 46–7; in Padua, 58; recalled to England, 60; and JE's smallpox, 66; on life in Oxford, 67; on JE's bethrothal and marriage, 74–5

Thirty Years War (1621–48), 20–1, 23

Thornhill, James, 302

Thurland, Edward, 119

Thynne, Lady Isabella, 93

Tillotson, John, Dean of St Paul's (*later* Archbishop of Canterbury), 273

Tivoli, Italy, 54

Tom (gardener), 291

Tompion, Thomas, 250

Tooke, Benjamin, 243

Tories: emergence as party, 272

Tours, France, 42

Tradescant, John, the Elder, 41, 148, 252

Travers, Samuel, 293

Triplet, Dr Thomas, 144

Tuke, Sir Charles, 209, 263

Tuke, George, 73, 257

Tuke, Mary, Lady (*formerly* Sheldon): marriage to Samuel, 209; in Paris, 215; Mary Evelyn stays with at Windsor Castle, 244; and John Evelyn Jr's marriage and children, 259–60; on death of Sir Richard Browne, 262; seeks position for John Evelyn Jr with duke of

York, 263; criticises court, 264; on JE's appointment as commissioner of Privy Seal, 270; Catholicism, 273; enquires about returning to England, 285

Tuke, Mary, the younger, 285

Tuke, Sir Samuel: exile after siege of Colchester, 85; in Paris, 99, 106; JE gives engraved portrait to, 104; writes to JE from The Hague, 105; in duke of York's entourage, 156, 160; returns to England, 156; in Breda with Charles II, 163; and preparations for Restoration, 164; arranges JE's audience with Charles II, 165; friendship with JE, 167; absent from Charles II's coronation, 170; on Mary's prospective position at court, 173; and improvements to Sayes Court, 183; and Mary's comments on JE's writing for Royal Society, 183; serves Henry Howard in Norwich, 183; and JE's disillusion with Charles II's regime, 184; on JE's concern for Dutch prisoners of war, 193; admiration for Louis XIV, 208; Catholicism, 208; remarries, 209; and Wren's visit to Paris, 214–15; JE informs of rebuilding of London after Fire, 219; brings prints of Paris gardens to JE, 229; deaths of wife and child, 229; on George Evelyn Jr, 229; Mary describes Sayes Court in winter to, 233; death, 243–4; gives beds and provisions for sick seamen in Third Dutch War, 242; and JE's Anglican convictions, 272; *The Adventures of Five Hours* (adapted from Spanish), 183–4

Tunbridge Wells, Kent, 122

Turkey Company: almshouses, 291

United Provinces (*also* Low Countries): architecture, 24–5, 175, 187; JE travels in, 24–5, 27–8, 331; *see also* Dutch

Upcott, William, 306

Urban VIII, Pope, 46, 49, 97

Vanbrugh, Sir John, 293

Vanbrugh, William, 293

Van Dyck, Sir Anthony, 35–6

Vaughan, Thomas, 138

Venice: JE in, 56, 59–60, 62; Carnival, 62; menaced by Turks, 69

Verney, Mary, Lady, 80

Verney, Sir Ralph, 71

Verrio, Antonio, 256, 273; *Triumph of the Black Prince* (painting), 271
Versailles: French court moves to, 39
Vesling, Johann, 62
Vesuvius, Mount, 52
Villiers, Lord Francis, 57
Virgil, 228
Virginia: JE receives plants from, 295
Vitruvius, 187–8, 300

Wadham College, Oxford, 132–3, 140
Wakeman, Sir George, 254
Walker, John, 295
Walker, Obadiah, 14
Walker, Robert, 85
Waller, Mary (*née* Bressy), 87
Waller, Edmund: in Italy and Switzerland, 60–2, 65–6; influence on JE, 62, 68; poems on Vesling and Rogers, 63; in France, 66–8, 75, 96, 100; plans journey to Spain with JE, 67; recipe for cure of lungs, 69; congratulates JE on marriage, 74; interest in self-powered engine, 75–6, 81; urges JE to return to England, 75; acquainted with de la Mothe le Vayer, 90; and JE's Lucretius translation, 103, 118; as advisor to Charles II, 106; pardoned by Rump and returns to England, 108, 118; JE discusses government with, 115; visits JE at Sayes Court, 117; accepts Commonwealth, 118, 241; at Hall Barn, 120, 191; invites George Evelyn to Hall Barn, 120–1; religious indifference, 120; and invitation to Browne to represent Commonwealth in Paris, 125–6; introductory poem to JE's Lucretius translation, 142–3; on commission to improve London, 178
Waller, Richard, 296
Waller, General William, 32
Wallis, John, 191
Walpole, Horace, 143n
Walter, Lucy, 97
Ward, Seth, 12, 132
Wase, Christopher, 113, 118, 120, 134, 141, 152, 241
Webb, John, 215
Whigs: emergence as party, 272
Whitehall Palace: plans for remodelling, 191, 271, 273
Wilkins, John: at Oxford, 132–4; intellectual circle, 137; JE entertains at

Sayes Court, 139; scientific interests, 140; returns to London, 167; in Royal Society, 169, 171, 200; and JE's scheme for naval hospital, 200–1; appearance, 296
William III (of Orange), King: courtship of Mary, 21, 32; marriage to Mary, 244; displaced from succession by birth of James, 273–4; invited to invade, 274–5; character and manner, 276; reign, 276–7; Sunderland writes to from Holland, 276; Sunderland greets on return from Holland, 277; and plans for Greenwich naval hospital, 294; death, 304
William and Mary College, Williamsburg, 295
Williamson, Sir Joseph, 199, 225, 234–5, 251, 265
Wilton House, Wiltshire, 134
Winchester Palace, 271
Windebank, Sir Francis, 4
Winthrop, John, the Younger, 181
Wise, Henry, 283, 287
Wood, Anthony à, 150, 288
Woodcote Park, Epsom, 83, 125
Worcester, Battle of (1651), 111
Worcester, Edward Somerset, 2nd marquess of, 81
Worsley, Benjamin, 146, 247
Wotton House, Surrey: as JE's home, 1–2; described, 2–3; George inherits, 17–18; JE buys pictures for, 26; garden and landscaping, 34–5, 104–5, 119, 129–30, 282–4, 292, 304; JE stays at in Civil War, 34–5; in Civil War, 40, 45; JE visits on return from France, 78; improvements, 104, 115–16, 130; JE visits with Mary, 127–8; social life at, 130, 204; in JE's *Elysium Britannicum*, 148; threatened by plague, 195; JE and Mary move to, 281–3, 287, 291–2, 303; entailment and dispute over, 283–4, 298–300; JE describes, 288; JE wants to redesign as Palladian villa, 289, 300; hurricane damage (1703), 297, 303; JE inherits and improves, 300–2, 304; JE's inventory of, 301–2; pork puddings, 302; Bohun's living at, 303–4; JE buried at, 305; Jack Evelyn inherits, 306
Wotton, Sir Henry: quoted, 127; on rewards of private gardens, 131; and John Beale, 158; on symmetry, 186, 301;

Wotton, Sir Henry (*cont.*)
    modesty over accomplishments, 187;
    advice on siting house, 256
Wotton, William, 141, 283, 296–7
Wray, Captain, 65–6
Wren, Sir Christopher: JE meets, 133; at
    Gresham College, 135; gives inaugural
    lecture at Royal Society, 168;
    experimental method, 169; and Royal
    Society publications, 184; and Pratt's
    architecture, 188; designs Sheldonian
    Theatre, 191; JE meets in Oxford, 191;
    and JE's plans for naval hospital, 199;
    visit to Paris, 214–15; and survey of old
    St Paul's cathedral, 216; plan for
    rebuilding London after Great Fire,
    219–21, 223; drafts plans for Royal
    Society building, 226; and new St Paul's
    Cathedral, 229; and Val-de-Grâce,
    Paris, 232; mathematical knowledge,
    249; presidency of Royal Society, 251;
    designs Royal Hospital, Chelsea, 262;

and revival of Royal Society, 265;
    informs JE of architectural trends, 289;
    and design of Turkey Company
    almshouses, 291; George Evelyn seeks
    advice from on mortar, 291; and
    building of naval hospital at Greenwich,
    293–4; visits Sayes Court to survey
    Peter the Great's damage, 298
Wren, William (Christopher's son), 262
Wyche, Sir Cyril, 281, 283, 289–90
Wyche, Mary, Lady (*née* Evelyn;
    George's daughter), 83, 261, 281, 283,
    287, 300

Yonge, James, 302
York, Anne, duchess of (*née* Hyde): as
    maid of honour to Mary Stuart, 78;
    marriage, 166, 210; move towards
    Catholicism, 208, 238; death, 238;
    Pepys meets, 238
York, Mary, duchess of *see* Mary of
    Modena, Queen of James II

Acknowledgements

My first and most considerable debt is to Frances Harris, head of modern historical manuscripts at the British Library. Without her unfailing encouragement, lightly worn scholarship and personal kindness, I would never have embarked on this book and more to the point, would certainly have never finished it. Early on, Douglas Chambers generously gave me copies of his transcriptions from Evelyn's letterbooks and he has been a friend and sounding-board ever since. Michael Hunter has kindly answered my questions and discussed Evelyn with me on several enjoyable occasions while Guy de la Bédoyère has been extremely helpful online.

Rather longer ago than I care to remember, Robert Baldock at Yale University Press sent me an email, its subject line 'welcome Mr Evelyn'. Here he is – for his tercentenary year. Candida Brazil has gamely and intelligently edited the material, on occasion bringing order to chaos, while Steve Kent found time to track down typefaces and distribute illustrations to excellent effect. I had a scrupulous and learned copy-editor in Robert Shore and every author's dream indexer in Douglas Matthews. Caroline Dawnay, my agent, has been gratifyingly eager to read what I have written. Then, just as the manuscript was nearing completion, Mary-Kay Wilmers of the *London Review of Books* commissioned a diary piece asking me to 'write about writing about Evelyn, and trees'. Finally, I became the diarist's diarist.

The list below is of those who have delved into archives or their own notes to reply to a request (which sometimes came out of the blue by email), or have made suggestions, shown me a book or building or helped me to track down a missing link. Thanks to you all, and to anyone who has slipped my memory, I can only apologise. Needless to say, none of those named above or below, bears any blame for my mistakes: Mavis Batey, Julian Bowsher, Colin Brent, Peter Clayton, Michael Cooper, Liz and Martin Drury, Diane Ducharme, Patrick Evelyn, Jenefer Farncombe, Mordecai Feingold, Robyn Gardner, Melissa Gold Fournier, Pem Goldschmidt, Patrick Goode, the Duke of

Grafton, Antony Griffiths, Peter Guillery, Robert Harding, Kate Harris, Kathy Haslam, Charles Hinde, Michael Horowitz, Ralph Houlbrook, Roger Hunt, Tom Jaine, Lisa Jardine, Sally Jeffery, Marika Keblusek, Mark Laird, Lucinda Lambton, Jill Leggatt, Prudence Leith-Ross, Philippa Lewis, Des McTernan, John-Michael Muller, Sister Mary Magdalene and Sister Mary Stephen, Sarah Mortimer, Stephen Pincus, Jenny Potter, Piers Pratt, Tim Raylor, Jenny Robinson, Elizabeth Rutledge, John and Nancy Safford, Andrew Saint, Amanda Saville, John Schofield, Dimitry Shvidkovsky, Alicia Schrikker, William Seward, the (separate!) staffs at the Registrar's office and children's day nursery in Southover Grange, Claire Tomalin, Amanda Vickery, Julian Watson, Ailsa Wildig, Donald Wintersgill, Christine Woollett, the late Giles Worsley, Alison Wright, Ann Young. The tercentenary conference, A Celebration of John Evelyn, held in April 2006 at Wotton House and organised by the Surrey Gardens Trust and the Garden History Society, was a gratifying reminder of how interest in John Evelyn is growing. The proceedings are to be published under that title.

I would like to acknowledge help from staff from many museums, archives and libraries, but in particular at the following: Duke Humfrey's Library, the Bodleian, Oxford; Boerhaaven Museum, Leiden; the Geffrye Museum, London; the National Monuments Record, Swindon; the Public Record Office (now the National Archives) at Kew; the India Office Library and the Patents Collection at the British Library; the London Metropolitan Archive; Norfolk Record Office, Norwich; Flintshire Record Office, Hawarden; the Royal Society; Maisons-Laffite, Ile de France; John Rylands University Library, Manchester; the British Museum, department of Prints and Drawings; the Society of Antiquaries; the Royal College of Physicians; the Royal Institute of British Architects drawings collection at the Victorian and Albert Museum; East Sussex Record Office, Lewes; the Beinicke Library, Yale and, as always, the inimitable London Library. This book has been dependent on the Evelyn material held at the British Library, in both the Department of Manuscripts and the Department of Rare Books. To the staff there, always so courteous and helpful, my particular thanks.

Finally, the repercussions of a book fall heavily on those closest to the writer. Living with a person with an approaching deadline and distant preoccupations is not much fun. I can only try to make it up to my friends and family afterwards. Above all, I owe much to my husband Michael, whose judicious eye on the page, alert to cliché and obfuscation, is always apt and helpful and to my Susannah who, like Evelyn's own Susanna, is the best possible reminder that after the storm comes the sun.

Photographic Acknowledgements

British Library Board: figs 1, 14, 20; plates 15–17, 20, 29. Robert Harding: figs 4, 5, 9, 10; plates 13, 24. Trustees of the British Museum: figs 7, 8; plate 12. Guy de la Bédoyère (after John Evelyn) fig. 17. Yale Center for British Art, Paul Mellon Collection: fig. 18; plates 2, 23. The Earl of Pembroke and Montgomery: Wilton House, Salisbury, fig. 22. The John Rylands University Library, Manchester: plate 1. Ailsa Wildig: plate 4. Sir John Soane's Museum, London: plate 5. Private collection: plates 7–10. The Marquess of Bath, Longleat House, Warminster, Wiltshire (photograph: Photographic Survey, Courtauld Institute): plate 11 . Royal Society: plate 18. Ashmolean Museum, Oxford: plate 19. The Collection of Prideaux Place: plate 27. RIBA Library, Drawings Collection: plate 28.